FOUNDATIONS OF A PLANNED ECONOMY
1926–1929

A HISTORY OF SOVIET RUSSIA

The following volumes have been published:

A HISTORY OF SOVIET RUSSIA

FOUNDATIONS OF A PLANNED ECONOMY 1926-1929

★ ★

VOLUME TWO

BY

EDWARD HALLETT CARR
FELLOW OF TRINITY COLLEGE, CAMBRIDGE

THE MACMILLAN COMPANY
NEW YORK, NEW YORK

The Macmillan Company
866 Third Avenue, New York, N.Y. 10022

First published in 1971 by The Macmillan Press, Ltd.,
London and Basingstoke

Library of Congress Catalog Card Number: 71-80789

FIRST AMERICAN EDITION 1972

Printed in the United States of America

CONTENTS

TABLES

PREFACE

THE second volume of *Foundations of a Planned Economy, 1926–1929* is designed as the political counterpart of the first volume, which was devoted to the economic history of this period and was written jointly by Professor R. W. Davies and myself. The main theme in the present volume has been to show how the repercussions of the transition from NEP to full-scale planning, and above all of the intense pressures of rapid industrialization, spread over the structure of party, government and society, and moulded them into new shapes not foreseen by those who made the revolution. What happened has been, and can be, interpreted either as a consummation or as a frustration of the purposes of the revolution. It partook of the dual and ambiguous character of all great historical transformations.

From a certain standpoint it might be said that the first volume of *Foundations of a Planned Economy* is a study of achievements, and the second of costs. It is tempting to ask the hypothetical question whether the results could not have been achieved at a lesser cost, or — still more unrealistically — whether, if the costs had been foreseen, the results would have been achieved or attempted. But the very conception of a social or national balance-sheet of achievements and costs seems inappropriate and misleading. The main beneficiaries of an historical process are seldom or never those on whom the costs have fallen; and the model of the balance-sheet dissolves into an irreconcilable conflict of interests and purposes between different groups — a challenge to the illusion that every problem has a solution which will be free from ambiguity, free from suffering, free from injustice, free from tragedy. The historian can only do his best to present the picture in all its aspects as a single whole, and, though well aware that the presentation will necessarily reflect his own provisional judgment, leave the ultimate verdict to the longer perspective of future generations.

No historian can hope to cover every department of the social and political life of a vast country even for the briefest period. Most of the topics treated in this volume imposed themselves; others have been selected — perhaps a little capriciously. It will be open to critics to point out omissions. The gravest omission of which I am conscious is my failure to deal in any detail with the so-called national question. This is in fact a whole series of different questions, since the problems of, say, Ukrainian or Armenian nationalism have little in common with those of Uzbek or Buryat nationalism — not to mention still more remote and less developed regions. Lack of linguistic competence and of access to local material must for the present put this subject out of reach of the ordinary historian. Nearly all books and articles hitherto published on it have been marked not only by an inadequacy of sources, but by an unconditional and uncritical acceptance, either of the beneficent influence of the USSR on the nationalities incorporated in it, or of the claims and grievances of spokesmen of these nationalities, which reveals them as vehicles of propaganda rather than of scholarship. It may be many years before these questions can be treated in any way adequately or dispassionately.

In preparing this volume I have been conscious of the same debts as before to personal friends and to institutions for indispensable assistance in my work. The extent of my indebtedness, both to individuals and to the libraries which generously minister to my needs, increases with every volume ; but I may perhaps excuse myself from repeating the list recorded in the preface to the previous volume. I should like, however, to add some further names to the list, and to express my warm thanks to Tamara Deutscher for letting me see the letter from Max Eastman to her husband quoted on p. 16, note 2 ; to Professor T. H. Rigby of the Australian National University for allowing me to borrow my Table No. 53 from his work on *Communist Party Membership in the USSR*, as well as for other valuable indications on party statistics ; to Mrs Narkiewicz, whose study of the Smolensk archives helped me to unravel the complications of the " Smolensk scandal " (pp. 136-141) ; and, last but not least, to Professor Yuzuru Taniuchi of the University of Tokyo, who patiently read drafts of the chapters on rural administration, and put generously at my disposal his unrivalled knowledge of this question.

Abbreviations and titles formed from initial letters have become an accepted part of modern speech and writing. For those which I have used the reader is referred to the List of Abbreviations on pp. 985-991 of Vol. 1 and to the supplementary list on pp. 495-496 of the present volume. References in footnotes to " Vol. 1 " relate to Vol. 1 of *Foundations of a Planned Economy, 1926-1929* ; previous instalments of the History are quoted by their titles. References to the works of Lenin are to the second Russian edition, unless another edition is specified. I am once more very much indebted to Mr Douglas Matthews for the preparation of the Index, and to Miss Jean Fyfe for carrying the main burden of typing my manuscript.

I have begun work on Volume 3, which will deal with Soviet foreign relations in the period 1926-1929. Unfortunately Professor Avakumović has been unable for personal reasons to continue the collaboration on which I had counted for this volume ; and this will somewhat delay progress.

June 15, 1971   E. H. Carr

PART II

THE RULING PARTY

CHAPTER 39

THE UNITED OPPOSITION

TROTSKY returned to Moscow in the latter part of May 1926 in a fighting mood. The first business was the cementing of the alliance between the two opposition factions adumbrated on the eve of Trotsky's departure for Berlin.[1] The process was not free from embarrassments. It was comparatively easy for Trotsky, who rated the future of the party above personal differences and resentments, to come to terms with Zinoviev and Kamenev, who were conscious of their helplessness in face of Stalin without Trotsky's support. It was more difficult for Trotsky's followers and admirers in Moscow — men like Preobrazhensky, Smilga, Radek and Mrachkovsky[2] — to range themselves with Zinoviev's Leningrad lieutenants — Evdokimov, Bakaev and Lashevich — who had so recently participated in the hounding of Trotsky. It was most difficult of all for the rank and file of both groups, which had been schooled to regard themselves as representing opposite poles of thought in the party, and to exchange the bitterest invective, to unite in a fellowship of reconciliation under a joint leadership. The process was complicated by the secrecy with which it had to be conducted. Visits were exchanged between the two groups and between the two capitals. An eye-witness has recorded a visit of Smilga to Leningrad, where he addressed a tightly packed meeting of 40 persons in a worker's lodgings. The Trotskyite leaders hesitated over a proposal to exchange lists of adherents — partly from fear of betrayal, partly perhaps from reluctance to reveal their numerical weakness. In Leningrad, the organized Trotskyites did not exceed ten, with some twenty sympathizers ; the Zinovievites numbered

---

[1] See *Socialism in One Country, 1924–1926*, Vol. 2, pp. 172-176 ; the approximate date of Trotsky's return is fixed by a letter of May 22, 1926, evidently written in Moscow (Trotsky archives, T 877).

[2] For Mrachkovsky's objections to the alliance see *Socialism in One Country, 1924–1926*, Vol. 2, p. 172, note 2.

five or six hundred.[1]   In Moscow the numbers were doubtless
larger and better balanced.   According to reports preserved in the
party archives, opposition committees and bureaus were also set
up in Tula, Kharkov, Nikolaev, Odessa and Tiflis, and an " underground military bureau " was created for work in the Red Army.[2]
But the united opposition remained a movement rich in leaders
and weak in active supporters.   No estimate put the number of
the latter at more than a few thousand.   Some members of the
former Democratic Centralism and Workers' Opposition groups
also joined the united opposition, though these groups appear
to have retained some independent existence.[3]

The new opposition set out to create an organization, though
little is known of this except what was uncovered or alleged by the
authorities.[4]   Secret meetings took place.   Documents attacking
party policy, as well as secret documents of the Politburo, were
sent out to provincial centres.   An active campaign, including
underground meetings and the distribution of illegal literature,
went on throughout the summer in the Moscow party organization.[5]   An energetic member of the opposition named Belenky
organized an opposition meeting on June 6, 1926, in a forest
near Moscow, which was addressed by Lashevich, deputy
People's Commissar for War.   According to a perhaps exaggerated
party report, Lashevich said that the aim was not to provoke
discussion, but " to bring the central committee to its knees ".[6]
The meeting was quickly divulged to the authorities; and on
June 8, 1926, a commission of the party central control commission
examined Lashevich, Belenky and others concerned.   Zinoviev

---

[1] The most detailed source for this phase is V. Serge, *Le Tournant Obscur*
(1951), pp. 101-102 ; the writer as a foreigner had no formal affiliation, but was
associated with the Leningrad Trotskyites.

[2] *Voprosy Istorii KPSS*, No. 5, 1958, p. 129 ; No. 6, 1959, p. 35.

[3] For these groups see *The Bolshevik Revolution, 1917–1923*, Vol. 1,
pp. 195-200.

[4] According to a delegate at the fifteenth party conference in October 1926,
the opposition was organized with committees, members' dues, instructors, and
a cypher and communications system (*XV Konferentsiya Vsesoyuznoi Kommunisticheskoi Partii (B)* (1927), p. 696) ; Uglanov on the same occasion called
Kamenev " a sort of secretary general of the illegal central committee of the
opposition " (*ibid.* p. 626).

[5] *Voprosy Istorii KPSS*, No. 2, 1967, pp. 124-125.

[6] A. Bubnov, *Partiya i Oppozitsiya* (1926), p. 20 ; this report was made to
a party meeting in Leningrad on July 29, 1926.

refused an invitation to attend on the plea that he was busy
preparing theses for the party central committee on the re-
elections to the Soviets.[1]   Lashevich admitted that the meeting
had taken place, and that he made a report to it, but refused to
name the other participants; Belenky admitted nothing.   The
presidium of the central control commission on June 12, 1926,
adopted a resolution severely reprimanding Lashevich and
Belenky.   It recommended the removal of Lashevich from his
post as deputy People's Commissar for War, and proposed to the
forthcoming session of the party central committee to expel him
from the committee, of which he was a candidate member.   It
warned both men that any renewal of their fractional activities
would lead to immediate expulsion from the party.   Five other
participants received reprimands and warnings of varying degrees
of severity.[2]   Special attention was given by the party leaders
to the Red Army, where Trotsky's influence was still feared:
three generals, Muralov, Putna and Primakov were relieved of
their posts on the score of opposition sympathies.[3]   Other less
conspicuous reprisals were doubtless undertaken.

Preparations were now in train for the session of the party
central committee in July 1926, at which the united opposition
would make its first open appearance.   The authorities decided
to strike a first blow at the opposition at its most vulnerable point
— its association with former members of the Workers' Opposition, which had been condemned since 1921 by Lenin and by
every other party leader.   Some time in 1924 the party central
control commission had come into possession of a letter written
early in that year by Medvedev, a former member of the group,
to a party comrade in Baku, criticizing a resolution of the Baku
party committee.   The letter attacked NEP as a sacrifice of the
worker to petty bourgeois interests in town and country, described
a small-scale peasant economy as " a petty bourgeois utopia ",
demanded a concentration of resources on heavy industry, and
was prepared for concessions to " international capital " if foreign
aid could be obtained for industrial development.   It denounced

---

[1] This was stated by Rykov in his speech of July 26, 1926 (see p. 11, note 1
below).
[2] *VKP(B) v Rezolyutsiyakh* (1936), ii, 118-121 ; it was omitted from later
editions of this work.   [3] Trotsky archives, T 2990.

the policies pursued in Comintern and Profintern as placing insufficient reliance on the proletariat, and claimed that the Workers' Opposition was the only group in the Soviet Union which represented the interests of the worker.[1] The letter was submitted to a meeting attended by all the party leaders except Trotsky, held on August 17-19, 1924, which decided to publish it in *Bol'shevik* with an official reply; Zinoviev was asked to draft the reply.[2] Thereafter the whole matter was forgotten till, on July 10, 1926, a few days before the party central committee was to meet, *Pravda* devoted an article to a slashing attack on Medvedev's letter, now two-and-a-half years old, as an example of the Right danger in the party. On the following day Trotsky wrote to the Politburo protesting against the exhumation of the letter;[3] and on July 17, 1926, Medvedev wrote a letter to *Pravda* (which failed to publish it) complaining of falsifications and distortions of his original letter in the article.[4]

The party central committee met on July 14, 1926, and remained in session for ten days. The occasion was marred by the sudden death on July 20, 1926, of Dzerzhinsky, who had just delivered an angry attack on Pyatakov for pressing too hard the claims of industrialization.[5] The committee passed resolutions on the recent elections to the Soviets, on the grain collections, and on housing.[6] But the topic which bulked largest in the minds of

[1] The letter is in the Trotsky archives, T 804; it was written after Lenin's death about the time of the formation of the British Labour government. It was never published; but quotations from it appeared in articles refuting it, and disputes arose about the accuracy of some parts of the text (see note 4 below). Medvedev also endorsed Shlyapnikov's article in *Pravda*, January 19, 1924 (see *The Interregnum, 1923-1924*, p. 125, note 1), which he described as " our article ".

[2] These facts are taken from Zinoviev's statement to the party central committee of July 19, 1926 (see p. 8 below) and Bukharin's speech of July 28, 1926 (see p. 11, note 1 below). For the meeting of August 17-19, 1924, see *Socialism in One Country, 1924-1926*, Vol. 2, pp. 6-7; it is not clear whether the decision was actually taken by the meeting or by the group of seven (the " secret Politburo ") set up by it. [3] Trotsky archives, T 2993.

[4] *Ibid.* T 885. Two months later *Bol'shevik* published an article by Shlyapnikov which repeated the substance of Medvedev's protest, and was followed by a long and polemical reply signed " V.L. " (*Bol'shevik*, No. 17, September 15, 1926, pp. 62-73, 74-102); V.L. alleged that some passages in the letter of 1924 had been omitted in a version supplied by Medvedev to the central control commission in 1926. [5] See Vol. 1, pp. 281-282.

[6] See pp. 274-275 below; Vol. 1, pp. 5-6, 613.

the delegates was the struggle for power in the party. Uglanov, the secretary of the Moscow provincial party committee, had been particularly active in making propaganda against the opposition.[1] On the eve of the session, Zinoviev and Trotsky sent a note to the Politburo expressing the fear that the party central committee " will be faced with a one-sided discussion initiated in fact from above ", and thought that such a discussion " can only do the party great harm ".[2] When the committee met, Zinoviev made a statement admitting that the Trotskyite opposition of 1923 had been right in its warnings of danger ; and Trotsky withdrew the charge of opportunism levelled at Zinoviev and Kamenev in *Lessons of October*.[3] The united opposition was thus formally constituted. Neither side remained on the defensive. The major document of the opposition was a declaration signed by the thirteen opposition members of the party central committee, including Zinoviev, Kamenev, Krupskaya and Trotsky, explaining their vote against the resolution on the Soviet elections.   It attributed fractionalism to the growth of " bureaucratism ", which was in turn the product of " the lowering of the specific weight of the proletariat in our society " and of the rise of the *kulak* : " the political and cultural self-consciousness of the proletariat as the ruling class " had been fatally undermined. After dealing with labour, industry and agriculture, the declaration returned to the issue of fractionalism, and denounced the persecution of the opposition : to lead the party did not mean " to strangle it by the throat ".[4]

[1] Trotsky had recently taken exception to a provocative speech of Uglanov on " inner-party democracy " (see p. 119 below).

[2] Trotsky archives, T 884 ; the document carries a note in Trotsky's hand-writing, " Apparently written by Zinoviev ".   Whatever Zinoviev may have hoped, Trotsky is unlikely to have entertained the illusion that a clash could be avoided.

[3] Both statements were quoted by Stalin (*Sochineniya*, viii, 237) ; according to a later report Zinoviev described his participation in the struggle against Trotsky as the greatest mistake of his life, and Orjonikidze called out : " Why did you fool the whole party ? " (*The New International* (N.Y.), August 1934, p. 42).   For Trotsky's *Lessons of October* see *Socialism in One Country*, Vol. 2, pp. 8-10.

[4] Trotsky archives, T 880 ; for the sections on agriculture, industry and labour see Vol. 1, pp. 5-6, 279-280, 521.   The declaration was not included in the official records of the session, and was circulated to members of the committee only at the time of the fifteenth party conference three months later (*XV Konferentsiya Vsesoyuznoi Kommunisticheskoi Partii (B)* (1927), p. 624).

The reaction of the party leadership to the opposition campaign was understandably sharp. No detail was neglected. Zinoviev was censured for his failure to carry out the decision of August 1924 to reply to Medvedev's letter to Baku, and retorted in a formal declaration of July 19, 1926, first, that the decision had not been seriously intended (it had been completely forgotten for nearly two years), and secondly, that it had been taken not by a properly constituted party organ, but by an illegal fraction.[1] The committee took no formal decision on the Medvedev affair. The main battle occurred over a majority draft resolution " On the Affair of Lashevich and Others and on the Unity of the Party ". Kuibyshev and Stalin dwelt on the inadmissibility of disunity and factions in the party.[2] A counter-draft signed by five members of the opposition, including Smilga, Rakovsky and Osinsky, describing the affair as " one of the dangerous phenomena " which had grown out of the soil of party repression, and condemning both it and the conditions which had provoked it,[3] was brushed contemptuously aside. The resolution adopted on the last day of the session endorsed the report and recommendations of the presidium of the central control commission of June 12, 1926, adding the details that Belenky had visited Odessa and established an opposition group there with a secret cypher, and that Lashevich had proposed to organize an opposition central committee " for the struggle against the party ". The principal novelty was the direct incrimination of Zinoviev. Since Belenky was an official of IKKI, it was reasonable to infer that the machinery of Comintern had been used for fractional purposes. The opportunity was taken to recall an incident cryptically referred to as " the affair of Guralsky and Vuiovič ", which had already incurred the censure of the party delegation to IKKI. In January 1926, after the débâcle at the fourteenth party congress, Guralsky, long a *protégé* of Zinoviev, and Vuiovič, a Yugoslav who worked in the secretariat of IKKI and was a supporter of the

---

[1] Trotsky archives, T 886 ; according to Bukharin's speech of July 28, 1926 (see p. 11, note 1 below), Zinoviev said : " As you are directing your fire against the Left, I thought it inconvenient to attack the Leftist comrade Medvedev ".

[2] For quotations from their unpublished speeches see *Voprosy Istorii KPSS*, No. 6, 1959, pp. 31-32.

[3] Trotsky archives, T 883 ; no record of the debate was published.

opposition, sent Gertrud Gessler, an official of IKKI, to Berlin, Paris and Rome, on a mission to persuade foreign communists not to vote resolutions condemning the opposition and supporting the party central committee ; Gessler had betrayed her employers and informed the Politburo. On this indirect but sufficiently damning evidence, Zinoviev was expelled from the Politburo ; and the recommendation to deprive Lashevich of his candidate membership of the party central committee, as well as of his official post as deputy People's Commissar for War, was also approved.[1]

The defeat of the opposition was unmistakable and crushing. A supplementary declaration by the 13 signatories of the main opposition declaration scarcely appeared to contest the verdict on Lashevich, but rather feebly complained that the opportunity had been seized to involve Zinoviev in it; "the 'affair' of comrade Lashevich has been converted into the 'affair' of comrade Zinoviev".[2] At the end of the session it was announced that Zinoviev would be replaced in the Politburo by Rudzutak. The promotion of Rudzutak and the death of Dzerzhinsky left only three remaining candidate members of the Politburo: Petrovsky, Uglanov and Kamenev. It was now decided to raise the number to eight by the election of Orjonikidze, Andreev, Kirov, Mikoyan and Kaganovich.[3] A minor blow to the opposition was the dismissal of Pyatakov from his post as deputy president of Vesenkha.[4] Lashevich presumably recanted, and was leniently treated, being appointed assistant to the president of the board of the Chinese Eastern Railway.[5]

----

[1] *KPSS v Rezolyutsiyakh* (1954), ii, pp. 280-286 ; the Gessler incident is described from party archives in *Voprosy Istorii KPSS*, No. 6, 1959, pp. 29-30. For Guralsky see *The Interregnum, 1923–1924*, pp. 211, 241 ; *Socialism in One Country, 1924–1926*, Vol. 3, pp. 104, 301, 497. Comintern affairs will be discussed in a subsequent volume.

[2] Trotsky archives, T 880.

[3] *Pravda*, July 25, 1926.

[4] See Vol. 1, p. 282. According to N. Ipatieff, *Life of a Chemist* (Stanford, 1946), p. 426, Trotsky at this time lost his membership of Vesenkha, where he had been president of the Scientific–Technical Administration ; but he had not apparently played any rôle there for at least two years.

[5] *Izvestiya*, November 21, 1926. When he died in Harbin in 1928 (*Pravda*, September 9, 1928), *Pravda* published a laudatory obituary notice by Unshlikht containing the following passage : " In one of the complex and difficult moments in the development of our revolution, M. M. wavered and abandoned the

An interesting minor episode marked the session. As commonly happened when feelings were inflamed, the opposition in its major declaration on "bureaucratism" quoted Lenin's "testament" and its postscript, and taunted the leaders with concealing these documents from the party. Stalin met the challenge by proposing that the next party congress should be invited to reverse the decision not to publish them taken at the time of the thirteenth party congress in May 1924, and to authorize the publication of the testament and the postscript in the *Leninskii Sbornik*. This was agreed.[1] Stalin also read to the committee Lenin's notes of December 30 and 31, 1922, on the national question; these were included in the official record of his speech.[2]

The campaign against the opposition was continued with increased vigour after the end of the session. A leading article in *Pravda* concentrated its fire on Zinoviev in order to justify the penalty imposed on him:

> If a member of the Politburo of the central committee of our party . . . decided to place himself at the head of Lashevich's illegal group, if comrade Zinoviev directed the attack of this group against the party, if comrade Zinoviev used the apparatus of IKKI for fractional interests, . . . if comrade Zinoviev placed fractional discipline above the discipline of the Bolshevik party, the plenum could not leave this schismatic act without consequences.[3]

fundamental Bolshevik line, but happily not for long. He honestly and frankly confessed his errors " (*ibid.* September 12, 1928).

[1] Quoted from unpublished archives in *Pyatnadtsatyi S"ezd VKP(B)*, i (1961), p. xxvii; for the decision of May 1924 see *The Interregnum, 1923-1924*, pp. 360-361.

[2] *Pyatnadtsatyi S"ezd VKP(B)*, ii (1962), 1659, note 317; Trotsky had criticized Stalin's attitude on the national question (*XV Konferentsiya Vsesoyuznoi Kommunisticheskoi Partii* (*B*) (1927), p. 84), and probably referred to Lenin's notes. For these "notes" (really three instalments of a single document) see *The Interregnum, 1923-1924*, pp. 262-263. According to a later statement by Trotsky, Stalin also read the letter to Trotsky of March 5, 1923; he misread the conclusion of the letter, substituting " with communist greetings " for " with best comradely greetings ", and Trotsky corrected him (*The New International*, N.Y., August 1934, p. 42). But Trotsky may conceivably have confused this with some other occasion; the statement that Stalin read Lenin's testament at this session is certainly erroneous. For Lenin's letter to Trotsky of March 5, 1923, see *The Interregnum, 1923-1924*, pp. 265-266.

[3] *Pravda*, July 27, 1926; the same article reverted to the Medvedev–Shlyapnikov faction, describing it as " an ultra-Right grouping ", which had begun " to *stink* of real Menshevism ".

Rykov, in his speech of July 26, 1926, to the Moscow party organization after the session, explained that, whereas the party's disagreements with Trotsky were graver than with Zinoviev, it was Zinoviev who had committed the unforgivable offence of organizing " schism in the party ". Bukharin, in the corresponding report to the Leningrad party organization on July 28, 1926, on the results of the session, impartially attacked the opposition in all its forms and manifestations.[1] The Moscow party organization, the central committee of the Ukrainian party, and the bureau of the Komsomol central committee, were among the organizations which came out with resolutions in support of the decisions of the party central committee.[2]

Further isolated reprisals were undertaken. The resolution of the party central committee on elections to the Soviets contained a passage referring to " counter-revolutionary agitation in favour of having special peasant, in reality *kulak*, parties and unions ", and asserted with emphasis " the inadmissibility, in the conditions of the dictatorship of the proletariat, of the existence of two or more political parties ".[3] No names were mentioned, and no action proposed. But after the end of the session *Pravda* brought the alleged agitation for a peasant group or party into connexion with Zinoviev's plea at the fourteenth party congress six months earlier for toleration of " former groups ", and described it as " a slide towards Trotskyism on the part of the new opposition " ;[4] and the party journal published, with an unusually strong editorial disclaimer, an article by the notorious party heretic Ossovsky, who argued that, so long as the Bolsheviks constituted the unique party in a socially diversified and predominantly peasant country, it could never be a truly united party. Its defects were attributed to its too comprehensive character ; and the moral was that room should be found for other parties.[5] A long article in *Pravda* by Slepkov, one of Bukharin's disciples, denounced Ossovsky's

---

[1] Rykov's and Bukharin's speeches were published in *Pravda* August 1, 3, 1926 ; they were reprinted together in a pamphlet, A. Rykov and N. Bukharin, *Partiya i Oppozitsionnyi Blok* (1926).   [2] *Pravda*, July 27, August 6, 11, 1926.

[3] *KPSS v Rezolyutsiyakh* (1954), ii, 271-272.

[4] *Pravda*, July 30, 1926 ; for Zinoviev's plea see *Socialism in One Country, 1924-1926*, Vol. 2, p. 142.

[5] *Bol'shevik*, No. 14, July 31, 1926, pp. 59-80 ; the editorial note, placed at the head of the article (not, as usual, at the foot of the first page), explained that " the thoughts and ideas developed in it have nothing in common with

views; and a few days later the expulsion of Ossovsky from the party was announced.[1]   Trotsky and Kamenev somewhat illogically voted in the Politburo against the decision, protesting against the attempt to attribute Ossovsky's views to " the opposition in general ", and condemning his expulsion as " a half-disguised, artificially organized blow at the opposition ".[2]   Simultaneously with these events, a decree of TsIK and Sovnarkom of August 14, 1926, relieved Kamenev of his post as People's Commissar for Internal and Foreign Trade, and appointed Mikoyan in his place.[3]   Shortly afterwards the secretariat of IKKI announced measures taken against Guralsky and Vuiovič; Guralsky was removed from Comintern work, and Vuiovič reprimanded. Vuiovič none the less continued his opposition activities in the executive committee of the Communist Youth International (IKKIM), of which he was secretary, till the president of IKKIM relieved him of his post and debarred him from further participation in KIM.[4]

Though the united opposition had now become a political entity, it suffered from the lack of any clear programme.   It was cemented by hostility to the ruling group in the party, and by little else.   The failure of the general strike in Great Britain and the results of the Pilsudski coup in Poland had been a serious set-back to official hopes and policies.   But the opposition hesitated, or did not wish, to enter this contentious field.   The party archives contained lurid reports of attempts to form underground opposition groups in the principal cities throughout the USSR.[5]   But these appear to have had little substance.   The defeat of the opposition at the July session and the threat of further reprisals, the constant harrying of opposition speakers at meetings, and their failure to rouse mass support, created the

Bolshevism–Leninism ".   For Ossovsky's previous article on price policy see *Socialism in One Country, 1924–1926*, Vol. 1, p. 317.

[1] *Pravda*, August 8, 14, 1926.
[2] Trotsky archives, T 2997; *XV Konferentsiya Vsesoyuznoi Kommunisticheskoi Partii (B)* (1927), pp. 500-501.
[3] *Pravda*, August 15, 1926.
[4] *Izvestiya*, September 28, 1926.
[5] *Voprosy Istorii KPSS*, No. 6, 1959, p. 35.

usual friction between those who thought that they had gone too far and those who thought that they had not gone far enough.[1] The latter view, though not shared by Trotsky himself, was taken by many Trotskyites, as well as by members of the Democratic Centralism and Workers' Opposition groups, who openly preached the formation of a new party. On the other hand, the Zinovievites — or at any rate Zinoviev and Kamenev — put loyalty to the party above all else, and still hoped to propitiate the majority. The excellent harvest, the good progress of the grain collections, and the increase in industrial wages[2] made the attacks of the opposition seem captious and irresponsible. A mood of underlying pessimism was revealed in a remarkable memorandum penned by Trotsky in or about September 1926. This contained the prophecy that the defeat of the united opposition would be followed by " the inevitable conversion into an opposition of the old group in the central committee ". A new quarrel would occur in which " Kaganovich will unmask Rykov, Uglanov Tomsky, and Slepkov, the Stens and co. will dethrone Bukharin ". Trotsky added that " only a hopeless blockhead can fail to see the inevitability of this prospect ".[3]

It may have been some dim consciousness that the situation was moving against them which caused a feverish outburst of activity by the opposition leaders at the end of September 1926, coinciding with the publication in *Bol'shevik* of the " Maizlin " article against Bukharin.[4] Trotsky's first " fractional " appearance was said to have been at the party cell of workers on the Kazan railway on September 30, 1926.[5] On the following day, Radek, Pyatakov, Zinoviev and Trotsky spoke at a party meeting in the Aviapribor factory in Moscow.[6] This initiative quickly provoked official action to nip it in the bud. On October 2, 1926, the

---

[1] A statement by Trotsky evidently intended for publication, minimizing differences within the united opposition, is preserved in the Trotsky archives, T 3003; this may be identical with the leaflet mentioned by Uglanov in *XV Konferentsiya Vsesoyuznoi Kommunisticheskoi Partii (B)* (1927), pp. 626-627.

[2] See Vol. 1, pp. 488-489, 522-523.

[3] Three drafts of this memorandum exist in the Trotsky archives (T 891, 3001, 3002).   [4] For this see Vol. 1, p. 10.

[5] *Voprosy Istorii KPSS*, No. 6, 1959, p. 36.

[6] *Pravda*, October 3, 1926; Molotov and Bukharin thought of attending the meeting, but decided not to (*XV Konferentsiya Vsesoyuznoi Kommunisticheskoi Partii (B)* (1927), p. 670).

Moscow party committee under the leadership of Uglanov, by a majority of 78 to 27, passed a resolution which condemned the Aviapribor demonstration as " a crime against the party ", charged the opposition with seeking " to fasten a discussion on the party ", and invited the party central committee to call the opposition to account.[1] On the following day, the opposition leaders rashly protested to the Politburo against the " bureaucratism " of the Moscow committee and the support given by party policy to the *kulak* and to the petty bourgeoisie;[2] the Politburo at once replied with a decision condemning the appearance of Trotsky, Zinoviev and Pyatakov at the Aviapribor factory as a breach of party discipline, and bringing the offence to the notice of the party central committee and central control commission.[3]

By this time, the failure of the campaign had become evident; and on October 4, 1926, the opposition leaders made what was in effect an appeal for terms of surrender.[4] Zinoviev, however, gained courage, or recknessness, from a desperate situation. On October 7, 1926, he appeared at a party meeting at the Putilov factory in Leningrad and demanded to speak. He was given 15 minutes, and made a " demagogic " appeal for an immediate increase in wages. His speech ended amid shouts of indignation from party stalwarts; and other spokesmen of the opposition were refused a hearing.[5] On the following day, the Politburo took note of " the heretical speech discrediting the party and the central committee " delivered by Zinoviev at the Putilov factory, and condemned this " unheard of violation of the elementary principles of party life ".[6] Other meetings of a similar kind

---

[1] *XV Konferentsiya Vsesoyuznoi Kommunisticheskoi Partii (B) (1927)*, p. 625; the text of the resolution was published in *Pravda*, October 3, 1926, which also gave prominence to the expulsion from the party by the Moscow party control commission of two members, and the censure of two others, for fractional activities.

[2] *XV Konferentsiya Vsesoyuznoi Kommunisticheskoi Partii (B) (1927)*, pp. 497, 625; the text has not been published.

[3] *Spravochnik Partiinogo Rabotnika*, vi (1928), i, 474.

[4] *Bol'shevik*, No. 19-20, October 31, 1926, p. 21; Zinoviev was afterwards reproached with having " made a declaration to the Politburo with a proposal for peace ", and the next day left for Leningrad to agitate against party policy (*XV Konferentsiya Vsesoyuznoi Kommunisticheskoi Partii (B) (1927)*, p. 691).

[5] *Pravda* and *Izvestiya*, October 8, 1926; the official resolution was carried by a majority of 1375 to 25.

[6] *Spravochnik Partiinogo Rabotnika*, vi (1928), i, 474-475.

appear to have been held in other factories. The opposition leaders, in the derisive words of Orjonikidze, " ran from one factory to another, from Moscow to Leningrad, from Leningrad to Moscow ".[1] Discussions behind the scenes were obstinate and uncompromising; and on October 11, 1926, at a further meeting of the Politburo Stalin, premising that " the opposition has suffered a severe defeat ", curtly announced his conditions. The opposition must unconditionally accept decisions of party organs; must openly recognize that its fractional activity had been " erroneous and harmful to the party " ; must disavow supporters at home like Ossovsky, Medvedev and Shlyapnikov; and must disavow supporters abroad like Ruth Fischer, Urbahns and Maslow, and cease to support the fractional struggle against the Comintern line in foreign communist parties. The opposition remained free to express its views within the limits of the party line. Much play was made at these meetings with a letter addressed by Trotsky to his supporters in September 1926 arguing that the proposals of the opposition provided the only " way out from the present severe crisis " ; in fact, the crisis had failed to materialize.[2] Finally, on October 16, 1926, six opposition leaders — Zinoviev, Kamenev, Pyatakov, Sokolnikov, Trotsky and Evdokimov — signed a declaration which appeared in the press on the following day. The economic issues on which the opposition campaign had mainly turned were not touched on, and the opposition was able to believe that it had abandoned no position of principle. But Stalin's conditions — obedience to party decisions, renunciation of fractional activities, and disavowal of supporters — were accepted *in toto*. It fell little short of unconditional surrender.[3] The party central committee recorded

---

[1] *Pyatnadtsatyi S"ezd VKP(B)*, i (1961), 433. *Pravda*, October 8, 1926, reported several meetings of factory cells at which workers had passed resolutions denouncing the opposition; at one of them Evdokimov and Nikolaeva were refused a hearing. According to an official party count, at meetings in Moscow 52,950 party members voted for resolutions condemning the opposition, 171 against, and 87 abstained; in Leningrad the corresponding figures were 33,927, 325 and 126 (*Pravda*, October 17, 1926).

[2] Stalin's speech of October 11, 1926, is in *Sochineniya*, viii, 209-213 (its first publication); Trotsky's letter was quoted by Stalin at the fifteenth party conference from the unpublished records of the two Politburo meetings (*ibid*. viii, 354).

[3] *Pravda*, October 17, 1926; statements of the signatories to the Politburo protesting that they signed " by way of party discipline " are preserved in the

the receipt of this declaration in a long and grudging statement which reviewed the events of the last few weeks, and rubbed salt in the opposition's wounds. This was published in *Pravda* on the same day as the opposition declaration. The two documents marked, in the words of *Pravda*, " the complete, absolute and magnificently sustained victory of the party over the united opposition ".[1]

By an unhappy coincidence for the opposition, this act of submission was followed two days later by the first publication in full, in the *New York Times* of October 18, 1926, of Lenin's so-called testament. There is no proof that Trotsky was privy to the publication, and the timing was almost certainly an accident. But Trotsky had been responsible for divulging the existence of the document to Eastman. Its publication could be regarded as a reversal of his attitude a year earlier when, at the behest of the Politburo, he had denied its authenticity.[2] This occurrence can hardly have failed to inflame Stalin's resentment. The leaders of the opposition had evidently supposed that, by signing the declaration of October 16, 1926, they would escape further controversy and censure at the forthcoming party conference. On or about October 21, 1926, it was decided in the Politburo that theses refuting the views of the opposition should be submitted by Stalin to the conference.[3] Trotsky seems to have felt that the opposition had allowed itself to be tricked into a meaningless surrender which had gained nothing. In an angry scene in the

Trotsky archives, T 896, 897. In a later note of uncertain date directed against the Democratic Centralists Trotsky defended the declaration of October 16, 1926, and declared that anyone who did not accept it " has no right to claim any kind of solidarity with us " (*ibid.*, T 961).   [1] *Pravda*, October 20, 1926.

[2] For the testament see *The Interregnum, 1923–1924*, pp. 258–259, 263 ; for Trotsky's statement of July 1, 1925, see *Socialism in One Country, 1924–1926*, Vol. 2, pp. 64–65. According to Eastman's own account, the text published in 1926 " was copied from the original retained by Krupskaya herself when she turned over the document to the party, and was brought to France by an emissary of the opposition and delivered to Boris Souvarine " (unpublished letter to I. Deutscher of April 20, 1956). Eastman arranged for publication in the *New York Times*. The fee was paid to Souvarine " for the cause of the French opposition " (*Byulleten' Oppozitsii* (Paris), No. 19, March 1931, pp. 38-39) ; this was mentioned at the ninth IKKI in February 1928 as an additional grievance (*Pravda*, February 12, 1928).

[3] The theses were said to have been drafted by Stalin " between October 21 and 25 " (Stalin, *Sochineniya*, viii, 384, note 75, 399).

Politburo he called Stalin " the grave-digger of the revolution ".[1]
The party central committee, meeting on October 23, 1926,
reacted sharply to the growing tension. It had before it a petition
from a delegation of IKKI, signed by representatives of ten
communist parties, asking that Zinoviev should no longer function as head of Comintern.[2] The Committee at once adopted
a resolution censuring Trotsky, Zinoviev, Kamenev, Pyatakov,
Evdokimov, Sokolnikov and Smilga, members of the central
committee, and Nikolaeva, a candidate member, for breaches of
party discipline ; excluding Zinoviev from all work in Comintern ;
and depriving Trotsky of his membership, and Kamenev of his
candidate membership, of the Politburo.[3] The central committee
also approved Stalin's theses on the opposition, which were
published in *Pravda* on October 26, 1926. The theses noted that
the opposition, in spite of its formal submission, had not renounced
" its errors of principle ", and described its views as " a *social-
democratic deviation* in our party on the fundamental question of
the character and prospects of our revolution ". They called for a
" decisive ideological struggle " against this deviation, and for a
recognition by the opposition of the erroneous nature of its
opinions ".[4] Trotsky prophetically observed that the adoption
of these theses by the conference would inevitably lead to the
expulsion of the opposition leaders from the party — a conclusion
which Stalin found it prudent to reject.[5]

When the fifteenth party conference opened on October 26,
1926 — the day of the publication of the theses — the opposition
leaders rather pathetically sought to maintain their interpretation
of the compromise of October 16 by refusing to speak in the
economic debate.[6] While the debate was in progress, negotiations

---

[1] The scene is described from the recollections of Trotsky's wife in V. Serg.,
Vie et Mort de Trotsky (1951), pp. 180-181 (where it is mis-dated 1927).
Exactly what provoked the outburst is conjectural ; but the phrase was certainly
authentic, being quoted by Bukharin a few days later at the conference (*XV
Konferentsiya Vsesoyuznoi Kommunisticheskoi Partii (B)* (1927), p. 578).

[2] *Voprosy Istorii KPSS*, No. 6, 1959, p. 38.

[3] *KPSS v Rezolyutsiyakh* (1954), ii, 290-291 ; the resolution was not
published at the time, though its tenour was known in the party.

[4] The theses are reprinted in Stalin, *Sochineniya*, viii, 214-233.

[5] *Ibid.*, viii, 293.   [6] For this debate see vol. i, p. 11.

were conducted behind the scenes, under the authority of the Politburo, with Shlyapnikov and Medvedev, as the result of which the two dissidents were induced to sign on October 29, 1926, a declaration renouncing their errors. Medvedev's "letter to Baku" was described as containing "a number of grossly erroneous opinions", and the "polemical tone" of Shlyapnikov's article in *Bol'shevik* of September 15, 1926, as "inadmissible". The offenders condemned their own past "fractional" activities, and recognized party decisions as "unconditionally binding". Molotov read this declaration to the party conference, prefaced by a statement from the party central committee and central control commission welcoming this "further collapse of the opposition bloc"; and the declaration and statement appeared on the following day in the press.[1] Then, on November 1, 1926, Stalin finally launched his theses in a speech which turned out to be one of his most comprehensive and relentless denunciations of the united opposition, sparing neither Trotsky's ancient differences with Lenin, nor Zinoviev's and Kamenev's recent tergiversations.[2] The three opposition leaders all spoke in reply. Kamenev, argumentative and cautious, suffered a few mocking interruptions. Trotsky made his last major speech to a party audience in terms of unyielding defiance, and with undiminished oratorical power. He was listened to in silence, and his time was more than once prolonged to enable him to finish. Zinoviev derisively recalled Bukharin's rôle in the Left opposition of 1918. But the tone of his speech was plaintive and pleading; if, he protested, he had been told that it was undesirable "in the interests of peace" for the opposition to offer explanations, he would not have spoken. He was constantly interrupted and in the end howled down.[3] Rudzutak pointed out that the opposition had renounced its fractional activities ("so long as no more fractional activity comes to light"), but not its erroneous views.[4]

---

[1] *XV Konferentsiya Vsesoyuznoi Kommunisticheskoi Partii (B)* (1927), pp. 417-419; *Pravda*, October 31, 1926.

[2] Stalin, *Sochineniya*, viii, 234-297.

[3] For these speeches see *XV Konferentsiya Vsesoyuznoi Kommunisticheskoi Partii (B)* (1927), pp. 463-492, 505-535, 555-577; Trotsky's notes for his speech are in the Trotsky archives, T 3014, and a fuller elaboration of his views at this time was contained in an unpublished memorandum, *ibid.* T 3006.

[4] *XV Konferentsiya Vsesoyuznoi Kommunisticheskoi Partii (B)* (1927), p. 546.

Bukharin made the principal speech in support of Stalin, and outdid his master in coarse and cynical mockery of the fallen foe.[1] Stalin's concluding speech, almost as long as the first and still sharper in tone, dwelt once more on the inconsistencies of the opposition, mocked Trotsky's diagnosis of a " severe crisis ", and brutally completed the discomfiture of his adversaries. In the course of his speech he announced that Krupskaya, who had been associated with the opposition (she had signed the opposition declaration of July 1926), had severed her connexion with it; Krupskaya herself remained silent.[2] The theses were unanimously adopted.[3] At the end of the conference, Kuibyshev, who had succeeded Dzerzhinsky as president of Vesenkha, was replaced as president of the central control Commission by Orjonikidze.[4] The defeat of the opposition was accompanied by disciplinary measures against its supporters. According to a later statement of Yaroslavsky, 88 members of the party were called to account by the Moscow control commission in the autumn of 1926.[5] If, however, sentences of expulsion were pronounced at this time, no publicity was given to them.

The work of harrying the opposition was continued before an international audience when the seventh enlarged IKKI met on November 22, 1926. Zinoviev, by way of complying with the decision of the party central committee, sent a formal letter to the secretariat of IKKI asking to be relieved of his presidency of IKKI and of his other functions in Comintern ; this was read and approved at the first sitting.[6] But he apparently intimated his intention to speak during the session. On December 7, 1926, Stalin delivered a long report on " The ' Russian ' Question ", repeating his indictment of the record, past and recent, of the opposition leaders.[7] At the end of the speech a declaration was read on behalf of the Russian delegation to the effect that an appearance by Zinoviev would be " in substance an appeal to

[1] *Ibid.* pp. 577-604.   [2] Stalin, *Sochineniya*, viii, 298-356.
[3] *XV Konferentsiya Vsesoyuznoi Kommunisticheskoi Partii (B)* (1927), p. 757 ; of " hundreds of thousands " of workers who attended factory meetings in Leningrad after the conference only 27 voted against the resolution, and 69 abstained (S. Kirov, *Izbrannye Stat'i i Rechi* (1944), p. 65).
[4] *Pravda*, November 5, 1926 ; he also became People's Commissar for Rabkrin (see p. 294 below).   [5] *Pravda*, February 1, 1927.
[6] *Puti Mirovoi Revolyutsii* (1927), i, 14-15.
[7] Stalin, *Sochineniya*, ix, 3-61.

IKKI against decisions of the VKP(B) ", and as such " in-
opportune " ; it was recalled that Trotsky had refused to speak at
the fifth congress of Comintern in 1924. Remmele, the KPD
leader, who was in the chair, ruled that it was for the opposition
to decide whether to appear or not.[1] Encouraged by this permission, Zinoviev, Trotsky and Kamenev all spoke — in that
order. Zinoviev dilated for an hour and a half on the incompatibility of " socialism in one country " with the teachings of Marx,
Engels and Lenin, who were copiously quoted, and on the
dangers of degeneration in the party ; he seems to have been
heard without serious interruption.[2] Trotsky argued that the
opposition speeches were not an appeal to IKKI against the party
or a breach of the opposition declaration of October 16, 1926.
He asked for two hours' speaking time, was given one hour, and
was evidently surprised when the president resolutely stopped him
at the end of that time " at the most interesting point " ;[3] he
had in fact said nothing new or particularly effective. Kamenev's
speech was the most coherent of the three — perhaps because he
read it from a prepared paper. He identified the views of the
opposition with Leninism, and was frequently interrupted with
indignant protests.[4] Bukharin answered Trotsky, and Stalin
wound up the debate,[5] his second speech being longer and more
vindictive than his first. The resolution submitted by Stalin, and
unanimously approved by the enlarged IKKI, described the
opposition as representing " a Right danger within the VKP(B),
sometimes masked with Left phrases ", and dwelt on its association with other oppositions, Russian and international ; it specifically endorsed the resolution of the fifteenth party conference
condemning the opposition, which was appended to it as an
annex.[6]

---

[1] *Puti Mirovoi Revolyutsii* (1927), ii, 44 ; for Trotsky's abstention in 1924
see *Socialism in One Country, 1924–1926*, Vol. 2, p. 6, Vol. 3, p. 91.
[2] *Puti Mirovoi Revolyutsii* (1927), ii, 58-83 ; for the duration of the speech
see *ibid.* ii, 104. In a leading article on the following day, *Pravda* denounced
Zinoviev's " attempt to create an *international* platform for all opposition
elements hostile to the VKP " as contrary to the promises made in the declaration
of October 16 (*Pravda*, December 9, 1926).
[3] *Ibid.* ii, 94-106 ; for an excerpt from the undelivered part of the speech see
Trotsky archives, T 3016.   [4] *Puti Mirovoi Revolyutsii* (1927), ii, 193-205.
[5] *Ibid.* ii, 106-121 ; Stalin, *Sochineniya*, ix, 62-151.
[6] *Kommunisticheskii Internatsional v Dokumentakh* (1933), pp. 680-690. A

The last stages of the proceedings were embittered by a trivial scandal. In his second speech Stalin revived a story, which had been rejected by the party central committee at the time (or dismissed as irrelevant — the record was not quite clear on the point), that in April 1917, after the abdication of the Tsar, Kamenev had joined with a group of Siberian exiles in sending a congratulatory telegram to the Grand-Duke Michael as " first citizen of the republic ". Kamenev rose to deny the allegation ; Stasova, formerly secretary of the party central committee, rebutted his denial ; and Stalin repeated the statement. For some minutes the two men stood shouting abuse at each other. Kamenev then declared that he would appeal to the international control commission.[1] A number of testimonies were prepared, supporting or refuting the allegation ; and these were eventually included in the records of the session. The split was strictly on party lines : Kamenev had the support of such well-known dissidents as Zalutsky, Smilga, Medvedev and Shlyapnikov.[2] The dispute never seems to have reached the international control commission. But, coupled with the "grave-digger of the revolution " incident, it illustrated the degree of mutual exasperation between Stalin and the opposition leaders at the end of 1926. The year which had seen the formation of the united opposition and Stalin's almost effortless victory over it had enormously raised his authority and his prestige. He had emerged head and shoulders above the other party leaders, and speculations were current at home and abroad about his outlook and significance. *Le Temps* hailed the downfall of Zinoviev in the summer of 1926 as the end of " the dictatorship of the proletariat " and of " the humiliating tutelage of the Red International ", and as a triumph for Stalin's policy of moderation.[3] Chamberlain told a meeting

---

foreign communist recently arrived in Moscow has left his impressions of the speakers : Bukharin was " pretentious ", Zinoviev " verbose ", Stalin ponderous but impressive, Trotsky " exceptionally intelligent and subtle ", but too " diplomatic ", Kamenev " clear and sober ", but weak in conclusions ; the opposition still seemed unaccountably optimistic (A. Ciliga, *Au Pays du Grand Mensonge* (1938), pp. 17-18.

[1] Stalin, *Sochineniya*, ix, 77 ; *Puti Mirovoi Revolyutsii* (1927), ii, 341-344.
[2] *Ibid.* ii, 352-367 ; a denial of the allegation by Zinoviev, Smilga and Fedorov, all of whom were present at the party conference of April 1917, appeared in the journal of the German opposition (*Mitteilungsblatt* (*Linke Opposition*), No. 3, February 1, 1927).   [3] *Le Temps*, July 27, August 8, 9, 1926.

of the Imperial Conference in London on October 20, 1926, that
Stalin was " the central figure in Russia today ", that he seemed
" very much alive to the necessity of putting his own house in
order ", and that a move " away from internationalism " might be
cautiously expected, at any rate as a long-term prospect.[1] Everywhere Stalin seemed less extreme than Trotsky or Zinoviev, less
truculent, less eager to fan the flames of revolution, a man of the
" golden mean ".[2] In the Soviet Union, where the first revolutionary wave had begun to ebb, this reputation stood him in good
stead, and blunted resistance to his growing monopoly of power.

The winter of 1926–1927 brought a deceptive truce in party
strife. The majority rested on the laurels of its successful
economic policy and of its triumph over the opposition at the
fifteenth party conference; the united opposition discovered no
favourable ground for resuming the struggle. At the Moscow
provincial party conference in January 1927 Yaroslavsky remarked
that " hardly anyone has said a word about the opposition " —
which he professed to regard as a favourable sign — and tried to
fill the gap by denouncing a secret circular distributed in Odessa
by a " group of members of the VKP(B) and VLKSM standing
on the platform of comrade Trotsky ".[3] In the same month
Kamenev lost his last post in Moscow as director of the Lenin
Institute, where he was replaced by Skvortsov-Stepanov,[4] and
was appointed Soviet representative in Rome. The party central
committee, at an unusually peaceful session of February 1927,
passed unanimous resolutions on the organization of industry, the
reduction of retail prices and elections to the Soviets. Two minor
members of the opposition, Nikolaeva and Bakaev, read declarations confessing their past errors and rallying to the opinion of the
majority, thus setting an example which was to be widely followed
in the future.[5] But the undercurrent of animosity and suspicion

---

[1] *Documents on British Foreign Policy*, Series 1 A, ii (1968), 947; for an
earlier diagnosis of Stalin's importance see a Foreign Office memorandum of
June 16, 1926 (*ibid.* ii, 106).
[2] The phrase is quoted from I. Deutscher, *Stalin* (1949), p. 295.
[3] *Pravda*, January 25, 1927.
[4] *Pyatnadtsatyi S"ezd VKP(B)*, ii (1962), 1629, note 98.
[5] The declarations and a leading article on them were published in *Pravda*,

remained, and was stirred by the increasing preoccupation of the party with the menace of the capitalist world. A half-hearted attempt was made to implicate the Trotskyite opposition, through its supporters abroad, in the scandalous revelations in December 1926 of Soviet–German arms transactions — the first tentative charge of disloyalty against the opposition.[1] A letter from Yaroslavsky to Trotsky of February 27, 1927, accused the opposition of encouraging underground conspiratorial activities.[2] The poor showing made by the opposition at the February session of the party central committee, and its evident inclination to seek compromise solutions, disconcerted the rump of the Democratic Centralists led by Sapronov and V. M. Smirnov. In February or March 1927 the group surreptitiously circulated a long memorandum, which reproached the opposition with having " disorganized the revolutionary section of the party " by voting for the majority resolutions, and was far more drastic in tone than any previous utterance. It spoke of " the liquidation of the party which has been successfully begun ", and foresaw the conversion of the central committee into " a peculiar type of Bonapartist government ". It refused to believe in the possibility of a rift in the party leadership between the Centre (" Stalin and Co. ") and the Right (" Rykov, Kalinin etc. "), and regarded this " illusion " as the source of the " waverings and errors " of the united opposition.[3]

The lull was, however, short-lived. Strife flared up again over the affairs of China, which were the subject of a sharp letter

February 15, 1927; for Nikolaeva's declaration see Vol. 1, p. 685. Yaroslavsky later named Krupskaya and Zalutsky with Nikolaeva and Bakaev as having left the opposition at this time (*Pravda*, July 22, 1927). For Krupskaya see pp. 19 above, 30-31 below; Zalutsky announced his secession from the opposition in a statement to the party central committee of March 11, 1927 (*Pyatnadtsatyi S"ezd VKP(B)*, ii (1962), 1646, note 200), but by December 1927 had rejoined it, and was expelled (see p. 49 below). Belenky, one of the ring-leaders of the opposition in July 1926 (see pp. 4-5 above), also recanted (*Pravda*, May 4, 1927).

[1] References to this episode, which will be discussed in a subsequent volume, are found in the Trotsky archives, T 912, 913.

[2] *Ibid*. T 924; for Trotsky's reply see T 929.

[3] Two versions of the memorandum are in the Trotsky archives, T 963, 964, the latter being a signed version dated June 27, 1927; Yaroslavsky in *Pravda*, July 22, 1927, dated the circulation of the first draft February-March 1927. For its presentation to the party central committee see p. 26 below.

from Trotsky to the Politburo and the party central committee
on March 31, 1927. During the next two months the situation
in China went from bad to worse, and Trotsky bombarded the
Politburo and the party central committee with protests.[1] The
secretariat withheld the stenographic record of Stalin's speech on
China delivered to the Moscow party organization on April 5,
1927; and Trotsky's indignant and unavailing demands for it
were reinforced by the complaint that he had been refused the
record of the session of the party central committee of July 1926.[2]
An article in *Pravda* on April 29, 1927, attacked Radek's views on
China and " the opposition headed by Radek ", without naming
any other names. On May 12, 1927, the Politburo decided not to
publish articles submitted by Trotsky on the Chinese situation
to *Pravda* and *Bol'shevik;* this was taken as proof that " the
Politburo does not want discussion ".[3] Meanwhile the opposition
renewed its campaign of protest. On May 9, 1927, Zinoviev at a
mass meeting in honour of the fifteenth anniversary of *Pravda*
broached the issue of party dissensions, and blamed *Pravda* for
boycotting the views of the opposition.[4] On the next day the
bureau of the Moscow party committee passed a resolution
denouncing Zinoviev's speech, and this was followed by a similar
resolution of the Leningrad party committee. Finally, the party
central committee came out with a resolution condemning
Zinoviev's action as a breach of the opposition's undertaking of
October 16, 1926, and referring it to the central control commission.[5]

A few days later the meeting of the eighth enlarged IKKI,
which opened on May 18, 1927, offered the opposition an occasion
for a further assault on official policies before an international

[1] The Chinese question will be discussed in a subsequent volume.

[2] Trotsky archives, T 943, 944.   [3] *Ibid.* T 3059.

[4] The text of the speech was not published, but it was frequently referred to
in subsequent controversy, e.g. by Orjonikidze at the fifteenth party congress
(*Pyatnadtsatyi S"ezd VKP(B)*, i (1961), 434, cf. *ibid.* ii, 1652, note 244); a
particular cause of offence was that non-party people were present at the
meeting.

[5] These resolutions, with protests from various other bodies, all appeared in
Pravda, May 13, 1927; the bureau of the Komsomol central committee issued
a similar resolution (*Spravochnik Partiinogo Rabotnika*, vi (1928), ii, 151).
Krupskaya apparently wrote to Zinoviev reproaching the opposition with
" fractiousnesss " (buza); Trotsky sent a reply defending the opposition
attitude (Trotsky archives, T 951).

audience. Bukharin was in charge of the proceedings, and reported on the Chinese question. Trotsky delivered two caustic speeches, and found his main supporter in the Yugoslav delegate, Vuiovič. Stalin, who had contemptuously absented himself during Trotsky's first speech, retorted that IKKI could not afford to convert its work on more important issues into " work on the question of Trotsky ",[1] and replied with a long and laboured defence of party policy in China. A resolution passed at the end of the session declared that the attitude of Trotsky and Vuiovič was incompatible with membership of IKKI, and formally empowered the presidium to expel them if their fractional activities continued.[2] Bukharin, in a report to the Moscow party committee on the proceedings, declared that Trotsky and Vuiovič, for all their criticisms, had " made literally not a single practical proposal ". His speech broadened out into a general attack on the opposition and on Trotsky, going back to his differences with Lenin in 1917, and at the end of the meeting a resolution was passed demanding the expulsion of Trotsky and Zinoviev from the central committee.[3]

It was while this stormy session was in progress that the united opposition launched its most impressive pronouncement to date — a declaration signed by 83 leading members of the opposition. This was forwarded to the Politburo on May 26, 1927, with a covering letter signed by Evdokimov, Zinoviev, Smilga and Trotsky, two members of each wing of the united opposition.[4] Though the covering letter showed that it had been

[1] Stalin, *Sochineniya*, ix, 282-283 ; the speeches of Trotsky, which were omitted from the unpublished stenographic record on the plea that they had been sent to Trotsky for correction and not returned in time (Trotsky archives, T 958), are preserved *ibid.* T 3061, and were published in *Die Fahne des Kommunismus*, No. 15, June 24, 1927.

[2] *Kommunisticheskii Internatsional v Dokumentakh* (1933), p. 745 ; a protest against this resolution as " an indubitable and incontestable Rightist deviation from Marxism, from Leninism ", is in the Trotsky archives, T 3060, and was published in *Die Fahne des Kommunismus*, No. 15, June 24, 1927. The proceedings of the session will be discussed in a subsequent volume.

[3] *Pravda*, June 18, 1927 ; the report was delivered on June 4, 1927. For Manuilsky's report to the party *aktiv* in Leningrad see *Leningradskaya Pravda*, June 4, 1927 ; Trotsky complained that, in spite of a ban on a publication of speeches delivered at the session, Manuilsky had quoted passages from his speech (Trotsky archives, T 959).

[4] The declaration and the covering letter are in the Trotsky archives T 941,

written under the impulse of the Chinese fiasco and the breach of
relations with Great Britain, the declaration also dealt with a
variety of economic questions,[1] demanded full publicity for the
opposition platform in advance of the forthcoming party congress,
and denounced the campaign against Zinoviev's speech of May
9, 1927, as a prelude to an attempt to remove him from the party
central committee. It accused the party leaders of substituting
" the petty bourgeois ' theory of socialism in one country ' " for
" a Marxist analysis of the real situation of the proletarian
dictatorship in the USSR ", and of favouring " Rightist, non-
proletarian and anti-proletarian elements " inside and outside the
party.

The declaration of the 83, which was *prima facie* a breach of
the opposition undertaking to abandon fractional activities, was
afterwards recognized as a landmark;[2] and from this point the
struggle continued almost without intermission to the final climax.
The declaration prompted the Democratic Centralists to forward
their protest, which mustered 15 signatures, to the party central
committee;[3] and a document prepared by a " buffer group ",
which still believed in the possibility of reconciliation with the
majority, circulated in opposition circles, and secured 40 signatures; it was finally communicated to the central committee in
the latter part of July 1927.[4] Acute nervousness about foreign

955; both were published in German translation in a pamphlet *Der Kampf um
die Kommunistische Internationale* (1927), pp. 149-164. The declaration was
open for further signatures throughout the summer; according to an opposition
letter to the Politburo of October 18, 1927, published in *Die Fahne des Kommunismus*, No. 35, November 11, 1927, 863 additional signatures were obtained.
Kamenev at the fifteenth party congress in December 1927 claimed " about
3000 signatures "; but Uglanov retorted that half the signatories had withdrawn
(*Pyatnadtsatyi S"ezd VKP(B)*, i (1961), 284).

[1] See Vol. 1, pp. 24-25, 687.

[2] Trotsky defended it, in a letter of August 12, 1927, to an unidentified
correspondent abroad (probably Krestinsky or Antonov-Ovseenko), who
thought it needlessly provocative (Trotsky archives, T 996); and Zinoviev also
defended it in a cautious vein (*ibid.* T 957).

[3] Slepkov in *Pravda*, July 9, 1927, dated it June 2, 1927; the final copy in
the Trotsky archives (see p. 23, note 3 above) is dated June 27, 1927.

[4] This document was referred to in Yaroslavsky's series of articles in *Pravda*
(see p. 30 below), and its delivery to the central committee reported in the last
of them.

affairs, and the fear of foreign intervention, mounted throughout the summer; and, for the first time for more than two years, a shortage of foodstuffs was experienced in the cities.[1] Covert reprisals against the opposition were multiplied; many of its supporters were quietly assigned to remote posts at home or abroad.[2] When on June 9, 1927, Smilga left Moscow to take up an appointment at Khabarovsk, so large a crowd collected at the Yaroslavl station to see him off that the occasion turned into a public demonstration of sympathy for the opposition; and both Zinoviev and Trotsky addressed the multitude.[3] Any indication of mass support for the opposition struck the party leaders in a sensitive spot, and counter-action was decided on. Zinoviev and Trotsky were indicted before the party central control commission by Shkiryatov and Yaroslavsky, both faithful Stalinists and members of the commission, who proposed their expulsion from the party central committee. A leading article in *Pravda* openly accused the opposition of disloyalty to the Soviet state.[4]

On June 24, 1927, Zinoviev and Trotsky appeared before the presidium of the central control commission. Both were in a fighting mood. Nothing is known of Zinoviev's speech except

[1] See Vol. 1, pp. 699-700.

[2] The memorandum by Trotsky cited in note 4 below named members of the opposition assigned to diplomatic posts abroad : Krestinsky was in Berlin, Rakovsky, Pyatakov, Preobrazhensky and V. Kosior in Paris, Kamenev and Glebov-Avilov in Rome, Antonov-Ovseenko and Kanatchikov in Prague ; Ufimtsev and Semashko in Vienna, Kopp in Stockholm, Mdivani in Paris, Kollontai in Mexico and Kraevsky in Argentina. A letter from Zinoviev, Evdokimov, and Trotsky of June 29, 1927, to the party central committee protested against the number of members of the opposition in diplomatic posts (quoted in *Bol'shevik* No. 23-24, December 31, 1928, p. 15) ; and Zinoviev in a letter of August 27, 1927, protested against the appointment of Safarov to Constantinople (Trotsky archives, T 999).

[3] The incident was cited in the resolution of the party central committee of August 9, 1927 (see pp. 32-33 below). In a letter to a correspondent of July 16, 1927, Trotsky denied rumours that he had made a speech attacking " the dictatorship of usurpers " ; his " speech " had been confined to the words : " The dangers to our country are great, the times are difficult, and each of us must be a doubly faithful son of Lenin's revolutionary party " (Trotsky archives, T 980). A report in the party archives put the crowd at no more than 300 (*Voprosy Istorii KPSS*, No. 5, 1958, p. 136).

[4] *Pravda*, June 22, 1927. A long reply by Trotsky on behalf of the opposition, pointing out that the attack rested on " the identification of the socialist state with the Stalinist group ", is in the Trotsky archives, T 3075 (for another copy with amendments by Zinoviev and Evdokimov, dated July 1, 1927, see *ibid.* T 970) ; there is no evidence whether it was ever despatched.

that he attacked Stalin's policy on the national question, presumably with reference to Lenin's still unpublished notes on the subject.[1] Trotsky, brushing aside the formal charges, which seem to have been confined to the appeal to IKKI and the incident at the Yaroslavl station, accused the commission of " exploiting the danger of war in order to harry the opposition and prepare for its break-up ". The most novel and striking passage in his speech was an approach from a fresh angle to the analogy of the French revolution and the alleged Soviet thermidor. Solts, a leading member of the commission, had remarked that the declaration of the 83 was liable to lead " to arrests and the guillotine ". Trotsky, pursuing the analogy, reminded his audience that the then " thermidorians and Bonapartists — the Right Jacobins " — had begun to shoot " the Left Jacobins — the then Bolsheviks ", and he asked Solts " which chapter you propose to open by the destruction of the opposition ". It was a bold and dangerous fantasy; and in a second speech delivered in reply to the debate Trotsky seemed concerned to attenuate the analogy with the French revolution.[2] The proceedings ended with a resolution of the presidium reviewing the misdeeds of the opposition, and in particular the breaches by Zinoviev and Trotsky of the undertaking of October 16, 1926, to renounce fractional activities, and submitting to the coming joint session of the party central committee and control commission " the question of the removal of comrades Zinoviev and Trotsky from membership of the central committee of the VKP(B) ".[3] Trotsky multiplied

---

[1] Extracts from Zinoviev's speech were quoted from an unpublished stenographic record of the session in *Pravda*, September 7, 1927.

[2] Both speeches were published in a much abbreviated form in L. Trotsky, *Stalinskaya Shkola Falsifikatsii* (Berlin, 1932), pp. 133-164; according to a note by Trotsky, passages were omitted which " could not have been comprehensible to the foreign reader without detailed explanations ". Fuller texts from the original stenographic record are preserved in the Trotsky archives, T 3160 (though Trotsky afterwards referred to " enormous omissions and distortions " in the stenographic record — see *ibid.* T 967). In the stenographic version of the first speech, Trotsky insisted that there was a concerted plan to expel Zinoviev and himself from the central committee; Yaroslavsky had been at work long before the affair of the Yaroslavl station.

[3] *Pravda*, June 26, 1927; the same issue carried a leading article entitled " A Warning ", which accused the opposition of treating the declaration of October 16, 1926, as " a scrap of paper ".

his protests. In a letter to the party central committee of June 27, 1927, he denounced the attempt to solve the party crisis by " mechanical repression of the opposition ", and indignantly noted that " *the central committee is openly resorting to the aid of the state apparatus against members of the party* " ;[1] and on the following day, in a letter to Orjonikidze, while purporting to recognize that the eradication of the opposition from the party was only a matter of time, he protested against rumours said to have been spread by Shkiryatov of an intention to expel Trotsky and 20 of his supporters.[2] From this time the press began to report resolutions of local party organizations demanding the expulsion of Trotsky and Zinoviev.[3]

The argument most calculated to excite prejudice against the opposition was the charge that it was seeking to weaken the Soviet power in face of a hostile capitalist world. Trotsky, in a letter to Orjonikidze of July 11, 1927, attempted to dispel this prejudice by invoking a famous precedent :

> The French bourgeoisie at the beginning of the imperialist war had at its head a government without rudder and without sails. The group of Clemenceau was in opposition to this government. Notwithstanding the war and the war censorship, notwithstanding the fact that the Germans were within 80 kilometres of Paris (Clemenceau said: " Precisely because of this "), he waged a furious struggle against bourgeois feebleness and indecision and for imperialist ferocity and ruthlessness. Clemenceau did not betray his class, the bourgeoisie ; on the contrary, he served it more faithfully, more firmly, more decisively, more intelligently than Viviani, Painlevé and co. The further course of events proved this. The group of Clemenceau came to power and by a more consistent, more unscrupulous, imperialist policy secured victory for the French bourgeoisie.[4]

The vision of a resolute and efficient Trotsky replacing a bungling and rudderless Stalinist government was provocative ; and for many months Trotsky was exposed to the taunt of hoping for an attack on the Soviet Union by the capitalist nations, which would

[1] Trotsky archives, T 3074.   [2] *Ibid.* T 965.
[3] See, for example, *Pravda*, July 6, 1927.
[4] Quoted in Stalin, *Sochineniya*, x, 52.

afford him the longed for opportunity to seize power.[1] While
Trotsky was aggressive and arrogant, Zinoviev showed the usual
symptoms of indecision. In a feeble attempt to demonstrate his
orthodoxy, and ingratiate himself with the authorities, he wrote an
article against Ustryalov and Kondratiev, which was published,
with a contemptuous editorial note, in the issue of *Bol'shevik* for
July 15, 1927.[2]

The party central committee was to meet at the end of July
1927; and the heat was now on. Slepkov denounced the " new "
platform of the Democratic Centralists, which he branded as
" neo-Menshevism ".[3] Yaroslavsky, in a series of four massive
articles in *Pravda*, took the whole opposition movement since
October 1926 as his target.[4] Maretsky refuted the slander of a
Soviet thermidor.[5] The claim of the opposition to represent the
original Bolshevik standpoint prompted the bureau of the Society
of Old Bolsheviks to issue a statement dissociating itself from the
views of the opposition leaders and demanding their expulsion
from the party central committee.[6] The session of the committee,
which lasted from July 29 to August 9, 1927, was evidently as
arduous as it was prolonged, though its records have not been
published and its course cannot be followed in detail. The
major debate was on international affairs. Theses were put forward by Bukharin, and counter-theses by Zinoviev. Both Trotsky
and Stalin spoke on August 1, 1927.[7] Trotsky's speech was not
lacking in provocation. He attacked Bukharin, Stalin and Molotov,
and ended with the dramatic exclamation : " For the socialist
fatherland ? Yes. For the Stalin line ? No. " On the next
day Krupskaya in mild but unambiguous terms dissociated
herself from the opposition. Some comrades were so concerned

---

[1] Trotsky attempted to answer this charge in a long unpublished memorandum of September 24, 1927, in the Trotsky archives, T 3092.

[2] For the article and the note see Vol. 1, p. 31.

[3] *Pravda*, July, 9, 12, 1927.   [4] *Ibid.* July 22, 23, 24, 26, 1927.

[5] *Ibid.* July 24, 29, 1927 ; a promised continuation did not appear, probably
because the topic had been sufficiently ventilated in the central committee.
For the controversy about a Soviet thermidor see pp. 427-428 below.

[6] *Izvestiya*, August 3, 1927.

[7] For a brief extract from Zinoviev's speech and his counter-theses see the
Trotsky archives, T 987, 988. Trotsky's speech is in L. Trotsky, *Stalinskaya
Shkola Falsifikatsii* (Berlin, 1932), pp. 165-179 (omitting a final paragraph, which
is in the Trotsky archives, T 3080), Stalin's in *Sochineniya*, x, 3-59.

with " this or that negative fact " that " they do not see the
construction that is going on in the country ". The opposition
was divorced from " real life ", and had " no roots in the masses " :
this was why the masses refused to follow it. In the previous year,
at a time of " marked stabilization ", she had supported the
opposition in its effort to draw attention to certain dangers. Now,
in the hour of danger from without, it was necessary to rally round
the authority of the party central committee.[1] Manuilsky compared Trotsky with Barère, and turned the tables by accusing
him of preparing a thermidor.[2] Molotov alleged that the opposition favoured only " conditional defence " of the fatherland, and
that its policy aimed at " insurrection against the party and the
Soviet power ".[3] After these controversial demonstrations, the
theses were duly adopted.[4] It was perhaps significant that the
issues of substance on which the battle was joined now related
mainly or exclusively to international affairs. On domestic
issues of economic policy, the rift between the majority and the
opposition was insensibly narrowing and becoming unreal.

The most bitter struggle turned, however, on the charges
against Trotsky and Zinoviev of violating party discipline, which
were the last item on the agenda ; to censure, and eventually to
expel, his rivals and critics had now become Stalin's major
objective. The tactics were those which had proved successful
in October 1926 — to wrest the maximum concessions from the
dissidents by holding out to them the hope of an agreement, and
then to pronounce the concessions inadequate ; and, while Trotsky
may have seen through the manœuvre, Zinoviev fell an easy
victim, and drew Trotsky with him along this barren path.
Zinoviev and Stalin both spoke on August 5, 1927, and Trotsky
on the following day.[5] Zinoviev was accused by Stalin of " gross

---

[1] The speech was featured prominently, and apparently verbatim, in *Pravda*,
August 3, 1927.   [2] Trotsky archives, T 3083.
[3] For a protest of 13 members of the opposition against this charge see *ibid.*
T 993.   [4] *KPSS v Rezolyutsiakh* (1954), ii, 359-372.
[5] Zinoviev's speech is not available ; he was quoted as having said that the
opposition differed from the majority on " theoretical, political, international,
economic, inner-party, Comintern and organizational " questions (*Pyatnadtsatyi
S"ezd VKP(B)*, i (1961), 195), and accused Stalin of following an incorrect
policy in the national question and of a " centrist " attitude, balancing between
Right and Left (*Pravda*, September 7, 1927). Stalin's speech is in *Sochineniya*,
x, 60-84, Trotsky's in the Trotsky archives, T 3085.

disloyalty " in attempting to return in his speech to the issues of
foreign policy which had already been disposed of ; and Trotsky
was constantly interrupted by demands to stick to the point. The
debate was carried on, in an increasingly tense atmosphere, by
lesser contenders. Finally, as the result of this fierce struggle, the
opposition was induced, on August 8, 1927, to make a declaration
under three heads. It vindicated the unconditional loyalty of the
opposition to the national defence of the Soviet Union and to the
international rôle of the workers' state, and dissociated itself from
the charge that the party leadership had entered a stage of
thermidorian degeneration, though it continued to detect " thermidorian elements " in the situation ; it denounced attempts to
create a dissident communist party in Germany ; and it categorically rejected all policies tending to create a second party in the
Soviet Union or to split the VKP(B). On this basis it called for a
cessation of repressive measures against the opposition, and for a
period of orderly preparation for the forthcoming fifteenth party
congress.[1] On the next day Stalin grudgingly went through the
declaration line by line, stressing every ambiguity, every reserva-
tion with which the opposition had tried to mitigate its humiliation ; the opposition had, he admitted, made a " retreat ", but
what it offered was not " peace in the party ", but " a temporary
armistice ".[2] Trotsky complained briefly — and in vain — that
the opposition declaration had been split into two halves : what
it conceded had been taken, what it asked in return was rejected.[3]

The resolution adopted on the same day " On the Violation of
Party Discipline by Zinoviev and Trotsky " revealed Stalin's
masterful hand. It rehearsed in detail the sins of the opposition
since 1923, and especially since October 16, 1926, when the united
opposition had professed to renounce its fractional activities. The
committee summoned the opposition to abandon the " semi-
defeatist " attitude implicit in Trotsky's " Clemenceau " thesis

[1] The declaration was published with the resolutions of the session in *Pravda*,
August 10, 1927. Trotsky later compared the declaration of August 8, 1927,
with the declaration of October 16, 1926 (both in essence documents of surrender),
as turning-points in the history of the united opposition (Trotsky archives,
T 3109). The diplomatic incident arising from Rakovsky's signature of the
declaration will be described in a subsequent volume.

[2] Stalin, *Sochineniya*, x, 85-91.

[3] Trotsky archives, T 3086.

and the slander about a thermidorian degeneration in the party
and the government, and to desist from its attempts to split
Comintern and to split the Russian party; it was in response to
this summons that the opposition had made its declaration of
August 8. While far from regarding this as adequate, the central
committee believed that it might " constitute a certain step towards
peace in the party ". It therefore decided to remove from the
agenda the question of the expulsion of Zinoviev and Trotsky
from the committee, and to substitute for it " a severe reprimand
and warning ". The remainder of the resolution was occupied
with warnings of the consequences of any further breach of
discipline.[1] The resolution, according to a later statement of
Orjonikidze, was forced with difficulty on a reluctant central
committee, which would unanimously have preferred immediate
expulsion.[2] Party meetings in Moscow and Leningrad, the former
addressed by Rykov, the latter by Bukharin, endorsed the decision
of the central committee and condemned the opposition; in
Moscow the resolution was voted unanimously, in Leningrad by
a majority of 3500 to 6.[3] The central committee of the Komsomol
greeted the decision in enthusiastic terms, and accused the
opposition of trying to build up a Trotskyite fraction in the
Komsomol.[4]

In opposition circles, the resolution was variously judged.
Zinoviev welcomed it in a characteristically extravagant outburst
of wishful thinking.[5] Radek believed that fear of opinion " in
broad sections of the party activists and the party bureaucracy "
had prevented Stalin from expelling Zinoviev and Trotsky from
the central committee.[6] On the other hand, Joffe, in a letter to
Trotsky of August 12, 1927, expressed strong disapproval both of
the manner and of the matter of the opposition declaration of
August 8, and foresaw no favourable ending.[7] Trotsky himself
drew the conclusion that the danger resided both in the Right

---

[1] *KPSS v Rezolyutsiyakh* (1954), ii, 387-394.
[2] *Pyatnadtsatyi S"ezd VKP(B)*, i (1961), 435.
[3] *Pravda*, August 12, 1927.
[4] *Oppozitsiya i Komsomol* (1927), pp. 133-143.
[5] See the draft of a speech in the Trotsky archives, T 995; it does not
appear for what occasion it was designed, or whether it was ever delivered.
[6] *Ibid.* T 998.
[7] Trotsky archives, T 994.

wing of the party (Rykov, Kalinin, Voroshilov, Sokolnikov) and in
the centre (Stalin), and put no faith in a rift between them.[1] The
cleavage between the two sectors of the opposition grew sharper.
A letter from the Zinovievites of August 15, 1927, contained
a thinly veiled warning against " light-hearted and adventurous
tactics " which might lead to the ultimate disaster of " the
exclusion of the opposition from the party ". The Trotsky group
on August 30, 1927, reproached its partner with reluctance " to
disarm in the struggle against an imaginary Trotskyism ".[2] On
the eve of its severest ordeal, the opposition no longer spoke with
a united voice.

The party central committee had fixed December 1, 1927, for
the opening of the fifteenth party congress.[3] An article by
Yaroslavsky, significantly entitled " The Party will not Repeat
the Mistake of 1920 ", tellingly recalled an occasion on which
Lenin, criticizing Trotsky's view of the trade unions, pointed to
the harm done by a "broad " discussion of the question.[4] Trotsky,
undeterred by the portents, confidently set to work to prepare
an opposition " platform " for the congress, which was delivered
to the party central committee early in September. On September
6, 1927, the opposition addressed a communication to the Politburo
and the central committee. It protested against the continued
persecution to which members of the opposition were subjected,
including the interruption of their meetings by hooligans;
demanded the return of banished members of the opposition
to participate in the pre-congress debate; and requested that the
" platform ", which bore the signature of 13 opposition leaders,
should be printed and circulated with other documents in advance
of the congress.[5] The platform was submitted to a joint meeting

[1] Memorandum " On the Results of the August Plenum " in Trotsky
archives, T 998; an extract was published in *Byulleten' Oppozitsii* (Paris), No.
3-4, September 1929, p. 35.
[2] These letters, which are not otherwise known, were quoted in the statement
of Zinoviev and Kamenev in *Pravda*, January 27, 1928 (see p. 54 below).
[3] *KPSS v Rezolyutsiyakh* (1954), ii, 394.
[4] *Pravda*, August 10, 1927.
[5] Trotsky archives, T 1010; a draft is preserved *ibid*. T 1007, and a printed
copy, apparently damaged by fire, *ibid*. T 1008. The platform was published

of the Politburo and the party central control commission on September 8, 1927, at which Stalin delivered a long speech, and the opposition was denied the right to reply. A decision was apparently taken to bring the platform to the knowledge of the party.[1] This was tantamount to a refusal to distribute the document in the usual way, and the opposition prepared to circulate its platform illicitly.

The authorities reacted swiftly. On September 11, 1927, *Pravda* published a leading article which described the opposition demand to " legalize their fraction before the congress and give it the right to act as it pleases " as " simply ridiculous ", and made it clear that the pre-congress rights of the opposition would be restricted to the presentation of counter-theses to the official theses. On the night of September 12–13, 1927, the OGPU unearthed in the house of one Sherbakov, a non-party man, an illicit press which was being used to duplicate the opposition platform. Four or more party members, including Mrachkovsky, Preobrazhensky and Serebryakov, were found to be implicated. Among those engaged in the work was a former Wrangel officer ; this was held to justify the description of the affair as " a military conspiracy ". These facts were reported by the OGPU to the central control commission of the party on September 13, 1927. On September 23, 1927, before any disciplinary action had been taken, Zinoviev, Smilga and Petersen wrote to the central control commission asking to be informed of the identity of the former Wrangel officer and whether he had been arrested ; the OGPU admitted in reply that he was one of their regular informants.[2] On September 28, 1927, the presidium of the Moscow party control commission expelled from the party 14 members involved, including Mrachkovsky, who " directed the work of the illegal printing-press " : it was an aggravation of the offence that " non-party bourgeois intellectuals " had participated in the

in an English translation in L. Trotsky, *The Real Situation in Russia* (n.d. [1928]), pp. 23-195 ; according to *Pyatnadtsatyi S"ezd VKP(B)*, ii (1962), 1649, note 224, it was delivered on September 3, 1927.

[1] Trotsky archives, T 1015, 1027 ; no records of this meeting were published.

[2] This account is taken from the opposition protest to the Politburo of October 1, 1927 (see p. 37, note 1 below) ; for Stalin's cynical admission that the " Wrangel officer " was an OGPU agent see *Sochineniya*, x, 187. The opposition continued to issue a daily bulletin in some form down to the time of the fifteenth party congress (*Pyatnadtsatyi S"ezd VKP(B)*, i (1961), 145, 431).

work.[1] The party central control commission, to which the resolution was submitted for confirmation, approved it, merely substituting a " severe reprimand " for expulsion in the cases of two minor offenders.[2] Preobrazhensky, Serebryakov and Sharov, who were not among the 14, now made a statement to the control commission accepting a share of responsibility for the printing-press ;[3] and a few days later the two first were also expelled from the party.[4] Mrachkovsky, who was treated as the ringleader, was arrested by the OGPU. These events appear to have aroused some popular excitement. An observer reported that " people are again gathering in groups in the streets and openly blaming the authorities ".[5]

Meanwhile, on September 27, 1927, the presidium of IKKI held a dramatic meeting which lasted from 9.30 p.m. to 5 a.m. Trotsky who spoke for two hours, delivered a flaming indictment of Stalin's policies at home and in Comintern. Stalin replied in a predictable vein, and was followed by Bukharin, Thälmann, Manuilsky and Kuusinen. Trotsky devoted a brief second speech, in reply to Kuusinen's attack, to the story of his relations with Lenin. A resolution to exclude Trotsky from IKKI was proposed by Murphy, a long-standing but undistinguished member of the CPGB, who himself a few years later left the party; it was carried with two dissentients.[6] A resolution expelling Rakovsky and Vuiovič from IKKI was then carried without dissent: Trotsky was said to have refused to submit to the discipline of the party, and Vuiovič to have declared in advance that he would not recognize the decisions of the forth-coming party congress.[7] The opposition continued to press its challenge. On October 1, 1927, Smilga, Bakaev, Evdokimov, Zinoviev and Trotsky wrote to the Politburo demanding a special

[1] *Pravda* and *Izvestiya*, September 29, 1927 ; this was the first mention of the affair in the press.
[2] *Pravda*, September 30, 1927.
[3] *Pyatnadtsatyi S"ezd VKP(B)*, i (1961), 435.
[4] *Pravda*, October 13, 1927 ; an undated protest by Preobrazhensky against his expulsion is in the Trotsky archives, T 1005.
[5] *Sotsialisticheskii Vestnik* (Berlin), No. 19(161), October 7, 1927, p. 14.
[6] The scene is described in J. T. Murphy, *New Horizons* (1941), pp. 274-277 ; Trotsky's speeches are in the Trotsky archives, T 3094, 3095, Stalin's in *Sochineniya*, x, 153-167.
[7] *Pravda*, October 1, 1927 ; Trotsky archives, T 1018.

commission to investigate the charges arising out of the discovery of the secret printing-press; and a few days later the opposition issued a manifesto " to all members of the party " calling for the publication of documents.[1] About this time mass defections from the opposition were announced in the press. *Pravda* of October 11, 1927, under the heading " The Trotskyite Opposition Disintegrates ", printed declarations by six party members (all but one of them workers) renouncing their association with the opposition. The same issue announced the defection from the opposition of 25 members of the Georgian party, and the discovery of " an underground fractional group " in the North Caucasian region, leading to the expulsion of two members and the recantation of six others.[2]

The situation was now overshadowed by the approaching celebrations of the tenth anniversary of the revolution. When the TsIK of the USSR met in Leningrad on October 15, 1927, Trotsky and Zinoviev clashed with the party majority over the seven-hour day — unfavourable ground on which to fight.[3] At the demonstrations which followed the session, when crowds of workers filed past tribunes filled with party and Soviet celebrities, Trotsky and Zinoviev, by accident or design, mounted a tribune a little apart from the rest; and the crowds, whether out of curiosity or of sympathy, gathered round them, abandoning the official leaders.   Trotsky and Zinoviev are said to have accepted this as an omen of mass support for the opposition.[4] These hopes proved illusory. The joint session of the party central committee and central control commission of October 21–23, 1927, found the party leadership poised for a fresh assault. On the eve of the meeting *Pravda* accused the opposition of creating the apparatus of a new party.[5] The principal business of the session was to

[1] Trotsky archives, T 1019, 1021; the letter to the Politburo and the manifesto were published in translation in *The New International* (N.Y.), November 1934, pp. 120-124.

[2] For other defections see *Pravda*, September 27, October 12, 1927; *Izvestiya*, October 11, 1927, listed more than 20 signatories of the declaration of the 83 who had dissociated themselves from it.   [3] See Vol. 1, pp. 497-498.

[4] The scene is described in L. Trotsky, *Moya Zhizn'* (Berlin, 1930), ii, 278 ; V. Serge, *Le Tournant Obscur* (1951), pp. 112-113.

[5] *Pravda*, October 20, 1927 ; a defector from the opposition was said to have revealed the existence in the Urals of an organized Trotskyite group dating back to 1924 (*ibid.* November 23, 1927).

approve theses for presentation to the fifteenth party congress
on work in the countryside and on the five-year plan.[1] But it
also had before it the question of the limits of discussion in the
party in preparation for the coming party congress, and a proposal
to expel Trotsky and Zinoviev from the party central committee.
On the very day when the session opened, Trotsky, indefatigable
as ever, took advantage of what was apparently a routine question-
naire from the bureau of party history about the personal participation of members of the party in the October revolution to send to
it a detailed and scorching exposure of " a few dozen examples "
of the slanders and distortions to which his revolutionary record
had been exposed in party polemics. Trotsky was able to produce
many documents showing himself in alliance with Lenin at one
time or another against almost all the other party leaders, and
concluded with an account of Lenin's final break with Stalin, and
with a curt but fierce denunciation of his rival.[2] This broadside
was bound to inflame an already super-charged atmosphere.

At this joint session Smilga and Evdokimov, who spoke for
the opposition on the economic issues, were constantly interrupted.[3]
Menzhinsky, Dzerzhinsky's successor as head of the OGPU,
reported on the illegal activities of the opposition and its alleged
plans for armed insurrection.[4] On the third day of the session,
Stalin introduced the proposal to expel Trotsky and Zinoviev
from the central committee. Conscious of his strength, and
determined to use it ruthlessly, he opened with a striking
manœuvre. By way of forestalling the sneers of the opposition,
he quoted the passage in the postscript to Lenin's testament
directed against himself. While Lenin had criticized the political
and ideological errors of other leaders, Stalin had been accused
only of " rudeness ". " Yes, comrades," Stalin now retorted, " I
am rude in regard to those who rudely and treacherously destroy
and split the party."[5] The remainder of the speech, the most
personal and most vindictive attack on which he had yet ventured,

---

[1] See Vol. 1, pp. 35, 870-871.
[2] *Stalinskaya Shkola Falsifikatsii* (Berlin, 1932), pp. 13-100; an English
translation is in L. Trotsky, *The Real Situation in Russia* (n.d. [1928]), pp.
199-315.   [3] See Vol. 1, p. 35.
[4] *Voprosy Istorii KPSS*, No. 6, 1959, p. 40.
[5] Stalin, *Sochineniya*, x, 175; for the postscript to the testament see *The
Interregnum, 1923–1924*, p. 263.

illustrated this thesis and set the tone for the debate. Zinoviev's and Trotsky's speeches were broken up by constant jeering interruptions. While Trotsky was speaking, a glass was thrown at him from the tribune (" it is said, by comrade Kubyak "). Yaroslavsky hurled a volume of the control figures at his head ; another volume was thrown at him by Shvernik during Bukharin's subsequent speech.[1] Rakovsky intended to speak on the French diplomatic crisis ; but the debate was closed before his turn came.[2] After the turmoil, the central committee unanimously adopted two resolutions. The first referred to the opposition platform and to the decision of the Politburo of September 8, 1927, to make it available to members of the party, but limited the rights of the opposition to the publication, in discussion sheets which formed supplements to *Pravda*, of counter-theses and amendments to the official theses.[3] The second resolution pronounced the sentence of expulsion on Zinoviev and Trotsky from the central committee, and submitted to the fifteenth party congress the whole question of the " fractional activity " of the Trotskyite opposition and of the Democratic Centralists.[4] When Bukharin reported on the session to a meeting of 6000 party members in Leningrad, Evdokimov and Bakaev spoke on behalf of the opposition, but registered only two dissentient votes.[5]

The campaign was continued with unabated vigour. On

[1] These incidents were described by Trotsky in a note to the secretariat protesting against the omission of any mention of them in the official record (Trotsky archives, T 1032) ; Zinoviev's and Trotsky's speeches with innumerable interruptions, but without mention of the scandalous incidents, were printed in *Pravda*, November 2, 1927, *Diskussionnyi Listok* No. 2 ; Trotsky's speech in the form in which he intended to deliver it is preserved in the Trotsky archives (T 3100), and was published in L. Trotsky, *The Real Situation in Russia* (n.d. [1928]), pp. 3-19. Kubyak was appointed to the secretariat after the fifteenth party congress (*Pravda*, December 20, 1927) ; in February 1928 he became People's Commissar for Agriculture of the RSFSR (see Vol. 1, p. 58).

[2] For the intended speech see Trotsky archives, T 1042.

[3] *KPSS v Rezolyutsiyakh* (1954), ii, 430-431 ; for the decision of September 8, 1927, see p. 35 above. The discussion sheets contained a limited amount of opposition material, well flanked with official articles ; the first appeared on October 30, 1927.

[4] *KPSS v Rezolyutsiyakh* (1954), ii, 431 ; a protest of October 23, 1927, from the nine remaining opposition members of the central committee, including Kamenev, Rakovsky and Smilga, against the expulsion of Zinoviev and Trotsky from the committee, and of " hundreds who think with us " from the party, was published in *Die Fahne des Kommunismus*, No. 35, November 11, 1927.

[5] *Pravda* and *Izvestiya*, October 27, 1927.

November 1, 1927, *Pravda* published for the first time, with fac-
similes, Lenin's letters of October 18 and 19, 1917, in which, on
the eve of the revolution, he had condemned the faint-heartedness and treachery of Zinoviev and Kamenev, denounced them as
" strike-breakers ", and proposed their exclusion from the party.[1]
The tactics employed in the party central committee were applied elsewhere, and opposition speakers at party meetings were
increasingly harried and interrupted. According to a statement of
the Moscow party control commission, Kamenev spoke for an
hour and ten minutes in the party cell of one factory and for 40
minutes in another ; and substantial time had been allocated in
other places to speeches by Radek, Rakovsky and Smilga.[2] But
at one Moscow party meeting Uglanov was said to have conducted
a claque of interrupters by signalling from the platform with his
order paper.[3] The same tactics were extended to the Komsomol,
where the opposition was also said to have created its own " illegal,
conspiratorial organization " and to have circulated " an anti-
party, anti-Leninist Komsomol platform, which was, so to speak,
the programme of a new Trotskyite youth league ".[4] At a meeting
of the Moscow Komsomol organization on October 26, 1927,
Kamenev and Rakovsky were systematically interrupted by an
organized claque.[5] In the Ukraine there were few Zinovievites,
but a hard core of Trotskyites was active. Rakovsky visited
Kharkov, Dniepropetrovsk and Zaporozhie early in November
1927, and attempted to address meetings. Here, too, he was
apparently refused a hearing ; and party meetings throughout
the Ukraine passed resolutions condemning the opposition by
overwhelming majorities.[6]

---

[1] For these letters see *The Bolshevik Revolution, 1917–1923*, Vol. 1, p. 97.
Stalin in his speech of October 23, 1927, stated that the party central committee
in July 1926 had taken a decision to print these letters (*Sochineniya*, x, 175) ;
there is no other evidence of this, and it seems unlikely that any decision
authorized the publication of the letters in advance of Lenin's testament,
publication of which awaited a decision of the congress (see p. 10 above).
A leading article in *Pravda*, November 4, 1927, drove home the analogy by
denouncing as " strike-breakers " all who disseminated slanders about " thermidor " and " the degeneration of the party ", and thus sought to hamper the
work of socialist construction in the USSR and to " *demoralize the international
proletariat* ".   [2] *Pravda*, November 12, 1927.
[3] *Pyatnadtsatyi S"ezd VKP(B)*, i (1961), 185-186.
[4] *Ibid.* i, 256.   [5] Trotsky archives, T 1034.
[6] *Pyatnadtsatyi S"ezd VKP(B)*, i (1961), 152-153 ; ii, 1631-1632, notes

The personal feud between Stalin and Trotsky, which had been openly declared since the autumn of 1926, when Trotsky called Stalin " the grave-digger of the revolution ", reached its highest pitch of intensity at this time. Inspired by Trotsky, the attacks of the opposition tended more and more to be directed against the person of Stalin, and by their very concentration helped to crystallize Stalin's position as the acknowledged party leader. Stalin became identified with the party. As Molotov claimed, the persecution (travlya) of Stalin by the opposition was " simply a means of masking its malicious attacks on the central committee and on the party "; Lenin's critical remarks about Stalin were used as a weapon against the party line. The same article contained the first hints of fear lest the opposition might resort to methods of terror against party leaders :

> To exacerbate the struggle by personal attacks and denuncia-
> tions against individuals may serve as a direct incitement to
> criminal terroristic designs against party leaders.[1]

And in another article of the same period Molotov referred to " hitherto childish, but already open, assaults (naskoki) on Soviet legality ", and observed that " a certain Left SR odour exudes from the opposition cess-pit "; he accused the opposition of setting up centres of illegal activity in various places.[2] It is difficult to be sure how far such pronouncements reflected genuine anxieties bred by the acrimony of the struggle, and how far they were simulated to justify the active employment of the OGPU against the opposition.

This was the moment when the opposition displayed its greatest public activity. But, in face of official propaganda and intimidation, it made little impression on the mass of party members. The highest estimate of those adhering to the opposi-tion platform was from 5000 to 6000.[3] In a memorandum of

---

115-117. Shortly afterwards Vuiovič was in the Ukraine, collecting signatures for a declaration of protest against the expulsion of Trotsky and Zinoviev (*ibid.* i, 190).

[1] *Pravda*, November 1, 1927.   [2] *Ibid.* November 5, 1927.

[3] V. Serge, *Mémoires d'un Révolutionnaire* (1951), p. 243. Stalin in a speech of November 19, 1928, said that " about 6000 voted against our platform at the time of the discussion before the fifteenth party congress "; an interrupter called out " 10,000 ", and Stalin rejoined that there might have been 20,000 sympathizers with the opposition who did not vote. This passage, reported in

November 2, 1927, Trotsky, perhaps scenting faint-heartedness in the Zinovievite camp, argued that any attempt at the forthcoming congress to expel the opposition would arouse the indignation of the workers ; " the exclusion of the opposition in thousands would mean the necessity for thousands of arrests ". Trotsky still believed that " the Stalin–Molotov fraction " would shrink from this extreme course. Boldness and courage were the most effective weapon against the mounting persecution.[1] The celebration of the anniversary of the revolution in Moscow on November 7, 1927, was expected to provide an opportunity for demonstrations similar to those which had occurred spontaneously in Leningrad in the previous month. But the police evidently now had orders to break up processions, and banners with opposition slogans were seized and destroyed.[2] When Trotsky toured the city in the company of Kamenev, Muralov and Smilga, militiamen fired into the air behind the car ; and the car was damaged by a gang of " Fascists ". When the group entered the apartment of Smilga, outside which floated banners with portraits of Lenin, Zinoviev and Trotsky and the slogan " Let us fulfil Lenin's testament ", the police forcibly broke into the apartment and tore down the banners.[3] Similar scuffles between police and opposition demon-

---

Pravda, November 24, 1928, and in a separate publication of the speech under the title *Ob Industrializatsii Strany* (1928), p. 45, was omitted from the text of the speech in Stalin, *Sochineniya*, xi, 245. According to N. Popov, *Outline History of the Communist Party of the Soviet Union* (Moscow, 1934), ii, 323, " the opposition received about 6000 votes as against 725,000 who voted for the theses of the central committee " ; this presumably represented a count taken at party meetings. *The History of the CPSU(B): Short Course* (Engl. transl. 1939), p. 285, reduced the number of dissentients to 4000.

[1] Trotsky archives, T 3101.
[2] Two of the banned opposition slogans were " Against opportunism, against a split — for the unity of Lenin's party " and " Turn the fire on the Right — against the *kulak*, the nepman and the bureaucrat " (Trotsky archives, T 3103) ; among other slogans put out by the opposition at this time were " Down with Ustryalovism " and " Down with Thermidor " (*Pyatnadtsatyi S"ezd VKP(B)*, i (1961), 287).
[3] For the account of Kamenev, Muralov and Smilga see Trotsky archives, T 1047 ; for Trotsky's own accounts *ibid.* T 1048, 3103. A photograph of the door of Smilga's apartment showing the damage done is preserved *ibid.* T 1086. An incident earlier in the day, when Preobrazhensky and Smilga appeared on the balcony of the headquarters of a district Soviet in the centre of Moscow to greet the demonstrators, and were dragged from the balcony by militiamen who broke into the house and destroyed the banners, is described *ibid.* T 1050. Preobrazhensky, in his repentant speech to the seventeenth party congress of 1934,

strators marked the day in Leningrad, where Zinoviev made an appearance.[1]

The provocation now seemed to have gone far enough. The Moscow party committee, in a resolution of November 9, 1927, diagnosed the counter-demonstration as proof of the determination of the opposition to found a separate party, and pronounced the expulsion of Trotsky, Zinoviev, Kamenev and Smilga from the party to be urgently necessary.[2] Two days later, the party central committee issued a statement condemning the appearances of Trotsky, Zinoviev, Kamenev, Smilga and others on the streets of Moscow and Leningrad, and " the attempts of the opposition to carry the party discussion beyond the limits of the party " ;[3] and *Pravda* published resolutions of local party organizations demanding the expulsion of Trotsky and Zinoviev from the party.[4] On the next day Trotsky and Zinoviev attended a session of the presidium of the central control commission. Faced by a demand to desist from " the organization of illegal anti-party meetings ", they staged a " demonstrative walk-out "; and a joint session of the party central committee and the central control commission decided to expel Kamenev, Smilga, Evdokimov, Rakovsky and Avdeev from the central committee and six other members of the opposition from the central control commission, and to expel Trotsky and Zinoviev from the party.[5] In a protest against the expulsions addressed to the central control commission, 31 members of the opposition none the less reaffirmed their determination to renounce fractional activity and not to

recalled that he had shouted himself hoarse from the balcony with cries of " Long live the world leader of the proletarian revolution, Trotsky " (*XVII S"ezd Vsesoyuznoi Kommunisticheskoi Partii* (*B*) (1934), p. 238).

[1] V. Serge, *Mémoires d'un Révolutionnaire* (1951), pp. 246-247.

[2] *Pravda*, November 10, 1927.

[3] *Izvestiya Tsentral'nogo Komiteta VKP(B)*, No. 42-43 (215-216), November 15, 1927, p. 1 ; on the same occasion a ban is said to have been pronounced on meetings between party members in private apartments (Trotsky archives, T 3105).

[4] *Pravda*, November 11, 1927.

[5] *Ibid.* November 15, 1927. This decision is variously dated ; Orjonikidze at the fifteenth party congress a month later, quoting only the decision on the expulsions from the central committee and the control commission, dated it November 12 (*Pyatnadtsatyi S"ezd VKP(B)*, i (1961), 7) ; the resolution of the congress on the opposition dated the decision to expel Trotsky and Zinoviev from the party November 14 (*KPSS v Rezolyutsiyakh* (1954), ii, 489).

form a second party.[1] The rout was complete. At party meetings
throughout the country, opposition spokesmen no longer dared to
show themselves, and 99 per cent of those present were recorded
as voting for the official line.[2] On November 15, 1927, Trotsky
punctiliously informed the secretariat of TsIK that he had vacated
his official apartment in the Kremlin; owing to the illness of his
son, his son and his wife would be obliged to remain for a few
days longer.[3]

The interval of rather more than two weeks between the
expulsion of Trotsky and Zinoviev and the meeting of the fifteenth
party congress was marked by a personal tragedy — the suicide
of Joffe. The immediate occasion for the act was a refusal of the
party authorities to sanction a journey abroad for medical treatment which had been recommended by the physicians.[4] But the
profounder cause was stated in a letter which he left addressed
to Trotsky:

> In my present state I cannot endure a situation in which the
> party silently tolerates your exclusion from its ranks, even though
> I am absolutely certain that sooner or later a crisis will oblige the
> party to cast off those who have led it to such a disgrace. In this
> sense my death is a protest against those who have led the party
> to such a situation that it cannot react in any way to this
> opprobrium.[5]

[1] *Pyatnadtsatyi S"ezd VKP(B)*, i (1961), 145; ii, 1630, note 109; neither
the text nor a list of signatories has been available.

[2] *Izvestiya Tsentral'nogo Komiteta VKP(B)*, No. 45-46 (218-219), December
27, 1927, p. 1.

[3] Trotsky archives, T 1053; the exodus of Zinoviev (carrying a death-mask
of Lenin), Radek, Kamenev and Sokolnikov is described in V. Serge, *Le Tournant
Obscur* (1951), pp. 139-141. The mention of Sokolnikov may be an error;
Sokolnikov announced at the congress that he had left the opposition " some
months ago ", and was rewarded by re-election to the party central committee
(*Pyatnadtsatyi S"ezd VKP(B)*, ii (1962), 1132, 1414); his defection from the
opposition does not appear to have been announced in the Soviet press, but was
reported in *Sotsialisticheskii Vestnik*, No. 18 (160), September 22, 1927, p. 13.

[4] Many months earlier, on January 20, 1927, Trotsky had written to Semash-
ko asking for travel facilities for Joffe on grounds of health (Trotsky archives,
T 918); a medical bulletin attributed his suicide to deteriorating health
(*Izvestiya*, November 18, 1927).

[5] The original letter was seized by the OGPU; after protests, a photostatic
copy was handed not to Trotsky, but to Rakovsky (L. Trotsky, *Moya Zhizn'*
(Berlin, 1930), ii, 283). The complete text of the letter is in the Trotsky
archives, T 1054, and was published in *Bol'shevik*, No. 23-24, December 31,
1927, pp. 145-151. A translation of a slightly abbreviated version circulated by

The pall-bearers at the funeral on November 19, 1927, were Chicherin, Litvinov, Karakhan and Enukidze; Joffe's diplomatic, rather than his party, standing was emphasized. Chicherin delivered a eulogy of the deceased. Lezhava spoke for the government, followed by a number of other orators, including Trotsky and Rakovsky. The presence of the opposition leaders attracted a sympathetic crowd, estimated by Trotsky at not less than 10,000, which hemmed in the speakers.[1] It was Trotsky's last public appearance in Moscow.[2] Trotsky himself was undaunted. On November 21, 1927, when Zinoviev and Kamenev showed increasing symptoms of nervousness, and had begun once more to dissociate themselves from their too resolute ally, Trotsky wrote a circular letter to Preobrazhensky, Pyatakov, Radek, Rakovsky and Eltsin — all survivors of the opposition of 1923 — begging them to confirm their recollections of the confessions made by Zinoviev and Kamenev in 1926 of the manner in which they had invented the legend of " Trotskyism ". Trotsky collected the replies, and eventually published them in exile.[3]

The Moscow provincial party conference which opened on November 20, 1927, provided a further opportunity to harry the dejected opposition leaders. Kamenev and Rakovsky both spoke. The latter, soured by his forced recall from Paris,[4] taunted the majority with failure to react more sharply to foreign provocation (" they did not defend me "), though he apparently admitted or implied that this might have meant war. When Rozengolts and Karakhan accused him of playing with the threat of war, he claimed that his words had been misunderstood or distorted. This did not save him from a fierce attack by Bukharin, who accused him

the opposition at the time is in L. Trotsky, *The Real Situation in Russia* (n.d. [1928]), pp. 325-332 ; Yaroslavsky taunted the opposition with the omissions, which were designed to cloak Joffe's pessimism about its prospects (*Pyatnadtsatyi S"ezd VKP(B)*, i (1961), 396).

[1] *Pravda* and *Izvestiya*, November 20, 1927, both reported the funeral, with a picture of the *cortège*; neither mentioned Trotsky. For descriptions see L. Trotsky, *Moya Zhizn'* (Berlin, 1930), ii, 284 ; L. Fischer, *Men and Politics* (1946), p. 94 ; Trotsky's speech is in the Trotsky archives, T 3108.

[2] Yanson at the fifteenth party congress in the following month offered the surly comment that " the last, most conspicuous, demonstration of political activity of the opposition took place in a cemetery " (*Pyatnadtsatyi S"ezd VKP(B)*, i (1961), 530).

[3] L. Trotsky, *Stalinskaya Shkola Falsifikatsii* (Berlin, 1932), pp. 101-109.

[4] This episode will be discussed in a subsequent volume.

of " sabre-rattling ", wanting to move troops to the Polish frontier and pronouncing " the dangerous word ' war ' ", and connected these threats with Trotsky's " Clemenceau thesis ". Bukharin also charged Kamenev with " lack of principle ", and exclaimed that " only cowards or political charlatans can behave like that ". Yaroslavsky, who alleged that the opposition had " several " illicit printing-presses, and distributed leaflets " in large quantities through the post " and in the factories, demanded the complete " *organisational annihilation* " of the opposition.[1] The conference adopted a resolution once more condemning the opposition and identifying its policies with Menshevism.[2] On the day the conference ended, Bukharin spoke on the same inexhaustible theme to the presidium of IKKI, which approved a resolution branding the activity of the opposition as " an obstacle to the interests of the international workers' movement and a betrayal of the Communist International ".[3] In the last week of November 1927 the Ukrainian and White Russian parties held congresses at which they passed resolutions condemning the opposition and endorsing the disciplinary measures taken against it.[4]

The fifteenth party congress opened on December 2, 1927. During the previous five weeks, eleven discussion sheets had appeared as supplements to *Pravda :* and these had carried two sets of opposition " counter-theses "[5] and a few other opposition documents. The opposition, with Trotsky, Zinoviev and several of the lesser leaders already out of the party, had nothing to hope from the congress, and could taste the bitterness of defeat even before the proceedings began. A few hours before the opening of the congress, Kamenev, I. N. Smirnov and Smilga visited Orjonikidze and asked for a preliminary discussion with members

---

[1] The speeches, other than those of Kamenev and Rakovsky, were fairly fully reported in *Pravda* and *Izvestiya*, November 23, 24, 26, 27, 1927 ; Stalin at the fifteenth party congress remarked that Rakovsky " made a fool of himself on the question of war " (*Sochineniya*, x, 354).

[2] *Pravda*, November 24, 1927.

[3] *Ibid.* November 24, 1927.

[4] *Ibid.* November 23, 26, 1927.

[5] See Vol. 1, pp. 34, 36.

of the Politburo: this was refused.[1] At the opening session
Orjonikidze reported a recommendation of the central control
commission that 12 members of the opposition should be removed
from their positions as members of the central committee or
control commission, and warned that further fractional activity
was incompatible with membership of the party; the time had
come to put an end to a situation in which " an insignificant
group of comrades, comprising in all 0·5 per cent of the whole
party " should " destroy the unity of the party and split the
party of Lenin ". The congress appointed a special commission
of 65 senior party members to study the documents and report
to the congress.[2] On the following day, 121 members of the
opposition, including those expelled from the party, addressed to
the presidium of the congress a declaration in which they reaffirmed
that they had no " differences of programme " with the party,
undertook once more to end their fractional activities, pleaded
for the reinstatement of those expelled and the release of those
arrested, and announced in advance their submission to decisions
of the congress.[3] But this did not help them. On the same day,
Stalin, having dealt with foreign and domestic policy, devoted the
third section of his opening report to the opposition, playing over
again — for the last time — the familiar themes of the past two
years. The opposition leaders rejected the possibility of " the
victorious building of socialism in our country ", accused the
party of a " thermidorian degeneration ", and denied the socialist
character of the revolution. He ended with an uncompromising
demand that they should " renounce their anti-Bolshevik views,
openly and honestly before the whole world ", or leave the party;
and " if they do not go, we will throw them out ".[4]

The depleted opposition, exposed to this bludgeoning, made
a weak showing, though Kaganovich professed to fear that it
would attempt some fresh manœuvre " in the style of August 8
or October 16 ". Rakovsky's attempt to address the congress

---

[1] *Pyatnadtsatyi S"ezd VKP(B)*, ii (1962), 1393.   [2] *Ibid.* i, 7-9.
[3] *Ibid.* ii, 1596-1598; Yaroslavsky quoted a statement by a member of the
opposition showing that the declaration was a compromise between a group
which wanted to capitulate, and a group led by Trotsky which wanted to
continue the struggle (*ibid.* i, 393-394). It was published in *Pravda*, December
20, 1927, with other opposition documents.
[4] Stalin, *Sochineniya*, x, 325-351.

on foreign affairs was constantly interrupted — among others by Kaganovich and Bukharin. He infuriated his audience by quoting newspapers of western countries to show that they regarded the opposition as presenting a greater revolutionary threat to the capitalist world than did the official line. Evdokimov read from a prepared paper, and was met by the taunt that Trotsky had written it for him. Kamenev aroused angry retorts by claiming that his only aim was " the reconciliation of the opposition with the party " ; and impatient interruptions greeted his plea for the release of Mrachkovsky and other imprisoned members of the opposition.[1] Rykov replied sharply to Kamenev, whom he charged with insincerity and evasion ; and Tomsky poked fun at the different attitudes of the opposition leaders :

> When they need a man of war, a war-horse, they launch Trotsky . . . When they need peace, they launch Kamenev. When a tear has to be shed, they launch Zinoviev.

Yanson claimed that the measures taken against the opposition had evoked widespread enthusiasm in the party, and dealt a blow at the " cult of personality ".[2] Stalin, in a brief reply to the debate, rejected both Kamenev's speech and the opposition declaration of December 3, 1927, as inadequate tokens of surrender.[3] The resolution adopted on December 7, 1927, on Stalin's report, pending the conclusions of the special commission, declared that the opposition had "become objectively a factor in the anti-Soviet struggle ", and that " membership of the Trotskyite opposition and propagation of its views is incompatible with remaining in the ranks of the Bolshevik party ".[4]

This resolution, and the activities of the special commission behind the scenes, finally dissolved the united opposition into its two component sections. On December 10, 1927, two further declarations were handed to the commission. The Zinovievite declaration, signed by Kamenev, Bakaev, Avdeev and Evdokimov, reaffirmed the belief of the group in the rightness of its views,

---

[1] *Pyatnadtsatyi S"ezd VKP(B)*, i (1961), 155, 206-214, 259-262, 279-285 ; Orjonikidze quoted an opposition bulletin of November 26, 1927, demanding the release of Mrachkovsky (*ibid.* i, 431).
[2] *Ibid.* i, 285-296, 333, 530.
[3] Stalin, *Sochineniya*, x, 368.
[4] *KPSS v Rezolyutsiyakh* (1954), ii, 441.

but unconditionally accepted the decisions of the congress, " however onerous they may be ". The Trotskyite declaration, signed by Muralov, Rakovsky and Radek, also accepted the abandonment of all fractional activity, but asserted the right of individual party members " to defend before the party within the limits of the statute . . . our views set out in the platform and the theses ".[1] Neither document was free from ambiguity and embarrassment ; and Orjonikidze professed to see " no great difference " between them.[2] But they pointed the way to deeper divergences to come. Pyatakov, at this time attached to the Soviet mission in Paris, was summoned to Moscow to be cross-examined by the special commission. He explained that he did not approve of such illegal activities as the secret printing-press and the November 7 demonstrations, but that these had been forced on the opposition by the official régime ; he added that he still regarded the opposition platform as correct, and that the rest of the party would shortly come round to it.[3] On the basis of these documents and enquiries, the commission drafted a resolution expelling from the party 75 " active workers of the Trotskyite opposition ", including Kamenev, Pyatakov, Radek, Rakovsky, Smilga and Zalutsky. On December 18, 1927, after Smilga had been allowed to read to the congress a declaration, in his own name and in those of Muralov, Rakovsky and Radek, protesting against their expulsion,[4] the resolution was adopted without further debate by the congress.[5] In the general eagerness to denounce and destroy the united opposition, little attention was given to the rump of the Democratic Centralists, who presented to the congress on December 4, 1927, an uncompromising declaration, attacking both economic and party policies, and describing the Red Army as

[1] Both declarations were published in *Pravda*, December 20, 1927, and ar in *Pyatnadtsatyi S"ezd VKP(B)*, ii (1962), 1599-1600. Copies in the Trotsky archives, T 1061, are labelled respectively " Theses of Zinoviev " and " Theses of Trotsky " ; it may be presumed that Zinoviev and Trotsky respectively had a share in drafting them.

[2] *Pyatnadtsatyi S"ezd VKP(B)*, ii (1962), 1392.

[3] *Ibid.* ii, 1393.

[4] *Ibid.* ii, 1398-1400 ; an appeal against the expulsions signed by Trotsky, Rakovsky, Radek and other leading Trotskyites, and addressed to the presidium of IKKI and to foreign communist parties, was published in *Die Fahne des Kommunismus*, No. 3, January 20, 1928.

[5] *Pyatnadtsatyi S"ezd VKP(B)*, ii, (1962), 1395-1397 ; *KPSS v Rezolyutsiyakh* (1954), ii, 488-490.

" an instrument for a Bonapartist coup ". The declaration was not published or included in the records of the congress, and only casual references were made to it.[1] But the resolution expelling the 75 members of the united opposition also provided for the expulsion of 15 members of " the group of Sapronov " as being " flagrantly counter-revolutionary ". A clean sweep had been made of the last organized opposition groups in the party.[2]

The Zinovievite wing of the united opposition had remained silent when the resolution of expulsion was voted. On the following day, December 19, 1927, Kamenev brought to Rykov a declaration signed by 23 expelled members of the opposition, including himself and Zinoviev, which he asked leave to read to the congress. Kamenev was refused admission, but the declaration was read by Rykov from the chair. It included a recantation of the " anti-Leninist views " of the opposition, recognized as " errors " the setting up of the secret printing-press, the November 7 demonstration, and the link with the dissident Maslow–Fischer group in Germany, and asked once more for reinstatement in the party. But this almost abject surrender made no impact. Rykov, in the name of the presidium of the congress, proposed not to examine the declaration, but to instruct the party central committee and central control commission to receive only individual applications for reinstatement from former members of the opposition, and to postpone consideration of them till six months had elapsed after their receipt. The congress adopted a resolution in this sense.[3] Zinoviev and Kamenev had been ignominiously told to wait.

A minor episode of the congress was the decision to print Lenin's testament. The proposal had been submitted to the congress by the party central committee in July 1926,[4] and had

---

[1] The declaration is in the Trotsky archives, T 1060; Tomsky, one of the few to mention it at the congress, remarked that " nobody has spoken of it here from the tribune, and it is not worth speaking about, since this group is a group of die-hards, people who have lost all perspective " (*Pyatnadtsatyi S"ezd VKP(B)*), i (1961), 331).

[2] The number of rank-and-file members expelled at this time seems to have been quite small. According to Moscow party archives, most members of the opposition " renounced their anti-party activities and dissociated themselves from Trotskyite views "; only in exceptional cases was the penalty of expulsion applied (*Voprosy Istorii KPSS*, No. 2, 1967, p. 127).

[3] *Ibid.* ii, 1417-1419; *KPSS v Rezolyutsiyakh* (1954), ii, 491.

[4] See p. 10 above.

again been mentioned by Stalin in his speech to the central committee on October 23, 1927.[1] The congress had nearly run its course when Orjonikidze, replying to the debate on the work of the central control commission, devoted " two words " to this question, and proposed to remove the ban on the publication of the testament. Even then the congress " forgot " to vote a resolution on the subject till Petrovsky issued a reminder from the chair. Rykov then formally proposed to publish the testament and Lenin's other " unpublished letters on internal party questions " ; the testament was, however, not to be published in the *Leninskii Sbornik* — the original proposal — but added to the stenographic records of the congress.[2] A part of the testament and the post-script were in fact printed in the daily bulletin distributed to delegates at the congress.[3] But they did not appear in the press, or in the official record of the congress published in the following year. The " other unpublished letters ", which Stalin had read to the party central committee in July 1926,[4] do not seem to have been published at all. Once the opposition had been crushed, the pressure for further disclosures petered out.

In the new Politburo elected by the party central committee after the congress Zinoviev and Trotsky were replaced by Rudzutak and Kuibyshev, both good Stalinists. The full membership of the Politburo now consisted of Bukharin, Voroshilov, Kalinin, Kuibyshev, Molotov, Rykov, Rudzutak, Stalin and Tomsky.[5] One of its first decisions, which followed hard on the end of the congress and the splitting of the opposition, was to deport Trotsky and his principal supporters from Moscow.[6] But here a strange anomaly occurred which showed clearly the hesitation of the

---

[1] Stalin, *Sochineniya*, x, 176.

[2] *Pyatnadtsatyi S"ezd VKP(B)*, i (1961), 610, 623.

[3] *Ibid.* ii, 1659, note 310 ; the bulletin has not been available.

[4] See p. 10 above ; the first effective publication of all these documents took place in 1956.

[5] *Pravda*, December 20, 1927.

[6] According to a message from Paul Scheffer to the *Berliner Tageblatt* of January 6, 1928, " 30 prominent leaders of the opposition " were informed by the OGPU of the decision on January 3 ; and on the following day the highest leaders — Trotsky, Muralov, Rakovsky and Radek, together with Kamenev and Zinoviev — were " invited in the name of the party to leave Moscow " (P. Scheffer, 7 *Years in the Soviet Union* (Engl. translation from German, 1931), p. 192) ; Scheffer had an interview with Trotsky on January 15, 1928 (*ibid.* pp. 204-205).

leaders — or at any rate of some of them — in applying this
drastic, and potentially unpopular, measure.[1] For a year or more
members of the opposition had been discreetly kept out of the
way by distant appointments, at home or abroad. Though
Trotsky and his colleagues had been expelled from the party, and
were in theory no longer amenable to party discipline, it was
proposed to apply the same procedure to them. They were
informed by the party authorities that they would be offered " work
in a number of remote places ".[2] This they accepted in principle,
demanding only that the work should be appropriate, and climatic
conditions congenial; on this ground they objected to a proposal
to send Trotsky to Astrakhan and Rakovsky to Ust-Sysolsk.
Orjonikidze, as president of the Orgburo, was willing to discuss
these objections, and referred them to Kosior. But here some
harsher hand intervened. Trotsky was summoned to the offices
of the OGPU, and refused to attend on the ground that the
conversation with Kosior was pending. This refusal was treated
as tantamount to a withdrawal of his voluntary acceptance of an
appointment; and the OGPU notified him that he would be
deported under art. 59 of the criminal code relating to counter-
revolutionary activities.[3]

The departure was fixed for the evening of January 16, 1928.
But the news became known; and so large a crowd gathered at

[1] In a letter to an unnamed correspondent, Trotsky afterwards related that a
day or two before his departure from Moscow he was visited by a " party
dignitary (sanovnik) ", who told him that, though the party policy was correct,
" the party régime is not without faults ", and that, " though we condemn the
opposition, we are embarrassed by the deportations " (Trotsky archives, T 3161);
according to a report from Moscow, Stalin pretended to have voted in the
Politburo against Trotsky's deportation, which took place after he had left for
Siberia (ibid. T 1588; for Stalin's Siberian tour see Vol. 1, pp. 50-51).

[2] Many of the deportees were in fact assigned to official posts; Rakovsky at
Astrakhan was employed as a " specialist-economist " in Gubplan (the provincial
planning department) at the maximum party salary (though no longer a member
of the party) of, for this zone, 180 rubles a month (Byulleten' Oppozitsii (Paris),
No. 85, July 1933, pp. 24-25). Sosnovsky worked in the local planning
commission in Barnaul (Trotsky archives, T 1119), Shtykgold as a " specialist "
in Vologda (ibid. T 1127). Later, however, some members of the opposition
were said to be earning a living as building workers (Byulleten' Oppozitsii (Paris),
No. 6, October 1929, p. 27).

[3] These proceedings were described in detail in a memorandum, presumably
written by Trotsky himself, and addressed to Orjonikidze and to the Politburo
with a copy to IKKI (Trotsky archives, T 1092).

the station that it was found prudent to postpone the departure — ostensibly for two days. On the next day, January 17, 1928, Trotsky, resisting to the last, was smuggled away in a special train which awaited the express at a station some miles out of Moscow. His destination was Alma Ata, the capital of Kazakhstan, on the extreme confines of the USSR about 160 miles from the rail-head at Frunze. The last part of the journey was made by truck and sleigh. Trotsky and his family reached Alma-Ata on January 25, 1928.[1] Two days after his departure an official *communiqué* announced that 30 active members of the opposition, including Trotsky, Radek, Smilga and I. Smirnov, had been expelled from Moscow.[2] Rakovsky was sent to Astrakhan, Radek to Tomsk and then to Tobolsk; most of the other leading Trotskyites were scattered over Siberia.[3] The equivocations of Zinoviev and Kamenev won for them the mild sentence of banishment to Kaluga, a provincial capital some 800 miles south-west of Moscow; and even this sentence does not seem to have been strictly enforced.[4]

[1] The deportation was described in a circular letter of February 28, 1928, from Trotsky to his supporters (Trotsky archives, T 1161), and in an account written by his wife in L. Trotsky, *Moya Zhizn'* (Berlin, 1930), ii, 285-297.

[2] *Pravda*, January 19, 1928.

[3] For lists of the places of residence of the principal exiles see Trotsky archives, T 1079, 1081.

[4] According to a statement by Kalinin six months later, they " live formally in Kaluga, but are very often in Moscow " (*Bednota*, June 9, 1928); in July 1928 Kamenev, having just regained his party membership, was living in an apartment in Moscow (see p. 65 below).

CHAPTER 40

REALIGNMENTS, 1928

THE banishment of its leaders from Moscow hastened the dissolution of the united opposition, which had set in immediately after the sentences of expulsion pronounced by the fifteenth party congress. On January 15, 1928, *Pravda* published, with suitable expressions of indignation, two letters or manifestoes, purporting to emanate from followers of Trotsky, which spoke openly of the " betrayal " of the opposition by Zinoviev and Kamenev, drew a sharp line between the opposition and the "capitulators", and discussed the attitude of various foreign opposition groups (notably that of Maslow and Ruth Fischer) to the split; the need was stressed for common international action by the opposition. Some days later, a letter appeared in *Pravda* from Zinoviev and Kamenev, who emphatically reaffirmed that they had " parted company with the group of L. D. Trotsky ", and summed up the differences which had divided the two wings of the united opposition. Their disagreement with Trotsky, which they traced back to August 1927, turned on their attitude to the possibility of a " second party "; at the fifteenth congress the only choice had been " to capitulate to the idea of the VKP(B) or to capitulate to the idea of a second party ". The platform of the opposition was " a document which contradicted the policy of the party central committee all along the line ". The only motto now could be, " Back into the party and back into Comintern ". *Pravda*, in publishing the statement, called it " a decisive step which facilitates the return to the party of all who take their stand on this position ".[1] Trotsky confined himself to a sarcastic comment on " the two knights who, by a malicious irony of fate, both turn out to be Sancho Panzas ".[2]

[1] *Pravda*, January 27, 1928.
[2] Trotsky archives, T 1179; contemptuous comment by Maslow and Ruth Fischer in Berlin was reported in *Pravda*, February 11, 1928.

The first nine months of 1928 were a period of confusion and uncertainty in party alignments. The first conspicuous defectors from the Trotskyite wing of the opposition were those employed in diplomatic posts abroad.[1] Pyatakov in a letter dated February 28, 1928, referred to his past attitude as a " mistake ", dissociated himself from the opposition platform of September 1927, and petitioned for readmission to the party.[2] Trotsky described him as a man who, in order to escape from contradictions, " makes a suicidal jump into a river ".[3] Krestinsky, whose position as Soviet representative in Berlin had precluded any active participation in opposition affairs, was a sympathizer with Trotsky's views. But, when questioned by the party central control commission, he wrote on March 22, 1928, enclosing copies of his correspondence with Trotsky, to assure the commission that he had never had any " organizational link " with the opposition, and had now made " an ideological break " with it.[4] On April 4, 1928, Antonov-Ovseenko, a long-standing friend and supporter of Trotsky, and now Soviet representative in Prague, wrote a letter to Stalin which appeared a few days later in *Pravda*. He referred to letters which he had written on October 28, 1927, to the Politburo and to Trotsky, expressing his general agreement with the political line of the party central committee and his disapproval of opposition attacks on it, but criticizing the " organizational policy " of the committee. Further consideration had led him to retract this criticism and to accept unconditionally the party line.[5]

The defeat of the opposition and the exile or recantation of its leaders came at a moment when the crisis of the grain collections was forcing a reappraisal of the official party line and undermining

---

[1] If R. Fischer, *Stalin and German Communism* (Harvard, 1948), p. 604, is correct in reporting the attendance of " 20 Russian comrades from the various embassies and legations " at an opposition meeting in Berlin at the beginning of December 1927, the Soviet diplomatic corps was a breeding-ground of opposition ; this would be a natural result of the practice of using foreign appointments as a way of getting rid of trouble-makers (see p. 27, note 2 above).

[2] *Pravda*, February 29, 1928 ; by accident or design, the letter was published under the headline " Declaration of Comrade Pyatakov ", though he had in fact been expelled from the party.   [3] Trotsky archives, T 3112.

[4] Trotsky archives, T 1232 ; an extract from the letter was published in *Pravda*, April 8, 1928.

[5] *Ibid.* April 8, 1928 ; for Antonov-Ovseenko's earlier support of Trotsky see *The Interregnum, 1923–1924*, pp. 324-325. Antonov-Ovseenko's defection was referred to in a letter of Trotsky of May 26, 1928 (Trotsky archives, T 1530).

the unity of the majority group in the Politburo. In the spring of
1927 the Democratic Centralists had recognized no significant
difference between Right and centre in the party, and Trotsky
had appeared to agree with them.[1] But later Trotsky, in the
opposition platform of September 1927, distinguished sharply
between two trends in the party — " a frank and open drift to the
Right ", based on support for " the ' economically powerful '
middle peasant ", and " the ' centrism ' of the official apparatus ",
which was concerned primarily with administration, sought to
stifle discussion, and looked at the party " from the top down ".
As leaders of the former group Trotsky named Rykov, A. P.
Smirnov, Kalinin, Petrovsky, Chubar and Kaminsky, with Tomsky
and other trade union leaders as auxiliaries ; of the latter, Stalin,
Molotov, Uglanov, Kaganovich, Mikoyan and Kirov. Bukharin
was seen as " wavering from one side to the other ". The two
groups were " consolidated by their common hostility to the
opposition ". But " to cut off the opposition would inevitably
accelerate the conflict between them ".[2] This acute prediction
was quickly justified. Even before the end of 1927 the careless
optimism with which the year had opened was beginning rapidly
to evaporate. Bukharin, whose position later became the most
sensitive barometer of the changing climate, seems to have been
the target rather than the author of the first moves. By the time
the fifteenth party congress met in December 1927, the rôle of
Stalin's most faithful lieutenant, which he performed with so
much fervour at the fifteenth party conference in the previous
year,[3] had been usurped by Molotov. Bukharin's long report on
the affairs of Comintern was largely theoretical, and not designed
to provoke controversy. But it was criticized in the debate,
guardedly by Lozovsky, and more openly by Shatskin and
Lominadze. Shatskin accused Bukharin of glossing over the
Rightest errors of foreign communist parties, and thought that
" the Right danger in the ranks of our supporters and of our
parties is very great ". Lominadze, just back from China, where
he had been one of Stalin's principal agents on the eve of the

[1] See pp. 23, 34 above.
[2] L. Trotsky, *The Real Situation in Russia* (n.d. [1928]), pp. 122-124; for
an earlier version of this prediction see p. 13 above.
[3] See p. 19 above.

ill-fated Canton rising, emphatically agreed with Shatskin, and declared that, " if communist parties have committed mistakes in the past two years, they have always committed Right mistakes ".[1]   Bukharin, in his reply, argued at some length against Shatskin and Lominadze that " the centre of gravity " of the opposition lay in "*Trotskyite groupings* " and that the Right danger was a transitory phenomenon.[2]   This did not prevent Lozovsky and Shatskin from addressing notes to the presidium of the congress — the former convicting Bukharin of error on a point of fact, the latter, much sharper in tone, accusing him of misrepresentation of Shatskin's party record.[3]   These exchanges must have revealed to the initiated that Bukharin no longer enjoyed the unconditional protection of the top leaders.   The rout of the opposition had made Bukharin expendable.

In the first months of 1928 the grain collections crisis and the increasing pressures of industrialization drove the party majority — the group now firmly crystallized round the personality of Stalin — towards policies hitherto associated with Trotsky and his followers.   It may be significant that neither Rykov nor Bukharin was among the leaders who undertook missions to the countryside to bring in the grain.   Bukharin, though he can hardly have been blind to symptoms of declining favour, long hesitated to challenge official policies.   At the ninth IKKI in February 1928, when the first signs of a turning away from the Right in Comintern were plainly visible, he defined Trotskyism as " nothing but the ' Left ' wing of the Social-Democratic party ", and placed the entire emphasis on the Trotskyite danger ; and the committee obediently recorded its satisfaction that " the fifteenth congress of the VKP(B) decisively put an end to the Trotskyite opposition by excluding it from the ranks of the party ".[4]   But Bukharin, in his report on the recent session of the party central committee to the Leningrad party organization on April 13, 1928, while deprecating " a tendency to neglect a sense of moderation, to skip over necessary stages through which we must inevitably pass ", remained safely within the party line, defending the " extra-

---

[1] *Pyatnadtsatyi S"ezd VKP(B)*, i (1961), 728, 729-730.
[2] *Ibid.* i, 835-839.
[3] *Ibid.* ii (1962), 1593-1596.
[4] *Kommunisticheskii Internatsional v Dokumentakh* (1933), p. 746 ; Bukharin's report was summarized in *Pravda*, February 17, 1928.

ordinary measures ", and trouncing both the defeated opposition
and the heresies of Kondratiev.[1] It was Rykov who first emerged
as the potential focus of dissent, differing publicly from Stalin
in his assessment of the " extraordinary measures ".[2] Only in
May 1928 did Bukharin begin openly to express his misgivings,
and then only in private memoranda which did not go outside
the Politburo.[3] The " Right opposition " still lacked determination, cohesion and a leader. Trotsky in a memorandum written shortly after his arrival in Alma-Ata clearly diagnosed the
situation :

> The opposition plan has been defeated ; the Stalin group has
> no plan ; the Rightists are afraid for the present to speak aloud
> of their real intentions.[4]

Belief in the threat from an increasingly powerful Right wing
in the party was an important factor in the growing disunity of the
exiled members of the opposition. Difficulties of communication
impeded any effort to maintain a united front. Correspondence
between them, and between them and Moscow, was inordinately
slow, though in the first months it does not seem to have been otherwise interfered with. Early in March 1928 Trotsky recorded the
receipt of a " first large packet of letters from Moscow ".[5] The
first of the exiles to recant were a group of Zinovievites, which
was headed by Safarov and included, among others, Vardin,
Tarkhanov and Vuiovič ; Safarov in a letter of March 31, 1928,

---

[1] *Pravda*, April 19, 1928 ; for Kondratiev see Vol. 1, pp. 20-22.

[2] See Vol. 1, pp. 60-61. Trotsky, in a memorandum written early in
1928 (cited in note 4 below), referred to " the Stalin-Rykov struggle ", and
somewhat fancifully saw it as " a struggle between the two apparatuses " of
party and state, with the Right predominant in the latter. In June 1928 he
referred to " Rykov's faction " (Trotsky archives, T 1588), and on September 12,
1928, writing to an unnamed supporter of the Right opposition, called him a
" Rykovite " (*ibid.* T 3161). *Sotsialisticheskii Vestnik* (Berlin), No. 20(186),
October 28, 1928, p. 3, belatedly reported that the new Right opposition
consisted of Rykov, Kalinin and Tomsky, and " according to some people "
Bukharin.   [3] For these see Vol. 1, p. 72.

[4] Trotsky archives, T 3019 ; it was published in *Die Fahne des Kommunismus*,
No. 51, December 21, 1928 ; No. 52, December 28, 1928.

[5] Trotsky archives, T 1179 ; in September 1928 a letter from Paris reached
Rakovsky in Astrakhan in ten days (*Cahiers du Monde Russe et Soviétique*, i, No. 4
(July-December 1960), p. 625). Presently complaints began to be heard of
non-receipt of letters (Trotsky archives, T 1613) ; for later restrictions see
pp. 82–83 below.

to the party central control commission appealed on behalf of the
group for reinstatement in the party.[1] In April 1928 Preobrazhensky, who had already engaged Trotsky in controversy on
the Chinese question, forwarded to him a long memorandum
entitled " The Left Course in the Countryside and Its Prospects ",
in which, after reviewing the alternatives of a consistent Left
course and a surrender to the *kulak*, he proposed that the opposition should ask official permission to hold a conference of opposi-
tionists in an attempt to bring about an alliance between the
opposition and the party centre against the Right.[2] Trotsky
found himself torn between two wings of his followers — the
" conciliators " who believed that Stalin should be supported
against the Rightist heresies of Rykov and Bukharin, and those
who believed that the apparent movement of official policy to the
Left was no more than a temporary zigzag, and would soon be
" compensated by steps to the Right ".[3]

Recantations based on the assumption that the majority had
now come round to policies formerly preached by the opposition[4]
were a source of embarrassment, and met with varying responses.
The central control commission rejected the declarations of
Safarov, Vardin and Tarkhanov as " unsatisfactory ".[5] Early in

[1] Trotsky archives, T 1249. According to Trotsky, Safarov, when he arrived
in Berlin from Constantinople in November 1927, loudly " proclaimed the
advent of thermidor ", and, on reaching Moscow and hearing a " cautious-
capitulatory speech " from Zinoviev, fell on him in a rage ; Safarov was, however, notoriously unstable — " a caricature variety of the Bukharin species "
(*ibid.* T 1530). For statements by Tarkhanov and Vardin see *ibid.* T 1355, 1599.
For Tarkhanov see *Socialism in One Country, 1924–1928*, Vol. 2, p. 103 ; for
Vardin, *ibid.* Vol. 2, p. 80 ; the recantation of Sarkis, another Zinovievite, was
recorded in *Pravda*, May 13, 1928.
[2] *Ibid.* T 1262 (for the covering note of April 23, 1928, to Trotsky see *ibid.*
T 1349) ; for the correspondence about China see *ibid.* T 1189.
[3] The latter view was expressed in an undated report received by Trotsky
from Moscow in the spring of 1928 (Trotsky archives, T 1175) ; Trotsky believed
that, at the session of the party central committee in April 1928 (see Vol. 1,
pp. 50-59), the Rightists had administered a rebuff to Stalin, and understood
that Bukharin had privately described Stalin as representing a " Trotskyite
danger " (Trotsky archives, T 1588).
[4] Manuilsky vigorously contested this assumption at the sixth congress of
Comintern in July 1928 (*Stenograficheski Otchet VI Kongressa Kominterna*
(1929), v, 56-57).
[5] *Pravda*, June 7, 1928 ; according to a letter in the Trotsky archives, T 1985,
Vardin had, however, been amnestied and was back in Moscow in the middle of
July 1928.

June 1928 Yaroslavsky published an article in *Pravda* headed " No Compromises ", in which he reminded doubters in the opposition ranks that the six-month limit fixed by the fifteenth party congress was about to expire, and that only those who made an unequivocal recantation (Zinoviev, Kamenev, Sarkis and Pyatakov were mentioned as examples) could hope for readmission to the party;[1] and on June 22, 1928, the party central control commission decided to reinstate in the party nearly 40 expelled members of the opposition, including Zinoviev, Kamenev, Evdokimov, Bakaev and Zalutsky.[2] The hesitations of the leaders, added to the pressure of official persecution, completed the disintegration of the rank and file. In the six months after the fifteenth party congress, 2270 members of the opposition were expelled from the party for opposition activities, and 3098 recanted and returned to their allegiance to the official line. Among those who recanted the proportion of workers was said to have been particularly high.[3]

The summer of 1928 was a crucial period in the turn of the party towards the Left and towards more uncompromising policies of industrialization, and in Stalin's growing mastery over the party organization. Stalin at this moment was keenly preoccupied with the balance of power in the party leadership; and for a brief moment Kalinin found himself in a strategic position. Hitherto his background and his inclinations had ranged him on the side of conciliation of the peasant, even of the well-to-do peasant. In the opposition platform of September 1927 he was bracketed with Rykov and A. P. Smirnov as supporters of " a frank and open drift to the Right ".[4] If, as might have been expected, Kalinin had now taken his stand with Rykov, Bukharin and Tomsky, this would have accounted for four votes in a Politburo of nine, and Stalin would have depended on the votes of Kuibyshev, Molotov, Rudzutak and Voroshilov to maintain a bare majority. It is not known what process of persuasion was

---

[1] *Pravda*, June 8, 1928.

[2] *Ibid.* June 29, 1928; Zinoviev celebrated his return by writing a non-controversial article on Austro-Marxism which was published in *Bol'shevik*, No. 16, August 31, 1928, pp. 15-28.

[3] *Ibid.* No. 4, February 28, 1929, pp. 28-29.   [4] See pp. 34–35 above.

applied to Kalinin, and whether it proved easy or difficult.[1] What
is clear is that in the summer of 1928 Kalinin rallied to the view
of the majority, and that this was conclusive for the balance of
forces in the leadership. About the same time Stalin, by means
equally obscure, bound closely to himself the volatile Voroshilov.
Henceforth a firm majority of six in the Politburo confronted the
three potential dissidents.

But Stalin, a master of tactics, paid no less attention to the
control of other points of power and influence in the party machine.
At the end of May 1928, when Bukharin was beginning to air his
dissent in the Politburo, Stalin took an occasion to address the
students of the Institute of Red Professors, hitherto Bukharin's
faithful disciples, in terms cautiously but unmistakably critical
of the views now advanced by Bukharin.[2] The next objective
was to secure control of the principal party organs, *Pravda* and
Bol'shevik, in which, through Bukharin and his supporters, the
influence of the Right had hitherto predominated. This operation
was apparently carried out during the few days before the meeting
of the party central committee on July 4, 1928. Little transpired
in public of what went on behind the scenes. The issue of
Bol'shevik for May 31, 1928, carried a colourless unsigned leading
article on self-criticism, written by one of Bukharin's followers,
Slepkov. At the session of the Moscow party committee on
June 30, 1928, Molotov criticized the article for treating self-
criticism too lightly and called it a " mistake " ; he apparently
named Slepkov as the author of the article, though the name did
not appear in the published report of his speech. On the following
day Slepkov submitted a statement to the Moscow party committee alleging that all the members of the editorial board of
Bol'shevik except Molotov had approved the article, and that
Molotov, having asked that proofs of the issue should be sent to
him before publication, had raised no objections ; and a few days

---

[1] Kalinin is said to have told Zinoviev in January 1929 that " he [Stalin]
talks about Left actions, but very soon will be obliged to carry out my policy in
triple measure, . . . that is why I support him " (*Byulleten' Oppozitsii* (Paris),
No. 1-2, July 1929, p. 16); Kalinin was an amiable man, addicted to wishful
thinking.

[2] For this address see Vol. 1, p. 73 ; for a confused and tendentious account
of the meeting by one who was present see A. Avtorkhanov, *Stalin and the Soviet
Communist Party* (1959), pp. 1-10.

later the statement was repeated in a letter from Slepkov which
was published in *Pravda*. Molotov replied, also in a statement to
the Moscow party committee and in a letter to *Pravda*, that he
had not seen the proofs of the issue in question, since he was
absent on leave in the Crimea ; and, since this fact was known to
Slepkov, he accused Slepkov of having " deliberately said what
was untrue ". He concluded by demanding that the matter
should be referred to the party central control commission.[1] The
first part of an article by the Bukharinite Goldenberg in the issue
of *Bol'shevik* for June 15, 1928, promised a continuation in the
next issue ;[2] this never appeared. In *Pravda* long articles
by Maretsky and Astrov on June 30 and July 1 and 3, 1928, were
silently countered on July 3, 1928, by Stalin's letter to " comrade
S.".[3] What lay behind these apparently trivial occurrences was
a severe shake-up in the editorial control of both journals.
Slepkov, Maretsky, Astrov and Zaitsev were convicted of having
failed to " stand up against the pressure of the petty bourgeoisie ",
and having practised " secret resistance " to the party line. In
July 1928 the party central committee " strengthened the editorial
collegium of *Pravda* " by some unspecified appointments —
notably, it would appear, Krumin and Saveliev — though it was
only in September 1928 that, after a struggle, a new bureau of
the party cell in *Pravda* was elected, composed of " the most
determined comrades capable of guaranteeing a correct party
line ", and the newspaper brought firmly under control.[4]

[1] *Pravda*, July 4, 1928 (Molotov's statement), July 5, 6 (Slepkov's and
Molotov's letters, both referring to their earlier statements to the Moscow party
committee) ; the central control commission, pronouncing some days later on
the Molotov-Slepkov affair, found that Molotov, having been absent from
Moscow, had no opportunity of making any observations on Slepkov's article,
and reproved Slepkov for having failed to check his allegation (*Izvestiya
Tsentral'nogo Komiteta VKP(B)*, No. 23(244), July 31, 1928, p. 13). According
to a report which reached Trotsky (Trotsky archives, T 1588), Slepkov had
attempted to undermine Kirov's position in Leningrad.

[2] *Bol'shevik*, No. 11, June 15, 1928, pp. 8-20.

[3] See Vol. 1, pp. 75-76 ; in *Pravda*, July 7, 1928, an article by Kritsman
praising the extraordinary measures, and treating them as an example of the
offensive against the *kulak* proclaimed by the fifteenth party congress, was
followed by a long and argumentative editorial note — perhaps from the pen of
Astrov — referring to " innumerable letters received by the editors, which
surely reflect the voice of the masses ", as evidence that the extraordinary
measures had weakened the alliance with the peasantry as a whole.

[4] This account was given retrospectively in *Pravda*, August 4, 1929 ; a

Similar changes occurred in the control of the party's principal theoretical journal, *Bol'shevik*. The editorial board, ever since its inception in 1924, had included Kamenev and Yaroslavsky. But the journal had been under the effective editorship of Bukharin, the recognized theorist of the party, and of his disciples, most of them products of the Institute of Red Professors. After the fifteenth party congress in December 1927, its board was composed of Astrov, Bukharin, Molotov, Slepkov and Yaroslavsky, three Bukharinites and two henchmen of Stalin. In June 1928 Krinitsky was added to the board, making the balance even. In August 1928 Slepkov was removed, and Bauman and Popov were added; thenceforward the control was firmly in Stalinist hands.[1] Bukharin's formal status had not been affected. But his real authority had disappeared; and his prestige had been sapped by his failure to protect his subordinates. Meanwhile, the first open attack on the leadership by a member of the party central committee was delivered by Frumkin in his letter to the Politburo of June 15, 1928. Frumkin's letter, though concerned with economic policy, was a direct challenge to the authority of the majority in the Politburo and in the party central committee. It is perhaps significant that, while the original intention was to send a reply to Frumkin in the name of the committee, Stalin hurriedly took the matter into his own hands, and replied to Frumkin in his own name.[2]

The session of the party central committee from July 4 to 12, 1928, was a crucial moment in the struggle between the leadership and the new Right group. The debate on the grain collections was sharply contested; and Bukharin and his supporters were

thorough purge of the party cell took place in July 1929, when 15 members were sent to less responsible work. Other references to the shake-up in *Pravda* in the summer of 1928 appear in a report in the Trotsky archives, T 2442 and in *Voprosy Istorii KPSS*, No. 4, 1960, p. 68; reports reaching Trotsky at the time were that Yaroslavsky had been sent to *Pravda* to keep an eye on Bukharin, and Slepkov had been appointed head of the Agitprop section of the party committee in Yakutsk (Trotsky archives, T 1558).

[1] Each issue of *Bol'shevik* printed a list of the editorial board; but the changes in its composition were belated, and did not reflect the actual position. Astrov formally remained a member of the board till June 1929, and Bukharin throughout the period of his disgrace. For Krinitsky see p. 406 below.

[2] This was stated by Bukharin to Kamenev in the conversation of July 11, 1928 (see pp. 65-66 below); for the Frumkin-Stalin correspondence see Vol. 1, pp. 74-75.

subject to frequent interruptions. Though an open clash between leaders was avoided, Rykov criticized Kaganovich, who was a henchman of Stalin; and Molotov attacked Astrov. Tomsky for the first time came out openly on the side of Bukharin and Rykov.[1] The resolution finally adopted was a compromise which led many to suppose that victory had gone to the Right.[2] It was decided that no member of the Politburo other than Bukharin should speak at the forthcoming sixth congress of Comintern;[3] and on July 30, 1928, when the congress was already in session, a solemn declaration was signed by all members of the Politburo, and sent to the sixth congress of Comintern then in session, protesting " against the dissemination of any kind of rumours about disagreements between members of the Politburo of the VKP(B) ".[4] Stalin was always sensitive to the importance of key appointments: Kaganovich changed places with Kosior, the former becoming a member of the party secretariat, the latter secretary of the Ukrainian party.[5] It seems to have been at this moment that Stalin turned his attention to the Moscow party organization, whose secretary-general Uglanov was reported to have remarked to a Komsomol leader that Stalin was strangling the party and must be got rid of. The beginning of a stubborn struggle for the control of the Moscow organization was afterwards dated back to this time.[6] In spite of the formal assurance that no divisions of opinion existed among members of the Politburo, the difference in tone between the speeches in which Rykov and Stalin commented on the decisions of the session on agricultural policy was sufficiently indicative of the character and sharpness of the conflict.[7] When the proceedings were afterwards discussed in

---

[1] Tomsky later dated back the beginning of his errors to this session, when he thought it necessary " to mitigate the strife which had arisen in the countryside by means of concessions to the middle peasantry " (*XVI S"ezd Vsesoyuznoi Kommunisticheskoi Partii (B)* (1931), p. 143).

[2] See Vol. 1, pp. 80-82.

[3] Trotsky archives, T 2442; according to this report, Lominadze opposed the decision — presumably in order to advertise his support of Stalin.

[4] *KPSS v Rezolyutsiyakh* (1954), ii, 558-559.

[5] *Pravda*, July 13, 1928; for Bukharin's explanation of the move see p. 66 below.

[6] Trotsky archives, T 2442; according to a statement made three months later in the Moscow provincial party committee, the question of Uglanov's removal was first raised by Stalin in July 1928 (*ibid.* T 2811).

[7] See Vol. 1, pp. 76-79.

factories and party cells, references were made to Molotov's attack on Slepkov (Slepkov was said to have written a further reply which *Pravda* had refused to publish, and which was being circulated illegally), to the differences between Stalin and Rykov and to "unprinted correspondence between members of the Politburo" (meaning, no doubt, Bukharin's memoranda of May and June), and the question was asked why Bukharin, contrary to his usual practice, had made no public speech to party members after the end of the session.[1]

But the most lurid light on the situation in the party at this time is shed by Kamenev's record, divulged only six months later, of his conversations with Sokolnikov and Bukharin on July 11, 1928 — the day before the session of the central committee ended. On July 9, 1928, Sokolnikov had written to Kamenev asking for a meeting, and adding mysteriously that " *this would be extremely important* ".[2] Sokolnikov appeared in Kamenev's apartment at 9 a.m. on July 11, 1928, and proceeded to give Kamenev an account of what had happened in the party central committee. Kalinin and Voroshilov had gone over to the majority. Bukharin had identified the official policy with that of Preobrazhensky; Rykov had attacked Kaganovich. "Stalin's line was defeated." Bukharin had twice said (presumably in private to Sokolnikov) that he would now " give up Stalin for Kamenev and Zinoviev " ; he wanted to see Kamenev, and hoped for " a bloc to remove Stalin ". At 10 a.m. Bukharin arrived " without ringing ", and Sokolnikov apparently withdrew.[3] Bukharin was "exceedingly

---

[1] For this report see Vol. 1, p. 83, note 3.

[2] The record in the Trotsky archives, T 1897, contains (1) Sokolnikov's letter, (2) the conversation with Sokolnikov, (3) the conversation with Bukharin, (4) supplementary notes to (3). It is a poorly typed document, slovenly in style and sometimes incoherent; the section on the conversation with Bukharin (which is by far the longest) is marked " Copy of a copy ". The main part of the record bears the note " 6 o'clock July 11 ", but (4) is dated " night of July 11–12 ". Versions of (3) appeared in *Sotsialisticheskii Vestnik* (Berlin), No. 6 (196), March 22, 1929, pp. 10-11, and of (2) and (4) *ibid.* No. 9 (199), May 4, 1929. These versions were incomplete, and not quite accurate ; some corrections, apparently designed to clear up confusions and obscurities of the original, seem to have distorted its meaning.

[3] The record, which is confused at this point, says that Sokolnikov " went away towards the end ". But it seems clear that Kamenev and Bukharin were alone throughout their conversation ; and Bukharin is reported as saying : " I arranged with Sokolnikov to come in again before my departure ".

excited and distressed ", and talked for an hour; " at times his lips twitched nervously ". His main theme was that the struggle had reached a point at which Kamenev and Zinoviev, " and probably the Trotskyites ", would " inevitably be drawn into it and play an important rôle in the decision ". Rykov and Tomsky, who alone knew of his meeting with Kamenev, agreed with him that they would rather have Kamenev and Zinoviev than Stalin in the Politburo. For weeks Bukharin had had no talk with Stalin (this did not appear to tally with remarks of Stalin to him which he quoted: " You would ruin the nerves of an elephant ", and " You and I are Himalayas, the rest are nonentities "); and in the Politburo incivilities like " Nonsense! " and " Liar! " had been exchanged. Bukharin recognized Stalin's tactics: " he has yielded now in order to cut our throats ". Stalin's immediate aims were to take control of *Pravda*, and to replace Uglanov, " who is wholly with us ", by Kaganovich. The Leningraders wavered. Andreev (who would be recalled from the North Caucasian region),[1] Yagoda and Trilisser were named as being against Stalin. On the other hand, Stalin had bought over the Ukrainians (meaning, primarily, Skrypnik) by promising to withdraw Kaganovich from the Ukraine. Orjonikidze " came to see me and swore loudly at Stalin, but at the decisive moment turned tail ". Stalin boasted that he had Kamenev and Zinoviev " in his pocket "; he would probably try to buy them with " high appointments ". Bukharin showed a special animosity against Molotov, " who instructs me in Marxism, and whom we call ' stone bottom ' ". The total impression made on Kamenev by Bukharin was of a doomed man, conscious of his own helplessness. " What can you do when you have such an opponent — a Genghis Khan ? " Stalin, Bukharin repeated, " will wait for *us* to start a discussion and will then cut our throats ". In fact, Stalin was even stronger than Bukharin imagined. He was able to crush the new Right dissidents without making the smallest concession to either wing of the old united opposition. The offers of " high appointments " to Kamenev and Zinoviev never came.

[1] Andreev had been appointed secretary of the party committee of the North Caucasian region in April 1928, when he was succeeded as member of the Orgburo by Bauman.

Meanwhile the approach of the sixth congress of Comintern, which was to meet in the middle of July 1928, provoked further waverings in the opposition camp. In June, Preobrazhensky, apparently without consulting his colleagues in exile, forwarded a statement of policy to the congress which ended with an appeal for re-instatement in the party.[1] About the same time, Radek, acting in ignorance of Preobrazhensky's *démarche*, circulated to Trotsky and seven other opposition leaders a memorandum for the congress which, in default of time to reach agreement, he proposed to send in on his own account. Its essential point was the assertion that " the ' fault ' of the opposition lay in the fact that it sounded the alarm earlier than the leadership of the party ". The implication was that the current official line conformed to the programme of the opposition ; this supported the conclusion that the opposition should be readmitted to the party.[2] Trotsky, true to his posture of proud defiance, sent independently to the congress a massive document which took the form of a critique of Bukharin's draft programme, and was completed on the eve of the congress with a polemical postscript entitled *What Next ?* The whole document breathed an unqualified condemnation of the Stalinist line and admitted no thought of concession or conciliation.[3] While Trotsky alone was responsible for it, his prestige caused it to be commonly regarded as a formal pronouncement of the opposition ; and Radek and Smilga (who had signed the Radek declaration) were persuaded to declare their adhesion to it, though Radek afterwards said that he had done so before he had seen the text.[4] This episode brought clearly into view the growing rift between the two wings of the opposition — the would-be conciliators and the irreconcilables — which Trotsky strove vainly to bridge.[5] All reports circulating in Moscow pointed to

[1] Trotsky archives, T 1594.
[2] *Ibid.* T 1780 ; in a handwritten letter to Trotsky of June 24, 1928, Radek tried to excuse himself for taking independent action (*ibid.* T 2046). Trotsky at once sent a circular letter to his supporters in terms coldly critical of " the theses of comrade Radek " (*Byulleten' Oppozitsii* (Paris), No. 1-2, July 1929, pp. 11-14).
[3] The Russian text is in the Trotsky archives, T 3123 ; in an English translation it is familiar as L. Trotsky, *The Third International after Lenin* (N.Y., 1936).
[4] This was explained by Radek in a memorandum circulated to members of the opposition in September 1928 (Trotsky archives, T 2441).
[5] The rift between Trotsky and Radek was evidenced by an immensely

a coming break in which Stalin would stand for policies of rapid industrialization against a Right opposition ;[1] and it was difficult to resist the conclusion that the old opposition should now rally to the defence of the new official line. For a time, the proceedings of the July session of the party central committee, which appeared to end in a curbing of Stalin's shift to the Left, lent encouragement to the irreconcilables. Trotsky, in a note on " The July Plenum and the Right Danger ", described Rykov's speech to the Moscow party organization of July 13, 1928, as " the report of a victor ", though he added that the victory over Stalin had been won, " it is true, with the help of Stalin himself ", and a little later, in a letter to Smilga, Trotsky argued that Stalin had sustained " a big tactical, though not a strategic, defeat ".[2] Kamenev was on record as thinking that Stalin had been " greatly weakened ", though he shrewdly added that " the apparatus still apparently in the hands of the centre is fairly strong ".[3] But these hopeful speculations did little to mitigate the disarray into which the old opposition had fallen.

The sixth congress of Comintern which met in Moscow from July 17 to September 1, 1928, marked a further stage in the discrediting of Bukharin. On the eve of the congress — evidently about the same time as his meeting with Kamenev — he invited Humbert-Droz, the Swiss member of the Comintern hierarchy

long memorandum written by Radek in the summer of 1928 on the theory of the proletarian dictatorship ; this was devoted to a critical examination of Trotsky's views since 1905, and ended by expressing the fear that the continued exclusion of the opposition from the party would keep it " without influence on the policy of the Soviet Government " (Trotsky archives, T 2324). Trotsky wrote to Radek on October 20, 1928, reminding him of recent pronouncements by him of a very different tenour (*ibid.* T 2820) ; on the following day he addressed a long circular letter to his supporters in which he again tried, with diminishing conviction, to build a common platform for the opposition (*ibid.* T 3146 ; *Die Fahne des Kommunismus*, No. 1, January 4, 1929).

[1] A foreign communist living in Moscow at this time recorded that, " when in 1928 the Stalin group and with it the whole party declared for war against private capitalism, I believed at first that this meant the proletarian and revolutionary rebirth of the communist party " (A. Ciliga, *Au Pays du Grand Mensonge* (1938), p. 82).

[2] Trotsky archives, T 3126, 2480.

[3] *Ibid.* T 2630.

who was already suspect of Rightist sympathies, to visit him in the Kremlin, and revealed the clash in the Politburo on the agrarian question, representing Stalin as having " capitulated " to the Trotsky-Zinoviev line. What may have passed between the two men on the issues confronting Comintern is not recorded.[1] When the congress met, Bukharin circulated the customary theses on the tasks of Comintern and the work of IKKI, which he was to present to the congress, without — according to a later statement of Stalin — having followed the normal procedure of submitting them in advance to the party delegation. The delegation hurriedly met, and insisted on no less than 20 amendments to the theses, thus advertising to the foreign delegates that Bukharin no longer enjoyed the full confidence of his own party.[2] During the congress, the " Neumann-Lominadze group " intrigued against Bukharin in the corridors.[3] Hints, or something more than hints, of Bukharin's fall from grace were given to leading members of foreign delegations. Stalin is said to have told Foster, the leader of the American delegation, that " his differences with Bukharin extended over a long period, but that the time had come when Bukharin's Right deviations could no longer be tolerated ". Another American delegate described the situation as follows :

> There were two congresses going on at the sixth world congress. One was the official congress over which Bukharin presided. . . . Then there was the corridor congress called together by Stalin ; . . . through it a devastating campaign was carried on against Bukharin as a Right-winger.[4]

From the platform of the congress Bukharin dutifully asserted, both in his main report on the tasks of IKKI and again in his reply to the debate, that in Comintern " the *Right deviation* now

---

[1] Unnumbered and undated memorandum in French in Humbert-Droz archives headed " My Relations with the Group of Rightists and Conciliators (Versöhnler) ", shown by internal evidence to have been written after the seventh congress of Comintern in 1935 ; Comintern affairs will be discussed in a subsequent volume.

[2] For Stalin's account of this episode see *Sochineniya*, xii, 19-23 ; the main charges against Bukharin were his failure to explain that the current stabilization of capitalism was insecure, and offered the prospect of " a new revolutionary upsurge ", and his omission, in speaking of the danger of a Right deviation, to say anything of the danger of appeasement of Right deviationists.

[3] See Humbert-Droz's memorandum cited in note 1 above.

[4] B. Gitlow, *I Confess* (N.Y., 1940), pp. 503, 507.

presents the central danger ", and that " the chief danger is, beyond doubt, the Right danger ".[1] But he drew no conclusions from the formula; and nobody hinted at its application to the Russian party. The theses adopted by the congress, while admitting that in some communist parties (for example, the Chinese) the danger of ultra-Leftism might still predominate, proclaimed that " the main line of deviations from the correct political position is to the Right ".[2] But Bukharin did not succeed in dispelling the impression of his own personal predilection for the Right, especially in the controversies raging in the German party. Bukharin could no longer protect his friends. The time would come when he would no longer be able to protect himself.[3]

Meanwhile any hint of a Right danger in the Russian party was sedulously avoided. On August 22, 1928, when the congress had already been in session for five weeks, Varga delivered a long report on the economic achievements and problems of the Soviet Union, and Manuilsky a review, entirely devoted to the Trotskyite opposition, of the situation in the Russian party.[4] These were followed next day, not by a debate, but by a series of prepared statements made on behalf of groups of foreign delegations, all laudatory of official policy and all sharply condemning the Trotskyite standpoint. A commission was appointed to draft a resolution on the subject.[5] The resolution, which was unanimously adopted without discussion on the last day of the congress, hailed " the successes of socialist construction in the Soviet Union " and endorsed the resolutions of the fifteenth party congress of December 1927 and of the ninth IKKI of February 1928 on the expulsion of members of the opposition from the party. A separate resolution proposed by Kolarov, and also adopted without discussion, pronounced it " superfluous to discuss with enemies of the

[1] *Stenograficheskii Otchet VI Kongressa Kominterna* (1929), i, 58, 610.
[2] *Kommunisticheskii Internatsional v Dokumentakh* (1933), p. 792.
[3] In the autumn of 1928 Bukharin opposed the official line, and supported the Right, on two issues in the German party, the proposed sanctions against Thälmann for attempting to cover up the Wittorf scandal, and the expulsion of Brandler and Thalheimer from the party ; this was part of Stalin's case against him (Stalin, *Sochineniya*, xii, 23-26). These questions will be discussed in a subsequent volume.
[4] *Stenograficheskii Otchet VI Kongressa Kominterna* (1929), v, 3-53, 55-85.
[5] *Ibid.* v, 86-96.

Communist International the counter-revolutionary political content of the Trotskyite platform ", since this had been decisively rebutted by the whole party, and rejected " the request of Trotsky, Radek, Sapronov and the other excluded persons for reinstatement in the party ".[1] Bukharin, who had borne the brunt of the work of the congress during its first five weeks, and presented its two major reports, took no part in these proceedings against the opposition. But in the report of the proceedings given a few days later to a party meeting in Moscow, he once more explained that, after the defeat of the Trotskyites, " the central phenomenon and the decisive danger within Comintern is the *Right* danger ".[2] It was Bukharin's last appearance as a major spokesman of party policy. Trotsky contemptuously compared his utterances at the congress to " bubbles emitted by a drowning man ", and remarked that the number of hours which he talked at the congress was " in inverse ratio to his influence, which declined from day to day " ; Stalin was successful in winning over three-fourths, if not nine-tenths, of the " apparatus-men " of the visiting foreign delegations.[3]

As Bukharin moved more and more decisively into the opposition camp, Molotov emerged as the leading theorist — under Stalin — of the party. The month of September 1928 was one of great activity for Molotov.[4] With the taking over of *Pravda* and *Bol'shevik* and the disgrace of Slepkov, Astrov and Maretsky, the Institute of Red Professors, long the preserve of Bukharin, had changed its ideological complexion.[5] It was apparently in September 1928 that Molotov found himself defending the cautious party line against three Red professors of the ultra-Left, Kostrov, Shatskin and Lominadze, of whom the two last were prominent in the Komsomol, and who now

[1] *Ibid.* v, 135-136 ; *Kommunisticheskii Internatsional v Dokumentakh* (1933), pp. 870-872, 873-874.   [2] *Pravda*, September 12, 1928.

[3] Trotsky archives, T 3129, p. 26, T 3146.

[4] Stalin appears to have been on holiday at the time ; he returned to Moscow on October 3, 1928 (*Izvestiya*, October 5, 1928).

[5] An undated letter of August or September 1928 from a Moscow Trotskyite reported that " under the flag of self-criticism Stalin has conquered the Institute of Red Professors " (Trotsky archives, T 2442) ; a re-election of the party cell in the institute was said to have eliminated supporters of Uglanov, and " the Bukharin school was expelled from the walls of the institute " (*Bor'ba Klassov*, No. 8-9, 1931, p. 28).

demanded permission to attack the Right leaders by name. Molotov was emphatic that no names should be used in attacks on the Right, and thought that the recent ultra-Left tone of *Komsomol'skaya Pravda* should be moderated. He admitted that "fractional" remarks by Uglanov against Stalin had been reported; but it was difficult to remove him at the moment. Molotov gave an assurance that the Right group in the Politburo was confined to Rykov, Bukharin and Tomsky, and that Kalinin supported the majority.[1] In the middle of September *Pravda* intervened to reprove the Moscow party committee for passing a resolution, on a report by Uglanov, which concentrated its attention on the Trotskyite opposition and neglected the offensive against the *kulak*.[2] A leading article in *Pravda* of September 18, 1928, headed "Comintern on the Struggle against Right Deviations" plainly hinted at the application of the Comintern theses to the Russian party. On September 22, 1928, Molotov addressed a conference of newspaper editors and, at the end of a mainly non-controversial speech, quoted the decision recently recorded by the sixth congress of Comintern "to intensify the struggle against Right deviations and against a conciliatory attitude to such deviations". He went on to remark that Trotskyism was "only one of the varieties of opportunism in our conditions", and cited the exhortation of the July session of the party central committee to press on with the campaign against the *kulak*. The resolution adopted by the conference after Molotov's speech was even more precise:

> It is essential to strengthen the ideological-political struggle against attempts to revive Trotskyism. At the same time it is essential to conduct a more resolute ideological struggle against the other opportunist perversions of the party line mentioned in the resolution of the July session of the party central committee, treating this struggle against open and half-open opportunist waverings as a main task, on the basis of the directive of the sixth congress of Comintern to intensify the struggle against Right deviations.[3]

[1] Trotsky archives, T 2533; for the campaign of *Komsomol'skaya Pravda* against the trade unions see Vol. 1, p. 553.
[2] See Vol. 1, pp. 88-89.
[3] Molotov's speech appeared in *Pravda*, September 26, 1928, the resolution *ibid.* October 3, 1928.

The balance had, however, to be preserved. Though in the top levels of the party the main challenge now came from the Right, " Trotskyism " had not entirely lost its appeal to the rank and file. Party circles were full of rumours. One, said to have been spread by " the Bukharin school ", was that " Stalin is carrying out the policy of the ' Trotskyites ', and is preparing an alliance with them ".[1] Speakers still appeared from time to time to uphold the cause of the Trotskyite opposition in party cells and factory meetings ; and in September 1928 a campaign was conducted for the release of Trotsky from Alma Ata on grounds of health.[2] Kamenev is said to have told two Trotskyites in Moscow in September 1928 that, if Trotsky were to issue an appeal " Call me, and we will work together ", he and his supporters would be welcomed back to the party and to responsible posts.[3] Official reports of the autumn of 1928 noted renewed activity by " the former Trotskyite opposition " in a factory district in Moscow, and an increased distribution of leaflets.[4] While most opposition documents were typed or multigraphed sheets, the occasional appearance of a printed manifesto bore witness to the possession of an illicit printing-press.[5] These activities called for counter-measures. A circular of the party central committee of September 26, 1928, signed by Molotov instructed regional and provincial party committees to react more sharply against Trotskyite manifestoes and demonstrations. " Active anti-party elements " among the workers were to be transferred from large to small enterprises, where they would do less harm, and were not to be admitted to the Red Army. Underground anti-party and anti-Soviet activities, especially among workers, were to be met by " decisive measures of revolutionary repression ". On the following day the Politburo called for " appropriate measures " against recent Trotskyite demonstrations.[6] This was no idle

---

[1] Trotsky archives, T 2442 (an anonymous report of September 1928 from Moscow).   [2] Trotsky archives, T 2534, 2535, 2560.

[3] Trotsky archives, T 2630. A record of this conversation appears to exist in the party archives ; Kamenev was reported to have advised his interlocutors to enter the party, to take state or trade union posts, and to wait till " the crisis matures " (*Voprosy Istorii KPSS*, No. 3, 1968, p. 49).

[4] Trotsky archives, T 2854, 2897.

[5] For poorly printed opposition manifestoes dated October 1928 and November 7, 1928, see *ibid*. T 2698, 2865 ; the latter was printed in 1000 copies.

[6] Trotsky archives, T 2674.

threat. On the night of October 21, 1928, more than 100 opposi-
tionists were said to have been arrested in Leningrad, Kharkov and
Moscow; and further waves of arrests followed in Kiev and
Leningrad.[1] The party leaders, at the moment of grappling with
the new Right opposition, were unwilling to incur any imputation
of relaxing the struggle against Trotskyism on the other wing.
The Zinovievites were less stubborn and recalcitrant. By the
end of 1928 it was reported that " almost the whole ' Leningrad
opposition ' has returned to the ranks of the party ".[2]

[1] Trotsky archives, T 2829, 2849, 2850.
[2] *Bol'shevik*, No. 2, January 31, 1929, p. 23.

CHAPTER 41

THE RIGHT DEVIATION

D URING the next few weeks, the simmering crisis at length boiled over. It is impossible to determine on the existing evidence, and may never have been clear, which group took the initiative in bringing the dispute to breaking point. Did Bukharin, or those with whom he acted, decide that a stand must now be made ? Or did Stalin decide at a given moment to nip in the bud the new opposition from the Right ? Perhaps no such decision was consciously taken on either side. But Bukharin was the most articulate, and intellectually best equipped, member of the Right wing; and the issue inevitably took the form of a clash between the groups of which Stalin and Bukharin were respectively the figureheads. By common consent the publication in *Pravda* on September 30, 1928, of Bukharin's *Notes of an Economist* was a political event; the article was the manifesto of the new Right.[1] Even Trotsky, who thought the article " a document not only of theoretical nullity, but of political helplessness ", marked the importance of the moment in one of those ironically condescending phrases which he habitually reserved for Bukharin :

> He has put his foot into cold water, but is still afraid to step into it. He stands and shivers — with courage.[2]

And Smilga, having demolished Bukharin's economic arguments, asked in bewilderment :

> How could it happen that a man who had deserved so well of the working class, who had worked long years under Lenin's leadership, the author of several interesting books, should have sunk to the shameful rôle of the theorist of those elements in the

[1] See Vol. 1, pp. 89-90, 317-319.
[2] Trotsky archives, T 3146.

VKP which are dragging the party and the whole working class
into the thermidorian abyss ?[1]

Rumours had for some time been circulating in Moscow of
Bukharin's secret visit to Kamenev in July and of his readiness to
" give up " Stalin and Molotov for Kamenev and Zinoviev.[2] It
is inconceivable that the party leaders were unaware of these
manœuvres, or failed to lay their plans to frustrate them. Such
precautions were scarcely needed. Bukharin lacked altogether the
astuteness and organizing skill of the politician. In conversation
with Humbert-Droz he insisted on the importance of remaining
within the limits of party legality and not forming a fraction.[3]
At this crucial juncture he left Moscow on a delayed vacation after
his exertions at the congress of Comintern. Before departing for
the Caucasus, Bukharin had made a perfunctory attempt to
regulate the tactics of his group. He would write articles for
Pravda from Kislovodsk ; Rykov would keep watch over economic
policy ; Uglanov, who was " in a very pugnacious mood ", was
instructed to keep quiet.[4] Unfortunately, Uglanov had already
compromised himself by his indiscretions at the session of the
Moscow provincial party committee in September. The committee's letter of October 2, 1928, admitting the shortcomings
of its September resolution was evidently regarded as inadequate.

[1] For Smilga's memorandum of October 23, 1928, see Vol. 1, p. 90 ; a
rebuttal of Bukharin's article, which it did not specifically mention, by the
economist Leontiev, appeared in *Pravda*, November 4, 1928. Bukharin in
conversation with Tasca referred to two replies to his *Notes of an Economist* by
Smilga and Preobrazhensky, the first hostile in tone, the second " the only one
which was interesting from the point of view of doctrine " (*Annali, 1966* (Milan,
1966), p. 656) ; Preobrazhensky's reply has not been traced.

[2] They were mentioned in a circular letter of Trotsky to his supporters of
October 21, 1928 (Trotsky archives, T 3146).

[3] See memorandum in Humbert-Droz archives cited p. 69, note 1 above.

[4] This account, given by Bukharin in a conversation with Kamenev in
January 1929, was reproduced in a note signed " G.G." in *Byulleten' Oppozitsii*
(Paris), No. 1-2, July 1929, pp. 15-17 ; since the published document is a record
made by an anonymous Trotskyite of Kamenev's account of the conversation,
the margin of error (apart from any suspicion of hindsight in Bukharin's story)
is large, and this source must be treated with caution. Bukharin wrote *Notes of
an Economist* in the last week of September 1928 ; the latest identifiable reference
in it is to an article in *Ekonomicheskaya Zhizn'*, September 21, 1928. He
probably left Moscow about the time of its publication on September 30, 1928.
An article by him in honour of Pokrovsky's birthday, which appeared in *Pravda*
on October 25, 1928, was dated " Kislovodsk, October 21 ". He returned to
Moscow in the first week of November 1928 (see p. 78 below).

When the committee met again on October 18, 1928, Uglanov, though he sponsored a fresh resolution retracting the errors of its predecessor, still seemed half-hearted in his penitence.[1] Stalin in his speech on the occasion for the first time specifically pointed to the Right deviation as the major danger, but (if the record is accurate) sedulously refrained from mentioning names. He admitted that in the party central committee there were " some, it is true very insignificant, elements of a conciliatory attitude to the Right danger ", and referred to the stenographic record of the July session of the committee as evidence of this.   But he categorically maintained that " in the Politburo there are neither Right nor ' Left ' nor conciliators ", and denounced rumours of deviations in the Politburo as "slanders ".[2] Uglanov momentarily saved himself by completely reversing his earlier position, denouncing the Right danger and praising Stalin.[3] But the session, at which no other representative of the Bukharin group ventured to appear, was an unmitigated set-back for the group, and paved the way for the elimination of its influence in the Moscow party organization. *Pravda*, which had hitherto treated the " Right danger " with cautious circumspection, now described the struggle against it as " the most important task for the whole coming period ."[4] The session of the Moscow party committee was followed by resolutions of Moscow district party organizations concerning the Right danger, and by meetings at which Uglanov himself came under heavy fire ; at one of these he pleaded pathetically that this had been the first error committed by the Moscow organization for four years.[5] It was ironically noted that, on the anniversary of the revolution on November 7, 1928, slogans which had been used a year earlier by the old opposition, and condemned as heretical, reappeared as official slogans in the struggle against the Bukharinites: " Down with the *kulak*, the nepman, and the

---

[1] For these proceedings see Vol. 1, pp. 90-92.
[2] Stalin, *Sochineniya*, xi, 235-236.
[3] This was presumably the occasion when, in the words of an eye-witness, Uglanov " made a pitiful recantation and confession of his sins, promising with tears to toe the party line in the future, praising Stalin's clear-sightedness, and delivering himself of all the rest of the routine hokum " (A. Barmine, *One Who Survived* (1965), p. 170).
[4] *Pravda*, Oct. 20, 1928.
[5] *Ibid.* October 23, 24, 1928.

bureaucrat ", " Fire to the Right ", " We will fulfil Lenin's
behests ".[1]

A session of the party central committee, at which Rykov was
to present a resolution on the five-year plan, was convened for
November 16, 1928. At the end of October, Rykov, in accordance
with the usual practice, prepared a draft resolution for submission
to the Politburo. At this point, Bukharin, knowing Rykov's
weakness and fearing that Stalin would " twist him round his
finger in the Politburo ", decided to hasten his return from the
Caucasus, flying by rapid stages. The authorities vetoed this
plan (regular aeroplane traffic scarcely existed in the Soviet Union
at this date), and he was obliged to complete his journey by train,
arriving in Moscow on the day after the Politburo had deliberated.[2]
Here his worst fears were confirmed. Rykov's draft resolution
had been amended in the Politburo to raise the allocations to
industrial development and to the Sovkhozy and kolkhozy, and
Rykov had accepted the changes.[3] Bukharin now put forward 11
demands, some of them economic, others relating to the removal
from key positions of certain Stalinist nominees, notably Krumin,
who was now de facto editor of Pravda. Among his demands was
a proposal to issue in the party organ a firm denial of " unfounded
talk about political disagreements in the Politburo ". Stalin also
wished to avoid a head-on collision, and proposed the appointment
of a commission of the Politburo consisting of Rykov, Bukharin,
Stalin, Molotov and Orjonikidze to consider the demands.
Bukharin's own account, relayed at second hand, is the main
authority for what followed. Delaying tactics were employed.
Bukharin, by way of an ultimatum, forced the commission to
meet; and an open quarrel occurred between him and Stalin,
apparently over Krumin's appointment. Bukharin left the room,
and handed to Stalin's secretary a prepared document announcing
his and Tomsky's resignation from the Politburo. When Stalin

[1] Trotsky archives, T 2850 ; for the 1927 slogans see p. 42 above.
[2] See the source cited p. 76, note 4 above ; Bukharin returned in time to
speak at the anniversary celebrations of November 7, 1928, when he mentioned
that he had just arrived in Moscow (Pravda, November 10, 1928). The speech
was intended to be non-controversial; he spoke of industrialization as " the
focus of all our work ", but added that " our country is a petty bourgeois
country . . . and will remain so for a considerable period ".
[3] See Vol. 1, pp. 92, 325.

received this, " his hands trembled, he turned pale, and said
that he was willing to make concessions ". Eventually it was
agreed to remove Krumin and two other Stalinists. On the
economic issues Bukharin had less success, being dissuaded by
Pyatakov from pressing this issue against Stalin, " the one man
who can still command obedience ". The theses of Rykov were
adopted in their amended form. But a somewhat incongruous
conclusion was added to them dealing with " deviations of various
kinds within the party ". These were described as a " Right
(openly opportunist) deviation " and " social-democratic, anti-
middle-peasant, super-industrialist tendencies (Trotskyism) ".
But the danger of the " Right openly opportunist deviation "
was firmly declared to be " at the present time the chief danger in
the VKP(B) ". This part of the resolution was, according to
Bukharin's own story, drafted by Bukharin himself in order to
" let the party know that I am not a Rightist ".[1]

When the party central committee met, Stalin dealt at length
with the situation in the party. The victory of the Right deviation
would, he explained, mean " the ideological destruction of our
party, the unleashing of capitalist elements, and an increase in the
chances for a restoration of capitalism ". Its adherents were to be
found " in the apparatus of our Soviet and economic, cooperative
and trade union institutions, and also in our party apparatus,
especially in its lower links in the countryside " ; Frumkin was its
typical representative. Having held the balance by a passage on
the " Left " deviation and the need to fight on both fronts,

---

[1] This account is derived from the source cited p. 76, note 4 above. Tasca
reports Bukharin as saying that he drafted the whole resolution " from the first
line to the last " (*Annali, 1966* (Milan, 1966), p. 656) ; but this must be a mis-
understanding. Orjonikidze, at the sixteenth party congress in 1930, recalled
Bukharin's " seven points having the character of an ultimatum ", including his
demand for a denial of rumours of differences in the Politburo (*XVI S"ezd
Vsesoyuznoi Kommunisticheskoi Partii (B)* (1931), p. 326). Bukharin is also said
to have demanded that Thälmann, the KPD leader, should be called to order for
criticizing his theses at the sixth congress of Comintern, and that Neumann,
the IKKI delegate, who had supported Thälmann, should be recalled from
Berlin (Stalin, *Sochineniya*, xii, 25). All sources agree that Bukharin and
Tomsky tendered their resignations and then withdrew them ; according to the
resolution of February 9, 1929 (see p. 89 below), Rykov also resigned. Bukharin
seems to have told Tasca that he gave way because Tomsky and Rykov de-
serted him (*Annali, 1966* (Milan, 1966), p. 658). For Rykov's draft resolution
see Vol. 1, pp. 92-93, 325 ; the concluding section of the resolution on deviations is in *KPSS v Rezolyutsiyakh* (1954), ii, 538-540.

Stalin returned to the Right. The resolution was correct in recommending the *ideological method* of struggle against the Right, since he did not believe that the Right deviation yet constituted a fraction. Organizational measures were not excluded, but should at present play a subordinate rôle. Stalin referred to Uglanov as a self-confessed supporter of the Right, but named none of the other leaders.[1] The resolution was unanimously adopted; and a formal decision was taken that all members of the Politburo should affirm in their public utterances the unity of the Politburo and the absence of disagreements within it.[2] The traditional reports on the proceedings to large Moscow and Leningrad party meetings were made on November 30, 1928, by Molotov and Rykov respectively (Bukharin's absence was significant). Molotov cited Frumkin as a representative figure of the Right deviation, but, like Stalin in the committee, mentioned no other names. He spoke of the need to cleanse the party of alien elements and indicated that the question of a party purge would be put before the forthcoming party conference. Rykov's emphasis was different. He, too, attacked Frumkin and the Right deviation. But he quoted with disapproval a reference in *Komsomol'skaya Pravda* to " elements which are dragging us along the path of a bourgeois-democratic restoration ", and indignantly declared that no such elements existed in the party. He appeared to dismiss the necessity for a purge :

When we speak of Right deviations, we understand deviations within the party, which must at the present stage be overcome by ideological struggle.

And, while formally maintaining the fiction of unanimity, he went far to admitting the existence of dissent among the leaders :

Decisions have been adopted unanimously, in the commis-

---

[1] Stalin, *Sochineniya*, xi, 270, 286-287. A month later, when German party delegates in the presidium of the IKKI quoted this speech as an argument against the application of reprisals to the German Right, Stalin repeated that " the Rightists in the VKP(B) do not yet represent a fraction and, incontestably, they carry out loyally the decisions of the central committee of the VKP(B) " ; this was not true of the German Right (*ibid.* xi, 307).

[2] Stalin, *Sochineniya*, xi, 321; a leading article in *Pravda*, November 25, 1928, emphasized that the resolution had been unanimously sponsored by the Politburo and unanimously adopted by the central committee.

sion of the Politburo, in the Politburo itself and in the plenum of
the central committee. Of course, we have disputes on particular
specific questions of our policy, our economic, cultural and other
construction. Under Ilich and with his participation, we also
quarrelled with one another, but nothing but good came of
this. . . . You elected us to the central committee, we were
elected to the Politburo — for what ? To discuss, dispute and
decide. But, if deviations are seen in every quarrel, then put
dolls or tailors' dummies there.[1]

If Bukharin persuaded himself that his tactics had resulted in
a victory for his cause, or had at least secured him a respite,
he was quickly disillusioned. In fact each successive compromise
only drew the noose tighter round the neck of the dissidents.
Scarcely had the session of the party central committee ended
when — even before Molotov and Rykov had delivered their
reports on it — the leaders completed their purge of the Moscow
party organization. At a meeting of the Moscow party committee
on November 27, 1928, Molotov stressed the need to struggle not
only against " the Right danger ", but against " a conciliationist
attitude to the Right danger " ; and the committee resolved on a
number of changes in personnel. Uglanov, the chief secretary
of the committee, was relieved of his post " at his own request ",
together with another secretary ; Molotov and Bauman were
appointed in their place ; and numerous other changes were made
in the personnel of the committee and of its administrative
sections. A provincial party conference was to be held in January,
following county and district conferences, to endorse these
appointments.[2] Three days later, the Moscow party meeting which
listened to Molotov's report on the session of the party central
committee went out of its way to express its approval of the
changes in the Moscow organization.[3] These moves were
patently designed to eliminate supporters and potential supporters
of Bukharin and Rykov, and to place the key Moscow organization

[1] Molotov's and Rykov's reports appeared in *Pravda*, December 4, 1928.
[2] *Pravda*, November 28, 1928 ; *Pravda* subsequently wrote of these
proceedings that " the party masses corrected the party line, and disciplined its
individual leaders " (*ibid.* January 12, 1929). For Uglanov's appointment as
People's Commissar for Labour see Vol. 1, pp. 555-556.
[3] *Pravda*, December 1, 1928 ; for Molotov's report see p. 80, note 3 above.

under the firm direction of the party majority in the person of
Molotov. Rykov and Bukharin were for the moment untouched.
If Tomsky was punished by eviction, at the eighth trade union
congress of December 1928, from his long-standing leadership
of the Soviet trade unions,[1] this was because he himself forced
the issue by resigning.

Having thus demonstrated his power against his new rivals
on the Right, Stalin turned to deal a final blow at his old enemies
on the other flank. Zinoviev and Kamenev, after a series of self-
inflicted humiliations, no longer counted, and could be ignored.[2]
But Trotsky, stubborn and articulate, was still a focus of disaffec-
tion; and the activity of his supporters had appeared to increase
in recent months. A memorandum of Stalin written at this time,
but not published till many years later, drew a sharp distinction
between " the former Trotskyite opposition within the VKP(B) "
and " the present anti-Soviet Trotskyite underground organization outside the VKP(B) ", and argued that " the ' liberal '
attitude towards those engaged in the underground Trotskyite
organization, sometimes exhibited by individual members of the
party, is completely inadmissible ".[3] Yaroslavsky responded to
the signal with a series of virulent articles in the party journal,
once more trouncing the opposition, poking fun at the dissensions
within it, and gloating over the number of defectors who had
asked for reinstatement in the party.[4] On November 10, 1928,
a decision was apparently reached to stop the political correspondence of all the exiles, with the exception of Preobrazhensky,
Radek, Ishchenko and Serebryakov, who were rightly believed

[1] See Vol. 1, pp. 559-560.

[2] Kamenev, by way of demonstrating his loyalty, wrote an article entitled
"New Style, Business Style", on the reconstruction of industry, which appeared
in *Pravda*, November 16, 1928; according to the report cited p. 76, note 4
above, Zinoviev and Kamenev had conversations with Orjonikidze in December
1928, presumably with a view to their re-employment in party or government
service, but these came to nothing.

[3] Stalin, *Sochineniya*, xi, 317. The memorandum is approximately dated by
a reference to Trotsky's circular letter of October 21, 1928 (see p. 76, note 2
above); it clearly preceded the decision to expel Trotsky from the USSR.

[4] *Bol'shevik*, No. 23-24, December 31, 1928, pp. 13-24; No. 2, January 31,
1929, pp. 14-31; No. 4, February 28, 1929, pp. 18-28.

to be moving towards recantation and submission; and at the
beginning of December 1928 Trotsky protested against an
" absolute postal blockade for more than a month ".[1] On December 16, 1928, the representative of the OGPU in Alma-Ata visited
Trotsky, and made a formal statement. Trotsky's supporters,
he declared, were engaged in counter-revolutionary activities,
which were directed by Trotsky. In these circumstances, the
OGPU required from him " a categorical undertaking " to abstain
from all political activity; otherwise it would be necessary to
bring about his " complete isolation from political life " — a
decision which would raise the question of a change in his place of
residence. Trotsky formally refused to answer unless the statement were put in writing. In fact, he replied in the form of a
letter addressed on the same day to the party central committee
and to IKKI, which combined a blunt refusal of the demand
with a merciless denunciation of " the fraction of Stalin " and all
its works.[2]

In face of this defiance two courses of action were open to the
Politburo: to place Trotsky in strict confinement or to expel him
from the Soviet Union. The course of the debate which must
have taken place is not known. According to one account,
Bukharin, Rykov and Tomsky voted against expulsion, and
another member of the Politburo — perhaps Kuibyshev — argued
against it in private.[3] But expulsion may well have seemed the
milder and less invidious, as well as the more convenient, alternative. It effectively ended the existence of an organized Trotskyite opposition in the Soviet Union. That Trotsky's presence
abroad might prejudice Soviet relations with foreign countries
probably occurred to nobody at a time when these relations did
not seem very important.[4] At the turn of the year 315 supposed

[1] Trotsky archives, T 2850, 2912.
[2] The letter was published in L. Trotsky, *Chto i kak Proizoshlo* (Paris, 1929),
pp. 57-65; it presumably reached neither of the addressees. The account was
repeated in L. Trotsky, *Moya Zhizn'* (Berlin, 1930), ii, 308-313.
[3] *Byulleten' Oppozitsii* (Paris), No. 1-2, June–July 1929, p. 3; the adverse
vote of Bukharin, Rykov and Tomsky is confirmed by a letter in the Tasca
archives (*Annali, 1966* (Milan, 1966), p. 648).
[4] Some members of the opposition were so puzzled by the decision that they
suspected a plot to have Trotsky assassinated either on the journey or on arrival
in Turkey (see letters from Pascal and Nin in the Tasca archives (*Annali, 1966*
(Milan, 1966), pp. 648-649).

Trotskyites were rounded up, and deported to various destinations.[1]
On January 18, 1929, the special conference of the OGPU — a
standing body to deal with important political offenders — resolved
to "banish citizen Trotsky L. D. from the territories of the
USSR ". The decision was based on art. 58 of the criminal code ;
the charge was one of " criminal activity, taking the form of the
organization of an anti-Soviet party, the action of which has been
directed recently to provoking anti-Soviet demonstrations, and
to preparing an armed struggle against the Soviet power ". On
January 20, 1929, the decision was presented to Trotsky in
Alma Ata. Two days later, the party travelled through intense
cold, on the road by which they had come almost exactly a year
earlier, to the railhead at Frunze, and transferred to a special
train. En route, after long delays, Trotsky learned that his
destination was Constantinople. He embarked at Odessa on
February 10, 1929, and reached Constantinople two days later.[2]
A last minute appeal by Trotsky to be allowed to go to Germany
rather than to Turkey would apparently have been granted by the
Soviet authorities. But the German Government, to Trotsky's
intense indignation, refused a visa.[3]

Trotsky's expulsion from the Soviet Union was not immediately announced, though the news must have spread rapidly
among party members, at any rate in the capital. On January 24,
1929, *Pravda* published a leading article, said to have been written
by Stalin, arguing that the Trotskyites had completed their
evolution from an " underground anti-party group " to an " underground anti-Soviet group ", and that this development justified
and necessitated measures taken by the OGPU.[4] A month later
at the Moscow provincial party conference Yaroslavsky referred
casually to " Trotsky's banishment " as something which would
evidently be familiar to his hearers.[5] Full publicity was eventually
given to Trotsky's first contacts with the outer world. Yaro-

---

[1] *Annali, 1966* (Milan, 1966), p. 648.
[2] L. Trotsky, *Chto i kak Proizoshlo* (Paris, 1929), pp. 16-17; *id. Moya
Zhizn'* (Berlin, 1930), ii, 313-317.
[3] *Byulleten' Oppozitsii* (Paris), No. 1-2, July 1929, pp. 5-8.
[4] The evidence for Stalin's authorship is the inclusion of the article in
Stalin, *Sochineniya*, xi, 313-317, where the editors inexplicably describe it as
" printed for the first time "; except for one or two trivial verbal corrections,
the texts are identical.
[5] *Pravda*, March 2, 1929; the speech was delivered on February 26, 1929.

slavsky, in an indignant article printed both in *Pravda* and in *Bol'shevik* entitled " Mr. Trotsky in the Service of the Bourgeoisie : or the First Steps of L. D. Trotsky Abroad ", noted that the exile's first action on arrival in Constantinople (now for the first time publicly mentioned as his destination) had been to send a respectful telegram to the president of the Turkish republic. The centre-piece of the article was a facsimile of the front page of the *Daily Express* of February 27, 1929, with the banner headline " Trotsky's Own Story of his Exile from Russia ".[1] A fortnight later a second article dealt faithfully with further contributions from Trotsky's pen to the *Daily Express*, to the syndicated American press and to several European newspapers. Trotsky was described with withering scorn as " a *gentleman* who, without blinking, takes tens of thousands in gold from the reactionary bourgeoisie " ; and Trotsky's son, also in Constantinople, was quoted as saying that his father would devote the proceeds of the articles to the dissemination of writings by opponents of Stalin.[2] The frenzied anger exhibited in these articles may have been prompted by a sudden and belated recognition how powerful an antagonist the Soviet Government, by its decision to exile Trotsky, had let loose on the world. It set the tone for all Soviet dealings with and about Trotsky throughout the ensuing decade.

Before Trotsky had left Soviet soil, Stalin was again faced with the struggle against the Right opposition. At the turn of the year Bukharin had two further secret meetings with Kamenev, the first together with Pyatakov, who was apparently in hospital at the time, the second, which took place on January 10, 1929, in the

[1] *Pravda*, March 8, 1929 ; *Bol'shevik*, No. 5, March 15, 1928, pp. 60-69.

[2] *Pravda*, March 22, 1929 ; according to an article by Yaroslavsky in *Pravda*, May 30, 1929, Radek and Smilga expressed disapproval of Trotsky's contributions to the bourgeois press, and Muralov retorted that Marx and Engels had justified, and engaged in, this practice. Trotsky himself compared his action to Lenin's recourse to German aid in 1917 to return to Russia, and said that he had merely " used the sealed train of the bourgeois press to tell the truth to the whole world " (*Byulleten' Oppozitsii* (Paris), No. 1-2, July 1929, p. 4). Trotsky was said to intend to devote his profits to the publication of writings of Lenin, as well as of proceedings of party congresses and conferences and other party documents (*Pravda*, May 12, 1929) — a project partly fulfilled in L. Trotsky, *Stalinskaya Shkola Falsifikatsii* (Berlin, 1932).

company of Tomsky, at the villa of Shmidt, the recently deposed
People's Commissar for Labour, who, however, was not present.
The first meeting was inconclusive: Bukharin presented a
preliminary draft of an economic programme, which met with some
criticism. At the second meeting, Bukharin produced an uncompleted programme of 16 pages, which Kamenev judged to be
" further to the Right than Bukharin's theses of April 1925 ".
Most of the conversation turned on the attitude to be adopted
at the forthcoming meeting of the party central committee.
Kamenev advocated a strong line, and the " collective resignation "
of Rykov, Bukharin and Tomsky was canvassed.[1] These exchanges may have strengthened Bukharin's faltering resolution ;
and from this time he rode for a fall. The fifth anniversary of
Lenin's death provided the occasion for some muffled exchanges.
The custodians of the Lenin archives produced, and printed in
Pravda on January 18, 1921, an unpublished lecture " On the
State " delivered by Lenin in 1919. In his peroration Lenin
spoke of the use made of the state by the proletarian dictatorship :

> We have taken this machine away from the capitalists, taken
> it for ourselves. With this machine, or with a club, we shall
> smash exploitation of every kind ; and when no possibility of
> exploitation remains in the world . . . only then, when no
> possibilities of this remain, shall we hand over this machine to be
> broken up.[2]

This was an emphatic reiteration of the point on which Lenin
had more than once crossed swords with Bukharin.[3] Its significance at this moment could not be missed. Bukharin's contribution consisted of two pronouncements which implicitly — though
still not openly — challenged the line of the party majority. The
relatively uncontroversial article which appeared in *Pravda* on
the eve of the anniversary, January 20, 1929, on *Lenin and the
Tasks of Science in Socialist Construction*, appeared to repeat the

---

[1] Both meetings were briefly described by Bukharin at his trial in 1938
(*Report of Court Proceedings: Anti-Soviet " Bloc of Rights and Trotskyites "*
(Moscow, 1938), pp. 386-387). This is the sole source for the first meeting ;
the second meeting is narrated in greater detail in the report cited p. 76, note 4
above, which refers to " several meetings " between Kanenev, Bukharin and
Pyatakov at this time.

[2] Lenin, *Sochineniya*, xxiv, 377.

[3] See *Socialism in One Country, 1924-1926*, Vol. 1, pp. 164-166.

favourable diagnosis of capitalist development rejected at the sixth congress of Comintern :

> We live in an epoch in which the militant forces of capitalism, of its technology, of its science, of its economy are once more growing.

Far more serious was the speech delivered by Bukharin at a great party meeting in the Bol'shoi theatre on the anniversary itself, and immediately published under the title *Lenin's Political Testament*. Bukharin relied on copious, but carefully selected, quotations from Lenin's writings to discount the idea that events were moving towards an aggravation of the class struggle or " a third revolution ". On the contrary, it was in the conception of a constantly diminishing class conflict that he sought " the theoretical basis of definition of our great tactical task ".[1]

Bukharin's speech, delivered on so solemn an occasion, could hardly be ignored by the party leaders. But the immediate provocation which hastened the renewal of party dissensions was the publication by the Trotskyites as a leaflet on January 20, 1929 — presumably with the purpose of creating trouble — of Kamenev's record of his conversation with Bukharin of July 11, 1928. The substance had no doubt been known for some time to Stalin. Now he could no longer affect to ignore it. After three days of debate in the Politburo, copies of the record were distributed to members of the party central committee and high party officials ; and Bukharin and Kamenev, summoned to appear before Orjonikidze as president of the central control commission, admitted its substantial accuracy.[2] Bukharin, now hopelessly compromised, drew fresh courage from despair. On January 30, 1929, at a joint session of the Politburo and the presidium of the party central control commission,[3] he made a declaration of which a few extracts were later quoted in full :

> Serious burning questions are not discussed. The whole country is in anguish over the question of bread and supplies,

[1] For these pronouncements see Vol. 1, pp. 206-207 ; among the numerous commemorative items published in *Pravda* on January 20 and 22, 1929, were non-controversial articles by Pyatakov, Kamenev and Zinoviev — a tribute to their renunciation of the opposition.

[2] *Byulleten' Oppozitsii* (Paris), No. 1-2, July 1929, p. 17.

[3] According to A. Avtorkhanov, *Stalin and the Soviet Communist Party*

but conferences of the ruling proletarian party say nothing.
The whole country feels that something is amiss with the
peasantry, but conferences of the proletarian party, of *our* party,
say nothing. . . . On the one hand, there is a hail of resolutions
(in identical terms) about deviations. On the other hand, there
are millions of rumours and gossipings about Rightists —
Rykov, Tomsky, Bukharin etc. This is petty politics, not the
politics which in a time of difficulties tells the working class *the
truth about the situation*, stakes everything on the masses, hears
and feels *the needs of the masses*, and carries on its work in unity
with the masses.[1]

The declaration protested against an agrarian policy which led to
the decline of agriculture and the impoverishment of the country ;
against an intolerably rapid tempo of industrialization which
required the levying of " tribute " from the peasantry ; and
against a party régime of unconditional discipline and submission
to party decisions. Bukharin made a direct attack on Stalin,
though without naming him :

> We are against the decisions of party leadership being taken
> by a single person. We are against the replacement of the
> control of a collective organ by the control of an individual,
> however authoritative.[2]

Tomsky and Rykov " demonstratively adhered " to the declaration ; and the three threatened to resign from their posts if
party policy were not modified. In the course of the discussions,
Rykov withdrew, or did not repeat, his threat of resignation ; the
other two appear to have stood firm.[3] Stalin made more than one
speech, in which he reminded his audience that Lenin had written
of Bukharin in 1916 as " devilishly unstable in politics ", and
recalled Lenin's severe treatment of offences against the party
committed by Shlyapnikov and by Tomsky himself. He now
branded Bukharin's *Notes of an Economist*, which a few weeks

(1959), p. 115, the four members of the central control commission attending
the meeting were Orjonikidze, Yaroslavsky, Shkiryatov and Solts — all
Stalinists — to whom Enukidze was added at Bukharin's request.
    [1] *XVI S"ezd Vsesoyuznoi Kommunisticheskoi Partii (B)* (1931), p. 325.
    [2] *Ibid.* pp. 201-202.
    [3] Information about what passed at the session must be pieced together
from Stalin's speeches and from the text of the resolution (see two following
notes).

earlier he had treated with relative indulgence, as " an anti-party, eclectic article, designed to slow down the development of industry ". He attacked " the Right opportunist, capitulationist platform " of the dissidents, clearly branding Bukharin as the ringleader.[1] On February 7, 1929, the majority proposed a compromise formula, under which Bukharin would recognize his conversations with Kamenev as " a political error ", would renounce the allegations in his declaration of January 30 — that the central committee was carrying out a policy of " military-feudal exploitation of the peasantry " and implanting a bureaucratic régime in the party — as having been made " on the spur of the moment, in the heat of controversy ", and would withdraw the declaration and the accompanying threat of resignation.[2] This was rejected. On February 9, 1929, Bukharin's declaration was re-affirmed jointly by himself, Tomsky and Rykov in a statement henceforth known as " the platform of the Bukharin group ".[3] On the same day, the joint session passed a resolution condemning Bukharin and Sokolnikov for their conversations with Kamenev, and Tomsky and Rykov for having been privy to them and failed to divulge them. The resolution not only refuted in detail Bukharin's errors of policy, but reviewed at length past instances of his disloyalty to the party, going back to the days of the Brest-Litovsk treaty. No member of the party — not even Trotsky — had ever incurred so searing a denunciation in an official document. But Stalin, conscious perhaps of the extent of the support still enjoyed by Bukharin in some sections of the party, was plainly reluctant to resort to extremes, or to bring the issue into the open. The resolution refused to accept Bukharin's and Tomsky's resignations, and imposed no sanctions.[4] Nothing appeared in

---

[1] The " brief note " in Stalin, *Sochineniya*, xii, 318-325, is evidently a conflation of two or more speeches. For Lenin's characterization of Bukharin see Lenin, *Sochineniya*, xxix, 229 ; for the sins of Shlyapnikov and Tomsky see *The Bolshevik Revolution, 1917-1923*, Vol. 1, p. 208 ; Vol. 2, pp. 324-325.

[2] The compromise formula was quoted by Stalin at the party central committee in April 1929 (*Sochineniya*, xii, 6-7).

[3] Rykov is said to have been half-hearted in his adhesion, and to have signed the joint declaration only after an " ultimatum " by Bukharin, Tomsky and Uglanov (A. Avtorkhanov, *Stalin and the Soviet Communist Party* (1959), p. 121).

[4] The resolution was published for the first time in *VKP(B) v Rezolyutsiyakh* (4th ed. 1933), ii, 521-530, with the omission of one paragraph condemning Bukharin for having spoken of the hopeless position of the currency ; the

the press, and no immediate report was made to the party central
committee, so that the unity of the party leadership remained
officially intact.

The Moscow provincial party conference which met almost
immediately after these proceedings was also of unusually long
duration, lasting from February 23 to March 6, 1929, and received much publicity in the press. Though the forms of unity
were preserved by including Bukharin, Rykov and Tomsky in
the honorary presidium of the conference, it was made the
occasion for a massive attack on the Right deviation and for a
demonstration, after the troubles of the previous autumn, of the
unshakable fidelity of the Moscow organization to the party line.
Molotov, who made the major report to the conference, sharpened
the image of the deviators as a hostile fraction within the party ;
and the resolution unanimously adopted at the end of the debate
on the report dwelt on this point :

> The conference considers that the political formation of a
> Right deviation in the form of a special line radically different
> from that of the party, and the prevalence of waverings in the
> sense of this deviation, constitute at the present moment a direct
> threat of fractional anti-party activity by the Rightists and by
> elements conciliatory towards them.[1]

Yaroslavsky made a report on party organization in which he
quoted a famous passage from one of Lenin's last articles *How to
Reorganize Rabkrin* stressing the duty of the party central control
commission to discipline offenders " without regard to persons "
— a hint that deviators in high places would no longer be spared.[1]
A few days later a party conference at Leningrad, which was
addressed by Voroshilov, passed a similar resolution demanding
" decisive measures on the part of the central committee to put

complete text appeared for the first time in *KPSS v Rezolyutsiyakh* (1954), ii,
556-567.
    [1] Molotov's report was published in *Pravda*, February 26, 27, 1929, and as
a separate pamphlet entitled *Ob Uspekhakh i Trudnostyakh Sotsialisticheskogo
Stroitel'stva* ; for the resolution see *Pravda*, February 27, 1929. According to
Byulleten' Oppozitsii (Paris), No. 1-2, July 1929, p. 17, Bukharin, Rykov and
Tomsky were attacked by name at the conference, but the names were kept out
of the record.
    [2] *Pravda*, March 2, 1927 ; for the quotation see Lenin, *Sochineniya*, xxvii,
405.

an end to the fractional activity of Right deviators and conciliators ".[1]

The next stage in the slow humiliation of Bukharin and his
group was not reached till active preparations began for the
sixteenth party conference, which was to meet in the latter part
of April, preceded by a meeting of the party central committee.
The first blow was the rejection by the Politburo of Rykov's
draft theses on the five-year plan, and the priority given to the
report on agriculture by Kalinin, whose conversion to the views
of the majority had earned him this promotion.[2]   By way of
reprisal, Bukharin, Tomsky and Rykov abstained in the Politburo
from the votes on Kalinin's theses and the revised theses on the
five-year plan.[3]   But this was a mere prelude to the proceedings
of the central committee, which lasted from April 16 to 23, 1929.
Bukharin, Rykov and Tomsky all spoke at length in defence of
their views on agricultural policy, on relations between proletariat
and peasantry and on the maintenance of NEP.[4]   Stalin, in a
massive reply, trained his heaviest artillery on Bukharin.   He
began by impatiently dismissing sentimental appeals to past
friendship (Bukharin had read extracts from intimate letters
exchanged in the past) ; the Bolsheviks were not " a family circle ",
but a political party.   A section of the speech, devoted to " Bukharin as theoretician ", rehearsed the story of his early controversies with Lenin, and quoted Lenin's verdict on him in the testament.   Another section headed " On Loyalty and Collective
Leadership " (both catchwords used by Bukharin) dealt faithfully
both with Bukharin's recent contacts with Kamenev and with
his campaign against Lenin at the time of the Brest-Litovsk
treaty.[5]   The committee in its resolution once more condemned

---

[1] *Pravda*, March 9, 10, 1929 ; Voroshilov's address was reprinted in K.
Voroshilov, *Stat'i i Rechi* (1937), pp. 287-325.

[2] See Vol. 1, pp. 248-250.   On March 30, 1929, the tenth anniversary of
Kalinin's appointment to succeed Sverdlov as president of TsIK and titular
head of state, was celebrated in the press with photographs, reminiscences, and
a mass of congratulatory messages ; at a meeting at which Stalin, Mikoyan and
Molotov figured prominently, Petrovsky proposed to create, in honour of the
anniversary, 100 studentships at agricultural and technical colleges for workers,
batraks and poor peasants (*Pravda*, March 30, April 2, 1929 ; *Bednota*, March 30,
31, 1929).

[3] Stalin, *Sochinenya*, xii, 6.   [4] See Vol. 1, p. 250.

[5] Stalin, *Sochineniya*, xii, 1-2, 69-79, 99-101 ; for Stalin's speech see Vol. 1,
pp. 250-251.

Bukharin's declaration of January 30, 1929, and the declaration of Bukharin, Tomsky and Rykov of February 9, 1929, and confirmed the Politburo decision of the same day, which was thus for the first time officially communicated to a large representative party organ. It rehearsed once more, with accumulated emphasis, the offences of the group. Noting specifically that " Bukharin, Rykov and Tomsky have not confessed their mistakes ", it again formally condemned their views and actions, and decided to deprive Bukharin and Tomsky of the posts occupied by them in *Pravda*, in Comintern, and in the trade union central council.[1] But the failure to publish the resolution bore witness to a still persistent reluctance to bring this split completely into the open. At the immediately following sixteenth party conference, where Kalinin introduced the resolution on agriculture, Rykov still appeared as one of three *rapporteurs* on the five-year plan.[2] Many speakers at the conference denounced the Right deviation ; and several of them attacked Bukharin by name. On the eve of the ending of the conference, Molotov " at the request of the delegates " made a two-hour report on the proceedings of the party central committee, and proposed a brief resolution noting " the departure of Bukharin's group from the general party line in the direction of a Right deviation ", and approving the decision taken by the committee in regard to it. The resolution, which was adopted by acclamation without debate, was printed in the bulletin distributed to conference delegates. But it did not appear in the official record of the conference published later in the year ; and the passages in which delegates had made personal attacks on Bukharin were also omitted or so modified as to exclude Bukharin's name.[3] Denunciations of the Right deviation

---

[1] *KPSS v Rezolyutsiyakh* (1954), ii, 549-566 ; this resolution, like its predecessor (see p. 89 above), was first published in *VKP(B) v Rezolyutsiyakh* (4th ed. 1933), ii, 515-521.

[2] See Vol. 1, pp. 252, 892.

[3] For the resolution see *KPSS v Rezolyutsiyakh* (1954), ii, 614-615 ; for a brief note of Molotov's report see *Shestnadtsataya Konferentsiya VKP(B)* (1962), p. 584. The passages in speeches attacking Bukharin by name were first published *ibid.* pp. 305 (Shlikhter), 319 (Lominadze), 352-353 (Roshal), 371-373 (Streltsov), 383-385 (Lyubchenko) ; this material was omitted or modified in *XVI Konferentsiya Vsesoyuznoi Kommunisticheskoi Partii (B)* (1929). The apparent absence of open attacks at the conference on Bukharin, Rykov and Tomsky led in some quarters abroad (see, for example, an article in *Die Fahne*

were multiplied in the press, and opinions and slogans known to be those of Bukharin were held up to opprobrium.[1] At the end of the conference, Uglanov was relieved of his posts as candidate member of the Politburo and member of the secretariat, and succeeded in both by Bauman.[2] But none of the major culprits was directly attacked. In June 1929 Bukharin delivered a major speech at a congress of the League of the Godless to an enthusiastic audience.[1]

The attempt of the party leaders, however half-hearted and ineffective, to draw a formal veil of secrecy over the defection of Bukharin, Rykov and Tomsky from the party line, contrasted sharply with the blaze of publicity in which the campaign against the united opposition had been conducted. When Bukharin at the session of the party central committee in April 1929 affirmed that his group did not constitute an " opposition ", Stalin bluntly retorted that this was untrue.[4] Nevertheless a distinction was drawn. The resolutions of the central committee and of the sixteenth party conference in the same month spoke of a " Right deviation (uklon) " ; it was only later that the term " Right opposition " came into common use — and then apparently not in official party documents.[5] The decision of April 1929 to remove Bukharin from his posts in *Pravda* and in Comintern was not published. Rykov remained president of Sovnarkom, having perhaps earned this indulgence by occasional falterings in his resistance to the party line.[6] A proposal said to have been made

des Kommunismus, No. 19, May 24, 1929) to the erroneous belief that a compromise had been reached.

[1] A sly article in *Pravda*, May 21, 1929, convicted the anonymous Right deviators of heresy on the strength of quotations from past speeches of Rykov and Tomsky.

[2] *Pravda*, April 30, 1929.

[3] *Ibid.* June 12, 1929 ; for the congress see p. 392 below.

[4] Stalin, *Sochineniya*, xii, 96.

[5] It appeared in a headline in *Pravda*, April 25, 1929, but its use at this time was exceptional. Tomsky, in his penitent speech at the sixteenth party congress in June 1930, remarked that " a parallel with the Trotskyites and Zinovievites is here completely out of place, and it is no accident that comrade Stalin did not draw such a parallel " (*XVI S"ezd Vsesoyuznoi Kommunisticheskoi Partii (B)* (1931), p. 144).

[6] Rykov later claimed that he had reacted to the Kamenev-Bukharin conversation " with the severest censure, and at once declared this ", but did not specify at what time or to whom (*XVI S'ezd Vsesoyuznoi Kommunisticheskoi Partii (B)* (1931), p. 149).

by "some comrades" to remove the three dissidents from the
Politburo was resisted by Stalin as unnecessary "at the present
time ".[1] No question arose of expelling any of them from the
party — as Trotsky, Zinoviev and Kamenev had been expelled
— or of banishing them from Moscow. Different reasons probably
accounted for the distinction. Stalin had been genuinely frightened of Trotsky's fighting qualities and of his potential appeal to
the masses of factory workers — the rank and file of those who
had made the revolution; and, when Zinoviev and Kamenev
joined Trotsky, he fought back with every weapon at his disposal.
The three leaders of the new party Right were not fighters ; they
had little following in the factories ;[2] they neither could nor
would organize a mass opposition. The party machine was now
more efficient and more ruthless. The quarrel could be confined
to the top ranks of the party. On the other hand, Bukharin
enjoyed widespread popularity and sympathy in the party.
Kalinin's speech at the sixteenth party conference in April 1929
showed a keen apprehension of the personal support which Bukharin might yet be able to muster. Among the Rightists there
were, he admitted, "idealistic people who will die for the Soviet
power "; though "inwardly inspired by idealistic impulses to
preserve and strengthen the proletarian dictatorship ", they
drifted towards the Right deviation. Such people were " *the most
dangerous element for our party* ". The Right conception was
" a poison . . . which gradually seeps into the communist, drop by
drop ".[3] Bukharin appealed to those party members and officials

---

[1] Stalin, *Sochineniya*, xii, 107.

[2] According to a report in the Trotsky archives, the Right opposition had less
mass appeal than the Trotskyites, but had some support "especially among
workers in the textile industry, and those connected with the countryside "
(Trotsky archives, T 2852).

[3] *Shestnadtsataya Konferentsiya VKP(B)* (1962), pp. 300-303 ; for the
identification of Bukharin with party support for " the *kulak* stratum in the
village " see p. 186 below. Krupskaya, having dissociated herself from the
united opposition (see pp. 30-31 above), was evidently one of those who sympathized with Bukharin. Writing in *Pravda*, January 20, 1929, on the kolkhozy, she stressed Lenin's unwillingness to use coercion against the middle
peasant ; and Bukharin wrote the first of several articles celebrating her
sixtieth birthday (*ibid*. February 27, 1929). She did not speak at the sixteenth
party conference in April 1929. At the sixteenth congress in 1930 she referred
to the Right deviation as " the chief danger " ; but, when repeatedly challenged to speak about Bukharin, Tomsky and Rykov, she criticized the two

who had turned their back on the storm and stress of revolution, and now wanted to conserve and enjoy rather than to innovate. Most of all, he appealed to party workers in the countryside, who shared his sympathy for the peasant.[1] These were few in number, and most of them probably, in the party sense, weaker brethren. Yet it was on them that the party must rely to carry out its crucial policies in the countryside. To alienate this group of party workers by too brusque reprisals against Bukharin would be dangerous. At every step Stalin took particular care to make it appear that it was Bukharin and his partners, not the party majority, who made the breach inevitable.

The sentence pronounced at the party central committee in April 1929 was none the less inexorable, and marked the end of the Right opposition as a political factor. It was in the field of Comintern that Bukharin's disgrace was first made known to the world. When the tenth IKKI met on July 3, 1929, neither Manuilsky nor Kuusinen, who made the main reports, mentioned Bukharin or the deviation in the Russian party. But, when the session was a week old, Molotov in the course of a long speech referred to the declaration of Bukharin, Tomsky and Rykov of January 30, 1929, as showing that, " in spite of oral protestations, they favour the Rightists and protect the conciliators ", and criticized a recent review by Bukharin of a German economic treatise as being a veiled attack on " our socialist economy " and in line with " the Right deviation ".[2] Thus encouraged, Manuilsky and Kuusinen both took up the attack in their replies to the debate;[3] and Remmele, the German delegate, proposed a draft resolution, the final text of which was to be settled by the political secretariat, condemning Bukharin's deviation and

---

last very mildly and did not mention Bukharin at all (*XVI S"ezd Vseoyuznoi Kommunisticheskoi Partii (B)* (1930), pp. 211, 213-214).

[1] An article in *Izvestiya Tsentral'nogo Komiteta VKP(B)*, No. 1(260), January 16, 1929, pp. 1-4, signed N.B., complained that local organizations did not take Right deviation seriously, and were not taking steps against it and stressed the need " *to develop the struggle against the Right danger* " ; old party members will not have overlooked the piquant coincidence that Bukharin's early articles of 1915 and 1916 were signed N.B.

[2] *Protokoll: 10 Plenum des Exekutivkomitees der Kommunistischen Internationale* (1929), pp. 422-423, 435 ; the review appeared in *Pravda*, June 30, 1929.

[3] *Ibid.* pp. 576-578, 627-631.

approving the decision of the party central committee of April 23,
1929, to remove Bukharin from the presidium of IKKI and to
debar him from participation in Comintern affairs.[1] This resolution, unlike the other resolutions adopted at the session, was not
immediately published in *Pravda*, which confined itself to recording without comment the removal of Bukharin from the presidium
of IKKI.[2] But a decision taken in the international forum of
IKKI could not remain a secret. On August 14, 1929, the central
committee of the German Communist Party, in a resolution
endorsing the proceedings of IKKI, referred to Bukharin as " the
chief representative of a cowardly opportunism in the VKP ";[3]
and on August 21, 1929, *Pravda* at length printed the July resolution of IKKI denouncing Bukharin and removing him from the
presidium. Three days later a moderately worded article rehearsed Bukharin's errors.[4] *Pravda* followed this up with an
article by the economist Leontiev condemning Bukharin's review
which Molotov had criticized some weeks earlier.[5] From this
time denunciations of the " Right opportunists " in the press
and at party meetings were regularly coupled with the name of
Bukharin. When in November 1929 the party central committee
at length removed Bukharin from the Politburo, and once again
censured and warned Rykov and Tomsky,[6] the victims had long
forfeited any semblance of authority or credit.

The exiling of Trotsky completed the disintegration of the old
opposition which had begun in the summer of 1928. Trotsky's
deportation had been followed by intensive measures of repression

---

[1] *Protokoll: 10 Plenum des Exekutivkomitees der Kommunistischen Internationale* (1929), pp. 876-877; *Kommunisticheskii Internatsional v Dokumentakh*
(1933), pp. 911-913. [2] *Pravda*, July 21, 1929.

[3] This resolution was published *ibid.* August 22, 1929.

[4] *Ibid.*, August 24, 1929; the article recognized " the immense services of
comrade Bukharin when he fought for many years in our ranks side by side
with V. I. Lenin ", but also drew attention to his " immense errors " when, in
company with Trotsky, he had opposed Lenin.

[5] *Ibid.*, August 27, 1929; for the review and Molotov's criticism see p. 95
above. Leontiev had written in the previous year in rebuttal of Bukharin's
Notes of an Economist (see p. 76, note above).

[6] *KPSS v Rezolyutsiyakh* (1954), ii, 662-663; the recantation of Bukharin,
Rykov and Tomsky dated November 12, 1929, was published in *Pravda*,
November 29, 1929.

against his supporters. Opposition reports spoke of a wave of
" January arrests " in industrial centres; and an " isolator " was
established in the former convict prison in Tobolsk, to which
100 members of the opposition were sent in the first three months
of 1929.[1] During the sixteenth party conference of April 1929,
38 Trotskyites, in a declaration to the presidium, formally renounced their adhesion to the opposition platform, condemned
Trotsky's pronouncements in the foreign bourgeois press, and
asked for " the most favourable conditions " for their return to the
party.[2] Serebryakov, who claimed that he had severed his links
with the opposition early in 1928, and Drobnis, a former Democratic Centralist, renounced their errors and petitioned for readmission.[3] More important was the joint recantation of three
outstanding intellectual figures of the opposition. Almost a year
earlier Preobrazhensky and Radek had taken the first steps on
this stony road,[4] and were now joined by Smilga, till recently
numbered among the irreconcilables. Yaroslavsky, in an article
in *Pravda*, quoted at length a letter written by Radek in Tomsk on
May 19, 1929 (and presumably intercepted by the authorities) to a
friend in " the Smilga fraction " of the opposition. The aim of
Radek and his friends, he now explained, had been " to turn the
face of the opposition to the party . . . so that it might really become
the Left wing of the party ". This line had been rejected by
Trotsky who wished to form a separate " All-Union Union of
Bolshevik-Leninists ", and who now described the Soviet régime
in terms appropriate to the Noske-Scheidemann régime in
Germany or to Macdonald in Great Britain. Radek opined that
" neither I nor you nor Evgenii [Preobrazhensky] have today
anything in common with these [views] ", and concluded:

> We saw in the cadres of the opposition a cadre of defenders
> of the October revolution. That dream is finished. . . . This is
> the hard, cruel truth, but it is better than illusion.[5]

In June 1929 Radek and Smilga were allowed to return together to
Moscow.[6] Here they were joined by Preobrazhensky; and on

---

[1] *Byulleten' Oppozitsii* (Paris), No. 1-2, July 1929, pp. 17-18.
[2] *Pravda*, April 28, 1929; further lists of some 30 seceders from the
opposition appeared *ibid.* May 17, 1929.   [3] *Ibid.* June 28, 30, 1929.
[4] See pp. 59, 67 above.   [5] *Pravda*, May 30, 1929.
[6] *Byulleten' Oppozitsii* (Paris), No. 6, October 1929, p. 25.

July 10, 1929, the three signed a declaration addressed to the
party central control commission, which was published three
days later in *Pravda*. The signatories announced that they had
broken " ideologically and organizationally " with Trotsky and
his supporters, and withdrew their signatures from all " fractional
documents " ;   confessed that the fifteenth party congress had
been right to reject the opposition platform, and that the policy
of the party central committee " was, and remains, Leninist " ;
and begged to be readmitted to the party.[1] Trotsky, more moved
by this than by any of the earlier defections, published a lengthy
article headed " A Wretched Document ", in which he called it
" a document of political and moral degeneration " ; his bitterest
comment was reserved for Radek " who began ever since February
1928 to look for motives for capitulation ".[2] Some consolation
was found in the adhesion of no less than 500 faithful members of
the opposition to a declaration issued on August 22, 1929, by
Rakovsky, V. Kosior and Okujava; this accepted the general
line of the five-year plan, but protested against a degree of pressure
on the workers which divided them from the party, demanded
" party democracy ", and refused to believe that socialism could
be victorious except on an international scale. Trotsky published
the declaration in his journal, together with an open letter approving it.[3]

The harsh conditions of banishment in remote, isolated and
climatically inhospitable regions undoubtedly hastened the disintegration of the opposition. But another factor inspired the
painful heart-searchings to which the exiles continuously subjected
themselves. The core of the programme of the united opposition
since its formation in 1926, and of Trotsky's criticisms of the
official party line since 1923, had been the belief that the party

---

[1] *Pravda*, July 13, 1929; lists of other members of the opposition who
adhered to the declaration of the three, containing 32 and 125 names respectively,
were published *ibid.* July 21, 28, 1929.

[2] *Byulleten' Oppozitsii* (Paris), No. 3-4, September 1929, pp. 5-11; the
article, dated July 27, 1929, was first published in *Die Fahne des Kommunismus*,
Nos. 30, 31, 32, August 16, 23, 30, 1929.

[3] *Byulleten' Oppozitsii* (Paris), No. 6, October 1929, pp. 3-8. The declaration
was written from Saratov, to which Rakovsky had been transferred from
Astrakhan ; by way of reprisal for the declaration, the " Saratov group " was
broken up, and Rakovsky sent to Barnaul (*ibid.* No. 7, November-December
1929, p. 13).

majority was lukewarm in its promotion of essential policies of industrial development and indulgent to the interests of the well-to-do peasant. Now that the party line had been reversed, and the majority was outbidding the opposition in its commitment to rapid industrialization, what meaning or consistency could be found in continued resistance ? Only a few stalwarts, like Trotsky himself and Rakovsky, were so firmly entrenched in hostility to the régime, and to the methods employed by Stalin to dominate the party, that the particular policies pursued at the moment seemed almost irrelevant. Many felt that new industrial power was being created and new potentialities built up, that constructive work was going forward of which they approved, and in which they earnestly desired to participate. Confession of past errors and miscalculations was in some measure genuine, and was in any case a small price to pay. I. N. Smirnov, one of those who recanted, used language which must have expressed the feelings of many :

> I cannot stand inaction. I want to build. In a barbarous and often stupid way the central committee is building for the future. Our ideological differences have little importance compared with the construction of great new industries.[1]

Pyatakov had urged Bukharin to moderate his opposition to Stalin as " the one man who can still command obedience ".[2] Nor were such feelings confined to repentant members of the opposition. An uncommitted observer recorded many years later an impression of officials and directors outbidding one another in a kind of " administrative ecstasy " for the plan :

> The psychology common to all thoughtful Bolsheviks in those days might be expressed somewhat as follows. Stalin's iron fist is hard to bear. His narrow vision is costing the country dear, as are his tyrannical methods. But, in spite of apparently insoluble difficulties, . . . the man's indomitable will is giving Russia a new industrial equipment.[3]

The ambivalence which divided the opposition also infected the whole party. The coarse brutality of Stalin's methods was condoned as the price of Stalin's achievement.

[1] V. Serge, *Mémoires d'un Révolutionnaire* (1951), p. 274.
[2] See p. 79 above.   [3] A. Barmine, *One Who Survived* (1945), p. 173.

CHAPTER 42

THE PARTY FRAMEWORK

(a) Membership

THE number of party members and candidates (the latter now being regularly included in party statistics) for the first time topped the million mark at the beginning of 1926,[1] and continued to advance steadily.[2] On October 14, 1926, the party central committee, perhaps inspired by the forthcoming population census in December, announced a census of party members;[3] the existing party tickets were to be withdrawn in the new year, and new tickets issued in March and April 1927.[4] Members more than three months in arrears with their dues were automatically excluded.[5] A census with obligatory re-registration of all members of the party performed some of the functions of a purge,[6] though the atmosphere of the two operations differed widely; an article in *Pravda* was headed " A Party Census, not a Purge ".[7] It was the first general review of the whole party membership since the purge of 1921,[8] though on the present occasion the motive dominant in 1921 — desire to reduce the size of the party — was conspicuously absent. The date fixed for the census was January 10, 1927. It was originally contemplated that local party organizations would have sent their returns to party

---

[1] See *Socialism in One Country, 1924–1926*, Vol. 2, p. 177.

[2] Table No. 52, p. 474 below.

[3] *Spravochnik Partiinogo Rabotnika*, vi (1928), i, 601-602; for the population census see pp. 419-420 below.

[4] *Spravochnik Partiinogo Rabotnika*, vi (1928), i, 547.

[5] *K XV S"ezdu VKP(B)* (1927), p. 330.

[6] The two operations had been equated in article 13 of the famous 21 conditions of admission to Comintern drawn up in 1920, which required communist parties " to conduct periodical purges (re-registrations) of the individual membership of party organizations in order systematically to cleanse the party of petty bourgeois elements which inevitably fasten on to it "; for the 21 conditions see *The Bolshevik Revolution 1917–1923*, Vol. 3, pp. 193-195.

[7] *Pravda*, December 22, 1926.

[8] See *The Bolshevik Revolution, 1917–1923*, Vol. 1, pp. 205-207.

headquarters in Moscow by February 1. But large numbers of party members failed to register promptly; the returns did not reach Moscow; and on March 28, 1927, the party central committee decided to extend the date of registration to May 15, and of the receipt of the final returns to June 1.[1] By a decision of the central committee of July 4, 1927, all who had not registered by that time were automatically excluded from the party.[2]

The census gave an opportunity for a thorough review of the party membership. When the local party organizations were instructed to make returns on the eve of the census, the number on their books was 1,192,458. The number of members who re-registered in the census was 1,147,014; the 45,000 who failed to re-register were said to have been mainly new recruits since 1924 and candidates not yet admitted to full membership.[3] The census classified members by place of occupation as follows :

Workers	484,622
Rural	264,964
In Institutions	228,230
In Educational Establishments	67,001
Military	94,067
Individual	5,135
Other	2,455
	1,147,074[4]

---

[1] *Izvestiya Tsentral'nogo Komiteta VKP(B)*, No. 10-11 (183-184), March 21, 1927, p. 2 ; No. 13(186), April 8, 1927, p. 4.

[2] *Spravochnik Partiinogo Rabotnika*, vi (1928), i, 665.

[3] *Sotsial'nyi i Natsional'nyi Sostav VKP(B)* (1928), pp. 4-5 ; of the 45,000, about two-thirds were workers, and one-third peasants ; the proportion of employees was negligible. This represented more than the normal annual wastage ; only 1 per cent left the party in 1924 and 1·97 per cent in 1926 (*Izvestiya Tsentral'nogo Komiteta VKP(B)*, No. 24-25(197-198), June 30, 1927, p. 7 ; No. 32-33(205-206), August 31, 1927, pp. 13-14). The percentage of members failing to register varied from 2·2 in the Moscow organization to 12 in Stalino ; the party central committee resolution of March 28, 1927, attributed the high percentage of non-registration " in some textile and mining districts " to insufficient care in the past in admitting candidates and to methods of mass recruitment (*Pravda*, April 1, 1927).

[4] *Sotsial'nyi i Natsional'nyi Sostav VKP(B)* (1928), p. 36 ; the sum of the items falls short of the total by 1000.

Apart from a very small minority of individuals, all party members
were enrolled in cells, and candidates in groups : these were in
principle based on their place of work or their occupation. The
party census classified members and candidates by type of cell
or group to which they belonged.[1] Urban membership increased
from 314,000 in 1922 to 840,000 in 1927, rural membership from
201,000 to 307,000 ; the party was still urban to the extent of
73·2 per cent.[2] The largest urban unit was the Moscow city
organization with 123,000 members, followed by the Leningrad
city organization with 93,000.[3] Moscow province had 130,049
members or 2·85 per cent of the population, Leningrad province
101,202 or 3·62 per cent ;[4] these were by far the highest ratios of
party membership to population. Of the 129,417 members of
Moscow city party organization on October 1, 1927, 67·5 per
cent were workers by social situation, 5·4 per cent peasantry, and
25·8 per cent employees ; no less than 40,673 are said to have
been activists " participating in the collective leadership of the
Moscow party organization ".[5]

A breakdown of the returns by nationality showed that Great
Russians, Poles, Baltic peoples and Jews had since 1922 lost a
little of their relative preponderance. The principal gainers were
the Ukrainians and White Russians; but almost all the smaller
nationalities slightly increased their very low percentages.[6] In
all national republics and regions (with the single exception of the
Armenian SSR), the proportion of non-Russians in the national
party was lower in 1927 than their proportion in the population ;
but in most cases the proportion had risen since 1922.[7] The
policy of increasing native representation clashed to some extent

---

[1] Party cells were classified as workers, rural, non-producer (i.e. employees), Red Army and national (E. Yaroslavsky, *Chistka Partii* (1929),
pp. 10-25). The average membership of rural party cells in 1929 was 14, of
factory cells 67 (*Bol'shaya Sovetskaya Entsiklopediya*, xi (1930), 535) ; a factory
cell might have as many as 1500 members (E. Yaroslavsky, *Chistka Partii*
(1929), p. 10).

[2] *Sotsial'nyi i Natsional'nyi Sostav (VKP(B))* (1928), p. 18 ; for the term
" urban " see pp. 270-272 below ; only 23 per cent of members were classified
as " rural " (see p. 179 below).   [3] *ibid.* p. 22.

[4] *Sotsial'nyi i Natsional'nyi Sostav VKP(B)* (1928), p. 20.

[5] *Voprosy Istorii KPSS*, No. 2, 1967, p. 126.

[6] See Table No. 53, p. 476 below.

[7] *Sotsial'nyi i Natsional'nyi Sostav VKP(B)* (1928), p. 118.

with the policy of increasing the worker component, since the non-Russian population everywhere in this period consisted predominantly of peasants ; among indigenous party members of all national republics the ratio of workers was lower, and of peasants higher, than among non-indigenous members. The proportion of women in the party rose from 8 per cent in 1922 to 10·5 per cent in the census of 1927. But the proportion was unevenly spread. Of Jewish members 23 per cent, of Lettish members 18·1 per cent and of Russian members 11·3 per cent were women ; the corresponding percentages of Bashkir, Kirgiz and Tajik women were 2·5, 0·9 and 0·7 respectively.[1] The proportion of employees by social situation among women members and candidates was 35·4 per cent as against 22·4 per cent for all party members and candidates ;[2] but the proportion of employees by present occupation among women members was only 33·2 per cent as against 41·3 per cent for the party as a whole.[3] Of employees by social situation, women were more likely than men to enter the party ; but, once admitted, women were less likely than men to become, as a result of their admission, employees by occupation. The proportion of women was always higher among candidates than among full members. Of members and candidates only 0·8 per cent (1·4 per cent of women) had higher education ; nearly all these were employees by social situation. 7·9 per cent had middle, 62·8 per cent lower, and 26·1 per cent only home, education. 2·4 per cent were illiterate ; a majority of these came from republics of Central Asia and from the Azerbaijan and Dagestan republics. 40·8 per cent had received some kind of party education, most of them in *politgramota* schools.[4]

Throughout the later nineteen-twenties preoccupation with the social composition of the party was increasingly acute. The drive for the admission of more peasants to the party, initiated at

---

[1] *Ibid.* pp. 138-139.
[2] E. Smitten, *Sostav VKP(B)* (1928), pp. 19-20.
[3] *Ibid.* pp. 26, 23.
[4] E. Smitten, *Sostav VKP(B)* (1920), pp. 59-65 ; in Kazakhstan, Kirgizia, Uzbekistan and Turkmenistan the illiteracy rate among party members ranged from 27 to 45 per cent (*Sotsial'nyi i Natsional'nyi Sostav VKP(B)* (1928), p. 145). For the educational status of party members see p. 157 below.

the end of 1924,[1] had petered out a year later. It never commanded unconditional approval in the party; and, though Stalin at the fourteenth party congress in December 1925 repeated the complaint that " the percentage of peasants in our party is still very insignificant " and that " on this side things are still not very good ",[2] the current was now setting sharply against a policy of concessions to the peasantry. Attention was drawn to the abuses of rural recruitment. The Astrakhan party organization was censured for the indiscriminate admission to the party of employees and seasonal workers; in the admissions for 1925 the proportion of employees had risen from 12 to 22 per cent.[3] The Penza organization had gone in for a policy of mass recruitment (61 per cent more members were admitted in 1925 than in the previous year) by " the method of requisition ".[4] In Smolensk province, as late as 1927, groups of 20 or 30 were being admitted to the party collectively: this encouraged the enrolment in the party of " casual elements which very quickly fell away ".[5] Rural party members, apart from other shortcomings, were untried and inexperienced. At the time of the party census of 1927 one-third of members of rural party cells were of less than one year's standing, and two-thirds of less than three.[6]

In 1926 the reaction had already begun to manifest itself. In the second half of 1925 131,661 persons had been admitted to the party as candidates, and 113,943 as full members; 39·6 per cent of the former and 12·6 per cent of the latter were peasants. In the first half of 1926 the totals fell to 95,344 and 71,043 and the percentages of peasants to 25·5 and 6·98 respectively.[7] Meanwhile the aim enunciated in the great days of the Lenin enrolment by the thirteenth party congress of May 1924, and by the four-

---

[1] See *Socialism in One Country, 1924–1926*, Vol. 2, p. 179.

[2] Stalin, *Sochineniya*, viii, 347.

[3] *Izvestiya Tsentral'nogo Komiteta VKP(B)*, No. 14(135), April 12, 1926, p. 3 ; a similar increase in the proportion of employees in the local organization was reported from Archangel (*Spravochnik Partiinogo Rabotnika*, vi (1928), ii, 220).

[4] *Izvestiya Tsentral'nogo Komiteta VKP(B)*, No. 16-17(137-138), May 3, 1926, pp. 4-5.

[5] *Ibid.* No. 24-25(197-198), June 30, 1927, p. 8.

[6] *Sotsial'nyi i Natsional'nyi Sostav VKP(B)* (1928), p. 85.

[7] For the 1925 figures see *VKP(B) v Tsifrakh*, v (1926), 6, 8 ; for those of 1926 see Table No. 54, p. 477 below.

teenth party conference a year later, that more than half the party should consist of " workers from the bench ",[1] had been partly eclipsed by the temporary enthusiasm for the admission of peasants. It had derived no credit from its endorsement by the Leningrad opposition on the eve of the fourteenth party congress in December 1925 ;[2] and the congress had been content to call in general terms for " a policy directed to . . . drawing more workers into the party, and persistently raising the specific weight of the proletarian element ".[3]   But the question was not forgotten. Molotov told the Orgburo in October 1926 that the social composition of the party had not changed in the first half of the year ; in view of the steady growth of the proletariat, this was not enough.   He reverted to the earlier injunction that more than half the party should be made up of workers actually engaged in production.   Meanwhile stricter criteria should be used in judging applications for membership from peasants, especially from middle peasants and those " bordering on middle peasant status " ; evidence should be required that such applicants " play a really active part in public life in support of the Soviet régime ".[4] A resolution of the party central committee of December 31, 1926, noted the many defects which required attention.   Insufficient discrimination was shown in admitting rural members ; such significant criteria as " membership of this or that social group, public activity, political consciousness etc." were neglected. Employees were admitted under the guise of workers or peasants. The proportion of workers from the bench in the party had not risen throughout 1926 above 41 per cent.[5]

This issue brought to the surface the long-standing ambiguity in party statistics.   Ever since the Lenin enrolment had called for the admission to the party of " workers from the bench ", the conventional classification of party members by " social situation " had become increasingly anomalous and misleading.[6]   From the

---

[1] See *The Interregnum, 1923–1924*, p. 354 ; *Socialism in One Country, 1924–1926*, Vol. 2, pp. 115-116.

[2] See *ibid.* Vol. 2, pp. 115-116.

[3] *KPSS v Rezolyutsiyakh* (1954), ii, 201.

[4] *Izvestiya Tsentral'nogo Komiteta VKP(B)*, No. 47-48(168-169), December 2, 1926, pp. 1-2.

[5] *Ibid.* No. 1(174), January 10, 1927, pp. 2-3.

[6] See *Socialism in One Country, 1924–1926*, Vol. 2, pp. 178-182.

beginning of 1927, as the result of an instruction of the statistical section of the party central committee,[1] party statisticians began to offer, in addition to the classification by "social situation", a subsidiary classification by "type of occupation", which provided a separate heading for *batraks*, distinguished between peasants engaged exclusively in agriculture and those who worked simultaneously in administration, or as artisans or craftsmen, or as hired labourers, and recorded separately artisans, students and unemployed.[2] The discrepancies brought to light by the comparison could no longer be ignored. On January 1, 1927, the criterion of social situation showed a party consisting of 56·1 per cent workers, 26·3 per cent peasants, and 16·2 per cent employees; the criterion of occupation revealed 38·1 per cent of workers, 11·7 per cent of peasants exclusively engaged in agriculture and 34·2 per cent of employees.[3] The relative relevance of the two criteria was never openly discussed. The question whether the environment of a party member's earlier years, or that of his present job, was a more significant factor in assessing his qualifications and attitudes did not invite speculation by party managers or statisticians, at any rate in public. But one obvious conclusion was that classification of party members by social situation very much understated the number of employees, if reckoned in terms of present occupation, and correspondingly inflated the number of workers and peasants; and this result was welcome to those who wished to maintain untarnished the official image of a workers', or workers' and peasants', party.

In arguments about the social composition of the party the

---

[1] *K XV S"ezdu VKP(B)* (1927), p. 7.

[2] See Table No. 52, p. 474 below; a slightly simpler classification "by type of occupation" had been used for those admitted to the party in 1925 in *VKP(B) v Tsifrakh*, v (1926), 7, 9. For some anomalies noted in 1925 see *Socialism in One Country, 1924–1926*, Vol. 1, p. 92.

[3] See Table No. 52, p. 474 below. The party census of 1927 showed still wider discrepancies, counting only 30 per cent of workers by occupation, 8·4 per cent of peasants exclusively engaged in agriculture, and 42·8 per cent of employees by occupation (*Sotsial'nyi i Natsional'nyi Sostav VKP(B)* (1928), p. 9); of members classified by social situation as workers less than half were engaged in manual work, 29 per cent were Soviet or trade union officials, and the rest fell into minor categories — 7 per cent Red Army, 5 per cent students, 2·5 per cent junior service personnel (*ibid.* p. 47). The discrepancies between party census figures and current party statistics were apparently due to changes in classification (see Table No. 52, p. 474 below, note 3).

batrak occupied an anomalous position. In theory, as a hired worker, he counted as a proletarian, and in party statistics tended to be grouped with the " workers ", though usually under a separate heading. In practice, he was often indistinguishable from the poor peasant.[1] Both those who wished to increase the proportion of workers, and those who wished to increase the proportion, among party members, of those engaged in agriculture, could espouse with good conscience the claims of the *batrak*. One of the grounds on which the opposition based its vote against the resolution on the elections to the Soviets at the session of the party central committee in July 1926 was the failure of the party to increase its activity among the *batraks* and poor peasants.[2] The opposition again raised the issue in its declaration of October 3, 1926, and incurred the charge of seeking to make capital out of it.[3] The same demand was repeated in the opposition counter-theses for the fifteenth party congress, which called on the party to " put itself at the head of the *batraks* ", to convene congresses of *batraks* and poor peasants, and to create " a union of the village poor " under party leadership.[4] But on the spot the demand seemed less realistic. Vserabotzemles, the trade union which was supposed to organize agricultural workers, was notoriously ineffective; and, at the time of its third congress in May 1927, only 23·3 per cent of all *batraks* and agricultural workers belonged to it.[5] Only 42 per cent of *batraks* could both read and write, another 6 per cent being able to read but not write.[6] The *batrak*, far from being a welcome recruit, could find no sponsors for an application for party membership, and, when examined by the party cell, could not answer a single question about the party statute.[7] Under pressure from the centre, the number of *batraks* in the party rose slowly from 0·5 per cent of the total party membership on

---

[1] See Vol. 1, p. 136.
[2] For this vote see p. 7 above.
[3] *Bednota*, October 7, 1926; for the declaration see p. 14 above.
[4] For the counter-theses see Vol. 1, p. 34.
[5] E. Smitten, *Sostav VKP(B)* (1928), p. 47; for Vserabotzemles see Vol. 1, pp. 140-141, and *Socialism in One Country, 1924–1926*, Vol 1, pp. 314-315.
[6] *Na Agrarnom Fronte*, No. 10, 1929, p. 165. In the Ural region, the percentage of illiterate *batraks* rose from 51·7 in 1926 to 55·8 in 1928; it was higher among females than among males, and lowest among young workers (*ibid.* No. 9, 1929, p. 90; many children were included in the category).
[7] *Bednota*, November 11, 1927.

January 1, 1925, to 1·3 per cent two years later.[1] Only 1·4 per cent of the members of Vserabotzemles were at this time members of the party.[2] A resolution of the party central committee of February 1927 once more urged the admission to the party of Sovkhoz workers, *batraks*, and other agricultural and timber workers.[3]

The year 1927 showed a renewed and strengthened preoccupation with the need to increase the worker contingent in the party; and the party census provided ammunition for the campaign. The average proportion of workers in major industries enrolled in the party was 10·5 per cent, varying from a maximum of 13·5 per cent in the oil industry to a minimum of 6·2 per cent in the textile industry, which was largely staffed by women. Membership was highest in the skilled industries, and lowest in those requiring a preponderance of heavy unskilled labour; it was only 7·5 per cent in iron-smelting and 7·7 per cent in coal mining.[4] On the other hand the ratio of semi-skilled and unskilled to skilled workers was higher among candidates than among full members:

	Skilled	Semi-skilled	Unskilled
Members	62·8	24·3	12·9
Candidates	52·6	26·7	20·7
All	60·0	25·0	15·0[5]

This indicated an unwelcome trend. The fourteenth party congress in December 1925, while seeking to "increase the specific weight of the proletarian core" of the party, had issued a warning against "excessive inflation of the party ranks and their

[1] *Izvestiya Tsentral'nogo Komiteta VKP(B)*, No. 26-27 (199-200), July 11, 1927, p. 4; a sample check in 1926 showed that *batraks* provided only 2·3 per cent of the membership even of rural party cells (*Spravochnik Partiinogo Rabotnika*, vi (1928), ii, 343).

[2] *Sotsial'nyi i Natsional'nyi Sostav VKP(B)* (1928), p. 97.

[3] *Pravda*, March 3, 1927; most *batraks* recruited into the party were said to be Sovkhoz workers (*Bol'shevik*, No. 9-10, May 31, 1929, p. 78).

[4] *Sotsial'nyi i Natsional'nyi Sostav VKP(B)* (1928), p. 51; about one quarter of worker members of the party were employed in transport (*ibid.* p. 61). For detailed figures of the proportion of party members in different industries in 1929 see *Sostav Fabrichno-Zavodskogo Proletariata SSSR* (1930), pp. 88-100.

[5] *Sotsial'nyi i Natsional'nyi Sostav VKP(B)* (1928), p. 65.

saturation with semi-proletarian elements not schooled in the
trade unions or in proletarian organization in general ".[1] The
rising proportion of semi-skilled and unskilled among newly
recruited candidates, though explicable in terms of the rapid
expansion of the labour force, aroused anxiety.[2] The resolution
of the party central committee of December 31, 1926, again drew
attention to the shortage of skilled workers in the party.[3] Another
disconcerting feature was that the ratio of party members among
workers in small industrial enterprises was higher than in large-
scale enterprises, ranging from 14·5 per cent in enterprises employing less than 30 workers to 8·8 per cent in enterprises employing
more than 3000.[4] Geographically, the best figures came from
Leningrad where 19 per cent of all industrial workers were party
members ; in Moscow the corresponding proportion was only
9 per cent.[5] In the preparations for the fourth Union Congress
of Soviets in May 1927 attention was given to the inclusion among
the delegates of a suitable proportion of workers from the bench
and peasants from the plough.[6]

In the second half of 1927 the social composition of the party
became a bone of contention in the last stages of the struggle
with the united opposition. Trotsky, in the opposition platform
of September 1927, drew attention to the presence in the party
of " no small number of ' worker ' bureaucrats — former workers,
that is, who have lost all connexion with the toiling mass ", and
proposed that for the next two or three years, " as a general rule ",
only workers from the bench and hired workers from agriculture
should be admitted to the party. Members of other social groups,
including poor peasants, should be accepted " only on a basis
of strict personal selection ".[7] A resolution of the party central

---

[1] *KPSS v Rezolyutsiyakh* (1954), ii, 81.
[2] *Izvestiya Tsentral'nogo Komiteta VKP(B)*, No. 24-25(145-146), June 28,
1926, p. 11 ; Malenkov, at this time an official of the party central committee,
commented that the semi-skilled worker now provided the most reliable recruits
to the party, and issued a warning against " a stratum of liberal workers " to be
found among the skilled workers (*Bol'shevik*, No. 21-22, November 30, 1926,
p. 48).   [3] For this resolution see p. 105 above.
[4] *Sotsial'nyi i Natsional'nyi Sostav VKP(B)* (1928), p. 77 ; pre-census
statistics showed a still larger discrepancy (*Bol'shevik*, No. 12, June 30, 1926,
pp. 62-63).   [5] E. Yaroslavsky, *Chistka Partii* (1929), p. 11.
[6] *Sovetskoe Stroitel'stvo*, No. 5-6, May–June 1927, p. 6.
[7] L. Trotsky, *The Real Situation in Russia* (n.d. [1928]), pp. 123, 127-128 ;

committee of October 13, 1927, " On the Regulation of the Growth
of the Party in Connexion with the Party Census ", set forth
five aims : increased recruitment of workers, especially in large
factories, and especially of activists already engaged in Soviet,
trade union or other public work ; a strengthening of Komsomol
activity among young workers ; increased recruitment of women
workers, especially in the textile industry ; increased enrolment
of *batraks* and poor peasants, especially those active in Vserabotzemles, in poor peasant groups, or in Soviet or cooperative work ;
and restraint, and a careful verification of credentials, in admitting
employees to the party. It included a specific demand (sometimes
referred to as a " two-year plan ") that within the next two years
the proportion of workers in the party membership should reach
50 per cent.[1] A further resolution of November 4, 1927, welcomed
the admission to the party, on the occasion of the tenth anniversary
of the revolution, of politically active workers, and launched the
slogan : " All leading men and women workers into Lenin's
party ".[2] This came to be known as the " October enrolment ".
At the fifteenth party congress in December 1927, 71·3 per cent
of the delegates were workers by social situation — the highest
proportion yet attained at any party congress.[3] But 58·2 per cent
of all delegates, and 66 per cent of the voting delegates, were
party officials of various grades ; and the number of " workers
from production " — and *a fortiori* of peasants — must have been
quite small.[4] The report submitted by the party central committee to the congress drew attention to " the unsatisfactory
organisation of party work in enterprises, and particularly the
weakness of work on the shop floor " ;[5] and Kosior, speaking at

Shlyapnikov, the leader of the former workers' opposition, also demanded the
admission of more workers into the party (*Pravda*, November 22, 1917,
Diskussionnyi Listok No. 6).

[1] *Izvestiya Tsentral'nogo Komiteta VKP(B)*, No. 39(212), October 22, 1927,
pp. 5-6.

[2] *Ibid.* No. 41(214), November 9, 1927, p. 11 ; *Pravda*, November 5, 1927,
which also printed this resolution, reported several declarations by groups of
workers in different factories of their intention to apply for membership of the
party.

[3] *Bol'shaya Sovetskaya Entsiklopediya*, xi (1930), 538.

[4] *XVI S"ezd Vsesoyuznoi Kommunisticheskoi Partii (B)* (1931), p. 599 ; at
the sixteenth congress in 1930 only 13·6 per cent of the delegates were " workers
from production " and 1·3 per cent " peasants from the plough ".

[5] *K XV S"ezdu VKP(B)* (1927), p. 15.

the congress on party organization, explained the apparent reduction in the proportion of workers from the bench in the party membership as due to changes in classification. This did not prevent Bakaev, the spokesman of the opposition, in a speech subjected to derisive interruptions, from holding Stalin personally responsible for the influx of peasants into the party, and insisting that the proportion of workers from the bench had fallen to 31 per cent.[1] The resolution of the congress noted the success of the " October enrolment ", and called for " the constant recruitment into the party of men and women workers from production ";[2] and in January 1928 the party central committee adopted yet another resolution stressing the importance of the recruitment of " workers from production ".[3]

This recruiting campaign had only a limited success in changing the social composition of the party. But, like the Lenin enrolment of 1924, it altered the party image in another respect by increasing the preponderance in it of new recruits who had no personal experience of the party's heroic years, and had shared neither its tribulations nor its triumphs. By 1927 the number of " undergrounders " who had been members before the revolution was less than 9000, and almost 60 per cent of the membership had been recruited in the last three years.[4] Trotsky in the opposition platform of September 1927 protested against " an extremely significant process of pushing out the old party men, who lived through the underground period, or at least through the civil war ", and introducing in their place " new elements distinguished chiefly by their unquestioning obedience ".[5] But the process owed more to the erosion of time, and to the demand to bring more workers into the party, than to the expulsion of a few

---

[1] *Pyatnadtsatyi S"ezd VKP(B)* (1962), i, 110-111, 375-376, 405 ; Bakaev also reverted to the unrealistic proposal of the Leningrad opposition two years earlier that 90 per cent of party members should be workers from the bench (see *Socialism in One Country, 1924-1926*, Vol. 2, pp. 116-118).

[2] *KPSS v Rezolyutsiyakh* (1954), ii, 440.

[3] *Izvestiya Tsentral'nogo Komiteta VKP(B)*, No. 3(224), January 30, 1928, p. 6.

[4] *Bol'shaya Sovetskaya Entsiklopediya*, xi (1930), 538 ; on the other hand, down to the fifteenth party congress of December 1927 inclusive, less than 10 per cent of those elected to the party central committee had joined the party since 1917 (*ibid.*).

[5] L. Trotsky, *The Real Situation in Russia*, (n.d. [1928]), p. 116.

leaders of the opposition. When Trotsky went on to call " the school of the young " a school of " revisionists ",[1] he was probably tilting at Bukharin's pupils in the Institute of Red Professors. But the words could have been given a wider application, and made an ironical comment on the days when Trotsky had appealed to the young to rejuvenate the party.[2] The members of the younger generation now entering the party were more matter-of-fact and perhaps more cynical, less ideological and less revolutionary, than their predecessors.

The October enrolment proceeded throughout the winter of 1927–1928. In the last quarter of 1927, 88,454 persons were admitted to the party as candidates (more than double the number for any previous quarter of the year), and 44,464 transferred from candidate to full member status; for the first quarter of 1928 the corresponding numbers were 80,523 and 41,701.[3] After this the pace slackened, though admissions as candidates amounted to 180,000 in the first three quarters of 1928, 67·7 per cent being workers, including *batraks*.[4] On April 1, 1928, the proportion of workers from production in the party membership was said to have reached 40·9 per cent. The attainment of the 50 per cent target proclaimed in the autumn of 1927 still, however, seemed remote. An unusually frank analysis of the reasons for the frequent reluctance of workers to join the party appeared in the journal of the party central committee in the autumn of 1928. Workers often felt that the lower party organs (with which alone they came in touch) were unable " *to struggle against defects in the work of economic, Soviet or other organs* ", or to protect the interests of the workers. Party representatives failed to support demands made by workers at production conferences in the factories; non-party activists were sometimes more eager than party members to take up workers' grievances. Minor causes were the number of meetings which party members were required to attend, and the bad impression made by drunkenness, hooliganism

---

[1] L. Trotsky, *The Real Situation in Russia* (n.d. [1928]), p. 121.

[2] See *The Interregnum, 1923–1924*, pp. 325-326.

[3] *VKP(B) v Tsifrakh*, viii (1928), 24, 26, ix (1929), 36.

[4] *Ibid.* ix, 26-29; it was alleged that some entrants were students of employee origin who intended to make their career as employees, but who had gone to work in a factory for three months in order to acquire the status of " workers from production " (*VIII Vsesoyuznyi S"ezd VLKSM* (1928), p. 84).

and other offences of party members.[1]   On the other hand, employees clung to the assurance of a party card as a guarantee of status, counting on " advantages in their employment which are in one way or another bound up with membership of the party as the ruling party ".[2]

The session of the party central committee of July 1928 foreshadowed the impending rift with Bukharin and the Right opposition in the party, which seemed likely to find its main support in the rural party organizations.[3]   These fears inspired fresh attention to the problem of the composition of the party.   An article by Malenkov early in August 1928 pointed out that workers from the bench still formed only 41 per cent of the party membership, and proposed that, in order to raise this proportion to the prescribed level of 50 per cent, 80 per cent of new recruits to the party should be workers from the bench.[4] The central committee, at its session of November 1928, followed up this initiative.   It noted in its resolution that 61 per cent of the members of the party were workers by social situation, but only 42 per cent " workers engaged in production " ;   and it demanded that, in order to attain the 50 per cent level by 1930, 80 per cent of those admitted to membership in the next two years should be " workers from production ".   It also concerned itself with the rural membership of the party.   In rural party organizations, " the specific weight of proletarian elements is still entirely insignificant, and cadres of kolkhoz members simply do not exist ". It called once again for the admission to the party of " agricultural workers and *batraks*, the best activists among the poor peasantry, and kolkhoz members ".[5]   An instruction of the party central

---

[1] *Izvestiya Tsentral'nogo Komiteta VKP(B)*, No. 32(253), October 31, 1928, pp. 2-3.   An anonymous note of May 1928 in the Trotsky archives, T 1390, emanating from the Kremenchug wagon works, referred to apathy towards the party among workers ; in October 1927 only 12 out of 3000 workers in the factory applied to join the party, and 6 of these were rejected.

[2] *Izvestiya Tsentral'nogo Komiteta VKP(B)*, No. 32-33(205-206), August 31, 1927, p. 12 ; this explained why so few employees had failed to re-register in the party census (see p. 101, note 3 above).

[3] For this session see pp. 63-64 above.

[4] *Izvestiya Tsentral'nogo Komiteta VKP(B)*, No. 24(245), August 10, 1928, pp. 1-3.

[5] *KPSS v Rezolyutsiyakh* (1954), ii, 545-547.   The latest figures available when this decision was taken were those up to July 1, 1928 ; in the third quarter of 1928 the percentage of workers from production admitted to the party was

committee to local party organizations of January 7, 1929, required that 90 per cent of those admitted to the party in industrial
regions, about 70 per cent in agricultural regions, and about 60
per cent in national autonomous republics and regions, should
be workers from production or *batraks*. Particular stress was laid
on the recruitment of workers " with a long record of work on
production in large-scale enterprises ".[1]

These pious intentions, as on previous occasions, remained
largely unfulfilled. They were, however, now overtaken by the
party purge foreshadowed at the time of the grain collections
crisis of January–March 1928, announced at the November 1928
session of the party central committee, and formally approved
by the sixteenth party conference of April 1929.[2] But, while the
purge undoubtedly removed known supporters of the Right as
well as members unsatisfactory on other grounds, and appears
to have fallen most heavily on rural organizations, it did not in the
long run substantially affect either the steady growth of the party
or its social composition. The proportion of peasants in the
party membership was not significantly reduced, and the rise in
the worker component did no more than keep pace with an
expanding industrial labour force. The total membership of
the party rose from 1,147,074 in 1927 to 1,304,471 in 1928 and
1,532,362 in 1929. The proportion of workers by social situation
rose from 55·7 per cent in 1927 to 61·4 per cent in 1929, and the
proportion of workers by present occupation rose from 40·9 per
cent in 1928 to 43·4 per cent in 1930.[3] But these changes were

---

68·6. Party statisticians calculated that, in order to reach the 50 per cent target
by January 1, 1931, at least 360,000 workers would have to be recruited by that
date and the admission of other categories restricted to 90,000 (*Izvestiya
Tsentral'nogo Komiteta VKP(B)*, No. 2-3(261-262), January 31, 1929, p. 23).

[1] *Pravda* February 5, 1929; *Izvestiya Tsentral'nogo Komiteta VKP(B)*,
No. 4(263), February 15, 1929, pp. 8-10; the instruction was, however, qualified
a few weeks later by a characteristic warning against following " the line of least
resistance " and pursuing number at the expense of quality (*ibid.* No. 10(289),
April 12, 1929, pp. 1-2). Complaint was made of " a significant leakage " of
members recruited in the mass campaigns of the winter of 1927–1928 (*ibid.* No. 7
(266), March 20, 1929, p. 11).

[2] For the purge see pp. 142-147 below.

[3] See Table 52, p. 474 below; Kaganovich at the sixteenth party congress
in May 1930 gave the following percentages of " workers from production " in
the party : fourteenth congress 35·7, fifteenth congress 40·8, sixteenth congress
48·6 (*XVI S"ezd Vsesoyuznoi Kommunisticheskoi Partii (B)* (1931), p. 83).

the natural result of the increased proportion of workers in the population rather than a specific consequence of the purge; and thereafter the discriminatory basis of recruitment was gradually relaxed.

(b) The Party Machine

The growth in the size of the party continued to be reflected in the increasing size of the main party organs. At the fourteenth party congress in December 1925, 655 voting delegates and 641 delegates with consultative rights represented a party comprising 643,000 members and 445,000 candidates. At the fifteenth congress two years later the party comprised 887,233 members and 348,957 candidates; the two categories of delegates had increased to 898 and 771 respectively. The numbers of the party central committee elected by each congress rose from 63 full members and 43 candidates in 1925 to 71 full members and 50 candidates in 1927; the membership of the central control commission increased from 164 to 195. The Politburo elected by the central committee after the fourteenth congress consisted of nine members, including Zinoviev, and five candidates, including Kamenev and Dzerzhinsky. After July 1926, when Zinoviev and Kamenev were expelled, and Dzerzhinsky died, the number of members was maintained at nine (Rudzutak replacing Zinoviev), but the number of candidates was raised to eight, at which level it was kept by the fifteenth congress in December 1927. The membership of the Orgburo was raised from 11 to 13, that of the secretariat remained constant at five. Of all these bodies the Politburo was now the only one where important debates took place, and contested issues of policy were fought out. But in matters of organization the secretariat was all-powerful. The Orgburo was now little more than a mouthpiece of the secretariat; and Orgraspred, the personnel department of the party, was an organ of the secretariat. The secretariat was under Stalin's

The target of over 50 per cent was said to have been reached in the Ukraine (where the proportion of industrial workers in the party was always high) by January 1, 1930 (*Voprosy Istorii KPSS*, No. 5, 1960, p. 123); in the Kharkov department, where 93·3 per cent of those admitted in 1928 were workers from production, it was hoped to reach a proportion of 55 per cent by January 1, 1931 (*Izvestiya Tsentral'nogo Komiteta VKP(B)*, No. 7(266), March 20, 1929, p. 10).

complete control; and it was through this control that he consistently dominated the Politburo, though the processes by which
he achieved this result were sometimes obscure, and down to
1929 his authority in the Politburo was not yet absolute.[1]

The party institution whose rôle changed most markedly in
this period was the central control commission.[2] Since its
amalgamation with the People's Commissariat of Workers' and
Peasants' Inspection (Rabkrin) in 1923,[3] the commission had
performed two functions of control — over the party, and over the
state, administrative machines. The amalgamation had been a
symptom of the gradual merger of the powers of the party with
those of the state, and had helped to promote it. But the two
functions were kept distinct; and the central control commission
decided by a resolution of April 1926 not to extend the amalgamation to the Rabkrins and control commissions of the Union
republics.[4] The joint organization in its capacity as supervisor
of the state bureaucracy was commonly referred to by the old
name of Rabkrin of RKI. While, however, this work was extensive and important, and abundantly publicized, it yielded pride
of place to the work of the commission in regard to the party —
its function before the amalgamation.[5] It was this work which
became increasingly conspicuous and important in the years after
1926. The struggle with the opposition, and the growing fre-
quency of the application of disciplinary measures culminating
in expulsion from the party, enhanced the rôle of the body in
which disciplinary authority was vested. But, with the apparent

---

[1] For the earlier history of these institutions see *Socialism in One Country,
1924–1926*, Vol. 2, pp. 196-199. The totals of members quoted above are
derived from the official records of the fourteenth and fifteenth congresses; the
totals of party membership announced on these occasions were generally in
excess of those recorded in current party statistics (see Table No. 52, p. 474
below).

[2] For the local control commissions see *Socialism in One Country, 1924–1926*,
Vol. 2, p. 217; their total membership in October 1926 amounted to 3619
(*Pravda*, October 26, 1926).

[3] See *The Bolshevik Revolution, 1917–1923*, Vol. 1, p. 228; *The Interregnum,
1923–1924*, p. 264.

[4] *Spravochnik Partiinogo Rabotnika*, vi (1928), ii, 295-297.

[5] According to the revised party statute of January 1926, it was no longer the
commission as a whole, but " the party collegium " of the commission, which
dealt with " matters concerning an infringement of party ethics " (*KPSS v
Rezolyutsiyakh* (1954), ii, 252).

accretion of its power, the independence of the commission diminished. Nothing now remained — except the meaningless formality of the direct election of the commission by the party congress — of the original conception of an authority which would exercise independent control over the major party organs as well as over rank-and-file party members. In 1921 the party central committee and control commission had sat jointly to consider, at Lenin's instigation, the expulsion of Shlyapnikov from the party.[1] This joint procedure had, however, been treated as exceptional, or perhaps as an ominous precedent, and was not repeated for several years. The session of the party central committee of January 1925, which censured Trotsky and relieved him of his military posts, was marked by " the participation of members of the central control commission " ; the same formula was repeated for the session of October 1925.[2] The session of the party central committee of April 1926 took place " with the participation of members of the presidium of the central control commission ".[3] The session of July 1926, which witnessed the first open appearance of the " united opposition " and the first disciplinary measures against it, was the first since 1921 to be described as " a joint plenum of the central committee and the central control commission of the VKP(B) ".[4]

During the next few years most of the major sessions of the party central committee took this form.[5] The central control commission had become in essence a department of the central committee, and took over some of the most controversial and sensitive work of the committee. The appointment of Orjonikidze in the autumn of 1926 as president of the central control commission in succession to Kuibyshev[6] brought to the commission a vigorous personality, a respected old party member, and a close associate of his fellow Georgian Stalin. New emphasis fell on the responsibilities of the commission. The duty of party members to " inform " on members seeking to form " ideological groupings " incompatible with the party line had been loudly proclaimed

---

[1] See *The Bolshevik Revolution, 1917–1923*, Vol. 1, p. 208.
[2] *KPSS v Rezolyutsiyakh* (1954), ii, 106, 173.
[3] *Ibid.* ii, 258.   [4] *Ibid.* ii, 268.
[5] For the history of these joint sessions see *Voprosy Istorii KPSS*, No. 10, 1965, pp. 73-79.
[6] See p. 19 above.

at the fourteenth party congress in December 1925.[1] Of some
minor amendments in the party statute affecting the central
control commission, which were adopted at the fifteenth congress
two years later, the most important was a new clause providing
that party members refusing to reply to questions put to them by a
control commission were liable to immediate expulsion.[2]   In
the elections to party organs at the end of the congress, when
changes in the personnel of the party central committee were
kept to a minimum, more than one-third of the members elected
to the central control commission at the fourteenth congress two
years earlier were replaced.[3] This suggested a desire to re-shape
the commission for its increasingly responsible rôle.

The institution which, itself unchanged, drew fresh strength
from all these changes, and notably from the successive increases
in the numbers of the party and of its principal organs, was the
secretariat of five, grouped closely round the dominant personality
of the general secretary.[4] By 1927 the secretariat was organized
in nine sections — an organization and distribution section
(Orgraspred), an agitation and propaganda section (Agitprop), a
press section, the political administration of the Red Army
(PUR), an information section (whose function it was to keep
members of the party informed about the activities of the central
committee, and the central committee about the work of local
party organizations and local opinion), a section for activities
among women workers and peasants, a statistical section, a section
for party history (Istpart), and a business and financial section.
This was the power-house of a large and expanding " apparatus "
of paid party workers all over the country, through which the party
organs — and in part also the organs of government — were

---

[1] See *Socialism in One Country, 1924–1926*, Vol. 2, pp. 220-221.

[2] *KPSS v Rezolyutsiyakh* (1954), ii, 491 ; for the original text see *ibid.* ii,
252-253.

[3] For the lists see *VKP(B) v Rezolyutsiyakh* (1936), ii, 81-82, 267-269 ; they
were omitted from later editions of this work. Of members of the central
committee only ten were not re-elected : these included Dzerzhinsky and
Krasin, who had died, and seven leading members of the opposition who were
expelled from the party.

[4] The last " independent " member of the secretariat was Evdokimov,
appointed after the fourteenth party congress in January 1926 as a gesture of
appeasement to the Leningrad opposition, but removed in April 1926 (see
Socialism in One Country, 1924–1926, Vol. 2, pp. 151, 174).

directed, controlled, recruited and purged. Uglanov, in a report
to the Moscow organization in June 1926, defined the functions
of "inner-party democracy" in terms which plainly left the initiative in the hands of the apparatus and its secretariat:

> To present promptly and correctly to the party organization
> for solution the fundamental tasks confronting the party and the
> country; to draw into the discussion and solution of these
> questions the broad masses of party members; promptly and
> correctly to expound to the proletariat the fundamental questions
> of socialist construction; to test modifications of our policy by
> the reactions of the working class and of its separate sections, and
> in the light of this test to modify the party line.[1]

Trotsky, in a long unpublished memorandum to the Politburo,
angrily denounced this formula as a theory of " party bureaucratism as a system " and " the dictatorship of the apparatus ",
since " a class with a disintegrated vanguard (and absence of free
discussion, of control over the apparatus, of election, means the
disintegration of the vanguard) can become only an object of
leadership for a centralized apparatus; indeed " the Stalinist
formula of the class dictatorship, opposed to the dictatorship of
the party, leads inevitably to the dictatorship of the apparatus ".[2]
The decay of the party and the growth of the party bureaucracy —
two facets of the same process — were the constant theme of the
opposition during this period. But the immense complexity of
the tasks confronting party and government, the poverty of the
ruling group in resources of every kind, the primitive level of the
mass of the population, the lack of trained and experienced
administrators — all pointed in the same direction. Bureaucracy
stepped into the shoes of democracy.[3] Kaganovich's sardonic
comment that " Menshevism and Trotskyism never understood
the importance of the party apparatus "[4] had some substance.

A party institution which acquired some importance at this
time was that of so-called " instructors " or " responsible instructors " — party officials sent out from the centre to make sure

[1] *Pravda*, June 4, 1926.
[2] Trotsky archives, T 2986; for Stalin's rejection of " the dictatorship of
the party " see *The Bolshevik Revolution, 1917–1923*, Vol. 1, pp. 230-232.
[3] For this process see pp. 291-292 below.
[4] *Izvestiya Tsentral'nogo Komiteta VKP(B)*, No. 4(263), February 15, 1929,
p. 1.

that party rules and instructions were understood and applied
by local organizations. In view of the thin party cover in many
regions, and the primitive level of education and political consciousness among most newly joined recruits, such guidance was
palpably necessary. By a resolution of March 28, 1927, the
party central committee proposed to establish a regular organization of " instructors " to be sent from higher to lower party units
in order to initiate them in the right methods of carrying out
party work.[1] This was hailed at the fifteenth party congress in
December 1927 as a " great achievement ", though regret was
expressed at the rapid turnover of instructors and difficulty in
obtaining them.[2] Both the grain collections crisis of 1928 and the
rift with the Right opposition brought the weaker rural party
organizations into the centre of the picture and enhanced the
importance of the instructors. A conference of the Orgburo in
December 1928 received and debated a report on the instructors'
work and functions.[3] This resulted in a resolution of the central
committee of January 14, 1929, calling for a concentration of the
work of the instructors on four " fundamental questions " :
support for industrialization and for the reconstruction of agriculture; support for " workers' democracy ", self-criticism, and
the struggle against bureaucratism; the struggle against Trotskyism " and, in particular, against the Right deviation " ; and the
regulation of the growth of the party and the formation of cadres.
A programme was laid down for the investigation of certain
specific local organizations and for the appointment of instructors
to certain key localities.[4]

The increased efficiency of the central apparatus of the
secretariat was doubtless one source of its growing power. The

[1] *Izvestiya Tsentral'nogo Komiteta VKP(B)*, No. 13(186), April 8, 1927,
pp. 4-5 ; for an article on the system see *ibid.* No. 14-15(187-188), April 2, 1927,
pp. 9-10.
[2] *Pyatnadtsatyi S"ezd VKP(B)*, i (1961) 127-128 ; the figures quoted —
that 20 instructors had left during the year and 23 new ones been appointed —
do not suggest an institution of large dimensions. But the Agitprop department
of the central committee also on occasion sent out its own instructors (*ibid.* i, 128).
[3] For extracts from the report see *Izvestiya Tsentral'nogo Komiteta VKP(B)*,
No. 4(263), February 15, 1929, pp. 2-4, from the speeches *ibid.* No. 5-6(264-265),
February 28, 1929, pp. 8-10.
[4] *Ibid.* No. 4(263), February 15, 1929, p. 8.

Orgburo celebrated the " régime of economy " in public affairs by calling, on August 16, 1929, for strict economy and control of expenditure in local party organs. This was reinforced by a resolution of the party central committee of September 17, 1926.[1] The party statute required the election by every party congress of a revision commission to supervise the efficient working of central party institutions and the party accounts. According to the report made by Kursky, president of the revision commission, to the fifteenth party congress in December 1927, some rationalization had been effected in the apparatus of the central committee and its departments and of the secretariat. The number of employees had been reduced from the total of 767 at which it had stood two years earlier to 657, though, if the central control commission and the party historical section (Istpart) were included, the total would rise to 971. Of the employees of the central committee 16 per cent were non-party (Kursky remarked, by way of example, that the party had no statisticians of its own), though in the " basic sections " the proportion did not exceed 4–6 per cent.[2] In 1926–1927 the party had for the first time a centralized budget, replacing a system of block grants to local party organizations. Some over-spending had occurred, especially in lower rural organizations. But Kursky looked forward to the stricter execution of the centralized budget of 1927–1928, in which the expenses of the apparatus of the central committee had been cut by 8 per cent.[3] No figures were cited ; details of party finance were never discussed in public. It was a rare exception when the journal of the party central committee published a decision of the committee of August 9, 1928, to reduce the number of local officials by 2500, but to increase the salaries of lower local party workers up to the rank of secretary of a district or rural district party committee.[4] Local party

----

[1] *Izvestiya Tsentral'nogo Komiteta VKP(B)*, No. 39(160), September 17, 1926, pp. 1, 5 ; for the régime of economy see Vol. 1, pp. 334-336.

[2] *Pyatnadtsatyi S"ezd VKP(B)*, i (1961), 123 ; the figure of 767 was given to the fourteenth congress two years earlier (see *Socialism in One Country, 1924-1926*, Vol. 2, p. 200). The turnover seems to have been surprisingly large : since 1925 441 new appointments had been made, and 446 employees transferred elsewhere (*K XV S"ezdu VKP(B)*) (1927), p. 354).

[3] *Pyatnadtsatyi S"ezd VKP(B)*, i (1961), 124-125.

[4] *Izvestiya Tsentral'nogo Komiteta VKP(B)*, No. 27(248), September 10, 1928, pp. 6-8.

organizations were said by the party statute to derive their funds
" from members' dues, subsidies granted by higher party organizations and other receipts ". Members' dues were never a very
substantial source of revenue; and the centralized budget was
certainly a factor making for more effective and rigid control from
the centre over local organizations.

The function vested in Orgraspred of assigning party members
to key posts both in party and in Soviet or other public institutions
was well established by 1926.[1] To prevent the machine becoming
clogged by the mass of appointments to be made was now a major
problem; and in November 1926 the rule was laid down that
personal files should be kept only of party members holding
" nomenclature " posts, i.e. posts on a list of appointments for
which the approval of the central committee (or, in practice, of
Orgraspred) was required, and that the rest should be registered
in a uniform card-index.[2] In the two years which elapsed between
the fourteenth and fifteenth party congresses 8761 party members
had been appointed by Orgraspred, 7445 to " responsible "
posts; of these 1220 were to posts in the first two categories of the
nomenclature, and required the sanction of the central committee
(meaning, Kursky pointed out, of the Politburo, the Orgburo and
the secretariat).[3] The election of the principal officers to leading
local party organizations was now a lost cause; even the polite
fictions of the previous period[4] do not seem to have been kept up.
The opposition platform of September 1927 alleged that " the
genuine election of officials is in actual practice dying out ", that
members of provincial, county and district party committees were
now elected for two years or more, and presidents of provincial
committees and other provincial bodies appointed by the central
committee for three, five years or longer.[1] Bukharin, at the
joint session of the Politburo and the presidium of the central
control commission in January–February 1929, is said to have

[1] See *Socialism in One Country, 1924–1926*, Vol. 2, pp. 206-212.
[2] *Spravochnik Partiinogo Rabotnika*, vi (1928), i, 527-533; Orgraspred at
this time used a " Powers machine " (an early punch-card tabulator) for recording party members (*Pyatnadtsatyi S"ezd VKP(B)*, i (1961), 128).
[3] *Ibid.* i, 126; comparison with earlier figures (see *Socialism in One Country,
1924–1926*, Vol. 2, p. 204) suggests that something had been done to rationalize
and decentralize the machinery of appointment.
[4] See *Socialism in One Country, 1924–1926*, Vol. 2, p. 212.
[5] L. Trotsky, *The Real Situation in Russia* (n.d. [1928]), pp. 115-116.

observed that " in the twelfth year of the revolution we do not have one elected secretary of a provincial party organization ", and that " everything is done from above ".[1]

(c) Party and Government

Apart from the organization and control of the party itself, the party authorities were concerned to organize the means whereby the will of the party could make itself effective in the organs of government. The penetration of party members into Soviet organs and other public organizations was the principal instrument by which party control of governmental policy was assured. In representative Soviet organs the proportion of party members was generally highest at the highest levels. At third, fourth and fifth Union Congresses of Soviets in 1925, 1927 and 1929 party members and candidates constituted 80·0, 72·5 and 46·6 per cent respectively of all delegates.[2] In urban Soviets in 1929 46·1 per cent of delegates, in village Soviets only 10 per cent, were party members ; and the proportion in intermediate organs varied between these extremes.[3] The reasons for party predominance in particular organs no doubt varied. To be a delegate to a Union, or even to a republican, congress of Soviets meant an impressive and comfortable visit to the capital at public expense ; and in the competition for places party members obviously enjoyed an advantage.[4] On the other hand, the almost exclusive selection of party members as presidents of department or county, and district or rural district, executive committees, indicated that these were key posts in rural administration, reserved for reliable servants of the party.

Appointments to high administrative posts were a jealously guarded party preserve ; the rôle of Orgraspred, though less often discussed than in the preceding period,[5] was not less important.

---

[1] *Byulleten' Oppozitsii* (Paris), No. 1-2, July, 1929, p. 11 ; for this session see pp. 88-90 above.

[2] *S"ezdy Sovetov v Dokumentakh*, iii (1960), 68, 111, 149 ; the reduction in the proportion of party delegates in 1929 was no doubt a policy decision.

[3] For these figures see Table No. 55, p. 478 below.

[4] For detailed regulations laid down by the presidium of the TsIK of the RSFSR for the payment of allowances to delegates to congresses of Soviets, to sessions of TsIK or to conferences summoned by government organs see *Sovetskoe Stroitel'stvo*, No. 12(17), December 1927, pp. 126-127.

[5] See *Socialism in One Country, 1924–1926*, Vol. 2, pp. 203-205.

For appointments to 841 top posts in economic organs, and to 280 in People's Commissariats (so-called " nomenclature posts "), the approval of five authorities, including the party central commission, the trade union central council and the OGPU, was required, and the process often took several weeks.[1] By 1927 a high proportion of the leaders of industry — 75·1 per cent of presidents and members of boards of administration of Vesenkha trusts, 82·9 per cent of boards of administration of syndicates, and 96·9 per cent (in absolute figures all but three) of directors of major industrial enterprises under Vesenkha — were party members;[2] this preponderance was due partly to the promotion of party members to high industrial posts, and partly to the practice of conferring party membership on important industrialists. In the clerical and lower administrative grades, the picture was different. The following percentages of party members among employees of the People's Commissariats of the USSR and the RSFSR in Moscow were reported to the fifteenth party congress in December 1927:

USSR		RSFSR	
Narkomtorg	27·6	Narkomfin	17·0
Narkomfin	18·2	Narkomvnudel	17·8
Vesenkha	20·2	Narkomzem	14·4
Narkomput'	22·0	Narkomtrud	28·0
		Narkomyust	22·4 [3]

[1] *Bol'shevik*, No. 8, April 30, 1928, pp. 67-68.

[2] *Bol'shaya Sovetskaya Entsiklopediya*, xi (1930), 543 ; Kaganovich at the sixteenth party congress in June 1930 stated that 85 per cent of those holding top positions in industry, and 36 per cent of their deputies, were party members (*XVI S"ezd Vsesoyuznoi Kommunisticheskoi Partii (B)* (1931), p. 79. The percentage of party members among managers of syndicates, which gained in importance at this time (see Vol. 1, pp. 373, 639-641), rose from 72·2 in 1926 to 84·2 in 1928 ; of 770 directors of state enterprises in 1926, all but 167 were party members, of 766 in 1928 all but 82 (*Bol'shevik*, No. 8, April 30, 1928, pp. 61, 64).

[3] *Pyatnadtsatyi S"ezd VKP(B)*, i (1961), 446-447. Orjonikidze did not recall Molotov's warning two years earlier that, while the proportion of party members in Soviet administration was increasing, it was necessary to take into account " the quality of workers in the state apparatus and the question whether they have the necessary knowledge " (*XIV S"ezd Vsesoyuznoi Komunisticheskoi Partii (B)* (1926), pp. 72-73).

According to a statement made at the sixteenth party conference in April 1929, 11·7 per cent of all employees in Soviet institutions were party members, and 25 per cent of those engaged in administration, though this proportion fell to 14 per cent for those engaged in the administration of industry.[1] Among technicians and intellectuals the proportion of party members was still lower. Of 14,800 trade unionists registered in the RSFSR as " scientific workers " only 6 per cent belonged to the party,[2] and as late as 1934 only one-third of all members of the Union of Soviet Writers.[3]

It was no easy task, with the limited resources in man-power available, to establish a governmental machine responsible to party decisions. It was still more difficult to impress the image and discipline of the party on its ordinary members and through them to influence the non-party mass of the population. What was above all required was to create some basis of consent by making decisions comprehensible and acceptable. Much attention was given to an informal group or category known as the party *aktiv*, or party activists, the most energetic and politically most advanced members of the rank and file of the party, who carried on its business at the lower levels — in district and local party organizations, in factory and in village — and propagated its ideas. These were, in effect, the non-commissioned officers of the party.[4] In the Moscow party organization, the number of activists was said to have grown from 10,620 in 1925–1926 to 38,815 at the end of 1927 ; in Leningrad and Tula the *aktiv* was composed largely of

[1] *Shestnadtsataya Konferentsiya VKP(B)* (1962), pp. 458-459 ; these statistics apparently included candidates as well as full members of the party. A table which distinguished between members and candidates (*Komministy v Sostave Apparata Gosuchrezhdonii i Obshchestvennykh Organsizatsii* (1929), Tablitsa 1, p. 55), gives a clue to the prestige and importance of different occupations in party circles : a notably higher percentage of members than of candidates was engaged in party work (9·1 and 3·2), in trade union work (8·0 and 6·7) and in industry (14·8 and 9·7), a lower percentage in cultural and educational work (9·0 and 17·1) and in Soviet administration (11·8 and 17·9).

[2] See Vol. 1, p. 597.

[3] *Pervyi Vsesoyuznyi S"ezd Sovetskikh Pisatelei* (1934), p. 663.

[4] By way of economy, the paid party apparatus was to be reduced by utilizing " the unpaid work of party activists " (*KPSS v Rezolyutsiyakh* (1954), ii, 603) ; a similar *aktiv* in the Komsomol was described as " the skeleton or backbone on which the whole organization is supported " (*Oppozitsiya i Komsomol* (1927), p. 39).

new recruits to the party, a high proportion of whom joined its
ranks.[1] "Activists" operated both in party and in non-party
institutions. In every Soviet, trade union, industrial, commercial
or cooperative organ, communists combined to form a party cell
for common discussion and action ; and one of the most important
functions of members of the cell was to permeate and influence
their non-party fellow-workers. These efforts were not always
welcome. In 1927 the Moscow party committee tried the experiment of attaching a number of party activists to 83 Moscow
establishments of various kinds ; but neither the establishments
nor the trade unions representing workers in them would cooperate, and the experiment came to nothing.[2]

These efforts were reinforced by the demand, which had been
a key-point in the campaign for " the revitalization of the Soviets "
since the autumn of 1924, for the increased participation of
" non-party elements " in Soviet work.[3] As it was more and
more plainly recognized that the thin layer of qualified and devoted
party members was inadequate for the establishment of a workable
local administration, or for the vast range of tasks imposed by an
expanding economy, and that a large-scale recruitment of non-
party workers and peasants into Soviet work was required,
frequent appeals were made for the support of sympathizers
outside the party ; and from this was developed the conception
of a " non-party *aktiv* " consisting of energetic and well-disposed
non-party workers who were ready to cooperate with the party
activists. The concept applied at first mainly to work in the
countryside, where the party was weakest. In May 1926 a decree
of the Orgburo had linked the campaign to revitalize the Soviets
with " the formation round the Soviets and the cooperatives of a
non-party peasant *aktiv* under the leadership of the party " ;[4]
and, at the TsIK of the RSFSR six months later, the *rapporteur*
on the forthcoming Soviet elections spoke of the need to " create

---

[1] *K XV S"ezdu VKP(B)* (1927), p. 14.
[2] *Sovetskoe Stroitel'stvo*, No. 12(29), December 1928, pp. 9-10.
[3] See *Socialism in One Country, 1924–1926*, Vol. 2, pp. 321, 326-327.
[4] *Pravda,* June 24, 1926 ; for earlier appeals to non-party people see *Socialism in One Country, 1924–1926*, Vol. 2, pp. 328-329, 331-332, 334.

a broad non-party worker and peasant *aktiv* ".[1]   At the fifteenth
party congress of December 1927 Molotov defined " the non-
party peasant *aktiv* " as consisting of " all those workers in
Soviets, cooperatives, and krestkomy, women peasant delegates,
leading workers from the Soviet intelligentsia, sel'kors, and
peasants who actively participate in the public life of the countryside, and constitute a broad peasant *aktiv* " ;[2] and the resolution
on work in the countryside instructed the party " to direct special
attention to the formation and extension of a non-party poor and
middle peasant *aktiv* ".[3]   Attempts to group the *aktiv* round the
village Soviet were in part frustrated by the failure of the Soviets
to function effectively.   Demobilized Red Army men and the
rabsel'kors were often named as providing the reliable core of a
rural non-party *aktiv*, the numbers of which were estimated in
1928 at 1,500,000.[4]   Party and non-party activists were closely
associated in the control of rural organizations.[5]   But the social
composition of the Soviet *aktiv*, as of the party itself in the
countryside, was suspect.   Such incongruous figures as church
cantors were sometimes found in it, and it included very few
batraks.[6]   This picture seems more realistic than that of a congress
of activists of the Middle Volga region at which half the places
were said to have been reserved for *batraks*.[7]

Reliance on non-party activists was not, however, confined to
the countryside.   In the factories, in contrast to the party *aktiv*,
the Soviet activists were mainly " workers with a long record in
production ".[8]   At the fifteenth party congress Kosior noted that,

[1] *III Sessiya Vserossiiskogo Tsentral'nogo Ispolnitel'nogo Komiteta XII Sozyva*
(1926), p. 515.
[2] *Pyatnadtsatyi S"ezd VKP(B)*, ii (1962).
[3] *KPSS v Rezolyutsiyakh* (1954), ii, 486.
[4] *Sovetskoe Stroitel'stvo*, No. 12(29), December 1928, pp. 10-17 ; *SSR: Ot
S"ezda k S"ezdu (Aprel' 1927–Mai 1929)* (1929), p. 170 ; *Voprosy Istorii KPSS*,
No. 6, 1964, p. 58.   The last source puts the total in 1928 at 2 millions : all these
estimates seem highly speculative.
[5] *Vlast' Sovetov*, No. 28-29, July 17, 1927, pp. 5-6.
[6] *Sovetskoe Stroitel'stvo*, No. 12(29), December 1928, p. 10 ; No. 6(35),
June 1929, p. 78 ; one party commentator discovered two *aktivs* in the countryside — one grouped round the village Soviet, the other grouped round the land
community and the *skhod* and hostile to the Soviets (*Bol'sheviks*, No. 9, May 15,
1928), pp. 79-80).
[7] *Izvestiya Tsentral'nogo Ispolnitel'nogo Komiteta VKP(B)*, No. 7(266),
March 20, 1929, p. 28.   [8] *K XV S"ezdu VKP(B)* (1927), p. 34.

especially in Soviet economic institutions, " the operative part of
our apparatus (not counting the top leadership), the part on which
the whole work of the apparatus directly depends, . . . is built for
the most part on non-party people " : these included the specialists who provided the indispensable technical knowledge for the
process of industrialization.[1] It was in this period that pressure
became increasingly strong to confer party membership on
outstanding specialists and administrators and on the top
personnel of the Red Army. Membership of the party was both a
reward for important services and a pledge of loyalty. Since the
notion of a mass party was still unacceptable, it was necessary at
lower levels to reserve some posts of dignity, and even of minor
administrative importance, for sympathizing non-party activists.
As early as 1925 the campaign for the revitalization of the Soviets
had led to progressive increase in the proportion of non-party
workers and peasants elected to Union and republican congresses
of Soviets and central executive committees.[2] Early in 1927
Bauman in an article remarkable for the fact that it scarcely
mentioned the party at all, declared that " the state apparatus,
especially in the countryside, must become the organizer of the
peasant masses ". In the last two years " an *aktiv* has grown up
round the Soviets ". But " the increasing Soviet social consciousness (obshchestvennost') " and " Soviet democracy " were still
weak; and activists must identify themselves with the work of
Soviet organs.[3] *Pravda* coined the term "non-party communists"
for people " really devoted to the party who think it enough that
they consciously and conscientiously support the party ".[4] A
year later the functions of the Soviet *aktiv* were described as being
to galvanize the lower Soviet organs into activity, to provide
recruits for administrative posts, and draw other workers and
peasants into active Soviet work.[5]

The trade unions had always provided a meeting place for
party and non-party workers; and, when the fifteenth party
conference of October 1926, at the moment of transition from the

[1] *Pyatnadtsatyi S"ezd VKP(B)*, i (1961), 105.
[2] See *Socialism in One Country, 1924–1926*, Vol. 2, pp. 339-340 and p. 123
above.
[3] *Pravda*, February 20, 1927.
[4] *Ibid.* September 24, 1927.
[5] *Sovetskoe Stroitel'stvo*, No. 12(29), December 1928, p. 16.

" restoration period " to the period of " reconstruction " of industry, passed a resolution on the trade unions, it used the language not of party, but of class, and appealed for " an increased interest in the common tasks of the class as a whole and a more extensive drawing of the working masses into the whole task of socialist construction ".[1] A resolution of the party central committee of July 1927 called for adequate representation of non-party people at trade union and cooperative congresses.[2] At the fifteenth party congress in December 1927 Kosior complained that the trade union central council contained only 3 per cent of non-party members and the central committees of individual unions only 4 per cent; the proportion of non-party delegates at trade union congresses in the past year had varied from 19 to 25 per cent, having previously been much lower. Another delegate humorously retorted that in his factory, after party orders had been obeyed by electing eight non-party workers to the factory committee, six of the eight had joined the party.[3] Ryutin, later pilloried as a Right deviationist, wrote in the party journal in the summer of 1928 that 99·6 per cent of the trade union central council, and 100 per cent of its presidium, consisted of party members; the situation in individual trade unions was little better, though it had improved somewhat since the fifteenth party congress. He added the well-founded, but unorthodox, comment that increased party representation was not equivalent to increased worker representation.[4]

The assimilation of non-party to party activists led to a blurring of the line between the rank and file of the party and the masses of workers and peasants which had other unforeseen consequences. A new line of demarcation began to appear

[1] *KPSS v Rezolyutsiyakh* (1954), ii, 312 ; Enukidze at this time also offered encouragement to " the unorganized urban workers ", whose zeal was said to surpass that of " the leading stratum of the urban proletariat organized in the trade unions " (*Sovetskoe Stroitel'stvo*, No. 2, September 1926, p. 21).

[2] See Vol. 1, p. 547, note 2.

[3] *Pyatnadtsatyi S"ezd VKP(B)*, i (1961), 94, 161 ; on the eve of the tenth anniversary of the revolution, the party central committee issued an instruction to recruit into the party, " first and foremost, the non-party *aktiv* which has grown up in the trade unions, the Soviets, the cooperatives and other public organizations " (*Izvestiya Tsentral'nogo Komiteta VKP(B)*, No. 39(212), October 22, 1927, pp. 5-6).

[4] *Bol'shevik*, No. 15, August 15, 1928, p. 24.

between a highly articulated, politically conscious and increasingly authoritarian party central organization and a passive, dispersed and often bewildered party membership, less and less clearly distinguishable, in its political attitudes and in the rôle which it was called on to play, from other " loyal " elements of the population. The party as a whole was no longer a vanguard or *élite* leading the masses of workers and peasants; the vanguard was formed of party officials leading and directing both the party and non-party masses. As the party strode forward more and more urgently on the stony road of industrialization, and of the un-remitting pressure on all sections of the population necessary to enforce it, relations between the directing organs of the party and its members fell into the mould of orders from above and unquestioning obedience from below; and, as the whole popula-tion, together with the rank and file of the party, was mobilized for the gigantic task, the dictatorship of the party organization at length crystallized in the dictatorship of the single leader.

The blurring of the line between party and non-party activists was also part of a larger process. The growing together of party and state institutions, both being executive agents of a single policy decided by a supreme authority, had been significantly inaugurated by the amalgamation of the Rabkrin of the USSR with the party central control commission in 1923.[1] The fusion made slow but unmistakable progress in the ensuing period. A weighty pronouncement on the régime of economy, issued on August 16, 1926, in the joint name of the party central committee and Sovnarkom, signed by Stalin, Rykov and Kuibyshev — a high party official, a high state official, and one who combined both functions — no longer seemed an anomaly.[2] From 1929 onwards, it became a frequent practice to issue decrees in the joint name of the central committee of the party and of TsIK or the presidium of TsIK. The formal distinction was maintained. The rule that party members spoke with a single voice in non-party institutions was invoked against members of the opposition who carried their dissentient opinions beyond the strict limits of a party forum.[3] But, as the dividing line between rank-and-file members of the party and non-party sympathizers grew less sharp, little practical

[1] See p. 116 above.   [2] For this declaration see Vol. i, pp. 335-336.
[3] See, for example, p. 24, note 4 above.

distinction between party and state institutions remained, and it came to seem immaterial whether a decision or an instruction issued from a party or a non-party organ, or jointly from both. The dual authority merely added a certain binding solemnity to the pronouncement.

CHAPTER 43

PARTY DISCIPLINE

EXPULSIONS from the party, mainly on grounds of mis-conduct but often also for breaches of party discipline, had been a regular feature of party practice and had accounted for a large turn-over in membership. Resignations and expulsions from the party in 1926 and 1927 appear to have followed a more or less normal course. In the six years from 1922 to 1928 260,144 members left the party. The number leaving it in 1927 was close to the average for these years — 44,058; of these, 16,718 were expelled by decision of a control commission, 27,340 either resigned " voluntarily " or were " automatically " removed for failure to register or to pay their dues.[1] Of those expelled in 1927 36·8 per cent had been members or candidates before 1924 — a figure which lends only moderate support to the frequent assertion that most of those expelled were recent recruits; the proportion of workers among those expelled was slightly lower, and of peasants and employees slightly higher, than their proportion in the total party membership.[2] But from 1922 to 1927 this was routine business. No general purge of the party membership had been undertaken since that instituted at Lenin's instigation in 1921.[3]

[1] See Table No. 56, p. 479 below; no corresponding figures appear to have been published for 1926. The only earlier period for which it is possible to distinguish between those expelled and those leaving the party "voluntarily " or " automatically " is the second half of 1925, when voluntary or automatic leavers accounted for 71·5 per cent of the exodus (*VKP(B) v Tsifrakh*, v (1926), 12). The figures for 1927 suggest an increased readiness to resort to formal expulsion; but the procedures or the classification may not have been identical. The penalty of suspension for a limited period was abolished by decision of the central control commission of December 9, 1926 (*Spravochnik Partiinogo Rabotnika*, vi (1928), ii, 374).

[2] *VKP(B) v Tsifrakh*, viii (1928), 28-29. On May 6, 1926, the central control commission laid down rules for the readmission to the party of workers expelled for minor offences; a further resolution of August 24, 1927, restricted this facility to " workers from the bench " (*Spravochnik Partiinogo Rabotnika*, vi (1928), ii, 371-374).

[3] See *The Bolshevik Revolution, 1917–1923*, Vol. 1, pp. 205-207; the

Expulsions for fractional activities, though far less numerous than expulsions for other offences, were those which aroused controversy and played a sinister rôle in party history. Attention to questions of party discipline was always stimulated by opposition within the party. It was Rykov who, in the days when he defended the party line against the newly formed " united opposition ", reverted to an analogy used with effect by Lenin, and proclaimed that anyone who did not heed " the party discipline of the dictatorship of the proletariat was " worse than a " strike-breaker " who violated trade union discipline.[1] Trotsky, when protesting in the opposition platform of 1927 against the expulsion of " old party men " and the dictatorship of the party apparatus, added : " It goes without saying that, after the adoption of a decision, it is carried out with iron Bolshevik discipline ".[2] As the economic situation worsened and the struggle with the opposition grew tougher in the summer and autumn of 1927, party discipline became stricter and harsher. Yaroslavsky, speaking for the central control commission at the fifteenth party congress in December 1927, sought to allay anxiety about the recent wave of expulsions from the party. In the two years since the previous congress, 93,000 members had been called to account by control commissions for various misdemeanours, 83,000 had been interviewed, and 28,563 expelled. Those called to account amounted to 1·8 per cent of all members in 1926, and 1·6 per cent in 1927 ; those expelled were about 1 per cent in each year. The causes of expulsion included such routine offences as persistent failure to attend meetings or to pay dues. Drunkenness was still a serious evil. But Yaroslasvky offered a generally reassuring picture :

> Any party organization will tell you that *there have been in our party fewer of the discussions* which formerly sometimes devoured the organization. . . . *There have been fewer conflicts at the national level* — a lot fewer.

There had also been " far less drunkenness . . . fewer breaches of party discipline, and less extravagance and getting into

expulsion of adherents of the opposition in the first months of 1924 (see *The Interregnum, 1923–1924*, pp. 356-357) did not have the dimensions of a purge.
[1] A. I. Rykov and N. Bukharin, *Partiya i Oppozitsionnyi Blok* (1926), p. 17.
[2] L. Trotsky, *The Real Situation in Russia* (n.d. [1928]), p. 129.

debt ".[1] Yaroslavsky went on to deal more explicitly with the political expulsions. Since the previous congress 2031 members had been charged with " fractional activity " and 970 of these expelled (this provoked cries of " Too few ! "). The central control commission had shown great moderation. Of 75 members arraigned before it, it had expelled only 19 ; it had heard appeals against 146 sentences of expulsion pronounced by local commissions, and confirmed only 47 of them. Referring to the charge that the OGPU had been used against party members, Yaroslavsky remarked that " we have been obliged to take the GPU under our protection ". He concluded mildly :

> We have expelled the opposition from our ranks ; but we must strengthen self-criticism, permit in our own ranks conscientious, comradely self-criticism.[2]

Side by side with its pronouncements excommunicating the opposition, the congress, in its general resolution on the report of the central committee, called for " the development of inner-party democracy and of practical criticism of shortcomings both in the Soviet apparatus and in the party itself ".[3]

The fifteenth party congress of December 1927 occupied, in the issue of party discipline, as in the offensive against the *kulaks*,[4] an ambivalent and intermediate position. It approved the first large-scale expulsion of leading members of an opposition within the party, and of measures of police repression against some of them, while continuing to proclaim that no fundamental change of attitude was contemplated, and that the rights of "inner-party democracy" and criticism within the party were unimpaired.[5]

---

[1] *Pyatnadtsatyi S"ezd VKP(B)*, i (1961), 536-539. Yaroslavsky's statistics were admittedly incomplete ; the proportion of members expelled in 1927 was about 1·5 per cent.   [2] *Ibid.* i, 550-553.

[3] *KPSS v Rezolyutsiyakh* (1954), ii, 440.   [4] See Vol. 1, pp. 40-41.

[5] A significant minor change occurred at this time. Down to the end of 1927 lists of expelled members with a brief statement of the cause of expulsion, were regularly published in the journal of the party central committee ; in the first half of 1928 lists of those expelled by the party central control commission appeared in occasional supplements. In July 1928 the journal announced that it would in future publish every three months lists of those expelled by the central control commission, and that the names of those expelled by local control commissions would be published locally (*Izvestiya Tsentral'nogo Komiteta VKP(B)*, No. 23(244), July 1928, p. 13). But no further central lists appeared ; if local lists were published, they have not been traced.

As in the campaign against the *kulaks*, events occurring in the first months of 1928 set in motion radical changes in attitude and policy which, seen in retrospect, had been foreshadowed by much that had gone before, and notably by the pronouncements of the fifteenth party congress. The grain collections crisis, quickly followed by the revelations of the Shakhty affair,[1] created an atmosphere of alarm and suspicion in which the bogy of dissent within the party assumed frightening proportions, and had to be exorcized at all costs by the sternest measures.

The failure of the grain collections exposed a grave and long-standing deficiency in the rural organizations of the party. The fourteenth party conference in April 1925, at the height of the pro-peasant orientation, had called for " a partial check of rural district (and also county) party organizations in cases where the membership of the organizations is found to comprise corrupt elements alien to the party, which discredit the party in the eyes of the peasantry ";[2] and the fourteenth party congress in December 1925 invited the central control commission and Rabkrin to undertake a check of " the work of lower organs, both party and Soviet ", in the countryside.[3] But this had achieved little.[4] The weakness of the party in the countryside was twofold. Party members were few in number and poor in quality; and some party officials tended to sympathize with the *kulak* and the well-to-do peasant, especially at a time when these groups enjoyed a certain indulgence from the makers of policy in Moscow.[5] The inability or unwillingness of the party official to put pressure on the peasant who held the grain was blamed for the breakdown in the collections; and the resolution of the party central committee of February 13, 1928, called for " a checking and resolute purging of party ... organizations ".[6] Though no announcement was made, Stalin later claimed that elements favourable to the *kulaks* had been " purged from the party in the spring of this year ".[7]

[1] See Vol. 1, pp. 584-585.
[2] *KPSS v Rezolyutsiyakh* (1954), ii, 141.   [3] *Ibid.* ii, 209.
[4] I. Maslov, *KPSS v Bor'be za Ukreplenie Edinstva Svoikh Ryadov (1925-1927 gg.)* (1955), pp. 126-127.
[5] For the state of the party in the countryside see pp. 179-184 below.
[6] See Vol. 1, pp. 51-52.   [7] Stalin, *Sochineniya*, xi, 235.

More serious defalcations occurred in high places, and were severely dealt with. In the Crimean ASSR, advantage had been taken of the exceptional provision in the agrarian code, which allowed large estates devoted to specialized crops to be kept intact, to favour the retention of large estates.[1] In the winter of 1927–1928, Ibragaimov, who, as president of the Crimean TsIK, was held responsible for a long series of abuses, was arrested, brought to trial and shot on the charge of " a sharp *kulak* deviation in the policy and practice of the Crimean government ".[2] The Shakhty affair intensified the growing sense that all was not right with the party. An article in *Pravda* on March 10, 1928, a few days after the Shakhty scandal broke, diagnosed " crying defects " in every branch of public work; and in the following month the party central committee, in its resolution on the affair, spoke of " a blunting of communist vigilance, of revolutionary sensibility on the part of our party workers in face of class enemies ".[3] In the summer of 1928 the check was extended to eight large regional organizations; 2130 members were expelled from the party, in proportions varying from 6 to 18 per cent of the total membership of the organizations affected.[4] The campaign for greater vigilance brought to light major scandals in local party organizations.

The most widely publicized of these was what came to be known as the " Smolensk scandal ". The first signs of trouble in

---

[1] An article in the journal of the party central committee in August 1927 pointed out that an economy which was highly commercial and depended on labour-intensive crops was especially open to abuses, and complained of the weakness of the party and of the cooperatives in the Crimea (*Izvestiya Tsentral'-nogo Komiteta VKP(B)*, No. 30-31(203-204), August 10, 1927, p. 7). Leasing of land by well-to-do peasants took place on a large scale (Ya. Yakovlev, *K Voprosu o Sotsialisticheskom Pereustroistve Sel'skogo Khozyaistva* (1928), p. 35); on the other hand, 46·6 per cent of all peasants had no working animals, and 68·5 per cent no implements of cultivation (*ibid.* p. 51). A commission set up by the Crimean Sovnarkom in June 1927 brought to light many irregularities (*Na Agrarnom Fronte*, No. 3, 1928, p. 111).

[2] *Na Agrarnom Fronte*, No. 3, 1928, p. 23 ; a resolution of the Orgburo of August 8, 1928, darkly referring to these events was published in *Pravda*, August 10, 1928. On February 14, 1928, the Crimean regional party committee issued a directive for a revision of the size of holdings to be carried out in five months after consultation with technical experts (*Na Agrarnom Fronte*, No. 5-6, 1928, pp. 52-53) ; and in the summer of 1929 it was announced that " land reform " was in progress in the Crimea (*Bednota*, June 15, 1929).

[3] *KPSS v Rezolyutsiyakh* (1954), ii, 501.

[4] *Shestnadtsataya Konferentsiya VKP(B)* (1962), p. 592.

the Smolensk party organization appeared as a result of the grain crisis at the end of 1927. After the neglect of technical crops in 1926,[1] the peasants of the western region had been encouraged in 1927 to increase their production of flax under a promise that grain to feed the region would be forthcoming from elsewhere. With the fiasco of the grain collections in the autumn months of 1927, the promised consignments failed to arrive; and at meetings on December 28–29, 1927, the Smolensk provincial party committee confronted the ugly spectre of famine. Peasants were killing their animals, were grinding oats and flax-seed for food, and threatened " hunger demonstrations ". It was decided to send the secretary of the committee, Pavlyuchenko, to Moscow to press for grain deliveries.[2] He evidently had some success. At a conference of secretaries of county party committees on February 12, 1928, it was stated that, thanks no doubt to the improvement in the grain collections, a million puds of grain had been received in January 1928, and that it was hoped, with the approval of Narkomotorg, to purchase more grain on the free market. In distributing the official supplies, preference would have to be given to those who delivered flax.[3] The immediate crisis had been surmounted. But the party, in Smolensk as elsewhere, was badly shaken; and scapegoats had, no doubt, to be found. The gravest offender was apparently an old Bolshevik named Pokaln, whose wife was the daughter of a " speculator ", and had previously been married to a " speculator in valuta ". Pokaln, an official of the provincial gostorg, had drunk with boon companions, taken bribes and consorted with *kulaks*, so that " a *kulak* policy was pursued under the party flag " and " *kulak* corruption of rural communists " set in. On January 20, 1928, he was dismissed from his post of inspector of the flax trade;[4] and the charges against him fitted easily into the current theme of " the reinforced offensive against the *kulak* ".

[1] See Vol. 1, pp. 8-9.
[2] Smolensk archives, WKP 33, quoted by O. Narkiewicz in *Soviet Studies*, xx, No. 2, October 1968, pp. 237-239; the availability of these archives makes possible a fuller account of this episode than of others comparable to it, though the evidence is circumstantial, and perhaps not always reliable.
[3] *Ibid.* p. 238.
[4] The sole authority for Pokaln's misdemeanours is an article in *Bol'shevik*, No. 10, May 31, 1928, pp. 14-22; no mention of him has been traced in the Smolensk archives.

But Pavlyuchenko himself was not immune; he may have had enemies who denounced him to Moscow.[1] Two inspectors from the party central control commission arrived in Smolensk to conduct an enquiry.[2] Whether or not as a result of their investigations, a fresh scandal was unearthed in a local wood-working factory called Katushka, where Pavlyuchenko had worked for 12 years. Foremen, some of them party members, were alleged to have held drunken orgies, seduced women workers, and introduced a régime of bribery and corruption, workers being intimidated by fear of dismissal. On April 28, 1928, the provincial party committee examined the situation; in the course of the discussion the Katushka affair was significantly, if inappropriately, called " another Shakhty ", and one speaker added that " political conclusions must be drawn " from it. Two days later the bureau of the committee adopted a stern resolution, which was signed by Pavlyuchenko, dissolving the party cell in the factory, expelling a number of officials and other offenders from the party and dismissing the director of the factory.[3]

If this display of severity was designed to forestall further reprisals from the centre, it failed in its purpose. The party central control commission, having received the report of its two investigators, decided to intervene; and the presidium of the commission adopted on May 9, 1928, a resolution which received wide publicity in the press. It described what had happened in the Katushka factory as " a distortion of the class line ", and recommended that Pavlyuchenko and his principal coadjutors should be transferred to work in industry, and excluded from party work. Re-elections were to be held for the principal party posts in the province.[4] But, in the mood prevailing in the party

---

[1] Study of the Smolensk archives makes this conjecture plausible (*Soviet Studies*, xx, No. 2 (October 1968), p. 238, note 28).

[2] *Pravda*, May 18, 1923; *Bol'shevik*, No. 10, May 31, 1928, p. 20.

[3] The record of the meeting of April 28, 1928, and the resolution of April 30, 1928, are in Smolensk archives, WKP 33.

[4] *Pravda*, May 18, 1928; *Izvestiya Tsentral'nogo Komiteta VKP(B)*, No. 16-17(237-238), May 25, 1928, pp. 15-16. Indignant articles about the affair appeared in *Pravda*, May 9, 16, 20, 1928, and *Bednota*, May 18, 24, 26, 1928; for supplementary details from the archives see M. Fainsod, *Smolensk Under Soviet Rule* (1959), pp. 48-52. According to *Shestnadtsataya Konferentsiya VKP(B)* (1962), p. 813, note 276, the president of the provincial branch of the wood-workers' trade union was one of the guilty.

leadership in the spring and summer of 1928, these sanctions seemed altogether too mild. Yakovlev, deputy president of Rabkrin, declared in an article in *Pravda* that " we must decisively alter our attitude to members of the party who know about abuses and remain silent ".[1] An article in *Bol'shevik* stressed the political undertones of the affair. What had happened was attributed to " the acquisition by communists of a typically bourgeois ideology ", resulting in exploitation, degeneracy and the cult of individual good living. Pavlyuchenko, together with Panfilov, the head of the provincial party Agitprop, and Alekseev, president of the provincial trade union council, formed a group which, though not itself participating in the current malpractices, had turned a blind eye to them, and obstructed attempts to probe the scandal; Panfilov had pretended that the abuses in the Katushka factory had been confined to a handful of incidents spread over four years. Among those removed from their posts was Nikitin, president of the provincial control commission.[2]

Meanwhile, the central control commission had evidently decided to make an example of an organization which had, perhaps, not offended more gravely than many others. Yakovlev travelled in person to Smolensk, and on May 18, 1928, summoned a meeting of members of the provincial party committee and control commission together with active party workers from the province, more than a thousand in all. For this mass assembly Yakovlev drew a lurid picture of drunken and sexual orgies and corruption of every kind. He announced that 60 local party officials had already been arrested (and this was " not enough "), and that new elements had been imported into the province to strengthen the party organization; these included a new secretary of the provincial party committee and a new president of the control commission. Panic spread through the organization. The reported reaction of the rank and file was a demand for severer punishment of the offenders. But confidence in the party had evidently received a shock; and notes of anti-Semitism, traditional in this

---

[1] *Pravda*, May 16, 1928.

[2] For the article in *Bol'shevik* see p. 137, note 4 above; Yakovlev at the sixteenth party conference in April 1929 attributed scandals like that at Smolensk to the fact that local party leaders " grow together with class-enemy elements " (*Shestnadtsataya Konferentsiya VKP(B)* (1926), pp. 446-447).

region, were heard, the ever-present tendency being to equate
Jews and communists.[1] Yakovlev also visited Kardymovo, 30
miles from Smolensk, the centre of a rural district, and discovered
eight old landed estates and several *kulak* holdings which had been
left undisturbed.[2] On June 1, 1928, Borisov, the new secretary
of the party committee entered on his functions, having had an
interview with Stalin, from whom he obtained a promise of an
improvement in food supplies to the province. But further
unrest occurred among women workers in a textile factory owing
to the introduction of the three-shift system ; Borisov, when he
visited the factory, was shouted down by angry workers.[3] The
situation of the party evidently remained precarious. Sweeping
changes were made in the party personnel ; and new appointments
were announced to posts in the administration and in the trade
unions.[4] In August 1928 the central control commission decided
to send a representative of its presidium to supervise a special
check of local party and Soviet cells in the Smolensk party organization, and laid it down that non-party workers and peasants should
be invited to participate in the investigation.[5] It was not till
February 1929 that a joint resolution of the party central committee and the presidium of the central control commission could
speak of " the liquidation of the gangrene ", and record that " the
composition of the leading party organs — from the provincial
party committee to the bureau of the cells — has been almost
entirely renewed ". Of former members of the provincial party
committee, of the provincial Soviet executive committee, and of
the provincial trade union committee, only ten retained their
posts ; of ten secretaries of county and district party organizations
only two remained ; 476 party members had been called to account,
and 150 expelled from the party. The resolution ominously added

---

[1] *Pravda*, May 20, 1928 ; *Izvestiya*, May 22, 1928.
[2] *Ibid.* May 25, 1928.
[3] M. Fainsod, *Smolensk Under Soviet Rule* (1959), pp. 49-52 ; for the three-
shift system in the textile industry see Vol. 1, pp. 500-504.
[4] *Izvestiya Tsentral'nogo Komiteta VKP(B)*, No. 24(245), August 10, 1928,
p. 20.
[5] *Ibid.* No. 25(246), August 22, 1928, p. 7. At the sixteenth party conference
in April 1929 Yaroslavsky criticized the participation of non-party people in
party purges as a dangerous innovation (*Shestnadtsataya Konferentsiya VKP(B)*
(1929), pp. 607-608) ; this did prevent the precedent being followed in the 1929
purge (see p. 145 below).

that " the work of purifying the Smolensk province must in no sense be regarded as finished ".[1]

The growing economic tension, the Shakhty affair and the exposure of scandals in the party, combined to create a mood of alarm, and inspired a massive appeal from the party central committee to all party members and workers which appeared on the front page of *Pravda* on June 3, 1928, and continued to be quoted for several weeks as a major pronouncement. It deplored the growing laxity of party discipline, citing the Shakhty, Smolensk and Artemovsk affairs;[2] the novel feature was the demand for more " inner-party democracy " and for self-criticism within the party " from top to bottom " and " without regard to persons ". A resolution of the party central control commission of August 29, 1928, harped on the theme of self-criticism;[3] and a resolution on party affairs adopted by the central committee at its session of November 1928 spoke of the need for " severe self-criticism " in the party and " the bold and consistent application of proletarian self-criticism ", and especially commended this to the trade unions as a means of overcoming their bureaucratic defects.[4] Kalinin called self-criticism " a Russian habit " — witness Gogol

---

[1] *Pravda*, February 9, 1929; *Izvestiya Tsentral'nogo Komiteta VKP(B)*, No. 5-6(264-265), February 28, 1929, pp. 17-19. The journal of the party central committee continued to harp on the deficiencies of agricultural production in the Smolensk region, on the resistance of the peasants to collective cultivation, and on the low level of party and Komsomol work (*ibid.* No. 8-9(267-268), March 31, 1929, pp. 10-11).

[2] The shortcomings of the Artemovsk party organization had been investigated and dealt with, on a report by Bubnov, in a resolution of the party central committee of March 5, 1928: this convicted the local party organization of insufficient contact with the masses, weakness in combating " morbid phenomena in the sphere of the Soviet and economic apparatus ", and " unhealthy symptoms " of the formation of a clique among some responsible workers and of support for " certain corrupt elements "; instructions were given to " review the staff of leading party officials " (*Izvestiya Tsentral'nogo Komiteta VKP(B)*, No. 8(229), March 15, 1928, pp. 4-5); one of the troubles appears to have been failure to check absenteeism and " anti-spets " demonstrations in Yugostal and Donugol (*ibid.* No. 20-21(279-280), July 29, 1929, pp. 21-22). For Bubnov's report see *Pravda*, March 21, 1928. Trouble also occurred in the legal administration; the president of the court of the department was expelled from the party for drunkenness and violence (*Izvestiya*, February 8, 1928), and four other legal officials were arraigned before the Ukrainian Supreme Court (*ibid.* May 25, 1928).   [3] *Pravda*, September 2, 1928.

[4] *KPSS v Rezolyutsiyakh* (1954), ii, 541-542; for criticism of the trade unions see Vol. 1, pp. 553-555.

and Saltykov-Shchedrin; but he deprecated " merciless " and
" unqualified " criticism which took no account of achievements.[1]
Pravda a month later drew prominent attention to abuses
committed at a county party conference, where the local leaders
had stifled criticism by indulging in " the attribution of a Trotskyite deviation to party members who expressed an opinion about
the composition of a county committee ";[2] and the journal of
the party central committee cautiously sought to reconcile self-
criticism with party discipline:

> Genuine Bolshevik discipline can exist only *on the basis* of
> genuine democracy and self-criticism.[3]

Trotsky's tart comment on the whole campaign was that the
appeal for self-criticism contained " *a secret paragraph exempting
the central committee* — or, more accurately, the heads of the
Stalinist faction — *from the operation of criticism in general* ".[4]

The expulsion of the leaders of the united opposition at the
end of 1927 cleared the decks for action on the other front.
Everything was now geared to the struggle against the Right
deviation, which drew such strength as it had from rural party
organizations. These had long been suspect in the highest party
circles in Moscow, and felt the weight of party discipline in the
spring of 1928.[5] Reviews of seven provincial or regional party
organizations (of which Smolensk was doubtless one) in the course
of 1928 had led to the expulsion of 13 per cent of their members.[6]
Bukharin's supporters had been removed from the Moscow
organization in October and November 1928.[7] At a moment
when the still unpublicized rift with Bukharin and the Right
opposition was about to come into the open, the leaders judged
that the time was ripe for a major cleansing operation. At the

---

[1] *Sovetskoe Stroitel'stvo*, No. 11(28), November 1928, p. 7.
[2] *Pravda*, December 28, 1928; for reports of attempts by other local party
organizations to stifle criticism see *ibid.* January 9, 18, 1929.
[3] *Izvestiya Tsentral'nogo Komiteta VKP(B)*, No. 2-3(261-262), January 31,
1929, pp. 4-6.
[4] *Byulleten' Oppozitsii* (Paris), No. 3-4, September 1929, p. 7.
[5] See p. 135 above.
[6] *Shestnadtsataya Konferentsiya VKP(B)* (1962), p. 592.
[7] See p. 81 above.

session of the party central committee in November 1928, Molotov cautiously observed that " the development of self-criticism has paved the way for a party purge ", which was now " knocking at our door "; that many local party committees and control commissions wanted a purge; but that it was necessary to make careful preparations for it, and in the countryside to connect it with the recruitment of poor peasants and *batraks* into the party.[1] The resolution, which was mainly concerned with recruitment, argued that this should be " combined with a strict check on the present composition of the party and its most decisive *purging* of elements socially alien to it which have fastened themselves on it and become bureaucratized and corrupt ". It demanded " far firmer measures than those taken in recent years to purge party organizations, by expelling from them elements which used their membership of the ruling party for aims of personal greed and ambition, elements of petty bourgeois degeneration which mingled with *kulaks* etc.".[2] This was something less than a formal decision to conduct a general purge. But the leaders were now bent on this course. Early in the new year a circular was sent out from the central party control commission to local commissions informing them that the question of a purge would be considered by the forthcoming sixteenth party conference, and instructing them to prepare for it, and to pay special attention to the selection of the local commissions which would be set up to conduct it.[3] An article by Yaroslavsky in *Pravda* significantly marshalled Lenin's various pronouncements on the necessity of party purges.[4] In February 1929 Yaroslavsky gave the Moscow provincial party conference particulars of selective purges carried out by local control commissions. From a mass of statistics the significant fact emerged that of party members arraigned for drunkenness only 24 per cent were expelled from the party, and of those called to account for fractional activities 52 per cent. Of 3865 members questioned in the first half of 1928 about opposition activities,

---

[1] These remarks were quoted in *Izvestiya Tsentral'nogo Komiteta VKP(B)*, No. 2-3(261-2 62), January 31, 1929, pp. 1-2. The speech was not published; the report of a speech by Molotov to the Moscow provincial party committee in *Pravda*, November 28, 1928, did not mention the purge.

[2] *KPSS v Rezolyutsiyakh* (1954), ii, 546.

[3] *Pravda*, February 6, 1929; *Izvestiya Tsentral'nogo Komiteta VKP(B)*, No. 4(263), February 15, 1929, p. 16.   [4] *Pravda*, February 3, 1929.

2972 had renounced their link with the opposition, though some of these were found to have continued to circulate opposition literature. Yaroslavsky ended with the firm pronouncement:

> The party purge should be general; it should cover the whole of our party.

Bauman in his report to the conference also referred to " the general purge in the ranks of the party " which would follow the major party conference.[1]

The scene was now set for the formal announcement of the purge at the sixteenth party conference. On March 29, 1929, Yaroslavsky presented to a meeting of the Moscow party organization the theses which he was to present to the conference. His report was significantly weighted against the rural component in the party. He criticized factory workers who had retained a base in the countryside, and who thought of factory work " only as a means to enrich their rural economy "; the party in the countryside comprised " many small proprietors — with corresponding attitudes ".[2] Yaroslavsky made it abundantly clear that the main emphasis of the purge was to be ideological. What was required was a " *class* approach "; the member should be judged " from the point of view of his fulfilment of the tasks of the class struggle, . . . the tasks of the building of socialism ". Inquisitorial methods, such as the questioning of neighbours about a member's personal behaviour, were to be avoided; Yaroslavsky issued a warning " against the petty digging into the private life of party members, against the vulgarization of the purge ".[3] The theses were formally approved by the central control commission on the following day, and immediately published in *Pravda*.[4] They explained that in a period " associated with the socialist offensive against capitalist elements in town and country, with a sharpening of the class struggle ", the party was called on " to strengthen resistance to the influence of the petty bourgeois element, to make the party more uniform ". Special attention was to be given to rural party cells: it was necessary " to purge

[1] *Pravda*, March 2, 7, 1929; see also the articles by Yaroslavsky cited p. 82, note 4 above.

[2] E. Yaroslavsky, *Chistka Partii* (1929), pp. 13-14; this pamphlet contains the text of Yaroslavsky's report and of the theses.

[3] *Ibid*. pp. 29, 33.   [4] *Pravda*, March 31, 1929.

them decisively of class-alien elements which penetrated them and of those who mingled with *kulak* elements — with merchants, beys and clergy ". The purge, it was repeated, was designed " to make the party more uniform, to free it from everything non-communist ". Among those to be " mercilessly expelled " were " concealed Trotskyites, Myasnikovites, Democratic Centralists, and leaders of other anti-party groups ". The theses ended with a recommendation that the purge should be completed before the sixteenth party congress, then expected to meet at the end of 1929. Notwithstanding Yaroslavsky's criticism,[1] the precedent of the Smolensk purge of 1928 was followed ; and non-party workers and peasants participated in the purge by attending meetings at which the records of party members were discussed. An article in the journal of the party central committee justified this procedure — a curious example of the blurring of the distinction between party members and non-party sympathizers — on the ground not only that the judgement of " non-party activists " on the behaviour of party members was valuable, but also that it would permit the discovery of new elements to replace " communists who have become demoralized or turned into *kulaks* or bureau-crats ".[2] When the conference met on April 23, 1929, the presentation of the resolution embodying the theses was deferred, by accident or design, until the last day of the proceedings. Meanwhile, the text of the instruction to be issued to local control commissions had been agreed in consultation with the representa-tives of the commissions, so that Yaroslavsky was able to confront the conference with a *fait accompli*. This did not save him from some critical interruptions. In his speech he modified the previous emphasis on the political aspects of the purge, which figured largely in the theses and in the instruction, and dwelt mainly on such social abuses as drunkenness and on the minor eccentricities of party life.[3] No debate was held on the resolution, which was

[1] See p. 140, note 5 above.
[2] *Izvestiya Tsentral'nogo Komiteta VKP(B)*, No. 2-3(261-262), January 31, 1929, p. 1 ; Lenin had written in 1921 that the purge of that year had been carried out " by relying on the experience and the indications of non-party workers ", and commented that " to purge the party by taking account of the indications of non-party toilers is a great achievement " (Lenin, *Sochineniya*, xxvii, 12-13 ; this passage was quoted in the theses).
[3] *Shestnadtsataya Konferentsiya VKP(B)* (1962), pp. 589-611 ; the instruc-tion laying down detailed procedure was published in *Pravda*, May 17, 1929.

unanimously adopted without amendment.[1]   Letters of instruction on the conduct of the purge, signed by Yaroslavsky as
secretary of the party collegium of the central control commission,
were sent to national party organizations, and to cells in non-
production (Soviet and administrative) institutions, cells in
teaching institutions, rural cells and cells in the Red Army.[2]

The purge was carried out during the rest of the year 1929. As
had evidently been intended, it was applied with special rigour to
rural party cells. The examination extended to 128,000 rural
party members, or 80·8 per cent of the total number resident in the
countryside; of these 15·7 per cent were excluded from the party.
The purge fell less severely on members of party cells in factories
and workshops; of these 8 per cent were excluded.[3]   No
statistical record was published of the grounds of expulsion.
But it is reasonable to assume that known sympathizers with the
Right opposition, more numerous in the countryside than in
town and factory, were effectively eliminated. A preliminary
report showed that defects had been found even in " leading
personnel " (not more precisely defined); of this category 0·4 per

---

A later instruction from the central control commission on the purge of rural
party cells emphasized that an important test was " a strict application of the
class line " (*ibid.* June 1, 1929).

[1] *Shestnadtsataya Konferentsiya VKP(B)* (1962), p. 611; *KPSS v Rezolyutsiyakh* (1954), ii, 605-614.   Much play was made at this time with a scandal in
the Astrakhan party organization, which was of long standing and arose from
the survival of private capital in the fishing industry and in local trade generally,
involving the corruption and connivance of party and Soviet officials; in the
spring of 1929, 200 persons were put on trial, including 90 officials and 40 party
members (*Pravda*, May 29, 1929).   A report of the regional party committee
of the Lower Volga region spoke of " a complete growing together with private
capital " in the local party organization, as well as of " a growth of Trotskyite
tendencies "; and the party central committee in a resolution of May 27, 1929,
called for an extensive purge directed against " elements of direct moral
corruption as well as of an incorrect political line " (*Izvestiya Tsentral'nogo
Komiteta VKP(B)*, No. 16(275), June 14, 1929, pp. 13-15).   The Astrakhan
affair was specifically associated with the Right deviation in a report in *Bednota*,
May 31, 1929, and in a later report in *Izvestiya*, August 22, 1929; revelations
continued to appear in the press for some weeks afterwards (*Pravda*, May 31,
June 1, 23, August 30, 31, 1929).   Yaroslavsky at the sixteenth party conference
spoke of party scandals at Smolensk, Sochi, Artemovsk, Astrakhan and " a
whole series of other places " (*Shestnadtsataya Konferentsiya VKP(B)* (1962),
p. 338).   [2] *Izvestiya*, May 31, 1929.

[3] These particulars are derived from unpublished party archives quoted in
Voprosy Istorii KPSS, No. 6, 1964, p. 69; see also reports by Yaroslavsky in
Pravda, April 23, May 22, 1930.

cent had been expelled, and 4·7 per cent reprimanded. Figures from one locality, which may have been typical, showed that, of those expelled from the party in the purge, 42·1 per cent were expelled as " alien elements ", 25 per cent on grounds of moral delinquency, and 20·2 per cent of a passive attitude to party affairs; 56·5 per cent of those expelled had joined the party since 1926.[1] Kalinin scouted the notion that class alone was a decisive criterion:

> If a man shows himself alien to us in his practical work, clear him out, even if he is an arch-proletarian.[2]

In some places too much weight had been given to details of private life, and not enough to " the steadfastness of the party member and his capacity to resist petty bourgeois influences ".[3] According to the final figures given to the sixteenth party congress in the following year, the total number of expulsions during the purge was 130,000 or 10·2 per cent of those investigated. But, as a result of appeals to the central control commission, no less than 24·2 per cent of these were eventually reinstated, reducing the total of expulsions to 99,600. Of those excluded, 16·9 per cent were said to have been excluded as being " alien elements " or " linked with alien elements "; in addition to these " about 10 per cent " were excluded for offences against party discipline, such as " fractionalism ".[4]

[1] *Krasnaya Zvezda*, October 18, 1929.
[2] M. Kalinin, *Voprosy Sovetskogo Stroitel'stra* (1958), p. 441.
[3] *Izvestiya Tsentral'nogo Komiteta VKP(B)*, No. 28(287), October 10, 1929, pp. 4, 7.
[4] *XVI S"ezd Vsesoyuznoi Kommunisticheskoi Partii (B)* (1930), p. 340; *Voprosy Istorii KPSS*, No. 6, 1964, p. 70. No formal end of the purge was ever announced, and the figures given to the congress may have been incomplete; a total of 170,000 is quoted in S. Trapeznikov, *Kommunisticheskaya Partiya v Period Nastupleniya Sotsializma* (1961), pp. 38-39.

CHAPTER 44

PARTY EDUCATION

THE Communist Academy continued to function rather ineffectively as the senior official organ of party education and its ideological " centre ".[1] In November 1926 it acquired a new statute which defined its functions as study and research, " the struggle against bourgeois and petty bourgeois distortions of Marxism ", and the creation of " cadres of highly qualified workers in the field of the theory and practice of Marxism and Leninism ". It was responsible to the TsIK of the USSR, which had to confirm elections of new members.[2] As the economic and political situation grew more tense, ideological embarrassments were not slow to appear. After the publication of Preobrazhensky's *Novaya Ekonomika* in 1926, Pokrovsky, the president of the academy, took pains to explain that the academy had never endorsed the views expressed in it.[3] Differences of opinion evidently occurred at the session of the academy in January 1927, at which Pokrovsky firmly declared that it was the task of the academy to stand out for " the correct Leninist point of view ", and that " in science no neutrality of any kind is possible ".[4]

[1] See *Socialism in One Country, 1924–1926*, Vol. 2, pp. 186-187; for the Academy of Sciences, which continued to exist as a non-party rival of the Communist Academy, see Note F, pp. 452-455 below.

[2] *Vestnik Kommunisticheskoi Akademii*, xix (1927), 269-276. The following table gives the sums assigned in the budget of the USSR for 1926–1927 (in rubles) to various higher institutions of learning :

Communist Academy	1,138,285
Marx-Engels Institute	667,562
Communist University of Toilers of the East	1,592,376
Sverdlov University	1,076,148
Central Asian Communist University	753,368
Central Asian State University	2,101,959

(*Sovetskoe Stroitel'stvo*, No. 4(9), April 1927, p. 121 ; all these figures showed some increase over those of 1925–1926).

[3] See Vol. 1, p. 26, note 1.

[4] *Vestnik Kommunisticheskoi Akademii*, xx (1927), 295.

In July 1927 the academy, apparently for the first time, made a detailed report on its activities to the party central committee; and the committee passed a resolution describing it as " the centre of scientific work in communist thought ", and indicating that discussions of controversial questions in its journals or other publications should be " accompanied by an exposition on the part of the academy of the party point of view ".[1] An article by Milyutin, the vice-president of the academy, in *Pravda* led up to the conclusion that its success in the future depended " on the extent to which it will succeed in organizing in larger measure the theoretical resources of the party ".[2] The plan of work of the academy for 1927–1928 was drawn up " on the basis of directions given by the party ".[3]

The Communist Academy evolved slowly but surely on the lines thus laid down. Its annual meeting in March 1928 expelled its prominent opposition members — Preobrazhensky, Radek, Rakovsky, V. Smirnov and Trotsky.[4] At the ensuing conference of Marxist-Leninist scientific research institutions,[5] Milyutin, vice-president of the academy, spoke complacently of the rôle entrusted to it by TsIK under its statute, and noted that " elements formerly alien and even hostile to Marxism are turning towards it "; he instanced the recent initiative of the chemists and the formation of associations of specialists to aid socialist construction.[6]

---

[1] *Spravochnik Partiinogo Rabotnika*, vi (1928), i, 687.

[2] *Pravda*, August 4, 1927. The conception was not new; in the early days of the academy Preobrazhensky invited it to become " the Gosplan of the field of ideology " (*Vestnik Sotsialisticheskoi Akademii*, i (1922), 9). At the sixteenth party congress in 1930 Pokrovsky more modestly called it " the theoretical party sub-centre ", and " the theoretical apparatus of the party ", the centre being the party central committee (*XVI S"ezd Vsesoyuznoi Kommunisticheskoi Partii (B)* (1931), p. 248).

[3] *Vestnik Kommunisticheskoi Akademii*, xxvi (2) (1928), 214.

[4] *Ibid.* xxvi (2) (1928), 216 ; Milyutin afterwards referred to the exclusion of certain members " for inactivity " and of others " on grounds of principle " (*ibid.* xxvi (2), p. 246). The academy had at this time about 70 members.

[5] The conference was held under the auspices of the Russian Association of Scientific Institutes of the Social Sciences (RANION), which had been formed in 1922 or 1923 in Moscow university ; one of the purposes of the conference was apparently to link RANION more closely with the Communist Academy (*ibid.* xxvi (2), 257-260). The Marx-Engels Institute and the Lenin Institute were among the institutes represented in RANION.

[6] *Ibid.* xxvi (2), 240 ; for the action of the chemists and the technicians see Vol. 1, pp. 583-584.

When, however, the conference showed signs of a sharp split between "mechanists" and "dialecticians" on the relations between philosophy and science, Milyutin refused to take up the issue or to brand the mechanists as "revisionists", and declared that the academy should keep open "the widest possibilities for different trends".[1]   More immediately topical was Milyutin's insistence on "the transition from individual work to collective work". The process of production ran from the initial individual report, through discussion of it and group working on the theme, to the "collective printed work".[2]   By the end of the nineteen-twenties the fashion of collective authorship was firmly established; and, though it was sometimes criticized as tending to diminish personal responsibility,[3] it continued — perhaps for that very reason — to spread.   In its earlier years the Communist Academy had published works of scholarship.[4]   As the task of instruction began to encroach on that of research, the emphasis shifted to text-books.   At the conference of Marxist research institutes in March 1928, Milyutin spoke scathingly of the low quality of many text-books used in vuzy and komvuzy; and another delegate remarked that "to publish a good Marxist text-book is no less important a job than to publish ten monographs".[5]   Later, the production of standard text-books on many subjects in conformity with the party line, and generally of collective authorship, became a regular function of the academy.

An early teaching activity of the academy had been the establishment of two-year courses in Marxism.[6]   In November 1926 the party central committee called for a further development of the courses.[7]   At the general meeting of the academy in January 1927, Pokrovsky, who referred to the courses as "a recognized method of mass education sponsored by the academy", declared that the present number of students was inadequate; and it was

---

[1] *Vestnik Kommunisticheskoi Akademii*, xxvi (2), 286.

[2] *Ibid.* xxvi (2), 241; Pokrovsky was afterwards quoted as saying at this time: "Individual creative activity in the field of history, as well as in other fields, is coming to an end; it is being replaced by collective activity. . . . We are now learning to work collectively; for bourgeois scholars it is difficult to work in this way" (*ibid.* No. 4-5, 1932, p. 58).   [3] *Ibid.* No. 3, 1932, p. 41.

[4] For a list of publications in 1926 see *ibid.* xvii (1926).

[5] *Ibid.* xxvi (2), (1928), 245, 273; for komvuzy see p. 153 below.

[6] See *Socialism in One Country, 1924–1926*, Vol. 2, p. 187.

[7] *Spravochnik Partiinogo Rabotnika*, vi (1928), i, 687.

later announced that funds had been provided to increase the
annual intake to 130.[1] A party order of April 7, 1927, limited
admission to party workers who had had party membership since
1919, and a record of five years' work in responsible provincial
party, trade union or Soviet posts.[2] Later the annual intake was
raised to 200, making a full complement of 400, of whom 30 per
cent were to be women. Provision was also made for a special
course for Komsomol members.[3] These courses were designed
to train the highest party intellectuals and officials.

The Institute of Red Professors, now under the direction and
influence of Bukharin, with Pokrovsky as its rector, maintained an
unimpeachably orthodox party line in the struggle against the
united opposition.[4] This won it favourable notice; and its
graduation ceremony on May 30, 1926, when 46 students graduated,
was graced by a speech from Molotov.[5] But concern was shown
to make the institute more practically useful. The party central
committee in a resolution of June 7, 1926, decided to increase the
length of the courses to four years, but to oblige students, from
their second year onwards, to take part in teaching in vuzy and
komvuzy.[6] A year later, on June 3, 1927, the committee called
for a revision of its programme " in order that more attention
may be paid to the bearing of its scientific work on the problems
facing the party ". The stipulation that students were to engage
in teaching from their second year onwards was repeated.
Agitprop was to ensure that graduates of the institute should be
employed in teaching, and not drafted to other employment.[7]
The report of the party central committee to the fifteenth party
congress in December 1927 remarked with satisfaction on the
link with Agitprop, in the form both of participation by Agitprop
in the affairs of the institute and of the use of graduates of the

---

[1] *Vestnik Kommunisticheskoi Akademii*, xx (1927), 289-290, 310.
[2] *Spravochnik Partiinogo Rabotnika*, vi (1928), i, 688.
[3] See p. 176 below.
[4] See *Socialism in One Country, 1924–1926*, Vol. 2, pp. 188-189.
[5] *Pravda*, June 2, 1926.
[6] *Spravochnik Partiinogo Rabotnika*, vi (1928), i, 711-712.
[7] *Ibid.* vi (1928), i, 565; later, the institute was said to have " begun to
train cadres also for the socialist economy and for the state apparatus " (*Partiinoe
Stroitel'stvo*, No. 24, 1931, pp. 2-3).

institute in Agitprop work.[1]   The scope of the institute was also
extended in 1927 at the suggestion of Pokrovsky by setting up an
evening communist university with courses lasting two or three
years.[2]

The year 1928 was an eventful one for the Institute of Red
Professors. It started quietly enough with a routine decree of the
party central committee on admission to the institute in the next
academic year. The proportion of workers was to be increased,
and candidates were required to qualify in the Russian language
and in mathematics ; the number of admissions for 1928–1929
was fixed at 400. This was followed in March 1928 by a circular
to all party organizations asking them to select candidates for
admission with higher political and academic qualifications.[3] But
Stalin's address at the institute in May 1928 seems to have been the
starting-point in a campaign which, in the course of the next few
months, destroyed the preponderant influence of Bukharin and
his supporters in the institute and made it a faithful and docile
instrument of the party majority.[4] The consequences for the
institute were devastating. According to a later report, the group
of " followers of the Right opportunist Bukharin school " which
had to be expelled from the institute was " not smaller " than the
group which had formed the " ideological nucleus " of the
Trotskyites in 1923–1924 ; and this meant that of the 236 graduates
of the institute from 1924 to 1929 many were found unsuitable
for appointments.[5] A meeting of the party cell on October 23,
1928, was a frankly political occasion. Krumin, the secretary of
the cell, boasted of the struggle waged against leaders of the
Moscow organization whose waverings had been " a symptom
of the Right danger ". Ryutin, one of the Moscow leaders just
removed from his post, was criticized by name. Krinitsky, the
head of the Agitprop section of the party secretariat, who attended
the meeting, called on the cell to " explain to the party masses the
essence and the danger of the Right deviation ".[6] Pokrovsky was

[1] *K XV S"ezdu VKP(B)* (1927), p. 159.
[2] *Kommunisticheskoe Prosveshchenie*, No. 1, 1930, pp. 61-62.
[3] *Izvestiya Tsentral'nogo Komiteta VKP(B)*, No. 5(226), February 22, 1928,
pp. 4-5 ; No. 9-10(230-231), March 26, 1928, p. 7.
[4] See pp. 61, 71, note 5 above.
[5] *Partiinoe Stroitel'stvo*, No. 2, 1930, p. 25.
[6] *Izvestiya*, October 25, 1928 ; for the trouble in the Moscow party committee

plainly unhappy at these developments. In an unpublished letter to Krinitsky, he described himself as " a bad rector — neither an administrator nor a political director ", and added that for the latter function a member of the party central committee was required; the institute was " too big and complex an institute for anyone of lesser party calibre ".[1] Hope was, however, felt for the future. When the party central committee reviewed the affairs of the institute in April 1929, it noted that the proportion of workers among the students had risen from 7 per cent at the first enrolment in 1921 to 40 per cent in 1929 (less than the 60 per cent called for in a party resolution of 1927). The institute was now divided into seven faculties — economic and agrarian, historical, party history, philosophical, law and administration, literary and scientific. It was decided to create a preparatory department to prepare suitable candidates for admission; 80 per cent of students in this department were to be workers and 20 per cent peasants.[2]

The Sverdlov University in Moscow and other universities and party institutions of higher education (komvuzy)[3] continued to expand their work, the aim of which was now unequivocally defined, by a resolution of the party central committee of April 22,

see pp. 72, 76-77, 81 above. It was perhaps significant that Ryutin had recently protested in the party journal against the overloading of scientific and technical institutions with party men, who were sometimes " dilettantes and know-alls " (Bol'shevik, No. 15, August, 15, 1928, pp. 28-29); for Krinitsky see p. 406 below.

[1] Voprosy Istorii, No. 6, 1969, p. 42.

[2] Izvestiya Tsentral'nogo Komiteta VKP(B), No. 13(272), May 14, 1929, pp. 25-26; for the resolution of 1927 see Spravochnik Partiinogo Rabotnika, vi (1928), i, 688.

[3] See Socialism in One Country, 1924–1926, Vol. 2, pp. 187-188. In May 1926 Pravda published the conditions of admission for 1926–1927 to the Sverdlov university, the Zinoviev university, and the Markhlevsky university of national minorities of the west (Pravda, May 13, 19, 20, 1926); two new komvuzy — North Caucasian and White Russian communist universities — founded between 1925 and 1927 brought up the total to 17, which, however, included such specialized institutions as the Tolmachev Military-Political Academy and the State Institute of Journalism (K XV S"ezdu VKP(B) (1927), p. 153). The number of communist universities rose from 21 with 5380 students in 1926–1927 to 62 with 15,667 students in 1927–1928; of other komvuzy from 18 with 7775 students, to 27 with 8835 students (SSSR : God Raboty Pravitel'stva 1927–1928 (1929), p. 484).

1927, as "to train qualified party officials ".[1] Bauman even feared "an over-production of ' official' communists ", and condemned party members who, having completed courses at komvuzy, wanted a job in Gosplan or Vesenkha or in a party committee, and were unwilling to work in a factory or in the countryside.[2] But other preoccupations seem to have prevailed. A Union conference of komvuzy drew up a new statute for these institutions which was duly approved by the party central committee on June 24, 1927. The rising " political and cultural standard " of new members of the party and the Komsomol was said to call for more intensive courses. But one aim was evidently to mobilize the komvuzy for the defence of party orthodoxy against the assaults of the opposition. "Attempts of some komvuzy to refrain from offering a special course in Leninism " were to be resisted (Marxism was no longer enough), and a struggle waged against various forms of " revisionism ". Among the subjects prescribed for study were the capitalist countries, especially England ; colonial and semi-colonial countries, especially China ; relations between proletariat and peasantry ; the ultra-Left enemies of Bolshevism ; and socialist construction in the USSR. The komvuzy were also to help in the organization of " evening communist universities, Soviet-party schools, and courses and circles for party and Komsomol activists ".[3] But much remained to be done. It was noted at this time that, in every 10,000 of the population, 43 in the United States entered higher educational institutions, 16 in France (this was said to include universities only), and 11 in the RSFSR (in the other component republics of the USSR the proportion must have been lower).[4] Only moderate successes attended the efforts to increase the proportion of workers, and to lower that of employees, enrolled in these institutions.[5] An article of 1928 was highly critical of work done in the communist universities. Students of economics

---

[1] *Sprachovnik Partiinogo Rabotnika*, vi (1928), i, 688-691.
[2] *Pravda*, March 29, 1927.
[3] *Spravochnik Partiinogo Rabotnika*, vi (1928), i, 673-675.
[4] G. Orjonikidze, *Stat'i i Rechi* (1957), ii, 119 ; these figures, provided by the Central Statistical Administration, were substituted for the incorrect figures actually quoted by Orjonikidze in his speech, as reported in *Pravda*, March 28, 1928.
[5] The following percentages (by social origin) were quoted for January 1 of the years named :

studying rural cooperatives " made calculations with invented figures supplied by cooperative officials " ; they had no means of checking the accuracy of the figures. The courses in political economy related to " a theory of abstract capitalism " : the theories of money taught to the student threw no light on " financial developments occurring in the Soviet economy ".[1]

Next in the hierarchy of party educational institutions came the Soviet-party schools, which were of several kinds.[2] Those with the highest educational qualifications were designed, like the komvuzy, for the training of higher party officials. Their growing importance was marked by a decree of the party central committee of June 28, 1926, to abolish first-grade (i.e. one-year) Soviet-party schools, except in the national republics, and to retain only two-year schools ; at the same time the committee instructed regional and local party committees to exercise " real control and political direction " over the schools.[3] A further decree of May 20, 1927, limited admissions in principle to party members of two years', or Komsomol members of three years', standing : not more than 25 per cent of the total enrolment might, by way of exception, be open to workers who could show a three-year record work in production. Not more than 10 per cent of the enrolment might consist of non-party students.[4] About 100 such schools existed in 1928 with 170,000 students ;[5] these turned out " propagandists, party workers and workers in political education ", but not " workers for mass Soviet organs ". Of those completing courses in 57 Soviet-party schools in the RSFSR in 1926 only 4 per cent went into Soviet work.[6] The gap

	1927	1928	1929
Workers	24·2	25·4	30·3
Peasants	23·3	23·9	22·4
Employees	52·5	50·7	47·3

(N. Dewitt, *Soviet Professional Manpower* (1955), p. 315.)

[1] *Kommunisticheskoe Prosveshchenie*, No. 5, 1928, pp. 33-37 ; this was described as a discussion article.

[2] See *Socialism in One Country, 1924–1926*, Vol. 2, pp. 189-191.

[3] *Spravochnik Partiinogo Rabotnika*, vi (1928), i, 684.

[4] *Ibid.* vi, i, 686 ; this compared with a limit of 25 per cent imposed in 1925 (see *Socialism in One Country, 1924–1926*, Vol. 2, p. 191).

[5] *Sotsialisticheskoe Stroitel'stvo SSSR, 1934*, p. 406.

[6] *Sovetskoe Stroitel'stvo* No. 12(29), December 1928, p. 129.

was filled partly by local initiative. Courses for instruction for
Soviet workers were organized by rural district or district executive
committees ; these included courses for poor peasants, *batraks*
and women members of Soviets, and especially for presidents and
secretaries of rural Soviets.[1] The courses for secretaries of district
(formerly county) party committees originally set up in 1923[2]
appear to have prospered. On October 2, 1926, Molotov gave the
opening address to the fourth series of courses, denouncing
Trotsky and the opposition bloc.[3] By 1927 the number of students
had risen from an initial 200 to 430. Places were reserved for
students from outlying regions, including small national groups.
Only party members of worker or peasant origin, who had completed five years of party membership and three years of responsible party work, were eligible for admission.[4] All training
institutions for party or Soviet officials seem to have been
loosely classified as Soviet-party schools. The number of Soviet-
party schools in this broad sense increased from 353 with 35,130
students in 1926–1927 to 593 with 45,010 students in 1927–
1928.[5]

The successive crises and growing pressures of the first months
of 1928 had, however, their repercussions on party education. A
writer in the journal of Narkompros in 1928 described material
conditions at Soviet-party schools as " the most vulnerable
sphere of our work ". Premises were bleak, crowded and dirty ;
food was badly prepared and served in badly organized kitchens
and refectories. For anyone who hoped to find in the schools
" a model of conditions in a socialist society " this was disillu-
sioning.[6] A conference of directors of Soviet-party schools was
held in May 1928,[7] but did not put an end to searching criticism.
A decree of the party central committee complained that the
courses were not closely enough connected with current party
work, and that an insufficient proportion of workers and *batraks*

---

[1] *Sovetskoe Stroitel'stvo* No. 12(19), December 1928, pp. 20-24; this
account complained, however, that " so far there is no kind of system in the
work of training and no regular forms ".
[2] See *Socialism in One Country, 1924–1926*, Vol. 2, p. 209.
[3] *Izvestiya*, October 5, 1926.
[4] *Spravochnik Partiinogo Rabotnika*, vi (1928), i, 691-694.
[5] *SSR: God Raboty Pravitel'stva, 1927–1928* (1929), p. 484.
[6] *Kommunisticheskoe Prosveshchenie*, No. 4, 1928, p. 69.
[7] *Ibid.* No. 5, 1928, p. 30.

was recruited. Theoretical studies were to be reduced, and those relating to economic development, to party problems and to practical local conditions expanded. Students were to be selected by the schools, on the recommendation of party committees and in consultation with Agitprop and Narkompros. A year's preparatory correspondence course before admission was recommended.[1] How far this decree was effective it is difficult to discover. But on July 1, 1929, the party central committee called for yet another reorganization of the Soviet-party schools, and repeated many of the same criticisms.[2]

Apart from the specific need to train party and Soviet workers, party opinion continued to be troubled by the low level of political understanding and consciousness in rank-and-file members, especially as the party strove to draw more and more workers and peasants into its ranks. The party census of 1927 revealed the poor educational standing of party members:

	Members	Members and Candidates (in percentages)	Women
Higher Education	0·9	0·8	1·5
Secondary Education	7·3	7·9	13·7
Elementary Education	63·2	62·8	45·8
Home Education	26·4	25·8	36·2
Illiterate	2·2	2·7	2·8[3]

[1] *Pravda*, September 7, 1928; *Kommunisticheskoe Prosveshchenie*, No. 5, October–November 1928, p. 30, which commented that " the task of training qualified lower village workers on the front of the cultural revolution has fallen to the Soviet-party schools ".

[2] *Izvestiya Tsentral'nogo Komiteta VKP(B)*, No. 20-21(279-280), July 29, 1929, p. 22; Kaganovich at the sixteenth party congress in 1930 treated both the decree of August 1928 and the decree of July 1929 as landmarks in the development of the schools (*XVI S"ezd Vsesoyuznoi Kommunisticheskoi Partii (B)* (1931), p. 85).

[3] *Izvestiya Tsentral'nogo Komiteta VKP(B)*, No. 32-33 (205-206), August 31, p. 2 ; for illiteracy in the party see p. 103 above. The problem of illiteracy in the population still engaged attention ; in 1927–1928 42,177 schools had been established for illiterate or semi-literate adults with 1,318,043 pupils (*Osnovnye Itogi Raboty Pravitel'stva SSSR k Perevyboram Sovetov 1928–29 g.* (1928), p. 151).

A party directive of May 16, 1927, revealed a preoccupation with party education at elementary levels. For those lacking the rudiments of political education, only the course in *politgramota* was to be obligatory in party schools; a choice was to be offered of a number of voluntary subjects, including administration, finance and agriculture. More attention was to be given to study circles and discussion groups.[1] Kosior, in his report to the fifteenth party congress in December 1927, spoke with satisfaction of the expansion of " voluntary groups " and the rapid growth of evening schools;[2] and a resolution of the Agitprop section of the party central committee dwelt on the need to educate the mass of recruits from the October enrolment.[3] As the scope broadened, the number of schools and courses designed to cope with the deficiency in political training continued to multiply:

	No. of Schools, Study Groups and Courses	No. of Students	Percentage of Party Members	Percentage of Women
1927–1928	42,543	754,568	62·2	16·4
1928–1929	48,202	862,649	53·8	18·2
1929–1930	52,315	1,177,013	43·6	21·4[4]

The initial friction between Glavpolitprosvet, the department of Narkompros, and the Agitprop section of the party central committee, with their respective regional and local organs, was now a thing of the past. When rural travelling schools, Soviet-

[1] *Izvestiya Tsentral'nogo Komiteta VKP(B)*, No. 19(192), May 23, 1927, p. 12; for the Orgburo report on which the decree was based see *ibid.* pp. 1-3.
[2] *Pyatnadtsatyi S"ezd VKP(B)*, i (1961), 116-117.
[3] *Pravda*, December 23, 1927. For the October enrolment see p. 110 above; only 22·9 per cent of the new recruits had taken a course in *politgramota* (*Izvestiya Tsentral'nogo Komiteta VKP(B)*, No. 8(229), March 15, 1928, p. 7).
[4] *Partiinoe Stroitel'stvo*, No. 11-12, 1930, pp. 48-49. A slightly different return for 1927–1928 recorded 21,516 schools with 678,850 students in towns, and 19,415 rural schools with 252,618 students; 70·3 per cent of the students in town schools, and 49·5 per cent in rural schools, were party members or candidates (*VKP(B) v Tsifrakh*, viii (1928), 36-37). The declining percentage of party members was probably due in part to the greater expansion in rural areas and in part to the policy of encouraging non-party people; according to Kaganovich, only from one-quarter to one-third of those enrolled were actually studying (*XVI S"ezd Vsesoyuznoi Kommunisticheskoi Partii (B)* (1930), p. 35).
[5] See *Socialism in One Country, 1924–1926*, Vol. 2, pp. 192-193.

party evening schools, and evening courses at komvuzy, were transferred by the decree of the party central committee of May 20, 1927,[1] to the Soviet budget, this was merely a matter of administrative convenience, and perhaps also a reflexion of the extent to which these facilities were now also open to non-party students. The forms of instruction available in town and country varied from courses for active party members and Soviet-party schools to evening schools, rural travelling and stationary *politgramota* schools, study circles for " self-education ", and circles for worker and peasant women.[2] The short-course evening Soviet-party schools established in 1925[3] increased in number from 929 with 42,811 students in 1927–1928 to 1619 with 74,468 students in 1928–1929, and were described as " the form of middle-level party education best suited to the needs and demands of the basic mass of members of our party ".[4] But the results of these efforts seem to have been limited. Yaroslavsky in the autumn of 1928 wrote that party members, and especially candidates, received practically no political education[5]; and at the sixteenth party congress in June 1930 delegates continued to deplore the lack of literacy among party cadres in the countryside, and the " extremely low percentage " of party members who had any " serious ideological training ".[6]

Apart from party members, the education of non-party people who were willing to collaborate with the party began to attract attention. In August 1928 the party central committee again stressed the importance of elementary *politgramota* courses, and encouraged the enrolment of non-party people.[7] By this time the line between party members and the so-called " non-party *aktiv* " was blurred, especially in the countryside. What was now at stake, though policies were still confused and organization lacking, was nothing less than " the mass training of the whole *aktiv* ".[8] A substantial resolution of the party central committee

---

[1] For this decree see p. 155 above.
[2] *K XV S"ezdu VKP(B)* (1927), pp. 146-148; *VKP(B) v Tsifrakh*, viii (1928), 36-37.   [3] See *Socialism in One Country, 1924–1926*, Vol. 2, p. 194.
[4] *Partiinoe Stroitel'stvo*, No. 11-12, 1930, p. 52.
[5] *Bol'shevik*, No. 20, October 31, 1929, p. 15.
[6] *XVI S"ezd Vsesoyuznoi Kommunisticheskoi Partii (B)* (1931), pp. 93, 341.
[7] *Pravda*, August 11, 1928.
[8] *Sovetskoe Stroitel'stvo*, No. 12(29), December 1928, p. 22.

of June 21, 1929, comprising a programme of mass party education for the coming year, stressed the importance of including not
only new recruits to the party, but " the non-party worker and
batrak-poor peasant *aktiv* ".[1]

[1] *Izvestiya Tsentral'nogo Komiteta VKP(B)*, No. 20-21 (279-280), July 29,
1929, pp. 19-20.

CHAPTER 45

THE KOMSOMOL

THE stormy seventh congress of the Komsomol in March 1926 had ended in the rout of the dissident minority, and in resolutions affirming the subordination of the Komsomol to party leadership and vigorously condemning the party opposition.[1] In the ensuing period membership of the Komsomol continued to grow steadily, approaching the two-million mark at the eighth congress in March 1928.[2] Its social composition was, however, a subject of the same controversy which had raged in these years round the composition of the party.[3] To increase the intake of members from the countryside had been accepted Komsomol policy since 1924. It always aroused discontent, especially when in 1925 it began to be associated with the policy of indulgence for the well-to-do peasant.[4] But for some time the official line was unchanged. A resolution of the fourteenth party congress in December 1925 had advocated " the organization in the Komsomol of the best middle peasant elements, with the support of the poor peasant and the *batrak* ", though " without forcing the pace and with suitable restraint on the growth of the RLKSM in the countryside " ; fear of the middle peasant was to be " decisively condemned ".[5] This formula was adopted by the seventh Komsomol congress in March 1926, which instructed the organization " to aim in the countryside, as hitherto, at including all young *batraks* and the broad masses of young poor peasants, and at the same time, with the support of the *batrak* and the poor peasant, to continue to draw into the league the best part of the young middle peasantry ". Another resolution declared that the Komsomol *aktiv* in the countryside should " consist of proletarian and semi-proletarian (poor peasant)

---

[1] See *Socialism in One Country, 1924–1926*, Vol. 2, p. 161.
[2] See Table No. 57, p. 480 below.   [3] See pp. 103-111 above.
[4] See *Socialism in One Country, 1924–1926*, Vol. 2, pp. 98-104.
[5] *KPSS v Rezolyutsiyakh* (1954), ii, 237.

strata, and also of the best strata of middle peasants loyal to the party and the league ".[1] A resolution of the Komsomol central committee of December 1926, while noting that the proportion of *batrak* members had risen from 9·5 to 11 per cent, complained that Komsomol recruiting in the countryside had been based on " too much forcing of growth and too little individual selection ", and that rural members of the Komsomol included " a disproportionately high percentage of employees ".[2]

When the fifth Komsomol conference met in March 1927, the party policy of support for the well-to-do individual peasant had begun to weaken and the issue was formulated in less conciliatory terms. The Komsomol in all its activities in the countryside was " to observe a clearly defined class line, helping the party to defend the interests of the *batrak* and the poor peasant, and strengthening the alliance of the poor peasant with the middle peasantry against the *kulak* " ; it was also to support the peasant who was engaged in " raising the level of the peasant economy on cooperative principles ". On the other hand, measures were to be taken to prevent " a reduction in the worker and *batrak* core of the organization by means of . . . a necessary restraint on the growth of the league in the countryside, and also by means of greater limitation on the admission of employees and of the intelligentsia ".[3] A circular of the Komsomol central committee of March 4, 1927, tightened up restrictions on the admission to the Komsomol of children of those deprived of electoral rights ;[4] another circular three months later pronounced proletarianization (orabochenie) to be " one of the most important guarantees of correct, party-oriented leadership of Komsomol organizations ".[5] Trotsky, in the opposition platform of September 1927, alleged that Komsomol was " filling up in the country with the middle and well-off peasant youth ", and was " being transformed into one of the sources for the dilution of the party with petty bourgeois elements ".[6] The party central committee, in an uneasy resolution of October 3, 1927, noted a sharp rise in the number of

---

[1] *VLKSM v Rezolyutsiyakh* (1929), pp. 235, 257.
[2] *Spravochnik Partiinogo Rabotnika*, vi (1928), ii, 75-76.
[3] *VLKSM v Rezolyutsiyakh* (1929), pp. 284-285.
[4] *Spravochnik Partiinogo Rabotnika*, vi (1928), ii, 147-148.
[5] *Ibid.* vi, ii, 158.
[6] L. Trotsky, *The Real Situation in Russia* (n.d. [1928]), pp. 135-136.

peasants in the Komsomol, a slight decline in the proportion of workers, and an insufficient rise in the number of *batraks*. The need was stressed to check the unduly rapid turnover in membership, and, " in view of the miscellaneous social composition of the Komsomol ", to strengthen the party core and to guarantee " proletarian leadership ".[1]

The crisis of the grain collections in the first months of 1928 drove home the same moral; Bukharin's report to the eighth Komsomol congress in May 1928 was full of criticism of the quality of the Komsomol membership and of injunctions to improve it.[2] More than 50 per cent of the rural membership of the Komsomol was said to be middle peasant, and less than 30 per cent poor peasant (or *batrak*); the rest was well-to-do peasant and *kulak*.[3] Chaplin, while rebutting Bukharin's more extreme criticisms, made some interesting disclosures on Komsomol membership in the towns and factories. He admitted that highly skilled workers did not enter the Komsomol or were unwilling to undertake responsible work there, and that, at the other end of the scale, Komsomol work was weak among the unskilled. The majority of members were drawn from the semi-skilled workers.[4] The general resolution of the congress repeated the demand of the sixth congress to recruit all young workers into the Komsomol. The resolution on work in the countryside called for " a certain restraint " in admitting middle peasants: that part only of the middle peasantry was to be admitted which " has shown its devotion to the interests of the party and the league, actively helps the cause of collectivization and of work among poor peasants and *batraks*, and leads the struggle against the *kulaks* ". That Komsomol organizations in the countryside should have hitherto grown largely through the recruitment of employees was described as " abnormal " ; more effort must be made to recruit " agricultural workers, *batraks* and poor peasants ".[5]

---

[1] *Izvestiya Tsentral'nogo Komiteta VKP(B)*, No. 41(214), November 9, 1927, pp. 11-12.   [2] See p. 174 below.

[3] *VIII Vsesoyuznyi S"ezd VLKSM* (1928), p. 252; later in the year a sample census showed 28·7 per cent poor peasants and *batraks*, 52·1 per cent middle peasants, 15·6 per cent well-to-do peasants, and 3·6 per cent *kulaks* (*Pravda*, June 1, 1929).

[4] *VIII Vsesoyuznyi S"ezd VLKSM* (1928), pp. 272-273 ; for similar tendencies in the party see pp. 108-109 above.

[5] *VLKSM v Rezolyutsiyakh* (1929), pp. 313, 339-340.

Special problems were created by the overlap between membership of the Komsomol and membership of the party, and by the recognized position of the Komsomol as a recruiting ground for the party. The party itself was still a youthful party. In 1927, 25 per cent of members were under 25, 54 per cent under 30, and 97 per cent under 50.[1] The party census revealed that 204,190 party members, or 17·8 per cent of the total membership, were also members of the Komsomol; by an odd anomaly, a further 8·1 per cent of party members, though below the age of 24, did not belong to the Komsomol. Of those enjoying dual membership 26·1 per cent were returned as workers, 7·6 per cent as peasants, 30·5 per cent as employers and 19·1 per cent as Red Army personnel.[2] Between 1926 and 1928 one-third of new recruits to the party were members of the Komsomol.[3] But this left undecided the fate of members of the Komsomol, who, on attaining the upper statutory age-limit of 23, had not been admitted to the party. These were generally students, peasants or employees who had difficulty in gaining admission to the party owing to the priority given to workers;[4] they were said to have numbered 123,000 on January 1, 1926, 225,000 on January 1, 1927, and 313,000 on October 1, 1927.[5] The fifth Komsomol conference in March 1927 proposed that they should find a place in " the cultural-economic work of the party and the state (central control commission and Rabkrin, Soviets, cooperatives etc.) " — presumably as a prelude to striking them off the lists of the Komsomol.[6] Kosior at the fifteenth party congress in December 1927, estimated that the

[1] Bol'shaya Sovetskaya Entsiklopediya, xi (1930), 541.

[2] E. Smitten, Sostav VKP(B) (1928), pp. 70-72; the rapid rise of party membership in the next two years reduced the proportion of Komsomol members in the party to about 10 per cent at the end of 1928 (Izvestiya Tsentral'-nogo Komiteta VKP(B), No. 5-6(264-265), February 28, 1929, p. 8; the absolute number remained approximately constant at 210,945).

[3] For detailed figures see A. Shokhin, Kratkaya Istoriya VLKSM (1928), p. 120; Izvestiya Tsentral'nogo Komiteta VKP(B), No. 7(260), March 20, 1929, p. 9; Chaplin claimed at the fifteenth party congress in December 1927 that the Komsomol had down to that time contributed 300,000 recruits to the party (Pyatnadtsatyi S"ezd VKP(B), i (1961), 256).

[4] Spravochnik Partiinogo Rabotnika, vi (1928), ii, 114; of 28,431 Komsomol admissions to the party in the October enrolment of 1927 79·7 per cent were factory workers (VKP(B) v Tsifrakh, viii (1928), 22).

[5] Izvestiya Tsentral'nogo Komiteta VKP(B), No. 7(266), March 20, 1929, p. 10.   [6] VLKSM v Rezolyutsiyakh (1929), pp. 285-286.

number of over-age members of the Komsomol would reach 350,000 by January 1928, 36 per cent being (by social situation) workers, 39 per cent peasants, and 25 per cent employees. But he offered no solution other than the proposal that they should be used in public work.[1] A delegate at the eighth Komsomol congress in May 1928 thought that they should be assigned to work which would give them an opportunity to prove their suitability for party membership and secure the necessary sponsors.[2] The resolution of the party central committee of November 1928 aggravated the problem by narrowing still further the avenues of admission to the party for those occupational categories to which most over-age members of the Komsomol belonged.[3] Continued efforts were reported to place over-age Komsomol members in Soviet, cooperative, trade union or other public work.[4] It appears, however, that many members, at any rate in rural areas, were tacitly allowed to retain their membership beyond the age of 23, if they failed to achieve party status. Many Komsomol officials, including probably all at higher levels, were party members; and a considerable proportion of these must also have been over age. This anomaly was increasingly reflected in the age of the delegates elected to congresses, nearly all of whom were party members. At the seventh Komsomol congress in March 1926, only 21 per cent of voting delegates were aged 23 or over; at the eighth congress in May 1928 50·8 per cent of voting delegates (or 53·7 per cent of all delegates) had passed that age.[5] At a time when complaint was made of " an abnormal turnover " in the ranks of the Komsomol[6] the interests of stability in the organization were doubtless served by turning a blind eye to the statutory age limit.

[1] *Pyatnadtsatyi S"ezd VKP(B)*, i (1961), 109.

[2] *VIII Vsesoyuznyi S"ezd VLKSM* (1929), p. 197.

[3] See p. 113 above; *Izvestiya Tsentral'nogo Komiteta VKP(B)*, No. 5-6(264-265), February 28, 1929, pp. 25-26, carried both the complaint of a " Marxist-economist ", who had been a Komsomol member since 1920, but was unable to secure admission to the party owing to the ban of November 1928, and the discouraging reply of the authorities.

[4] *Ibid.* No. 7(260), March 20, 1929, p. 10.

[5] *VII S"ezd Vsesoyuznogo Leninskogo Kommunisticheskogo Soyuza Molodezhi* (1926), p. 490; *VIII Vsesoyuznyi S"ezd VLKSM* (1928), p. 547; for the party membership of delegates see Table No. 57, p. 480 below.

[6] *VLKSM v Rezolyutsiyakh* (1929), p. 312; Bukharin at the fourteenth

By the spring of 1927 economic problems had begun to dominate the Soviet scene. The formidable tasks of industrialization loomed ahead, and the campaign for " rationalization " was in full swing.[1] To improve the efficiency of the juvenile worker, and to harness him to the furtherance of these campaigns, was now a major preoccupation of the Komsomol. At the fifth Komsomol conference in March 1927 Stalin made his first appearance at a Komsomol assembly to deliver a brief speech, half of it devoted to these topics, and half to current events in China, which threatened to throw discredit on party policy.[2] The operative clauses of the main resolution of the conference opened on a stern note :

> The most important task of the VLKSM in socialist construction is to help the party, the economic organs and the trade unions in the organization of production, in technical improvements, in raising the productivity of labour and lowering the cost of industrial goods by drawing into the whole of this work the mass of workers and young workers. Special attention must therefore be given to strengthening practical cooperation between Komsomol and trade unions, . . . to explaining to young and adult workers the significance and essence of socialist rationalization, to encouraging inventions, to facilitating the close cooperation of young workers with specialists and foremen, and to struggling against reactionary moods of opposition to rationalization, which are still found in backward groups of workers and young workers.

This was to be accompanied by a determined defence of the interests and the living standards of the young worker, which was also described as a " most important task " of the Komsomol.[3] The explicit mention of the purpose common to Komsomol and trade unions, followed by the enumeration of points on which the unions showed small sympathy for the special claims of the young

party congress had noted that from January to August 1925, 565,000 admissions to the Komsomol had been accompanied by 110,000 resignations, and associated this with " an absolute decline of discipline in our ranks " (*XIV S"ezd Vsesoyuznoi Kommunisticheskoi Partii* (*B*) (1926), p. 815).

[1] See Vol. 1, pp. 340-344.

[2] Stalin, *Sochineniya*, ix, 193-202 ; events in China will be discussed in a subsequent volume.

[3] *VLKSM v Rezolyutsiyakh* (1929), p. 284.

worker, pointed to the sharp rivalry between the two organizations
which was to burst out in the near future.[1] The general resolution of the conference was followed by a special resolution on the
struggle against bureaucratism, and by another " On the Participation of Youth in Productive Life and on the Economic Work of
the VLKSM ", which detailed Komsomol policy in such matters
as the training of young workers, unemployment and wages.[2]
The conference was afterwards said to have marked " the starting-
point in the turn of the league to production ".[3] The fifteenth
party congress in December 1927 named the Komsomol, side by
side with the trade unions and the cooperatives, as " one of the
chief helpers of the party " in overcoming cultural and technical
backwardness and building the socialist order.[4]

Importance had always in theory been attached to the educational functions of the Komsomol. But the fourteenth party
congress in December 1925 seems to have been the first occasion
on which primary emphasis was placed on this aspect of the
organization. Bukharin spoke anxiously of the indifference of
many of the young to the Komsomol, and put part of the blame on
leaders who failed to realize that " talks about lofty subjects
unconnected with daily life do not ' catch on ' any more ", and that
it was not enough to repeat slogans like " international revolution"
and " Red Army ".[5] The resolution of the congress alleged that
the thirteenth congress eighteen months earlier had " turned the
rudder towards pure ' politics ' ", and that it was now necessary
to assert the primacy of " cultural-economic work ".[6] A resolution of the seventh Komsomol congress of March 1926 stated in
unequivocal terms the reasons for this change of emphasis :

Cadres of *new* young workers are arising among whom we are
faced with conducting an enormous work of organization and
education. New strata of youth (to a large extent those who
filter into industry from the countryside) represent for the most

[1] See Vol. 1, pp. 552-553.
[2] *VLKSM v Rezolyutsiyakh* (1929), pp. 287-296 ; for the struggle against
bureaucratism see pp. 296-298 below.
[3] *Malaya Sovetskaya Entsiklopediya*, ii (1934), 550.
[4] *KPSS v Rezolyutsiyakh* (1954), ii, 467.
[5] *XIV S"ezd Vsesoyuznoi Kommunisticheskoi Partii (B)* (1926), pp. 818-819.
[6] *KPSS v Rezolyutsiyakh* (1954), ii, 235 ; the description of the resolution
of the thirteenth congress (*ibid.* ii, 84) seems hardly justified.

part raw material which had not passed through the school of
proletarian struggle under capitalism, of civil war, or of public
work.[1]

Much of this education was thought of in terms of Marxist
ideology, of the party line, and of political work. In November
1926 the Komsomol central committee denounced Leftists who
alleged that the Komsomol had been " depoliticized ".[2] In 1926,
and again in 1927, Komsomol members were reproached with an
apathetic attitude to membership of the Soviets, and failure to
discharge their duties when elected to them.[3] Among charges
brought against the Komsomol organization at this time were
" non-payment of members' dues, poor attendance at meetings,
insubordination when subjected to league discipline, infiltration
of alien elements into the organization, and ' dead souls ' who
belong only in name to the league ".[4] Even where their loyalty
was not in question, the undisciplined enthusiasm of Komsomol
members sometimes gave trouble. In Azerbaijan, where they
played a vigorous part in Soviet work, their activities were said to
have a " disturbing character ", and they despised dull routine ;[5]
Pravda commented with mild irony on "the purely youthful
swing (razmakh) " with which they took up the slogan of self-
criticism.[6] Bukharin at the fourteenth party congress of December
1925 criticized Komsomol members who waged a kind of " ideological guerrilla warfare " against society, thought it unbecoming
for a communist to take off his hat when he entered a house, and
fell into the mood of " cocking a snook " and " spitting wherever
you go ".[7] The central committee of Komsomol in November
1926 passed a resolution condemning " slovenliness and dis-
organization in work and in personal life ".[8]

---

[1] *VLKSM v Rezolyutsiyakh* (1929), p. 234.
[2] *Spravochnik Partiinogo Rabotnika*, vi (1928), ii, 194.
[3] *VII S"ezd Vsesoyuznogo Leninskogo Kommunisticheskogo Soyuza Molodezhi*
(1926), p. 36 ; *Spravochnik Partiinogo Rabotnika*, vi (1928), ii, 167-168. In
1929 7·6 per cent of members of city Soviets, 6·4 per cent of members of village
Soviets, and 7·3 per cent of presidents of village Soviets, were Komsomol
members ; percentages in the executive committees were much lower (*Bol'shaya
Sovetskaya Entsiklopediya*, xi (1930), 542).
[4] *Oppozitsiya i Komsomol* (1927), p. 72.
[5] *Sovetskoe Stroitel'stvo*, No. 12(17), 1927, p. 78.
[6] *Pravda*, May 19, 1928.
[7] *XIV S"ezd Vsesoyuznoi Kommunisticheskoi Partii (B)* (1926), p. 824.
[8] *Spravochnik Partiinogo Rabotnika*, vi (1928), ii, 160.

These deficiencies soon came, however, to be seen as the symptoms of a deep-seated malaise. The suicide of the young poet Esenin, following bouts of heavy drinking and sexual licence, in December 1925 made an enormous impression. Interpreted as a gesture of revolutionary protest against the humdrum life of the day, it inspired " a wave of suicides among the young ",[1] which excited deep concern among party leaders. The critic Sosnovsky, later a member of the opposition, denounced Esenin's influence in the columns of *Pravda* as a source of hooliganism among the young.[2] At a meeting held in the Meyerhold theatre to discuss the question, Voronsky tried to rescue Esenin's name from its association with hooliganism and pessimism; Polonsky maintained that Esenin, whose early poems reflected joy in life, had later become infected with influences of the church and the peasantry. But a report of the meeting recorded the impression that " Esenin's poetry has not only not lost its halo, but its charm has scarcely been shaken ".[3] Bukharin did his best to break the spell. In a caustic article in *Pravda* entitled *Malicious Observations* he described the cult of Esenin as " the most harmful phenomenon of our literary age and most deserving of castigation ". Esenin had been called " the peasant poet of a transitional epoch, who perished because he could not adapt himself to it ". In fact, Esenin represented " the repulsive traits of the Russian countryside and of the so-called ' national character ' " — violence, lack of discipline etc. The cult, which had become " a harmful social force ", was the result partly of the survival of a bourgeois attitude to work, and partly of " the astonishingly monotonous ideological fare " offered by the party to the young. Communists and workers in general were " not walking abstractions, but people of flesh and blood "; a party manual could not compete with the poetry of Esenin. The trouble was that even proletarian poets had ceased to produce creative work, and had been " turned into critics, organizers and politicians ".[4]

---

[1] I. Bobryshev, *Melkoburzhuaznye Vliyaniya sredi Molodezhi* (2nd ed. 1928), pp. 96-97.

[2] *Pravda*, September 19, 1926; Mayakovsky, who had been attacked by Sosnovsky in the past, thought that the article would " do more for the circulation of Esenin's hooligan verses than all the books put together " (*Lituraturnoe Nasledstvo*, lxv (1958), 38).

[3] *Izvestiya*, December 22, 1928.   [4] *Pravda*, January 12, 1927.

The problem was discussed in the latter part of February 1927 at a well attended meeting of the literary section of the Communist Academy. Lunacharsky read reports indicating that almost all the young were " infected with lack of faith (bezverie) ". This was commonly attributed to an impression that the situation was no longer revolutionary, and that the revolutionary movement had suffered " partial defeat ". Lunacharsky drew encouragement from the British general strike and miners' strike and from the growth of the Chinese nationalist movement (the disasters of the spring and summer of 1927 still lay ahead).

> Can these events [he asked] going on before our eyes infect us with pessimism and lack of faith ?

In a second speech, he described the " Eseninshchina " as " the most organized ... external expression of the desire to create some kind of ideology of pessimism ". Preobrazhensky spoke of the " intolerable triteness and boredom " of proceedings at Komsomol meetings. Sosnovsky said that the young were stuffed with political literature, and that when they encountered human feelings in Esenin's poems it was like " escaping from a cellar that reeks of rotten cabbage and entering the fresh air " ; conventional forms of recreation were rejected as fit only for " tootlhess hags and old men ". Polonsky carried the diagnosis further :

> There is little respect for man because there is little respect for oneself. There is no will-power, no desire to create a good strong type of new man ; ... even the Komsomol still does not breed the man who could serve as a model. In our time, when it is said that the quality of shoes, galoshes and other manu- factured goods must be improved, we must *first of all improve the quality of socialist man.*[1]

Mayakovsky, who spoke twice, tried to dissociate Esenin from the mood of cynicism : " what we are now making of Sergei Esenin

---

[1] *Upadochnoe Nastroenie sredi Molodezhi : Eseninshchina* (1927), pp. 13, 57, 69-70, 88-89 ; this was a record of speeches delivered at the meeting. An abbreviated text of Lunacharsky's speech is in A. Lunacharsky, *Sobranie Sochinenii*, ii (1904), 342-347. Polonsky's personal impressions were recorded in an unpublished letter to Gorky at Sorrento on February 16, 1927 : " War has been declared on Esenin. I don't approve. It's bad. Last year he was praised to the skies, today he is hooted. It's always like that with us " (quoted from the Gorky archives in V. Pertsov, *Mayakovsky v Poslednye Gody* (1965), p. 114).

is a monstrosity ". He attacked Bukharin for directing his shafts not against " Eseninism ", but against " Esenin himself in his own person ".[1] A few days later, and in more cautious official language, the fifth Komsomol conference sounded the same note of anxiety about the states of mind prevalent " in backward strata of young workers ". These included " egalitarian moods " and " an incorrect attitude to specialists and foremen " ; young peasants were alleged to display jealousy of the towns and an inclination to oppose the interests of the peasantry to those of the working class ; students succumbed to " pessimistic petty-bourgeois moods (Eseninshchina etc.) ". Such " anti-proletarian " tendencies were said to be encouraged by " opposition elements in the party and the Komsomol ", and " an unceasing struggle on ideological front " was called for in order to counter them.[2]

Hooliganism and debauchery, as well as political disillusion-ment, among the young continued to trouble the authorities. Yaroslavsky, in a moment of frankness at the fifteenth party con-gress in December 1927, explained that few Komsomol representa-tives had been invited to the celebrations of the tenth anniversary of the revolution, at which foreigners were present, because it would have been impossible to prevent them from getting drunk.[3] Drunkenness and debauchery were charges frequently brought against members of the Komsomol drafted for work in the countryside ; and references occur to the unscrupulous Komsomol bureaucrat who made a career by fawning on his superiors and denouncing and persecuting those beneath him.[4] Bukharin at the eighth Komsomol congress in May 1928 described drunken orgies presided over by the secretary of the Komsomol organization

[1] V. Mayakovsky, *Polnoe Sobranie Sochinenii*, xii (1959), 312-320 ; Mayakovsky in 1926 had written a well-known poem *To Sergei Esenin*, and in an article detected in Esenin's last years " a clear attraction to the new ", " an evolution from Imaginism towards VAPP ", and " an evident sympathy for us (the men of Lef) " (*ibid.* xii, 94-95 ; this part of the article first appeared in the Tiflis newspaper *Zarya Vostoka*, June 5, 1926).

[2] *VLKSM v Rezolyutsiyakh* (1929), p. 283. For " egalitarianism " see Vol. 1, pp. 529-531 ; for attitudes to specialists see Vol. 1, pp. 578-580, 589.

[3] *Pyatnadtsatyi S"ezd VKP(B)*, i (1961), 538 ; a decree of the party central committee of February 1928 forbade members of the party and the Komsomol to visit casinos or play games of chance for money (*Izvestiya Tsentral'nogo Komiteta VKP(B)*, No. 5(226), February 22, 1928, p. 6).

[4] I. Bobryshev, *Melkoburzhuaznye Vliyaniya sredi Molodezhi* (1928), pp. 74-75.

in Sochi, where Komsomol girls were put at the disposal of
Komsomol youths; dancing-classes in Leningrad were said to be
a means of dragging Komsomol girls into " the mire of debauchery ".[1] Even if such lurid pictures are discounted, sufficient
evidence exists of youthful violence, debauchery and cynicism to
build up a formidable indictment of failure to curb even flagrant
abuses.[2] This was the one short-lived period when sexual
problems became a favourite theme of Soviet fiction.[3]

The Komsomol was one of the targets of the united opposition,
which connected its problems with the decay of the old family
structure, and the rise of " the new family " based on " completely
new relations between two independent individuals who play the
rôle of independent builders of society ". In its declaration to the
party central committee in July 1926 it accused the Komsomol
leaders of " bureaucratism ", and of attempting to replace worker,
poor peasant and *batrak* members by elements of the intelligentsia
and the bourgeoisie.[4] While party control over the Komsomol
organization and its leaders was now firmly established, and was
not again seriously threatened, the opposition kept up its attacks
and clearly enjoyed support among the rank and file; and charges
against the opposition of setting up an illegal organization and
circulating " an anti-party, anti-Leninist Komsomol platform "[5]

---

[1] *VIII Vsesoyuznyi S"ezd VLKSM* (1928), pp. 25, 72.

[2] I. Bobryshev, *Melkoburzhuaznye Vliyaniya sredi Molodezhi* (2nd ed. 1928),
which was widely quoted at the time, was full of stories of such incidents, but
said little to justify the reference to " petty bourgeois influences " in the title.
In May 1928 unusual publicity was given to a squalid case of suicide by a young
woman after an orgy in a hotel room; the principal culprit was a member of the
Federation of Soviet Writers (*Izvestiya*, May 23, 1928).

[3] The two most famous literary reflections of this mood, Malashkin's novel
Luna s Pravoi Storony and Romanov's story *Bez Cheremukhi*, date from 1927.
Polonsky, editor of *Novyi Mir*, in which most of Romanov's stories appeared,
deplored his preoccupation with sex, but admitted that "' sexual themes ' are
now the most fashionable themes " (*Izvestiya*, April 3, 1927); in a further
article he regretted that these subjects were not treated in relation to the decay
of the old family and the liberation of women, but became simply " a photo-
graphic picture of erotic anecdotes " (*ibid.* April 7, 1927).

[4] For the declaration see p. 7 above; for references to the Komsomol see
also *XV Konferentsiya Vsesoyuznoi Kommunisticheskoi Partii (B)* (1927),
pp. 686-687, and *Oppozitsiya i Komsomol* (1927), pp. 31-32.

[5] See p. 40 above.

were at most a melodramatic exaggeration of what took place. Restiveness in the Komsomol organizations in Moscow, Kharkov and Georgia was attributed to opposition intrigues; members of the Georgian Komsomol were said to have founded " a league of defenders of inner-party democracy named after comrade Trotsky ".[1] The opposition platform of September 1927 declared that what the party demanded of the Komsomol was "' obedience ' and readiness to bait the opposition " ; it attacked the preponderance of " petty bourgeois elements " in the Komsomol, and the growth of bureaucratism and " paid officialdom ".[2] The declaration of the Democratic Centralists, also prepared for the fifteenth party congress of December 1927, accused the Komsomol of fostering " not genuinely proletarian revolutionaries ", but " docile officials of the state and party apparatus ", and complained of " repressions applied to dissidents ".[3] The congress itself, absorbed in the struggle against the opposition and the preparation of the five-year plan, made only incidental references to the affairs of the Komsomol. The claim that, at Komsomol meetings held in advance of the congress to discuss " contentious questions ", 99 per cent of those present had voted " for the party, against the opposition ",[4] suggested that the tactics employed at party meetings had been no less successful in those of the Komsomol. Chaplin, in his report to the eighth Komsomol congress in May 1928, remarked that, in the two years since the previous congress, " the overwhelming bulk of Komsomol strength and activity had to be diverted from creative work to the struggle against the opposition ".[5]

---

[1] *Oppozitsiya i Komsomol* (1927), pp. 3-15 ; for the trouble in Kharkov see *ibid.* p. 84. The Georgian opposition was mentioned in an article by Chaplin in *Pravda*, August 20, 1927, which also referred to attacks by " opposition groupings " in the Komsomol on such points as the iron-clad minimum for juveniles and the wages tariff for learners (for these questions see Vol. 1, pp. 474-480); these attacks found an echo in " backward, conservative attitudes among backward strata of the working class and the young workers ", which opposed rationalization and alleged that the workers were being exploited.

[2] L. Trotsky, *The Real Situation in Russia* (n.d. [1928]), pp. 134-139 ; it was noteworthy that throughout this period almost all delegates at Komsomol congresses and conferences were party members or candidates (see Table No. 57, p. 480 below), and had therefore a double commitment to the party line.

[3] *Oppozitsiya i Komsomol* (1927), pp. 58-59 ; for this declaration see pp. 49-50 above.   [4] *Pyatnadtsatyi S"ezd VKP(B)*, i (1961), 256-257.

[5] *VIII Vsesoyuznyi S"ezd VLKSM* (1928), pp. 2-3.

The expulsion of the opposition from the party ended serious resistance in the Komsomol. Henceforth the leaders of the Komsomol, as of the party, could count on unqualified acceptance of the party line. The eighth congress, held in May 1928, was the most orderly and uneventful yet seen in the history of the league. Bukharin's opening address on behalf of the party central committee was more critical than laudatory. Bukharin spoke firmly of " the task of industrial reconstruction and the task of organizing cooperative production in the countryside ". But he referred to the shortcomings in the social composition of the Komsomol, to the drunken and dissolute behaviour of some of its members, and to its failure to counter the insidious activities of preachers of religion. He distinguished between the experiences of three generations of Komsomol members. The first had suffered under " the policemen, the officials, the old officers " of the Tsar. The second had been through the civil war and " seen the class enemy with weapons in his hands ". The present generation lacked these experiences, and could see only " the glaring contradictions in our régime, contradictions which will not be quickly overcome ". In conclusion he dwelt on the need to improve party leadership in the Komsomol. He refused to admit that this had already been strengthened; on the contrary it might even have deteriorated.[1]

All these themes were reflected in the congress debates. Rukhimovich, a deputy president of Vesenkha, came to the congress to deliver a long report on industrialization.[2] The general resolution of the congress proclaimed it necessary to draw the Komsomol into " the business of socialist construction " : this would involve the eradication of " narrowness, routine and bureaucratism " in the leadership, and of " isolation and bureaucratism " in Komsomol organs. The voluntary character of the work required did not imply " renunciation of the obligatory demands made on Komsomol members by the statute of the VLKSM ".[3] A special resolution on industrialization reiterated these points.[4] Chaplin mildly attempted to take the edge off

<hr />

[1] *VIII Vsesoyuznyi S"ezd VLKSM* (1928), pp. 18-41.

[2] *Ibid.* pp. 344-369.

[3] *VLKSM v Rezolyutsiyakh* (1929), p. 312; Chaplin in his report also insisted on a reconciliation of the voluntary principle with the notion of " obligatory tasks " (*VIII Vsesoyuznyi S"ezd VLKSM* (1928), pp. 46-47).

[4] *Ibid.* pp. 319-330. A corresponding resolution on Komsomol work in

Bukharin's comments on party leadership by pleading that criticism should not be confined to issuing reproofs and commands, but should extend to assistance to the Komsomol in working out its problems.[1] One speaker complained that party directives were not always clear, and instanced a meeting at an enterprise in the Urals at which Komsomol delegates had inadvertently taken the wrong side because the local party cell had failed to apprise them of the party line. But the congress took cognisance of a protest against the action of the Tambov provincial party committee in seeking to impose its nominee as secretary of the Komsomol provincial committee; since no issue affecting the party line had arisen, this interference was condemned as " a violation of the principles of party leadership ".[2] The question of a revision of the programme of the Komsomol was removed from the agenda in order to await the expected debate at the forthcoming congress of Comintern on the Comintern programme.[3]

When Bukharin spoke for the party at the Komsomol congress in May 1928, the strains and stresses which were to lead to the emergence later in the year of the Right deviation were already making themselves felt. It was at this moment that Bukharin began to air his doubts in the secrecy of the Politburo, and Stalin moved quickly to capture the strong points where Bukharin's influence might prove dangerous.[4] Of these the Komsomol was one. Bukharin never had the personal hold of Trotsky on the young, and his cautious policies were less likely to appeal to them. But he was a popular figure, and had served for the last two or three years as the principal contact man for the party central committee in the Komsomol. Stalin's brief hortatory speech on the last day of the congress avoided controversial issues, and was clearly designed as a compliment to the Komsomol and a mark of Stalin's personal interest in it; and this was followed a few days later by a rather fulsome message to the Komsomol newspaper,

the countryside (*ibid.* pp. 330-340) was not debated in open session, but was drafted by a commission and formally approved by the congress (*VIII Vsesoyuznyi S"ezd VLKSM* (1928), p. 544); for Komsomol shortcomings in rural areas see pp. 182-183 below.
    [1] *Ibid.* p. 73.
    [2] *Ibid.* pp. 250-251, 599-600.
    [3] *VLKSM v Rezolyutsiyakh* (1929), p. 308 ; the Comintern programme will be discussed in a subsequent volume.
    [4] See pp. 61-63 above.

Komsomol'skaya Pravda, on the occasion of its third anniversary.[1]
Friction between Komsomol and trade unions was no novelty, and
had clearly marked causes. When in the summer of 1928 the
Komsomol became the spearhead of a campaign against the trade
unions, which was also a tactical move against the Right opposition,[2] the hand of Stalin or his henchmen was plainly discernible
in the process. Stalin cautiously guarded himself in an article on
self-criticism, which, while praising the Komsomol newspaper
Komsomol'skaya Pravda, reproved it for " a whole series of
intolerable caricatures " of the trade union leaders.[3] But the tenth
anniversary of the Komsomol in October 1928 brought a further
congratulatory message from Stalin;[4] and in the same month a
resolution of the Komsomol central committee deplored " a Right
danger in the Komsomol movement ", which was attributed to the
low intellectual calibre of the peasant element in the league.[5] A
decision of the Communist Academy, at the instigation of the party
central committee, to establish training courses for Komsomol
officials, in which some 30 students were enrolled,[6] was a further
recognition of the need to strengthen the ideological link between
party and Komsomol.

The preoccupation in the winter of 1928–1929 with the social
and ideological purity of the party drew attention to the neglected
problem of the overlapping membership of party and Komsomol,
10·5 per cent of whose members were now also party members.[7]
A critical article in the journal of the party central committee
concluded that " the party nucleus in the Komsomol fulfils weakly
its rôle of conveying party influence to the mass of Komsomol
members "; party members in the Komsomol " turn up their
noses at rank-and-file members ".[8] A long resolution of the party

---

[1] Stalin, *Sochineniya*, xi, 66–79. A. Barmine, *One Who Survived* (1945),
p. 170, treats Stalin's encouragement of *Komsomol'skaya Pravda* as a first move
to counter Bukharin's control of *Pravda*; for the dislodging of Bukharin from
Pravda see p. 62 above.

[2] See Vol. 1, pp. 552–557.   [3] Stalin, *Sochineniya*, xi, 136.
[4] *Ibid.* xi, 242–243.   [5] *Pravda*, June 1, 1929.
[6] *Deyatel'nost' Kommunisticheskoi Akademii, 1918–1928* (1928), p. 117;
the number was raised in 1929 to 50 (*Izvestiya Tsentral'nogo Komiteta VKP(B)*,
No. 7(226), March 20, 1929, p. 15).
[7] See pp. 164–165 above.
[8] *Izvestiya Tsentral'nogo Komiteta VKP(B)*, No. 5–6(264–265), February 28,
1929, p. 6.

central committee on February 11, 1929, " On Current Tasks of
the Komsomol and Tasks of Party Leadership of the Komsomol ",
covered every aspect of Komsomol work. Having described the
Komsomol as " the largest reserve of the communist party " and
" the closest auxiliary of the party ", it demanded the mobilization
of the masses of the young for " the fundamental tasks of socialist
construction and of the reshaping of our economy " ; industrialization, collectivization and mass cooperation in agriculture, defence,
and the struggle against bureaucratism were causes into which the
efforts of the young should be channelled. The resolution called
for increased recruitment of young workers, and for " a review of
the ranks of the league with a view to purge it of alien and corrupt
elements ". Finally, the party central committee was " con-
vinced that the Komsomol, under the leadership of the party, will
continue in future to be a disciplined Leninist organization ".[1]
The proposed " review " of Komsomol membership was carried
out in March 1929. Among the abuses discovered were false
descriptions of social origins (*kulaks* disguised as middle peasants,
sons of merchants as workers, and middle peasants as poor
peasants or *batraks*) and an inordinate number of " dead souls "
(as many as 48 per cent of the Smolensk Komsomol) ; disciplinary
measures were applied to those responsible, as well as to cases of
" drunkenness, sexual debauchery, hooliganism etc.".[2]   It may be
assumed that ideological purity was also not neglected, and that
deviators were strictly dealt with. The shake-up in the Komsomol
was at least as drastic as in the party. In the interval before the
next congress in 1931 nearly all the Komsomol leaders of 1928 had
been denounced and removed from their posts ; and of the 120
members elected to the Komsomol central committee at the eighth
congress in 1928 only 22 were re-elected at the ninth congress
three years later.[3]

The organization of Young Pioneers for children between the
ages of 10 and 14 established by the fifth Komsomol congress of

---

[1] *Ibid.* No. 8-9(267-268), March 31, 1929, pp. 15-17.
[2] *Ibid.* No. 16(275), June 14, 1929, pp. 2-4.
[3] *VIII Vsesoyuznyi S"ezd VLKSM* (1928), pp. 554-555 ; *IX Vsesoyuznyi
S"ezd VLKSM* (1931), pp. 439-440.

1922[1] grew rapidly. By March 1926, it had been extended to rural areas and claimed a total membership of 1,586,000.[2] By this time also a subsidiary organization of Little Octobrists had been formed for children under Young Pioneer age.[3] At the eighth Komsomol congress in May 1928 both Bukharin and Chaplin criticized the lack of attention paid by the Komsomol to the Young Pioneers organization, which had even suffered some decline in membership; Krupskaya spoke more indulgently, but deplored a tendency of the pioneers to foster individual competition among children rather than a collective spirit.[4] The congress urged Komsomol organizations to discard " an official, bureaucratic attitude to pioneer work ", and to form pioneer sections where this had not already been done. The " methods of work of Boy Scouts " with their insistence on " personal incentives and individual competitions " were rejected as " completely unacceptable for the communist education of children " ; and a half-way house was to be found between total " politicization " of pioneer work and neglect of " social-political education ".[5] A resolution of the party central committee of June 25, 1928, which prematurely claimed a membership of two millions (this may have included Little Octobrists), laid stress on the educational function of the movement and on the need to eradicate petty bourgeois and religious prejudices from the minds of the young.[6]

---

[1] *Pyatii Vserossiiskii S"ezd RKSM* (1927), pp. 346-348.

[2] *VII S"ezd Vsesoyuznogo Leninskogo Kommunisticheskogo Soyuza Molodezhi* (1926), pp. 4, 43-45, 455-456.

[3] *Ibid.* pp. 43-45, 455, 468.

[4] *VIII Vsesoyuznyi S"ezd VLKSM* (1928), pp. 40. 64, 496-497 ; any decline in members must have been temporary, since 1,792,000 pioneers were registered on January 1, 1929, and the total later rose to several millions (*IX Vsesoyuznyi S"ezd VLKSM* (1931), p. 362).

[5] *VLKSM v Rezolyutsiyakh* (1929), pp. 340-347.

[6] *Pravda*, July 14, 1928 ; the pioneers held their first " all-Union rally " in August 1929, when 7000 of them paraded in the Dynamo stadium (*Izvestiya*, August 19, 1929).

CHAPTER 46

THE PARTY IN THE COUNTRYSIDE

THE initial problem of the party in rural areas was the small-ness of its numbers. The census of December 1926 showed 82 per cent of the population of the USSR residing in the countryside. The party census of the first months of 1927 revealed that party members constituted 1·78 per cent of the total population, but only 0·52 per cent of the rural population.[1] Members of the party in the countryside, as in the towns, were organized in cells.[2] Of a total of 42,715 party cells and groups of candidates, 20,878 (or 48·9 per cent) were rural. But, since the average membership of rural cells was low (12·7), only 23·1 per cent of party members and candidates lived in the countryside and were enrolled in rural cells. The party coverage of 546,747 " rural inhabited points " in the Soviet Union was therefore extremely thin.[3] Of peasant households in 1927 only 0·7 per cent included a party member, and 1·1 per cent a member of the Komsomol;[4] and many villages can never have seen a communist except in the guise of an occasional visiting official. Active party members in the countryside were hopelessly overloaded with party work.[5]

Social analysis of the rural party membership presented the usual complexities. Of 264,055 rural members, 65,691 (24·9 per cent) were workers by social situation. But only 23,964 (9·1 per cent) were workers by occupation, and only 13,226 (5 per cent) were *batraks* or agricultural workers, most of the other workers by occupation being employed in industrial enterprises or in transport; no less than 24,169 workers by social situation were now employees by occupation. While 149,734 rural members (56·7 per cent) were peasants by social situation, only 111,688 (42·3 per cent)

---

[1] E. Smitten, *Sostav VKP(B)* (1928), pp. 12-13.
[2] See p. 102, note 1 above.
[3] *Sotsial'nyi i Natsional'nyi Sostav VKP(B)* (1928), pp. 79-81.
[4] *Sel'skoe Khozyaistvo SSSR, 1925–1928* (1929), pp. 134-135.
[5] *Derevenskii Kommunist*, No. 8(80), April 22, 1928, pp. 18-19.

were peasants by occupation; 84,880 (32·3 per cent) were exclusively engaged in individual agriculture, most of the other peasants by occupation combining agriculture with paid work elsewhere. The number of kolkhoz peasants was insignificant. While only 41,346 rural members (15·6 per cent) were employees by social situation, employees by occupation numbered 105,229 (39·8 per cent), being drawn about equally from peasants, workers and employees by social situation.[1] Of rural party members working as employees, 44 per cent were said to maintain some link with agricultural production, either by active or by financial participation.[2] But the official report of the party census drew attention to the ambiguities of classification which made rural party statistics particularly difficult to assess:

> The variety and complexity of social class relations in the Soviet countryside, and the weakness of the rural party organization itself, have hitherto hampered study of the classification of rural communists in current returns, and rendered the statistics of the party in the countryside the weakest section of party statistics.[3]

As late as April 1929, the journal of the party central committee repeated the complaint that " *party cells consist to a large extent of workers in the Soviet or cooperative apparatus unconnected with agriculture* "; in many rural areas only one-third of party members were engaged in agricultural work.[4] Allowing for uncertainties of classification and some overlapping, it is clear that the category of " rural communists " included no more than a small minority of peasants primarily engaged in the cultivation of the soil, and that attempts to increase the proportion of such peasants in the party ended in frustration.[5]

Complaints from Moscow of the weakness of the party in the countryside[6] turned, however, not so much on the inadequacy in

---

[1] See Table No. 58, p. 481 below; for the classifications of workers, peasants and employees by occupation see *Sotsial'nyi i Natsional'nyi Sostav VKP(B)* (1928), pp. 93, 101, 104. Particular stress was afterwards laid on the weakness of party representation in the kolkhozy (*Bol'shevik*, No. 9, May 15, 1928, p. 37; *Na Agrarnom Fronte*, No. 8, 1929, pp. 62-68); see also p. 187 below).   [2] E. Smitten, *Sostav VKP(B)* (1928), pp. 46-47.

[3] *Sotsial'nyi i Natsional'nyi Sostav VKP(B)* (1928), p. 78.

[4] *Izvestiya Tsentral'nogo Komiteta VKP(B)*, No. 11-12(270-271), April 24, 1929, p. 14.   [5] See pp. 103-104 above.   [6] See p. 135 above.

numbers, or ambiguity in status, of the rank-and-file membership
as on the failure of rural party organs to carry out effectively the
decisions of the central authorities or to secure their acceptance by
the peasant.   The official policy of indulgence to the well-to-do
peasant adopted in 1925, and the recruitment of rural party members from the upper strata of the peasantry, had bred a certain
identity of interest and status between the well-to-do peasants and
party members and officials in the countryside.   An enquiry by
the party central control commission in 1926 revealed that 17 per
cent of party members in rural areas were " economically secure "
(meaning, apparently, that they employed hired labour); the
proportion rose to 21 per cent in the North Caucasian region and
to 49 per cent in Siberia.   A Transcaucasian party member boasted
of the success of the party in recruiting middle peasants, and
declared that more than half the members of some party cells
employed *batrak* labour.[1]   In the spring of 1929, when one-sixth of
peasant households in the RSFSR had assets worth 800 rubles or
more, one-fourth of households headed by party members had
reached this standard.   In the Ukraine twice as high a proportion
of peasant party members as of non-party peasants employed hired
labour; application of other criteria produced similar results.
This was a deep-seated and easily explicable phenomenon.   " The
conditions of development of the petty bourgeois economy ", noted
the party journal, " have their effect even on the economy of the
rural communist ", so that it " *grows into a well-to-do or even
entrepreneurial economy* ".[2]   Budennyi told the fifth Union
Congress of Soviets in May 1929 that the " top level " of party
workers in the countryside consisted of " the agronomist, the
doctor, the Soviet official, the cooperative or credit official ", who
formed a " cultural élite " and showed themselves " thick-skinned
and wholly insensitive " to the *batrak*, the ordinary peasant or the
demobilized Red Army man.[3]   Nor were these conditions confined to the lowest party organizations.   " The leadership offered
to economic, cooperative and Soviet organizations by party

---

[1] *Na Agrarnom Fronte*, No. 10, 1928, pp. 82-83.
[2] *Bol'shevik*, No. 9-10, May 31, 1929, pp. 75-76, 82-89.
[3] *5 S"ezd Sovetov SSSR* (1929), No. 16, p. 6 ; of 31,400 agricultural specialists working in the countryside at this time, however, only 4·3 per cent were
members of the party and 3·3 per cent of the Komsomol (*Derevenskii Kommunist*,
No. 14(86), June 26, 1928, pp. 16-17).

committees from district level upwards " was said to suffer from
" substantially the same defects ".[1] A high proportion of secretaries of county party organizations were young and inexperienced.[2]
How far collaboration was promoted by well-to-do peasants joining
the party, and how far by party members drawing economic
advantages and a higher standard of living from their privileged
political status, can hardly be guessed. But it is clear that the
official policy of support for the well-to-do peasant was popular in
many party circles in the countryside, and was assiduously applied.

The shortcomings of party members were not mitigated by the
rural members of the Komsomol, who substantially outnumbered
party members,[3] and were a somewhat dubious adjunct to the
forces of the party in the countryside. The social composition of
rural cells of the Komsomol presented " a particularly unfavourable picture ";[4] here, according to the opposition platform of
September 1927, middle peasants were rapidly gaining ground at
the expense of *batraks* and poor peasants.[5] At the eighth Komsomol congress in May 1928, the principal *rapporteur* painted a
sombre picture of Komsomol work in the countryside. Some
Komsomol cells, under *kulak* pressure, had refused to participate
in grain collection and self-taxation campaigns. A *kulak* in
Tambov province had given a Komsomol member 50 rubles, with
15 rubles for himself, to bribe local officials to reduce his tax
assessment. Even the secretary of a Komsomol cell might
" become assimilated to alien elements, and walk out with the
daughter of a *kulak*, a priest or a mill-owner ", preferring to
associate with " more so-called ' cultured ' strata "; and " a
majority of well-to-do peasants in the ranks of the Komsomol play
the rôle of sub-*kulaks* ".[6] A critical resolution of the party central

---

[1] *Na Agrarnom Fronte*, No. 10, 1928, p. 81.
[2] *Pyatnadtsatyi S"ezd VKP(B)*, i (1961), 178.
[3] The party census recorded nearly 49,000 Komsomol cells in the countryside with 1,100,000 members (*Sotsial'nyi i Natsional'nyi Sostav VKP(B)* (1928),
p. 81); the greater success of the Komsomol in attracting recruits in the
countryside suggests that it may have had an appeal to the younger generation
of peasants in revolt against its elders.
[4] *Na Agrarnom Fronte*, No. 10, 1928, p. 83.
[5] L. Trotsky, *The Real Situation in Russia* (n.d. [1928]), p. 136.
[6] *VIII Vsesoyuznyi S"ezd VLKSM* (1928), pp. 66-67; the resolution of the
congress complained that the Komsomol, in following the injunction to recruit
the " best middle peasants ", had interpreted " best " not in a class sense, but

committee of February 11, 1929, spoke of " the rural Komsomol organization " as " the weakest and most backward sector of Komsomol work ".[1]

The failure of the grain collections in the winter of 1927–1928, and the need for " extraordinary measures " to enforce deliveries, drew the attention of the top party leaders to these defects. Indeed, just as the crisis encouraged the tendency to denounce all recalcitrant peasants as *kulaks*, so it encouraged the branding of all party members who resisted the new policies as friends of the *kulaks*, and disloyal to the party. Stalin, during his Siberian tour in January–February 1928, spoke angrily of officials who remained on friendly terms with *kulaks* because *kulaks* " have cleaner houses and eat better ".[2] The central committee instruction of February 13, 1928, observed that the party line in a large number of regions had been " distorted ", and that " elements alien to the party " had recently appeared in party organizations ; such elements " see no classes in the countryside, do not understand the foundation of our class policy, and strive to carry on their work in such a way as to offend nobody in the countryside, to live at peace with the *kulak*, and in general to keep their popularity among ' all strata ' in the countryside ". The leading article in *Pravda* of February 15, 1928, which heralded the change in policy towards " *kulak* strata " in the countryside, also attacked the shortcomings of party members and organizations.[3] A report of the party central committee noted cases of failure to collect stocks of grain held by *kulaks* and of oppressive measures against middle and poor peasants, a tendency to " turn a blind eye " to abuses, and " the presence in some cells of class-alien elements which openly protect the *kulaks* " ;[4] and the resolution adopted by the committee referred once more to " individual elements in the party, especially in the countryside, which had failed to oppose an adequate resistance to the *kulaks* ".[5] In the lower party organizations, according to Stalin, " a whole batch of communists in the rural districts and

---

in a general cultural sense, and had admitted to the Komsomol " *kulak* and other elements socially alien to the league " (*VLKSM v Rezolyutsiyakh* (1929), p. 332).
  [1] For this resolution see pp. 176-177 above.   [2] Stalin, *Sochineniya*, xi, 4.
  [3] For the instruction and the article see Vol. 1, pp. 51-53 and p. 135 above ; both were believed to have been written by Stalin.
  [4] *Izvestiya Tsentral'nogo Komiteta VKP(B)*, No. 12-13(233-234), April 17, 1928, pp. 1-4.   [5] *KPSS v Rezolyutsiyakh* (1954), ii, 265.

villages came out against the policy of the party, going as far as a link (smychka) with *kulak* elements "; and " 'letters ', ' declarations ' and other documents from a number of workers in our party and Soviet apparatus ", expressing disapproval of the extraordinary measures, were evidence of " an attraction towards a Right deviation ".[1]   In the Barnaul department of Siberia party members held back grain and supported a " hostile *kulak* agitation " against the party; even judges and procurators hesitated to apply art. 107.[2]   In the Smolensk province, where two rural district party committees were reported to have joined in the opposition of the peasants to self-taxation and to the grain deliveries, the provincial party committee commented on the generally poor performance of local party organizations.[3]   " The environment ", observed an official spokesman at the fourteenth All-Russian Congress of Soviets in May 1929, " sometimes sucks in even party men ".[4]

Numerous devices were tried to remedy the shortcomings of party work in the countryside. The peasant committees of mutual aid made meagre and sporadic contributions to rural economic life.[5] The groups of poor peasants were an ineffective attempt to create a focus of support for the régime within the administrative machine of the Soviets, and to mobilize the poor peasant against the *kulak*.[6] More hope was placed in the method of despatching groups of party workers from the towns to rural areas. The institution of " patronage " had been brought into play at the time of the elections to Soviets at the beginning of 1927, when it was said, doubtless with much exaggeration, to have mobilized the services of more than a million workers and to have covered four million peasant households (a population of 20 millions); " patronage " workers, after careful instruction, had spent from one to two weeks in the countryside.[7]   The institution reappeared in the critical months of 1928, when Bauman addressed the *aktiv* of patronage

---

[1] Stalin, *Sochineniya*, xi, 235; for an eloquent description of the corrupting influence of " alien elements " in the party see *Derevenskii Kommunist*, No. 18, September 28, 1929, pp. 3-4.   [2] Trotsky archives, T 1230.

[3] M. Fainsod, *Smolensk under Soviet Rule* (1959), p. 47; for alleged collusion with *kulaks* as one of the causes of the notorious " Smolensk scandal " see p. 137 above.   [4] *XIV Vserossiiskii S"ezd Sovetov* (1929), No. 15, p. 7.

[5] See Note G, pp. 456-458 below.

[6] See Note H, pp. 459-463 below.

[7] *Pravda*, January 13, 1927; for the earlier history of " patronage ", see *Socialism in One Country, 1924-1926*, Vol. 2, pp. 343-344.

workers in Moscow.[1] But of the members of "workers' brigades" and trade union groups sent to the countryside during this period to reinforce inadequate party resources only a few seem to have been associated with this moribund organization.[2] Work in the countryside, more than any other branch of party work, exhibited the characteristic vice of relying on occasional mass campaigns interspersed with long intervals of inactivity and apathy.[3] The most effective support for party policy in the countryside came not from the peasant, but from the "rural intelligentsia" of teachers, doctors and agronomists, who collaborated with party and Komsomol members in their efforts "to implant culture in the masses" and to counteract the influence of "ecclesiastical-*kulak* and sectarian cliques".[4]

Acute dissatisfaction in Moscow with the attitude and performance of a large number of rural party organizations coincided with the rift between the party majority and the Right opposition, which widened steadily throughout 1928. The policy of support for the well-to-do peasant, haltingly proclaimed in Moscow from 1925 till 1927, and whole-heartedly endorsed by most party authorities in the countryside, now became the policy of Bukharin and his fellow-deviators. Propaganda against Rightist leanings in rural party organizations became more intensive. The resolution of the party central committee of November 1928 passed a sweeping condemnation:

> In the composition of rural organizations, the specific weight of proletarian elements still remains absolutely minute, and the number of kolkhoz members is negligible. In certain cases, they are found to include a considerable proportion of well-to-do peasants, and sometimes also elements which have drawn near to the *kulaks*, degenerated and become completely alien to the working class.[5]

Articles in the journal of the party central committee noted " the presence in our party of a certain number of Right, flagrantly

[1] *Pravda*, August 2, 1928; for a further appeal see *ibid*. November 15, 1928.
[2] *Izvestiya Tsentral'nogo Komiteta VKP(B)*, No. 11-12(270-271), April 24, 1929, pp. 9-13; for the workers' brigades see Vol. 1, pp. 261-262.
[3] G. Konyukhov, *KPSS v Bor'be s Khlebnymi Zatrudneniyami* (1960), p. 10; for this tendency see Vol. 1, p. 516.
[4] *SSSR: Ot S"ezda k S"ezdu (Aprel' 1927–Mai 1929)* (1929), p. 131.
[5] *KPSS v Rezolyutsiyakh* (1954), ii, 546-547.

opportunist elements ", and " the appearance among rural communists of the attitudes of the large proprietor ".[1]   *Pravda* in
December 1928 asserted that in the countryside many communists
" see no classes, no class struggle, and want to live at peace with
the whole population and hurt nobody ", and described a village in
the Ukraine which had been dominated for the past year by a *kulak*,
thanks to " the identification of the top party people with the *kulak*
stratum in the village ".[2]   Party convention still prohibited the
naming of names.   But few persons of authority in the party, at
whatever level, can have remained unaware that Bukharin was
the target of these attacks ; and many of those who held these
views probably looked to him as the potential leader of their
cause.[3]

As the crisis deepened, and collectivization — though still on a
voluntary basis — came to be more widely recognized as the only
way out, criticism at the centre of the attitudes of rural party
organizations became more vocal.   *Pravda* attributed the failure
of the grain collections of 1928–1929 to " the corruption of the
local apparatus by *kulak* elements " and " *the absence of any serious
organizational work on a mass scale among the poor and middle
peasant* sectors of the countryside ".[4]   Complaints began to focus
on the lukewarmness of local party officials and members towards
the kolkhoz movement, which had never been popular in the

[1] *Izvestiya Tsentral'nogo Komiteta VKP(B)*, No. 24(255), November 22,
1928, pp. 5, 10 ; the article from which the second quotation is taken related
specifically to the Ukraine.

[2] *Pravda*, December 19, 1928 ; Shlikhter, People's Commissar for Agriculture of the Ukrainian SSR, at a local party conference in December 1928,
quoted letters in this sense from numerous rural party members : " The struggle
with the *kulak* . . . is at an end ; the *kulak* is a small man in the countryside "
(from the Ural region) ; " there is no clearly defined *kulak* type in the village ;
the *kulak* is not dangerous " (from the Moldavian ASSR) ; " the kulak scarcely
exists any more, and where he exists his influence is small " (from the Ukraine)
(A. Shlikhter, *K Itogam Noyabr'skikh Plenumov TsK VKP(B) i TsK KP(B)U*
(1929), pp. 42-43). This was, broadly speaking, what Bukharin had said at the
party central committee in July 1928 (see Vol. 1, p. 79).

[3] M. Fainsod, *Smolensk under Soviet Rule* (1959), pp. 211-212, quotes from
the local party archives a party member who said : " I agree with Bukharin's
line on the question of the development of agriculture ".

[4] *Pravda*, March 9, 1929. A leading article *ibid.* June 1, 1929, attributed the
weakness of the grain collections to Right deviationists ; and Andreev, reporting
to the party central committee from the North Caucasian region, admitted that
" pressure on the *kulak* was not always guaranteed in sufficient measure to
satisfy the requirements of the party line " (*ibid.* July 7, 1929).

circles now branded as the Right deviation.[1] Pressure was applied
to rural party members to give active support to the movement.
An article appeared in the journal of the party central committee in
January 1929 under the title " Organize a Kolkhoz or Leave the
Party ", and was followed by another declaring that " the party
member must once for all take the initiative in the collectivization of
agriculture ".[2] Kubyak, fresh from a visit to Kazakhstan, complained of " anti-kolkhoz attitudes " prevailing in party circles
there ; kulak opposition had been connived at by the local
authorities, who, no doubt on grounds of efficiency, " take away
from the kolkhozy the tractors which we send them ".[3] Failure
of rural communists to join kolkhozy remained a common source
of scandal ; the case was quoted of a well-to-do peasant who was a
party member, and who declared that he would rather give up his
party ticket than enter the kolkhoz.[4] The indictment may have
been inflated for political reasons, and abuses less common than
was suggested. It seems clear that in the new kolkhozy formed
after January 1, 1928,[5] the proportion of party members was
higher than in the old kolkhozy.[6] The converse complaint
was heard that, in kolkhozy where party cells had been formed,

[1] For the weakness of party membership in the kolkhozy see p. 113 above ;
for Bukharin's earlier attitude see Socialism in One Country, 1924–1926, Vol. 1,
p. 221.

[2] Izvestiya Tsentral'nogo Komiteta VKP(B), No. 1(260), January 16, 1929,
pp. 5-8 ; No. 5-6(264-265), February 28, 1929, p. 21. The first article was by
Vareikis, a former Bukharinite, and was clearly intended to announce his
conversion to the official line ; the second criticized it as too mild and half-
hearted.

[3] Bednota, March 24, 1929 ; this was evidently the basis of the charge that
in Kazakhstan " a kulak ideology is being applied by the [agricultural] specialists "
(Trudy Pervoi Vsesoyuznoi Konferentsii Agrarnikov-Marksistov, i (1930), 141).

[4] Pravda, June 1, 1929 ; Bednota, June 27, 1929. Further examples are
quoted in M. Fainsod, Smolensk under Soviet Rule (1959), pp. 214-215.

[5] See Vol. 1, pp. 166-169, 171-180.

[6] A sample investigation of kolkhozy in Siberia and in the Volga and North
Caucasian regions in 1928 showed 18 per cent of members of communes, 4·9 per
cent of artels and 6·1 per cent of TOZ, as party members (Na Agrarnom Fronte,
No. 10, 1929, p. 113) ; party representation in the administrative organs of the
kolkhozy was also higher than in the ordinary membership — 41·5 per cent in
communes, 13·8 per cent in artels and 11·4 in TOZ (Kolkhozy SSSR: Statisti-
cheskii Spravochnik (1929), p. 41, Table 17). By the summer of 1929, 18·3 per
cent of rural party members had joined kolkhozy (Derevenskii Kommunist,
No. 18, September 28, 1929, p. 2), and 20 per cent in the Ukraine ; but these
were said to belong to the well-to-do stratum (Na Agrarnom Fronte, No. 8, 1929,
p. 66).

" communists occupy all the leading posts ", and that " there is no difference between the bureaus of the party cells and the management organs of the collectives ".[1]   But the party purge initiated in the spring of 1929, which fell more sharply on rural than on urban members,[2] may be fairly regarded as one of the preliminaries or pre-conditions of large-scale collectivization.

In the summer of 1929 the failures of the party organization in the countryside were far more conspicuous than its successes. Over the vast expanse of the USSR, party coverage of predominantly rural regions and rural institutions was so thin as to be often non-existent. Whether the party sought to control or to woo, its man-power and its points of contact were hopelessly inadequate for the task.[3] Much of what happened in the countryside in the nineteen-twenties can be accounted for by sheer lack of numbers and resources ; as an exiled member of the opposition noted, the weaker the local party cell, the more ready it was to resort to " marked administrative pressure " and abuses of all kinds.[4] But much that was done was also due to lack of comprehension of peasant interests and peasant mentality. The party, in its composition as in its ideology, was essentially urban ; it was not only Trotsky who looked down on the peasant. The régime which it created and inspired appeared in the countryside as an alien power, sometimes beneficent, more often menacing, but always remote. The peasant, mused Kalinin in 1927, was more of an individualist than the worker ; he lived in isolation with his family. The party worker required " an immense amount of energy, will and perseverance " to make any impression on the rural population.[5] The young peasant, demobilized from the Red Army and now a party member, who returned to the village, wearing a suit " like a brother of Chamberlain " and arguing in favour of the kolkhoz, was received with derision : " You are not

---

[1] *Na Agrarnom Fronte*, No. 8, 1929, p. 72 ; in order to make party influence in the kolkhozy more effective, the party central committee on April 12, 1929, issued an order that party workers in the kolkhozy should remain at their posts for not less than three years (*Bednota*, April 21, 1929).

[2] See p. 146 above.

[3] *Izvestiya Tsentral'nogo Komiteta VKP(B)*, No. 11-12(270-271), April 24, 1929, p. 14.

[4] *Byulleten' Oppozitsii* (Paris), No. 3-4, September 1929, p. 18 ; the writer was Sosnovsky.

[5] M. Kalinin, *Voprosy Sovetskogo Stroitel'stva* (1958), p. 349.

one of us ; get out of here ".[1] The two cultures did not meet.
The country had effective ways of retaliating against infiltration
from the town.   Kalinin at the sixteenth party conference of April
1929 feared " the replenishment of the working class by migrants
from the countryside ", and thought that " through this channel
hesitations are transmitted to the working class, and thence to
particular strata of the party " ;[2] and Molotov a few weeks later
made the point more explicit:

> The influence of the petty-bourgeois factor extends not only
> to the middle peasant elements in our rural organizations . . . ;
> this factor puts its stamp on a certain number of party pro-
> letarians, especially those who have close connexions with the
> countryside.[3]

However strong or weak the justification, deep suspicion continued
to be felt in Moscow of the attitude not only of the peasant, but of
the comparatively rare party member who had direct contact with
him.   When at the end of the year the plunge was taken into mass
collectivization, the main agents of enforcement were not the thin
stratum of doubtfully reliable party officials established in the
countryside, but detachments of devoted communists and of
police sent out from the cities.   It was, if not a " revolution from
above ", at any rate a revolution from without.   This accounted in
part for the blind and brutal character of the operation.

[1] *5 S"ezd Sovetov SSSR* (1929), No. 16, p. 4.
[2] *Shestnadtsataya Konferentsiya VKP(B)* (1962), p. 299; for Bukharin's
comment on this theme see Vol. 1, p. 456.
[3] *Pravda*, July 20, 1929.

PART III

THE SOVIET STATE

CHAPTER 47

UNION AND REPUBLICS

(a) The Constitutional Structure

THE structure of the USSR remained unchanged during this period: no additions were made to the six Union republics established before 1926.[1] Of the Union republics the RSFSR occupied a unique position both as the matrix out of which the USSR had been created and as the model for the other republics. It comprised more than two-thirds of the population of the Union (nearly 101 millions out of 147 millions at the 1926 census, the Ukrainian SSR having 29 millions of the remainder); and, though all the languages of the Union were equal in theory, Russian was in practice, and was bound to be, its common language.[2] Even after the adoption of a revised constitution in 1925, the RSFSR could scarcely be said to function as an entity distinct from the USSR. An official commentator claimed that, whereas at the twelfth All-Russian Congress of Soviets in May 1925 the line of demarcation had not yet been clearly drawn, at the time of the thirteenth congress two years later " the government of the RSFSR already occupied a fully defined and specific place among our central organs ".[3] Yet its anomalous, and clearly subsidiary, status continued to be felt. When its fourteenth congress met in May 1929, so many comments were made on the poor standing of the RSFSR that Rykov felt bound to offer some defence, pointing to the

[1] See *Socialism in One Country, 1924–1926*, Vol. 2, p. 231; the Tajik autonomous republic, since 1925 a unit in the Uzbek SSR, became the seventh Union republic in 1931.

[2] Skrypnik complained that Ukrainian was hardly ever spoken in the TsIK of the USSR, and that, when it was, the official stenographers had difficulty in recording it (*4 Sessiya Tsentral'nogo Ispolnitel'nogo Komiteta Soyuza SSR 4 Sozyva* (1928), No. 7, p. 22); on the still rarer occasions when other languages were spoken, interpreters were apparently provided.

[3] *Vlast' Sovetov*, No. 15, April 10, 1927, p. 1; for the situation in 1925 see *Socialism in One Country, 1924–1926*, Vol. 2, pp. 255-256.

abundant representation of the RSFSR in institutions such as STO
and the People's Commissariats. But he admitted " the absence, in
the composition of administrative organs, and especially in practical work, of a clear distinction of functions between Union organs
and those of the RSFSR ", and spoke jocularly of his own dual
capacity as " Rykov of the USSR " and " Rykov of the RSFSR ".[1]
At the end of the session Rykov was relieved of his post as president of the Sovnarkom of the RSFSR, and replaced by Syrtsov.[2]
Syrtsov admitted a little later that " the situation of the RSFSR is
unique and specific, " and had to be handled with " the greatest
political tact ", since the RSFSR did not constitute " a finished
whole " like the other republics.[3]

In the other republics, the process of constitution-making, or
of the adaptation of pre-Union constitutions to the new Union
status, was accompanied by extensive friction, though the constitutional question rarely came into the open, and was never more
than a side-issue in a struggle which took other forms. It was
afterwards alleged that between 1926 and 1928 " the revision of
the constitutions of the Union republics proceeded in conditions of
struggle against Trotskyite-Rightist elements and their nationalist
allies ", who tried to secure "' constitutional safeguards ' for the
unimpeded development of capitalist elements under cover of
NEP ".[4] The charge is sufficiently indicative of the forces at work.
The advance of planning and industrialization strengthened the
pressure for every form of centralization, and intolerance of any
resistance to it on national grounds ; and the party struggle made
it easy to identify this resistance, more or less plausibly, with the
opposition in the party. The struggle was most acute in the
Ukrainian SSR, where the execution of the decision of the ninth
Ukrainian Congress of Soviets in May 1925 to prepare an amended

    [1] *XIV Vserossiiskii S"ezd Sovetov* (1929), No. 4, p. 2.
    [2] *Izvestiya*, May 19, 1929.
    [3] *XVI S"ezd Vsesoyuznoi Kommunisticheskoi Partii (B)* (1931), p. 221 ; the
occasion was a proposal made at the sixteenth party congress in June 1930 (*ibid.*
p. 165), but not pursued, to merge the People's Commissariats of the RSFSR
with those of the USSR. From *Kommunisty v Sostave Apparata Gosuchrezhdenii
i Obshchestvennikh Organizatsii* (1929), p. 95, it appears that institutions of the
RSFSR, including People's Commissariats, administrative organs, trusts and
syndicates, were commonly classified for statistical purposes, like similar institutions of the USSR, as " central institutions ".
    [4] *Sovetskoe Gosudarstvennoe Pravo*, ed. A. Vyshinsky (1938), p. 110.

text of the constitution[1] was subjected to prolonged delays. Among other peculiarities, the amended draft prepared by the Ukrainian TsIK apparently retained the text of the Declaration of Rights of the Toiling and Exploited People, which no longer figured in the contribution of the RSFSR in 1925, and defined more precisely the categories of those excluded from electoral rights.[2] The tenth Ukrainian Congress of Soviets in April 1927 postponed the issue for further discussion;[3] and it was not till May 1929 that the constitution received the final approval of the eleventh congress. The result was, in part, a compromise. The firm assertion of the entry of the Ukrainian SSR into the USSR as an "independent treaty state", limited only in matters reserved to the USSR under its constitution, was retained. This was a stronger affirmation of formal independence and sovereignty than appeared in the constitution of any other Union republic. But its original insistence on class principles as the basis of the constitution was toned down. In these respects, the Ukrainian constitution of May 15, 1929, moved cautiously nearer to the 1925 constitution of the RSFSR.[4] The White Russian SSR acquired its revised constitution on April 11, 1927.[5] Meanwhile, the Transcaucasian SFSR and its three constituent republics had also revised their constitutions.[6] In Central Asia the question was not the revision of old constitutions, but the provision of constitutions for new republics. The Uzbek constitution was adopted by the second Uzbek Congress of Soviets on March 30-31, 1927, the Turkmen constitution by the second Turkmen Congress of Soviets on the same date.[7] Both had the peculiar feature of omitting from the list of People's Commissariats the People's Commissariat of Internal Affairs (Narkomvnudel); and the significance of the omission was made plain when in the following year the presidiums of TsIK of the two republics issued decrees abolishing the respective

---

[1] See *Socialism in One Country, 1924–1926*, Vol. 2, pp. 259-260.

[2] See statement by Skrypnik in *Izvestiya*, November 14, 1926; for the 1925 constitution of the RSFSR see *Socialism in One Country, 1924–1926*, Vol. 2, pp. 253-255.   [3] *S"ezdy Sovetov v Documentakh*, v (1964), 198-199.

[4] *Ibid.* v, 227-242. The history of the Ukraine during these years has still to be written; the complexity of the situation is crudely simplified in much tendentious material from both sides.

[5] See *Socialism in One Country, 1924–1926*, Vol. 2, p. 262.

[6] See *ibid.* Vol. 2, pp. 264-265.

[7] *S"ezdy Sovetov v Dokumentakh*, vii (1965), 118-139, 533-547.

Narkomvnudels, and distributing their functions between other commissariats, the organization section of TsIK, and a central administrative section attached to Sovnarkom.[1] This action was challenged on constitutional grounds by the procurator of the Supreme Court of the USSR. The TsIK of the USSR, having received a verdict of the Supreme Court, proceeded " very cautiously " and requested the TsIKs of the two republics to reconsider their decision and revise their constitutions.[2] The republics obediently decided to reinstate the commissariats as from October 1, 1928;[3] and a corresponding amendment was made in the Uzbek constitution in May 1929.[4]

The system of autonomous republics and regions within the major republic had been devised by the RSFSR between 1920 and 1922 to give constitutional form to the national aspirations of its non-Russian peoples ; and though, after the creation of the USSR, the same principle was applied on a smaller scale by other Union republics, it remained primarily a problem of the RSFSR. In the period 1926-1929 only one new autonomous republic was created by the promotion to that status of the Kirgiz autonomous region. The change was first canvassed, probably not without higher sanction, in a petition of the autonomous region to the TsIK of the RSFSR on February 1, 1926. The presidium of TsIK reported favourably on it to the session of TsIK in November 1926, which also heard an appeal from the Kirgiz delegate, speaking in Kirgiz. A formal resolution to create an Kirgiz ASSR was then adopted.[5] The new ASSR was proclaimed at a first Kirgiz Congress of Soviets on March 7, 1927.[6] Its statute was approved by the TsIK and Sovnarkom of the RSFSR in April 1927, and the republic was formally brought into being by decree at the thirteenth All-

---

[1] *Sovetskoe Stroitel'stvo*, No. 8(25), August 1928, pp. 60, 62 ; a proposal to abolish the Narkomvnudel of the RSFSR was extensively discussed in the Narkomvnudel journal and at a representative conference in 1924 (*Vlast' Sovetov*, No. 2, May 1924, pp. 62-77 ; No. 5, August 1924, pp. 84-99), but made no further progress.   [2] *Sovetskoe Stroitel'stvo*, No. 7(24), July 1928, pp. 99-101.

[3] *Ibid.* No. 12(29), December 1928, pp. 164-165.

[4] *S"ezdy Sovetov v Dokumentakh*, vii (1965), 200-202.

[5] *Tret'ya Sessiya Vserossiiskogo Tsentral'nogo Ispolnitel'nogo Komiteta XII Sozyva* (1926), pp. 151, 839-840 ; *id.: Postanovleniya* (1926), pp. 66-71.

[6] *S"ezdy Sovetov v Dokumentakh*, iv, ii (1963), 456-657.

Russian Congress of Soviets in the same month.[1] The Cherkessian national department, formed in the spring of 1926 on the creation of the North Caucasian region, was converted two years later into an autonomous region, being one of seven such units included in the North Caucasian region.[2] The total number of autonomous republics on January 1, 1929, was 15 and of autonomous regions 16.[3]

Article 44 of the revised constitution of the RSFSR of May 11, 1925, provided that congresses of Soviets of the ASSRs should adopt constitutions for " confirmation " by the TsIK of the RSFSR, and " final confirmation " by the congress of Soviets of the RSFSR. The difficulties of constitution-making in the autonomous republics were comparable to those experienced in some of the Union republics, and produced the same readiness to postpone awkward constitutional issues to an indefinite future. The Volga German ASSR was first in the field, and its congress of Soviets in January 1926 approved a draft constitution, under which the People's Commissariats of the republic were unconditionally responsible to its TsIK, the TsIK elected delegates directly to the TsIK of the USSR, and the subordination of the autonomous republic to the RSFSR, of which it was a constituent member, was studiously played down.[4] The immediate sequel of this bold effort is not recorded ; but the Volga German ASSR seems to have remained without a constitution.[5] Other autonomous republics struggled to emulate this initiative. At various dates in 1926 and 1927 the congresses of Soviets of the Yakut, Buryat-Mongol, Bashkir, Karelian and Tatar autonomous republics adopted draft constitutions, sometimes explicitly in a provisional form, for submission to the RSFSR.[6] But the only republic to emerge successfully from this ordeal appears to have been the Dagestan ASSR, whose congress of Soviets adopted an approved constitution on

[1] *Sobranie Uzakonenii, 1927*, No. 31, art. 205 ; *S"ezdy Sovetov v Dokumentakh*, iv, i (1962), 81-82.
[2] *Sobranie Uzakonenii, 1928*, No. 49, art. 371 ; for the North Caucasian region see *Socialism in One Country, 1924–1926*, Vol. 2, pp. 287-288, and p. 229 below.
[3] *Administrativno-Territorial'noe Delenie SSSR* (8th ed. 1929), p. 3.
[4] *Vlast' Sovetov*, No. 16, April 18, 1926, pp. 3-5.
[5] No document of this republic is included in *S"ezdy Sovetov v Dokumentakh*, iv, i (1962), ii (1963), or in official collections of constitutional enactments.   [6] *Ibid.* iv, ii, 57-58, 244, 336, 372, 553-554.

April 5, 1927.[1] Of the autonomous republics included in other Union republics, the Moldavian ASSR in the Ukrainian SSR acquired its constitution in 1925,[2] the Nakhichevan ASSR in the Azerbaijan SSR in April 1926,[3] the Abkhazian ASSR in the Georgian SSR in October 1927 ;[4] the Tajik ASSR in the Uzbek SSR in April 1929.[5]

(b) Legislative Powers

Relations between the USSR and the Union republics under the constitution of the USSR had been abundantly discussed in 1924 and 1925, mainly in the context of Ukrainian claims to maintain a real, and not purely formal, constitutional independence.[6] In the ensuing period public debate in the organs of the USSR no longer took place. But controversy was endemic in a situation where constitutional rules were so ill defined and held in such scant respect. The fundamental difference between Soviet constitutional and legal theories and those current in the bourgeois world was a constant theme of Soviet writers :

> Legal rules are designed for the planning of the economic and political life of the country, and they are nothing but the planning policy of the state. Therefore, in applying this or that legislative rule, one must start not only from the fixed forms and letter of the law, but from the content embodied in the rule, i.e. from the substance of the policy which the said rule is carrying out.

It was emphasized that this implied decisions based not on individual caprice, but on a collective conception of the end in view.[7] Enukidze remarked on one occasion that the USSR " acts as

---

[1] *S"ezdy Sovetov v Dokumentakh*, iv, i (1962), 1031-1048.

[2] See *Socialism in One Country, 1924–1926*, Vol. 2, p. 261.

[3] *S"ezdy Sovetov v Dokumentakh*, vi (1964), 335-343 ; for an article explaining the historical reasons for the establishment of this minute autonomous republic with a population of only 105,000, and its constitutional relations with the Azerbaijan SSR, see *Sovetskoe Stroitel'stvo*, No. 3(32), March 1929, pp. 106-114.

[4] See *Socialism in One Country, 1924–1926*, Vol. 2, p. 265 ; the Ajarian ASSR, also in the Georgian SSR, does not seem to have had a constitution till 1937.   [5] *S"ezdy Sovetov v Dokumentakh*, vii (1965), 363-384.

[6] See *Socialism in One Country, 1924–1926*, Vol. 2, pp. 235-251.

[7] *Sovetskoe Stroitel'stvo*, No. 9(26), September 1928, pp. 17-18.

guardian of the Union republics in matters of Soviet construction ".[1] No formal limitation of the powers of the Union was consistent with this view. The enumeration in the first constitution of the RSFSR in 1918 of the powers enjoyed by the All-Russian Congress of Soviets and TsIK had been illustrative, not exhaustive.[2] The enumeration in art. 1 of the constitution of the USSR was held to have the same incomplete character, which was not nullified even by the explicit provision of art. 3 that " the sovereignty of the Union republics is restricted only within the limits laid down in the present constitution ". As one commentator remarked, " a strict interpretation of art. 1 of the constitution would place the supreme organ of the USSR in a situation of contradiction with its fundamental tasks ".[3]

The Union had from the first few inhibitions about legislating on matters which appeared to fall within the scope of the republics ; if an excuse was required, it was provided by the need for uniformity. When the constitution entitled the Union to promulgate " foundations " or " fundamental principles " of legislation in various fields to be enacted by the republics, this did not imply a distinction between abstract principles enunciated by the Union and their concrete application by the republics, but between enactments of primary importance, which formed the " backbone " of legislation on the given topic and which were within the competence of the Union, and secondary enactments which could be left to the republics.[4] A decree of the USSR of January 30, 1925, on authors' rights was an early and much quoted example of such legislation.[5] While the other Union republics apparently applied the decree without question, the RSFSR by a decision of February 20, 1925, postponed the enforcement of the decree in its territory till such time as it could prepare its own legislation on the question. The authorities of the USSR requested the cancellation of the decision.[6] What happened next is not clear ; it was not till October 11, 1926, that a decree of the RSFSR on authors'

---

[1] *Vsesoyuznoe Soveshchanie po Perevyboram Sovetov v 1929 g.* (1928), p. 105.
[2] See *The Bolshevik Revolution, 1917–1923*, Vol. 1, pp. 132-133.
[3] *Sovetskoe Stroitel'stvo*, No. 5-6(22-23), May–June 1928, p. 22.
[4] *Ibid.* No. 7(36), July 1929, pp. 83-84.
[5] *Sobranie Zakonov, 1925*, No. 7, art. 57.
[6] *Sovetskoe Stroitel'stvo*, No. 9(26), September 1928, p. 15 ; No. 6(35), June 1929, p. 23.

rights, more elaborate than that of the USSR, was finally issued.[1] In 1928 new " foundations " were promulgated by the USSR, thus presumably conceding the competence of the republics to legislate on the subject in detail.[2] The existing limit of 10,000 rubles on inheritance was removed by a decree of the USSR of January 29, 1926. On the other hand, each Union republic had its own civil code, and the RSFSR, by decree of April 6, 1928, amended its civil code in order to extend the category of persons to whom bequests could be made by will — a significant instance of the haphazard character of these procedures.[3] The constitution of the USSR had laid down no rules or procedures for the conduct of Soviet elections ; such provisions were embodied in the constitutions of the republics, or left by these constitutions to their respective TsIKs. When an important instruction on the forthcoming elections to the Soviets was issued by the TsIK of the USSR on September 28, 1926,[4] detailed legislation was left to the Union republics. In practice, however, intervention went far beyond these limits. For the elections the Union authorities set up a central electoral commission to regulate electoral procedure and to issue uniform rules on the qualifications of voters. When the TsIKs of the RSFSR and the Ukrainian SSR issued instructions which clashed with those of the central commission, they were quickly called to order by a decision of the presidium of TsIK of the USSR and obliged to comply.[5] But victory did not always go to the central authorities. A curious instance is recorded of a decree of the TsIK of the USSR of May 23, 1928, on a delimitation between Union and republican legislative competence on taxation and tax revenues, which a year later was " still unpublished in view of fresh disagreements which have arisen regarding it ".[6]

---

[1] *Sobranie Uzakonenii, 1926*, No. 72, art. 567.

[2] *Sobranie Zakonov, 1928*, No. 27, art. 245.

[3] *Sobranie Zakonov, 1926*, No. 6, art. 37 ; *Sobranie Uzakonenii, 1928*, No. 47, art. 355 ; for other examples of Union legislation on matters of civil law see *Sovetskoe Stroitel'stvo*, No. 7(24), July 1928, pp. 131-132.

[4] *Sobranie Zakonov, 1926*, No. 66, art. 500 ; a precedent had been set in the previous elections by a decree of January 1925 (see *Socialism in One Country, 1924–1926*, Vol. 2, pp. 330-331).

[5] *Sovetskoe Stroitel'stvo*, No. 1(6), January 1927, pp. 114-115 ; discrepancies in the electoral legislation of the Ukrainian, White Russian and Transcaucasian republics were discussed in an article in *Izvestiya*, October 30, 1926. [6] *Sovetskoe Stroitel'stvo*, No. 6(35), June 1929, p. 26.

More complicated than the problem of the delimitation of legislative competence between Union and republics was the related issue of the manner in which Union legislation took effect. Article 19 of the constitution of the USSR provided that " all decrees, decisions and orders issued by TsIK are to be carried out immediately throughout the whole territory of the USSR ". A concession to practical necessity was made in a further decree of TsIK and Sovnarkom of February 5, 1925, which laid down that decrees of TsIK or its presidium, and of Sovnarkom and STO, should come into force in the capitals of the Union republics or in subordinate local centres on the date of receipt of the official text of the decree.[1] A writer in the journal of Narkomyust, who borrowed from a legal philosopher the hypothesis of " a dialectical correspondence of centralization and decentralization in the Soviet system ", endeavoured to disentangle the complex relations of Union and republican legislation. Some Union enactments came into effect directly throughout the Union. Some took the form of directives to the republics which resulted in republican legislation. Sometimes the Union issued a law, and the republics followed suit, often incorporating provisions of the Union law in their own enactments ; in such cases, there appeared to be two valid legislative instruments.[2] The attitude of the Union authorities was at the outset elastic and cautious. A decree of the USSR of October 1924 on military crimes remained ineffective for more than a year pending its incorporation in the criminal codes of the republics. The Union decree of February 25, 1927, on state crimes, though promulgated after discussion with the RSFSR and presumably with other republics, had to await inclusion in the criminal codes of the republics before it could be implemented.[3] A common formula in Union decrees was for the TsIK of the Union to " propose " to the TsIKs of the republics to issue the requisite order or decree ;[4] this, though no doubt tantamount to an instruction, preserved the form of republican initiative.

[1] *Sobranie Zakonov, 1925*, No. 8, art. 75.

[2] *Ezhenedel'nik Sovetskoi Yustitsii*, No. 44-45, November 28/December 5, 1928, pp. 1138-1141.

[3] *Sovetskoe Stroitel'stvo*, No. 7(36), July 1929, pp. 78-79, where the dispute with the RSFSR about authors' rights (see pp. 199-200 above) is also cited ; for the decrees on military and state crimes see pp. 352-354 below.

[4] See, for example, the decree of the USSR on urban Soviets of February 8,

The screw was, however, gradually tightened. A further decree of June 1, 1927, distinguished between decrees which were simply directives for republican legislation, decrees which by their nature required republican legislation to carry them out, and other Union legislative enactments, including " foundations " and " fundamental principles " and formal instructions to amend republican legislation; these " other " enactments, unless they contained some indication to the contrary, were to be carried out by the republics within two months.[1] But this did not put an end to controversy. The Transcaucasian SFSR adopted the practice, where the question of competence seemed doubtful, of re-issuing in its own name decrees already promulgated by the TsIK or Sovnarkom of the USSR; and the other republics sometimes followed the same course. This practice was, however, condemned on an appeal by the procurator of the Supreme Court on the ground that it cast doubt on the validity of the original enactment and implied that the organs of the Union had no legislative, but only directive, functions.[2] Failure of the republican authorities to carry out, or to carry out punctually, decisions of the highest organs of the Union inspired a further decree of the presidium of the TsIK of the USSR of May 19, 1928, drawing attention to this abuse, and demanding that measures should be taken to end it.[3] The examples given suggested that bureaucratic procedures or sheer incompetence were the main causes of failure. But Orjonikidze, in a speech at the eighth trade union congress in December 1928, also attacked constitutional quibbles as a source of delay:

This or that republic, picking on some point in a resolution of Sovnarkom, or referring to the constitution or the preroga-

1928 (*Sobranie Zakonov, 1928*, No. 10, art. 86); the same formula was used by the RSFSR in issuing instructions to autonomous republics and regions (*Sobranie Uzakonenii, 1928*, No. 47, art. 356).

[1] *Sobranie Zakonov, 1927*, No. 32, art. 326; the decree was said to have been prompted by disputes with the Ukrainian SSR (*Sovetskoe Stroitel'stvo*, No. 6(35), June 1929, pp. 23-24).

[2] *Sovetskoe Stroitel'stvo*, No. 9(26), September 1928, p. 14; the mining code promulgated by the USSR on November 3, 1927 (*Sobranie Zakonov, 1927*, No. 68, arts. 687, 688) was re-enacted by the RSFSR (*Sobranie Uzakonenii, 1928*, No. 133, art. 871) and the Ukrainian SSR, but not by the other Union republics, which apparently accepted the Union enactment as valid.

[3] *Sovetskoe Stroitel'stvo*, No. 7(24), July 1928, pp. 115-117; for examples of delay see *ibid.* pp. 103-115.

tives of the Union republics, holds up the execution of a resolution for long months.[1]

Relations between organs of the USSR and organs of the Union republics were defined in a way which made friction unavoidable. The unconditional right of the TsIK of the USSR to suspend decrees of the congresses of Soviets, TsIKs or other organs of the republics was firmly asserted in the constitution (arts. 20, 31, 32). Article 59 of the constitution also recognized the right of the TsIKs of the republics or their presidiums to suspend any decree or ordinance of the TsIK or Sovnarkom of the USSR which might contravene the constitution or the existing legislation either of the Union or of the republics; but, since interpretation of constitutional questions was vested ultimately in the TsIK of the Union, the overriding authority of that organ was not impaired.[2] Commentators in Moscow frankly admitted that the formal rights of the republics were often overridden, since their strict enforcement would have been impracticable. The People's Commissariats of the USSR committed " frequent infringements of the rights of the Union republics in their departmental activities and in the coordination of measures carried out by them, or coordinated these only with the corresponding People's Commissariats of the RSFSR, while neglecting coordination with the other Union republics".[3] The unified People's Commissariats of the USSR felt no obligation to act through the corresponding commissariats of the republics, and issued orders direct to subordinate organs in the territory of the republic: this practice was defended by the presidium of TsIK.[4]

Whatever the constitutional position, the forces which, since the first days of the Soviet constitution, had made for the centralization of power in a strong unitary state,[5] continued to work, and were strengthened by the advent of planning and industrialization, and by the pressures which these engendered. Significantly, the presidium of TsIK ruled that decisions of STO, which

---

[1] *Vos'moi S"ezd Professional'nykh Soyuzov SSSR* (1929), p. 268.

[2] Even where the interpretation was formulated by the procurator of the Supreme Court, it had no validity till it had been confirmed by the presidium of TsIK (see p. 339 below).

[3] *Sovetskoe Stroitel'stvo*, No. 9(26), September 1928, p. 13.

[4] *Ibid.* No. 6(35), June 1929, pp. 24-25.

[5] See *The Bolshevik Revolution, 1917–1923*, Vol. 1, pp. 126-140.

was frequently responsible for major planning decisions, were not
subject to suspension by the republics under art. 59.[1]   The
authorization accorded to the Union by the constitution to lay down
" foundations " of legislation in various fields had served to establish a predominant influence of the Union authorities over such
vital matters as land utilization, judicial organization and procedure and criminal law.[2]   The Union authorities were responsible
under the constitution for a " single state budget of the USSR "
and for a " general plan of the whole national economy of the
Union ".   Where no such constitutional provision could be invoked, anomalous devices were sometimes applied to bring about a
necessary centralization of authority.   To supervise the medical
services of the Red Army the Union authorities set up a military
health department which was attached to the People's Commissariat of Health (Narkomzdrav) of the RSFSR, the USSR having
no such organ, and whose decisions were carried out locally
through the Narkomzdravs of the Union republics.[3]   By 1928
such arrangements were rarely scrutinized from the standpoint
of constitutional propriety.   What counted were the practical advantages of central control and direction.

(c) Union and Republican Organs

No major institutional changes occurred in this period.   The
Union Congress of Soviets functioned as a widely representative
biennial forum of more than 2000 delegates and candidates for
public pronouncements and carefully organized debates ; following the third congress in May 1925, fourth and fifth congresses
were held in the spring months of 1927 and 1929.   Between the
congresses, the central executive committee (TsIK) elected by the
congress held three or four sessions, somewhat less formal than the
congresses, but attended by more than 800 delegates and candidates.   For these sessions a standard procedure was gradually
established.   A general report by Rykov, as president of the

---

[1] *Sovetskoe Stroitel'stvo*, No. 6(35), June 1929, p. 26.
[2] For land utilization see Vol. 1, pp. 106-109 ; for the other two matters see
pp. 337, 348 below.
[3] *Sovetskoe Stroitel'stvo*, No. 2(19), February 1928, pp. 36-37 ; for a note
on the constitutional ambiguities of this solution see *ibid*. No. 5-6(22-23), May–
June 1928, pp. 172-173.

Council of People's Commissars, on the activities of the government was a regular first feature. Once a year the People's Commissar for Finance delivered his report on the budget, with a co-report by the president of the budgetary commission of TsIK (the only standing commission). Frequent features were a report by the chief delegate of one of the Union republics on the affairs of his republic, and reports by the People's Commissars in charge of agriculture, industry and foreign affairs. The reports on foreign affairs, delivered in this period by Litvinov, were often addressed primarily to a foreign audience. All these reports were commonly, though not invariably, followed by debates in which points of substance were sometimes raised, and minor amendments made in resolutions submitted; but no vote was ever taken. The two chambers into which TsIK was divided, the Council of the Union and the Council of Nationalities, sat together to hear, and sometimes to debate, these reports. But some separate sessions were always held, rather — it would seem — to mark the independent rôle of the second chamber, in whch the non-Russian nationalities were heavily over-represented, than for any practical purpose.

The experience of TsIK continued, however, to illustrate the tendency of authority, and the effective transaction of business, to pass from the large representative assembly to the select presidium appointed by it.[1] Between the well publicized sessions of TsIK, the presidium held frequent meetings which were not regularly reported,[2] except in the form of decrees issued by the presidium, or jointly by the presidium and Sovnarkom. Constitutional procedure required that such enactments should be submitted for confirmation to the next session of TsIK. But this quickly became a formality. The original budgetary statute of October 29, 1924, had been debated and adopted by the full TsIK; and, when an amended statute to widen the budgetary powers of the republics was discussed by TsIK in April 1926, it was assumed that the same procedure would be followed.[3] What happened was quite

[1] For the presidium of TsIK see *Socialism in One Country, 1924–1926*, Vol. 2, pp. 241-243.

[2] The presidium appointed at the session of TsIK in April 1926 held 12 meetings in May–July 1926, and dealt with 315 questions, of which some 65 were financial (*Sovetskoe Stroitel'stvo*, No. 1, August 1926, p. 126); but even such bare announcements of business transacted were rare.

[3] See *Socialism in One Country, 1924–1926*, Vol. 2, pp. 459-460, 534.

different. In February 1927 it was reported to the budgetary commission of TsIK that an amended statute had been drafted, and
was being applied on an instruction of the presidium of TsIK.[1] In
May 1927 the new statute was formally promulgated in the name
of TsIK and Sovnarkom.[2] Nearly a year later, in April 1928, a
Ukrainian delegate at the session of TsIK complained that the
statute had been approved only by the presidium, and demanded
its submission to the plenary session.[3] When at the same session
Enukidze cursorily reported 425 laws, 88 secret resolutions and 538
decisions of minor state significance adopted by the presidium
and by Sovnarkom, another delegate protested that all significant
decrees should be submitted separately to TsIK for discussion.[4]
Nobody contested the legitimacy of the proposal. But its fulfilment in practice would clearly have been impracticable. The protest was shelved, and the demand for a discussion of the budgetary
statute was postponed till the following session.[5] When TsIK
again met in December 1928, the issue of the budgetary statute
was once more postponed, and was apparently never raised again.
The protest against the blanket approval of decrees and decisions
of the presidium was renewed with diminished effect; and TsIK
once again confirmed without comment or discussion a long list of
enactments of its presidium.[6]

A specific constitutional point arose on the expulsion from
TsIK of Trotsky, Zinoviev, Kamenev, Rakovsky and four other
members of the opposition as a sequel to their expulsion from the
party at the fifteenth party congress in December 1927. Under the
1923 statute of TsIK, sentences of expulsion from TsIK could be
pronounced only by TsIK itself or by the congress of Soviets.
On December 30, 1927, the party fraction in the presidium of
TsIK passed a resolution requesting Kalinin to propose to the
presidium to exclude from TsIK the eight former party members
who had been expelled from the party; and the decision to expel
them was taken by the presidium on the following day.[1] The

---

[1] *Plenum Byudzhetnoi Komissii TsIK Soyuza SSR* (1927), p. 28; *Vestnik
Finansov*, No. 8, 1927, p. 5.
[2] *Sobranie Zakonov, 1927*, No. 27, art. 286.
[3] *3 Sessiya Tsentral'nogo Ispolnitel'nogo Komiteta Soyuza SSR 4 Sozyva*
(1928), pp. 118–123.   [4] *Ibid.* pp. 709, 712-714.   [5] *Ibid.* pp. 709, 712-714.
[6] *4 Sessiya Tsentral'nogo Ispolnitel'nogo Komiteta Soyuza SSR 4 Sozyva*
(1928), No. 1, p. 6; No. 33, pp. 17-19.

decision on this occasion was simply reported by Enukidze to the next session of TsIK in April 1928, with a somewhat laboured explanation that " continued presence in the ranks of TsIK is unthinkable for a communist who has lost the confidence of his party ".[2] A similar procedure was adopted for the expulsion of members of the opposition from the TsIK of the RSFSR.[3]

Unlike the presidium of TsIK, the separate presidiums of the two chambers had no legislative powers.[4] But, while the presidium of the Council of the Union remained a formal and inactive body,[5] the presidium of the Council of Nationalities, though without constitutional warrant, made vigorous attempts, by way of compensation for the fading prestige of the council, to assert its independent identity. At the end of June 1927 it held for the first time a two-day session, and decided to meet every three weeks for the remainder of the year.[6] With most of its members dispersed in various parts of the Soviet Union, this ambitious programme was not carried out. But between this date and the fifth Union Congress of Soviets in May 1929 it held 19 meetings, and debated a variety of topics relating to the national republics and regions.[7] Among the items discussed by it during this period were reports from Vesenkha on " national " industries ; from the White Russian republic on the employment of native White Russians in the administration ; on the new Turkic alphabet ; from the ZSFSR on national problems in Transcaucasia ; from the co-operatives on their activity and organization in national republics and regions ; and from Komzet on the settlement of Jewish workers.[8]

---

[1] *Izvestiya*, January 3, 1928.

[2] *3 Sessiya Tsentral'nogo Ispolnitel'nogo Komiteta Soyuza SSR 4 Sozyva* (1928), pp. 705-706 ; the normal procedure of a decision by TsIK itself was illustrated by the expulsion of one Rogachev in November 1926 for an official misdemeanour (*III Sessiya Vserossiiskogo Tsentral'nogo Ispolnitel'nogo Komiteta XII Sozyva: Postanovleniya* (1926), p. 270).   [3] *Izvestiya*, January 3, 1928.

[4] See *Socialism in One Country, 1924–1926*, Vol. 2, pp. 242-243.

[5] According to Skrypnik, it never met (*4 Sessiya Tsentral'nogo Ispolnitel'nogo Komiteta Soyuza SSR 4 Sozyva* (1928), No. 7, p. 28).

[6] *Sovetskoe Stroitel'stvo*, No. 7(12), July 1927, pp. 123-127.

[7] B. Kul'besherov, *Deyatel'nost' Soveta Natsional'nostei i ego Presidiuma* (1929), pp. 24-25.

[8] *SSSR: Ot S"ezda k S"ezdu (Aprel' 1927–Mai 1929)* (1929), p. 143 ; for the discussion on the cooperatives see *Sovetskoe Stroitel'stvo*, No. 12(29), December 1928, pp. 170-173.

Such modifications as were made in the machinery of government in this period tended to enhance the authority of the Union over the Union republics. Of the three tiers of People's Commissariats,[1] the Union commissariats, which had no counterpart in the republics and represented the plenitude of central power, gave rise to no difficulties. The unified commissariats, where Union and republican organs with the same name and function existed side by side, provided the most delicate situation. The formation of the People's Commissariat of Trade (Narkomtorg) through an amalgamation of Narkomvnutorg and Vneshtorg[2] prompted a decree of July 9, 1926, which distinguished between its foreign trade functions, in respect of which it, like Vneshtorg, enjoyed the status of a Union commissariat, and its internal trade functions, in respect of which it was a unified commissariat. But the decree also contained some far-reaching provisions on internal trade. The People's Commissariat of Trade of the RSFSR was to act in the RSFSR as " plenipotentiary " of the Narkomtorg of the USSR, which was also authorized to issue instructions direct to organs of the RSFSR and of its autonomous republics and regions on matters relating to the grain collections, grain prices, or the financing of the collections. Other agricultural products were handled by the Narkomtorg of the RSFSR, subject to directives from the Narkomtorg of the USSR. The latter was also empowered to draw up " delivery plans " (plany zavoza) for industrial goods.[3] A further decree a year later made these powers still more explicit.[4] This was a remarkable example of the way in which practical convenience dictated a simplification and centralization of the cumbrous device of the unified commissariats: it is, however, noteworthy that it applied only to the RSFSR and not to the other Union republics.

The non-unified republican commissariats which had no Union counterpart — Internal Affairs, Justice, Education, Health, Agriculture and Social Security — represented what remained of the

---

[1] See *Socialism in One Country, 1924–1926*, Vol. 2, pp. 257-260.

[2] See *ibid.* Vol. 1, p. 451.

[3] *Sobranie Zakonov, 1926*, No. 48, art. 347. The dual status of the Narkomtorg of the USSR as both a Union and a unified commissariat was held to require an amendment of the constitution; this was adopted at the fourth Union Congress of Soviets in April 1927 (*S"ezdy Sovetov v Dokumentakh*, iii (1960), 142).   [4] *Sobranie Zakonov, 1927*, No. 44, art. 442.

formal autonomy of the republics; and the form was jealously preserved. When the Uzbek and Turkmen SSRs abolished their People's Commissariats for Internal Affairs they were firmly told that such action was unconstitutional and compelled to reinstate them.[1] A proposal by Ryazanov in March 1928 to establish a Union People's Commissariat of Education was greeted with so much disapproval that he substituted a plea for a Union scientific centre or committee.[2] But in all these fields the central organs of the USSR constantly intervened with what were, in fact, overriding powers. A commentator in the journal of TsIK observed that it was "impossible to speak of everything subject to the direct management of the non-unified commissariats of the Union republics as falling within the exclusive competence of these republics", since "direct management" was also exercised by the Union authorities by way of planning and of the budget.[3] In the RSFSR it was observed that, since the People's Commissariats of the USSR had been formed in practice by taking over those of the RSFSR, "a certain conservatism among the directors and workers" in these commissariats had led to their retaining operational functions which should have belonged to the RSFSR, instead of confining themselves to the directive functions conferred on them by the constitution.[4] The immense importance and intractability of agricultural problems made it impossible to maintain in practice the formal autonomy of the republican Narkomzems. Since the formation of the Union the Narkomzems of the republics had held periodical conferences to coordinate their policies; and at one of these conferences in 1925 a resolution was adopted which not only sought to regularize this procedure, but drew attention to the need to represent and defend agricultural interests in organs of the USSR, and empowered the Narkomzem of the RSFSR to undertake this task on behalf of the Narkomzems of the other republics.[5] By a decree of the USSR of July 19, 1927,

---

[1] See pp. 195-196 above.
[2] *Vestnik Kommunisticheskoi Akademii*, xxvi (2) (1928), 253, 291.
[3] *Sovetskoe Stroitel'stvo*, No. 2(7), February 1927, pp. 35-36.
[4] *Izvestiya*, January 25, 1927.
[5] *Sovetskoe Stroitel'stvo*, No. 2(19), February 1928, pp. 38-40; according to this article similar conferences had been held by other non-unified republican commissariats, but it seems clear that outside agriculture the system was less developed. For a conference of Narkomzems in November 1926 see Vol. 1, p. 9.

legislative sanction was given to conferences of Narkomzems, and the Narkomzems of the republics were instructed to organize similar conferences of Narkomzems of the autonomous republics within their domain.[1] The existence of this machinery explains why it was possible to delay till the end of 1929 the creation of a Narkomzem of the USSR. The same problems encountered by the non-unified commissariats of the Union republics *vis-à-vis* the organs of the USSR were reproduced in the relations of non-unified commissariats of the autonomous republics to the Union republics.[2] But here too forms were generally preserved. A proposal to abolish the Narkomyusts of the autonomous republics was discussed and rejected at a conference of Narkomyusts of the RSFSR in June 1927.[3] The factors which made these constitutional controversies largely unreal, even to those who took part in them, were the strength of the economic forces making for centralization, the disparate character of the units of the USSR which made uniform solutions inappropriate and unworkable, and, above all, the rôle of the unified party, becoming more and more the focus of ultimate decisions on every major issue.

Relations between the presidium of TsIK of the USSR and the Sovnarkom of the USSR were veiled in the same formal obscurity as in the earlier years of the Union.[4] But friction between them seems to have been rare ; both found their place in a vast and expanding governmental machine. From the beginning of 1926 it was common practice for important decrees of the USSR to be issued in the joint names of TsIK (or its presidium) and Sovnarkom.[5] In the more restricted scope of the RSFSR the juxtaposi-

[1] *Sobranie Zakonov, 1927,* No. 45, art. 459.

[2] For a somewhat academic discussion of relations between non-unified People's Commissariats of the RSFSR and those of the autonomous republics see *Sovetskoe Stroitel'stvo,* No. 1(6), January 1927, pp. 92-106.

[3] *Ezhenedel'nik Sovetskoi Yustitsii,* No. 25, June 29, 1927, p. 754 ; the same proposal was repeated a year later in the journal of Narkomyust by the president of the supreme court of the Dagestan ASSR, and rebutted by a member of the collegium of the Narkomyust of the Volga German republic (*ibid.* No. 29, August 7, 1928, pp. 808-810; No. 49-50, December 24, 1928, pp. 1238-1242).

[4] See *Socialism in One Country, 1924-1926,* Vol. 2, p. 245.

[5] According to *Sovetskoe Gosudarstvennoe Pravo,* ed. A. Vyshinsky (1938), p. 302, laws which " laid down norms of political and economic life " were promulgated in this way ; but not all these decrees answered to this description.

tion of TsIK and Sovnarkom sometimes proved more embarrassing. Kalinin in May 1928 spoke of a "struggle" between Narkomvnudel and the organization section of TsIK, and attempted to define the situation in confused language which revealed its ambiguity :

> The presidium of TsIK carries out chiefly the organizational part [of the work of TsIK], and the main work of administration falls to Sovnarkom. Sovnarkom in reality carries out the immediate work, the presidium is the organ of legislation, direction and control. Sovnarkom executes, so to speak, the tasks laid down by the presidium of TsIK.[1]

The issue was most acute in the small national autonomous republics and regions. The administrative machinery of the autonomous republics was a replica of that of the Union republics, and that of the autonomous regions was modelled on the arrangements of the great regions of which they formed miniature units. The introduction of the "régime of economy " of 1926 [2] caused a critical eye to be cast on these provisions. A campaign was launched in the press to reduce the inflated and costly administrative apparatus of the autonomous republics and regions. The attempt " to approximate national autonomous units . . . to sovereign Union republics " was condemned. Independent Sovnarkoms and People's Commissariats were not required for these lesser units, and could be replaced by the presidiums and sections of their Soviet executive committees.[3] A passage in a resolution of the party central committee of July 1926, which urged the need to draw into the work of the Soviets " the toilers of the more backward *national republics and regions* ", was rather captiously quoted in support of TsIK as " *the mass organ whch realizes to its full extent the principle of Soviet democracy* " against the Sovnarkom as a purely adminis-

---

[1] M. Kalinin, *Voprosy Sovetskogo Stroitel'stva* (1958), pp. 360-361.

[2] See Vol. 1, pp. 334-335.

[3] *Pravda*, January 7, 1927; *Sovetskoe Stroitel'stvo*, No. 1(6), January 1927, pp. 18-22; *Vlast' Sovetov*, No. 12, March 20, 1927, p. 6. Rather half-hearted rejoinders appeared in *Sovetskoe Stroitel'stvo*, No. 2-3(7-8), February–March 1927, pp. 130-132; *Vlast' Sovetov*, No. 17-18, May 1, 1927, pp. 30-31. Examples of extravagant institutions maintained by autonomous republics were quoted in *Sovetskoe Stroitel'stvo*, No. 2-3(7-8), February–March 1927, p. 133, No. 5-6(22-23), May–June 1928, p. 51. Art. 47 of the constitution of the RSFSR of May 11, 1925, specifically recognized the right of autonomous republics to curtail the number of their People's Commissariats.

trative organ.[1] Rykov at the thirteenth All-Russian Congress of
Soviets in April 1927 again drew attention to the excessively elaborate administrative machines of the autonomous units, which he
attributed to amibition to imitate the structures of the USSR or
the RSFSR.[2] A conference on the question organized by Rabkrin
in the same month led to substantial changes. Several autonomous units, including the Karelian and Bashkir autonomous
SSRs, adopted the method of amalgamating the Sovnarkom with
the presidium of the Soviet executive committee; others formally
maintained the separate organs, but amalgamated the administrative staffs attached to them; other reforms were also recorded.[3]
But such developments were certainly not uniform.[4] At the fifteenth party congress in December 1927 Orjonikidze produced a
table showing the reductions effected in the administrative apparatus of autonomous republics and regions. Staffs had everywhere
(except in the newly created Cherkessian autonomous region) been
cut by percentages varying from 11·7 to 34; the chief economies
had been realized by reducing the number of sections of the
administration.[5] Another defect mentioned at this time in the
North Osetian autonomous region was " slowness in changing
over the conduct of business to the Osetian language, and inadequate recruitment of Osetians into the state apparatus ".[6]
Language difficulties must have been endemic in many autonomous
regions, and contributed to the inflation of administrative staffs.

[1] *Sovetskoe Stroitel'stvo*, No. 2-3(7-8), February–March 1927, p. 137. For
the resolution of July 1926 see pp. 274-275 below; the passage quoted as in
KPSS v Rezolyutsiyakh (1954), ii, 278.

[2] *XIII Vserossiiskii S"ezd Sovetov* (1927), p. 38.

[3] *Sovetskoe Stroitel'stvo*, No. 7(12), July 1927, pp. 42-47.

[4] An account of the administration of the small Nagorny-Karabakh autonomous region in the Azerbaijan SSR in 1928 described the regional Sovnarkom
as " concentrating in itself the whole work of administering the region and
enjoying the rights of the presidium of TsIK "; since the president of TsIK
was also the president of Sovnarkom, the two institutions virtually coalesced
(*ibid.* No. 10(27), October 1928, pp. 105-106; whether details of the regional
People's Commissariats given in this account are a blueprint of what was
supposed to happen or a factual record of what did happen, and how far this
region was typical of others, cannot easily be established).

[5] *Pyatnadtsatyi S"ezd VKP(B)*, i (1961), 459; the figures for different
regions do not appear to have been always strictly comparable. The process of
reduction was said to be still incomplete (*ibid.* i, 526).

[6] *Sovetskoe Stroitel'stvo*, No. 12(17), 1927, p. 118.

CHAPTER 48

REGIONALIZATION

THE process of administrative reorganization of the territory of the USSR known as regionalization (raionirovanie), on lines laid down by the twelfth party congress in 1923, had made considerable progress by 1926. The Ukrainian, White Russian, Uzbek and Turkmen SSRs had been organized as regions; the Ural, North Caucasian, Siberian and Far Eastern regions had been established, all within the RSFSR.[1] In the Union republics other than the RSFSR regionalization had not involved the creation of a new major territorial unit, and excited no jealousies. The regions of the RSFSR established in 1925 and 1926 covered sparsely inhabited areas where existing administrative structures were weak. In the more developed areas of the RSFSR the vested interests of the old province, county and rural district were far more powerful; and the attempt to scrap these units in favour of a new structure of regions, departments and districts encountered keen resistance, which seems to have been sufficient to hold back the further progress of regionalization throughout 1927. When the Sovnarkom of the RSFSR in March 1927 considered a report from Rabkrin pressing for the completion of the reform, A. P. Smirnov led a delaying action, and the resolution adopted on the subject was equivocal.[2] In that year only the Leningrad region was constituted, coming into existence on August 1, 1927.[3] The fifteenth party congress in December 1927 paid little attention to regionalization, but slipped one significant sentence into its resolution on the five-year plan:

> In order to obtain the greatest possible coverage of the economic life of the country with planned leadership, the

---

[1] For these developments see *Socialism in One Country, 1924–1926*, Vol. 2, pp. 280-292.   [2] *Izvestiya*, April 1, 1927.
[3] *Sobranie Uzakonenii, 1927*, No. 80, art. 536; No. 82, art. 547. For a full picture of regionalization up to this time, including names and population totals of departments and districts see *Sovetskoe Stroitel'stvo*, No. 2(19), February 1928, pp. 61-81.

congress considers it indispensable to complete the regionalization of the whole country within the coming five-year
period.[1]

Under the rising prestige and impetus of planning, and in tense
atmosphere of the grain collections crisis, regionalization was now
hastily pressed forward. The month of May 1928 saw the formation of three important new regions of the RSFSR — the Central
Black-Earth region comprising the central agricultural provinces
with its capital at Voronezh;[2] the Middle Volga region with its
capital at Samara;[3] and the Lower Volga region with its capital
at Saratov.[4] On January 14, 1929, five new regions were created:
a Northern region with its capital at Archangel, which included
the Komi autonomous region; a Western region with its capital
at Smolensk; a Nizhny-Novgorod region; a Central Industrial
region with Moscow as its capital; and an Ivanovo-Voznesensk
region.[5] Finally the hitherto non-regionalized Transcaucasian
federal republic was brought into line and the process of regionalization set in motion by the regional party committee in March
1929.[6] The number of regions in the RSFSR increased from
three on January 1, 1926, to eight on January 1, 1929, and the
number of provinces was reduced from 47 to 16; corresponding
changes occurred in the numbers of the subordinate units of

[1] KPSS v Rezolyutsiyakh (1964), ii, 465.

[2] Sobranie Uzakonenii, 1928, No. 54, art. 406; for further decrees fixing
its boundaries and its division into departments and districts see ibid. No.
96, arts. 616, 617. The first regional party conference and first regional
congress of Soviets took place early in August 1928 (Istoricheskie Zapiski, li
(1955), 199).

[3] Sobranie Uzakonenii, 1928, No. 54, art. 407; for the decree fixing its
boundaries see ibid. No. 118, art. 744. The first congress of Soviets of the
Middle Volga region was reported in Bednota, September 11, 1928.

[4] Sobranie Urakonenii, 1928, No. 56, art. 421; for decrees fixing its
boundaries and divisions see ibid. No. 96, arts. 615, 618. Fhe formation of
this region had been preceded by an extensive controversy, no less than four
rival schemes having been canvassed; these were discussed in a series of
articles in Planovoe Khozyaistvo, No. 4, 1928, pp. 247-286.

[5] Sobranie Uzakonenii, 1929, No. 10, art. 116; for the decree fixing their
boundaries see ibid. No. 41, art. 438. The Central Industrial region was
re-named the Moscow region (ibid. No. 41, art. 437). Kalinin addressed the
first congress of Soviets of the Ivanovo-Voznesensk region on July 15, 1929
(M. Kalinin, Voprosy Sovetskogo Stroitel'stva (1958), pp. 440-445).

[6] Voprosy Ekonomicheskogo Raionirovaniya SSSR, ed. G. Krzhizhanovsky
(1957), p. 241.

the two systems.[1] In April 1928 the TsIK of the RSFSR adopted a statute of " regional, department and district congresses of Soviets and their executive committees ".[2]

While Rykov described the North Caucasian region, at its first congress of Soviets, as " so to speak, a state within a state ",[3] any attempt to involve regionalization in constitutional issues was avoided ; and only one such issue in fact arose — the status of the autonomous republics. The incorporation in the new regions of autonomous regions or departments (the North Caucasian region included no less than seven) encountered no objection of principle, though a spokesman of the North Caucasian region at the TsIK of the RSFSR in November 1926 described the national question as " the fundamental and most complicated of all our questions ", and a resolution was passed that a member of the presidium of the regional executive committee should be deputed to take charge of it.[4] But the incorporation of autonomous republics was still regarded, even in Gosplan, as " untimely and inappropriate ".[5] The Moldavian ASSR had formed part of the Ukrainian SSR, and the Tajik ASSR of the Uzbek SSSR, since 1924,[6] so that here regionalization involved no change in status. But the extension of regionalization to areas of the European RSFSR where the feelings of national minorities were keener, or more readily found institutional expression, posed the problem in an acute form. Even before the formation of the Middle Volga region, protests had been registered against the intervention of the provincial authorities at Samara in the economic affairs of the Tatar and Chuvash ASSRs.[7] In response to these sentiments, the original proposals of Gosplan to include the Karelian ASSR in the Leningrad region, the Tatar and Chuvash ASSRs in the Middle Volga region, the Bashkir ASSR in the Ural region, and the Buryat-Mongol ASSR in a

[1] See Table 58, p. 481 below.
[2] *Sobranie Uzakonenii, 1928*, No. 70, art. 503.
[3] *III Sessiya Vserossiiskogo Tsentral'nogo Ispolnitel'nogo Komiteta XII Sozyva* (1926), p. 262.
[4] *Ibid.* pp. 264, 879.
[5] *Planovoe Khozyaistvo*, No. 5, 1926, p. 194.
[6] See *Socialism in One Country, 1924–1926*, Vol. 2, pp. 261, 268.
[7] *Pyatyi S"ezd Sovetov Tatar'skoi SSR* (Kazan, 1925), pp. 24-25, quoted in W. R. Batsell, *Soviet Rule in Russia* (N.Y., 1929), p. 648 ; the Chuvash ASSR had just been promoted to republican status (see *Socialism in One Country, 1924–1926*, Vol. 2, p. 257).

Siberian region, were all dropped.[1] Circumstantial evidence suggests a sharp struggle over the inclusion of the Volga German ASSR in the Lower Volga region. But the formation of that region in May 1928 was followed on June 19, 1928, by a unanimous vote of a congress of Soviets of the autonomous republic in favour of entry into the region.[2] On June 28, 1928, two decrees of the RSFSR were issued. The first defined the conditions of entry of an autonomous republic into a " regional union " and the rights enjoyed by it, which included the right of secession from the region at any time on a vote of its congress of Soviets. On the other hand, the economic plan of the region was binding on an autonomous republic included in it; and disputes between republican authorities and those of the region were referred to the Sovnarkom or the TsIK of the RSFSR. The second decree confirmed the decision already taken by the congress of Soviets of the Volga German ASSR providing for the incorporation of the republic in the Lower Volga region.[3] A few months later a further decree of the RSFSR regulated relations between autonomous regions and the new regions in which they were incorporated. The autonomous regions retained independent administrative rights in all domestic matters, other than those of economic and financial policy, and the right of appeal to the Sovnarkom or presidium of TsIK of the RSFSR against budgetary provisions of the regional authorities affecting them, but did not enjoy the formal right of secession.[4] National autonomy, and the constitutional forms in which it was embodied, remained valid within the limits imposed by economic necessities. The decree of January 14, 1929, creating the five new

---

[1] *Voprosy Ekonomicheskogo Raionirovaniya*, ed. G. Krzhizhanovsky (1957), pp. 312, 322.

[2] *Sovetskoe Stroitel'stvo*, No. 10(27), October 1928, p. 14.

[3] *Sobranie Uzakonenii, 1928*, No. 79, art. 544; No. 80, art. 550. The incorporation of autonomous republics into regions continued to excite controversy, and was defended on the ground that " *the formal independence of small*, in particular, culturally backward, republics does not help to bring out their potentialities for economic and social-cultural development " (*Sovetskoe Stroitel'stvo*, No. 11(40), November 1929, p. 85); but a critic protested that this formula " sets up an opposition between economic regionalization and the national policy of the Soviet power " (*ibid*. No. 1 (42), January 1920, p. 64). The authors of the first five-year plan claimed that " the national principle and the principle of economic regionalization merely complement each other " (*Pyatiletnii Plan Narodno-Khozaistvennogo Stroitel'stva SSSR* (1929), iii, 11).

[4] *Sobranie Uzakonenii, 1928*, No. 137, art. 889.

regions contained a clause which affirmed that " autonomous regions entering into the composition of the above regions retain all rights conferred on them by the decrees creating them and by subsequent legislation ".[1]

With the simultaneous progress of regionalization and planning, the interdependence of the two processes was well established. Regionalization had been conducted " on the basis of the work of Goelro and Gosplan " ; this was what distinguished it from such merely administrative rearrangements as were carried out by bourgeois governments.[2] The compilers of the control figures for 1928-1929 in the autumn of 1928 declared regionalization " an ever more urgent and essential pre-condition of the planned direction of the building of the national economy of the USSR " ;[3] and the five-year plan pronounced that " only in this way can the highest coefficient of effectiveness of social labour be attained ".[4] Some of those who sponsored regionalization certainly thought of it as a step towards decentralization. Its association with planning made it in practice a process of centralization, and served to strengthen the hands of the central authorities. It was also an instrument for the extension of the control and influence of industry over the countryside, by promoting both the creation of new industrial units and the mechanization and collectivization of agricultural production. The agricultural expert of Gosplan noted that it was in the Ukraine, in the northern Caucasus and in the Urals, where regionalization had come earliest, that the greatest progress had been made in the reorganization of agriculture in large mechanized units ;[5] and Rykov, at the moment of the adoption of the plan, looked forward to the development of the regions into " regional producer combines ".[6] Finally the sixteenth party congress in 1930 authoritatively summed up the whole process :

> The completion of the economic regionalization of the country significantly speeds up the industrialization of formerly

[1] For this decree see p. 214 above.
[2] *XV Let Sovetskogo Stroitel'stva* (1932), p. 158.
[3] *Kontrol'nye Tsifry Narodnogo Khozyaistva na 1928–1929 god* (1929), p. 22.
[4] *Pyatiletnii Plan Narodno-Khozyaistvennogo Stroitel'stva SSSR* (1929), iii, 9.
[5] M. Vol'f, *Puti Rekonstruktsii Sel'skogo Khozyaistva* (4th ed., 1929), p. 89.
[6] *XIV Vserossiiskii S"ezd Sovetov* (1929), No. 4, p. 5.

backward areas, of frontier areas and national republics, creates
there new industrial and proletarian centres, and facilitates a
more correct and practical distribution of industry and agriculture over the whole territory of the USSR.[1]

[1] *KPSS v Rezolyutsiyakh* (1954), iii, 13-14.

CHAPTER 49

LOCAL ADMINISTRATION

(a) The Lower Soviets

THE process of regionalization and the practical need to decentralize an overloaded and far-flung administration led to a growing preoccupation in the middle and later nineteen-twenties with the need to grant effective powers to the lower Soviet organs. In constitutional doctrine, these powers were unlimited; the slogan " All power to the Soviets " had never been revoked.[1] The third Union Congress of Soviets in May 1925 declared that " the Soviets, as organs of government, should stand in fact at the head of all economic and cultural construction in the Soviet republic, and direct it ".[2] In January 1927 a writer in the journal of TsIK repeated that " all Soviets and executive committees, as organs of self-administration and administration, in the strict sense of the constitution of the USSR, embody the full plenitude of power ", and were technically " sovereign ".[3] The RSFSR statute of urban Soviets had called the Soviet " the supreme organ of power " in its territory.[4] Petrovsky, the president of TsIK of the Ukrainian SSR, boldly wrote that the urban Soviet " embodied " the dictatorship of the proletariat, and was concerned with " the whole sum of economic, political and cultural questions of the whole urban population and, first and foremost, of the proletariat ";[5] and Kaganovich, at an election conference in 1928, found it proper to stress that the Soviets were not merely mass organizations, but organs of government.[6] But the doctrine of dual subordination meant that lower Soviet organs

[1] See *Socialism in One Country, 1924–1926*, Vol. 2, pp. 304-305.
[2] *S"ezdy Sovetov v Dokumentakh*, iii (1960), 77.
[3] *Sovetskoe Stroitel'stvo*, No. 1(6), January 1927, pp. 27-28.
[4] For this statute see *Socialism in One Country, 1924–1926*, Vol. 2, pp. 360-361.
[5] *Sovetskoe Stroitel'stvo*, No. 1(6), January 1927, pp. 6-7.
[6] *Vsesoyuznoe Soveshchanie po Perevyboram Sovetov* (1928), p. 10.

were responsible not only to their own electors but to the Soviet
organ immediately superior to them; and this implied a chain of
authority handed down from the centre. Slogans of " decentralization " and " local self-government ", where they took the form
of resistance to central authority, were exposed as reactionary.[1]

The practical importance of local Soviets, though entirely
divorced from dreams of sovereignty, was none the less great. The
theme of the " revitalization of the Soviets" as a means of bringing about the active participation of the masses in Soviet work[2]
was constantly repeated. " Our chief task ", said Kalinin at the
TsIK of the RSFSR in November 1926, is " *to draw the broad
masses into Soviet construction*, i.e. to revitalize the Soviets ."[3]
When the opposition in its counter-theses for the fifteenth party
congress accused the party of promoting " an empty administrative
' revitalization ' of Soviets ", Bauman vigorously defended the
process as a stimulant of mass activity.[4]   In April 1928 Enukidze,
though no longer using the term " revitalization ", treated the
Soviets as an indispensable instrument in the realization of planning:

> We shall not be able to build any kind of socialism unless we
> have strong village and urban Soviets constructed on a uniform
> system.[5]

Some means had to be found of providing for minor local needs;
and the local Soviets were indispensable agents for the execution
and enforcement of centrally planned policies. Both functions
required the establishment of contacts with the population and
the winning of some measure of its confidence.

Regionalization, while it did not touch either the republican
administrations at the top, or the rural and urban Soviets which
formed the base of the Soviet pyramid, radically affected the intermediate levels of the whole structure. Throughout the USSR

[1] This was the theme of a long article in *Sovetskoe Stroitel'stvo*, No. 2,
September 1926, pp. 122-141.
[2] See *Socialism in One Country, 1924-1926*, Vol. 2, p. 368.
[3] *III Sessiya Vserossiiskogo Tsentral'nogo Ispolnitel'nogo Komiteta XII
Sozyva* (1926), p. 4.
[4] *Pravda*, November 15, 1927, *Diskussionnyi Listok* No. 4; for the counter-
theses see Vol. 1, p. 34.
[5] *3 Sessiya Tsentral'nogo Ispolnitel'nogo Komiteta Soyuza SSR 4 Sozyva*
(1928).

the old hierarchy of province, county and rural district was gradually superseded. But the process was not uniform. The administrative changes resulting from regionalization varied substantially
in different parts of the USSR. In all the Union republics, except
the RSFSR, the republic had become a region for the purposes of
the new scheme. This no doubt made it easier for the planners
and economic managers at the centre to extend their control over
the republics. But no new territorial units were created ; the old
provinces disappeared ; and the normal three-tier administrative
structure within the republic consisted of department (replacing
the county), district (replacing the rural district) and village Soviet.
In the RSFSR a large number of regions, replacing a still larger
number of provinces, had been formed within the republic, thus
creating a cumbrous four-tier structure of region, department,
district and village Soviet. But the most persistent argument invoked against regionalization was that, by enlarging the size and
diminishing the number of lower administrative units, it widened
the gap between organs of administration and masses of population. The increase in size and reduction in number of the lower
administrative units, which had begun before regionalization was
undertaken, were intensified by it.[1] The complaint was sharply
voiced by a delegate from the North Caucasian region at the TsIK
of the RSFSR in November 1926 :

> In practice the result is not to bring the government closer
> to the population, but to increase the distance, since for every
> trifle the inhabitant of the Cossack settlement or the village
> must travel tens of versts to the district or the department.[2]

Orjonikidze at the seventh trade union congress in December 1926
made himself the spokesman of the decentralizers. Village Soviets
had no powers ; and the peasant who used to visit the rural district
(volost') centre for his business now had to go to the more remote
centre of the district (raion).[3] In a report to the party central

---

[1] See *Socialism in One Country, 1924–1926*, Vol. 2, pp. 294-297.
[2] *III Sessiya Vserossiiskogo Tsentral'nogo Ispolnitel'nogo Komiteta XII
Sozyva* (1926), p. 267 ; it was stated that, whereas on July 1, 1923 (1926 is a
misprint), there were 462 counties in the RSFSR, not including the autonomous
republics, the number had been reduced by November 10, 1926 to 228 (*ibid.*
p. 443).
[3] *Sed'moi S"ezd Professional'nykh Soyuzov SSSR* (1927), p. 460.

control commission in February 1927 Orjonikidze again attacked
the degree of centralization inherent in the scheme:

> By regionalization we wanted to bring the Soviet power
> nearer to the population. But we have so curtailed the rights
> of the districts that, in the result, questions which were formerly
> decided by the county executive committee are now decided by
> the department.[1]

The interplay between the demands of centralization and decentralization coloured all the controversies of these years about
the intermediate Soviet structure.

The status of the region itself was not established without some
difficulty. At the session of the TsIK of the RSFSR in November 1926 a lengthy debate was devoted to the affairs of the North
Caucasian region, the most powerful of the new regions. Some
ardent supporters of regionalization feared that any devolution of
power to the lower Soviet organs would leave the region too weak.
If departments had taken over the role of the former provinces,
and districts of counties, what remained for the region?[2] The
argument implied that the region should recoup itself through a
larger devolution of powers from the republic; and a demand ran
through the debate for an extension of the powers of the region,
for the guarantee of adequate revenues for the regional budget,
and even for an independent regional budget.[3] This view, however, encountered resistance from those who thought that the
administrative structure should be simplified by curtailing the
functions not of the republic, but of the regions. The fourth
Union Congress of Soviets in April 1927 amended the constitution
by providing that, in regionalized areas, delegates to the republican
congresses of Soviets should be elected by the department (okrug)
congresses of Soviets: what was noticeable here was the transfer
of this function from the provincial, not to the regional, but to the

---

[1] *Sovetskoe Stroitel'stvo*, No. 2-3(7-8), February–March 1927, p. 76; for
the same complaint from a peasant in a discussion organized by the newspaper
Krest'yanstkaya Gazeta in the autumn of 1927 see *Krest'yane o Sovetskoi Vlasti*
(1929), pp. 172-173.

[2] *III Sessiya Vserossiiskogo Tsentral'nogo Ispolnitel'nogo Komiteta XII
Sozyva* (1926), pp. 370-372.

[3] *Ibid.* pp. 255, 283 ; see also *Sovetskoe Stroitel'stvo*, No. 1(6), January 1927,
p. 31, No. 8-9(13-14), August–September 1927, pp. 28-30.

department, congress.[1]   Party as well as Soviet institutions had to
be adapted to the new territorial divisions.   Regulations issued in
September 1927 in preparation for the fifteenth party congress
prescribed that delegates, who had hitherto been elected by provincial party congresses or conferences, should in the regionalized
areas be elected by a congress or conference of the department.[2]
These provisions appeared to foreshadow a move to by-pass the
region as a political unit, leaving the region to exercise purely
economic functions.   Kalinin, speaking in the TsIK of the
RSFSR in April 1928, looked forward to the acquisition by the
regions of independent budgets.[3]   But six months later he was
insisting on the need " to strengthen the independence of department budgets ".[4]   In fact, as the authority of the planners grew,
and as the process of regionalization made progress, more and
more planning power passed into the hands of the region.   But, in
the matter of local administration, more functions seem to have
been acquired by the intermediate and lower Soviet organs.

The best index of the gradual devolution of powers to lower
Soviets was the growth of local budgets.   While all budgets
increased, the share of the regional budget in the total " local
budget " of the region declined everywhere between 1925-1926 and
1928-1929, except in the North Caucasian region, where it achieved
a modest rise of 4·5 per cent.[5]   The battle for rural district
budgets was won in Moscow in the spring of 1925.[6]   The decree
of the USSR of April 1926 on local finances prescribed a system
of budgets for districts, rural districts and urban Soviets (rural
Soviets were still excluded);   these were to be considered the
" fundamental local budgets ", the higher local budgets (i.e.
those of region, department and county) being " regulating

---

[1] S"ezdy Sovetov v Dokumentakh, iii (1960), 140-141 ;   Enukidze observed
that the change " maintained the link of the highest organ of the USSR with the
lower congresses of Soviets ", but offered no further explanation (SSSR: 4
S"ezd Sovetov (1927), pp. 582-583).
[2] Pravda, September 25, 1927.
[3] II Sessiya Vserossiiskogo Tsentral'nogo Ispolnitel'nogo Komiteta XIII
Sozyva (1928), pp. 527-528.
[4] III Sessiya Vserossiiskogo Tsentral'nogo Ispolnitel'nogo Komiteta XIII
Sozyva (1928), No. 18, pp. 8-9.
[5] Voprosy Ekonomicheskogo Raionoiovaniya SSSR, ed. G. Krzhizhanovsky
(1957), pp. 328-329 ; the " local budget " was the total of all budgets below
republican level.
[6] See Socialism in One Country, 1924–1926, Vol. 2, pp. 460-461.

budgets ".[1] Conditions on the spot made it uncertain how far these intentions would be realized in practice. A report on 15 rural districts in the province of Saratov in the autumn of 1926 showed that only eight of these had " real " budgets of their own; few rural districts had any revenues beyond the tax receipts assigned to them. Worse still, " inability to keep accounts and sometimes a flagrantly criminal attitude to financial resources " were described as " the plague spot of our rural economy ". In some places, teachers' wages were six months in arrears, and fears were expressed of a " breakdown in the whole rural district economy ".[2]

Though improvement was precarious and patchy, local budgets increased rapidly in the ensuing years. Between 1925-1926 expenditure borne on local budgets almost doubled. The largest item was social and cultural expenditure (i.e. health and education): this doubled during the period. Expenditure on the national economy increased more than two-and-a-half times, while administrative expenses remained fairly stable. A large and increasing share of revenue (more than half from 1926-1927 onwards) came from the state budget, whether in the form of direct subventions or by way of deductions allowed to the local authorities from state taxes collected, or from state loans subscribed, in their area; local revenues, including local taxes and receipts from economic enterprises, increased more slowly.[3] How far this comparatively orderly picture of a working budgetary system corresponded to the infinitely varying conditions of life in the Soviet countryside in the nineteen-twenties can hardly be judged. Local Soviet organs handled increasingly large sums for a variety of purposes. But the bulk of these funds was received by them from higher republican or regional authorities, to whom they were responsible; except in a formal sense, they did not have independent budgets of their own. The net result of the changes in local government in these years was to enlarge the functions, and enhance the importance, of the lower Soviet organs, but at the same time to increase their dependence on the central authorities.

The extent of the power and functions exercised by local

[1] See *Socialism in One Country, 1924–1926*, Vol. 2, pp. 464-465; a corresponding decree of the RSFSR was issued in November 1926 (*Sobranie Uzakonenii*, 1926, No. 92, art. 668. For the pressure for village Soviet budgets see pp. 256-259 below.

[2] *Izvestiya*, October 30, 1926.   [3] See Table No. 60, p. 483 below.

Soviets varied enormously, and formal enactments are an uncertain guide to what happened on the spot. In April 1925, limited legislative powers were formally conferred by decree of the RSFSR on rural district and district executive committees ; among the taxes which local authorities were permitted to levy on their own account were taxes on buildings, on freight traffic by rail or water, and on turnover in local markets.[1] A decree of the RSFSR of June 28, 1926, purported to systematize the powers of rural district and district executive committees, and of urban and village Soviets, to issue binding orders and regulations : these were confined mainly to emergencies and elementary necessities, fires, epidemics, sanitary regulations etc.[2] Emergency powers had already been conferred even on village Soviets, which continued, with or without authorization, to impose labour service for necessary local work.[3] The central authorities, especially Narkomfin, tenaciously resisted every extension of the powers of local organs whose competence was not unreasonably suspect.[4] In 1926 the Sovnarkom of the RSFSR was said to have annulled rights granted by the North Caucasian regional authorities to district executive committees and village Soviets.[5] But the powers enjoyed and exercised *de facto* by local organs were determined by the habits and needs of the localities quite as much as by decrees handed down from Moscow; and the process of devolution continued.

In the spring of 1927, when the campaign for budgets for village Soviets was already gathering momentum,[6] a general review of the powers of local Soviet organs in the RSFSR was undertaken. Rabkrin prepared a draft statute " On the Rights and Obligations of Local Organs of Soviet Government " designed to systematize and extend their powers.[7] Basing itself on this

[1] For these decrees, see *Socialism in One Country, 1924–1926*, Vol. 2, p. 460 ; Rykov later attributed deficits in local budgets to the falling off of taxable private trade (*XLI Sobranie Upolnomochennykh Tsentrosoyuza* (1928), pp. 280-281).

[2] *Sobranie Uzakonenii, 1926*, No. 39, art. 304.

[3] See *Socialism in One Country, 1924–1926*, Vol. 2, pp. 310-311, 463-464.

[4] Critics continued to complain that orders issued by the local authorities were often ill-considered and unworkable, and did not " correspond to the tasks of current policy " (*Sovetskoe Stroitel'stvo*, No. 6(35), June 1929, p. 69).

[5] *III Sessiya Vserossiiskogo Tsentral'nogo Ispolnitel'nogo Komiteta XII Sozyva* (1926), p. 267.   [6] See pp. 256-258 below.   [7] *Izvestiya*, May 15, 1927.

project, the TsIK of the RSFSR issued on July 23, 1927, a decree
which was not mandatory, but constituted a programme or directive for future action. It sought to define the powers of legislation
and enforcement to be exercised by Soviet organs, and to extend
their budgetary rights. The decree was said by a commentator to
" provide a firm economic and juridical basis for the activity of
local organs, and thereby create prerequisites for the active participation of the masses in administration and for a successful struggle
to improve and simplify the state apparatus ".[1] Three months
later a formal statute of the RSFSR was issued defining the powers
of district or rural district executive committees and of urban and
village Soviets. District and rural district executive committees
were entitled to issue obligatory decrees to ensure order and security and the protection of public property, sanitary measures, and
the regulation of trade and markets. Soviets of towns with a
population not exceeding 5000 enjoyed the same rights as district
executive committees ; but this did not apparently apply to village
Soviets. For infringements of these enactments district and rural
district executive committees could impose fines not exceeding
three rubles or five days' forced labour, village Soviets fines of one
ruble or two days' forced labour.[2]

The way was now clear for the promulgation by the RSFSR of
a formal statute of regional, department and district executive
committees with a similar, though less elaborate, statute of provincial, county and rural district organs in provinces which had
not yet undergone the process of regionalization ; these were
adopted by the TsIK of the RSFSR on April 6, 1928. The chain
of subordination was clearly laid down. The congress of Soviets
at each level was convened by the executive committee of the level
immediately above it ; and an executive committee had the power

---

[1] *Sobranie Uzakonenii, 1927*, No. 79, art. 533 ; *Sovetskoe Stroitel'stvo*, No.
12(17), December 1927, p. 68. It was " not an administrative act, but had a
directive character " (*ibid*. p. 58).

[2] *Sobranie Uzakonenii, 1927*, No. 120, art. 812 ; the decree is dated
November 21, 1927, but according to *Sovetskoe Stroitel'stvo*, No. 12(17),
December 1927, p. 130, was adopted by the presidium of TsIK on October 24,
1927. It had been under discussion since June 1926 (*ibid*. No. 1(18), January
1928, p. 45). Further decrees of the USSR of January 4, 1928 (*Sobranie
Zakonov, 1928*, No. 5, art. 42) and of the RSFSR of April 30, 1928 (*Sobranie
Uzakonenii, 1928*, No. 50, art. 379) elaborated these provisions in complicated
and probably quite unrealistic detail.

to annul or suspend any decision of a lower executive committee or congress of Soviets. Delegates to department (okrug) congresses of Soviets were to be elected by urban and factory Soviets in the ratio of one to 1000 electors, and by district congresses of Soviets in the ratio of one to 5000 inhabitants. Smaller towns, but not towns which were department capitals, also sent delegates to district congresses of Soviets. Regional executive committees were entitled to extend special rights to village Soviets covering more than 3000 inhabitants and having independent budgets.[1] An article in *Izvestiya* explained that one of the purposes of the statute was to make local Soviet organs responsible to the regional Soviet executive committee, and to strengthen the authority of the regions in questions of economic policy and trade.[2] But even in the RSFSR this apparently uniform system was not effective, and exhibited wide differences of practice at the lower levels. In the Ural region the department was said never to have become more important than the old county. In the North Caucasian region, and also apparently in the Middle and Lower Volga regions and in Siberia, the department was the pivot of the whole structure.[3] In the Ukrainian and White Russian SSRs the department never became important, and the district was the effective unit of administration.[4] Most of the autonomous republics dispensed with the department and were content with the district (sometimes called the " canton ") and the village Soviet as subordinate units.[5] In the Transcaucasian, Uzbek and Turkmen republics lower Soviets (with some notable exceptions, such as the urban Soviets of Baku, Samarkand and Tashkent[6]) remained embryonic or non-existent throughout the nineteen-twenties. The *rapporteur* at a

---

[1] *Sobranie Uzakonenii, 1928*, No. 70, art. 503; No. 94, art. 606; for the discussion of these decrees see *II Sessiya Vserossiiskogo Tsentral'nogo Ispolnitel'-nogo Komiteta XIII Sozyva* (1928), pp. 360-452. On one point the statute corrected an inadvertent error in the constitution of the RSFSR, which prescribed for elections from urban Soviets a ratio of one deputy to 1000 inhabitants (instead of electors); urban Soviet elections had always been based on place of employment, not place of residence.

[2] *Izvestiya*, March 30, 1928.

[3] O. Konstantinov, *USSR po Raionam: Severnyi Kavkaz* (1928), pp. 36-37; S. Trapeznikov, *Istoricheskii Opyt KPSS* (1965), p. 67; *XVI S'ezd Vsesoyuznoi Kommunisticheskoi Partii (B)* (1931), pp. 116-117.

[4] *Sovetskoe Stroitel'stvo*, No. 5-6(10-11), May–June 1927, pp. 28-29.

[5] *Voprosy Ekonomicheskogo Raionirovaniya*, ed. G. Krzhizhanovsky (1957), p. 322.   [6] See pp. 267-268 below.

conference of heads of organization sections of executive committees of autonomous republics and regions held in May 1928 declared emphatically that " *in districts with a native population the only task at present is to organize the Soviets themselves* ".[1] But nowhere had the intermediate Soviet organs, between the republican or regional organizations above and the village or urban Soviets below, any substantial elective or representative character. Where they existed at all, they were convenient links in an administrative chain, but never exercised any independent function.[2]

Below the level of autonomous national republics and regions, provision was made for national minorities in the form of national departments (okrugs) and national districts (raions) as well as of national village Soviets.   While the eastern non-Slav peoples of the USSR were probably the most extensive beneficiaries of these arrangements, the principle applied to all sufficiently compact minority groups.   In the RSFSR, the ethnographically varied Middle Volga region included one (Mordvin) national department, 22 national districts and 1187 national village Soviets.   The Chita department of the Far Eastern region included two Buryat-Mongol national districts.   The Central Black-Earth region included several Ukrainian national departments, districts and village

---

[1] *Izvestiya*, May 23, 1928.

[2] The following totals of intermediate units were officially recorded on January 1, 1929:

	RSFSA	Ukr. SSR	White Russian SSR	ZSFSR	Uzbek SSR	Turkmen SSR
Departments (Okruga)	115	40	8	—	10	3
Districts	1618	584	101	—	89	34
Counties	143	—	—	49	6	—
Rural Districts	1405	—	—	150	40	—

The average population of a department in the RSFSR at this date was 583,888 and of a district 44,814, but this covered variations, depending mainly on population densities, of from 1,013,340 and 62,622 respectively in the Central Black-Earth region to 230,799 and 26,759 in the Far Eastern region (*Administrativno-Territorial'noe Delenie SSSR* (8th ed. 1929), (pp. 12, 21). In 1930 the department in the RSFSR was abolished, leaving the district as the major unit of administration within the region ; the other Union republics, where the department had never been an effective unit, presumably followed suit.

Soviets.[1]   In the North Caucasian region, which included seven national districts, expenditure on national minorities was said in 1926 to have increased three or three-and-a-half times in the past three years, with a consequent diminution of national tensions.[2] In the parts of the region inhabited by Cossacks so-called " horde (stanitsa) Soviets " took the place of village Soviets, and were apparently active and efficient ; the Cossack Soviet covered a larger population than the normal village Soviet, and was said " to resemble . . . in the scope of its work a rural district executive committee ".[3] The fourteenth All-Russian Congress of Soviets in May 1929 advocated a further extension of national administrative units " in localities inhabited by national minorities ".[4] In the Ukrainian SSR, 872 national Soviets — Russian, German, Polish and Jewish — existed in 1926–1927, and an increase was planned for the two following years ; in the White Russian SSR, a total of 36 national Soviets in 1926 increased to 66 — Russian, Ukrainian, Polish, Lettish and Jewish — in 1927.   In the Ukraine 56 Jewish national village Soviets existed in 1926–1927, and 89 were planned for 1928–1929 ; in White Russia 18 existed in 1926 and 23 in 1928.[5] The main purpose of these national minority units — the transaction of business in the national language — was at first imperfectly fulfilled ; formidable obstacles must have been encountered. But it was claimed in 1929 that " in this respect also achievements are now substantial ".[6]

Proposals were frequently discussed for the creation of a larger autonomous Jewish national unit, though such proposals conformed imperfectly to the normal pattern, owing both to the territorial dispersal of the Jewish minority and to the fact that no national unit which was or could be contemplated would accommodate more than a fraction of the Jewish minority in the USSR.   On September 4, 1926, moved perhaps by symptoms of a recrudescence of popular anti-Semitism,[7] the central bureau of Jewish sections of

---

[1] These examples are quoted from *RSFSR : Ot S"ezda k S"ezdu (Aprel' 1927–Mai 1929)* (1929), p. 16.

[2] *III Sessiya Vserossiiskogo Tsentral'nogo Ispolnitel'nogo Komiteta XII Sozyva* (1926), pp. 265-266.

[3] *Ibid.* pp. 294-297 ; a large stanitsa might comprise 10,000 or 15,000 inhabitants (*ibid.* p. 267).   [4] *S"ezdy Sovetov v Dokumentakh*, iv, i (1962), 138-139.

[5] *SSSR : God Raboty Pravitel'stva, 1927–28* (1929), p. 35.

[6] *SSSR : Ot S"ezda k S"ezdu (Aprel' 1927–Mai 1929)* (1929), p. 120.

[7] See pp. 395-398 below.

the party adopted a resolution on " the desirability of establishing an autonomous Jewish territory ". The resolution included a warning against " a nationalist inflation of Jewish territorial autonomy ", and denounced the bourgeois nationalist aspirations of Zionism ; the end in view was to make " the Jewish poor a part of the universal cause of socialist construction ".[1] This policy secured the influential support of Kalinin who, in a speech of November 17, 1926, attributed the drive for the settlement of Jewish workers on the land primarily to " economic necessity ", but also to " the wish to maintain one's nationality ". He went on :

> The Jewish people faces a great task, that of preserving its nationality; and this requires the transformation of a considerable part of the Jewish population into a compactly settled agricultural peasantry numbering at least several hundred thousand. Only thus can the Jewish masses hope for the survival of their nationality.[2]

This unexpected intervention led to a controversial debate at the conference of party Jewish sections which met in the following month ; advocates of territorial autonomy clashed sharply with those Jewish communists who, looking forward to the total assimilation of all nationalities into an international socialist community, openly criticized Kalinin's speech, and rejected any solution that encouraged and perpetuated Jewish nationalism.[3] The policy of territorial autonomy which temporarily prevailed had from the first less than wholehearted support from influential sectors of the Jewish community and from the Soviet authorities. In 1927 a small Jewish " national district ", peopled mainly by Jewish settlers, was organized in the Kherson department of the Ukraine, near the mouth of the Dnieper.[4] Other Jewish colonies

---

[1] Quoted from a Yiddish source in S. Schwarz, *The Jews in the Soviet Union* (Syracuse, 1951), p. 121 ; for the Jewish sections see p. 393 below.

[2] *Izvestiya*, November 25, 1927.

[3] For quotations from an incomplete Yiddish record of the debate see S. Schwarz, *The Jews in the Soviet Union* (Syracuse, 1951), pp. 122-128.

[4] According to a report published a year later, it had a population of over 16,000 of whom 85 per cent were Jews, comprising 4 old Jewish settlements, and 22 settlements of new immigrants. It included 7 village Soviets, 6 of them Jewish, 1 Ukrainian, and had not only a district executive committee (RIK), but a district congress of Soviets. The original 20 party members or candidates had increased to 31 party members and 23 candidates ; Komsomol members numbered 204. Leasing of land and hiring of labour were prevalent, but steps

were settled in the southern Ukraine and in the Crimean ASSR;
some of these had " national " village Soviets. But, in the restricted area available, none of them was of significant size or
acquired national district status.

A more ambitious project was now under way. In the summer
of 1927 a mission from Komzet surveyed the large, remote and
sparsely inhabited region of Birobijan in the Far East, and pronounced it suitable, after preparatory clearing to·make it fit for
cultivation, for Jewish settlement.[1] The promotion of migration
to the Far East was a matter of general concern at this period,[2]
and was not unconnected with growing political and military
apprehensions about the Far Eastern situation. On March 28,
1928, the presidium of TsIK of the USSR assigned to Komzet " for
the needs of mass settlement by Jewish toilers " free lands in the
Birobijan district on the Amur river in the Far Eastern region.
After making provision for the organization of the prospective
migrants, the decree ended with a declaration that, in the event of
favourable results of this settlement, " the possibility of the formation on the territory of the said district of a Jewish national
administrative-territorial unit " would be kept in view.[3] Di-
manshtein, long the most prominent spokesman for Jewish
interests in the party, cautiously commented that the project was
designed " not for any kind of nationalist purposes, from which we
are far removed, but for concrete goals connected with socialist
construction in our country ".[4] Lack of preparations on the spot,
and lack of enthusiasm among its promoters, made the project a

had been taken to prevent " strong " settlers and *kulaks* from monopolizing free
land.   Of 17 kolkhozy 3 were *artels*, 9 machine-tractor societies and 5 TOZy;
of members of kolkhozy 65 per cent belonged to committees of poor peasants.
The picture drawn is of a fairly prosperous community with the number of
cattle and pigs increasing and some specialized fruit-growing.   National
separatism and anti-Semitism were hopefully said to be on the wane (*Sovetskoe
Stroitel'stvo*, No. 10(27), October 1928, pp. 107-118).

[1] S. Schwarz, *The Jews in the Soviet Union* (Syracuse, 1951), pp. 174-175;
for Komzet see Vol. 1, p. 933. The plan must have been mooted as early as 1926
when Smidovich, the president of Komzet, told a Jewish-American visitor that
he regarded Siberia as too remote for Jewish settlement (J. N. Rosenberg, *On the
Steppes* (N.Y. 1927), p. 24).

[2] See Vol. 1, p. 931.

[3] *Sovetskoe Stroitel'stvo*, No. 4(21), April 1928, pp. 63-64.

[4] Quoted in S. Baron, *The Russian Jew under Tsars and Soviets* (N.Y. 1964),
p. 231.

dismal failure;[1] and, though Birobijan in 1934 acquired the constitutional status of an autonomous region,[2] it never became an effective Jewish national unit.

An extreme example of the difficulty of setting up organs of local administration in the remoter regions of the Soviet Union was provided by the so-called " small nationalities of the north ".[3] The Komi, occupying the north-eastern corner of European Russia on the fringes of Siberia, formed an autonomous region, and the Yakuts in the north-eastern sector of Siberia an autonomous republic, both within the RSFSR. Between them were to be found more than 20 separate tribes or peoples, some of them not numbering more than a few thousand, many of them nomadic, engaged mainly in hunting, fishing and reindeer-herding.[4] In 1924, after the abolition of the People's Commissariat of Nationalities,[5] the presidium of the TsIK of the RSFSR set up a " committee of the north ", whose function was " to assist in the planned organization of the small nationalities of the north in economic, in administrative and judicial, and in cultural and health matters ", and to assure them the equality of rights guaranteed by the constitution of the RSFSR.[6] In February 1925, the committee received a formal statute, Smidovich, an important party official, being appointed its president. Local committees subordinate to it were set up in Archangel, Tomsk, Irkutsk, Tobolsk, Krasnoyarsk and other administrative centres; these committees included representatives of the small nationalities.[7] One of the first tasks

---

[1] Catastrophic conditions in 1928–1929 are described in an article in *Sovetskoe Stroitel'stvo*, No. 5(46), May 1930, pp. 117-123.

[2] *Sobranie Uzakonenii, 1934*, No. 19, art. 114.

[3] For the difficulties of establishing Soviet machinery in other backward regions see *Socialism in One Country, 1924–1926*, Vol. 2, pp. 364-365.

[4] For an enumeration of the small northern nationalities based on the 1926 census see F. Lorimer, *The Population of the Soviet Union* (Geneva, 1946), p. 60; for a more up-to-date classified list see M. Sergeev, *Nekapitalisticheskii Put' Razvitiya Malykh Narodov Severa* (1955), pp. 227-228.

[5] See *The Bolshevik Revolution, 1917–1923*, Vol. 1, p. 285.

[6] *Sobranie Uzakonenii, 1924*, No. 57, art. 556. The full name was " committee for cooperation with the nationalities of the northern borderlands "; it should not be confused with the " committee for the northern sea route ", which was concerned with the opening of the Arctic route and development of trade.

[7] *Sobranie Uzakonenii, 1925*, No. 12, art. 79; No. 18, art. 113.

of these committees was the sending out of expeditions to collect information about these little known peoples.[1]

The result of these activities was the issue by the TsIK and Sovnarkom of the RSFSR on October 25, 1926, of what was described as " a temporary statute on the administration of the native peoples and tribes of the northern regions of the RSFSR ". It purported to provide an administrative framework for peoples " leading a wandering, nomad or semi-nomad way of life, occupied mainly in hunting, fishing and reindeer-herding, and also, in so far as they are not organized separately in special republics and regions, those leading a settled life and occupied in hunting sea mammals ". It included a list of the peoples concerned, who were to be found in Archangel province, in the Ural, Siberian and Far Eastern regions, in the Komi autonomous region and in the Yakut and Buryat-Mongol ASSRs. The system was copied from the local rural institutions established elsewhere. A tribal assembly and tribal Soviet replaced village *skhod* and village Soviet; the district native congress and executive committee replaced the normal district congress of Soviets and executive committee. Exceptions from these arrangements were allowed with the agreement of the committee of the north. One such exception was recorded in the statute; where no literate person was available, oral decisions of the tribal assembly and Soviet were recognized.[2] The word " temporary " in the title of the statute suggested some doubt of its finality. Conversion of primitive peoples from nomadic to settled life was always regarded as a civilizing mission, and a proper aim of Soviet policy.[3] Insistence on the tribal unit of administration, and the attempt to combine this with the territorial unit, was later renounced as an error. Tribal organization was a synonym for the authority of the tribal chief; it was now already in decay, and often gave place to the territorial unit — not, perhaps, without official encouragement. An article by

---

[1] M. Sergeev, *Nekapitalisticheskii Put' Razvitiya Malykh Narodov Severa* (1955), p. 227.   [2] *Sobranie Uzakonenii*, *1926*, No. 73, art. 575.

[3] A decree of the USSR of October 1, 1926, requested the TsIKs of the Union republics to allocate land to gypsies desirous of " going over to a settled way of life " (*Sobranie Zakonov*, *1926*, No. 67, art. 507); it was not till February 20, 1928, that the RSFSR issued a decree making the desired provision and passing on a similar request to the autonomous republics (*Sobranie Uzakonenii*, *1928*, No. 28, art. 203).

Smidovich of October 1928, said to be an expanded version of a
report approved by an enlarged plenum of the committee of the
north, argued strongly that the native peoples, in spite of nomadic
habits, had a keen sense of territorial demarcation, regarded certain
areas of land and water (for fishing) as their possession, and would
not trespass on those of other tribes. The next stage of development should therefore be territorial organization. Territory should
be assigned to tribal congresses of Soviets, and carefully delimited
from that of neighbouring peoples. Documents of entitlement to
" working utilization for their livelihood " of the assigned territory would then be issued to the native tribal executive committee
of Soviets by the regional executive committee.[1]

In the years between 1926 and 1929 either tribal or territorial
Soviets were apparently formed in most, but by no means all, of
these areas.[2] Between 1925 and 1930 participation of the population in elections to Soviets was said to have increased from 15-20
per cent to 40-50 per cent.[3] Resistance, whose extent and persistence it is difficult to measure, was offered by primitive native
populations to these unfamiliar arrangements. " Traditions of
obedience to the personal power of a tribal chief " made it difficult
to understand the very notions of election, collective decision and
self-government; any institution was personified in the absolute
power of its head. The admission of women to any kind of assembly was repugnant. At most the ban might be relaxed for a widow
who was head of a family. The creation, and the first steps, of any
new political institution had to be guided by Russian party workers;[4] and Soviets as organs of local administration in these remote
regions must have involved an unusually large element of make-
believe. But they were also part of a slow and immensely difficult
process of education, modernization and integration designed to
draw backward peoples into a more advanced economy and
society.

[1] *Sovetskoe Stroitel'stvo*, No. 10(27), October 1928, pp. 5-13.
[2] M. Sergeev, *Nekapitalisticheskii Put' Razvitiya Malykh Narodov Severa*
(1955), pp. 231-232, 237-239; this account, based on a wide range of published
and unpublished material, seems to be the best available. In a decree of
October 14, 1927 (see p. 235 below), " tundra and island Soviets " are mentioned as an alternative to tribal Soviets.
[3] *Ibid.* p. 245.
[4] *Ibid.* pp. 235-237.

The task of creating a judicial system was complicated not only by a clash, familiar in other backward territories of the Soviet Union, between native custom, notably in matters relating to marriage and the status of women, and the principles of Soviet law, but by inability or unwillingness to distinguish between administrative and judicial functions. A proposal to confer judicial rights on native Soviets was mooted by the committee of the north in the autumn of 1926, but resisted by Narkomyust; and in the following year a revised plan embodying various safeguards was introduced.[1] A ruling of the TsIK of the USSR of June 1, 1927, authorized as a temporary measure the entrusting of judicial functions to native administrative organs of the northern region. Local customs were to be applied " in so far as these do not contradict the principles of Soviet legislation ". Jurisdiction was to be both criminal and civil, but did not extend to major crimes or to matters concerning " infringement of the interests of the State ". An appeal was to be allowed to higher Soviet organs.[2] This decision was implemented by a decree of the RSFSR of October 14, 1927, which, with the same specified reservations, conferred judicial powers in certain regions on " native tribal (or tundra or island) Soviets " and on native Soviet executive committees. Proceedings were to be conducted publicly in the local language or dialect; decisions and sentences were to be recorded, as a general rule, in writing. Sentences of up to one year of forced labour could be pronounced, but a limitation was placed on heavier penalties; " measures involving torture, mutilation, beatings and insults to personal dignity " were " unconditionally prohibited ".[3] At first Russian judges sat with native assessors, and the work was gradually transferred to purely native organs. Things went easily when native customs were applied; but clashes occurred over such questions as women's rights and marriage customs. The right of appeal helped to sap the hitherto undisputed authority of tribal authorities.

It is easier to appreciate the good intentions behind these measures than to assess their effectiveness. The committee of

---

[1] *Sovetskoe Stroitel'stvo*, No. 8-9(13-14), August–September 1927, pp. 112-113.

[2] *Sobranie Zakonov, 1927*, No. 32, art. 330.

[3] *Sobranie Uzakonenii, 1927*, No. 111, art. 746.

the north at a session in March 1929 congratulated itself that its work was " getting on to steady, planned rails ", and spoke of an extension of " native Soviets ", of trading points and co-operatives, of medical services, and of budgets and rights of self-taxation for Soviet district committees.[1] A fairly realistic account later in the same year admitted that a majority of the population of the northern regions was still nomadic or semi-nomadic. The process of " Sovietization " had made slow progress : " many of these Soviets exist only in name, a large number of them depend exclusively on the work of their presidents ". Dealing with nomadic people, the Soviets had no clearly defined territory to administer ; even boundaries between departments, regions and republics often cut across tribal units. Throughout the area 125 schools with 3500 pupils were said to have been set up. Other recorded achievements are less impressive ; the establishment of peasant committees of mutual aid is likely to have remained an empty gesture. The general picture is of a search for new forms of economy and society, inculcated by measures which doubtless comprised education, persuasion and compulsion in varying proportions.[2]

(b) Land Community and Skhod

The one constituted authority in the countryside which had survived the revolution was that of the *mir* and of its traditional *skhod*. The *obshchina* or *mir*, commonly known in Soviet documents by the general term " land community ",[3] was the ancient association of peasant, originally serf, households of a given property or locality. The *skhod*, or village meeting of heads of households, was its organ.[4] After the emancipation of 1861, it took on certain public functions. It became collectively responsible for the collection and payment of taxes, and exercized powers of discipline over its members.[5] Apart from the collection of state taxes,

---

[1] *Izvestiya*, April 2, 1929.

[2] *Sovetskoe Stroitel'stvo*, No. 9(38), September 1929, pp. 106-118 ; for a later and more general account see M. Sergeev, *Nekapitalisticheskii Put' Razvitiya Malykh Narodov Severa* (1955), pp. 241-245.

[3] See Vol. 1, p. 119.

[4] See *Socialism in One Country, 1924-1926*, Vol. 2, p. 307, note 4.

[5] For a review of the functions of the *obshchina* in the period after 1861 see

the *mir* operated a system of " self-taxation "[1] for local purposes, and also had receipts from property and undertakings leased
or operated by it. Part of these revenues was used by the *mir* to
maintain services and administration; part was transferred for
similar purposes to the rural district budget.[2]

The first effect of the revolutions of 1917, bringing a sharp
reaction against the consolidated individual holdings of the Stoly-
pin reform, was to restore the authority of the *mir*.[3] The agrarian
code of 1922[4] made the public status of the *mir* quite explicit by
including three chapters (arts. 42-64) on the composition, the
administrative organs and the rights and obligations of " land
communities ". The *skhod* or assembly had the right to possess
" elective organs ", and to appoint a president and a secretary, as
well as a " plenipotentiary " (upolnomochennyi) to perform
necessary executive functions, though, where the boundaries of
the *mir* coincided with the territory of the village Soviet, these
functions could in fact be discharged by the Soviet. In practice,
the " plenipotentiary " (a pompous disguise for the *starosta*, or
elder, of the *mir*, who had existed from time immemorial, who
presided at meetings of the *skhod*, and whose title was still in
current use) was commonly appointed president of the village
Soviet, thus ensuring both conformity with the code and the
punctual execution by the Soviet of decisions of the *mir* or its
skhod.[5] When the TsIK of the RSFSR adopted the agrarian code
in October 1922, a delegate put in a *caveat* that the land community
must not be allowed to " replace the village Soviets or other
Soviet organs ".[6] The warning was justified by the sequel. In
the rivalry for effective control of local administration in the

---

Entsiklopedicheskii Slovar', ed. Brokgaus-Efron, xxiv (1898), 216-221, and of the
village community which was commonly, but not always, coterminous with the
obshchina, *ibid.* xxix (1900), 377-385 ; one of the recurrent themes of Stepniak,
The Russian Peasantry (1888), was the encroachment of the central government
on the traditional self-government of the *mir*.

[1] See Note I, pp. 464-468 below.

[2] In 1905 nearly 40 per cent of the revenue was transferred to rural district
budgets (*Vestnik Finansov*, No. 4, 1927, pp. 58-60).

[3] This process is described in detail in P. Pershin, *Agrarnaya Revolyutsiya v
Rossii*, ii (1966), 221-337.

[4] See *The Bolshevik Revolution, 1917–1923*, Vol. 2, p. 296.

[5] *Vlast' Sovetov*, No. 44, November 1, 1925, p. 17.

[6] *IV Sessiya Vserossiiskogo Tsentral'nogo Ispolnitel'nogo Komiteta IX
Sozyva*, No. 2 (Oct. 26, 1922), p. 3.

countryside between the village Soviet, backed by the tenuous resources of party and governmental power, and the *mir*, rooted in the immemorial habits of the peasant community, nearly all the advantages were at first on the side of the latter. The statute of village Soviets of October 1924[1] had spoken, optimistically but unrealistically, of the subordination of the *skhod* to the Soviet. Supervision over the proceedings of the *mir* was entrusted by the agrarian code of 1922 to the rural district executive committee. This marked its status as a public body, but avoided subordinating it to the new-fangled village Soviet, at this period rarely an effective organ. These conditions testified to the continued predominance of the *skhod* in local affairs. As late as 1927, " rural district executive committees again and again refer important questions of local economic life to the *skhods* over the head of the village Soviets ".[2]

The issue was complicated by the reduction in the number of village Soviets, and the " enlargement " of the area and population covered by each, which had gone on spasmodically since 1922.[3] This gradually broke down the territorial identity of the village Soviet and land community or *mir*, and the interchangeability of officers and functions between them, which had been contemplated in the 1922 agrarian code. By 1928 an average of four land communities were included in a village Soviet;[4] and various devices were in use to meet this discrepancy. Sometimes the " plenipotentiaries " of all the land communities in the area were elected deputies to the village Soviet.[5] Article 45 of the 1922 code authorized " unions " of land communities. These seem to have been uncommon. But one case was quoted from Saratov province in which a number of land communities had formed a union and completely taken over the functions of the village Soviet.[6] In

[1] See *Socialism in One Country, 1924–1926*, Vol. 2, p. 322.

[2] *Izvestiya Tsentral'nogo Komiteta VKP(B)*, No. 29(202), July 30, 1927, p. 3 ; the supervision of the rural district over the *mir* was, however, a dead letter (M. Rezunov, *Sel'skie Sovety i Zemel'nye Obshchestva* (1928), p. 47) and was abrogated in 1927 (see p. 255 below).

[3] See *Socialism in One Country, 1924–1926*, Vol. 2, pp. 297-298.

[4] *3 Sessiya Tsentral'nogo Ispolnitel'nogo Komiteta Soyuza SSR 4 Sozyva* (1928), p. 751 ; *4 Sessiya Tsutal'nogo Ispolnitel'nogo Komiteta Soyuza SSR 4 Sozyva* (1928), No. 12, p. 22.

[5] *Vlast' Sovetov*, No. 23-24, June 17, 1928, pp. 40-41.

[6] *Sovetskoe Stroitel'stvo*, No. 4(21), April 1928, p. 35.

general, the "enlargement" of the village Soviets, by empha-
sizing their separateness from the *mir*, and by making more tenuous and more remote their direct contacts with the mass of the
population, seems to have enhanced the independence and importance of the land community and its *skhod*.[1]

This trend the policy-makers were determined to reverse.
The plan for local administration at the lowest levels in the
countryside, which had taken shape by 1926 in the minds of the
central authorities in Moscow, aimed at replacing the *mir* by the
village Soviet as the effective public authority in the countryside,
and transforming the *skhod* into a Soviet organ — the smallest
unit in the Soviet administrative structure. The struggle to bring
about these results, which continued for at least three years in varying conditions and with slight success, was symptomatic of the rift
between the thinking of party leaders and constitutional lawyers
in Moscow and the traditional practices of the countryside, and of
the difficulty of establishing points of contact between them. The
plan called for two institutional changes. In the first place, the
skhod in its capacity as the general assembly of the *mir* must be
transformed into a citizen assembly exercising public functions;
or, alternatively, a clear distinction must be drawn between the
skhod when acting as general assembly of the *mir* and the *skhod* as
general assembly of citizens. Secondly, the *skhod* in the latter
sense must be placed in a position of subordination to, and dependence on, the village Soviet as the administrative unit immediately
above it. In practice, these processes merged into one another,
and presented the same problem. The exaltation of the Soviet and
the transformation of the *skhod* could be effected only by pressure
from the higher authorities and in defiance of all the resources and
traditions of the *mir*.

The struggle began in earnest when in August 1926 a draft
statute for the *skhod* was issued by the TsIK of the RSFSR for
purposes of discussion. It described the *skhod* as " a general
assembly of citizens ", thereby plainly distinguishing it from the
traditional *skhod*. The *skhod* was to be convened by the village
Soviet, to which it was made subordinate and responsible for its

---

[1] See *Socialism in One Country, 1924–1926*, Vol. 2, pp. 354-356.

decisions.[1] These proposals provoked a formidable debate in the press. The *mir* enjoyed a substantial measure of support in party, and still more in Soviet, circles.[2] On August 17, 1926, the Narkomzem of the RSFSR issued an instruction quoting the agrarian code to show that " the land community is in no way subject to control by the village Soviet ", and that any attempt by the Soviet to call the *mir* to account was unconstitutional.[3] A leading article in the peasant newspaper argued strongly against the subordination of the land community to the village Soviet in agrarian questions.[4] On the other hand, the journal of Narkomvnudel published a forthright article, attacking the hypothesis that the village Soviet and the *skhod*, as the organ of the *mir*, had equal rights. The village Soviet was the organ of government; the *skhod* had merely the same status as peasant committees of mutual aid, the Ukrainian komnezamozhi, or the cooperatives. The article carried, however, an editorial note that questions of the competence of the *skhod* and the land community were still " open to discussion ".[5] A common complaint against the draft was that the definition of relations between village Soviet and land community was not sufficiently precise.[6] The view that wider powers should be given to the *skhod* clashed with the view that more control over the *skhod* by the village Soviet was desirable.[7] The ambition of the reformers was " to thrust the *kulak* out of his last stronghold in the countryside, and to transform the *skhod* into a regularly functioning mass organization of poor and middle peasants ".[8] The debate was raised from republican to Union level; and the statute which emerged in the form of a decree of the USSR of March 14, 1927, represented on paper a major victory for those who sought to subordinate the *skhod* to the village Soviet. Protocols of the *skhod* were to be submitted to the Soviet, which might within a week

[1] The draft was announced in *Bednota*, August 13, 1926, and published *ibid.* August 29, 1926.   [2] See Vol. 1, pp. 122-126.

[3] *Na Agrarnom Fronte*, No. 5, 1928, p. 68; another statement by Narkomzem in the same sense is quoted in M. Rezunov, *Sel'skie Sovety i Zemel'nye Obshchestva* (1928), pp. 52-53.   [4] *Bednota*, September 11, 1926.

[5] *Vlast' Sovetov*, No. 32-33, August 15, 1926, pp. 3-4.

[6] *Ibid.* No. 39, September 26, 1926, pp. 3-6; No. 42, October 17, 1926, p. 4; No. 48, November 28, p. 18.

[7] *Ibid.* No. 47, November 21, 1926, pp. 3-4; No. 48, November 28, 1926, p. 19.

[8] *Sovetskoe Stroitel'stvo*, No. 5, December 1926, p. 47.

protest to the higher Soviet authority against any decision of the
skhod and suspend its operation; decisions that were accepted
were carried out by the village Soviet. The *skhod* was referred to
in the decree as the "general assembly of citizens", and was
carefully differentiated from the "general assembly of members
of the land community" functioning under the agrarian code;
each was explicitly forbidden to trespass on the functions of the
other. Otherwise relations between the two assemblies or *skhods*
were veiled in obscurity.[1]

The attempt to establish two separate *skhods*, or to draw a
constitutional distinction between two different capacities of the
skhod, was too far removed from common sense to be comprehensible to a peasant community, and proved a fiasco. The situation
was diagnosed in December 1927 by an official commentator:

> There is not even a distinction between the very conception
> of "the *skhod* of the land community" and the *skhod* as a
> general assembly of citizens. What exists is simply the *skhod*,
> at which all village questions, questions of cultivation, and,
> therefore, of tenure, as well as administrative and cultural
> questions, are decided.[2]

The *skhods* of citizens, wrote another commentator, "for the most
part do not meet, and most frequently of all are replaced by the
skhods of the land communities ".[3] In a majority of villages, a
year after the decree, no delimitation had taken place.[4] The issue

---

[1] *Sobranie Zakonov, 1927*, No. 51, art. 333 ; for this decree see also *Socialism
in One Country, 1924-1926*, Vol. 2, p. 355.

[2] *Izvestiya*, December 15, 1927 (art. by Karp); the words were repeated
textually without acknowledgment by another writer in *Sovetskoe Stroitel'stvo*,
No. 5-6(22-23), May–June 1928, p. 69.

[3] *Derevenskii Kommunist*, No. 5-6(77-78), March 14, 1928, p. 28.

[4] M. Rezunov, *Sel'skie Sovety i Zemel'nye Obshchestva* (1928), p. 24; the
statute was admitted not to have "brought about any radical change in the
desired direction " (*Na Agrarnom Fronte*, No. 5, 1928, p. 68). The journal of
Narkomyust, in two articles of 1929 deploring the failure to establish "revolutionary legality " in the countryside (*Ezhenedel'nik Sovetskoi Yustitsii*, No. 25,
June 29, 1927, pp. 758-761 ; No. 26, July 6, 1927, pp. 787-790) drew a lurid
picture of administrative chaos. Land communities practised "systematic
intrusion into the sphere of village Soviets and general assemblies (*skhods*) ",
dealing with " a series of administrative, economic and other questions entirely
unconnected with questions of land utilization and consolidation ". *Skhods*
dealt with questions pertaining either to the land communities or to the village

of the dual status of the *skhod* first became acute over questions of membership. Before the revolution the *skhod* was an assembly of heads of *dvors*. Article 52 of the agrarian code specifically laid down that all members of a " land community " over the age of 18 were members of the *skhod*; but this rule, though basic to all Soviet constituent bodies, was in many — probably in most — regions ignored by the *mir*, where the " dominant rôle " was still played by the head of the household, or, if he was incapacitated, by his eldest son.[1] The tension was aggravated by a further anomaly of membership. In 1925 — and increasingly from 1926 onwards — the attempt was made to interpret strictly the constitutional rules on the disfranchisement of employers of hired labour, traders and other similar categories;[2] and the decree of March 14, 1927, prescribed that only men and women " who under the constitution of the USSR enjoy electoral rights " could be members of the *skhod* established under the decree. The incompatibility of Soviet principles with those of the *mir* was starkly revealed, since it would have been unthinkable to exclude from the *skhod* any well-to-do peasant who played a prominent rôle in the *mir*.[3]

The drafting of the General Principles of the Utilization and Consolidation of Land introduced a fresh complication. The proposal was made to confer membership of the *skhod* on *batraks*, smiths and rural artisans, even when these held no land. This proposal was endorsed, after some debate, by a meeting of peasant delegates to the TsIK of the RSFSR in November 1926,[4] and was embodied in art. 48 of the final version of the principles two

Soviets; " in particular, they do not shrink from giving directives to the village Soviet, sometimes treating it as their own subordinate technical apparatus ". All three organs sometimes arrogated to themselves the functions of the courts (*ibid.* No. 25, June 29, 1927, p. 760).

[1] *Izvestiya*, December 15, 1927; *Na Agrarnom Fronte*, No. 5, 1928, p. 64; M. Rezunov, *Sel'skie Sovety i Zemel'nye Obshchestva* (1928), p. 41, which concludes that, " in a majority of cases, the *skhod* is an assembly of heads of households ", and that " young people and women very rarely appear at the *skhod* ".

[2] See *Socialism in One Country, 1924–1926*, Vol. 2, pp. 328-331, and pp. 278-280 below.

[3] An article in *Vlast' Sovetov*, No. 21, May 23, 1926, p. 5, made the point that any increase in the number of disfranchised persons emphasized the difference between the village Soviet and the *skhod*.

[4] *Na Agrarnom Fronte*, No. 11-12, 1926, pp. 127-130.

years later.[1] Yet the admission of such persons was fundamentally repugnant to the traditions of the *skhod* as an assembly of households holding land in the *mir*. The directives issued by the party central committee on October 20, 1927, for the drafting of the general principles contained stipulations that " proletarian and semi-proletarian elements in the countryside (*batraks*, shepherds, smiths etc.) " should be voting members of the " general assembly (*skhod*) " of the *mir*, and that persons disqualified as electors in Soviet institutions should also lose their vote in the *skhod*;[2] and the second demand was echoed in the resolution of the fifteenth party congress two months later.[3] But these pronouncements remained ineffective. So long as the prevalent form of land-holding for the vast majority of peasants was through the *mir*, and so long as official attitudes to the *mir* were ambivalent, party and Soviet attempts to dictate rules of membership and voting procedures to the traditional *skhod* were abortive. Neither of the two alternative solutions — to force the traditional *skhod* into the mould of a Soviet institution, or to set up a Soviet *skhod* side by side with the existing institution — was really practicable. The Gordian knot could not be unravelled.

The issue which underlay all discussions about the status of the *mir* and of its *skhod* and their relation to the village Soviet was the class struggle and attitude to be adopted to the well-to-do peasant. The *mir*, as a community of land-holding households, was naturally dominated by its prosperous and successful members, and was unlikely to conduct its affairs in a manner detrimental to their interests. The peasant newspaper in the summer of 1926 had called the *skhod* " the traditional hide-out (lavilka) of a handful of active peasants, mostly the richest of them ", and had asked : " Where better than in the *skhod* can one watch the struggle and the oppressive action of the rich? "[4] The *starosta* or " plenipotentiary " who executed its decisions was normally a well-to-do peasant or

---

[1] *4 Sessiya Tsentral'nogo Ispolnitel'nogo Komiteta Soyuza SSR 4 Sozyva* (1928), No. 12, pp. 73-77 ; for the principles see Vol. 1, pp. 106-108.
[2] For these directives see Vol. 1, p. 107.
[3] *KPSS v Rezolyutsiyakh* (1954), ii, 487.
[4] *Bednota*, August 21, 1926.

" even a *kulak* ", and " protected the interests of the *kulaks* ".[1]
At any rate down to 1928 self-taxation imposed by the *skhod* was
normally non-progressive and levied equally on rich and poor.[2]
Every attempt to modify the membership of the *skhod* by excluding those whom Soviet legislation sought to disqualify or by admitting landless *batraks* or artisans was obstinately resisted. At
the debate on the general principles in the Communist Academy in
1926 one speaker described the *skhod* as " a primitive moot or, if
you like, parliament in which the class struggle is conducted on the
subject of land distribution " ; another spoke of the *mir* as " very
often wholly and entirely in the hands of *kulaks* ".[3] It was " the
wealthy and strong section of the peasantry " which was active in
the *skhod*.[4] Poor peasants rarely found it worth while to attend
the *skhod* ;[5] and the land communities were said to have ham-
pered the formation of groups of poor peasants.[6] A case was
quoted from Siberia in which *kulaks* had expelled poor peasants
from the *mir*, and had themselves infiltrated the village Soviet.[7]
" Hitherto ", exclaimed Molotov at the fifteenth party congress in
December 1927, " . . . when we have revitalized the Soviet, the
kulak laid hands on the land community, and tried to dig himself in there ".[8] Both in the western part of the Ukraine and in
White Russia land communities were weaker than in the RSFSR.[9]
But in the Ukraine they were accused of interfering in the work of

---

[1] *Vlest' Sovetov*, No. 21, May 27, 1928, p. 28.
[2] See Note I, pp. 464-468 below.
[3] *Na Agrarnom Fronte*, No. 9, 1926, pp. 96, 106.
[4] *Vlast' Sovetov*, No. 21, May 27, 1928, p. 29 ; for much evidence of the
predominance of well-to-do peasants in the land community and in the *skhod* see
M. Rezunov, *Sel'skie Sovety i Zemel'nye Obshchestva* (1928), pp. 35-40.
[5] *Vlast' Sovetov*, No. 18, May 6, 1928, p. 21. This appears to have been the
basis of constant complaints of poor attendance at the *skhod*, which sometimes
fell to 10 or 15 per cent of those qualified (*SSSR: 4 S"ezd Sovetov* (1927), pp.
466-467 ; *III Sessiya Vserossiiskogo Tsentral'nogo Komiteta XII Sozyva* (1926),
p. 298) ; for statistics of attendance compiled by the Rabkrin of the RSFSR see
M. Rezunov, *Sel'skie Sovety i Zemel'nye Obshchestva* (1928), p. 42.
[6] *Vlast' Sovetov*, No. 22, June 3, 1928, pp. 12-13 ; for the groups of poor
peasants see Note H, pp. 459-463 below.
[7] *Istoriya Sovetskogo Krest'yanstva i Kolkhoznogo Stroitel'stva v SSSR*
(1963), p. 319.
[8] *Pyatnadtsatyi S"ezd VKP(B)*, ii (1962), 1217.
[9] In White Russia the land communities were " young in comparison with
the RSFSR ", and presented " no great threat of becoming an obstacle to the
work of the Soviets " (*Sovetskoe Stroitel'stvo*, No. 8(25), August 1928, p. 74).

village Soviets in the interests of *kulaks* and well-to-do peasants ; and even in White Russia the *skhod* was sometimes said to annul or override the decision of a village Soviet.[1]

The political independence of the *mir* and its *skhod* was in part the product of its financial independence. Article 64 of the agrarian code of 1922 had recognized the land community as a juridical person capable of acquiring property and entering into contracts. What was traditionally regarded as the common property of the village was vested in the *mir* which, at a time when no village Soviet possessed an independent budget, derived its revenues from dues paid for the use of common lands, vegetable plots, forests, water-rights, or the services of the village bull, as well as from levies imposed on its members, and out of these revenues, and of the traditional system of self-taxation, defrayed the cost of essential public services. " The traditional belief in the *skhod* as the owner of the communal property of the village " prevented the village Soviets from taking over such minor rural economic enterprises as " mills, smithies etc. . . . ".[2] Above all the authority of the *skhod* was recognized by the peasant (and especially, no doubt, by the well-to-do peasant), who showed " a positive reaction to self-taxation " for such purposes as the building of schools and wells.[3] As pressure increased for the provision of social and cultural amenities in the villages, this task also fell, with the approval or acquiescence of the Soviet authorities, on the only local organ which disposed of funds and of means of raising them. On June 24, 1926, the Soviet executive committee of the North Caucasian region encouraged land communities to accumulate capital funds for " cultural, educational and other social purposes ", and provided that such funds were the "inde-

---

[1] *Ibid.* No. 2(19), February 1928, p. 28, No. 8(25), August 1928, p. 73 ; a report from the Ukraine quoted " examples where land communities, fallen under the influence of *kulaks*, undermined or sometimes annulled measures taken by village Soviets in defence of the interests of weak and poor peasants " (*ibid.* No. 12(17), December 1927, p. 19).

[2] M. Rezunov, *Sel'skie Sovety i Zemel'nye Obshchestva* (1928), pp. 9-22, gives a factual review, largely derived from local sources, of the confused and by no means uniform financial situation of the land communities ; the renting of land, followed by self-taxation, were the two largest sources of revenue of the land community (*ibid.* p. 12), though self-taxation is said to have been the major source in all but the largest communities (*Vlast' Sovetov*, No. 22, June 3, 1928, p. 21).

[3] *Sovetskoe Stroitel'stvo*, No. 5-6(22-23), May–June 1928, p. 155.

feasible property " of the community and could not be included in the village or regional budget.[1] Even when the village Soviets began by slow degrees, and with great variations in practice, to acquire budgets of their own,[2] their financial resources were insignificant in comparison with those of the *mir*. According to a rather vague statement of Enukidze at the fifteenth party congress in December 1927, the total annual budgets of " land communities and other unions of peasants " amounted to 80 or 100 million rubles, while those of the 2300 village Soviets which alone had budgets reached only a paltry 16 millions.[3] This state of affairs perpetuated the subordination of the Soviet to the *mir* and its organs, which was the precise opposite of what party and Soviet authorities at the centre had desired or contemplated. The *skhod* frequently voted subsidies for the upkeep and the services of the village Soviet, including the pay of its president and secretary.[4] Little distinction seemed to be made between the financial status and functions of the two organs :

> All kinds of compulsory levies continued to exist in the countryside ; they were taxes in their nature and were imposed by the local authorities. Moreover, local Soviets directly participated in the imposition of self-taxation, and questions of imposing various levies were usually discussed at the peasant meeting on the initiative of the local authorities.[5]

In the Volga German autonomous republic a combined village budget was established, involving a virtual amalgamation of *mir* and Soviet organs.[6] In Azerbaijan " some mingling of functions " occurred between *skhod* and village Soviet, so that " village Soviets

---

[1] *Izvestiya*, October 30, 1926 (art. by Kruglov).

[2] See *Socialism in One Country, 1924–1926*, Vol. 2, pp. 462-464.

[3] *Pyatnadtsatyi S'ezd VKP(B)*, ii (1962), 1246 ; for the amounts raised by " self-taxation " see Note I, pp. 464-468 below. For village Soviet budgets see pp. 256-258, and Table No. 62, p. 485 below.

[4] *Vlast' Sovetov*, No. 37, September 12, 1926, p. 24 ; *Sovetskoe Stroitel'stvo*, No. 2-3, February–March 1927, p. 107.

[5] *Vestnik Finansov*, No. 4, 1927, pp. 60-61.

[6] *Sovetskoe Stroitel'stvo*, No. 5-6(22-23), May–June 1928, p. 10. By a decree of the republic of July 21, 1926, income from free lands was transferred to the village Soviet budget (*Na Agrarnom Fronte*, No. 5, 1928, pp. 75-76) ; a spokesman of the republic hailed with satisfaction this diversion of local revenues from the *mir* to the village Soviet (*Vlast' Sovetov*, No. 30, July 24, 1927, p. 9).

sometimes try to solve questions connected with the self-taxation of the peasantry ".[1] But the general picture was fairly summed up in a report prepared in 1927 for the Orgburo by the Institute of Soviet Construction of the Communist Academy :

> *The economically independent land community takes the village Soviet under its guardianship.* The material dependence of the village Soviet on the land community puts a brake on the further development and revitalization of the work of the Soviet and of its sections, and on the other hand is the basis for the taking over of the work of the village Soviet by the land community *skhod*.[2]

As late as May 1929 an official spokesman at the fourteenth All Russian Congress of Soviets painted the same picture :

> The village Soviet remains naturally dependent on the land communities, receiving very large grants from them.[3]

The institutions of the *mir* were not only financially stronger than those of the Soviet, they were also more efficient and more active. The " complete incompetence " of the village Soviet in comparison with the *skhod* of the land community was notorious.[4] The *mir* could at any rate draw on the shrewd self-interest of the well-to-do and successful peasant in coping with practical problems. Meetings of the *skhod* were far more frequent than those of the village Soviet or of its presidium.[5] The *skhod* was " formally, in its organization, far more of a mass organization than the Soviet " ; it attracted to itself " the growing activity of the peasant masses ".[6] It was " a fully established institution ".[7] Sometimes the *skhod* took it upon itself to appoint the electoral commission which drew up the list of voters for the village Soviet.[8] As the assembly of the *mir* it was ready to deal with any local issue which interested its members. Unlike the village

---

[1] *Sovetskoe Stroitel'stvo*, No. 5-6(22-23), May–June 1928, p. 159.
[2] M. Rezunov, *Sel'skie Sovety i Zemel'nye Obshchestva* (1928), p. 22.
[3] *XIV Vserosiiskii S"ezd Sovetov* (1929), No. 15, p. 14.
[4] *Vlast' Sovetov*, No. 48, November 28, 1926, p. 19.
[5] M. Rezunov, *Sel'skie Sovety i Zemel'nye Obshchestva* (1928), pp. 33-34.
[6] *Sovetskoe Stroitel'stvo*, No. 9(26), September 1928, p. 39; No. 5(34), May 1929, p. 107.
[7] *Ibid.* No. 5-6(22-23), May–June 1928, p. 158.
[8] *Ibid.* No. 12(29), December 1928, p. 100; for the electoral commissions see p. 275 below.

Soviet it was inhibited by no considerations of party or Soviet
orthodoxy; it was probably not exceptional to find that a *skhod*
appointed caretakers for the village church and collected funds for
its maintenance.[1] Kosior admitted at the fifteenth party congress
in December 1927 that 60-70 per cent of the discussions in the
mir, and only 10-20 per cent of those in the village Soviets, turned
on issues of local interest.[2] A report of Rabkrin about the same
time analysed the questions dealt with by the *skhods* of the land
communities — 39 per cent agrarian-economic, 16 per cent administrative, 9 per cent social-cultural, 8 per cent welfare, 12 per
cent political and other — and concluded that the *skhod* was the
" primary link in peasant self-government ".[3] The party journal
admitted that its prestige stood higher than that of the Soviets;
it constituted " a second organ of government ".[4] It was still
commonly assumed that the *skhod* took decisions, and the village
Soviet acted as its executive organ.[5] It was claimed that the
ancient customs and traditions of the countryside had been " almost untouched " by the revolution; " the characteristic feature
of the old ' moot ' that everything was decided by the *mir* has been
preserved by the land community up to our time ".[6] Another
commentator a few weeks later drew the same realistic picture:

> *The village* skhod *continues to occupy the predominant posi-
> tion in the life of the village* . . . The general meetings of citizens
> (*skhods*) function as organizations completely fused with the land
> communities.   No possibility exists of drawing any visible line
> of demarcation in the activity of these two organizations.[7]

The *mir* remained the stronghold of peasant solidarity against the
Soviet power.   Milyutin, who at the session of TsIK in April 1928
spoke cautiously of " an absence of regulation of relations " between the *skhod* and the village Soviet, admitted at the following

---

[1] M. Rezunov, *Sel'skie Sovety i Zemel'nye Obshchestva* (1928), p. 31; for
some specimen agendas of village Soviets and land communities for purposes of
comparison see *ibid.* pp. 28-29.

[2] *Pyatnadtsatyi S"ezd VKP(B)*, i (1961), 100.

[3] *Vlast' Sovetov*, No. 18, May 6, 1928, p. 21; *Derevenskii Kommunist*, No.
5-6(77-78), March 14, 1928.

[4] *Bol'shevik*, No. 9, May 15, 1928, pp. 80-81.

[5] *Izvestiya*, December 15, 1927, p. 3 (art. by Karp).

[6] *Vlast' Sovetov*, No. 21, May 27, 1928, p. 28.

[7] *Sovetskoe Stroitel'stvo*, No. 12(29), December 1928, p. 73.

session in December 1928, that " the land community is master "
and that " the village Soviet sits on one side ".[1]

The extreme reluctance of the party leaders to proceed to direct
action against the *mir* was a tribute to its unbroken hold over the
mass of the peasantry.[2]   Voices were still heard to argue that the
influence of the well-to-do peasant could be broken not by a direct
assault from without on the land community and its *skhod*, but
only by waging a class struggle within it,[3] and that the *mir* would
be superseded only when " the historical transition of agriculture
to a higher stage of development " led to " a dying out of its
economic presuppositions ".[4]   As late as the spring of 1929 the
agricultural expert of Gosplan protested against a growing tendency to identify the *mir* with the village Soviet, claiming that the
former should perform the separate and subordinate functions of
a " producer cooperative ".[5]   But the grain crisis, and increasing
pressure to extend and strengthen collective cultivation, prompted
more and more directly hostile action against the *mir* as the focus
of resistance to the forced grain collections, and more violent
assaults on its authority.   At the critical moment of the battle for
the grain in the winter of 1928–1929, a decree on the collective
use of land authorized any member of a land community who
desired to join a neighbouring kolkhoz of any type to transfer to
the kolkhoz the land assigned to him by the community, which had
no right to veto or obstruct such transfer.[6]   When the drive for
mass collectivization of agriculture was finally launched, decrees
were issued by the USSR and by the RSFSR liquidating the land
communities in areas of mass collectivization.[7]

(c) *Rural Soviets*

The village Soviets, even when a halt had been called to the
process of their enlargement,[8] remained the weakest link in the

---

[1] *3 Sessiya Tsentral'nogo Ispolnitel'nogo Komiteta Soyuza SSR 4 Sozyva*
(1928), p. 729 ;   *4 Sessiya Tsentral'nogo Ispolnitel'nogo Komiteta Soyuza SSR
4 Sozyva* (1928), No. 12, p. 21.   [2] See Vol. 1, pp. 125-126.
   [3] *Bol'shevik*, No. 13-14, July 31, 1928, p. 101.
   [4] M. Rezunov, *Sel'skie Sovety i Zemel'nye Obshchestva* (1928), p. 54.
   [5] *Na Agrarnom Fronte*, No. 4, 1929, p. 10.
   [6] *Izvestiya*, February 16, 1929.
   [7] *Sobranie Zakonov, 1930*, No. 16, art. 172 ; *Sobranie Uzakonenii, 1930*,
No. 51, art. 621.
   [8] See *Socialism in One Country, 1924–1926*, Vol. 2, pp. 352-353.

chain of Soviet local government. Like the rural district (volost')
authority set up by the Tsarist government after the emancipation
as a unit of peasant self-government, the village Soviet was an artificial creation enjoying none of the prestige or efficacy of the traditional indigenous peasant unit, the *mir*. On January 1, 1929, there
were 72,163 village Soviets in the USSR (55,340 in the RSFSR) covering a population of 123.5 millions (85 millions in the RSFSR) ;
this meant an average of 1700 persons (1500 in the RSFSR) to one
village Soviet. Each village Soviet included an average of eight
" inhabited points " (nine in the RSFSR).[1] The average number
of elected members of a village Soviet was about 18.[2] A description
of what was apparently a fairly active village Soviet in 1926 indicated that it met once or twice a month ; that the average attendance was from 5 to 7 ; that not more than 15 per cent of the
questions discussed related to agriculture ; and that most of the
business was transacted by the president and secretary. In many,
especially in smaller, village Soviets, " collective action is lacking,
plenums meet very rarely, once or twice a year, and tend to have a
ceremonial, solemn character ".[3] As late as 1928 it was officially
admitted that there were still many " village Soviets whose plenums do not meet regularly, and where the work of the village
Soviet is equivalent to the work of its present and secretary ".[4]
Some village Soviets, in addition to the president and secretary,
appointed a presidium to act as their executive organ ; but this
does not seem to have been ordinarily found necessary.[5] A village

---

[1] See Table No. 61, p. 484 below; for an estimate of four land communities to a village Soviet see p. 238 above.

[2] *Sovetskoe Stroitel'stvo*, No. 12(29), December 1928, p. 17.

[3] *Ibid.* No. 6(35), June 1929, p. 80 ; in 1928 some village Soviets were said
to have met to elect a president and secretary, and then not met again for a year
(*ibid.* No. 8(25), August 1928, p. 71).

[4] L. Kaganovich, *Partiya i Sovety* (1928), p. 78. According to M. Rosnitsky,
Litso Derevni (1926), p. 30, the normal village Soviet consisted simply of a
president and secretary, of whom the latter was sometimes the more important ;
a Rabkrin report confirmed that as a rule " the whole work is done by the
president and secretary. . . . The presidiums of village Soviets replace the
plenums " (*Sovetskoe Stroitel'stvo*, No. 12(29), December 1928, p. 86).

[5] *Ibid.* No. 2-3(7-8), February–March 1927, pp. 96-97 ; *Vlast' Sovetov*,
No. 27, July 3, 1927, pp. 15–16. Some village Soviets appointed a " village executive officer " (sel'skii ispolnitel') who performed some of the functions of
a village policeman ; but, since an old man no longer capable of heavy agricultural work was often chosen for the post, he was not likely to catch a horse-thief
(*Ezhenedel'nik Sovetskoi Yustitsii*, No. 33, August 24, 1927, p. 1028).

Soviet which had within its jurisdiction several "inhabited points" or "settlements" might delegate one of its members as a plenipotentiary to deal with the affairs of a particular settlement.[1]

The average monthly pay of a president of a village Soviet rose from 20·1 rubles in 1926 to 22·2 rubles in 1927, and of a secretary from 18·9 to 21·5 rubles; these were pittances to supplement other sources of livelihood.[2] Workers left village Soviets for better paid posts in cooperatives, credit societies or Sovkhozy.[3] At the TsIK of the RSFSR in November 1926, the complaint was made that the president or "plenipotentiary" of the village Soviet responsible for transacting its business, who "is *de facto* the village Soviet", sometimes received no pay at all.[4] The rate of 25 rubles for a secretary attracted only "unsuitable secretaries, often barely literate and scarcely capable of reading even printed matter".[5] Communications were so poor that decrees and orders issued in Moscow took on an average 56 days to reach the lowest Soviet organs.[6] Roads had deteriorated since the revolution, and postal services were rudimentary; the number of "rural mail-carriers" (an institution unknown before the revolution) rose from 6938 in 1924–1925 to 19,161 in 1927–1928.[7] The telephone was scarcely known, and as late as 1930 the chief towns of some districts still had no telegraph.[8] Contacts with higher Soviet organs were confined to rare and occasional visits from represen-

---

[1] *Sobranie Uzakonenii*, 1927, No. 27, art. 284.

[2] *Sovetskoe Stroitel'stvo*, No. 12(29), December 1928, pp. 27-28; the monthly salary of a president of a rural district executive committee in 1927 was 71·8 rubles and of a secretary 53·8 rubles. By 1929 the average monthly pay of presidents of village Soviets in the RSFSR had risen only to 23·5 rubles and of secretaries to 22·7 (*ibid.* No. 5(34), May 1929, p. 116). For the wages of industrial workers in this period see Vol. 1, Table No. 25, p. 958. In 1928 50 per cent of village Soviets were said to have paid secretaries who were not members of the Soviet (*Sovetskoe Stroitel'stvo*, No. 12(29), December 1928, p. 17).

[3] *Ibid.* No. 5-6(22-23), May–June 1928, p. 164; the annual turnover of "basic workers" in village Soviets ranged from 45 to 100 per cent (*XIV Vserossiiskii S"ezd Sovetov* (1929), No. 15, p. 7).

[4] *III Sessiya Vserossiiskogo Tsentral'nogo Ispolnitel'nogo Komiteta XII Sozyva* (1926), p. 298.

[5] *Sovetskoe Stroitel'stvo*, No. 12(17), December 1927, p. 83.

[6] *Ibid.* No. 2, September 1926, p. 15.

[7] *Gosudartsvennyi Apparat SSSR, 1924–1928* (1929), p. 22.

[8] *Vlast' Sovetov*, No. 21, May 23, 1926, p. 31; No. 27, July 4, 1926, pp. 6-7; *XVI S"ezd Vsesoyuznoi Kommunisticheskoi Partii (B)* (1931), p. 165.

tatives of district or department executive committees.[1] The situation was worst in outlying regions where conditions were primitive, and local Soviets weakly developed. In Azerbaijan, outside the capital city of Baku, 68·1 per cent of deputies elected to Soviets in 1927, and 51·2 per cent of their presidents, were illiterate.[2] Nowhere in the Soviet hierarchy, as the journal of Narkomyust complained, was a " more or less juridically literate person " to be found below the rank of secretary of the rural district executive committee.[3] It was not surprising that the Soviets displayed " a lack of understanding how to organize work effectively on fundamental economic problems ".[4] The village Soviets, declared the party journal in 1928, were only post offices which " execute commissions for various administrative and judicial organs (issue of summonses, help in collecting taxes etc.) ".[5]

The shortcomings and low standards of the village Soviets were a matter of frequent concern. On June 30, 1926, the presidium of TsIK addressed a letter to the TsIKs of the Union republics, drawing attention to the poor qualifications of the personnel of village Soviets, and the inadequate supply of books, documents, forms and other requisites, and suggesting among other things that the salaries of personnel should be raised.[6] In the spring of 1927 the Narkomvnudel of the RSFSR demanded a rationalization of the work of the lower Soviet organs in the countryside — the district and rural district executive committees and the village Soviets; functions were to be more precisely defined, and care taken to recruit better staff.[7] The number of paid employees of village Soviets rose from 130,000 on May 1, 1926, to 140,000 on January 1, 1928 — a significant increase at any time when stren-

[1] *Sovetskoe Stroitel'stvo*, No. 3-4, October–November 1926, pp. 127-128, 130.

[2] *Ibid.* No. 12(17), December 1927, p. 81. For the USSR as a whole 12·7 per cent of members of village Soviets, and 2·8 per cent of their presidents, were illiterate (*ibid.* No. 12(29), December 1928, pp. 19, 23); for the RSFSR, excluding the autonomous republics, the figures were 10 and 1·6 per cent, for the autonomous republics 24 and 6·1 per cent (*ibid.* No. 5(34), May 1929, p. 110).

[3] *Ezhenedel'nik Sovetskoi Yustitsii*, No. 25, June 29, 1927, p. 760.

[4] M. Rezunov, *Sel'skie Sovety i Zemel'nye Obshchestva* (1928), p. 30 — a mildly worded verdict.

[5] *Bol'shevik*, No. 6, May 31, 1928, p. 46.

[6] *Ibid.* No. 4(9), April 1927, p. 53.

[7] *Vlast' Sovetov*, No. 22, May 29, 1927, pp. 11-12.

uous efforts were made to cut staffs elsewhere.[1] By 1928 a few
district or rural district executive committees had appointed " instructors " — no doubt, on the analogy of party " instructors " —
to visit village Soviets, and a plea was put forward for the extension and regularization of the system.[2] The plea is likely to have
been defeated by the lack of available personnel. Anxiety was
constantly expressed at the failure of the Soviets to inspire any
confidence in the population.

> The peasantry [ran one official report] looks on the village
> Soviet as an organ of compulsion, and expects from it only
> orders and instructions, in most cases not of a very popular
> kind.[3]

A resolution of the sixteenth party conference in April 1929 deplored the replacement of Soviet and other elected bodies " *by
their own top strata* (the presidium of the Soviet, or in the countryside very often simply by the president and secretary of the
Soviet) ".[4] This might lead to one of two evils.

> Peasants' enquiries [read one plaint] are not answered, the
> " bosses " higher up grumble about the poor quality of returns
> and reports, . . . urgent and important papers are added to the file
> unread, and the president begins his working day at 5 a.m. and
> finishes it at 12 o'clock at night.

Alternatively, the president " simply does nothing at all, and
waits for the first opportunity to leave work and bury himself in
his peasant farm ".[5] At the elections of January-March 1929, 95
per cent of the presidents of village Soviets were returned as poor
or middle peasants, 50 per cent had served in the Red Army, 25
per cent were members of the party or the Komsomol, and 1·2 per
cent were women ; 37·6 per cent of them were serving their first
term of office.[6] But this said little about their capacity for an
exacting job.

---

[1] *Gosudarstvennyi Apparat SSSR, 1924–1928* (1929), p. 5.
[2] *Sovetskoe Stroitel'stvo*, No. 9(26), September 1928, pp. 39–54 ; for party
instructors see pp. 119-120 above.
[3] *Izvestiya*, June 6, 1928.
[4] *KPSS v Rezolyutsiyakh* (1954), ii, 604.
[5] *Ibid.* No. 5(34), May 1929, p. 110.
[6] *Sovetskoe Stroitel'stvo*, No. 5(34), May 1929, pp. 109, 114.

From 1927 onwards, the strengthening of the village Soviet became a major preoccupation of party policy. Once the party had finally turned its back on the conciliation of the well-to-do peasant, and the " reinforced offensive against the *kulak* " was proclaimed, it seemed no longer possible to allow him to use the *mir* and its *skhod* as a citadel for the defence of his interests and a bulwark against the encroachments of the Soviet. Only as the village Soviets gained power and efficiency would it be possible to make them — what they had always been in name — the units of local administration; and the growing pressure for higher agricultural productivity, for improved crop rotations, for mechanization and land consolidation, for more collective cultivation, required an organization which would give the Soviet authorities some measure of control over the operations of the *mir*. The party central committee at its session in February 1927 insisted that " the Soviets must more and more become the organizational, political and economic centres for all worker and peasant public activity ".[1] The statute of the *skhod* of March 14, 1927, was a first attempt — unrealistic and abortive as it proved — to establish the authority of the village Soviet over the *mir*.[2] The Ukraine was always in advance of other parts of the Union in the development of local government, and the institution of the *mir* was less widespread and less deeply rooted. The tenth Ukrainian Congress of Soviets in April 1927 passed a resolution which demanded " the regulation of mutual relations of the village Soviets as organs of government with the land communities as social-economic village unions, by establishing an order in which the village Soviets would have full powers for directing the land communities ", and " a strengthening of the rôle of the village Soviet as the sole fully qualified organ of Soviet power in the village ".[3] As often happened in Soviet campaigns, recognition of the necessity of a certain course of action bred the optimistic assumption that this course could be, and was being, effectively pursued. An enthusiastic report in the journal of Narkomvnudel in the summer of 1927 claimed that " in the last two years village Soviets are becoming collective organizations, and abound in non-party peasant activists playing a direct

---

[1] *KPSS v Rezolyutsiyakh* (1954), ii, 357.
[2] See pp. 240-241 above.
[3] *S"ezdy Sovetov i Dokumentakh*, v (1964), 179-180; see also p. 257 below.

part in the work of the Soviet and its sections ".[1]   The peasant
newspaper, reversing its attitude of the previous year, demanded
that "the village Soviet should be master of the land ".[2]   On
September 27, 1927, a decree of the RSFSR formally amended the
agrarian code of 1922 by transferring to the village Soviet the right
of supervision over the proceedings of the land community conferred by the code on the rural district executive committee.[3]
On October 12, 1927, the TsIK of the Ukrainian SSR adopted a
decree enpowering village Soviets to review " all decisions of
general assemblies and administrations of land communities in
their territory, and to confirm and register them, or to suspend
them if they were not in accordance with the law" .[4]   A few days
later the party central committee issued its directives for the drafting of the general principles of land utilization, which referred to
the need for " an improvement in the mutual relations between
Soviets and land communities from the point of view of ensuring
the rôle of leadership by the Soviets ".[5]

The fifteenth party congress in December 1927 dealt with the
question in a desultory fashion which betokened the lack of any
practicable solution.   One delegate spoke of " elements of dual
power in our countryside ", with an allusion to the slogan " All
power to the Soviets " which had been invoked to overthrow the
" dual power " of 1917 ;[6] and Enukidze discerned " immense
gains " in the work of village Soviets since the previous year, and
cited " the more decisive step " taken by " our Ukrainian comrades " to establish the authority of the village Soviet over the land
community.[7]   The congress resolution called for " an improvement in relations between Soviets and land communities from the
point of view of assuring the directing rôle of the Soviets ".[8]   An

---

[1]   *Vlast' Sovetov*, No. 24-25, June 29, 1927, p. 21.
[2]   *Bednota*, June 16, 1927 ;   for the earlier pronouncement see p. 240 above.
[3]   *Sobranie Uzakonenii*, *1927*, No. 105, art. 706 ;   for this provision of the
code see p. 238 above.
[4]   *Zbirnik Uzakonen' ta Rosporyazhen'*, 1927, No. 47, art. 58 ;   the relevant
chapter is printed in M. Rezunov, *Sel'skie Sovety i Zemel'nye Obshchestva* (1928),
pp. 74-76.   [5]   For these directives see Vol. 1, p. 107.
[6]   *Pyatnadtsatyi S"ezd VKP(B)*, ii (1962), 1281.
[7]   *Ibid.* ii, 1242, 1245 ;   a commentator called the Ukrainian decree of
October 12, 1927, " a novelty for all the other Union republics " (*Sovetskoe
Stroitel'stvo*, No. 12(17), December 1927, p. 21).
[8]   *KPSS v Rezolyutsiyakh* (1954), ii, 486-487.

assurance that " significant improvements " had in fact occurred
in the work of the village Soviets[1] seemed to lack substance.
Kaganovich touched a crucial point when he insisted that " the
plenums of the Soviets should increase discussion of practical,
economic, administrative and day-to-day questions affecting the
broad masses of electors ", and give more attention to " questions
connected with the peasant economy and peasant life ".[2] But
nothing altered the hard fact that the land community and its
skhod handled most issues of vital importance to the day-to-day
life of the peasant,[3] and that the village Soviet was an unfamiliar,
ineffective and often unwelcome intruder.

The most controversial developments of the struggle revolved
round the issue of the financial autonomy of the village. The
establishment of independent budgets for village Soviets had been
actively canvassed in Moscow since 1925. Local practice outran
the pronouncements of legislators at the centre. The Volga German autonomous republic had introduced village Soviet budgets
in 1924 ; in the Ukraine they developed more rapidly than in
the RSFSR ; and the newly established regions tended to favour
their introduction.[4] In November 1926 the new statute of the
RSFSR on local finances cautiously pronounced in favour of independent budgets for " the village Soviets of economically strong
inhabited points ".[5] But Narkomfin continued to regard village
budgets with the utmost mistrust — ostensibly on the plea that
supervision of them involved extra work ;[6] and no Union legislation at this time sanctioned them. In 1926–1927 3 per cent of
village Soviets in the RSFSR had budgets, and 4·5 per cent in the
Ukraine ; in the other republics they were still virtually unknown.[7]

[1] *Pyatnadtsatyi S"ezd VKP(B)*, i (1961), 100.
[2] L. Kaganovich, *Partiya i Sovety* (1928), pp. 78-79.
[3] See pp. 247-248 above.
[4] See *Socialism in One Country, 1924–1926*, Vol. 2, pp. 461-465.
[5] *Sobranie Uzakonenii, 1926*, No. 92, art. 668.
[6] *Vsesoyuznoe Soveshchanie po Perevyboram Sovetov v 1929 g.* (1928), p. 66 ;
for Narkomfin objections see p. 225 above. The fear that local budgets would
be subject to " direct dependence on the will of the population ", and that this
was incompatible with the dictatorship of the proletariat (*Sovetskoe Stroitel'stvo*,
No. 4(21), April 1928, p. 44) was perhaps more often felt than openly expressed.
[7] See Table No. 62, p. 485 below. For village budgets before 1926 see

The case for village budgets received its strongest reinforce-
ment from the long struggle to replace the authority of the *mir*
and its traditional *skhod* by the authority of the village Soviet. If
the village Soviet was to exercise effective power, it must have
financial independence; and some progress was made in this
direction. A decree of the RSFSR of March 7, 1927, recognized
the rights of village Soviets having independent budgets to hold
and lease property, and to enter into contractual relations.[1]
The tenth Ukrainian Congress of Soviets in April 1927 voted to
accord independent budgets to all urban and workers' settlements,
and to village Soviets possessing the necessary economic prerequisites ; to hand over enterprises and property of local importance
to local Soviets; and to give village Soviets the right to settle
disputed questions of local significance.[2] A decree of the RSFSR
of July 18, 1927, purported to confer on village Soviets the right
to impose compulsory labour service for transport and necessary
public works; the provisions were to be elaborated by Narkomyust in consultation with the local authorities, and submitted to
Sovnarkom for confirmation.[3]

When Enukidze at the fifteenth party congress in December
1927 contrasted the insignificant number, and small volume, of
Soviet village budgets with the massive financial resources of the
land communities,[4] this was a clear call for action. If strong village
Soviets came in this period to be recognized as a necessary focus of
resistance to the *kulak* and of the offensive against him, it was also
apparent that an independent budget was a necessary condition of
a strong village Soviet. " The power to take decisions ", wrote

---

Socialism in One Country, 1924–1926, Vol. 2, pp. 461-464 ; the total of village
budgets increased by 65 per cent in 1926–1927 (*Sovetskoe Stroitel'stvo*, No.
4(21), April 1928, p. 38). An analysis made in 1926 of newly introduced village
Soviet budgets in Kostroma county showed that their total amount varied from
700 to 4000 rubles ; that about 70 per cent — in some cases 100 per cent — of
their revenues came from taxation (deductions from the agricultural and other
taxes) ; that 68 per cent of their expenditure was on wages of Soviet officials and
employees (communal services were, no doubt, financed mainly by the *mir*) ;
and that some of these supposedly independent budgets were in fact drawn up
by the rural district executive committee (*Izvestiya*, October 30, 1926 — art. by
Tadeush).   [1] *Sobranie Uzakonenii, 1927*, No. 26, art. 172.
    [2] For this resolution see p. 254 above.
    [3] *Sobranie Uzakonenii, 1927*, No. 73, art. 500 ; final confirmation had
apparently to await a further decree of July 30, 1928 (*Sobranie Uzakonenii*, 1928,
No. 99, art. 625).   [4] See p. 246 above.

one commentator, " is enjoyed by those Soviets which have their own budgets and are economically powerful."[1] Rabkrin discovered that village Soviets with independent budgets interested themselves far more " in local questions and in institutions transferred to their budget ", and " discuss the needs of the population far more fully than those without budgets or on the rural district budget ".[2] From the North Caucasian region it was reported that, "where village Soviets have their own budgets, and are economically strong, they control the *skhods* ".[3] In July 1928, Sovnarkom passed a resolution recording that village Soviet budgets had yielded favourable results and calling for an expansion of the network.[4] Shortage of qualified personnel and obstruction from higher Soviet authorities were serious obstacles. Cases were quoted where, even after the principle of a village Soviet budget had been conceded, the budget was for practical reasons still drawn up by officials of the district or rural district executive committee; and, when the budget had been drawn up, it could be upset by a cut in the revenues receivable from higher Soviet organs.[5] Nevertheless, the number and proportion of village Soviets having their own budget increased substantially in 1927–1928, and some two-and-a-half times in each of the two following years; and the average size of the budget also increased. The most spectacular results were achieved in the RSFSR and the Ukrainian and White Russian SSRs; in the other, more primitive, Union republics, the rise was also steep, but from a lower level.[6] The proportion of village Soviets with budgets was higher in areas which had early been subject to regionalization, such as the Northern Caucasian region, than in areas which had lagged behind.[7] A resolution of the fourteenth All-Russian Congress of Soviets in May 1929 pressed for the completion of the system of village Soviet budgets by the financial year 1932–1933, this exhortation being significantly followed by the injunction " to sub-

[1] *Izvestiya*, December 15, 1927 (art. by Karp).
[2] *Sovetskoe Stroitel'stvo*, No. 4(21), April 1928, p. 39.
[3] *Ibid.* No. 5-6(22-23), May–June 1928, p. 69.
[4] *Pravda*, July 4, 1928; a decision was taken at this time to increase by 20 per cent the number of village Soviets in the White Russian SSR having their own budgets (*Sovetskoe Stroitel'stvo*, No. 1(30), January 1929, p. 37).
[5] *Vlast' Sovetov*, No. 8, February 26, 1928, p. 8; No. 22, June 3, 1928, pp. 6-7.   [6] See Table No. 62, p. 485 below.
[7] *Sovetskoe Stroitel'stvo*, No. 9(26), September 1928, pp. 139, 142-144.

ordinate the land communities to the leadership of the village Soviets ".[1]

The campaign to assert the authority of the village Soviets made slow progress. An innovation designed to make village Soviets effective and to draw some part of the population into their work was the formation of sections. The statute of village Soviets of the RSFSR of October 16, 1924, laid it down that the Soviet " in necessary cases forms commissions, and allots various tasks to individual citizens and groups of citizens " ;[2] and the conference on Soviet construction in the spring of 1925 passed a resolution calling for the establishment of sections in district or rural district executive committees, as well as in rural Soviets.[3] Sections of village Soviets are said to have appeared " spontaneously " on the basis of this resolution ;[4] but these must have been exceptional cases. It was not till March 21, 1927, that the TsIK of the RSFSR adopted a statute of " permanent commissions (sections) " of district or rural district executive committees and village Soviets; this named six basic sections — agricultural, cultural-educational, financial, health, local economy, and trade and co-operatives — though it was not assumed that all these would be set up in every Soviet. An important provision was that non-members of the Soviet were eligible for membership of sections, provided they were not persons deprived of electoral rights. One of the principal aims of the measure was to build up a non-party *aktiv* in the countryside.[5] But, like other efforts to promote political activity and consciousness among the peasants, the sections of village Soviets never came to life.[6] At the fifteenth party congress

---

[1] *S"ezdy Sovetov v Dokumentakh*, iv, i (1962), 134.

[2] For this statute see *Socialism in One Country, 1924–1926*, Vol. 2, p. 322.

[3] *Soveshchanie po Voprosam Sovetskogo Stroitel'stva, 1925 g.: Aprel'* (1925), p. 171 ; for this conference see *Socialism in One Country, 1924–1926*, Vol. 2, pp. 325-326.

[4] *Pravda*, September 27, 1927; *Sovetskoe Stroitel'stvo*, No. 12(29), December 1928, pp. 52-53.

[5] *Sobranie Uzakonenii, 1927*, No. 39, art. 250; this decree immediately followed the decree of the USSR on the *skhod* (see pp. 240-241 above), and was evidently part of a general drive to build up an effective Soviet administration in the countryside.

[6] *Izvestiya Tsentral'nogo Komiteta VKP(B)*, No. 29(202), July 30, 1927, p. 4.

in December 1927, Kosior accorded them a bare mention in his
report on organization; and Enukidze's claim of three million
members of sections of village Soviets in the whole USSR[1] was a
fantastic exaggeration. Averages of 1·3 sections per village Soviet
in the RSFSR and of 6·6 members per section were quoted by a
party commentator.[2] But a Rabkrin report of 1928 stated bluntly
that, in contrast to sections of urban Soviets, sections of rural
Soviets " in the majority of cases do not work " ;[3] and this was
amply confirmed by less formal reports.[4] An account which
quoted some isolated instances of useful work by sections attributed the general weakness to " the low cultural level of workers
in village Soviets, the absence of planning in the work of the sections and the size of the territory subject to the village Soviet (the
so-called enlarged Soviets) ".[5] The groups of poor peasants,
which, though organized by the party, were based on the rural
Soviets,[6] proved equally ineffective.

The " extraordinary measures " of the first months of 1928
exacerbated every social and institutional issue in the countryside.
They involved for the first time active and direct party intervention
in peasant affairs; and party cells worked through the village
Soviet, and notoriously held aloof from the *mir*.[7] After the grain
collections crisis of the first months of 1928 a commentator noted
that " the elected organs of land communities, which enjoy great
authority in the countryside, . . . often covertly or openly resisted
the carrying out of our measures ". Two conflicting groups strug-

[1] *Pyatnadtsatyi S"ezd VKP(B)*, i (1961), 100, ii (1962), 1246.
[2] *Bol'shevik*, No. 13-14, July 31, 1928, p. 102.
[3] *Sovetskoe Stroitel'stvo*, No. 12(29), December 1928, p. 90; the formation
of sections by urban Soviets had been prescribed in their statute of October 1925
(see p. 263 below).
[4] *Sovetskoe Stroitel'stvo*, No. 8(25), August 1928, pp. 32, 71 (" very few . . .
really work ", " do no work at all and exist only on paper ") ; No. 9(26),
September 1926, p. 39 ("absolute inactivity of the sections of [rural] Soviets").
[5] *Ibid*. No. 12(29), December 1928, p. 57.
[6] See Note H, pp. 459-463 below.
[7] *Izvestiya Tsentral'nogo Ispolnitel'nogo Komiteta VKP(B)*, No. 11-12(270-
271), April 24, 1929, pp. 13-14; complaints were constantly made in party
circles during 1928 that insufficient leadership was being given to the land
communities (see, for example, *Derevenskii Kommunist*, No. 5-6(77-78), March
14, 1928, pp. 28-30; *Bol'shevik*, No. 13-14, July 31, 1928, pp. 104-105).

gled against each other in the countryside — the Soviet *aktiv* and an *aktiv* organized by and around the *mir*.[1] The campaign against the land community was identified with the campaign against the *kulak* on the plea that the latter in practice dominated the *mir* ; the prestige of the *mir* could be sapped by depicting it as the preserve of the *kulak*. The strength of party animosity was reflected in the increasingly uncompromising tone of official pronouncements. A conference of party organizations in May 1928 made a recommendation that economic undertakings belonging to land communities should be put under the management of the village Soviet.[2] In June 1928 a report of Rabkrin recommended that village Soviets in the RSFSR should be given the right to abrogate decisions of the *skhod* of the land community, subject to an appeal to the district executive committee.[3] The final text of the general principles of land utilization adopted in December 1928 left no doubt of the intention of the legislators to treat the *mir* and its *skhod* as public organs, and to mark their formal subordination to the village Soviet. The chapter on, " The Land Community and the Village Soviet " deprived persons disfranchised under Soviet law of the right to vote in the *skhod* or to hold office in the *mir* (though they apparently retained their membership), and accorded full voting rights not only to all adult members of the *dvors* forming the land community, but to all *batraks*, shepherds, artisans and other persons employed by it. A provision in the agrarian code of 1922 which allowed the land community to be guided by " local customs where these are not in contradiction with the law " was replaced by one prescribing strict conformity with the law. The *mir* still exercised control over the utilization of land, and could take " measures to promote cooperation and collectivization in production ". But the decisions of its assembly could be vetoed by the village Soviet, subject to an appeal to the rural district, or higher, executive committee (articles 47-53).[4]

---

[1] *Bol'shevik*, No. 9, May 15, 1928, pp. 79-81 ; for the clash between the two *aktivs* see p. 127, note 6 above.

[2] *Izvestiya*, June 6, 1928.

[3] *Deyatel'nost' Organov Partiino-Gosudarstvennogo Kontrolya: Sbornik Dokumentor* (1964), pp. 134-137.

[4] For the general principles see Vol. 1, p. 108 ; according to *Bednota*, November 2, 1928, the article on the subordination of the land community to the village Soviet (art. 51) was strengthened on an initiative of the Sovnarkom of the RSFSR.

Such pronouncements contained, however, a large element of wishful thinking or plain make-believe. The village Soviet was still a politically unreliable, as well as an ineffective, instrument. The quality of employees of village Soviets was still low, and the turnover excessively large.[1] The well-to-do peasant was still over-represented in the village Soviet;[2] and the poor peasant, even when he was elected to the Soviet, had neither the time nor the transport to attend its meetings.[3] In the winter of 1928–1929 all the evidence goes to show that the predominance of the *mir* and its organs in the countryside had not been seriously shaken.[4] The campaign against them, like the campaign against the *kulak*, proved ineffective, and for the same reason: the great majority of middle peasants, and even of poor peasants, could not be mobilized in support of the towns, the workers or the government against the well-to-do peasant. How little had really changed was shown when, at the fourteenth All-Russian Congress of Soviets in May 1929, Kiselev scornfully remarked that " the material basis of the KKOV is immeasurably more solid than that of the village Soviets, which have no property ";[5] and the resolution of the congress once again demanded an extension of village budgets and more pay for presidents and secretaries of village Soviets, and stressed the need " to subordinate the land communities to a leadership of the village Soviets ".[6] It was one of the serious miscalculations by the authorities of the situation in the countryside that they overestimated the effect of a small infusion of party and governmental power in transforming the village Soviets into loyal and serviceable instruments of Soviet policy.

---

[1] *Izvestiya*, January 26, 1929 (art. by Ryskulov).

[2] See table in *Sel'skoe Khozyaistvo SSSR, 1925–1928* (1929), pp. 134-135, showing that representation in the village Soviet varied directly with wealth measured in terms of ownership of means of production.

[3] *SSSR: 5 S"ezd Sovetov* (1929), No. 16, p. 10; an investigation of 27 village Soviets in the Lower Volga region in 1928 showed that out of 386 members 112 were poor peasants, 158 middle peasants and 116 well-to-do peasants, but that, whereas 45 per cent of the well-to-do peasants and 40·5 per cent of the middle peasants attended meetings regularly, only 14·4 per cent of the poor peasants did so (*Sovetskoe Stroitel'stvo*, No. 2(31), February 1929, pp. 130-131).

[4] See pp. 248-249 above.

[5] *XIV Vserossiiski S"ezd Sovetov* (1929), No. 15, p. 16; for the KKOV see Note G, pp. 456-458 below.

[6] *S"ezdy Sovetov v Dokumentakh*, iv, 1 (1962), 132-134, 136.

(d) Urban Soviets

The term " urban Soviets " covered an even greater variety of institutions than the term " village Soviets ". In major cities of the RSFSR Soviets had led an active existence since the earliest days of the régime, and had received official sanction in statutes of January 1922 and October 1925.[1] Urban Soviets also functioned in many smaller towns and settlements.[2] The party central committee at the session in July 1926 had called for an improvement in the work of urban Soviets " especially in towns with an insignificant proletarian population " ;[3] in a small town containing few workers the Soviet normally consisted of " a group of employees ".[4] The situation in the Ukrainian and White Russian SSRs was similar. In the non-Slav areas of the USSR development was slower and followed rather different lines. Even in an important industrial centre like Baku, the Soviet as a large representative organ dated only from the end of 1926, in Tiflis only from the second half of 1927 ;[5] urban Soviets in Tashkent and Samarkand were first elected in January–February 1927.[6] The formation in large cities of district Soviets subordinate to the main urban Soviet seems to have taken place spontaneously without legislative sanction ; the statutes of urban Soviets of the Ukrainian and Transcaucasian republics, but not of the other republics, provided specifically for urban district Soviets.[7] Finally, a decree of the USSR of February 8, 1928,[8] sanctioned the formation of urban district Soviets in cities of over 100,000 inhabitants.

Throughout this period attempts were made to improve the efficiency of urban Soviets and make them more effective as mass representative organs of the workers. In July 1926 the party central committee, in its resolution on the just completed Soviet elections, noted the increased participation of unorganized workers and of the petty bourgeoisie in the urban Soviets, which were

---

[1] See *Socialism in One Country*, 1924-1926, Vol. 2, pp. 356, 360-361.
[2] See pp. 271-272 below.
[3] *KPSS v Rezolyutsiyakh* (1954), ii, 278.
[4] *Sovetskoe Stroitel'stvo*, No. 8-9(13-14), August–September 1927, p. 8.
[5] *Ibid.* No. 5-6(22-23), May–June 1928, p. 124.
[6] *Ibid.* p. 183.   [7] *Ibid.* No. 4(33), April 1929, pp. 123-124.
[8] See p. 265 below.

invited, " on the basis of their new ' statute '", to " strengthen the
recruitment into all their work of the toiling urban masses, and
first and foremost, of course, of the industrial workers ".[1] Some
advance could be registered in the work of larger urban Soviets.
Sessions became more frequent ; once or twice a month seemed to
be the norm. Attendance improved, and often reached 60 to 70
per cent of the deputies. A sample of 11 large urban Soviets in
1926 showed that only 24 per cent of deputies were workers from
the bench ; 36·9 per cent were workers by social situation now
employed in administrative posts, and 25 per cent employees.
Urban Soviets were far more practical and effective bodies than
village Soviets. Housing and social security were the questions
of major interest. Complaints related to the restriction of budgetary rights of the Soviets, and in general to failure to define
their powers and functions.[2] But by the beginning of 1927 only
the RSFSR and the White Russian SSR had statutes of urban
Soviets, and the Uzbek SSR promulgated a statute, apparently on
the model of the RSFSR, in January 1927.[3] The tenth Ukrainian
Congress of Soviets in April 1927 cautiously recommended an extension of rights of urban Soviets. They were to have independent
budgets which must, however, be confirmed by the department
(okrug) executive committee ; they were to be allowed to form a
presidium, whose functions must, however, be geared to those of
the presidium of the department executive committee in such a
way as to safeguard the direction of the work of urban Soviets by
the higher organs ; and all members of the Soviet were to be recruited for active work in commissions and sections.[4] But, here as
elsewhere, many officials were afraid of putting too much power in
their hands.[5] On July 11, 1927, the party central committee again

---

[1] *KPSS v Rezolyutsiyakh* (1954), ii, 269, 276 ; for Molotov's remarks about
the urban Soviets in his report to the committee see *Sovetskoe Stroitel'stvo*, No.
2, September 1926, p. 19.

[2] *Ibid.* No. 5, December 1926, pp. 10-17 ; sample tests of urban Soviets
in the RSFSR in 1928 showed 47 per cent of deputies as workers by social
situation and 37·9 per cent as workers from production (*Izvestiya*, May 23,
1928).

[3] *Sovetskoe Stroitel'stvo*, No. 5-6(22-23), May–June 1928, p. 186 ; the
Transcaucasian SFSR issued a statute of urban Soviets on February 20, 1928
(*ibid.* No. 5-6(22-23), May-June 1928, p. 118).

[4] *S"ezdy Sovetov v Dokumentakh*, v (1964), 181 ; for the sections see pp.
268-271 below.

[5] *Vlast' Sovetov*, No. 14, April 3, 1927, pp. 4-5.

stepped in with a long resolution on the revitalization of urban Soviets. It pointed out that only the RSFSR and the White Russian SSR had so far attempted to carry out the resolution of July 1926 by broadening the " material basis " of urban Soviets. The further measures required included (a) the separation of budgets of urban Soviets from those of the provinces, and the handing over to them of properties and enterprises ; (2) the setting up of Soviets in workers' settlements (poselki) of urban type and (3) the giving to urban Soviets of a share in the management of local enterprises run by higher Soviet organs. The party fraction in the TsIK of the USSR was to press for the enactment of these measures.[1] Even this took time. It was not till February 8, 1928, that TsIK at length issued its decree on urban Soviets, accompanied by a letter of exhortation to the TsIKs of the Union republics. All towns of 100,000 inhabitants and upwards, as well as all workers' settlements, were to have Soviets ; these were once again described as " the highest organs of power in the territory " ; they were to " decide " questions of local significance and " discuss " questions of higher policy. They were to take over " social and cultural institutions " run by state industrial enterprises (hospitals, baths, schools, etc.) They were recognized as juridical persons, and were to receive from the central executive committees of the republics authority to issue obligatory orders. The jealously guarded right to form executive committees was still withheld ; the urban Soviet could form only a presidium, which was subordinate to the presidium of the higher executive committee, or sections or commissions, which had no executive functions. An attempt was made to solve the knotty problem of the relation of urban Soviets to higher Soviet organs by providing that the executive committees of territorial units in which the towns were situated were " under an obligation to render an account of their work to the plenums of the urban Soviets ". The embarrassment of legislation by Union organs on matters which had hitherto been within the competence of the republics was betrayed in the accompanying letter addressed by the TsIK of the USSR to the

---

[1] *Spravochnik Partiinogo Rabotnika*, vi (1928), i, 634-635 ; the resolution was originally published in *Pravda*, July 19, 1927. Some of the pressure behind this resolution came from the North Caucasian region with its three large cities (Rostov, Krasnodar and Novorossiisk) (*Izvestiya*, July 20, 1927).

TsIKs of the Union republics ; this urged them to give all manner of support to the work of urban Soviets and their sections.[1] The decree clearly proved ineffective. A circular of the TsIK of the RSFSR of January 9, 1929, drew attention to cases of failure to give urban Soviets independent budgets and to hand over to them social and cultural institutions run by state industrial enterprises.[2]

The growth of urban Soviets had from the first been strongly contested. Provincial, county and rural district Soviet authorities in whose area a town was situated, obstructed the development, or even the formation, of urban Soviets.[3] The prohibition on the formation by urban Soviets of executive committees was due to fear that these might become effective organs of power. Relations between urban Soviets and the county (or department) and rural district (or district) executive committees covering the area in which the town was situated were notoriously delicate ; and from time to time efforts of urban Soviets to assert their independence of these authorities had to be checked.[4] Kosior at the fifteenth party congress in December 1927 admitted that the higher Soviet authorities frequently overrode or ignored the sections of urban Soviets,[5] and a year later Enukidze remarked that urban Soviets must " remain within the general system " ; otherwise there would be " dual power ".[6] In the non-Slav republics, where the whole Soviet administrative structure was weak or embryonic, different solutions were found. Whereas in the RSFSR and in the Ukraine urban Soviets, other than those in the largest cities, had to contend with the jealous opposition of the more powerful department or county, district or rural district Soviet organs, in the remoter regions urban Soviets, once these were created, became the most powerful Soviet administrative organs in their respective

---

[1] *Sobranie Zakonov, 1928*, No. 10, arts. 86, 87 ; according to an article in *Sovetskoe Stroitel'stvo*, No. 2(19), February 1928, p. 10, the decree for the first time gave urban Soviets " sources of revenue capable of guaranteeing the balancing of city budgets without a deficit ".

[2] *Vlast' Sovetov*, Prilozhenie No. 1, January 9, 1929.

[3] *Ibid.* No. 24-25, June 20, 1926, p. 1 ; No. 32-33, August 15, 1926, pp. 24-25. It was reported from Siberia that department executive committees " look on the urban Soviet as an unnecessary organ, and try in every way to circumvent it " (*Sovetskoe Stroitel'stvo*, No. 3(32), March 1929, p. 99).

[4] *Vlast' Sovetov*, No. 24-25, June 20, 1926, p. 4.

[5] *Pyatnadtsatyi S"ezd VKP(B)*, i (1961), 98.

[6] *Vsesoyuznoe Soveshchanie po Perevyboram Sovetov v 1929 g.* (1928), p. 104.

republics, serving as instruments of the Sovietization of the whole region, and exemplifying a pattern by which Soviet culture was carried from industrialized towns and factories into the country-side. The Kazan city Soviet, thanks to the absence of any pro-vincial executive committee, early acquired an independent posi-tion of authority in the Tatar ASSR.[1] The Baku Soviet, dealing with a population of 446,000, not only had two subordinate urban district Soviets representing factory districts remote from the city centre, but also had attracted to it three rural districts with a popu-lation of 77,000. The Baku city Soviet in effect replaced the non-existent county Soviet organization ; the rural district congresses of Soviets sent deputies to the urban Soviet.[2] The Baku Soviet enjoyed, doubtless in virtue of its special status, the unique pri-vilege of having an executive committee ; but an executive committee set up by the Taskhent Soviet was dissolved in January 1928, and the subordination of the Soviet to the executive com-mittee of the department reasserted.[3] Elsewhere in the Trans-caucasian SFSR urban Soviets were said to have performed the functions of non-existent county executive committees in the inter-val between county congresses of Soviets.[4] The Ashkhabad urban Soviet, which was first formed in 1926 in connexion with the regionalization of the Turkmen SSR, was directly responsible, no doubt in the absence of other effective Soviet organs, to the TsIK of the republic.[5] According to a decree of the Uzbek SSR on urban Soviets of January 1927, the larger urban Soviets such as Tashkent and Samarkand, were responsible to department execu-tive committees and the smaller to district executive committees, thus following the pattern common in the RSFSR. In April 1927 the district executive committee took the management of Tashkent

---

[1] See *Socialism in One Country, 1924–1926*, Vol. 2, p. 357.
[2] *Sovetskoe Stroitel'stvo*, No. 5-6(22-23), May–June 1928, pp. 124-125, 133.
[3] *Ibid.* No. 5-6(22-23), May–June 1928, pp. 124-125, 186. The Baku Soviet may have owed its special status in part to its ability to raise revenue from a tax of 0·5 kopeks per pud on oil produced in its territory (*ibid.* p. 125) ; most urban Soviets, even when they acquired independent budgets, needed financial help from the higher authorities in order to balance them.
[4] *Ibid.* No. 12(17), December 1927, p. 17.
[5] *Ibid.* No. 9(26), September 1928, p. 117 ; elsewhere in Turkmenistan, newly formed urban Soviets were said to have no executive powers and to be entirely subordinate to the department (okrug) authorities (*ibid.* No. 5-6(10-11), May–June 1927, p. 20).

hospitals out of the hands of the Tashkent Soviet; and the Samarkand Soviet was said to have suffered even more arbitrary interventions by its district executive committee.[1] Contrary to normal practice, Samarkand had two urban Soviets — one for the new city with a predominantly Russian population, the other for the old city with a native population; this anomaly was condemned as both unconstitutional and wasteful.[2] No conclusion can be drawn from the variety of these arrangements except their pragmatic character, the difficulty of distinguishing between those which were effective and those which were not, and the hazards of all generalizations about urban Soviets applicable to the USSR as a whole.

The most important development in the urban Soviets in this period was the extension of the system of " sections " or commissions. As the Soviets quickly grew too large for the transaction of current business,[3] it seemed at first that, following the precedent of TsIK, they would cede the effective exercise of power to their own presidiums. Such a trend was reported and documented in a Rabkrin report of 1928:

> In practice the decisive organs of urban . . . Soviets are the presidiums . . . Questions are brought before the plenum when they have been decided in practice by the presidium of the Soviet or the presidium of the executive committee; the plenums only confirm these decisions.[4]

But, perhaps through fear that the presidiums might aspire to the rôle of the banned executive committees, other counsels prevailed.

---

[1] *Sovetskoe Stroitel'stvo*, No. 5-6(22-23), May–June 1928, pp. 189-190.

[2] *Ibid.* No. 5-6(22-23), May–June 1928, pp. 186-188.

[3] The average number of members of an urban Soviet in the RSFSR in 1926 was 117 as against 84 in 1924–1925 (*Pravda*, October 26, 1926). But large and important urban Soviets might have a thousand or more members; Baku Soviet had 1208 members and 349 candidates in 1926–1927 (*Sovetskoe Stroitel'stvo*, No. 5-6(22-23), May–June 1928, p. 127).

[4] *Ibid.* No. 12(29), December 1928, p. 85. The examples quoted were of Soviets outside the RSFSR — Odessa, Dniepropetrovsk, Kremenchug, Tashkent and Baku; nearly one-half of the questions discussed at the 15 plenary meetings of the Odessa Soviet between March 1927 and March 1928 were " general political ", and not " business ", questions, the latter being handled in the presidium (*ibid.* No. 10(27), October 1928, p. 123).

The campaign for the revitalization of the Soviets had been based on the principle of drawing into Soviet work a maximum number of ordinary people.[1] It was contemplated, in art. 47 of the statute of urban Soviets adopted in October 1925,[1] that Soviets would set up at least five " sections ", for communal services, finance, education, health, and trade and cooperatives, to which sections for administrative and legal questions, and for questions of housing, labour, industry and social security, for military questions and for the work of Rabkrin, might eventually be added. In 1926 it was reported that 80 per cent of urban Soviets had established the prescribed five sections (including 30 per cent which also had additional sections) and 20 per cent had failed to establish all the five.[3] Much of the activity of the urban Soviets at this time revolved round the work of the sections. These were manned not exclusively, or perhaps even mainly, by elected members of the Soviet, but by " co-opted persons (vovlechenn-ye) ", the method of whose choice was not formally laid down, but who appear to have been for the most part workers. The numbers recruited in this way were quite large. In the RSFSR at the beginning of 1928 33,500 persons had been co-opted into the sections of 147 urban Soviets ;[4] in Moscow the total rose from 8400 in 1926 to 14,700 in 1927. The Leningrad Soviet in 1927, besides the five regular sections, had sections for administrative, agricultural and military questions : district Soviets in the city also established sections.[5] The Odessa Soviet, consisting of 1360 members and 426 candidates, had 552 co-opted persons in its eight sections, the

---

[1] This was the reason for the rapid turnover in membership, re-election for a second term being the exception rather than the rule ; in Moscow in 1927 73 per cent of the Moscow urban Soviets were new members, in Leningrad from 74 to 80 per cent, in Bryansk 96 per cent. The practice was criticized as unfavourable to the formation of a solid *aktiv* (*Izvestiya*, May 23, 1928). In the first decade of the régime 500,000 people were said to have been deputies at one time or another in one of the Moscow urban Soviets (*Sovetskoe Stroitel'stvo*, No. 5-6 (10-11), May–June 1927, p. 15) ; see also p. 285 below.

[2] See *Socialism in One Country, 1924–1926*, Vol. 2, pp. 360-361.

[3] *Vlast' Sovetov*, No. 44-45, November 7, 1926, pp. 35-36.

[4] *Sovetskoe Stroitel'stvo*, No. 12(29), December 1928, pp. 5-6 ; in Leningrad 66 per cent of those co-opted were workers, in Ivanovo-Voznesensk 80 per cent. Trade unions sometimes helped in selecting recruits for sections (*ibid.* No. 5-6, May–June 1928, p. 139). For Moscow, Krupskaya gave a total of 12,300 persons belonging to sections in 1925–1926 (*Pravda*, April 12, 1927) ; this presumably included urban district Soviets as well as the Moscow city Soviet.

[5] *Vlast' Sovetov*, No. 35-36, September 4, 1927, p. 27.

membership of which varied from 100 to 300; but the services of these were said to be inadequately used.[1] The Baku Soviet with 1327 members co-opted 791 workers into its sections.[2] Krupskaya reported that in the Moscow Soviets the most popular sections were those dealing with health, and that not enough attention was paid to education.[3] Narkomyust became interested in the establishment of legal sections, the function of which was to spread the understanding of law, to promote revolutionary legality, and to combat crime, corruption and bureaucratism; a competition was announced early in 1928 for the best " administrative-legal " section of a Soviet.[4] A decree of February 15, 1929, removed restrictions on the number of sections which might be set up.[5] As time went on, sections began to develop a life of their own, independent of the Soviets from which they emanated; they were " in substance not sections, i.e. parts, of the organ in question ", and consisted mainly not of deputies elected to the Soviet, but of electors recruited for this special work.[6] Presently, however, the sections themselves became too large for effective work, which was relegated to bureaus of the sections or to sub-sections.[7]

The dual purpose of these institutions was to improve the efficiency of administration and to increase the participation and interest of broad sectors of the population in this work. Conflicting reports make it difficult to assess how far, and in which proportions, these two aims were achieved in the urban Soviets. An article in *Izvestiya* complained that the sections, and the workers who participated in them, had too little contact with the departments of the Soviet;[8] from the Tver Soviet it was reported that only 37 per cent of those enrolled in the sections actually took part in the work.[9] In general, the sections of urban Soviets, in contrast

[1] *Sovetskoe Stroitel'stvo*, No. 10(27), October 1928, p. 122.

[2] *Ibid.* No. 5-6(22-23), May–June 1928, p. 130.

[3] *Pravda*, April 12, 1927; in general, the sections for trade and cooperatives and for finance were the least popular.

[4] *Ezhenedel'nik Sovetskoi Yustitsii*, No. 7, February 22, 1928, p. 193, No. 8, February 29, 1928, pp. 255-256.

[5] *Sobranie Zakonov, 1929*, No. 13, art. 111.

[6] *Sovetskoe Stroitel'stvo*, No. 8(25), August 1928, p. 31.

[7] *Ibid.* No. 10(27), October 1928, pp. 123-124.

[8] *Izvestiya*, May 23, 1928.

[9] *Sovetskoe Stroitel'stvo*, No. 12(29), December 1928, p. 8.

to those of rural Soviets, were said to work effectively.[1] The great
city Soviets of Moscow and Leningrad, and perhaps of other large
cities, with district Soviets subordinate to them, were comprehensive organizations enjoying a substantial amount of power and
prestige, and appear to have built up a substantial *aktiv* of Soviet
workers.[2] But favourable reports emanating from them probably
had little application to smaller urban Soviets in outlying regions.

The category of urban " inhabited points " possessing Soviets
was extremely varied, ranging from the " two capitals " (Moscow
and Leningrad) to small factory settlements ;[3] and definitions in
the legislation of the Union republics was not uniform.   The
RSFSR defined as "urban" all inhabited points with an adult population of more than 1000, of whom not more than 25 per cent were
engaged in agriculture.[4]   In a decree of the RSFSR of September 27, 1926, provision was made for the establishment of workers'
settlements (*poselki*) by decision of the executive committees of
autonomous republics, provinces or regions ; and this was followed
in 1927 by similar decrees providing for health-resort and resi-
dential (*dacha*) settlements.   These were in theory all entitled to
have settlement (*poselkovye*) Soviets.[5]   By Ukrainian legislation
an inhabited point with more than 3000 inhabitants could be
recognized as a " settlement (*poselenie*) of urban type " ;   10,000
inhabitants were required to constitute a town or city.[6]   In 1928
the Ukrainian SSR had 199 settlement Soviets, 48 in factory,
transport or mining settlements, 53 in " local " settlements (i.e.
non-peasant and non-worker settlements, lacking a defined class
character) and 98 in small towns which, falling short of the minimum population of 10,000 required to qualify for an urban

---

[1] *Ibid.* p. 89.   [2] *Izvestiya*, May 23, 1928.
[3] *Ekonomicheskoe Obozrenie*, No. 8, 1928, p. 140, classified 730 urban
inhabited points in the European provinces of the RSFSR under 13 different
heads.   [4] *Sobranie Uzakonenii, 1924*, No. 73, art. 726.
[5] *Ibid. 1926*, No. 65, art. 509 ; *id. 1927*, No. 56, art. 384 ; *id. 1928*, No. 8,
art. 70.   In the autumn of 1926 the number of urban settlements in the RSFSR
was 206 (*Sovetskoe Stroitel'stvo*, No. 3-4, October–November 1926, pp. 121, 126-
127) ; Moscow province had 38 workers' settlement Soviets in 1928 (*ibid.* No.
2(31), February 1929, p. 27.   For the vague term *poselok* see Vol. 1, p. 234,
note 1.
[6] *Zbirnik Uzakonen' ta Rosporyazhen'*, 1924, No. 9, art. 87.

Soviet, were allowed to have settlement Soviets.[1]   The White
Russian SSR recognized urban " localities " (*mestechki*) as well as
towns or cities, but apparently did not lay down limits of number
of inhabitants.[2]   Urban inhabited points throughout the USSR
were officially enumerated on January 1, 1929, as follows :

	RSFSR	Ukrain-ian SSR	White Rus-sian SSR	ZSFSR	Uzbek SSR	Turk-men SSR
Towns or Cities	506	80	29	54	35	8
Settlements (*pose-leniya*) of urban type	—	96	—	—	—	—
Localities	—	—	53	—	—	—
Workers' settle-ments (*poselki*)	263	—	—	—	3	— 3

The central authorities were concerned from time to time to
extend the network of Soviets in urban settlements.   The resolution of the party central committee on urban Soviets of July 11,
1927, called on the government to expedite the formation of
Soviets in workers' settlements ; and this injunction was repeated
in the decree of the USSR on urban Soviets of February 8, 1928.[4]
In the spring of 1928 the Shakhty affair focussed attention on the
miners' settlements of the Donbass region ; and the party central
committee in its resolution on the affair demanded an enquiry into
the settlement Soviets.[5]   The failure of settlement Soviets to
develop an independent economic status was attributed to the fact
that their public services were run either by the state or by the
enterprise (e.g. Donugol) to which they were attached.[6]   An investigation conducted by the Ukrainian authorities reported that

[1] *Sovetskoe Stroitel'stvo*, No. 10(27), October 1928, p. 34.
[2] *Zbor Zakonau i Zahadau BSSR, 1925*, No. 31, art. 293.
[3] *Administrativno-Territarial'noe Delinie SSSR* (8th ed. 1929), p. 12 ; this
classification omitted some smaller settlements (e.g. factory and *dacha* settlements) elsewhere classified as urban inhabited points.
[4] For the resolution and the decree see pp. 284-265 above.
[5] *KPSS v Rezolyutsiyakh* (1954), ii, 509 ; for this resolution see Vol. 1, p.
586.
[6] *Vsesoyuznoe Soveshchanie po Perevyboram Sovetov v 1929 g.* (1928), p. 124.

these Soviets would become effective only if they possessed independent powers and budgets of their own ; at present, they were
described as " nomadic organizations, without possessing even the
covered wagon needed for a nomadic life ". The conclusion was
" to endow the Soviets of the Donbass as quickly as possible with
a full measure of economic and administrative rights ".[1] But a
general account of the settlement Soviets in the spring of 1929
drew a discouraging picture. Few of them had budgets ; some
had presidiums, but many had no staff at all. They were bound to
lack authority so long as " the basic economy of the settlements is
under the control of the economic enterprises ". About the same
time the presidium of TsIK of the RSFSR decided to strengthen
the settlements of the Donets department by assigning to them
buildings, communal enterprises, and shops and warehouses
hitherto the property of Donugol, but not directly utilized in the
processes of production.[2] Settlement Soviets, though recognized
as being of an urban type, clearly shared much of the weakness of
village Soviets, and many of them were at the same primitive stage
of development.

    [1] *Sovetskoe Stroitel'stvo*, No. 10(27), October 1928, pp. 33-34 ; No. 11(28),
November 1928, p. 37.
    [2] *Ibid.* No. 5(34), May 1929, pp. 111, 173.

CHAPTER 50

THE ELECTORAL PROCESS

W HAT distinguished village and urban Soviets from all other Soviet organs was that they were elected by direct popular vote. Village and urban Soviets elected deputies to the district (or rural district) congress of Soviets; and the congress of Soviets at each level elected both deputies to the higher level congress and members of its own executive committee. But these elections, conducted in a closed forum, all had the character of nomination. Only the elections of deputies to village or urban Soviets, by inhabitants in the countryside, or by workers and inhabitants in factories and towns, were direct elections, where the element of nomination was tempered and influenced by popular choice. The amount of attention given by the central authorities to the elections to village and urban Soviets in 1927 and again in 1928–1929 was a measure of the importance attached to them as points of direct contact with the population which provided means of moulding popular opinion and welding it behind the régime.

(a) Soviet Elections, 1927

The *post-mortem* on the Soviet elections of 1925–1926 conducted at the session of the party central committee in July 1926 had sounded an ambiguous note. The disquiet widely felt in party circles about some aspects of the elections could not be openly expressed without playing into the hands of a vocal opposition. But certain guiding lines for the future clearly emerged in the text of the resolution. The party was to be increasingly active, especially in the countryside, and the class issue was to be more strongly emphasized; more non-party workers and more poor and middle peasants were to be drawn into Soviet work; and, most specifically, " the curtailment of the number of persons deprived of electoral rights ", which had been characteristic of the last elections, was to be decisively reversed by a more rigid application of the legal provisions on disqualification. Less realistically, the resolution called for greater participation by " the toilers of the more backward republics and regions ".[1] Belief in annual elections of deputies to Soviets still prevailed ;[2] and on September 28, 1926, the TsIK of the USSR issued detailed instructions for the Soviet elections to be held in the first months of 1927. In addition to the central electoral commission of the USSR, central electoral commissions were to be set up by the Union republics, including workers and peasants directly engaged in production, members of trade unions and of the Komsomol, and representatives of national minorities ; electoral commissions were to function at every level down to that of the town and village. The categories of those disqualified from voting were more precisely defined. Voting was to be open. These instructions were circulated to all the Union republics.[3] The presidium of TsIK decided to convene the fourth Union Congress of Soviets on April 15, 1927, and to begin the elections on January 1, 1927, so that they might be completed in time for the congress.[4]

The next months brought a flow of hortatory pronouncements on the forthcoming elections. The turn away from policies of conciliation of the well-to-do peasant brought about a new and ever shriller insistence on the class war in the countryside, and on the need to isolate the *kulak* by mobilizing the poor peasant and the *batrak* and by winning over the support of the middle peasant. A decree of the party central committee of November 15, 1926,[5] was followed on November 26, 1926, by a circular letter from the TsIK of the USSR to the TsIKs of the Union republics. This described the purpose of the campaign as being to cement the

[1] *KPSS v Rezolyutsiyakh* (1954), ii, 268-280 ; see also *Socialism in One Country, 1924–1926*, Vol. 2, pp. 362-364.

[2] The *rapporteur* at the TsIK of the RSFSR in November 1926 tentatively suggested that, while elections to Soviets should remain annual, elections to higher Soviet executive committees might take place every two years (*III Sessiya Vserossiiskogo Tsentral'nogo Ispolnitel'nogo Komiteta XII Sozyva* (1926), pp. 547-548).

[3] *Sobranie Zakonov, 1926*, No. 66, arts. 500, 501 ; for a decree of the RSFSR of November 4, 1926, elaborating these instructions, see *Sobranie Uzakonenii, 1926*, No. 75, art. 577.

[4] *Sovetskoe Stroitel'stvo*, No. 3-4, October–November 1926, p. 154.

[5] *Izvestiya Tsentral'nogo Komiteta VKP(B)*, No. 49(170), December 10, 1926, pp. 2-3.

alliance between workers and poor and middle peasants, and to achieve " the final liquidation of the political influence of the *kulaks* on the peasant masses ". Party workers were to be sent to the countryside to assist in the task.[1] In December 1926 a further instruction of the party central committee warned local party organizations to be on their guard against attempts by *kulaks*, nepmen and other bourgeois elements to influence the elections;[2] and the central committee in a resolution of December 30, 1926, embroidered the theme of a struggle between workers and *kulaks* to win over the middle peasant, whose support was crucial: to revitalize the Soviets meant " to draw into them the whole basic mass of the peasantry ".[3] Kalinin, perhaps deliberately adopting a milder tone, declared that " the most important slogan of the campaign " would be " we are building socialism in our country ".[4] But Molotov greeted the new year with an article arguing that the elections were destined to " show up more clearly class interests and class contradictions in the peasantry " and that the new Soviets would " reflect more fully *the influence of poor peasants and batraks* "; the result would be " the full control of the whole state apparatus by the working class ".[5] Less attention was paid to the class issue in the towns. But the TsIK of the RSFSR in November 1926 gave instructions " to strengthen the proletarian core in urban Soviets " and " to prevent the infiltration into urban Soviets of exploiting elements of the population ".[6]

As in all Soviet institutions, the desire to educate and instruct was an important factor. An elaborate system of " reports " was devised, under which, before the elections, representatives of executive committees reported on their work to lower Soviet organs. District or sometimes department executive committees reported to meetings of village Soviets; " anti-Soviet elements " were said sometimes to utilize these meetings for their purposes — presumably by heckling the speaker. Department executive committees were supposed to report in the same way to urban

[1] *Sobranie Zakonov, 1926*, No. 75, art. 594.

[2] *Izvestiya Tsentral'nogo Komiteta VKP(B)*, No. 50-51(171-172), December 24, 1926, pp. 1-2; the circular also appeared in *Pravda*, December 28, 1926.

[3] *Spravochnik Partiinogo Rabotnika*, vi (1928), i, 631-634.

[4] *Izvestiya*, December 18, 1926.

[5] *Pravda*, January 1, 1927.

[6] *Sovetskoe Stroitel'stvo*, No. 5, December 1926, p. 142.

Soviets, but generally confined themselves to circulating pamphlets and leaflets.[1]   The decisive moment in Soviet elections was the preparation of the list of candidates.   Alternative candidates rarely appeared, and the option of voting against the list was meaningless; those who came to vote voted for it.   But the drawing up of the list raised in an acute form the problem of reconciling the injunction to the party to exercise functions of leadership and the injunction not to resort to procedures of command and nomination which would antagonize non-party workers and peasants.   The principle was clearly enunciated : every candidate must be subjected to " a preliminary check in the non-party *aktiv* ", and then pass " through the filter of criticism by leading workers and peasants " in order to ensure the elimination of " worthless and unsuitable candidates, party or non-party ".[2]   What seems to have happened in practice was that a first list was drawn up by party or Komsomol organs, and agreed at a joint meeting of party and Soviet authorities : this was then discussed, modified and agreed in consultation with the local *aktiv*.[3]   Attempts were made by *kulaks* " to penetrate the Soviets and introduce *kulak* spokesmen ".[4]   The degree of pressure applied from above no doubt varied considerably from place to place.[5]   Party attitudes were not uniform.   While *Pravda* reported with satisfaction that the proportion of party members in village Soviets was increasing, Molotov condemned the packing of Soviets with " nominated candidates " as likely to divorce the Soviets from the mass of non-party peasants.[6]   The latter view came to prevail —

---

[1] *Ibid.* No. 4(9), April 1927, pp. 64-68.

[2] *Ibid.* No. 5, December 1926, pp. 6-7.

[3] *Ibid.* No. 7(12), July 1927, pp. 71-73 ; this account comes from the Ukraine, where elections in the rural areas were perhaps more efficiently organized than in the other republics.

[4] *Ibid.* No. 5, December 1926, p. 8 ; in a later report nepmen and *kulaks* were said to have organized " illegal pre-election meetings ", where they planned tactics and discussed candidates (*ibid.* No. 8(25), August 1928, p. 6).   Opposition was, however, less vocal than in the previous elections (*ibid.* No. 4(9), April 1927, p. 5).

[5] According to an optimistic report from the Ukraine, " the elections passed off without any kind of pressure or orders, which had not been absent from previous campaigns " (*ibid.* No. 7(12), July 1927, p. 73) ; Kaganovich boasted that " an almost complete end was made of the old method of command and administrative pressure, of war-time methods " (L. Kaganovich, *Partiya i Sovety* (1928), p. 70).

[6] *Pravda*, January 30, February 4, 1927.

at any rate, officially.   Another article in *Pravda* condemned attempts to fix high percentages of party members for election to Soviets as " incorrect and politically harmful ", and mentioned with disapproval urban Soviets where the percentage had risen from 35 to 74 and village Soviets where it had risen from 10 to 28.[1] The party central committee on March 15, 1927, passed a resolution insisting that, of those elected to county, provincial or central executive committees (where the proportion of party members would be higher than in lower Soviets), not less than one-third should be non-party.[2]

The most important concrete issue in the preparations for the new elections was that of the franchise.   In 1925–1926 the electoral lists had notoriously included many of those petty capitalist and bourgeois voters whom the constitution had purported to debar.[3]   The decree of the TsIK of the USSR of September 28, 1926, was an attempt to introduce greater stringency and greater uniformity into the process of drawing up the new lists.   It enunciated once more the main categories of those excluded from voting — employers of hired labour for purposes of profit, those living on unearned incomes or occupied in trade, and those disqualified, by reason of social status or occupation, under the existing republican constitutions.   The circular of November 26, 1926, admitted that the " extended interpretation " given to previous legislation had led to the granting of electoral rights to " persons deprived of this right under the constitutions of the Union republics and the constitution of the USSR ", and endeavoured to define more precisely the excluded categories.[4]   Molotov told a trade union audience in January 1927 that in the elections of 1925–1926 the proportion of those disfranchised had been only 1 per cent ;   in the forthcoming elections it must rise to 3-4, or, exceptionally, to 5-7 per cent.[5]

These repeated injunctions had their effect.   Local electoral commissions vied with one another in excluding suspect voters. In the towns, where the percentage of the disfranchised had previously been higher than in the countryside, a modest increase in

---

[1] *Pravda*, February 18, 1927.
[2] *Spravochnik Partiinogo Rabotnika*, vi (1928), i, 629.
[3] See *Socialism in One Country, 1924–1926*, Vol. 2, pp. 331-333.
[4] For these pronouncements see p. 275 above.
[5] *Bednota*, February 5, 1927.

the rate seems to have caused no trouble. But in the first weeks of 1927, complaints flowed in from the countryside of harsh and capricious interpretations of the instruction. Kalinin reported on these to the party central committee in February 1927 ;[1] and the committee in its resolution, while rehearsing the aims and tasks of the party in this " second *broad and open* campaign for elections to the Soviets ", added a significant rider :

> At the same time it is indispensable to pay particular attention to the correct application of the electoral instruction directed against the *kulaks*, and only against them. The correct application of the instruction should not drive away from the Soviet the middle strata in the countryside. To deprive the middle peasant of electoral rights is objectively a direct help to the *kulaks*. Every attempt at so broad an interpretation of the instruction as to bring the middle peasant into the category of those deprived of electoral rights must be regarded as a very gross political blunder.[2]

Pravda took up the cry, and protested especially against the disfranchisement of teachers in rural areas.[3] Kiselev in an article in *Izvestiya* expressed the fear that the link with the peasantry would be weakened by the election of too many *batraks*.[4] The peasant newspaper prominently featured a letter from Rykov to Enukidze pleading the cause of a peasant of Smolensk province unjustly disfranchised.[5] Other odd examples of discrimination were quoted. In Vyatka province men over 60 and women over 50 were disqualified as being too old to work ; cases occurred in Novgorod province where those cultivating no land or paying no agricultural tax were excluded from the lists.[6] Reports spoke of mass disfranchisement of well-to-do — and some less well-to-do — middle peasants.[7] The presidium of TsIK of the RSFSR issued a revised

---

[1] M. Kalinin, *Voprosy Sovetskogo Stroitel'stva* (1958), pp. 332-347.

[2] *KPSS v Rezolyutsiyakh* (1954), ii, 358.

[3] *Pravda*, February 17, 1927 ; according to a later report, 30 per cent of all teachers in one rural district were disfranchised on the ground that they were children of priests, or had relations with *kulaks* (*Sovetskoe Stroitel'stvo*, No. 8(25), August 1928, p. 10).

[4] *Izvestiya*, February 19, 1927.   [5] *Bednota*, March 10, 1927.

[6] *III Sessiya Vserossiiskogo Tsentral'nogo Ispolnitel'nogo Komiteta XII Sozyva* (1926), p. 523.

[7] *Sovetskoe Stroitel'stvo*, No. 4(9), April 1927, pp. 12-21 ; *Vlast' Sovetov*, No. 19, May 8, 1927, p. 22.

instruction not to disfranchise the following categories : peasants
engaged on seasonal work in towns who employed hired labour
during their absence ; workers in factories who retained land in the
countryside and employed labour to cultivate it ; artisans and
craftsmen ; members of *artels* hiring out their labour.[1] These
attempts to put a brake on the zeal of the enthusiasts had some
effect. While Molotov had advocated anything from a three-fold
to a seven-fold increase in the number of those disqualified, the
final figures showed that between two and three times as many
persons were disqualified from voting in 1927 as in 1925–1926,
and that, while increases occurred in every category, the heaviest
increase of all was due to the more rigorous exclusion of " dependants " of those disqualified.[2]

On April 14, 1927, *Pravda* announced the completion of the
elections in an atmosphere of official jubilation. Bauman, the
secretary of the Moscow party organization, described the elections
in Moscow city and province as " a kind of popular political fes-
tival, which, once again and still more closely, united the mass of
toilers round the proletarian dictatorship ".[3] A report from the
Ukraine averred that " the leadership of party and Soviet organs "
in the campaign had been more satisfactory than ever before, that
the authority of the party " grew and was strengthened during the
electoral campaign ", and that " the broad masses of the electors "
had displayed increased interest and activity.[4] Meanwhile, the
statisticians began to collate results. In the elections to urban
Soviets nearly 60 per cent of those qualified had voted, representing a substantial advance on the previous elections. In the elections to village Soviets, rather less than 50 per cent had voted ;
the proportions for the RSFSR (47·4 per cent) and for White

---

[1] *Pravda*, February 19, 1927. The employment of hired labour seems to
have been the main crux in determining who should, and should not, be disqualified ; an article in *Vlast' Sovetov*, No. 42, October 7, 1926, pp. 1-4, had
complained of the ambiguities of the original instruction of September 28, 1926,
on this point.

[2] See Table No. 63, p. 486 below. In the RSFSR nearly 40 per cent, in
the Ukraine nearly 50 per cent of those excluded were disqualified as members of
families of disqualified persons ; doubts were expressed about the legality of
some of these exclusions, which were apparently an innovation in these elections
(*Sovetskoe Stroitel'stvo*, No. 4(9), April 1927, pp. 6, 12, 70).

[3] *Pravda*, March 20, 1927.

[4] *Sovetskoe Stroitel'stvo*, No. 4(9), April 1927, pp. 75, 82-83.

Russia (46·4 per cent) were the same as in 1925–1926, and for the Ukraine (51·1 per cent) had actually declined.[1] The disqualification of the most active voters in previous elections may have contributed to this result. It seems clear that the régime was less successful in rallying mass support in the countryside than in the towns. The participation of " organized " (i.e. trade union) proletarian voters was said to have increased ; and statistics were quoted to show that activity in the countryside had " lagged behind the activity of the urban proletariat" .[2] The verdict on the elections in the rural areas was ambivalent. The attempt to drive a wedge between richer and poorer peasants had ended in failure, and helped to exacerbate relations between the régime and the peasantry as a whole. Statistics of those elected to village Soviets and to higher Soviet organs in the countryside showed at all levels a marked increase in the proportion of poor peasants, of " workers and *batraks* ", and of party and Komsomol members, and a decrease in the proportion of employees.[3] But, while Kaganovich claimed that in 1927 the poor peasant, and no longer the middle peasant, had been " to a significant extent the master in the elections ",[4] another commentator referred to " a distortion (peregib) . . . in the sense of a sharp increase in the representation of poor peasants and *batraks* in the Soviets at the expense of the middle peasants ", and thought that this reacted unfavourably on the bloc between poor and middle peasants.[5] The controversies on future policy which divided the party were reflected in divergent interpretations of the results of the elections.

[1] See Table No. 64, p. 487 below. The highest percentages in the 1927 elections to urban Soviets were said to have been registered by Red Army men (77) and by trade unionists (70) (*Osnovnye Itogi Raboty Pravitel'stva SSSR k Perevyboram Sovetov 1928–29 g.* (1928), p. 25) ; the important rôle of Red Army men in the elections was later emphasized by Enukidze (*Vsesoyuznoe Soveshchanie po Perevyboram Sovetov v 1929 g.* (1928), pp. 45-46).

[2] *Sovetskoe Stroitel'stvo*, No. 8-9(13-14), August–September 1927, pp. 9, 14 ; Kosior spoke at the fifteenth party congress in December 1927 of the " comparatively slow " growth of peasant activity in the elections (*Pyatnadtsatyi S"ezd VKP(B)*, i (1961), 100) — the comparison being presumably with the towns.

[3] See Table No. 65, p. 488 below.

[4] L. Kaganovich, *Partiya i Sovety* (1928), p. 72.

[5] *Sovetskoe Stroitel'stvo*, No. 5-6(22-23), May–June 1928, p. 163.

(b) Soviet Elections, 1929

The theory of annual elections to Soviets had not been discarded; and in the autumn of 1927, when all political activity centred round the celebration of the tenth anniversary of the revolution, it was still assumed that fresh elections would be held in the following spring. A resolution of the party central committee of September 5, 1927, called for elections between January and April 1928.[1] On November 19, 1927, the presidium of TsIK of the USSR resolved that the elections should take place on the same basis as in the preceding year, appointed a central electoral commission under the presidency of Enukidze, and issued a circular letter of instruction to the TsIKs of the Union republics.[2] *Pravda* declared in a leading article that, in view of " the aggressive economic course " now being pursued, the elections should take the form of " a political offensive " against the enemies of the proletariat.[3] The Turkmen SSR, with an enthusiasm born of inexperience, hastened to fix the beginning of its elections for December 20, 1927. The other republics pleaded that, in face of their many commitments on behalf of planning and socialist construction, they could not mount another electoral campaign so soon; and on January 6, 1928, an announcement suddenly appeared in the press that, in response to " petitions from various individual Union republics and regions of the RSFSR ", the elections had been postponed to the autumn. The Turkmen elections, having already begun, were allowed to go forward.[4] Unfortunately the autumn, on the strength of recent practice, was pre-empted for other campaigns — the elections to the boards of consumer cooperatives, rural and urban, the trade union campaign for the collective contracts in the factories, the elections to the peasant committees of mutual aid.[5] In the end, the elections to

[1] *Spravochnik Partiinogo Rabotnika*, vi (1928), ii, 634.
[2] *Sovetskoe Stroitel'stvo*, No. 12(17), December 1927, p. 104.
[3] *Pravda*, December 1, 1927.
[4] The suddenness of the decision is shown by the fact that *Bednota*, January 6, 1928, which announced the decision on a back page, carried on its front page a prominently featured article on the forthcoming elections; for the circumstances of the postponement see *Sovetskoe Stroitel'stvo*, No. 11(18), January 1928, pp. 41-43.
[5] *Izvestiya Tsentral'nogo Komiteta VKP(B)*, No. 34-35(207-208), September 17, 1927, pp. 1-2, 5.

the Soviets were not held till the first months of 1929 — two years after the previous elections.[1]

The election campaign was launched in earnest at a conference at which the USSR, the Union republics and local Soviet organs were all represented, meeting in Moscow from October 9 to 11, 1928. Kaganovich delivered a report on the political aims, and Enukidze on the practical problems, of the elections. A number of other speeches were made; and a record of the proceedings was circulated to local authorities.[2] Kaganovich explained once more that the party must not refrain " from leadership, from putting forward candidates ", but must not " crush the will of the electors ". He stressed the class issue, and the need to mobilize *batraks*, poor peasants and a majority of middle peasants against the *kulak*. At the same time the material interests of the electors — buildings, roads, bridges, schools — should not be neglected : " the whole sum of the practical needs of the worker's and peasant's life " should be discussed at electoral meetings. Enukidze admitted that instructions were sometimes ambiguous, that discrepancies existed between those of the USSR and those of the republics, and in particular repeated the warning " not to try at all costs to increase the percentage of those deprived of electoral rights ".[3] A circular from Narkomyust to local judicial authorities urged the need to protect the legal rights of workers and peasants, and to ensure that electoral lists were drawn up in conformity with the law.[4] Kalinin opened the public campaign in November 1928 in a speech of rather confused good will. The current slogan of

[1] The proposal to hold elections in the summer (see *Socialism in One Country, 1924–1926*, Vol. 2, p. 308) was revived at the TsIK of the RSFSR in November 1926, when 15 provinces wanted elections in summer, 26 in autumn and 14 in winter (*III Sessiya Vserossiiskogo Tsentral'nogo Komiteta XII Sozyva* (1926), p. 524; see also *Sovetskoe Stroitel'stvo*, No. 8-9(13-14), August–September 1927, p. 63) ; it was rejected, presumably on the ground that the peasant would be unable to leave his work.

[2] The reports and concluding remarks of Kaganovich and Enukidze and a few of the other speeches were published in *Vsesoyuznoe Soveshchanie po Perevyboram Sovetov v 1929 g.* (1928), which was presumably the document circulated ; for an account of the conference see *Sovetskoe Stroitel'stvo*, No. 11(28), November 1928, pp. 105-109. The text of Kaganovich's report diverges in places from the version in *Pravda*, October 24, 1928.

[3] *Vsesoyuznoe Soveshchanie po Perevyboram Sovetov v 1929 g.* (1928), pp. 17-18, 24-25, 39-41, 49.

[4] *Ezhenedel'nik Sovetskoi Yustitsii*, No. 36-37, September 30/October 7, 1928, p. 1008.

self-criticism meant, not " criticism for the sake of criticism ", or just making a noise, but the correction of so-called " inevitable mistakes ". The duty of "*personal criticism*" of candidates for election was linked with the vision of a new society:

> We are creating a new man, whose characteristic traits must be quite different from those of the man who grew up in the capitalist world.

He concluded with an appeal to recognize the activity of the communist party as " dictated by the interests of the working class and of the overwhelming majority of its faithful allies, the peasantry ".[1] Kalinin also delivered a report to the session of the TsIK of the USSR in December 1928, in which he contrasted the meaningless elections in bourgeois countries with Soviet elections, which were " a vast political school of immense significance ", which sought to " inspire the worker and peasant masses, to arm them with will and impulse for the struggle for communism, for the struggle for socialist construction "; and in his concluding speech he reverted to the absorbing preoccupation of the party leaders:

> *We must isolate the* kulak *politically, and steer into the struggle against the* kulak *the millions of non-party peasants.*[2]

The party central committee issued a new year manifesto to all party committees setting out the aims to be put before the electors: peace and an increase in the defence capacity of the USSR; maintenance of the tempo of industrialization; an increase in the yield, and the socialist reconstruction, of agriculture; and the struggle against bureaucratism.[3]

In the hope of establishing a sense of real contact between electors and elected, between the masses and their deputies in the Soviets, some attention was paid at this time to the right of recall. Under art. 75 of the constitution of the RSFSR of 1925, repeating the provision of art. 78 of the constitution of 1918, electors to Soviets could at any time recall a deputy elected by them and hold a new election; this right was specifically reaffirmed in the statutes of rural and urban Soviets. In the later nineteen-twenties

---

[1] *Sovetskoe Stroitel'stvo*, No. 11(28), pp. 5-14; this issue of the journal of TsIK was devoted entirely to the forthcoming elections.

[2] *4 Sessiya Tsentral'nogo Ispolnitel'nogo Komiteta Soyuza SSR 4 Sosyva* (1928), No. 27, p. 4.   [3] *Pravda*, January 1, 1929.

the practice had fallen into disuse, though Soviets sometimes themselves unconstitutionally expelled unsuitable deputies.[1] One advantage of the practice was to draw the maximum number of ordinary people into active participation in Soviet work; this was a goal in itself, as well as a safeguard against bureaucratism.[2] It was recorded that, during the first ten years of the revolution, 8,700,000 persons had at one time or another served as deputies to village Soviets and 800,000 to urban Soviets; nine millions had been elected to rural district (or district), county (or department) and provincial (or regional) congresses of Soviets, and 700,000 to the executive committees of these organs. Of all these more than 60 per cent had served only for a single term, the rapid turnover giving the opportunity for as many as possible to share the experience.[3] In November 1927 when new elections were projected, the TsIK of the USSR went out of its way to remind the Union republics of the importance of the right of recall;[4] and after this deputies were said to have been recalled in " a number of towns ".[5] In July 1928 a decree of the RSFSR described the right of recall as " one of the most important forms of Soviet democracy "; and local Soviets, trade unions, Krestkomy, and other public organizations were encouraged to bring before the electors, if the latter did not raise it on their own initiative, the question of the recall of deputies for neglect of duties or other forms of misconduct.[6] The right of recall was stressed by Kaganovich and Enukidze, as well as by other speakers, at the Union conference on the elections in October 1928.[7] In the following year, considerable numbers of members of urban Soviets were reported to have been recalled on grounds of " passivity and unsatisfactory work ".[8]

It is clear that the elections were more thoroughly organized than ever before. The number of electoral commissions was

[1] *Sovetskoe Stroitel'stvo*, No. 12(19), December 1928, pp. 96-97.
[2] See pp. 296-298 below.
[3] L. Kaganovich, *Partiya i Sovety* (1928), pp. 60-61.
[4] *Sovetskoe Stroitel'stvo*, No. 12(17), December 1927, p. 105.
[5] *Ibid.* No. 1(18), January 1928, p. 44.
[6] *Sobranie Uzakonenii, 1928*, No. 104, art. 657.
[7] *Vsesoyuznoe Soveshchanie po Perevyboram Sovetov v 1929 g.* (1928), pp. 19, 103.
[8] *SSSR: Ot S"ezda k S"ezdu (Aprel' 1927–Mai 1929)* (1929), p. 124; for figures from the Samarkand and Tashkent Soviets see *Sovetskoe Stroitel'stvo*, No. 5-6(22-23), May–June 1928, pp. 198-199.

increased, and the area covered by each reduced.[1] A decree of the presidium of the TsIK of the RSFSR laid down procedures for the checking and purging of lower electoral commissions,[2] which seem to have been extensively applied. In the Siberian region 2000 members of electoral commissions were purged, and the quotas of poor peasants, *batraks*, middle peasants and women increased.[3] More than 50,000 workers were despatched from towns and factories to the countryside to take part in the campaign. Electors marched to the voting assemblies in procession, headed by party or Komsomol members, with banners and music.[4] Confusion sometimes occurred over the voting procedure. Article 30 of the instruction of the USSR of September 28, 1926, provided that candidates who received " a majority of the votes of electors taking part in the vote " were elected. In some places this was taken to require a majority of electors present at its meeting, whether they voted or not ; in others, the candidate who received most votes was elected, though, where three or more candidates presented themselves, this might be a minority vote. A more common abuse was the practice of voting, not for candidates individually, but *en bloc* for a list of candidates.[5] This had been strongly condemned by Enukidze at the Union conference of October 1928,[6] but doubtless proved too convenient to be discarded. Voting was open, and the whole constituency generally voted at the same time, though cases were recorded in which voting assemblies went on for two or three days.[7]

The feature which distinguished Soviet elections in the countryside in the first months of 1929 from those two years earlier was the increase in tension due to the events of the intervening period. The " offensive against the *kulak* ", which had found its economic *raison d'être* in the grain collections, took political shape in the electoral campaign, when slogans of class warfare were loudly proclaimed, and attempts made to organize the *batrak*, and

---

[1] *Sovetskoe Stroitel'stvo*, No. 4(33), April 1929, p. 100.
[2] *Vlast' Sovetov*, Prilozhenie, No. 1, January 9, 1929, p. 12.
[3] *Sovetskoe Stroitel'stvo*, No. 12(41), December 1929, p. 3, which also gives an analysis of the final composition of the commissions in four republics.
[4] *SSSR: Ot S"ezda k S"ezdu (Aprel' 1927–Mai 1929)* (1929).
[5] *Sovetskoe Stroitel'stvo*, No. 12(29), December 1928, pp. 111-114.
[6] *Vsesoyuznoe Soveshchanie po Perevyboram Sovetov v 1929 g.* (1928), pp. 54-55.
[7] *SSSR: Ot S"ezda k S"ezdu (Aprel' 1927–Mai 1929)* (1929), pp. 130-131.

the poor and middle peasant, against the *kulak*. Resistance was certainly offered by well-to-do peasants, with support from large numbers of poorer peasants who sympathized with them rather than with the authorities. In one village in the province of Penza *batraks* were disfranchised as " non-working elements " because they had no land; and the president of another village Soviet asked contemptuously : " Can *batraks* really have voting rights? " [1] Open defiance was probably confined to remote and out-of-the-way regions. It was noted that " the nearer to the periphery, the worse the social composition of the electoral commissions ".[2] In some places, *kulaks* were said to have organized " underground ' electoral commissions ' ", and put forward lists of candidates. But the more usual method was to conduct propaganda urging peasants to boycott the elections.[3] Two circulars of Narkomyust in January 1929 reminded courts and procurators of their duty to take vigorous measures against persons attempting to prevent *batraks* and poor peasants from participating in the elections.[4] In Novgorod " hostile whisperings " were heard against the cooperatives and against the electoral commissions. In Stalino a worker, suborned by *kulaks*, declared at a meeting that " the Soviet Government has given us nothing and done nothing for us ", but was shouted down. In Tashkent, tinkers and baptists interrupted a meeting with shouting and whistling.[5] Houses of party and Soviet officials in the countryside were reported to have been burned down during the campaign; and hooligans broke up electoral meetings, " especially meetings of women ".[6] Such incidents were the basis of later allegations of a " *kulak* terror ".[7]

[1] *Sovetskoe Stroitel'stvo*, No. 5(34), May 1929, p. 133.
[2] *Izvestiya Tsentral'nogo Komiteta VKP(B)*, No. 36(257), December 15, 1928, p. 1. In Uzbekistan, Turkmenistan and Siberia large numbers of *kulaks* and similar types were members of electoral commissions (*Sovetskoe Stroitel'stvo*, No. 4(33), April 1929, p. 98); in some parts of the Transcaucasian SFSR unmarried women of 20 and upwards were classified as " nuns " and disqualified from voting (*ibid.* No. 5(34), May 1929, p. 134).
[3] *SSSR: Ot S"ezda k S"ezdu (Aprel' 1927–Mai 1929)* (1929), pp. 131-132.
[4] *Ezhenedel'nik Sovetskoi Yustitsii*, No. 4, January 31, 1929, pp. 95-96.
[5] *Izvestiya*, April 3, 1928.
[6] *Ezhenedel'nik Sovetskoi Yustitsii*, No. 5, February 7, 1929, pp. 97-98.
[7] *Sovetskoe Stroitel'stvo*, No. 5(34), May 1929, pp. 134-136; *Izvestiya Tsentral'nogo Komiteta VKP(B)*, No. 17-18(276-277), June 29, 1929, p. 12; the archives recorded " 144 terrorist acts " committed by *kulaks* in the Central Black-Earth region during the elections (*Istoricheskie Zapiski*, xli (1952), 225).

Statistically the election results were favourable. The percentage of electors disqualified had not risen significantly (except in Uzbekistan). Striking increases were recorded in the proportion of qualified electors who went to the poll, both for urban and for village Soviets, of women electors exercising their vote, and of women elected to Soviets.[1] Reports on the elections breathed, however, a note of dissatisfaction and anxiety. While they were in progress, an article in the journal of the party central committee deplored the neglect of work among poor peasants, and the neglect of the *batraks* by both party and trade union workers, and repeated the old charge that some party secretaries consorted with *kulaks*, and preached anti-Semitism and political freedom for *kulaks*.[2] The first returns inspired a resolution of the presidium of TsIK which, while noting some positive features, foreshadowed a determination to override the results where these proved unsatisfactory :

> Where representation of middle peasants on the one hand, and of *batraks* and poor peasants on the other, is insufficiently reflected in the Soviets, a check should be urgently carried out on the elections to these Soviets, and steps taken to remedy these defects.

It was necessary to apply strictly the rules of disqualification, and to " call to account those guilty of infringing the electoral law ".[3] On the eve of the elections, on January 7, 1929, the TsIK of the RSFSR had given a warning that the categories of disqualification were " in some places being too widely interpreted ".[4] On March 4, 1929, the presidium of the TsIK of the RSFSR issued a decree calling for a strict review of cases of deprivation of voting rights.[5] A substantial number of those appealing against

[1] See Table No. 65, p. 488 below.

[2] *Izvestiya Tsentral'nogo Komiteta VKP(B)*, No. 2-3(261-262), January 31, 1929, pp. 2-4 ; Kaganovich had already cited cases where Soviet officials from the district executive committee " arrive in a village, call on the *kulak*, drink with him, and then, naturally, do his business for him " (*Vsesoyuznoe Soveshchanie po Perevyboram Sovetov v 1929 g.* (1928), p. 12).

[3] *Pravda*, March 1, 1929. The same issue reported cases where elections had been annulled because too small a proportion of women had been elected ; this practice was denounced as " mechanical leadership ".

[4] *Izvestiya*, January 9, 1929.

[5] *Ibid.* March 5, 1929 ; a circular based on the decree was sent out on March 13, 1929 (*ibid.* March 14, 1929). The circular also referred to a decree of the USSR of March 4, 1929 ; this has not been traced, and may have been a mistake for the decree of the RSFSR.

disqualification were said to have been reinstated.[1]   But it is not clear how many elections were actually annulled.

The fifth Union Congress of Soviets in May 1929 was too much absorbed in economic issues to pay much attention to the elections. It praised in conventional terms " the significant growth in the activity of the broad toiling masses in town and country ", and attributed the success of the elections to the policy of revitalizing the Soviets and to " a strengthening of the lower Soviet apparatus ".[2]   But a party report alleged that, even after the elections, *kulaks* and merchants continued to sit in village Soviets.[3]   A resolution of the party central committee of June 3, 1929, summing up the results betrayed symptoms of anxiety.   The " growth of political consciousness of the industrial proletariat " and the help given by workers to the countryside was praised ;   a bloc was believed to have been established between poor and middle peasants.   Noteworthy features were the " sharpening of class struggle ", the " socialist offensive of the proletariat ", and the " growth of resistance of capitalist elements ".   On the other hand, work had been weak among *batraks* and poor peasants ; distortions had occurred in the party line ;   and some Soviet organizations had been in league with " the *kulak* top stratum ". The conclusion was a call " to remedy the evident defects of the electoral campaign in the work of the Soviets ".[4]   The elections of 1929 may be read as a last attempt by the party and the régime to undermine the resistance of the peasantry from within.   When this failed, the way was open for the direct and naked coercion of " revolution from above ".

[1] *Sovetskoe Stroitel'stvo*, No. 3(44), March 1930, p. 81.
[2] *S"ezdy Sovetov v Dokumentakh*, iii (1960), 155.
[3] *Izvestiya Tsentral'nogo Komiteta VKP(B)*, No. 14-15(273-274), May 31, 1929, pp. 1-3 ; it also appeared in *Pravda*, June 16, 1929.
[4] *Izvestiya Tsentral'nogo Komiteta VKP(B)*, No. 17-18(276-277), June 29, 1929, pp. 12-13.

CHAPTER 51

THE SOVIET BUREAUCRACY

BUREAUCRACY is a long-standing and widely resented evil
of modern society. Dislike and mistrust of bureaucracy
presided at the cradle of the French revolution, and nour-
ished anarchist and liberal creeds throughout the nineteenth century. Democracy, which meant the management of public affairs
by the people, was regarded as the very antithesis of bureaucracy,
which meant their management by the agents of some remote and
alien power. This picture seemed particularly apposite in Russia,
where an army of officials was the embodiment, for the mass of the
population, of a harsh and irresponsible autocracy. It was deeply
embedded in the thinking of the first Bolsheviks, and inspired the
vision in Lenin's *State and Revolution*, written on the eve of the
October revolution, and in Bukharin's and Preobrazhensky's
ABC of Communism written in 1919, of the replacement of a professional bureaucracy by ordinary citizens performing in rotation
the simplified tasks of administration.[1] But, when it came to party
organization, different principles emerged. Lenin, in *What is to
be Done?* written in 1904, distinguished between the firm " organizational principles " of revolutionary democracy and those of the
" opportunists " ; and, in taunting the latter with an attempt to
cloak anarchism under the name of democracy, he had boldly proclaimed that, on this hypothesis, " bureaucracy v. democracy is
the same thing as centralism v. autonomy ". Treating the party
congress as a " centre " from which rights and powers radiated,
he summed up :

Bureaucratism *versus* democratism, this is precisely centralism *versus* autonomism, and this is the organizational principle

[1] The idea was repeated as late as 1931 by a Komsomol leader : " Today you
are a blacksmith, tomorrow the president of a village Soviet ; today, you are a
young lathe-operator or locksmith, tomorrow the secretary of a Komsomol
committee " (*IX Vsesoyuznyi S"ezd VLKSM* (1931), pp. 57-58) ; this echoed a
famous passage in *Die Deutsche Ideologie* (*Karl Marx–Friedrich Engels :
Historisch-Kritische Gesamtausgabe*, Ier Teil, v, 22).

of revolutionary social-democracy as against that of opportunist social-democracy. The latter principle attempts to work
from below upwards, and therefore defends as far as possible
and wherever possible an autonomism, a democratism which
extends (among those whose enthusiasm outruns their reason)
to anarchism. The organizational principle of revolutionary
social-democracy works from above downward, and defends the
extension of the rights and plenipotentiary powers of the central
organ against the party.[1]

In the intervening period Lenin wrote much of the need for
autonomy and for " the state of the commune ". But, when he
faced practical problems on the eve of the seizure of power, he
reverted to his defence of centralism as a principle of authority.
" To demonstrate to Bolsheviks, centralists by conviction, by their
programme, and in the tactics of their whole party ", he concluded,
" the necessity of centralism, is to beat at an open door " ; and,
once the proletariat had taken over the state, " then we are fully
and unconditionally for strong government and for centralism ".[2]
The realism of Lenin's acceptance of strong central direction as a
condition of rational organization, later reflected in his enthusiastic
endorsement of " one-man mangament " in industry,[3] blended
uneasily with the idealism of his premises.

Other ambiguities beset the Bolshevik approach to the problem of bureaucracy. As the Soviet Government consolidated its
power, and gradually and at first insensibly spread its tentacles
over the country, the scope of its bureaucracy grew apace. The
officials who performed rudimentary, but essential, services for
the new régime were often the same people who had performed the
same functions for the old ; not everything had been uprooted by
the revolution. The constant preoccupation with bureaucracy in
Lenin's last writings manifested not only a dislike of bureaucracy
as such, but a profound apprehension that bureaucrats who inherited the habits and the culture of the old régime might overrun
and contaminate the new order.[4] But the trouble was not confined to old bureaucrats. Trotsky early in 1919 rounded on " the
new Soviet bureaucrat " as ignorant, self-important and envious,

[1] Lenin, *Sochineniya*, vi, 313-314.   [2] *Ibid.* xxi, 268.
[3] See *The Bolshevik Revolution, 1917–1923*, Vol. 2, pp. 187-191.
[4] See *Socialism in One Country, 1924–1926*, Vol. 1, pp. 117-119.

and described such officials as " a real menace to the cause of the communist revolution " and " real accomplices of counter-revolution ".[1] Bukharin, whose simple idealism died harder than that of the other leaders, spoke in November 1922 of the danger of creating " a colossal administrative apparatus " which would only " hinder the development of the forces of production ".[2] The dynamic of modern society, as well as the particular Soviet commitment to planning and socialism, decided otherwise. The struggle against bureaucracy had the same illusory character, and for much the same reasons, as the parallel struggle for decentralization.[3] Every attempt at reform drew more power to the centre, and increased the number and authority of those required to exercise it. Old prejudices were exorcized by a semantic device. Everyone denounced bureaucracy; " bureaucratism " was in constant use as a pejorative term. But everyone recognized the need for a body of qualified officials to administer party and Soviet institutions; and this came to be known, by a neutral term, as the party or Soviet " apparatus ". A quotation from Lenin, dating from April 1921, served as an appropriate text:

Without the " apparatus " we should have perished long ago. Without a systematic and obstinate struggle to improve the apparatus we shall perish before we have created a basis for socialism.[4]

The fifteenth party conference in October 1926 branded bureaucratism as " a great evil throughout the whole period of the existence of the Soviet Government ", which was becoming " even more dangerous at the present time ".[5] But the campaign against bureaucracy, thought it derived much of its flavour from the earlier strain of idealism, became in effect a campaign to prune and strengthen the apparatus, to purge it of abuses, and to fit it for the vital tasks entrusted to it.

In 1926 the campaign against bureaucracy, understood in this

---

[1] L. Trotsky, *Kak Vooruzhalas' Revolyutsiya*, i (1923), 170-172; long afterwards, Trotsky alleged that demobilized Red Army officers had introduced authoritarian methods into the administration (L. Trotsky, *The Revolution Betrayed* (Engl. transl. 1937), p. 90).

[2] *Protokoll des Vierten Kongresses der Kommunistischen Internationale* (1923), p. 417.

[3] For this see Vol. 1, pp. 351-354.   [4] Lenin, *Sochineniya*, xxvi, 312.

[5] *KPSS v Rezolyutsiyakh* (1954), ii, 297-298.

sense, entered a new phase. It became an integral part of the campaign for the " régime of economy ", and figured largely in the proclamations and pronouncements relating to it. The TsIK of the USSR at its session in April 1926, while proposing " a further increase in expenditure for cultural and economic needs ", demanded " a relative reduction in expenditure for purely administrative needs ";[1] and the party leaders in a more urgent appeal of April 25, 1926, called for "a severe reduction in the staffs of People's Commissariats, and especially in *khozraschet* establishments and cooperatives ".[2] The decree of June 11, 1926, formalized the demand ; and the joint declaration of August 17, 1926, expressed the demand for economy in monetary terms, calling for a reduction in the annual costs of administration of from 300 to 400 million rubles.[3] Decrees of June and July 1926 specified all-round cuts of 10 per cent.[4] These demands were accompanied by loud denunciations of bureaucratism. Lenin, in one of his last articles, had complained of the " miserably low " level of culture of Soviet administrators.[5] This theme was now constantly repeated. An article in the journal of Gosplan in July 1926 called bureaucratism " the inevitable consequence of the low level of our productive forces and culture ";[6] and Lebed, deputy People's Commissar for Workers' and Peasants' Inspection (Rabkrin), regarded the spread of culture as " the fundamental basis " of the struggle against it.[7] Trotsky, in the opposition platform of September 1927, concentrating on the party bureaucracy, declared that " our party régime is giving birth to an innumerable caste of genuine bureaucrats ", and called for a cutting down of " the present swollen budget of the party " and of " the salaries paid to the apparatus ".[8]

[1] *2 Sessiya Tsentral'nogo Ispolnitel'nogo Komiteta Soyuza SSR: Postanovleniya* (1926), p. 13.

[2] For this appeal see Vol. 1, p. 334.

[3] For the decree and the declaration see Vol. 1, pp. 335-356.

[4] *Sobranie Zakonov, 1926*, No. 54, arts. 395, 396.

[5] See *Socialism in One Country, 1924–1926*, Vol. 1, p. 118.

[6] *Planovoe Khozyaistvo*, No. 7, 1926, p. 12 ; the writer was Bazarov.

[7] *Pravda*, September 23, 1926 ; this was the basic theme of the articles on bureaucracy in *Bol'shaya Sovetskaya Entsiklopediya*, viii (1927), 480-489, and *Malaya Sovetskaya Entsiklopediya*, ii (1928), 936-939.

[8] L. Trotsky, *The Real Situation in Russia* (n.d. [1928]), pp. 124, 130 ; by way of aggravation Trotsky alleged that " one-fourth of those at the head of our party administration are former SRs or Mensheviks " (*ibid.* p. 114).

The appointment of Orjonikidze early in November 1926 to succeed Kuibyshev in the dual office of president of the party central control commission and People's Commissar for Rabkrin [1] provided a fresh stimulus for the campaign. On November 15, 1926, the party central committee followed this up with an instruction to party members, and " especially the control commissions and Rabkrin ", to work for " the eradication of bureaucratism, the introduction of strict economy in the expenditure of state funds, the simplification and cheapening of the apparatus ".[2] Orjonikidze's first major pronouncement on the question after his appointment took the form of a plan submitted to the presidium of the central control commission and approved by it. Both Soviet administration and the management of industry were to be reviewed in the search for economy and for improvement of quality.[3] In a speech to the seventh trade union congress in December 1926, he quoted instances of inflated staffs and failure to reduce them. He dwelt on the proliferation of book-keeping, on the duplication of functions, on " the flood of paper ". But he made no concrete proposals and concluded sagely with the familiar quotation from Lenin about the reform of the apparatus.[4] At the Moscow party provincial conference in January 1927 Stalin also touched on the question of bureaucracy, and quoted one of Lenin's last speeches to the effect that the two most important safeguards were " the choice of people " and " verification of the carrying out of decisions ".[5]

[1] See p. 19 above ; for the fusion of the two institutions see p. 116 above.

[2] *Izvestiya Tsentral'nogo Komiteta VKP(B)*, No. 49(170), December 10, 1926, pp. 2-3 ; it was also published in *Pravda*, December 9, 1926.

[3] *Ibid.* December 3, 1926 ; repeated articles on this topic appeared in *Pravda* in the next few days and weeks.

[4] *Sed'moi S"ezd Professional'nykh Soyuzov SSSR* (1927), pp. 447-462 ; for the quotation see p. 292 above.

[5] Stalin, *Sochineniya*, ix, 158 ; for Lenin's speech see Lenin, *Sochineniya*, xxvii, 255-259. Orjonikidze's report at the Moscow conference is in G. Orjonikidze, *Stat'i i Rechi* (1957), ii, 23-52. The problem of ensuring that decisions were promptly carried out remained acute throughout this period ; on May 19, 1928, the presidium of TsIK passed a resolution requiring that a date should be fixed for the carrying out of all its decisions ; if Sovnarkom, or the TsIK of any of the republics, thought that the delay was too short, it could petition for a prolongation within three days of the receipt of the decision (*Sovetskoe Stroitel'stvo*, No. 7(24), July 1928, pp. 115-117 ; for a list of outstanding decisions of 1925-1927 which had not been punctually executed see *ibid.* pp. 104-115).

" *The fundamental defect in our apparatus* " [declared Orjonikidze in December 1928] " *is either a devilish delay in the execution of our decisions or a complete ignoring of these decisions or a distortion of their class content.* "[1]

The session of the central control commission which opened on February 4, 1927, was devoted almost exclusively to this theme. The campaign against bureaucratism became at this time the special province of Rabkrin. Orjonikidze in his report explained the new organization of Rabkrin : the three hitherto existing sections — one for verification and control, one for rationalization, one for the study of problems — had been sub-divided into specialized groups. He noted " a new form of bureaucratic distortion " ; " the most arrant bureaucrats cry out louder than anyone against bureaucratism ". Orjonikidze quoted Lenin's famous proposal in the April theses of 1917 that officials should receive " the average wage of a good worker ". He read an unpublished memorandum on Rabkrin and letters to Kursky, the People's Commissar for Justice, and to I. K. Ezhov, an official of Vesenkha, on the abuses of bureaucracy, written by Lenin in 1921 ; these were published next day in *Pravda*.[2] As the emphasis shifted from the régime of economy to rationalization,[3] the campaign against bureaucratism lost nothing of its intensity. On August 30, 1927, Sovnarkom issued a directive to cut all administrative expenses by 20 per cent in the forthcoming financial year 1927–1928.[4] The demand was taken up by the party central control commission, and relayed to control commissions throughout the country.[5] At the fifteenth party congress in December 1927, Kosior complained that, though past injunctions had had some effect, work on the rationalization of the apparatus was still " weak ".[6] At the same congress, Rykov in his reply to the debate on the five-year plan offered some rather naive reflexions on the

[1] *Vos'moi S"ezd Professional'nyk Soyuzov* (1929), p. 267.
[2] The session was fully reported in *Pravda*, February 5, 6, 1927; for Orjonikidze's report see also *Sovetskoe Stroitel'stvo*, No. 2(7), February 1927, pp. 68-70. Lenin's memorandum on Rabkrin is in *Sochineniya*, xxvii, 14-20 (where it is erroneously said to have been printed for the first time in *Leninskii Sbornik*, viii (1929), 42-48); the letters to Kursky and Ezhov are in Lenin, *Sochineniya*, xxix, 403-404, 406-407. For Lenin's proposal on the pay of officials see *ibid.* xx, 89.   [3] See Vol. I, pp. 340-341.
[4] *Sobranie Zakonov*, *1927*, No. 53, art. 542.   [5] *Pravda*, October 1, 1927.
[6] *Pyatnadtsatyi S"ezd VKP(B)*, i (1961), 105.

bureaucracy. The practice by which high officials " mechanically " put their signature to other people's opinions encouraged " de facto irresponsibility "; it ought to be clear who bore responsibility for what. He concluded that the rate of socialist construction depended " on the quality of all our work ", and ended with an appeal for self-criticism.[1] The general resolution of the congress on the report of the party central committee called for a reduction of not less than 20 per cent in administrative costs in 1927–1928. It also proposed to abolish the special disciplinary courts for officials, and to bring those guilty of " criminal carelessness, inadmissible excesses or a bureaucratic attitude to business " before the ordinary courts.[2]

The original conception of the participation of the masses in the day-to-day work of administration as a guarantee against the evils of bureaucracy had never been quite extinguished. What was held to distinguish the dictatorship of the proletariat from other forms of government was its reliance on the active participation of the masses. This conception had helped to inspire the campaigns of 1925 and 1926 for the revitalization of the Soviets,[3] but seemed to have little to do with the campaign to reduce staffs and costs in the major organs of government dictated by the regime of economy.[4] It revived in 1927 with the shift to a more positive policy of rationalization. Molotov boldly proclaimed, on the occasion of the new elections to the Soviets, that the aim should be " the complete taking over of the whole state apparatus by the working class ".[5] In Orjonikidze's report to the central control commission in February 1927, prominence was given to the relations of bureaucracy with the population :

The growing activity of town and country demands a most conscientious, most serious attitude to the interests of the popu-

[1] *Pyatnadtsatyi S"ezd VKP(B)*, ii (1962), 1171-1172.
[2] *KPSS v Rezolyutsiyakh* (1954), ii, 443, 445.
[3] See *Socialism in One Country, 1924–1926*, Vol. 2, pp. 323-324, 326-327, 366-367.
[4] At the outset of the campaign, on June 9, 1926, the central control commission and Rabkrin issued a circular to control commissions on the duty to report on the results of their investigations to " the masses of workers and peasants " (*Spravochnik Partiinogo Rabotnika*, vi (1928), ii, 389); but this was not quite the same thing, and seems to have been a dead letter.
[5] *Pravda*, January 1, 1927.

lation. Every citizen of a Soviet republic ought to be able to get an answer to any question which he puts ; but this we do not have.

The Komsomol, at its fifth conference at the end of March 1927, joined in the hue and cry. In addition to a call in the general resolution " to draw the Komsomol, the masses of young workers, peasants, employees and students into the work of Rabkrin for the improvement of the state apparatus and the struggle against bureaucratism ", the conference passed a special resolution urging Komsomol members to support Rabkrin in its campaign against " bureaucrats and robbers of public funds ".[1] A resolution of the party central committee of May 9, 1927, on rationalization spoke more broadly of the need to draw the masses into the campaign.[2]

The resolution of the fifteenth party congress in December 1927 on the five-year plan, gave a fresh impetus to the movement by declaring that "work on the rationalization of the whole national economy had as its chief and decisive prerequisite *the broad involvement in it of the worker and peasant masses* ".[3] On January 19, 1928, the presidium of the commission decided to set up a joint complaints bureau under the Rabkrins of the USSR and RSFSR with a mandate to conduct investigations into complaints of abuses or maladministration by employees of the Soviet bureaucracy.[4] Zemlyachka, a veteran party worker, was appointed director of the bureau, which called for volunteers for the investigation of complaints, and enrolled more than a thousand workers : 20,000 complaints were investigated in the course of the first year. The practice was established of organizing teams of workers who made unannounced visits to public offices, and reported on their procedures and especially on their attitude to the public.[5] A report of March 1928 described " the drawing in of the masses " as " the one serious and one reliable means of combating bureaucratism ", and considered it " necessary that this apparatus should feel itself under proletarian control and, in general, under the control of the

---

[1] *VLKSM v Rezolyutsiyakh* (1929), pp. 284, 287-290.
[2] *Pravda*, May 15, 1927.   [3] *KPSS v Rezolyutsiyakh* (1954), ii, 466.
[4] *Deyatel'nost' Organov Partiino-Gosudarstvennogo Kontrolya : Sbornik Dokumentov* (1964), pp. 269-270.
[5] *Ibid.* pp. 282-296; *Voprosy Istorii KPSS*, No. 12, 1964, pp. 88-89. An appeal to workers, students and employees to volunteer for this work appeared in *Pravda*, June 16, 1928.

masses which it serves ".[1] The same month saw the appearance
in *Pravda* of the first special supplementary sheet devoted to the
work of Rabkrin ;[2] and supplements continued to appear perio-
dically in *Pravda* during the next two years. The second plenum
of the central control commission early in April 1928 spoke of the
need to draw the masses into the struggle against bureaucratism,
and to reduce administration costs by 20 per cent.[3] The eighth
congress of the Komsomol in May 1928 urged its members to
participate actively in the struggle of Rabkrin against bureaucratism ;[4] groups of Komsomol members recruited to participate
in these campaigns were afterwards known as " light cavalry ".[5]
At the eighth trade union congress of December 1928 Orjonikidze
appealed for cooperation of the temporary control commissions
with Rabkrin in securing the execution of decisions ;[6] and shortly
afterwards a joint instruction to this effect was issued by Rabkrin
and the trade union central council.[7]

The effort to build a link between the struggle against bureaucracy and the political consciousness of the masses was embodied
in the spring of 1928 in the new slogan of " self-criticism ".
This seems to have made a first unnoticed appearance in a speech
of Rykov, who spoke at the fifteenth party congress of " the self-
criticism of the whole party",[8] and was explained in a leading
article in *Pravda* on May 16, 1928 :

> The slogans of self-criticism means a revitalization of inner-
> party, Soviet and trade union *democracy*. It commits us to a

[1] *Deyatel'nost' Organov Partiino-Gosudarstvennogo Kontrolya : Sbornik Dokumentov* (1964), pp. 122, 125 ; for a further report of January 1929 on the bureau see *ibid.* pp. 282-296.

[2] *Pravda*, March 15, 1928.

[3] *Ibid.* April 13, 1928.

[4] *VLKSM v Rezolyutsiyakh* (1929), p. 335.

[5] *Deyatel'nost' Organov Partiino-Gosudarstvennogo Kontrolya : Sbornik Dokumentov* (1964), pp. 143-144, 151 ; the term " light cavalry " had been used — perhaps coined — by Bukharin at the eighth Komsomol congress in May 1928 (*VIII Vsesoyuznyi S"ezd VLKSM* (1928), p. 34), and was repeated by Yakovlev at the sixteenth party conference in April 1929 (*XVI Konferentsiya VKP(B)* (1962), p. 486).

[6] *Vos'moi S"ezd Professional'nykh Soyuzov* (1929), p. 315 ; for the temporary control commissions see Vol. I, pp. 569-572.

[7] *Deyatel'nost' Organov Partiino-Gosudarstvennogo Kontrolya : Sbornik Dokumentov* (1964), pp. 142-143.

[8] *Pyatnadtsatyi S"ezd VKP(B)*, ii (1962), 1169.

strengthening of mass control, to a more energetic, bolder, more systematic drawing of the masses into socialist construction.

The slogan had from the first an ambiguous character. Bukharin told the eighth Komsomol congress in May 1928 that " it does not in the least mean that you criticize somebody else; self-criticism means that you criticize yourself and allow others to criticize you ".[1] But a Leningrad delegate complained that top people, including the Komsomol central committee, were exempt from criticism; and this was not really answered by Stalin's insistence on criticism from below as well as from above.[2] An appeal by the central party committee " to all party members and to all workers " to engage in purposeful self-criticism in order to combat bureaucratism and promote socialist construction was published in *Pravda* on June 3, 1928; this included a section on the improvement of the Soviet apparatus. Three weeks later Stalin intervened with an article in *Pravda* to make it clear that self-criticism did not justify the substitution of "' critical ' shake-ups *from above* " for " mass criticism *from below* ".[3] A session of the central control commission in the last days of August 1928 had before it a report of Lebed on " Self-criticism and the Struggle to Reform the State Apparatus ", and adopted a cautious and ambiguous resolution. Party organizations were said to fear to draw the masses into the work of criticism, and to have paid insufficient attention to the slogan of self-criticism. But " the search for sensation, the irresponsible smearing of business managers and administrators " and " direct or covert persecution for inconvenient criticism " were alike condemned.[4] Several business managers appear to have written to the press complaining of the ill effects of the campaign on labour discipline; this was sharply rebutted as an attempt " to discredit the slogan of self-criticism itself in the guise of a struggle against distortions of it ".[5] Maxim Gorky, recently returned to the Soviet Union from abroad, came out against

[1] *VIII Vsesoyuznyi S"ezd VLKSM* (1928), p. 40.
[2] *Ibid.* p. 81; Stalin, *Sochineniya*, xi, 73.
[3] *Ibid.* xi, 138; the article appeared in *Pravda*, June 26, 1928.
[4] Reports of the session were published in *Pravda*, August 28, 29, 30, 31, 1928, the resolution on self-criticism *ibid.* September 1, 1928; the record of the session, published under the title *III Plenum TsKK Sozyva XV S"ezda VKP(B)* (1928), has not been available.
[5] *Pravda*, September 9, 1928.

" self-criticism " on the ground that it obscured the " immense
achievements " of the régime and gave a handle to bourgeois
critics.[1]

The results of the campaign for economy and rationalization
cannot be assessed with any degree of precision. In the spring of
1927, when the campaign was a year old, many optimistic estimates
were current. The liquidation of 200 branches of banks had resulted in an annual saving of 6-8 million rubles; of 95 Exchanges in
a saving of 10-11 millions ; of 645 trading agencies in Moscow alone
with a staff of 3000 in a saving of 14 millions ; the liquidation of
some transport organizations and the reorganization of others had
saved 4 millions ; a simplification of the apparatus of trusts and
Sovkhozy 2 millions. The apparatus of rural Soviet organs was
said to have been reduced by 80 per cent. The staff of Narkomfin,
amounting to 1680, had been cut by one-third.[2] The headquarters staff of Vesenkha was to be cut by 25 per cent.[3] At a
congress of the trade union of Soviet and trade employees in May
1927, Rykov and Figatner, the president of the union, heavily
stressed the need to improve and reduce the apparatus of Soviet
and trading institutions, but gave little precise information.[4]
In the Ukrainian SSR, the staffs of People's Commissariats were to
be cut by from 30 to 40 per cent, and of the territorial departments (okruga) by from 25 to 29 per cent.[5] The White Russian
SSR proposed to introduce " a functional structure of the apparatus ", involving a reduction in number of officials by from 30 to
50 per cent.[6]

Doubts were felt from the first about the reality of some of these
reductions. Figatner at the fifteenth party conference in October
1926 criticized estimates of 10 or 13 per cent reductions in the

[1] *Vos'moi S"ezd Professional'nykh Soyuzov SSSR* (1929), p. 275.
[2] See the reports by Lebed and Yakovlev, both deputy People's Commissars
for Rabkrin, in *Pravda*, April 16, May 4, 1927.
[3] *Torgovo-Promyshlennaya Gazeta*, August 29, 1926.
[4] *Pravda*, May 12, 1927. The number of employees covered by this union
was stated at the fifteenth party congress in December 1927 to be 963,000
(*Pyatnadtsatyi S"ezd VKP(B)*, i (1961), 519) ; it did not include employees in
transport or in industrial establishments.
[5] *Izvestiya*, July 30, 1927.
[6] *Sovetskoe Stroitel'stvo*, No. 5-6(10-11), May–June 1927, p. 27.

staffs of People's Commissariats, and declared that the true figure did not exceed 4 per cent; an interjection from Kosior provoked a scathing retort:

> Yes, comrade Kosior, you have the figures, and we know what is happening in the machine: that is the difference between us. They give you a reduction of dead souls, and we say that this reduction does not exist in real life.[1]

In the budget for 1926–1927 provision was made for a reduction of staff in Union organs by 8683; but this was soon overtaken by an increase of more than 58,000, of whom some 37,000 represented an expansion of existing organs and 20,000 the acquisition of new functions.[2] Complaints were heard, not only of the inflated numbers, but of the poor quality, of personnel. Rapid turnover of staff was a frequent source of inefficiency. The apparatus of Narkomindel owed its excellence to "the stability of the personal composition of its directing group". On the other hand, the apparatus of Vesenkha and (paradoxically) of Rabkrin had been subjected to constant reorganization, and was very poor. A decree of the presidium of TsIK of May 4, 1927, authorizing Rabkin to advise on staff reductions had encountered resistance on this score, and had been applied " with the greatest caution ".[3] The defects of Rabkrin were confirmed at the fifteenth party congress in December 1927 by Orjonikidze, who pointed out that it could not fulfil its task unless the party assigned to it " the best workers "; and Shkiryatov complained that good party workers were first sent to the economic organizations, and to Rabkrin only in the last resort.[4] A decree of the RSFSR instructing executive

---

[1] *XV Konferentsiya Vsesoyuznoi Kommunistichiskoi Partii (B)* (1927), p. 239.

[2] *Sed'moi S"ezd Professional'nykh Soyuzov SSSR* (1927), p. 449. A similar relation between reductions and additions was found in all the Union republics, except the RSFSR: here, doubtless as a result of transfer of functions to the USSR, the number of posts abolished (25,000) exceeded the number of new posts created (less than 20,000). The same figures, originally given by Orjonikidze to the seventh trade union congress in December 1926, were repeated by him a month later to the Moscow party conference (G. Orjonikidze, *Stat'i i Rechi* (1957), ii, 23-24).

[3] *Sovetskoe Stroitel'stvo*, No. 5-6(22-23), May–June 1928, pp. 60-61; for the decree see *ibid.* No. 5-6(10-11), May–June 1927, p. 150.

[4] *Pyatnadtsatyi S"ezd VKP(B)*, i (1961), 466, 594; two years later Orjonikidze was still complaining that the best party workers were not assigned to Rabkrin, but only " people with a party ticket dating from before the flood " (G. Orjonikidze, *Stat'i i Rechi* (1957), ii, 180).

committees to cut down the numbers of interdepartmental
commissions and conferences at all levels was apparently ineffective.[1]

Optimistic estimates gradually gave way to more realistic
assessments of the limits of possible reductions in the administrative apparatus. At the fifteenth party congress in December 1927
Orjonikidze admitted that the demands of the regime of economy
campaign had not been fully met, but pleaded that " we have
saved an awful lot ".[2] A decree of May 17, 1928, unlike its
predecessors in previous years, set only the modest aim of not
exceeding in 1928–1929 the administrative costs of 1927–1928.[3]
Orjonikidze, in a long review at the eighth trade union congress in
December 1928, admitted that " we cannot boast of great successes
in this matter ", and claimed only " the elimination of some
defects ".[4] Comprehensive statistics of the personnel of Soviet
institutions in these years showed that the progressive increase in
numbers was slowed down after May 1, 1926, but continued
throughout this period. Personnel employed in public administration (except in organs of public order and security), and in
economic institutions, including state trading and credit institutions, was reduced ; personnel employed in social and cultural
services, mainly education and health, increased.[5] Orjonikidze
gave to the sixteenth party congress in 1930 striking figures of
the reduction of the apparatus of the People's Commissariats of
the USSR and the Union republics, and of the central banks ; the
largest reductions of all were reported in departments of Narkomfin. Some economies at the centre may have been realized by the
transfer of functions to local authorities. Increases in local administrative staff had swallowed up the economies expected from
regionalization, and cuts in staff had been difficult. Administrative costs borne on local budgets rose in 1928–1929 by 18·5 per
cent ; it was explained that this was due to the payment of higher
salaries, not to the employment of larger staffs.[6] Costs of adminis-

[1] *Sobranie Uzakonenii, 1926*, No. 57, art. 445 ; *Sovetskoe Stroitel'stvo*, No.
5-6(22-23), May–June 1928, p. 54.
[2] *Pyatnadtsatyi S"ezd VKP(B)*, i (1961), 461.
[3] *Sobranie Zakonov, 1928*, No. 28, art. 257.
[4] *Vos'moi S"ezd Professional'nykh Soyuzov SSSR* (1929), p. 261.
[5] See Table No. 66, p. 489 below.
[6] *XVI S"ezd Vsesoyuznoi Kommunisticheskoi Partii (B)* (1931), p. 317.

tration in industry were, as Orjonikidze had previously admitted, difficult to ascertain, especially as trusts and factories were on *khozraschet*, and could juggle with administrative and operational costs. Vesenkha claimed that costs of administration in industry had been cut by 26 million rubles in 1926–1927 and by 58 millions in 1927–1928; but Rabkrin regarded estimates of 18 and 40 millions respectively as nearer the mark.[1] Costs of administration borne on the Union budget rose very sharply in 1926–1927, and declined slightly in each of the two succeeding years.[2] It cannot be estimated how much of the reduction was obtained by transfer of expenditure to other heads.

Besides the swollen numbers of the Soviet bureaucracy, its social composition continued to preoccupy party stalwarts. Since the days when Lenin wrote anxiously of the preponderance of former Tsarist and bourgeois employees in the Soviet apparatus,[3] time had mitigated the danger. Fears of sabotage by former Tsarist employees had at this time been largely overcome:

From the era of sabotage we are infinitely remote. The solid basis of our power compels the bureaucratic elements which we have to stick firmly to their duties.

Calculations had been made to show that regionalization, which substituted larger for smaller units of administration, would permit of a reduction of personnel; but figures from the Urals and the northern Caucasus, the first areas to be regionalized, showed that the process was uneven, and that, where staffs were temporarily reduced, they soon began to grow again (*Sovetskoe Stroitel'stvo*, No. 4(9), April 1927, p. 115; No. 5-6(10-11), May–June 1927, pp. 48-49).

[1] *Vos'moi S''ezd Professional'nykh Soyuzov SSSR* (1929), p. 262.

[2] See Vol. 1, Table No. 41, p. 974; the following table of costs of administration per head of population borne on the budgets of the Union republics included in the budget of the USSR showed both the reductions affected in 1927–1928 and the variations in costs between the republics:

	1926–27		1927–28	
	rubles	kopeks	rubles	kopeks
RSFSR	1	19	0	95
Ukrainian SSR	1	52	1	21
White Russian SSR	1	30	1	41
ZSFSR	2	42	1	95
Uzbek SSSR	1	96	1	56
Turkmen SSSR	1	26	2	45
USSR	1	35	1	07

(*Sovetskoe Stroitel'stvo*, No. 5-6(22-23), May–June 1928, p. 30.)

[3] See p. 291 above.

The enemy to be feared was not treason, but inertia.[1] Out of the 963,232 members of the trade union of Soviet and trade employees (which covered all Soviet administrative, and Soviet and cooperative economic, institutions), 267,415 had been in similar public or private employment in 1913. Of this latter total, 37·2 per cent worked in People's Commissariats, 47·7 per cent in Soviet or cooperative economic institutions, and 5·9 per cent in state or cooperative credit institutions. But of the 963,232 Soviet employees only 40,093, or 4·2 per cent, had been formerly employed in Tsarist institutions, though the proportion rose to 5·9 per cent for employees of People's Commissariats.[2] These figures did not seem unduly alarming. But the mood changed sharply in the spring and summer of 1928, when the publicity given to the Shakhty affair centred on the alleged disloyalty of former bourgeois " specialists ". Enukidze in October 1928 cautiously admitted that Soviet bureaucracy still contained " material from the old bureaucracy . . . former ministers, gendarmes, generals, etc."[3] The denunciation and dismissal of alien elements in administrative posts was now actively preached and pursued, especially in the small autonomous republics and in provincial and regional organizations, where they had hitherto escaped notice. At the eighth trade union congress in December 1928, Orjonikidze gave instances of the dismissal of considerable numbers of former landowners, high officials, White army officers, gendarmes, priests and merchants ; some of those dismissed were said to have found their way back to new appointments.[4] Yakovlev told a Moscow provincial party conference in February 1929 that, as the result of a recent investigation by Rabkrin, 48 " former officers of Kolchak, Denikin, Petylura etc.", out of a total staff of 268, had been dis-

[1] *Pravda*, March 31, 1927.

[2] *Gosudarstvennyi Apparat SSSR, 1924–1928* (1929), 59-60. These statistics are not precisely dated ; but, since some of them were quoted at the fifteenth party congress in December 1927 (*Pyatinadtsatyi S'ezd VKP(B)*, i (1961), 519), they were probably compiled in that year.

[3] *Vsesoyuznoe Soveshchanie po Perevyboram Sovetov v 1929 g.* (1928), pp. 113-114.

[4] *Vos'moi S"ezd Professional'nykh Soyuzov SSSR* (1929), pp. 269-270; for the autonomous republics see *ibid*. pp. 314-315. Much indignation was aroused over a former railway manager in Siberia under Kolchak, now said to be employed in Rabkrin ; according to Orjonikidze, he was employed in Narkomfin (*ibid*. p. 314).

missed from the wine and spirits trust Tsentrospirt. Unfortunately, added Yakovlev, " those whom we removed are finding their way back into snug posts " ; some of them were members of a trade union and drew unemployment benefit.[1]

The other side of the problem was the recruitment into the bureaucracy of loyal party members or active sympathizers, workers and peasants. Lenin looked forward to the training of " a mass of young people capable of radically transforming our apparatus " ;[2] and at a non-party meeting on February 9, 1920, he spoke of " the struggle against bureaucratism in our institutions ", and appealed to non-party workers to " come to the help of communists who are tiring under an unbearable burden ", and to " enter all state institutions in order to check the whole state apparatus ".[3] Earlier appeals by party leaders, from Lenin onwards, for the mass participation of workers in the struggle against bureaucratism had been based primarily on the supposition that the workers would check and supervise the bureaucrats, not that they would replace them, since bureaucracy itself was destined to disappear ; and a certain ambiguity on this point attended official pronouncements in the middle nineteen-twenties. The rapporteur on elections to the Soviets to the TsIK of the RSFSR at its session in November 1926 declared it " *essential, by drawing into the Soviets the great masses of workers and peasants, to remake our state apparatus with its bureaucratic deformations, to expel bureaucratism from it, to make it cheap, accessible, near and comprehensible to the masses* ".[4] Kalinin about the same time called the Soviets " the tool with the help of which workers and peasants keep the power in their hands and govern the immense state ".[5] The party central committee at its session in February 1927 hoped for an antidote to bureaucracy in

---

[1] *Pravda*, March 1, 1929.   [2] Lenin, *Sochineniya*, xxvi, 353.
[3] *Ibid.* xxv, 27-28.
[4] *III Sessiya Vserossiiskogo Tsentral'nogo Ispolnitel'nogo Komiteta XII Sozyva* (1926), p. 515.
[5] M. Kalinin, *Voprosy Sovetskogo Stroitel'stva* (1958), p. 220. Eighteen months later, in May 1928, Kalinin made a speech in precisely the opposite sense, defending a core of " narrow specialists " in Soviet administration ; " with us everyone knows everything and knows nothing ". This no doubt meant a " bourgeois structure " of administration ; but " we should borrow all that is best from this bourgeois structure " (*ibid.* pp. 363-364) ; the aim of this outburst was presumably to moderate the current campaign against the specialists (see Vol. 1, pp. 585-586).

the recruitment of " the best workers and outstanding peasants ",
party and non-party, into the Soviet apparatus. The trade unions
were to be the main channels for this promotion, which was to be
furthered not by shock campaigns, but by " systematic, persistent work ".[1] Komsomol members were invited, in a joint letter
from the party central control commission and the Komsomol
central committee, to participate in " the re-making of the state
apparatus ".[2]

Lip-service had long been paid to the principle of " promotion ". But progress was slow, owing no doubt to the small number and poor quality of available recruits. In the spring of 1928
the Shakhty affair powerfully stimulated the demand to train young
workers as engineers and specialists.[3] The suggestion was made
that workers should be given three or six months' leave of absence
from factories to work in government institutions, especially in
Rabkrin.[4] Izvestiya, making use of the current slogan, described
training for Soviet work as part of the " cultural revolution ".[5]
Orjonikidze, in his report to the eighth trade union congress in
December 1928, proposed that young workers from factory schools,
workers in the trade unions and men demobilized from the Red
Army should be recruited for the administrative staffs of Soviet
institutions and industrial and commercial establishments.[6] But
practical and psychological obstacles continued to impede the
process. A party report issued on the eve of the sixteenth party
conference in April 1929 drew attention to the limited success
achieved. The annual number of workers recommended by party
organizations for " promotion " rose from 7459 in 1925 to 14,500
in 1927–1928. But few of these had been accepted for responsible
posts. In the past four years, 13 trusts or syndicates and two
glavki, with a total administrative staff of 4992, including 1819
" responsible " officials, had accepted only 78 promotees put forward by party organizations. While the aim of " replacing worthless bureaucratic elements in the apparatus by workers " was
everywhere recognized, proposed appointments " come up against
resistance from the heads of the institutions ". The following

[1] Pravda, March 27, 1927.   [2] Izvestiya, October 4, 1927.
[3] See Vol. 1, pp. 593–596.   [4] Izvestiya, May 23, 1928.
[5] Izvestiya, August 2, 1928; for the slogan see pp. 406–407 below.
[6] Vos'moi S"ezd Professional'nykh Soyuzov SSSR (1929), p. 271.

table showed the position in some leading Soviet institutions.

	Total Staff	Promotees	Promotees Employed at Headquarters
Narkomfin	500	32	22
Gosbank	450	37	13
Narkompros	250	7	7
Narkomtrud	140	3	3
Narkomtorg	600	2	1[1]

Even Soviet officials of unimpeachable origins sometimes became " bureaucratized " and resisted change.[2] Stalin admitted at the eighth Komsomol congress in May 1928 that the trouble now came, not from the old bureaucrats, but from bureaucratism among communists.[3] Birman, the director of Yugostal, alleged that the source of bureaucratism in industry was the interference of Rabkrin and the trade unions, and was sharply reproved by Yakovlev at the sixteenth party conference in April 1929. But he replied with vigour, and evidently enjoyed some sympathy in the audience.[4]

The rift with the Right opposition sharpened every current controversy. Both sides eagerly attacked bureaucratism. Bukharin, in reporting to the Moscow party organization in September 1928 on the sixth congress of Comintern, quoted his comment at the fourth congress six years earlier on the danger of creating " a colossal administrative apparatus ".[5] In his *Notes of an Economist* in the same month he reiterated :

> We are far too centralized ; we must ask ourselves whether we cannot take a few steps towards Lenin's state of the commune.

[1] *Izvestiya Tsentral'nogo Komiteta VKP(B)*, No. 11-12(270-271), April 24, 1929, pp. 6-8.
[2] A. Fabrichny, *Chastnyi Kapital na Poroge Pyatiletki* (1930), p. 53.
[3] Stalin, *Sochineniya*, xi, 71.
[4] *Shestnadtsataya Konferentsiya VKP(B)* (1962), 459, 492-501.
[5] *Pravda*, September 12, 1928 ; for the earlier speech see p. 292 above.

And in the *Political Testament of Lenin* in January 1929 he quoted
Lenin to show that the cure for bureaucracy was " to return
to the deep historical sense of the (proletarian) dictatorship ",
i.e. to the workers.[1] On the other hand, the party central control
commission, after the session of the central committee in November 1928, ignoring the theoretical aspects of the debate, identified
the struggle against the Right danger with the struggle against
bureaucratism.[2] This was a significant moment. Though no
direct contact is known to have existed between the Right-wing
" deviators " in the party and the few former bourgeois or Menshevik non-party officials and specialists who still held responsible
positions in Soviet commissariats and economic institutions, the
conjecture that they sympathized with the criticisms of the rate of
industrialization expressed by Bukharin and his supporters was
plausible, and was indeed confirmed by their attitude on concrete
issues.[3] The drive to remove these " alien " elements from the
Soviet apparatus, which increased in intensity throughout 1928,
was reinforced by the drive against Rightist dissidents in the party,
and the two operations, inspired by a common purpose, began
insensibly to coalesce. Orjonikidze, in his report to the eighth
trade union congress in December 1928, spoke of the " purge " of
Soviet staffs in certain provinces, and declared that it was necessary
" to purge the apparatus of worthless and noxious elements " :
these included both traitors like the Shakhty specialists and idlers
who indulged in bureaucratic and corrupt practices.[4] The procedure and terminology hitherto current in the party were thus extended to the Soviet bureaucracy.

The further development of this theme had not long to wait.
In April 1929 *Pravda* published the text of a draft resolution approved by the party central committee for submission to the forthcoming sixteenth party conference " On the Achievements and
Next Tasks of the Struggle against Bureaucratism ". This was
the first specific resolution ever devoted by a major party assembly
to the problem of bureaucracy and contained a comprehensive

---

[1] For *Notes of an Economist* and the *Political Testament* see pp. 75, 87
above ; Stalin in April 1929 criticized Bukharin's view of the state as anarchist
or " semi-anarchist " (Stalin, *Sochineniya*, xii, 70-76).
[2] *Pravda*, November 27, 1928 ; for the session of the party central committee, see pp. 79-80 above.   [3] See Vol. i, p. 590.
[4] *Vos'moi S"ezd Professional'nykh Soyuzov SSSR* (1929), pp. 269, 271.

review of the subject. It connected the prevalence of " bureaucratic distortions " with " the intensification of the class struggle "
and the pressure of *kulaks*, urban bourgeoisie and bourgeois intelligentsia on the working class. It claimed that administrative expenses had been cut, under the régime of economy, by 300 million
rubles, and staffs reduced by 100,000 ; and " *hundreds and thousands of workers and employees* " had been drawn into the work of
Rabkrin. But the chief emphasis now appeared to rest on improving the quality rather than on reducing the number of bureaucrats.
Rabkrin was instructed to institute " *a purge of the Soviet apparatus* " in which the criterion was to be " the quality of work " and
not merely " class origin " ; and it was to begin in Soviet organs
" directly in contact with the toiling masses ". Officials found
unsuitable were to be transferred to lower posts, or removed altogether, temporarily or permanently, from Soviet administration.
More attention was to be given to the selection and training of
" promotees ", and directors of institutions were to take " *personal responsibility* " for providing favourable conditions of work
for them. On the other hand, no indulgence was to be shown to
" communists *who do not learn, and do not want to learn, seriously
the business of administration* ", and were content to " *rubber-
stamp other people's ideas and proposals* ". Inefficient communists
must be removed, and sent back to the kind of work for which they
were fitted ; the practice of shifting them round " *from institution
to institution, from district to district* " should be abandoned. The
resolution contained a short section on the need for " *the most
obstinate struggle against elements of bureaucratism in the party
itself* " — this was the only hint of a connexion between the purge
in the Soviet apparatus and the purge in the party ; and it ended
with the demand for " a mighty wave of self-criticism from below ",
once more described as " the decisive method of combating
bureaucratism ".[1] When the conference met at the end of April
1929, the draft resolution was presented by Yakovlev, deputy
People's Commissar for Rabkrin. He devoted the greater part of
his speech to practical problems of improving the administrative
apparatus. But, in a striking passage which purported to sum up
what had gone before, he declared with emphasis that the required
reform was " *an improvement of the state apparatus which would*

[1] *Pravda*, April 12, 1929.

make it capable of fighting against the kulak *and the nepman* ", and
that the essence of the process was to break the resistance of those
" elements of the bourgeois intelligentsia " who had hoped that
NEP would lead quickly back to a bourgeois-capitalist order ;
and in winding up the debate he for the first time openly linked
bureaucratism in the Soviet apparatus with the Right deviation in
the party :

> *He who is against industrialization, he who is against collec-*
> *tivization stands, whether he means or does not mean to, for the*
> *perpetuation of the roots of bureaucratism. . . . He who is against*
> *bureaucratism* (and 99 per cent of the party are against bureau-
> cratism, the broadest masses of the working class are against
> bureaucratism) *is also inevitably against representatives of any*
> *kind of Right deviation, however they may disguise their positions.*[1]

The resolution was adopted with minor verbal amendments, side
by side with another resolution on the purge in the party.[2]   A
joint resolution of the party central control commission and
Sovnarkom on the purge of state, cooperative and other public
organizations, drew an explicit distinction between the purge
undertaken for ideological reasons and measures of rationalization
and reduction of staffs.[3]   Kalinin, addressing a congress of the
trade union of Soviet trade employers on June 15, 1929, described
the aim of the purge as " the expulsion only of vicious elements
hostile to the Soviet power and of hopeless bureaucrats ".[4]   It was
announced that the purge would begin in Narkomfin, Narkomtrud
and Narkomyust on June 15, and in Narkomzem on July 10, 1919.[5]

The resolution of the sixteenth party conference included an
idealized description of what was meant by the slogan of " democratic centralism " :

[1] *Shestnadtsataya Konferentsiya VKP(B)* (1962), pp. 469, 482.
[2] *Ibid.* pp. 613-615.   For the final text of the resolution see *KPSS v
Rezolyutsiyakh* (1954), ii, 590-605 ; the accompanying resolution on the party
purge (see pp. 145-146 above) drew special attention to party cells composed
of employees working in Soviet, commercial or trade union institutions : " On
the composition of these cells, on the quality of their work, on the degree of their
party discipline, on their contact with the masses, depends the confidence of the
broad masses of party and non-party workers and peasants in the apparatus of
the Soviet state " (*KPSS v Rezolyutsiyakh* (1954), ii, 610).
[3] *Pravda*, June 2, 1929.
[4] M. Kalinin, *Voprosy Sovetskogo Stroitel'stva* (1958), p. 348.
[5] *Pravda*, June 8, 1929.

Local party and Soviet organs are under an obligation to carry out unswervingly party and governmental directives and decisions, at the same time putting before the central organs the question of any modification whose necessity is demonstrated by local experience. Only this *mutual control* of the decisions of the centre by the practice of the localities, and of the practice of the localities by the leadership of the centre, will permit both the realization of an unswerving fulfilment of proposals and resolutions of central institutions, and the introduction into them of the necessary corrections indicated by local experience.[1]

Some progress was undoubtedly made at this time towards improving the efficiency of the administrative machine and making it more accessible to the population. But this progress was compromised, and to a large extent nullified, by purges both in the party and in the Soviet apparatus which removed those bold enough to challenge the party line, and reduced those who remained to a rigid and uncritical obedience. Thus weakened and shorn of all initiative, the administrative apparatus became the instrument of the harsh and increasing pressures imposed by the policies of industrialization, so that the bureaucracy of the nineteen-thirties, though perhaps more efficient, was also more oppressive, than that of an earlier period.

[1] *KPSS v Rezolyutsiyakh* (1954), ii, 592.

CHAPTER 52

THE RED ARMY

(a) Military Preparedness

THE reforms associated with Frunze provided the basis of a permanent organization for the Red Army; and by the autumn of 1926 something had been done to improve its efficiency.[1] But it was the international crisis and war scare of the spring of 1927 which put the Red Army into the centre of the political picture. The theses of PUR for the ninth anniversary of the Red Army in February 1927 spoke apprehensively of British policy, and of " the need of serious preparation of the USSR for defence ".[2] Voroshilov's report on it to the fourth Union Congress of Soviets in April 1927 was the most comprehensive review of military needs and aims since the days of the civil war. Having dilated on the failure of the League of Nations and of " other auxiliary organs of imperialism " to ensure peace, and on the rising armaments expenditure of capitalist countries, he set forth four cardinal needs of the Soviet Union: (a) an efficient and well-equipped regular army, (b) adequate trained reserves of officers and men, (c) capacity to switch the national economy to the requirements of war, and (d) " psychological mobilization " of workers and peasants. He ended with an appeal to the country to be " on guard ".[3] A few days later the executive committee of Comintern adopted a lengthy resolution on " The Tasks of the Communist International in the struggle against War and the Danger of War ".[4] On June 1, 1927, the party issued an appeal to all party members for " exceptional attention to the Red Army, to questions of worker-peasant defence ".[5] The first week in July 1927 was announced as " defence week "; and this celebration,

[1] See Vol. 1, pp. 426-428.   [2] Izvestiya, February 10, 1927.
[3] SSSR: 4 S"ezd Sovetov (1927), pp. 531-540.
[4] Kommunisticheskii Internatsional v Dokumentakh (1933), pp. 699-717.
[5] Pravda, June 1, 1927.

which coincided with that of the fifth anniversary of the Soviet
constitution, was deemed such a success that it was prolonged for a
further week.[1] It ended on Sunday, July 17, 1927, with a mass
demonstration addressed by Bukharin, Voroshilov and Enukidze.[2]
The session of the party central committee of July–August 1927
injected the international danger into the struggle against the
opposition, though the resolution adopted by the session, while
stressing the need for preparedness and praising the response of
the workers to defence week, did not specifically mention the Red
Army.[3] Joint military and naval manœuvres in the neighbour-
hood of Odessa in September 1927 received unusual publicity.[4]
The tenth anniversary of the Red Army on February 22, 1928, was
celebrated with pomp and circumstance; and the order of the
Red Banner was awarded to Kalinin, Petrovsky and Rykov, as
well as to Unshlikht, Kirov, Vatsetis, Zof, and other military and
industrial leaders.[5]

The new factor to which increasing prominence was given at
this time was the development of heavy industry as the basis of
military power.

> We became accustomed during the civil war [wrote Tu-
> khachevsky] to think that we were beggars, poor and unarmed,
> and that our main weapon was only our revolutionary spirit. If
> this was partly true in the period of the civil war, the picture
> looks quite different at the present time.[6]

Voroshilov in his report to the fourth Union Congress of Soviets
in April 1927, while admitting that the Red Army lagged behind
the armies of western Europe in weapons and equipment, claimed
that Soviet military technology was advancing " in line with the
progress of the whole national economy, in proportion to our
industrialization ", and devoted the concluding section of his report to this theme. The adaptation of the economy to the needs

---

[1] *Izvestiya*, July 8, 10, 1928; party slogans for defence week had been
published in *Pravda*, June 29, 1927.   [2] *Ibid*. July 19, 1927.
  [3] *KPSS v Rezolyutsiyakh* (1954), ii, 359-364; for this session see pp. 30-33
above.   [4] *Izvestiya*, September 24, 25, 30, 1927.
  [5] *Ibid*. February 23, 1928; for a long article by Voroshilov on the occasion
see pp. 317, 326 below.
  [6] *Voina i Voennoe Iskusstvo*, ed. E. Gorev (1927), p. 135; the publication
of this volume of essays was symptomatic of the renewed interest in military
affairs.

of defence was one of " the most actual tasks ", in which not only
heavy industry, but transport, agriculture and the chemical industry had their parts to play.[1]   The Gosplan control figures
drafted in the autumn of 1927 referred to the need " to guarantee
the continuation of the forced tempo of industrialization, while
. . . increasing by all means the capacity of the country for defence ";[2] and at the fifteenth party congress of December 1927
Voroshilov, starting from the " accepted truth " that " a new
world slaughter threatens mankind with irrevocable inevitability ",
laid the strongest emphasis on the development of war industries:

> Enjoying undoubted success in forms of organization, in the
> training, education and military preparedness of Red Army
> men and of the officer corps, we have taken as our main goal
> and fundamental content of the five-year plan the raising of the
> technical strength of the Red Army to the level of first-class
> contemporary armies.[3]

The resolution of the congress called for the most rapid development of " those branches of heavy industry which increase in the
shortest possible time the economic power and defence capacity
of the USSR ".[4]   One of the party slogans for the tenth anniversary of the Red Army in February 1928 ran:

> Industrialization of the USSR is the foundation of its capa-
> city for defence. Proletarian, raise the productivity of labour.
> Strength the defence of your state.[5]

Looking back five years later on the history of the Red Army,
Voroshilov saw the year 1928 as a turning-point in its development, since the first five-year plan had involved its " radical
technical reconstruction ".[6]

While industrialization had pride of place, other conditions
necessary to transform the Red Army into an effective fighting force

---

[1] *SSSR: 4 S"ezd Sovetov* (1927), pp. 549, 554-560; for the development of
the armaments industry see Vol. 1, pp. 426-431.
[2] *Kontrol'nye Tsifry Narodnogo Khozyaistva SSSR na 1927-1928 god* (1928),
p. 15.
[3] *Pyatnadtsatyi S"ezd VKP(B)*, ii (1962), 974-992; for further quotations
from this speech see Vol. 1, p. 429.
[4] *KPSS v Rezolyutsiyakh* (1954), ii, 457.
[5] *Pravda*, February 11, 1928.
[6] K. Voroshilov, *Stat'i i Rechi* (1937), p. 561.

were not neglected. The basic decree on army organization of September 18, 1925, was re-issued in a revised and expanded form on August 8, 1928. The sharp distinction between regular and territorial units was maintained. More detailed regulations were laid down for pre-military training and for the call-up, and more emphasis was placed on the status and functions of the officer corps. The provision that " non-toilers " should be employed only in non-combatant service was retained, with the proviso that such persons should be subject to a special tax.[1] Recruitment appears to have presented no serious difficulties, Of those called up in 1927 92·16 per cent presented themselves voluntarily, and in 1928 94·56 per cent; in an army with a peasant component of 74·3 per cent these figures were regarded as satisfactory. Natives of Kazakhstan, of the Central Asian republics, of the Dagestan ASSR, and of the mountain regions of the northern Caucasus were called up for the first time in 1928.[2]

The status and functions of the officer corps as a distinct entity began at this time to assume a new importance in Soviet thinking. Voroshilov made a long speech at the graduation of young officers from military schools in 1926;[3] and the graduation ceremony of young officers from the military academy on July 2, 1927, was honoured by speeches from Rykov and Voroshilov.[4] The improvement in material conditions of Red Army men, and especially of officers, engaged the attention of the fourth Union Congress of Soviets in April 1927, which called for an increase in the Red Army budget for amenities, aimed at " a further improvement in the feeding, clothing and quartering of the troops, with particular attention to the improvement of the living accommodation of the officer corps ".[5] Increased pay and allowances for officers were announced to come into force on June 1, 1927.[6] On the tenth anniversary of the Red Army in February 1928, when further

---

[1] *Sobranie Zakonov, 1928*, No. 51, arts. 448, 449; for the 1925 decree see *Socialism in One Country, 1924–1926*, Vol. 2, p. 400. The tax on " non-toilers " was imposed by decrees of November 6, 1925, and December 31, 1926 (*Sobranie Zakonov, 1925*, No. 76, art. 577; *id. 1927*, No. 3, art. 31).

[2] *SSSR: God Roboty Pravitel'stva 1927–28* (1929), pp. 43-44, 47·

[3] *Izvestiya*, September 21, 22, 1926.   [4] *Ibid.* July 3, 1927.

[5] *S"ezdy Sovetov v Dokumentakh*, iii (1960), 138; see also *Socialism in One Country, 1924–1926*, Vol. 2, pp. 403-404.   [6] *Izvestiya*, May 22, 1927.

grants were promised to improve such amenities as radio, cinema and libraries, three million rubles were assigned to improve the living quarters of officers. The pay of both officers and rank and file was increased: " wages in the Red Army came nearer to the average wage level of industrial workers ".[1] In 1928 the Red Army disposed of 2458 apartment houses which provided accommodation for 63,220 officers and their families.[2] It seems clear that these measures taken at this time resulted in some all-round increase in living standards, but also in a widening of the gap between officers and men. Blomberg, the head of the German Truppenamt, when he visited the Soviet Union in 1928, was shown club rooms of the Red Army house in Moscow which were open to all Red Army men without distinction of rank. But he observed that " the officers corps is already distinguished by behaviour, manners, dress and needs from the great mass of the soldiers ", and concluded that the separation between them was unlikely to diminish.[3] A statute of July 13, 1928, laying down conditions of service for junior, senior and high-ranking officers was evidently designed to improve their status and to give security of tenure. Dividing the officer personnel into military, political, administrative, medical and veterinary categories, it detailed conditions and length of service in each rank, rates of pay, and criteria for promotion. The principle of promotion by seniority said to be " widely practised in bourgeois armies " was firmly rejected, and promotion by merit and qualification written into the statute.[4]

The problem of military discipline in a régime committed to egalitarian principles and to rejection of the brutal discipline of the Tsarist army[5] was solved by a gradual and cautious shifting of emphasis. Frunze shortly before his death had spoken against

[1] *Pravda*, February 23, 1928; *Osnovnye Itogi Raboty Pravitel'stva SSSR k Perevyboram Sovetov 1928–29 g.* (1928), p. 19.

[2] *SSSR: God Raboty Pravitel'stva 1927–1928* (1929), p. 50.

[3] See Blomberg's report in the archives of the *Auswärtiges Amt*, 9480/276226 (for an incomplete English translation of the report see *Slavonic and East European Review*, xl (1962), 218-241); at Kronstadt in 1929 one of two Red Army Houses was reserved for officers and rank-and-file " activists " (*Krasnaya Zvezda*, October 9, 1929).

[4] *Polozhenie o Prokhozhdenii Sluzhby Srednim, Starshim i Vysshim Nachal' stvuyushhim Sostavom* (1928); its main provisions are summarized in N. Pyatnitsky, *Voennaya Organizatsiya Gosudarstvennoi Oborony SSSR* (Paris, 1931), pp. 88-90, 93.

[5] See *Socialism in One Country, 1924–1926*, Vol. 2, pp. 404-405.

" mechanistic methods " of discipline and widespread disciplinary punishments.[1] Voroshilov in April 1927 was eloquent on the sensitiveness of the rank and file to " the slightest injustice " and on the need to cultivate close relations between officers and men.[2] The rapidly declining proportion of former Tsarist officers in the Red Army made this a problem primarily of the new generation of Soviet-trained officers.[3] It may be significant that the proportion of officers to rank and file was considerably higher in the Red Army than in the old Tsarist army or in most western armies.[4] The opposition platform of September 1927 drew a characteristic moral from the problem :

> The question of the mutual relation of classes in the country,
> and the true policy of the party in this sphere, has a decisive
> significance for the inner solidarity of the army and for the
> mutual relations between the commanding staff and the body
> of the soldiers.[5]

Voroshilov, in his article on the tenth anniversary of the Red Army in February 1928, emphasized, by way of distinction from the armies of the capitalist world, that officers and men of the Red Army " belong to one and the same class " ;[6] a few weeks later he told a conference of party cells in the Red Army that there were " too many reprimands and *far too little encouragement* ".[7] The Red Army newspaper explained the unduly harsh attitude of some junior officers to their men as due to inexperience and inadequate training :

> A considerable number of our young officers try to compensate for their ignorance by unnecessary strictness. The same can be said of our young officers who are group leaders in political education classes. Their insufficient general culture and the

---

[1] M. Frunze, *Sobranie Sochinenii*, iii (1927), 359.

[2] K. Voroshilov, *Oborona SSSR* (1927), pp. 76-77.

[3] By 1930 only 4500 former Tsarist officers — one-tenth of the whole officer corps — remained (N. Pyatnitsky, *Voennaya Organizatsiya Gosudarstvennoi Oborony SSSR* (Paris, 1931), p. 116) ; in the previous autumn, when a purge of Soviet institutions was in progress (see p. 310 above), Unshlikht issued an order deprecating any widespread movement to exclude former Tsarist officers (M. Fainsod, *Smolensk under Soviet Rule* (1959), p. 219).

[4] For comparative figures see N. Pyatnitsky, *Voennaya Organizatsiya Gosudarstvennoi Oborony SSSR* (Paris, 1931), pp. 113-114.

[5] L. Trotsky, *The Real Situation in Russia* (n.d. [1928]), p. 172.

[6] *Pravda*, February 23, 1928.   [7] *Ibid*. April 6, 1928.

lack of time and place for the preparation of the regular lessons affect both the conduct of the lessons and their assimilation.[1]

Even relations between senior and junior officers when off duty were subject to intolerably rigid habits of discipline. The junior remained silent or simply acquiesced " out of some involuntary sense of subordination and fear " ; and this, in the words of the Red Army newspaper, " eats away our unity, our comradely relations, and makes them rotten, formal, external and not genuine ".[2]

Much attention was, however, paid to the dangers of insubordination among party, and particularly Komsomol, members. " Questions of the military discipline of members of the party and the Komsomol ", declared the Red Army newspaper in March 1927, " are constantly in the centre of attention of the political organs " ; and it was reported that in 1926 290 party members had been arraigned for breaches of military discipline, and 70 of them excluded from the party.[3] A year later a warning was issued by the Komsomol central committee against " an idealization of the conditions of Red Army service ", which " may create in the recruit a false impression that the Red Army is simply a school, while completely forgetting its fundamental importance as the core of the armed forces of the Soviet Union ".[4] In 1929 the Red Army newspaper continued to protest against " an artificial division between Komsomol and military discipline " ; in the past year in one Caucasian brigade seven Komsomol members had been expelled, five put under arrest and 67 punished.[5] More intensive training of officers in military schools and academies, of which the Tolmachev Military-Political Academy was the most famous, was undertaken, and the usual efforts made to increase the intake of workers. The proportion of workers in the total admission rose from 39 per cent in 1927 to 56 per cent in 1928.[6] The weakness of educational background was blamed for the shortcomings of the finished product. " Cadets who pass out of our training schools lack the habits of command ", and " show slight acquaintance with

---

[1] *Krasnaya Zvezda*, March 6, 1928.   [2] *Ibid.* June 28, 1927.
[3] *Ibid.* March 25, April 7, 1927.   [4] *Izvestiya*, August 25, 1928.
[5] *Krasnaya Zvezda*, February 13, 1929.
[6] *SSSR: Ot S"ezda k S"ezdu (Aprel' 1927–Mai 1929)* (1929), p. 170; according to Voroshilov's anniversary article in *Pravda*, February 23, 1928, the proportion of workers, peasants and others in the Red Army in 1927 was respectively 22, 50 and 28 per cent.

army life ".[1]   Evening courses in general education were added
to the training in 1928.[2]   In all fields, however, progress had been
made.   A resolution of the party central committee of July 15,
1929, on " the state of defence of the USSR ", registered the ad-
vances realized in the last five years, and especially since 1927,
and looked forward to the creation in the next five years of " a
modern military-technical basis of defence ".   Contemporary
types of artillery and tanks, an air fleet, and " improvement of the
material conditions of life of the officer corps " were particularly
cited.[3]

The year 1928 was marked by the appointment of Shaposhnikov as chief of staff of the Red Army to succeed Tukhachevksy,[4]
who was transferred to the command of the Leningrad military
district.[5]   Tukhachevsky had led the offensive against Warsaw in
1920, and had clashed with the southern army command under
Egorov, Budennyi and Stalin;[6] and, though he had avoided any
involvement in opposition activities, his removal might be interpreted as an early attempt by Stalin to pay off old scores and to
place in key positions men on whose personal loyalty he could
count.   But more profound significance could also be read into
the change.   Tukhachevsky remained, as a soldier, the child of the
revolution.   His experience of the Tsarist army was limited to
brief service as a subaltern in the war.   He joined both the Red
Army and the party in 1918.   He eagerly embraced the view of the
Red Army as the striking-force of world revolution, and in 1920
propounded the still-born plan of an international military general
staff attached to Comintern.[7]   Not much survived of these extravagant ambitions when Tukhachevsky wrote the article on " War
as a Problem of Armed Conflict " for the first edition of the Soviet
encyclopaedia, except a firm insistence on the offensive as a primary
factor in Red Army strategy and tactics, though this did not lead

---

[1] *Krasnaya Zvezda*, April 3, 23, 1929.
[2] *SSSR: Ot S"ezda k S"ezdu (Aprel' 1927–Mai 1929)* (1929), p. 170.
[3] *KPSS o Vooruzhennykh Silakh Sovetskogo Soyuza* (1969), pp. 264-266.
[4] See *Socialism in One Country, 1924–1926*, Vol. 2, pp. 397-398, 414.
[5] The appointments were announced, with biographies and photographs of
both, in *Izvestiya*, May 6, 1928.
[6] See *The Bolshevik Revolution, 1917–1923*, Vol. 3, p. 214.
[7] See *ibid.*, Vol. 3, pp. 210-211.

to any depreciation of the importance of new weapons and technical equipment, or of the development of a powerful industrial base.[1] But, in so far as the revolutionary tradition was still alive in the Red Army or in party circles associated with military affairs,[2] Tukhachevsky was its spokesman. Shaposhnikov, eleven years Tukhachevsky's senior, had already made a career in the imperial army, and was a staff officer in the war. He rallied early to the Red Army, but never aspired to any but a professional rôle; he did not become a party member till 1930.[3] In 1924 he published an account of the Polish campaign of 1920, which appears to have been critical of Tukhachevsky's offensive strategy. Blomberg, whose visit to the Soviet Union in 1928 took place shortly after Shaposhnikov's appointment, spoke of the class character and political orientation of the Red Army, but noted that communist and non-communist army leaders were united in " an uninhibited faith in Russian nationalism ", and concluded:

> Purely military points of view step more and more into the foreground; everything else is subordinated to them.[4]

In a period when the earlier hypothetical function of the Red Army as the spear-head of world revolution had been subordinated to the specific duty to defend the frontiers of the USSR, the replacement of the brilliant, erratic Tukhachevsky by a solid non-political professional soldier had a certain logical consistency.

---

[1] *Bol'shaya Sovetskaya Entsiklopediya*, xii (1928), 576-598; the article, though not published till 1928, is likely to have been written while Tukhachevsky was still chief of staff. For the doctrine of the offensive see *Socialism in One Country, 1921–1926*, Vol. 2, pp. 386-388.

[2] Stalin in an article celebrating the tenth anniversary of the Red Army, called it " the army of liberation of the toilers " and declared that it was " reared in the spirit of internationalism, in the spirit of the unity of interests of the workers of all countries " (*Sochineniya*, xi, 21-26); and Voroshilov, at the Rabsel'kor conference in December 1928, called the Red Army " the leading armed detachment of the world proletariat " (*Izvestiya*, December 9, 1928). The international revolutionary tradition of the Red Army survived in a deliberately attenuated form in the Field Regulations of 1929; " The Red Army, in defending the USSR, by the very fact of its existence cooperates in the struggle of oppressed toiling masses of the whole world for their liberation " (quoted in N. Pyatnitsky, *Voennaya Organizatsiya Gosudarstvennoi Oborony SSSR* (Paris, 1931), p. 6).

[3] He spoke at the fourth Union Congress of Soviets in April 1927, using suitable quotations from Engels, on the importance of the industrial basis of military power (*SSSR: 4 S"ezd Sovetov* (1927), pp. 574-575).

[4] *Auswärtiges Amt*, 9480/276222-4.

(b) Army and Party

Ever since the thirteenth party congress in May 1924, it had been declared policy to increase the party component in the armed forces. From a percentage of party and Komsomol members variously stated at 12 or 15 in 1925,[1] it rose in 1929 to 29 per cent, or a total of 110,000.[2] Of 93,289 communists enrolled in military cells or groups at the time of the party census of January 1927, 43,336 were workers by social situation, 24,512 peasants and 23,676 employees.[3] What is clear is that a large proportion of these joined the party after, not before, being enrolled in the Red Army, and that the army increasingly became a channel through which the rank and file could be selected and groomed for party membership. In February 1926 PUR issued a directive for the recruitment of more workers from the army into the party;[4] of 22,261 communists demobilized in 1926, 18,432 or 82·8 per cent had joined the party while on service.[5] The still more rapid increase in the proportion of party members in the officer corps, which had started in the previous period,[6] continued, especially in the top ranks. A decree of the party central committee of July 15, 1927, called for a further increase of members of the party and the Komsomol in the entry to officers' schools.[7] Orjonikidze reported to the fifteenth party congress in December 1927 that, while the percentage of party and Komsomol members in the Red Army as a whole had risen from 22·8 in 1925 to 29·9 in 1926, the percentage in the officer corps had risen from 43·3 in 1925 to 47 in 1926 and 54 in 1927. The percentage among company commanders in 1926 was 52, among regimental commanders 51·2, among divisional

---

[1] See *Socialism in One Country, 1924–1926*, Vol. 2, p. 408, note 1.

[2] *Bol'shaya Sovetskaya Entsiklopediya*, xi (1930), 542 ; lower figures and percentages from other sources are quoted in T. Rigby, *Communist Party Membership in the USSR* (1968), p. 241. Figures for the Red Army normally included naval and air forces. Voroshilov in April 1927 gave the following percentages for units of the Red Fleet — party 20·36, Komsomol 21·48, non-party 58·16 (K. Voroshilov, *Oborona SSSR* (1927), pp. 131-132) ; in 1927 71 per cent of the officers of the Baltic fleet, and 90 per cent of those in command of ships, were " former gentry " (*Voprosy Istorii*, No. 12, 1964, p. 29).

[3] *Sotsial'nyi i Natsional'nyi Sostav VKP(B)* (1928), pp. 38-40.

[4] *Spravochnik Partiinogo Rabotnika*, vi (1928), ii, 189-191.

[5] *Izvestiya Tsentral'nogo Komiteta VKP(B)*, No. 13 (186), April 8, 1927, p. 8.

[6] See *Socialism in One Country, 1924–1926*, Vol. 2, p. 415.

[7] *Spravochnik Partiinogo Rabotnika*, vi (1928), ii, 180.

commanders 54·7 and among corps commanders 85.[1] The percentage among junior officers rose from 11·6 on January 1, 1926,
to 17·5 on January 1, 1927.[2] A statistical comparison of the rank
and function of party members of the armed forces in 1925 and
1929 confirmed that the largest increase, both absolute and propor-
tional, occurred in the number of party members of the officer
corps.[3] This made it easy to ensure that the highest posts in the
party cells in the Red Army were generally held by officers and
non-commissoned officers, and that the organization was effectively
controlled by them. A sample check made in the autumn of 1926
revealed that, of secretaries of party cells and of bureaus of party
organizations in the Red Army, 85-90 per cent were officers or non-
commissioned officers, and not more than 10-15 per cent rankers.[4]
This had at any rate the advantage of minimizing potential clashes
between military and party discipline. Unshlikht in a speech of
February 1927 tried to define the relation between party and non-
party officers and to calm the apprehensions of the latter :

> Our course is set not for a 100 per cent party officer corps,
> but for a guarantee of the leadership of our party in the Red
> Army. The best part of our non-party officers can be assured
> that their work will remain necessary to the Red Army and will
> find deserved appreciation and support from the leading Red
> Army organs.[5]

Two years later, after the prolonged troubles of the grain crisis, the
rôle of the non-party officer was expounded in a leading article in
the Red Army newspaper in less complimentary terms ; it was
necessary " to educate him in a socialist spirit, in order that he may
successfully discharge his function in the army of the proletarian
dictatorship ".[6]

---

[1] *Pyatnadtsatyi S"ezd VKP(B)*, i (1961), 441-442 ; according to Voroshilov
in February 1928, 48·1 per cent of the officer corps were party members, and
4·8 per cent members of the Komsomol (*Pravda*, February 23, 1928).

[2] *K XV S"ezdu VKP(B)*, (1927), p. 241.

[3] See Table No. 67, p. 490 below.

[4] *Krasnaya Zvezda*, April 29, 1927 ; nearly 80 per cent of party cells in the
Red Army had 15 or less members, and nearly all had 50 per cent or more of
officer members (N. Pyatnitsky, *Voennaya Organizatsiya Gosudarstvennoi
Oborony SSSR* (Paris, 1931), pp. 38-39).

[5] *Krasnaya Zvezda*, February 26, 1927 ; for a similar assurance by Frunze in
1925 see *Socialism in One Country, 1924–1926*, Vol. 2, p. 413.

[6] *Krasnaya Zvezda*, April 12, 1929.

Much attention was devoted to strengthening the party organization in the Red Army, on which the authority of the party over the army finally depended. Under a party resolution of December 20, 1924, a party cell was to be formed in any company, battery or squadron containing three or more party members.[1] A resolution of the Orgburo early in 1927 stressed the importance of improving the party organization, and especially in raising the qualifications of secretaries of party cells. More attention was to be paid to political education, to the study of decisions of party congresses, and to " timely explanation of the policy of the party and the Soviet Government ". A leading article in the journal of the party central committee accompanying the publication of the resolution attributed any shortcomings to the youth and inexperience of party members in the Red Army.[2] The measures taken at the time of the formation of the united opposition to counter fears of Trotsky's influence in the army had proved adequate.[3] On the eve of the fifteenth party congress in December 1927, the party central committee was able to boast that the opposition had found no support in party organizations in the Red Army, and that the number of party members in the army guilty of offences against party discipline had fallen to insignificant proportions.[4] To achieve military efficiency seemed essential to the survival of the Soviet Union in a potentially hostile world. To maintain party ascendancy over the army seemed essential to the survival of the régime. " To know how to reconcile party relations with relations of commander and subordinate ", mused the Red Army newspaper, " is a far from easy matter ".[5]

In pursuit of this dual aim, the key position was held by the Political Administration of the Red Army (PUR) and by the military commissars. The régime of economy had cut the number of political workers in the armed services in the autumn of 1926 from

---

[1] *Izvestiya Tsentral'nogo Komiteta VKP(B)*, No. 4(79), 1925, pp. 11-14.

[2] *Ibid.* No. 90(182), March 7, 1927, pp. 1-4.   [3] See p. 5 above.

[4] *K XV S"ezdu VKP(B)* (1927), pp. 244, 246; according to *Krasnaya Zvezda*, December 1, 1927, 0·19 per cent of party members in the Red Army voted for the opposition, and 0·2 per cent abstained, these proportions being lower than in the party as a whole.

[5] *Krasnaya Zvezda*, Feburary 12, 1928; cases of friction between party and non-party officers, arising from claims of the former to override decisions of the latter irrespective of military rank, continued to give trouble (*ibid*. September 25, October 11, 31, December 1, 1929).

14,672 to 11,490, and of commissars from 648 to 612.[1] But, in spite of the assumption that the commissars would be superseded at some date in the future by the introduction of " one-man command ",[2] the importance of political indoctrination under party control was never challenged. The rôle of PUR had been defined in art. 78 of the revised party statute adopted by the fourteenth party congress in December 1925 :

> General direction of party work in the Red Army and Red Fleet is carried out by the Political Administration of the Red Army as the military section of the central committee.[3]

It was a regular function of the commissars, as agents of PUR, to take control of party cells and organizations and act as the authorized channel of communication between the party and the military command. It was not unfair to call the political staff " the ' eyes ' and ' ears ' of the party in the army ".[4] A long instruction of PUR of August 19, 1927, on " the liquidation of political illiteracy " among party and Komsomol Red Army men entrusted the task to the political officers responsible to PUR in territorial as well as in regular units, in the Red Fleet and in military schools.[5] A further instruction to party cells in the Red Army was issued by the party central committee on November 1, 1928. Meetings of company cells were to be held not less than twice a month, of the regimental collective not less than once a month. Nomination of party officials was the rule ; only at the level of the company cell or the regimental collective was election still allowed. The commissar (or the holder of one-man command, where this had been established) had full authority over the party organization of his unit.[6] A standard work of 1929 emphasized the peculiar position of the party organization in the Red Army, which was only the " apparatus " of the commissars :

[1] *K XV S"ezdu VKP(B)*, (1927), pp. 238-239.
[2] See *Socialism in One Country, 1924-1926*, Vol. 2, pp. 409-410.
[3] *KPSS v Rezolyutsiyakh* (1954), ii, 254-255.
[4] N. Pyatnitsky, *Voennaya Organizatsiya Gosudarstvennoi Oborony SSSR* (Paris, 1931), p. 32.
[5] *Spravochnik Partiinogo Rabotnika*, vi (1928), ii, 201-208.
[6] *Izvestiya Tsentral'nogo Komiteta VKP(B)*, No. 33(254), November 13, 1928, pp. 6-10; according to *Krasnaya Zvezda*, February 12, 1928, election was permitted " only in the lower links (company or regiment) of the party organizations and party commissions "; the rest of the party apparatus was " appointed ".

The party organization has no right to interfere with their actions and is obliged to carry out instructions received from them and to render them help in all their work. Even in the event of disagreement with the instructions of the commissar, the political assistant or the one-man commander, the bureau of the party collective must carry them out, appealing for a final solution of controversial questions to the proper political organ.[1]

The Red Army newspaper again drew attention to the peculiar status of party organizations in the Red Army, where " the military commissar often has the right, acting on his sole responsibility, to suspend the carrying into effect of a resolution of the cell of the VKP, if the cell takes a decision not corresponding to the party line in the army ".[2] Apart from these functions, the commissars constituted a source from which, according to a perhaps exaggerated estimate of Voroshilov, " many hundreds of excellent officers, staff officers and other military specialists " had been drawn.[3]

The faltering steps taken in 1924 and 1925 to combine the military and political functions of the officer corps, and to supersede the duality of commander and commissar, by introducing one-man command had met with imperfect success.[4] Efforts continued through the winter of 1926–1927, and culminated in a directive issued on May 13, 1927, by the People's Commissar for War in his capacity as president of the Revolutionary Military Council. The directive applied to all the armed forces. It placed on the military commander the responsibility for " general political leadership for the purpose of complete coordination of military and political affairs in the unit " ; the " political assistant " was to be responsible for " all party-political work ", and to be head of the political organization ; the political assistant was to report to the commander on the political condition of the unit, and on all basic instructions received from higher political organs. The apparent effect of the directive was to apply throughout the Red Army provisions originally confined to units under one-man command. The commissar lost his function of control over the military com-

[1] N. Kharitonov, *Politicheskii Apparat Krasnoi Armii* (1929), p. 73.
[2] *Krasnaya Zvezda*, May 12, 1929.
[3] *Pravda*, February 23, 1928.
[4] See *Socialism in One Country, 1924–1926*, Vol. 2, pp. 379, 409–414.

mander ; his right to sign orders was restricted to those dealing with party-political work.[1] The directive caused consternation in party circles. Ostensible grounds of opposition were the impossibility of applying it in the immediate future to the Red Fleet, where the officers, and especially the high command, were still predominantly non-party, or to the national contingents of the Central Asian republic, in which political work was still all-important.[2] But, as the sequel revealed, the real obstacle was the stubborn resistance of the commissars to the gradual deflation of their rôle, and the influence which they still enjoyed in party circles.

The first focus of resistance seems to have been the Tolmachev Political-Military Academy in Leningrad, where the cadets in November 1927 addressed a letter to PUR protesting against the extension of the rights of military commanders and of one-man command as likely to bring about " a weakening of party leadership in the army " ; and copies were sent to army commands throughout the country. The only region known to have responded favourably to this protest was the White Russian command, where in the autumn of 1927 the commissars and their staffs passed a resolution against an extension of one-man commands. At first this agitation was brushed aside. Voroshilov, in his article on the tenth anniversary of the Red Army in February 1928, complacently observed that " the function of control and observation of the officer corps, the rôle of guardian and ' nurse ', which formerly constituted the main function of the commissar, is now passing into history ".[3] Soon, however, events took a more serious turn. On March 15, 1928, a party meeting of the Tolmachev academy, led by its commandant, passed a resolution condemning " the forcing of the pace in the introduction of ' one-man command ' ". A conference of secretaries of party cells at the end of March 1928 tried to pour oil on the waters; Voroshilov eulogized the " party-political staff " and disclaimed any plan " to liquidate the

---

[1] *Voprosy Istorii KPSS*, No. 12, 1964, pp. 332-333 ; *KPSS i Stroitel'stvo Sovetskikh Vooruzhennykh Sil* (1965), p. 155. The text of the directive has not been available.

[2] *Voprosy Istorii KPSS*, No. 12, 1964, p. 33 ; as usual in disputes on military matters, little was allowed to transpire in public. For the position in the fleet see p. 321 note 2 above.

[3] *Pravda*, February 23, 1928 ; for the beginnings of this change of functions see *Socialism in One Country, 1924–1926*, Vol. 2, pp. 410-411.

political officers ".[1]   But this did not prevent the commissars of
the White Russian military district from holding a further meeting
in May 1928, and passing a strongly worded resolution, which
spoke of " the depreciation and diminution of the rôle of the party-
political organs ", and criticized the attitude of the military commanders.[2]

In the crisis atmosphere of the spring and summer of 1928, the
main anxiety of the party authorities was to stave off any danger
that the discontent of the military commissars might find a link
with other disaffected elements in the party.   It will not have
escaped notice that the army in White Russia had also been a centre
of agitation against the forced grain collections of the first months
of 1928.[3]   Caution was needed in order to nip this movement of
protest in the bud without bringing fresh recruits to the forces of
opposition in the party ; and here the tradition which kept military affairs out of party quarrels probably helped the party leaders
to isolate the trouble.   On June 27, 1928, the Revolutionary-
Military Council in formal session adopted a decree " On the
Political and Moral Condition of the Red Army ", which was
accompanied by a directive from Bubnov, the president of PUR,
to the officer corps.   The resolution of the Tolmachev academy was
declared " not to correspond in some of its parts " to army requirements, and the White Russian resolution was described as " merit-
ing total condemnation ".   In spite of these verdicts, however, the
substance of the decree was comparatively mild, dwelling on such
familiar generalities as the need to strengthen the unity of the
commanding and political staff, to overcome the opposition within
the army, and to correct bureaucratic distortions.[4]   On October
23, 1928, when the new party struggle was coming to a head, Bubnov addressed the party *aktiv* of the Moscow garrison, which
passed a resolution expressing the need both to " finish off the
remnants of the Trotskyite opposition " and, above all, to resist
" the Right deviation, conciliation of it, and concealment of the

---

[1] *KPSS i Stroitel'stvo Sovetskikh Vooruzhennykh Sil* (1965), pp. 229-230 ;
Pravda, April 6, 1928.

[2] N. Kharitonov, *Politicheskii Apparat Krasnoi Armii* (1929), p. 60 ; *KPSS i
Stroitel'stvo Sovetskikh Vooruzhennykh Sil* (1965), p. 230.   [3] See p. 330 below.

[4] *Voprosy Istorii KPSS*, No. 12, 1964, pp. 34-35 ; Bubnov's directive
appears to be the document cited in *KPSS i Stroitel'stvo Sovetskikh Vooruzhennykh Sil* (1965), p. 231, note 3.

Right danger, from whatever source they come ".[1] But, so far as
the record goes, nothing was said to identify these dangers with
any movement of dissent in the army. A decision of the party
central committee of October 30, 1928, which specifically endorsed
the decree of June 27, 1928, and deplored the lack of unity between
political and military staffs, still struck an ambiguous note, demanding both " the unshakeable unity of command and political
personnel " and " the continuous strengthening of the directing
influence of the communist party in the army and the fleet ".
Finally on November 24, 1928, the Revolutionary Military Council
promulgated a Statute of Commissars, One-man Commanders
and Political Assistants to replace the temporary statute of July 30,
1925. The delimitation of functions proceeded on familiar lines.
Where full one-man command had not yet been established, commanders and commissars had joint responsibility for the political
and moral condition and the fighting capacity of the unit. Where
full one-man command had been established, the commander had
total responsibility and signed all orders, but the political assistant
also signed orders " directly relating to the political life of the
unit ".[2] What progress was made during this time towards the
establishment of one-man command, remains uncertain. By 1928
more than half the regimental and divisional commanders, and virtually all corps commanders, held one-man commands; among
them 70 per cent were party members who had joined the Bolsheviks before the October revolution.[3] According to Unshlikht, 52
per cent of all corps, divisional brigade and regimental commanders
in 1928 were party members, and 32 per cent held one-man commands.[4] Thus not all party members of high army rank held one-
man commands, though probably all who did were party members.
     The impression left by these long drawn out proceedings is
that, while the need for a single and unqualified authority in the
Red Army and in all its units was widely recognized, the strong

    [1] *Krasnaya Zvezda*, October 24, 1928.
    [2] For a narrative of these events, supported by references to unpublished
archives, see *Voprosy Istorii KPSS*, No. 12, 1964, pp. 33-36; an extract from
the resolution of the party central committee of October 30, 1928, is in *KPSS o
Vooruzhennykh Silakh Sovetskogo Soyuza* (1969), pp. 252-254. For the temporary statute of July 30, 1925, see *Socialism in One Country, 1924–1926*, Vol. 2,
p. 413.   [3] N. Kharitonov, *Politicheskii Apparat Krasnoi Armii* (1929), p. 52.
    [4] *Krasnaya Zvezda*, November 15, 1928.

and persistent repugnance of some party stalwarts, as well as of the commissars themselves, to anything that might seem to weaken party control over the army made it expedient for the party leaders to await the gradual merging of the officer corps with the party, through the dual process of the appointment of party members to military commands and of the recruitment of ranking officers into the party, rather than to court determined resistance by attempting to hasten unification. On the issue of substance, moderation prevailed. An article in *Pravda* once more distinguished between the two types of one-man command, and found satisfaction in the reflexion that the second type was increasing year by year.[1] Yet, as the struggle with the Right in the party assumed sharper forms, any toleration of overt dissent was rejected as dangerous. A party meeting in the Tolmachev academy on December 10, 1928, rescinded the resolution of March 15, 1928, as incompatible with the party line, and required its active sponsors to submit to party discipline;[2] and the party central committee, in a resolution based on a report of PUR of the same date, noted " a failure to bring promptly to light examples, reflected in the moods of different groups in the Red Army, of influence of *kulak* class elements in the countryside, and to react to them ", and demanded " a decisive struggle against all deviations in the ranks of party organizations from the correct party line ". The resolution did not identify the deviators. But a leading article accompanying its publication in the journal of the party central committee observed no such restraint, referring openly to " a part of the top political personnel of the White Russian military district " and " the collective of the Military-Political Academy ".[3] Voroshilov in his article in *Pravda* on the Red Army anniversary on February 23, 1928, after attacking the Right opposition, observed that " internal difficulties have left their mark on the Red Army ", producing " morbid phenomena both in the mass of the Red Army and in the officer personnel ", and briefly instanced the White Russian and Tolmachev protests. The whole controversy was wound up by a resolution of the party central committee of February 25, 1929,

---

[1] *Pravda*, February 23, 1929; for the two types see *Socialism in One Country, 1924–1926*, Vol. 2, p. 410.

[2] *Voprosy Istorii KPSS*, No. 12, 1964, p. 36.

[3] *Izvestiya Tsentral'nogo Komiteta VKP(B)*, No. 37-38(258-259), December 31, 1928, pp. 1-2, 8-9.

which recorded that the waverings and errors of the army opposition had been condemned by all party organizations in the army,
and by almost all those who had been guilty of them; the party
now had " cadres of a political staff entirely faithful to the party
and ideologically unwavering ".[1] None of the offenders seems to
have suffered immediate reprisals.[2] But the party purge of 1929
was vigorously applied to party cells in the Red Army, commissions
being appointed which received oral and written reports on members;[3] and those guilty of refractory behaviour were certainly
called to account. The authority of the party was vindicated, and
the deviators chastised. Yet, in so far as any principle was at stake,
the cause of party control over the armed forces, on which the deviators took their stand, emerged triumphant. It was only as the
military commanders and their staffs themselves became subject
to party discipline that the commissars, who had once been the sym-
bols and instruments of party control, were gradually superseded.

(c) Army and Population

The anomalous status of the Red Army as a major Soviet
institution of predominantly peasant composition had long been a
matter of anxiety in party circles. When after 1926 a reaction set
in against the pro-peasant orientation in Soviet policy, these
apprehensions increased. The growing tension in the economy
culminated in the grain collections crisis of the winter of 1927–
1928. Complaints were heard among Red Army men of peasant
origin about the low official prices for grain and the high prices for
industrial goods; and it was asked why peasants could not deliver
their grain to the private trader.[4] The political commissars in the
White Russian republic, already struggling to defend their rights
and their status, passed a resolution expressing anxiety about the
restiveness of well-to-do peasants in the army.[5] The Red Army

---

[1] *Izvestiya Tsentral'nogo Komiteta VKP(B)*, No. 8-9(267-268), March 31,
1929, pp. 13-14; *KPSS o Vooruzhennykh Silakh Sovetskogo Soyuza* (1969),
pp. 258-261. It was originally published in *Izvestiya*, March 22, 1929.

[2] Some of them fell victims to the purge eight years later on the score of their
actions at this time, being denounced retrospectively as " a White Russian–
Tolmachev anti-party grouping ", and accused of Trotskyism and of a Right
deviation (*Voprosy Istorii KPSS*, No. 12, 1964, pp. 36-37).

[3] *Izvestiya*, May 12, 1928.   [4] *Krasnaya Zvezda*, March 9, 1928.

[5] See Vol. 1, p. 57, note 8.

newspaper, at the height of the crisis, corroborated the view that the well-to-do peasant could constitute a menace ; cases occurred in which he took advantage of his position to indoctrinate his poor and middle peasant fellow-soldiers.[1] A few months later, on the occasion of the 1928 call-up, the same newspaper made a solemn pronouncement on the theme :

> Class-alien and socially dangerous elements and persons deprived of electoral rights penetrated into the army, albeit in small numbers. Undoubtedly attempts will be made this year, too, by these elements to penetrate into the ranks of the army. This should in no case be allowed.[2]

The picture was further darkened by the discovery of the Right deviation in the party. Unshlikht expressed his fears of the influence of the " petty bourgeois element ", and thought that the Right danger was greater in the army than elsewhere.[3] A few weeks later, he voiced the same concern at a conference in the autumn of 1928 on the occasion of the tenth anniversary of PUR :

> The real backbone of the worker-peasant army is the young peasant, who comes into the ranks of the Red Army with all the prejudices which exist in the countryside, who receives letters from the countryside fostering these prejudices. I start therefore from the point that the Red Army may be the source of strong pressure from the petty bourgeois element in the ranks of our party organization. Hence the danger that elements liable to Rightist inclinations may appear in the ranks of our party organization in the Red Army. And this danger is greater than in our civilian party organizations. We should therefore say here quite definitely : Be on your guard, comrades, unmask this pressure which arises from petty bourgeois elements, give it the decisive rebuttal it deserves.[4]

In the spring of 1929 the Red Army newspaper was still reporting pro-*kulak* and anti-collective trends in the army, even among officers and commissars.[5]

On the other hand, these apprehensions bred an acute consciousness of the need for mass propaganda to mitigate peasant mistrust, and of the unique opportunity provided by the Red Army for this work. The composition of the Red Army had always

---

[1] *Krasnaya Zvezda*, March 29, 1928.   [2] *Ibid*. August 10, 1928.
[3] *Ibid*. September 15, 1928.   [4] *Ibid*. November 15, 1928.
[5] *Ibid*. April 18, 1929.

imposed on it extensive educational functions. In the middle nineteen-twenties, total illiteracy among recruits was confined mainly to units of the smaller nationalities, but one-half of the recruits were at best semi-literate; only 0·2 per cent of them were still illiterate at the end of their service.[1] To instruct the recruit was as necessary a task as to teach him to march and shoot. Evening schools of general education were set up in military units. Like other national armies, however, the Red Army was also a school of loyalty. The enrolment of new recruits in the autumn was an occasion for ceremonial marching and patriotic speeches.[2] One of the slogans for a tenth anniversary in February 1928 called the Red Army " a school of socialism for millions of peasants and workers ".[3] Political instruction in small groups was an integral part of military training; and emphasis was laid on the military threat to the Soviet régime. [1] Red Army men were expected to emerge from their training as loyal and useful Soviet citizens — the better of them with rudiments of political understanding and aspirations to party membership. The correspondence of Red Army men with their families had been named by the thirteenth party congress of May 1924 as a way " to bring the countryside into touch with the current tasks of the Soviet state ".[5] Evidence of a somewhat later date reveals official encouragement and organization of such correspondence. At the time of the grain collections crisis of 1928, Komsomol members on a training ship sent in the space of three or four months " more than 2000 official registered letters, not counting a vast number of letters written home by Red Fleet men in the course of ordinary correspondence ".[6] In some units of the Red Army the writing of letters became a collective activity, and records were kept of the number of letters sent.[7] In the electoral campaign of 1927 the political organs of the

[1] *K XV S"ezdu VKP(B)* (1927), p. 250.
[2] For a description see M. Fainsod, *Smolensk under Soviet Rule* (1959), p. 339.   [3] For these slogans see p. 314 above.
[4] *K XV S"ezdu VKP(B)* (1927), pp. 257-258.
[5] *KPSS v Rezolyutsiyakh* (1954), ii, 56; a " bureau of soldiers' letters " attached to PUR " serves to watch our soldiers' moods, to carry out Red Army requests and petitions, to review information laid by them, and also guarantee an attentive attitude to them on the part of civil and military organs " (quoted from a Soviet source in N. Pyatnitsky, *Voennaya Organizatsiya Gosudarstvennoi Oborony SSSR* (Paris, 1931), p. 29).
[6] *Krasnaya Zvezda*, August 16, 1928.   [7] *Ibid.* January 22, 1929.

Red Army were said to have " performed a colossal amount of work ", especially by distributing posters in remote localities.[1]

It was confidently expected that Red Army men, when they had completed their service, would become a powerful instrument in the political education and organization of the masses. A resolution of the party central committee of March 7, 1927, noted with satisfaction " the growth of the authority and influence of party and Komsomol among non-party Red Army men . . . the creation of a near-party *aktiv*, . . . the training of activist workers in the countryside ".[2] A further resolution of October 14, 1927, called on members of the party and the Komsomol demobilized from the Red Army to work in Soviet, cooperative and other public institutions ; and the appeal was extended to " demobilized activists near to the party ".[3] Special courses were organized for those about to be demobilized in order to prepare activists for work in the countryside ;[4] and Kosior at the fifteenth party congress in December 1927 spoke of " the immense work " undertaken by the political organs of the Red Army " in preparing those demobilized to become, on their arrival in the countryside, valuable public workers ".[5] Bukharin at the Moscow provincial party conference a month earlier had dwelt on the prospect with exaggerated enthusiasm :

> The peasant who has passed through the communist school of the Red Army already has a certain kernel of proletarian training, of socialist training. We have the broadest masses drawn into state work, and the remoulding by these masses of the state apparatus. This process unmakes our basic classes, depeasantizes the peasantry and deproletarianizes the proletariat. It is an element in the dying out of state power itself.[6]

A year later the same process was described in more sober terms in the journal of TsIK :

> Absorbing into itself the mass of raw young peasants, the Red Army every year gives them back to the countryside

---

[1] *Sovetskoe Stroitel'stvo*, No. 12(29), December 1928, pp. 101-102.
[2] *Spravochnik Partiinogo Robotnika*, vi (1928), ii, 181.
[3] *Izvestiya Tsentral'nogo Komiteta VKP(B)*, No. 39(212), October 22, 1927, pp. 6-7.   [4] *K XV S"ezdu VKP(B)*, (1927), p. 258.
[5] *Pyatnadtsatyi S"ezd VKP(B)*, i (1961), 103.
[6] *Pravda*, November 24, 1927.

politically and culturally transformed. . . . Demobilized Red
Army men are often the most active element in rural social life.[1]

A further resolution of the party central committee of April 12,
1929, instructed PUR to make provision to train Red Army men
and junior officers about to be demobilized for work in party,
Soviet, or cooperative organs. Such work would include not only
administration and teaching, but work in kolkhozy and Sovkhozy
which would promote collective and cooperative forms of agriculture.[2] In the later nineteen-twenties the party was engaged in
a vital struggle to maintain its ascendancy over the Red Army and
to prevent the driving of a wedge between military efficiency and
party loyalty. It was in the course of this struggle that it developed
a more far-reaching ambition to use the army, like the trade unions,
as an instrument for the education and indoctrination of masses
and a pillar in the construction of the new Soviet society ; and the
weakness of the party, and the absence of effective Soviet institutions in the countryside, gave it a particular importance in relations between the régime and the peasantry.[3]

The society Osoaviakhim, founded in January 1927, was the
heir of three earlier civilian societies concerned with various aspects
of defence.[4] A congress of Aviakhim opened in January 17, 1927,
with an address by Rykov, who explained that the purpose of
the congress was to effect a merger with the Society for the Promotion of Defence (OSO).[5] A week later Voroshilov addressed
a joint session of the congress and the central council of OSO,
and the birth of a new joint organization was announced under the
title Osoaviakhim.[6] In April 1927 Osoaviakhim received the
accolade of the fourth Union Congress of Soviets, which called on
local Soviets to accord to it (and to the Supreme Council of Physical Culture) all manner of support.[7] While the earlier societies
had been primarily concerned with propaganda and populariza-

---

[1] *Sovetskoe Stroitel'stvo*, No. 12(29), December 1928, p. 15.
[2] *KPSS o Vooruzhennykh Silakh Sovetskogo Soyuza* (1969), pp. 262-263.
[3] For the prevalence of religious practices in the Red Army and the need to
counteract them see pp. 389-390 below.
[4] See *Socialism in One Country, 1924–1926*, Vol. 2, p. 419, note 8.
[5] *Izvestiya*, January 20, 1927.   [6] *Ibid.* January 27, 1927.
[7] *S"ezdy Sovetov v Dokumentakh*, iii (1960), 140.

tion, the war scare of 1927 stimulated movements to equip the civilian population for defence in the event of invasion. A circular of the trade union central council advocated " the broad development of the sport of shooting, of military clubs, and of popularization of military skills" and called this "a primary task of trade union organizations ".[1] Osoaviakhim was quickly swept into this movement. A decree of the party central committee of July 24, 1927, proclaiming a " defence week of Osoaviakhim ", spoke of the task of arming workers for defence; this resulted in the enrolment of numerous groups for various military and para-military activities, including aviation and chemistry, and in the collection of a fund of 11 million rubles, which was named " Our Answer to Chamberlain ", and served to provide 100 aeroplanes.[2] Membership in October 1927 had reached nearly 3 millions organized in 42,000 cells, 15·7 per cent being women, and 17·4 per cent party members.[3] The budget of the society for 1927–1928 amounted to 8·4 million rubles; nearly 20 million rubles had been collected for such purposes as the building of aeroplanes and airfields.[4] These figures, if in any way authentic, can have been achieved only by mass enrolments from the Komsomol, the trade unions, or other institutions, but were significant of the importance now attached to Osoaviakhim by the authorities. The young were trained in such para-military arts as flying, marksmanship and map-reading; at a later stage military training in field conditions was undertaken. Blomberg on his visit of September 1928 was struck by the extent of the organized participation of the population in an air-raid exercise in Kiev.[5] Osoaviakhim was mainly an urban institution; a resolution of the party central committee of March 19, 1928, complained of the weakness of the

---

[1] *Trud*, April 27, 1927.

[2] *K XV S"ezdu VKP(B)* (1927), pp. 267-286; *Voprosy Istorii*, No. 6, 1965, p. 47.

[3] *League of Nations: Armaments Year-Book*, v (1929), pp. 829-830; by social situation, 37·2 per cent were workers, 21·0 peasants, 26·5 employees, 6·7 students, 7·1 military, 1·5 others. The membership had risen to more than 5 millions two years later (D. Fedotoff White, *The Growth of the Red Army* (Princeton, 1944), p. 289).

[4] *Ibid.* p. 830; *Pravda*, February 23, 1928 (art. by Voroshilov). In 1930 the entrance fee was 20 kopeks, and the annual subscription from 20 kopeks to 3 rubles according to the wages of the member (*Krasnaya Zvezda*, May 15, 1930).

[5] *Auswärtiges Amt*, 9480/276233-4.

lower cells of the organization, especially in the countryside. The same resolution revealed some embarrassment over " the question of providing the population with small-calibre weapons, cartridges and sporting rifles " ; this was reserved for later discussion.[1] Other functions of Osoaviakhim were not neglected. In its early stages it was much occupied with the encouragement of the chemical industry, and especially with the provision of fertilizers for agriculture.[2] A scientific section of its central council was set up with S. Kamenev, the former chief of staff of the Red Army, as its president, and in June 1927 Oldenburg, the secretary of the Academy of Sciences, and other academicians attended a meeting to discuss the contributions of science to defence.[3] In an address to the council of Osoaviakhim in March 1928, Unshlikht rather surprisingly, according to the published report, concentrated on the application of aviation and chemistry to agriculture, and had little to say about their military uses.[4] Osoaviakhim sometimes undertook political functions. A circular issued by Unshlikht in November 1928 to its local branches urged them to participate actively in the forthcoming elections to the Soviets, and to make sure that questions of defence were kept to the fore in the campaign ; Budennyi made an appeal in the same sense.[5] The institution continued for some years to attract massive official publicity. But the extent of its actual contribution to national defence remains uncertain.

[1] *Pravda*, April 23, 1928.
[2] See Vol. 1, p. 239 ; for further examples of this side of its work see *Voprosy Istorii*, No. 6, 1965, pp. 46-48.
[3] *Izvestiya*, June 21, 1927.
[4] *Pravda*, April 4, 1928.
[5] *Izvestiya*, November 20, 1928.

CHAPTER 53

THE RULE OF LAW

THE constitution of the USSR of January 1924 reserved to the Union authorities the establishment of " the foundations of judicial organization and procedure, as well as of the civil and criminal legislation of the Union ".[1] To enunciate the foundations of civil law proved too exacting a task ; and the civil code of the RSFSR, which was imitated or borrowed *in toto* by the other Union republics,[2] held the field unchallenged till a much later date. The other tasks imposed on the Union by the constitution were more punctually discharged. After the stormy session of TsIK in October 1924,[3] decrees of the USSR were approved embodying " foundations " of judicial organization and of criminal legislation and criminal procedure.[4]

(a) Courts and Procurators

The foundations of judicial organization promulgated in October 1924 followed the lines laid down in the decrees of the RSFSR of 1922, when the first statute on courts was enacted, and the office of procurator of the RSFSR created ; these had been supplemented, when the USSR came into being, by the creation of a Supreme Court of the USSR and by the appointment of a procurator of the Supreme Court.[5] The foundations, proclaiming as their purpose " the realization of revolutionary legality ",[6] and resting firmly on the principle of a " single judicial system " for the Union, took over the existing three-tier system of courts — people's courts,

---

[1] See *The Bolshevik Revolution, 1917-1923*, Vol. 1, p. 404.

[2] For a review of differences between the civil codes of five Union republics and of the constituent republics of the Transcaucasian SFSR (which did not itself have a code) see *Sovetskoe Stroitel'stvo*, No. 7(24), July 1928, pp. 131-134.

[3] See *Socialism in One Country, 1924–1926*, Vol. 2, pp. 236-239.

[4] *Sobranie Zakonov, 1924*, No. 23, art. 203 ; No. 24, arts. 205, 206.

[5] See *Socialism in One Country, 1924-1926*, Vol. 1, pp. 80-85, Vol. 2, pp. 236-239.   [6] See *ibid.* Vol. 2, pp. 468-471.

provincial courts and supreme courts of the republic — which
was established by the RSFSR in 1922,[1] and adopted, though
no doubt with some shortcomings in practice, by the other Union
republics. The people's court, consisting of a people's judge and
two elected lay assessors, continued to conduct the day-to-day
administration of justice in the vast majority of minor crimes and
disputes, and represented the popular element in the Soviet system
of justice.[2] This principle was emphatically re-asserted by Yanson,
People's Commissar for Justice of the RSFSR, in February
1929, at a moment when harsher forms of justice were being
introduced for major crimes :

> Our court is a people's court. Our people's court is most
> closely linked with the population through the assessors. . . . We
> are wholly and completely under public supervision. A thou-
> sand threads unite us with the worker and peasant population.
> Our court can in no way be compared with the former courts,
> of this fact there can be no question at all.[3]

The provincial courts and supreme court of the republic functioned as courts of appeal, or as courts of first instance in cases of
major importance.

The foundations did not call for any immediate revision of the
RSFSR code of judicial organization. It was not till November
1926 that a revised code took account of the changes in the
administrative structure of the republic due to the progress of
regionalization. In regionalized areas, people's courts were to
function at the level of the district (raion), which replaced the
county ; higher courts were to function at the level of the region
(oblast' or krai), replacing the provincial courts ; but between the
regional courts and the district courts was inserted a new layer of
department (okrug) courts. The supreme court of the republic
underwent no substantial change.[4] This appeared to substitute a

---

[1] See *Socialism in One Country, 1924–1926*, Vol. I, pp. 80-82.

[2] In 1927 540,108 people's assessors were elected, 309,525 of them being
peasants, and 98,604 workers (*Osnovnye Itogi Rabochego Pravitel'stva 1928/29 g.*
(1928), p. 164).

[3] *Ezhenedel'nik Sovetskoi Yustitsii*, No. 9-10, March 8/15, 1929, p. 207 ;
for Yanson see p. 364 below.

[4] *III Sessiya Vserossiiskogo Tsentral'nogo Ispolnitel'nogo Komiteta XII
Sozyva : Postanovleniya* (1926), pp. 72-122 ; *Sobranie Uzakonenii, 1926*, No. 85,
art. 624 ; for the process of regionalization see pp. 213-215 above. Auto-

four-tier system for the old three-tier system of courts. The original intention may have been to squeeze out the regional and provincial courts between the department courts and the supreme court of the republic.[1] What in fact happened was that the provincial courts became the highest court of appeal from decisions of the department courts, and the supreme court of the republic acted as court of appeal only in major cases where the regional court had acted as court of first instance.[2] When the departments were abolished in 1930,[3] the original three-tier structure was reinstated.

The structure and functions of the lower courts of the republics were little affected by the imposition on them from above of the Supreme Court of the USSR. The Supreme Court enjoyed the prestige of having been created by the constitution of the USSR, which had already laid down its functions and composition. It was to be guided, as the foundations proclaimed, " by the interests of the Union as a whole and by those of the separate republics, whose sovereign rights it will maintain " — a phrase plainly designed to appease republican critics of its centralized authority. The court consisted of some 30 judges, but never sat as a whole. It exercised under its statute three distinct functions. Sitting as a so-called " plenum " of 15 judges,[4] it gave, at the invitation of the TsIK of the USSR, interpretations on points of law, or of compatibility with the constitution, arising out of appeals by lower organs or by the procurator against acts of Union republics or of People's Commissariats of the USSR. These interpretations, however, required confirmation by TsIK to establish their validity ; it was emphasized that this did not establish a right of judicial review in the western sense. Secondly, the Supreme Court acted as a court of appeal from decisions of lower courts, including the

nomous republics also had supreme courts, whose status was similar to that of regional courts ; but in small autonomous republics incorporated in regions (see pp. 215-217 above) no intermediate courts existed between the supreme court and the people's courts.
    [1] For the exclusion of the regions from the process of election to the Union Congress of Soviets see pp. 222-223 above.
    [2] *Ezhenedel'nik Sovetskoi Yustitsii*, No. 9-10, March 8/15, 1929, p. 202.
    [3] See p. 228, note 2 above.
    [4] The number fixed by the constitution at 11 was raised to 15 by the third Union Congress of Soviets in May 1925 to permit of the inclusion of one judge from each Union republic (*S"ezdy Sovetov v Dokumentakh*, iii (1960), 77).

supreme courts of the Union republics ; for this purpose, it formed several permanent panels, of which the civil collegium, the criminal collegium and the military collegium were the most active. Thirdly, it functioned exceptionally, through its collegia, as a court of first instance to try serious charges of state crimes against members of TsIK or other high officials, or other criminal cases of particular importance to the Union or to two or more of the Union republics ; such cases could be heard by either one of the permanent collegia or by a special court convened, on instructions from TsIK, for the purpose.[1] The Supreme Court was described in the constitution of the USSR as an organ " attached to TsIK " ; and this fairly designated its subsidiary status. Sandwiched between TsIK on one side and an increasingly active procurator on the other, its independent authority scarcely corresponded to the formal dignity with which it was invested. Attempts were made from time to time to secure an extension of its powers.[2] But it was not till July 1929 that a revised statute gave it the right, on its own initiative and without the intervention of the procurator, to challenge legislative acts of organs of the USSR and of the republics.[3] It is doubtful whether this change had much effect in practice.

The office which continuously expanded its authority and influence during this period was the procuracy ; and this extension of power accrued both to the procurators of the republics and to the newly appointed procurator of the Supreme Court. The office of procurator, which dated back to Peter the Great and had lapsed in 1917, was re-established for the RSFSR, after a personal inter-

[1] For the foundation and statutes of the Supreme Court see *Socialism in One Country, 1924–1926*, Vol. 1, pp. 84-85 ; for an account of the activities of the Supreme Court in 1928 see *SSSR: God Raboty Pravitel'stva, 1927-28* (1929), pp. 463-467. In that year the court held four plenary sessions and dealt with 63 items, of which 33 were cases of legality (conformity of administrative or legislative acts with the law or the constitution), 25 cases of judicial review and 5 organizational questions ; in addition, 5 major cases were dealt with by the the criminal collegium (including the Shakhty trial), 2 by the civil collegium, and 14 by the military collegium.

[2] See the discussion in *Ezhenedel'nik Sovetskoi Yustitsii*, No. 20, May 31, 1928, pp. 591-593. On the other hand, a discussion article in *Izvestiya*, June 2, 1928, proposed its abolition ; of its rudimentary functions, only the hearing by its military collegium of appeals from military courts was important, and this could be provided for in some other way.

[3] *Sobranie Zakonov, 1929*, No. 50, art. 445.

vention by Lenin, in May 1922. It became, in effect, a department
of Narkomyust, the People's Commissar for Justice of the RSFSR
being *ex officio* the procurator of the republic ; [1] and a similar office
was established by the other republics. The procurator of the
republic appointed provincial and regional procurators and assistant procurators directly responsible to him ; and a network of
assistant procurators and officials of the procuracy spread over the
county (or, where regionalization had been effected, department
and district) courts. The office of procurator had become, even
before the creation of the USSR, the symbol and instrument of the
uniform and centralized administration of law.[2] Article 14 of
the foundations of judicial organization adopted by the TsIK of
the USSR in October 1924 prescribed that the procurator's office
should be " organized on the basis of centralization and sole subordination to the procurator of the republic ". The ensuing years
brought increasing importance to the work of the republican procurator, and especially of the procurator of the RSFSR.[3]

When, under the terms of the constitution, a procurator of the
Supreme Court of the USSR was appointed in 1924, he inherited
this tradition, and might have seemed to represent, in the field of
judicial organization, the centralizing forces inherent in the constitution of the Union. He was directly appointed by TsIK ;
and the absence of a Narkomyust of the USSR gave him an independent position not enjoyed by the procurators of the republics.
His destiny, clearly foreshadowed from the outset, was to become
the supreme custodian of legality, and the supervisor of the

---

[1] Kursky, from 1922 to 1928, combined the two offices ; Krylenko, who was
deputy People's Commissar for Justice and principal *aide* of the procurator, in
effect exercised the functions of procurator. Yanson's subsequent comment
that Kursky was " somewhat aloof . . . from the courts ", and that the whole
collegium of Narkomyust was under " procuratorial constraint (zasilie) " seems
to have been a covert attack on Krylenko's influence (*Ezhenedel'nik Sovetskoi
Yustitsii*, No. 9-10, March 8/15, 1929, p. 202) ; down to 1928 Krylenko was
closely associated with the growing power of the procuracy.

[2] See *Socialism in One Country, 1924–1926*, Vo. 1, pp. 81-83.

[3] In May 1926 the Sovnarkom of the RSFSR asked for " a further planned
increase in the staffs of the procuracy ", so that every county should have at least
two procuratorial officials, one of them charged with tasks of " general supervision " (*Ezhenedel'nik Sovetskoi Yustitsii*, No. 31, August 1, 1926, p. 915) ;
in 1926 the procurator of the RSFSR reviewed 10,000 enactments of various
authorities, in 1927 16,000 (*Sovetskoe Stroitel'stvo*, No. 9(26), September 1928,
p. 11).

administration of law, throughout the Union. This was not, however, his initial position, and nearly ten years elapsed before he finally made good this claim. For the present his powers were limited. His title was significant: he was procurator not of the USSR, but of the Supreme Court of the USSR. He could act only through the Supreme Court. He could appeal to the Supreme Court against acts of organs of the Union, or against decisions of the supreme courts of Union republics, but not against acts of republican organs. He had no formal authority over the procurators of the republics. Throughout the nineteen-twenties, the post of procurator of the Supreme Court was occupied by Krasikov, a respectable, but colourless, jurist; and republican jealousies of Union authority, and the strong legal tradition entrenched in the Narkomyust of the RSFSR, stubbornly resisted any encroachment. When Solts, a member of the presidium of the party central control commission, who was also a judge of the Supreme Court, proposed in an article in the journal of TsIK the creation of a procurator of the USSR,[1] he was firmly rebutted by Kursky, the People's Commissar for Justice of the RSFSR;[2] and the proposal was not pursued. The procurator of the Supreme Court did, however, stake out his claim in two fields where the overriding powers of the Union were not contested — military affairs and security; one of his assistants was appointed as procurator to the military collegium of the Supreme Court, another as inspector of the OGPU.[3] Extended functions brought new prestige to the office and, no doubt, a larger and abler personnel; the procurator wielded ever wider influence behind the scenes.

This growing prestige of procuratorial authority was connected with a significant shift of emphasis in its scope and character. The procurator was the watchdog of legality. He initiated prosecutions, and instituted appeals to the supreme court of the republic against legally assailable decisions of lower courts. It is perhaps fair to assume that, during these years, the influence of the ubiquitous procurator was responsible for some improvement in the legal standards of justice in the people's courts. But it was also his function to review from the legal standpoint all actions and deci-

[1] *Sovetskoe Stroitel'stvo*, No. 2, September 1926, pp. 59-62.
[2] *Ibid.* No. 4(9), April 1927, pp. 97-102.
[3] For these functions see pp. 354, 357-358, 372 below.

sions of government organs, political as well as judicial, and to
appeal against them on grounds of law to the TsIK of the republic
or its presidium. To check the legality of what was done by the
courts became a less conspicuous part of the functions of the procurator than to check the legality of what was done by organs of
government, whether by way of legislative or of administrative
action. Both unconstitutional enactments and abuses committed
by officials came within his purview, and it was his function to
appeal against both; at the lower administrative levels his
intervention concerned mainly routine questions of finance and
taxation.[1] The campaign against " bureaucratism "[2] contributed
to the importance and popularity of the procurator. He was hailed
as the scourge of bureaucrats, the man appointed to hunt down
bureaucratic abuses; and this rôle more and more seemed to
eclipse his other functions. In the spring of 1927 the procuracy
was called on to play its part in the campaign to reduce prices;[3]
and an article of the period declared that " the organization of
activists in the countryside and their attraction into cultural-legal
work is the central point of the axis round which the separate parts
of the complex operations of the procuracy in the countryside
revolve ".[4]

This extension of the procuratorial function from the field of
law to that of administration soon became a subject of controversy.
Solts, in the article in which he advocated the creation of a procurator of the USSR, had also attacked the view that the procurator
should be concerned primarily, like a bourgeois procurator, with
the courts.

> The whole weight of procuratorial supervision [he declared]
> should be concentrated mainly, not on observing how far the
> work of this or that court or judicial organ parts company with
> this or that article of the code, but on a real watch over the
> activity of administrators, high and low, who often violate
> legality.

The procuracy, like Rabkrin, though in a different capacity,
should devote itself to oversight over the Soviet apparatus. Its

[1] *Vlast' Sovetov*, No. 44-45, November 7, 1926, pp. 23-24.
[2] See pp. 292-296 above.
[3] *Ezhenedel'nik Sovetskoi Yustitsii*, No. 20, May 25, 1927, pp. 598-600; for
this campaign see Vol. 1, pp. 684-688.   [4] *Ibid.* No. 26, July 4, 1926, p. 802.

role was to be comprehensive. Solts described it as " leaning on party and Soviet authority, on peasant and worker public activity, and extensively utilizing the press ".[1] Solts raised a further significant issue when in the same article he demanded close cooperation between the procuracy and the party control commissions at all levels : this would mean a real " party-political " link between the two organizations.[2] The amalgamation of the party central control commission with Rabkrin had given it a direct interest in Soviet administration ; and it was this aspect of its work which appeared to inspire Solts's article. But the call for cooperation between the control commission and the procurators had another meaning. The struggle against the united opposition began in earnest at the session of the party central committee in July 1926. Cooperation between the party central control commission and the procuracy, and between their subordinate organs at lower levels, was soon to become a vital link in this pattern, and illustrated the effect of the internecine party struggles in shaping political institutions.

The struggle which went on behind the scenes between the jurists, headed by Krylenko, who insisted on the function of the procuracy as one of legal interpretation, and the politicians and administrators, who wished to transform it, like other Soviet organs, into a supple instrument of party and Soviet policy, flared up at the fifteenth party congress in December 1927. Yanson called for " a little revolution " in the administration of justice. He complained that, in the hands of the procurators, concern for legality sometimes turned into " pedantry (bukvoedstvo) ", and that what were wanted were " more practical people " (" and fewer lawyers ", interjected Solts).[3] Krylenko, who encountered mocking interruptions, defended the legal work of courts and procurators in combating bureaucratism.[4] Shkiryatov directly attacked Krylenko for getting his priorities wrong. The business of law was to suppress crime, not to become embedded in niceties of legal interpretations.

---

[1] *Sovetskoe Stroitel'stvo*, No. 2, September 1926, p. 61 ; for this article see p. 342 above. Solts had sponsored the resolution on revolutionary legality at the fourteenth party conference in April 1925 (see *Socialism in One Country, 1924–1926*, Vol. 2, p. 469).

[2] *Sovetskoe Stroitel'stvo*, No. 2, September 1926, p. 60.

[3] *Pyatnadtsatyi S"ezd VKP(B)*, i (1961), 527.   [4] *Ibid.* i, 577–578.

Apart from the letter of the law [said Shkiryatov] — and I am for defending the law — but apart from the letter of the law there should be *proletarian revolutionary feeling* in the examination of any affair ; but for them sometimes the law is above everything.

Solts pursued the same argument a little less crudely. A judge was often a worker :

His proletarian feeling tells him that this is the right thing to do. The procurator says : Be this as it may, has such and such an article been carried out?

This happened because the procurators did not stick to their proper business — " to watch that the local authorities do not break the laws ".[1] The congress reflected a mood, but took no formal decision. The quarrel was patched up, and Krylenko was elected to the congress a member of the central control commission — an appointment which symbolized the strengthened link between the procuracy and party organs. But it was not long before a legal commentator would write of the supervisory functions of the procurator as " essentially political ".[2] Political elements began to complement, and even to eclipse, legal elements at an early stage.

The increasingly political character of the procuracy was illustrated by its association with the *rabsel'kor* movement. Since 1925 the *rabkors* and *sel'kors* had been encouraged to report abuses to Rabkrin or to the local procurator.[3] A leading article in *Pravda*

[1] *Ibid.* i, 591-593, 603-604. A similar argument was carried on simultaneously in the journal of Narkomyust ; while one writer attacked as " defeatists and liquidators " those who sought to place legal limits on procuratorial supervision, another protested against " investigations in depth " of rural executive committees by the procuracy, and maintained that these activities could only weaken the procurator's real legal functions (*Ezhenedel'nik Sovetskoi Yustitsii*, No. 45, November 21, 1927, pp. 1393-1396, No. 51, December 30, 1927, pp. 1590-1593). The most extreme case for the aggrandisement of the procuracy was stated in a discussion article in *Izvestiya*, May 26, 1928, which dismissed the distinction between the practical rôle of Rabkrin and the legal role of the procurator as " scholastic ", and wished the procurator to take over the functions of the People's Commissar for Justice.

[2] *Ezhenedel'nik Sovetskoi Yustitsii*, No. 24, June 30, 1928, p. 685.

[3] See *Socialism in One Country, 1924-1926*, Vol. 2, pp. 470-471.

on the eve of the third Union conference of *rabsel'kors* in May 1926
observed that " the work of such Soviet organs as the procuracy
cannot be imagined except in conjunction with the *rabsel'kors*,
who render great help in establishing revolutionary legality ".[1]
Representatives of the procuracy organized and attended local
conferences of *rabsel'kors*.[2] The number of " notes " from
rabsel'kors on which procurators in the RSFSR took action
increased from 58,891 in 1926 to 72,230 in 1927 ; in the list of
abuses dealt with in these notes the largest item was misdemeanours by officials, notably in the cooperatives.[3] But of notes sent
to the procurators by *rabsel'kors* in 1928 only 28 per cent were
confirmed by subsequent enquiry, though it was not clear whether
this was due to the unreliability of the reports or to the laxity of
the procurators.[4] By 1928 80,000 *rabsel'kors* representing 43
newspapers were said to be at work in the RSFSR, and 34,600
representing 69 newspapers in the Ukraine.[5] At a time when stress
was being laid on the rôle of the procurators in countering bureaucratism, the fifteenth party congress of December 1927 advocated " wide use of the *rabsel'kor* movement in the struggle with
bureaucratic distortions ".[6] As the activities of the *rabsel'kors*
multiplied, so also did the charges against them of spying on the
population ;[7] and a recrudescence of acts of violence against them
was reported in 1928.[8] On the other hand it was alleged that

[1] *Pravda*, May 23, 1926.

[2] *Ezhenedel'nik Sovetskoi Yustitsii*, No. 18, May 9, 1926, p. 559.

[3] *Ibid*. No. 23, July 23, 1928, pp. 668-669 ; this was confirmed in a report
from Vyatka province *ibid*. No. 4, January 31, 1928, p. 110. For a case of persecution of two *rabkor* by a factory management on which they had reported
adversely see Smolensk archives WKP 22 (report of bureau of Belsk county party
committee, September 28-29, 1926).

[4] *Ezhenedel'nik Sovetskoi Yustitsii*, No. 2, January 17, 1929, pp. 25-26.

[5] *Sovetskoe Stroitel'stvo*, No. 12(29), December 1928, p. 13. *Rabkors*
conducted campaigns in factories against drunkenness and absenteeism, and
sel'kors on grain collections, sowings, self-taxation, and contributions to state
loans ; wall newspapers were sometimes used as the medium (*ibid*. No. 2(31),
February 1929, pp. 93-94). [6] *KPSS v Rezolyutsiyakh* (1954), ii, 445.

[7] See *Socialism in One Country, 1924–1926*, Vol. 2, p. 470, note 6. On
May 3, 1927, the Narkomyust of the RSFSR issued an instruction on the treatment of charges of slander brought against *rabsel'kors* by persons or institutions
on whom they had reported (*Ezhenedel'nik Sovetskoi Yustitsii*, No. 19,
May 18, 1927, p. 591) ; this was evidently a frequent occurrence.

[8] See Vol. 1, pp. 97-98 ; for a description of surreptitious persecution of
rabsel'kors see *Ezhenedel'nik Sovetskoi Yustitsii*, No. 31, August 21, 1928, pp.
860-863.

rabsel'kors sometimes took money from peasants for giving them undercover advice on legal matters.[1]   When the fourth *rabsel'kor* conference met, two-and-a-half years after its predecessor, in November 1928, *Pravda* found it necessary to rebut the charge that the *rabsel'kors* were simply " legions of voluntary ' Soviet spies ' " and " police pens ", and claimed that the movement had helped to bring abuses to light and to further the class struggle and the work of socialist construction.[2]   The conference was addressed by Bukharin, Ulanova, Yaroslavsky and Voroshilov, and received extensive publicity in *Pravda*.[3]   The *rabsel'kors*, whatever their other functions, had become the unofficial " eyes " of the procurator in the countryside ; and as such they were part of a far-ranging movement of cooperation between Soviet and party organs, directed both to the defence of Soviet legality against administrative abuses and to the defence of party loyalties against opposition and dissent, in which legitimate and sinister functions were almost inextricably blended.

The growing power of the procuracy was marked by a decree of the RSFSR of January 30, 1928, which abrogated the rule that the People's Commissar for Justice should also be the procurator of the RSFSR.   Henceforth the People's Commissar would have two deputies, of whom one would be president of the supreme court of the republic and control the organization of the courts, and the other the procurator of the republic.[4]   Whatever the purpose of the decree (which professed to change nothing of substance), its effect was to make the procurator of the RSFSR less dependent on the republican administration, and more directly responsible to the procurator of the Supreme Court of the USSR, and thus to prepare the way for the welding of the whole procuratorial system into a single unit.   At the same time, the procurator secured a further accretion of power.   His rôle as prosecutor in criminal cases had always given him an important influence over the preliminary investigation ; and the revised code of the RSFSR of November

---

[1] *Ibid.* No. 42-43, November 14/21, 1928, pp. 1097-1100.
[2] *Ibid.* November 28, 1928.
[3] *Ibid.* November 29, December 4, 7, 8, 9, 1928.
[4] *Sobranie Uzakonenii, 1928*, No. 46, art. 343.

1926 on the organization of the courts provided that the preliminary investigation, though normally remaining in the control of the court, might in important cases be entrusted to the procurator.[1] This was the thin end of the wedge. An active campaign to place the preliminary investigation of all criminal cases under the control of the procurator had been carried on in 1927.[2] On March 15, 1928, the Narkomyust of the RSFSR issued a decree handing over the machinery of preliminary investigation " wholly and fully " to the procurator; and a conference of workers in the procuracy, meeting on the following day, adopted a resolution, which was formally endorsed by Narkomyust, calling for the full implementation of the decree.[3] The procurator had drawn into his net another facet of the administration of justice.

(b) The Criminal Code

The foundations of criminal legislation enunciated by the TsIK of the USSR simultaneously with the foundations of judicial organization, in October 1924, though modelled in form on the " leading principles " of 1919 and the criminal code of the RSFSR of 1922,[4] proved a turning-point in Soviet criminal law. Like all early Soviet legal edicts, they faced in two directions. In theory, they provided the most complete official embodiment of the sociological view of criminal law which dominated Soviet legal thinking in the nineteen-twenties. According to this view, which had also won increasing support in the western world, crime was a consequence not of moral guilt, but of social and psychological abnormalities amenable to treatment by remedial or educational measures. The most extreme form of this doctrine, popular in the Soviet Union in the nineteen-twenties, was " reflexology ", which taught that human behaviour could be explained in physiological terms, so that " all acts of men are determined " and " crime occurs in the way in which it is fated to occur ".[5] Repression

---

[1] For this code see p. 338 above.

[2] *Ezhenedel'nik Sovetskoi Yustitsii*, No. 23, June 15, 1927, pp. 689-690.

[3] *Ibid.* No. 14, April 16, 1928, pp. 420-422.

[4] See *Socialism in One Country, 1924-1926*, Vol. 1, pp. 71, 76-78.

[5] *Pod Znamenem Marksizma*, No. 7-8, 1926, p. 77; the article from which these quotations are taken was an attempt by two leading exponents of reflexology to reconcile it with dialectical materialism.

could be justified, not as punishment of the criminal, and not as a measure to correct his defects, but as a necessary defence of the social order against actions detrimental to it. The code of 1922, while it excluded the concept of guilt, retained the term " punishment ", speaking of " punishment and other measures of social defence " (art. 8). The foundations of 1924 logically abandoned " punishment ", and treated all forms of repression as " measures of social defence ". They stressed the validity of measures " of a medical-educational or medical kind " where measures " of a judicial-reformatory kind " were not applicable (art. 29). This led to a lenient attitude to ordinary crime, which might have been more widely applied if larger resources had been available, and fitted in with the conclusion, accepted by most Soviet jurists of the time (though no trace of it appeared in the foundations), that criminal law with its paraphernalia of codes, courts and measures of repression was the product of social and political disorders, and of the survival of elements hostile to the régime, and, like the state itself, would die away once these were eradicated.[1]

This approach encouraged, however, if it did not justify, a different practical conclusion. If offences dangerous to the social order became the main or sole target of " measures of social defence of a judicial-reformatory kind ", the nature of these offences called for measures of the utmost severity. The distinction between " state crimes " and other crimes was sharply emphasized in the foundations by the withdrawal of legislation on state crimes, as well as on military crimes, from the competence of the Union republics and its transfer to that of the USSR, and by the further stipulation that the presidium of TsIK might " in indispensable cases indicate to the Union republics the kinds of forms of crime for which the USSR deems it indispensable to apply the definite line of a single penal policy " (art. 3). The paramount needs of security once more favoured centralization. When the TsIK of the USSR adopted the foundations in October 1924, it invited the Union republics, not later than March 1, 1925, to revise their existing criminal codes in the light of them. But the echoes of the constitutional wrangle which had occurred in TsIK when the

---

[1] This view was propounded in a once authoritative work, E. Pashukanis, *Obshchaya Teoriya Prava i Marksizm* (1924), p. 19; for this aspect of the foundations see *Socialism in One Country, 1924–1926*, Vol. 2, pp. 433-434.

foundations were adopted[1] had scarcely died away ; and the interval proved too short.[2] It was not till October 1925 that a draft revised code approved by the Sovnarkom of the RSFSR was submitted to the TsIK of the RSFSR.[3] After a long and confused debate the session approved the draft in principle, but instructed its presidium to suspend its formal enactment, and to raise one disputed point with the TsIK of the USSR. The proposal to reserve to Union authorities legislative powers on counter-revolutionary crimes was accepted. But did this extend also to " crimes against the administrative order ", which under the 1922 code of the RSFSR were included in the same chapter? The TsIK of the RSFSR proposed that these should remain within the competence of the republics.[4] The effect of the proposal would have been to confine the authority of the Union to counter-revolutionary crimes and to restrict the new extended concept of " state crimes ".

While these leisurely debates were in progress, the TsIK of the USSR further demonstrated its interest in the field of security by issuing on August 14, 1925, a decree " on espionage, and also on the collection and transmission of economic information not open for publication ".[5] When, however, the whole issue came up once more at the session of TsIK in April 1926, opinions were still divided. The draft of a statute on state crimes, comprising both counter-revolutionary crimes and " crimes against the administrative order especially dangerous to the USSR " was provisionally approved, but was cautiously sent to the Union republics for their observations.[6] This action appears to have caused further hesitations in the People's Commissariat of Justice of the RSFSR,[7]

---

[1] See *Socialism in One Country, 1924–1926*, Vol. 2, pp. 236-239.

[2] No information is available for the republics other than the RSFSR, but it may be assumed that they lagged well behind it.

[3] The draft was published under the title *Proekt UK RSFSR s Ob"yasnitel'noi k nemu Zapiskoi* (1925).

[4] *Vserossiiskii Tsentral'nyi Ispolnitel'nyi Komitet XII Sozyva: Vtoraya Sessiya* (1925), pp. 404-411 ; *id. Postanovleniya* (1925), p. 65.

[5] *Sobranie Zakonov, 1925*, No. 52, art. 390. This was amplified by a further decree of April 27, 1926, enumerating items of secret information covered by the decree ; it was divided into three sections, of which the second was devoted to economic secrets — information regarding valuta, export and import plans, and industrial inventions (*Izvestiya*, October 9, 1926).

[6] *Sobranie Zakonov, 1926*, No. 30, art. 194 ; the term " state crimes " appeared in the title and preamble of the statute, but not in the text of the articles.

[7] An article in *Ezhenedel'nik Sovetskoi Yustitsii*, No. 36, 1926, p. 1057, ex-

and no observations were forthcoming. But the TsIK of the RSFSR at its session in November 1926, decided, pending a final pronouncement from the USSR, to bring into force on January 1, 1927, the code approved by it in principle in October 1925, retaining the chapter on counter-revolutionary crimes and crimes against the administrative order in the form (subject to minor drafting amendments) in which it had appeared in the criminal code of 1922.[1]

The RSFSR code of 1926 continued to assert (art. 9) that measures of social defence did not have the character of retribution (vozmezhdie) or punishment (kara).[2] But it retained and emphasized the distinction between crimes against the state or its officials, which were socially dangerous, and others, which might not be, and exhibited a marked leniency towards the latter. The maximum sentence for any crime not recognized as socially dangerous, including intentional homicide, was ten years to be served in a correctional labour camp. A novel provision was to the effect that where an act, recognized at the time of its commission as socially dangerous, had, in virtue of some change in the social-political environment or in the character of the accused, ceased to be socially dangerous at the time when it came up for investigation and judgment, it should not be subject to measures of social defence (art. 8).[3] On the other hand, the code allowed of the application of measures of social defence to persons who constituted a social danger through their connexion with a criminal milieu or through their own past activity, even though no specific act was alleged against them (art. 7). The death penalty by shooting was retained as an exceptional measure of defence for grave crimes

plained that the action of the Union authorities had delayed the promulgation of the RSFSR code.

[1] *Sobranie Uzakonenii, 1926*, No. 80, art. 600.

[2] The term " retribution " may have been a hit at the views of Pashukanis, for which see *Socialism in One Country, 1924–1926*, Vol. 1, p. 86 ; the choice of the highfalutin word " kara " was probably due to the fact that the ordinary word for punishment (nakazanie) had been used in the RSFSR code of 1922 (see p. 349 above).

[3] The original form of this provision was an amendment of the 1922 code in February 1925, which instructed the procurator and the court not to institute or to continue a criminal prosecution in cases where the alleged act, though technically falling within the terms of the code, could not " in respect of its consequences " be regarded as socially dangerous (*Sobranie Uzakonenii, 1925*, No. 9, art. 68).

against the administrative order (arts. 20, 21). Most of the crimes enumerated in the retained articles 58 and 59, if committed in an aggravated form, incurred the death penalty. A long section (arts. 60-108) followed on other crimes against the administrative order, and a further section (arts. 109-127) on crimes committed by officials. The continued leniency of the code towards ordinary crime made it possible to take the optimistic view, expressed in an article in *Izvestiya*, that it represented a further move against " the over-production of punishments ".[1] All in all, its preoccupation with questions of public order and security was the most conspicuous feature of the criminal code of the RSFSR of November 1926.

The promulgation of the criminal code of the RSFSR galvanized the authorities of the USSR into action. At the session of the TsIK of the USSR in February 1927 Krylenko made a report on the amendments in the " foundations " of 1924 necessary to bring them into line with the new criminal codes, and Krasikov on the proposed new statute on state crimes.[2] On February 25, 1927, two decrees were issued. One amended the foundations of 1924 by adding the category of " crimes against the administrative order most dangerous to the USSR " to that of " counter-revolutionary crimes " ; the other was a statute on " state crimes " — the controversial term which embraced both categories.[3] The statute was based mainly on the relevant articles of the 1922 criminal code of the RSFSR and of the draft revised code of 1925. Its main significance resided rather in the isolation of " state crimes " in a separate document emanating from the highest legislative authority than in its few innovations. State crimes were defined as " acts directed against any of the worker-peasant governments of the USSR or of Union or autonomous republics " ; another article included in the category of " worker-peasant governments " any workers' state not belonging to the Union. Three types of economic action were recognized as state crimes : wrecking (vreditel'stvo), diversion and sabotage. Any action committed " with the special intent to weaken the government and the func-

[1] *Izvestiya*, December 31, 1926 ; the author of the article was Shirvindt (see p. 367 below).
[2] *SSSR: Tzentral'nyi Ispolnitel'nyi Komitet 3 Sozvya: 3 Sessiya* (1927), pp. 118-145.
[3] *Sobranie Zakonov, 1927*, No. 12, arts. 122, 123.

tioning of the state apparatus " constituted " counter-revolutionary sabotage ". Though design or intent was frequently mentioned in these articles, this did not appear to be a necessary feature
of criminal action. The following section explicitly recognized the
possibility of " crimes against the administrative order committed
without counter-revolutionary intent which undermine the foundations of the state administration and the economic power of the
USSR and the Union republics ". Failure to report acts, or
attempted acts, of mass disorder, counterfeiting or banditry en-
tailed criminal responsibility. The statute was said to be enacted
" for inclusion in the criminal codes of the Union republics ".
The question whether it entered into force before such inclusion
remained apparently unresolved. The delay was now short. On
June 6, 1927, the RSFSR amended its criminal code by embodying
these provisions. Articles 1-14 of the statute (counter-revolutionary crimes) and arts. 15-17 (crimes against the administrative
order) now became arts. 58 (1-14) and 59 (1-13) of the criminal
code of the RSFSR.[1] The other Union republics introduced
criminal codes differing only in detail from the amended code of
the RSFSR.[2]

Military offences occupied a special place in Soviet criminal
law. Military transport tribunals and military tribunals had been
set up during the civil war ;[3] and the criminal code of the RSFSR
of 1922 contained a chapter on military crimes, negatively defined
as crimes which " by their nature and significance cannot be committed by civilians ". The contents of the regulation somewhat
belied the definition ; in addition to offences normally arising out
of military service, the crimes which were named, and for which
penalties were prescribed, included evasion of military service and
military espionage in its widest sense. Two years later, at a time
when the Red Army was undergoing a reorganization,[4] the newly

[1] *Sobranie Uzakonenii, 1927*, No. 49, art. 335.
[2] For a summary of the main differences see *40 Let Sovetskogo Prava* (1957),
i, 555-556.
[3] *Sobranie Uzakonenii, 1920*, No. 21, art. 112 ; No. 54, art. 236. The military transport tribunals were abolished in 1923 (*Sobranie Uzakonenii, 1924*, No.
13, art. 119) ; transport tribunals were re-established in 1930 (*Sobranie Zakonov,
1930*, No. 57, art. 611).
[4] See *Socialism in One Country, 1924–1926*, Vol. 2, pp. 395-397.

created USSR firmly asserted its jurisdiction over military crimes. Simultaneously with the promulgation of its foundations of criminal law in October 1924, the TsIK of the USSR issued a decree on military crimes, which did not differ substantially from the chapter in the 1922 code; and it also included in its foundations of judicial organization a provision for military tribunals under the supervision of a special procurator (art. 21).[1] Confusion and delay were caused by the refusal of the RSFSR and the other republics to carry out the new provisions till they had been formally incorporated in the codes of the republics — a step which nobody was in a hurry to take till the Union authorities once more intervened.[2] On August 20, 1926, a statute of the USSR on military tribunals and the military procuracy provided for a system of courts with a military procurator directly responsible to the procurator of the Supreme Court of the USSR, to dispense military justice.[3] In November 1926 the decree of the USSR of October 1924 on military crimes was incorporated textually as the concluding ninth chapter in the revised criminal code of the RSFSR.[4] Henceforth military crimes clearly belonged to the category of state crimes over which the organs of the USSR reigned supreme.

Particular difficulty was caused by the survival, in many non-Russian areas, whose customary way of life included such practices as polygamy, forced marriage or marriage by purchase, blood feuds and vendettas, and fraternal or tribal jursidiction, of local courts rendering judgments, in criminal as well as civil cases, on the basis of native, generally Muslim, law. The problem was most acute in the autonomous republics and regions of the RSFSR; and in the autumn of 1924 a conference, at which the republics and regions were represented, prepared a draft decree which was

---

[1] For the decree see *Socialism in One Country, 1924–1926*, Vol. 2, p. 441. The 69 military tribunals existing in 1925 were reduced to 36 in 1926 (*Sovetskoe Stroitel'stvo*, No. 1(6), January 1927, p. 113); but this was evidently a result of rationalization, not of diminished authority.

[2] *Ibid.* No. 2-3(7-8), February–March 1927, pp. 52-53.

[3] *Sobranie Zakonov, 1926*, No. 57, art. 413; three months later an amendment provided that personnel of the Red Army might be added to the tribunals as temporary members (*ibid.* No. 74, art. 577).

[4] For this code see pp. 351-352 above; the chapter on military crimes was revised and extended in January 1928 (*Sobranie Uzakonenii, 1928*, No. 12, art. 108).

designed to eliminate by slow degrees courts administering " customary " law. The government was to give no financial support to such courts ; they were to hear cases only with the consent of both parties ; and their judgments could be executed only on an order from a people's court, which was empowered to overrule them. The draft was sent to the local authorities concerned for discussion ; and no further action seems to have been taken on it for three years.[1] In 1924 the RSFSR added to its criminal code of 1922 special chapters relating to the Turkestani and Bashkir autonomous republics, and to several autonomous regions, which attempted to deal with these practices and vetoed the assumption by native courts of jurisdiction over criminal offences — an attack on the courts administering Muslim or customary law and on certain forms of tribal life ;[2] and in October 1925 it decided to add to the criminal code a new chapter dealing with " primitive " crimes in the territories of autonomous republics and regions.[3] But once again the difficulties proved formidable. When the revised criminal code of the RSFSR was approved in 1926, nothing was done to carry out these plans ; and the legal status of the supplementary chapters to a superseded code must have remained in doubt. Meanwhile, the creation of the Uzbek and Turkmen Union republics had raised the specific problem of Muslim courts in areas no longer under the jurisdiction of the RSFSR ; and on September 21, 1927, the TsIK of the USSR intervened with an instruction " On Shariat and Adat Courts ". This went somewhat further than the RSFSR code, formally depriving the Muslim courts of jurisdiction in criminal cases, and in disputes about land or labour, and prohibiting the establishment of any new Muslim courts. It made recourse to these courts in civil cases a matter of voluntary agreement between the parties, and forbade any governmental organ to enforce their rulings.[4] Marriage and the division of family property were the two major issues

[1] *Sovetskoe Stroitel'stvo*, No. 8-9(13-14), August–September 1927, p. 110.
[2] *Sobranie Uzakonenii, 1924*, No. 79, art. 787 ; in 1925 further chapters relating to the Buryat-Mongol and Kazakh ASSRs were added (*ibid. 1925*, No. 29, art. 212 ; No. 70, art. 554).
[3] *Vtoraya Sessiya Vserossiiskogo Tsentral'nogo Ispolnitel'nogo Komiteta XII Sozyva : Postanovleniya* (1925), p. 66.
[4] *Sovetskoe Stroitel'stvo*, No. 8-9(13-14), August–September 1927, pp. 110-111.

in which the authority of the customary courts was still commonly invoked, and blood-feuds and other primitive methods of retribution continued to present problems of criminal justice. In April 1928 the TsIK of the RSFSR added yet another chapter (chapter 10) to its criminal code of November 1926 under the title " Crimes Constituting Survivals of Primitive Ways of Life ", which was no longer particularized geographically, but dealt uniformly with these abuses.[1] The slow elimination of these survivals of primitive society was the result of the gradual dissolution of the society through contact with the modern world rather than of direct legislative action.

(c) Tightening the Screw

The dichotomy between state crimes, now firmly placed under the jurisdiction of the USSR, and ordinary crimes, over which the republics retained control, was reflected in the institutional arrangements, and in the penal policies which they were designed to apply. The Narkomyusts and ordinary courts of the republics, up to and including their supreme courts, exercised jurisdiction over ordinary crimes. The USSR had no Narkomyust and no ordinary courts ; and, while it was content to leave the republics to deal with minor state crimes, and all legislation relating to state crimes was written into the criminal codes of the republics, it exercised supreme jurisdiction over state crimes, and dealt directly with major state crimes, through organs responsible to it — the Supreme Court of the USSR, the procurator of the Supreme Court, and the Unified State Political Administration (OGPU). Of these the third ultimately became the most powerful as well as the most notorious. Even before the creation of the Union, the GPU of the RSFSR, though formally integrated into the judicial structure, had inherited much of the extra-judicial character of the defunct Cheka.[2] But, whereas the GPU was subordinate to the People's Commissariat of Internal Affairs of the RSFSR, its transformation into the OGPU of the USSR made it, like the procuracy, an independent organ, and enormously enhanced its authority;

---

[1] II Sessiya Vserossiskogo Tsentral'nogo Ispolnitel'nogo Komiteta XIII Sozyva: Postanovleniya (1928), pp. 31-35 ; Sobranie Uzakonenii, 1928, No. 47, art. 356.

[2] See The Bolshevik Revolution, 1917-1923, Vol. 1, pp. 180-181.

and, like the Supreme Court, it enjoyed the prestige of being named in the constitution.[1] Its activities in defence of security were ubiquitous, centralized and secret. Every crisis, every alarm, extended its activity and enhanced its prestige. When the Soviet representative in Warsaw was assassinated by a " white" *émigré* in June 1927, the OGPU was instructed " to take decisive measures for the defence of the country against foreign spies, *provocateurs* and murderers, together with their monarchist and white-guard allies ".[2] The bomb-explosion in the Leningrad party club on June 8, 1927,[3] was immediately followed by an order of the OGPU to shoot ten former monarchists on a charge of espionage against the USSR;[4] and a public trial of those implicated in the Leningrad affair, who were alleged to have been agents of the Finnish, Latvian, British and French secret services, was held in September 1927, and extensively reported.[5] In the running battle which marked the development of penal policy between the remedial measures seen by early Bolshevik thinkers as the right response to the social evil of crime, and still upheld throughout the nineteen-twenties by officials and legal advisers of the Narkomyust of the RSFSR, and the crude and brutal " measures of social defence " applied by the OGPU,[6] victory went to the latter.

The tenth anniversary of the OGPU, whose continuity with the original Cheka was thus openly recognized, inspired the issue on December 18, 1927, of proclamations by Voroshilov, as president of the revolutionary-military council, and by Menzhinsky, as president of the OGPU, and of much publicity celebrating the services of the institution in defending the revolution. The celebration, which included a military parade and a session of the Moscow Soviet addressed by Kalinin and Bukharin, marked the tougher attitude, now rapidly gaining ground, to offences against the state.[7] These were years when the Union was busy in every field asserting its centralized authority against the dispersed, often

---

[1] For its statute and functions see *Socialism in One Country, 1924–1926*, Vol. 2, pp. 442-444.   [2] *Izvestiya*, June 9, 1927.
[3] See Vol. 1, p. 295.   [4] *Pravda*, June 10, 1927.
[5] *Ibid*. September 16, 21-25, 1927; an OGPU communiqué on the charges was published *ibid*. September 2, 1927.
[6] For an instance of ambivalent attitudes even within the OGPU see *Socialism in One Country, 1924–1926*, Vol. 2, p. 445, note 5.
[7] *Izvestiya*, December 18, 20, 1927.

discordant, and sometimes obstructive, claims of the republics; the OGPU, firmly allied with the Supreme Court and its procurator, seemed to represent this authority in the administration of law. These were years of mounting economic and political pressures in every part of the Soviet system, when an entrenched regime became almost hysterically sensitive to rising unrest; and the OGPU reaped the support and prestige earned in such times by the proclaimed custodian of law and order. Finally, these were years of acute dissension within the party, when the authority of the ruling group was challenged by a numerous and articulate opposition and by demagogic appeals to popular discontent; once the distinction between disloyalty to the party and disobedience to the state had been effaced, the OGPU appeared on the party scene as the adjunct and instrument of the party central control commission.[1] The alliance of control commission, procurator of the Supreme Court and OGPU became the firm bulwark of the existing order; the efficiency and ruthlessness of the OGPU made it the main executive arm of the trinity. Law and order, masquerading under the brand-name of " revolutionary legality ", was the slogan of a nervous and insecure authority.

The practical, as well as the theoretical, problems of punishment had always weighed heavily on the Soviet authorities. The criminal code of the RSFSR of 1922 had relied, apart from some minor and some unrealistic punishments (for example, expulsion from the RSFSR), and the death penalty, which was reserved as an exceptional measure for counter-revolutionary crimes, on " deprivation of liberty with or without strict isolation " for a maximum of ten years, and " forced labour without detention under guard " for a maximum of one year — the former designed as a severe penalty for grave crimes, the latter as a mild penalty for lesser offences. Those sentenced to " deprivation of liberty " were handed over to the administration of places of confinement, whose close asssociation with the OGPU helped to determine the conditions of their punishment. The word " prison (tyur'ma) " had ugly connotations of an oppressive past; and the re-naming of prisons as " places of confinement "[2] did not remove the prejudice of the

---

[1] For the first symptoms of this process see *Socialism in One Country, 1924–1926*, Vol. 2, pp. 219-221 ; for later developments see pp. 35-36, 134 above.
[2] The word tyur'ma gradually crept back into use, though it was never

enlightened legislator against holding the offender in cruel and useless idleness behind locks and bars — a bourgeois practice which was constantly condemned.[1] This traditional prejudice, reinforced by serious overcrowding in the few conventional urban prisons, and by increased preoccupation with the national need for security, encouraged the view that the punishment of long-term offenders should take the form of forced labour in settlements designed for the purpose. To establish an adequate number of the reformatory labour colonies for which provision was made in the corrective labour code of the RSFSR of 1924[2] would have far outstripped available resources. In 1925–1926 33 agricultural colonies were said to have existed with a total area of 36,942 hectares, in 1927 1200 small workshops and 51 factories, the largest of these employing 3000 prisoners.[3] More rough-and-ready expedients were required. The experience of the OGPU since 1922 in establishing settlements in remote regions for persons exiled by administrative order for counter-revolutionary activities[4] fitted it to organize places of confinement in the same regions for ordinary criminals sentenced to deprivation of liberty by the courts. In course of time, these two types of establishments came to be assimilated in practice; and both were known, by the name originally used for places of confinement under the Cheka, as " concentration camps ". Different from these were the " isolators" , where prisoners were held in strict seclusion, but not normally subject to forced labour — if only because of the difficulty of organizing it. Throughout the nineteen-twenties political personages deported by administrative order of the OGPU, whether condemned merely to exile (ssylka)[5] or to confinement in an isolator, continued to

officially adopted; Tolmachev, People's Commissar for Internal Affairs of the RSFSR, apologized half-heartedly in 1928 for using " the old terminology " (*Ezhenedel'nik Sovetskoi Yustitsii*, No. 22, June 16, 1928, p. 646).

[1] Dostoevsky in *The House of the Dead* regarded the Russian system of mass deportation as more humane than the western system of individual confinement in closed prisons; " Soviet corrective labour policy," declared the Soviet encyclopaedia, " has nothing in common with bourgeois prison policy, which seeks to crush and destroy, morally and physically " (*Bol'shaya Sovetskaya Entsiklopediya*, xxix (1935), 600).   [2] See *Socialism in One Country, 1924–1926*, Vol. 2, p. 445.

[3] M. Isaev, *Osnovy Penitentsyarnoi Politiki* (1927), p. 159.

[4] See *Socialism in One Country, 1924–1926*, Vol. 2, pp. 431–432.

[5] Ssylka meant exile to a remote locality under the control of the OGPU; persons so exiled were normally obliged to accept local employment in order to keep themselves.

enjoy exemption from obligatory labour, though the principle that class enemies should be granted a privilege withheld from ordinary criminals condemned by the courts was obviously vulnerable to criticism.[1]

What contributed most to the breakdown of the Soviet penal system of the early nineteen-twenties was the impracticability of the penalty of forced labour " without detention " or " not under guard ". The principle enshrined in the criminal code of the RSFSR of 1922 that the minor offender should atone for his misdeeds by so many days of obligatory labour for the benefit of the community quickly ran into difficulties. The obvious method of employing such labour in existing enterprises or factories encountered the objection that this meant competition with free labour and the exclusion of the unemployed; and a decree of February 1923 ruled that such persons should, in default of other openings, be employed in economic enterprises attached to places of confinement.[2] The corrective labour code of the RSFSR of 1924[3] made elaborate provision for the application of sentences of forced labour without detention. Sentences were to be served in enterprises controlled by the administration of places of confinement, or in other enterprises if such were not available, under the direction of a provincial inspector: 25 per cent of the normal wage earned by such labour was to be deducted to defray administrative costs, the remainder being paid to the offender. But neither the labour colonies organized under the corrective labour code nor the forced labour camps for long-term prisoners established in remote regions by the OGPU were fitted to receive persons sentenced to short periods of forced labour without detention; and the number of petty criminals on whom this sentence was pronounced by the courts defied all attempts to carry it out in a rational way. The only offenders to whom this system could really be applied were urban workers, who were directed to continue in their existing jobs; in their case the penalty amounted to a small fine. Elsewhere the organization of useful work for convicted offenders in a society already riddled with unemployment was quite beyond available administrative or financial resources. In the countryside the

[1] See *Socialism in One Country, 1924–1926*, Vol. 2, pp. 446-447.
[2] See *The Interregnum, 1923–1924*, pp. 58-59.
[3] See *Socialism in One Country, 1924–1926*, Vol. 2, p. 445.

results were farcical. Forced labour for convicted peasants could rarely be organized; and, where jobs were available, 75 per cent of the normal wage was a reward far higher than the peasant had ever received for probably far more arduous labour.[1] Local branches of the forced labour administration failed to function. In Orel province in 1925 only 10 per cent of those condemned to forced labour could be put to work; in Siberia forced labour could not be organized at all.[2] A decree of the RSFSR of September 6, 1926, referring to the increasing difficulties of forced labour, re-iterated that convicted wage-earners should continue to work in their existing jobs, and attempted to place the responsibility for organizing forced labour for other offenders on regional and district executive committees;[3] this is unlikely to have proved effective. A sample check in 1927 purported to show that of forced labour days awarded by the courts in the first quarter of 1926, 48 per cent had actually been worked, and in the first quarter of 1927 65 per cent.[4] These estimates were probably exaggerated. The later verdict that forced labour without detention " did not constitute a serious measure of social defence ", since it was " completely un-organized ",[5] was not unfair.

The second disabling factor in Soviet penal policy — the scandalous overcrowding of " places of confinement " — was mainly a consequence of the first. The failure to organize forced labour without detention led to a multiplication of the alternative device of short-term sentences of deprivation of liberty and the over-loading of places of confinement. Places of confinement were crowded with short-term prisoners convicted of minor crimes. It was pointed out that, while the number of prisoners at the end of 1924 represented 120 per cent of the scheduled capacity of places of confinement, the ratios at the end of 1926 had risen to 177 per cent; on the other hand, the average length of sentence had fallen from one year and three months in 1924 to nine months in 1926.[6]

[1] For these problems see *Ezhenedel'nik Sovetskoi Yustitsii*, No. 18, May 9, 1926, pp. 557-558.   [2] *Ibid*. No. 16, April 28, 1927, p. 477.
[3] *Sobranie Uzakonenii, 1926*, No. 60, art. 462.
[4] *Ezhenedel'nik Sovetskoi Yustitsii*, No. 34, August 31, 1927, p. 1050.
[5] *Ibid*. No. 21, June 9, 1928, p. 620. The People's Commissar for Internal Affairs complained of " excessive indulgence and excessive liberalism " in the application of forced labour; it became a privilege, not a punishment (*ibid*. No. 22, June 16, 1928, p. 646).
[6] *40 Let Sovetskogo Prava,* ed. O. Yoffe (1957), i, 517.

Here, too, the peasant offender presented an intractable problem. Peasants held in places of confinement were commonly released " on leave " for field work during the harvest; this was said to apply even to murderers and those convicted of other crimes of violence.[1] More serious was the pressure to relieve the congestion by releasing prisoners long before their full term had been served; this prerogative was in the hands of the so-called " distributing commission ", which assigned prisoners to places of confinement.[2] Rabkrin in a report of September 1927 drew attention to the growing scandal of uncompleted sentences. The practice of premature releases was defended in *Izvestiya* by an official of Narkomyust, who argued that, if sentences of deprivation of liberty were pronounced " only when every other measure of social defence is absolutely inappropriate ", the problem of congestion would disappear, and was attacked in the journal of Narkomyust by another writer, who accused the distributing commission of behaving like a court of appeal.[3]

The argument about premature releases was significant of the deepening rift between those who maintained the earlier " humane " and " liberal " traditions of Narkomyust and of the corrective labour code and those who demanded a harsher penal policy in the interests of security. When Kursky, the People's Commissar for Justice, spoke of the need for severer penal measures and the curtailment of premature releases, a writer in the journal of TsIK called this view " mechanistic ", and thought that it " reduces to nothing the most precious achievements of the revolution in judicial policy ".[4] The issue was momentarily shelved by the proclamation, in the autumn of 1927, of a massive amnesty in honour of the tenth anniversary of the revolution, to include all those serving short sentences except recidivists.[5] The amnesty

[1] *Ezhenedel'nik Sovetskoi Yustitsii*, No. 24, June 22, 1927, pp. 734-736.

[2] See *Socialism in One Country, 1924-1926*, Vol. 2, p. 424, note 1.

[3] *Izvestiya*, November 2, 1927; *Ezhenedel'nik Sovetskoi Yustitsii*, No. 46, November 28, 1927, pp. 1428-1430.

[4] *Sovetskoe Stroitel'stvo*, No. 4(9), April 1927, p. 98.

[5] *Sobranie Zakonov, 1927*, No. 61, art. 620; the anniversary proclamation of October 15, 1927 (see Vol. 1, pp. 33, 496) had announced a proposal " to alleviate the measures of social defence imposed by verdicts of the courts or by administrative procedure in respect of all condemned persons, except active members of political parties whose aim is the destruction of the Soviet régime, and hardened swindlers (rastratchiki) and bribe-takers ".

covered 80,000 prisoners, 64,000 of them in the RSFSR; the proportion of prisoners amnestied was highest in the White Russian SSR (74 per cent) and lowest in Azerbaijan (19·3 per cent). Of those amnestied 35·8 per cent had been convicted of crimes against property and 22 per cent of hooliganism. Nearly all were serving relatively short sentences; hardly any prisoners serving sentences of five years or more were amnestied.[1] Another estimate put the total of those amnestied as high as 125,000. But the number of those in confinement quickly rose again, reaching 100,000 on July 1, 1928, and 123,000 on September 1, 1928.[2]

By this time the serious overcrowding of places of confinement, the scandal of premature releases and the impracticability of organizing forced labour without detention had all combined with the mounting political pressure to bring about a rapid change in the climate of opinion. The foundations of criminal law of October 1924, issued by the TsIK of the USSR within a few days of the corrective labour code of the RSFSR, made one significant addition to the catalogue of punishments in the RSFSR criminal code of 1922 — expulsion from a named locality in the USSR, coupled with an order prescribing or forbidding residence in any other named locality. The revised criminal code of the RSFSR of 1926 maintained this provision, and added a fresh penalty — " deprivation of liberty in corrective labour camps in remote localities of the RSFSR ". The code, like the foundations, maintained a limit of 10 years on all sentences; and it specified that sentences of deprivation of liberty might vary from one day to 10 years. Short-term sentences of deprivation of liberty for minor crimes became the most conspicuous target of the reaction that now set in. Cases were quoted of a sentence of three months' deprivation of liberty imposed for stealing a hen, or of six months for stealing a couple of ropes worth 15 rubles. Of those sentenced 80 per cent were guilty of petty crimes, and the overwhelming majority were workers or peasants; for such offenders deprivation of liberty was not an appropriate punishment.[3] On the other hand, serious crimes involving danger to state security merited far harsher penalties.

---

[1] *Sovetskoe Stroitel'stvo*, No. 3(32), March 1929, pp. 155-157.
[2] *Ezhenedel'nik Sovetskoi Yustitsii*, No. 46-47, December 12/19, 1929, pp. 1176-1177.
[3] *Ibid.* No. 8, February 28, 1929, pp. 170-171; a similar complaint was

According to Yanson, who seems to have taken the lead in the
matter, Narkomyust made a report in this sense in the autumn of
1927, and by the end of the year a resolution had been drafted to
give effect to it.[1] Solts at the fifteenth party congress in December 1927 declared that, if all sentences of the courts were to be
carried out, " we should have to spend millions on prisons ", and
protested againt a policy which " has filled our prisons with
workers and peasants for trivial offences ", while major questions
of security were neglected.[2]

But the issue of penal policy had now become an issue of
burning controversy in Narkomyust, where the older party
traditions were deeply rooted ; and it was not till Yanson succeeded Kursky as People's Commissar of Justice of the RSFSR
early in 1928 [3] that action was finally taken. On March 26,
1928, the presidium of TsIK and the Sovnarkom of the RSFSR
issued a far-reaching resolution " On Penal Policy and the Régime
of Places of Confinement ". As regards penal policy, it was " indispensable to apply severe measures of repression exclusively to
class enemies and professional criminals and recidivists (bandits,
fire-raisers, horse-stealers, persons of debauched habits, bribe-
takers and thieves) " ; severe sentences must be severely enforced,
without remission or mitigation. On the other hand, in dealing
with casual criminals, first offenders and those not socially dangerous, sentences of short-term deprivation of liberty should be replaced by lesser penalties, including forced labour not under
guard ; courts were encouraged to acquit even those who had
committed criminal acts " if the application of measures of social
defence is plainly inappropriate ". The corrective labour code
was to be amended in such a way as to permit of an extension of the
term, or of the application of fresh measures of social defence, for
incorrigible criminals. As regards corrective labour policy, forced
labour should in principle be unpaid and socially useful, and

made that too many petty offences were being brought before military courts
(*Krasnaya Zvezda*, November 16, 1929).

[1] *Ezhenedel'nik Sovetskoi Yustitsii*, No. 9-10, March 8/15, 1929, p. 195.

[2] *Pyatnadstsatyi S"ezd VKP(B)*, i (1961), 603-605 ; for Solts's other interventions in this debate see pp. 344-345 above.

[3] Kursky, who had been People's Commissar for Justice of the RSFSR
since 1918, was appointed Soviet representative in Rome in January 1928 ;
Yanson, like Solts, was a member of the party central control commission, and
had been a leading official of Narkomyust.

should represent " a real measure of repression " in comparison with public works organized by Narkomtrud for the unemployed. It was essential to organize the " banishment " (ssylka) of socially dangerous elements, where this sentence was pronounced, in such a way that it was a more effective penalty than mere transfer from one place of residence to another ; to keep casual criminals in places of confinement strictly separate from socially dangerous elements, and to grant no special privileges to the latter ; and to improve discipline in places of confinement. As regards investigation, steps were to be taken to expedite the judicial process ; and the establishment of " comradely courts " in factories, and " conciliation chambers " or arbitral tribunals in the villages, to deal with minor offences and disputes was approved. The People's Commissariats of Justice and of Internal Affairs were instructed to prepare legislation to give effect to these recommendations.[1] Though not in form a legislative enactment, and not published in the official collection of laws and decrees, the resolution was constantly quoted in the next twelve months as an authoritative pronouncement.

The resolution of March 26, 1928, was in form concerned with the mitigation of penalties for minor offenders as well as with the intensification of those for major state criminals. Its practical effect was, however, determined not so much by its ostensible purpose as by the atmosphere in which it was issued. During the past year economic tensions and the struggle against the opposition brought an ever increasing preoccupation with major " state crimes ". On the occasion of the tenth anniversary of the revolution in November 1927 Kalinin spoke appreciatively of " the organs of the GPU in which our best party comrades work ", and added that they were " comprehensible to the working masses ".[2] The tenth anniversary, a month later, of the OGPU prompted *Pravda* to a massive eulogy of the achievements and indispensability of the security organs as the scourge of class enemies and the defenders of law and order.[3] The instruction of March 26, 1928, was issued a few days after the first disclosure of the Shakhty affair, with cries

---

[1] *Ezhenedel'nik Sovetskoi Yustitsii*, No. 14, April 16, 1928, pp. 417-419 ; for comradely courts see Note K, pp. 471-473 below.

[2] M. Kalinin, *Voprosy Sovetskogo Stroitel'stva* (1958), p. 352.

[3] *Pravda*, December 18, 1927 ; for this occasion see p. 357 above.

of treason resounding on all sides,[1] and ushered in a period of acute tension in Narkomyust. " In no previous year ", Yanson reported, " were so many bureaucrats inside and outside the apparatus of the People's Commissariat of Justice called to account as in 1928 ";[2] and here, as elsewhere, victory went to the advocates of strong and ruthless measures.[3]   In the autumn of 1928 an authoritative article in the journal of Narkomyust spoke of the " organizational rift and breakdown of control " between judicial and penal organs, and attributed the delay in carrying out the instruction of March 26, 1928, to " liberal " interpretations of the corrective labour code.[4]

Pressure mounted steadily throughout the year.   In a decree of May 21, 1928, an attempt was made to tighten up the provisions of the 1924 corrective labour code of the RSFSR for forced labour not under detention ; a sharp distinction was now drawn between those sentenced for less than six months and those sentenced for longer periods.[5] On August 20, 1928, nettled by delays in putting these instructions into effect, Narkomyust sent a circular letter to local authorities reaffirming the need to limit the number of trivial prosecutions, to abandon the imposition of short-term sentences of deprivation of liberty, but to impose " severe sentences and long terms of deprivation of liberty " on " class enemies, recidivists and declassed elements ".   For professional criminals exile was an appropriate penalty.   Sentences of deprivation of liberty with strict isolation should be sparingly used, owing partly, perhaps, to administrative difficulties, and partly to inability to employ those in

---

[1] See Vol. 1, pp. 584-585.

[2] *Ezhenedel'nik Sovetskoi Yustitsii*, No. 9-10, March 8/15, 1929, p. 197.

[3] Fainblit, the official of Narkomyust who had written in *Izvestiya*, November 2, 1927, in defence of remissions of sentence (see p. 362 above), came out in March 1928 with an article in the Narkomyust journal arguing that the prevalence of early releases could proceed only from "a false theory of correction as the sole aim of our penal policy " (*Ezhenedel'nik Sovetskoi Yustitsii*, No. 11, March 21, 1928, p. 326) ; later he attacked other Narkomyust officials by name, and denounced the " grumblings of our liberals who ' defend ' the purity of Marxist principles " (*ibid*. No. 35, September 24, 1928, pp. 955-956). Such hurried conversions were probably not uncommon.

[4] *Ibid*. No. 40-41, October 31/November 7, 1928, pp. 1077-1079.

[5] *Sobranie Uzakonenii, 1928*, No. 57, art. 426.   In rural areas the Soviet executive committees were supposed to be responsible for organizing forced labour without detention (see p. 361 above) ; the decree of March 23, 1929 (see pp. 371-372 below) instructed regional authorities to apply the decree of May 21, 1928, more vigorously.

isolation on productive work.[1] On November 28, 1928, Narkom-vnudel issued, " by agreement with Narkomyust ", a long instruction on the organization of forced labour without detention, designed to take account of the decree of May 21, 1928. Its most significant provision was that a person sentenced to forced labour without detention for more than six months might, if suitable work was not available either in his present place of employment or in special establishments in the vicinity of his place of residence, be sent to serve his sentence in labour establishments elsewhere.[2] In such circumstances the distinction between forced labour without detention and forced labour in a camp might tend to disappear ; this was clearly a move in the direction of harsher penalties for long-term offenders. Shirvindt, head of the Narkomyust administration of places of confinement, who signed the instruction, had already been under attack in the Narkomyust journal as a covert liberal, and cannot have been happy at these developments. He now boldly replied to his critics by quoting article 26 of the criminal code of the RSFSR to the effect that punishment should be " free from any element of torture, and must not cause the criminal needless and superfluous suffering ", reaffirmed by the provision in art. 4 of the foundations promulgated by the USSR in 1924 that measures of social defence should not " pursue the aim of causing physical sufferings or of infringing human dignity", as well as art. 74 of the party programme calling for the " replacement of prisons by institutions of an educational character ". An " *anti-Marxist deviation* ", he concluded, was all the more dangerous when it " *marches under the banner of 100 per cent orthodoxy and of the struggle against liberalism* ".[3] But the humanitarian principles of penal policy, preached and to some extent practised, in the early years of the Soviet régime, had now been engulfed by the political and economic crisis.[4] The year 1929 opened

---

[1] *Ezhenedel'nik Sovetskoi Yustitsii*, No. 33, September 4, 1928, p. 919; a report from rural localities spoke of the " inertia of our judicial and procuratorial organs in applying instructions on penal policy " (*ibid*. No. 8, February 28, 1929, p. 19).

[2] *Ibid*. No. 9-10, March 8/15, 1929, pp. 233-238.

[3] *Ibid*. No. 48, December 28, 1928, pp. 1224-1225.

[4] The last open demonstration by supporters of these principles seems to have been at a conference of workers in penal institutions held in November 1928, which adopted a resolution on a report by Shirvindt expressing the view that " the idea of ' correction ' has proved its rationality ", and that what was

with a strongly worded circular signed by Yanson as People's Commissar for Justice of the RSFSR rehearsing previous instructions of the past year on forced labour, and complaining of failure to comply with them. The number of persons in the RSFSR under sentences of deprivation of liberty for less than one year had risen from 24,583 in March 1928 to 31,026 in December 1928. Henceforth people's courts were categorically forbidden to pronounce sentences of deprivation of liberty for less than one year. Any judge infringing this order could himself be brought to trial, and would " learn by personal experience what forced labour is like ". Alternative punishments to be imposed were " forced labour, fines, exile, and other measure of social defence ". Persons already serving sentences of deprivation of liberty for less than one year should be transferred to forced labour.[1]

As early as January 1928 it had been announced that a sixth All-Russian Congress of Judicial Workers would be held in the following May.[2] Prevailing uncertainties and controversies within Narkomyust were probably responsible for its postponement; and in the autmun it was announced that the congress would meet in February 1929.[3] Theses prepared in advance for adoption by the congress were submitted to a preliminary conference of judges and representatives of the procuracy at the end of November 1928, and some of them amended in the light of observations made.[4] The main theses — by Yanson on the work of Narkomyust, by Krylenko on the revision of the criminal code, and by Traskovich

required was " a further improvement and deepening of these methods and their combination with a real individualization of measures of social defence " ; the resolution of March 26, 1928, was apparently not mentioned. The conference was not reported, and the only information about it is derived from a critical account in *Ezhenedel'nik Sovetskoi Yustitsii*, No. 7, February 20, 1929, pp. 155-158.

[1] *Ibid.* No. 2, January 17, 1929, p. 48. Some party members protested against the " hooligan language " of this instruction ; Yanson defended it on the ground that " procurators have to be people with strong nerves " (*ibid.* No. 9-10, March 8/15, 1929, p. 209).

[2] *Ibid.* No. 1, January 10, 1928, p. 25 ; for the fifth congress in 1924 see *Socialism in One Country, 1924–1926*, Vol. 2, pp. 436–437.

[3] *Ezhenedel'nik Sovetskoi Yustitsii*, No. 36-37, September 30/October 7, 1928, p. 973.

[4] *Ibid.* No. 48, December 26, 1928, p. 1226.

on corrective labour policy — all stressed the need for a reduction in short-term sentences for trivial crimes, combined with sharper measures against major crimes and a sterner penal policy. An advance article in *Pravda* explained that Soviet criminal law and procedure was to be " submitted to a radical review ", and the civil code " cleansed from the abstract formulas of bourgeois law ".[1] When the congress met on February 20, 1929, Yanson presented his theses in an immensely long report, which covered the whole field of action of Narkomyust. Quoting the resolutions of the fifteenth party congress of December 1927, he proclaimed in his theses that " the task of the procuracy and of the courts is to struggle against, and to punish with greatest severity, any kind of attempt to restrain or prejudice the tempo of industrialization ". He rehearsed the main injunctions of the resolution of March 26, 1928, called for " a far-reaching development of forced labour on new principles ", and announced that Narkomyust had prepared a draft chapter to be included in the corrective labour code embodying the new approach. Finally, he spoke significantly of relations with party organs :

> The procuratorial and judicial organs must, as an invariable rule, maintain a close link with the party committee, and notify to it in good time any irregularity directed against the interests of the Soviet state.[2]

After a debate devoted mainly to expressions of approval, Yanson's report was duly endorsed by the congress.[3]

Krylenko's theses and report on the proposed revision of the criminal code attempted to straddle the old and new points of view. Krylenko had been at work on a revised criminal code since the autumn of 1927,[4] and had expounded his views to the collegium of Narkomyust, apparently without opposition, in the summer of 1928.[5] But the atmosphere had now changed ; and he spoke at the congress to a critical, and in part directly hostile, audience. He

---

[1] *Pravda*, February 20, 1929 ; for civil law see pp. 379-380 below.
[2] For the theses see *Ezhenedel'nik Sovetskoi Yustitsii*, No. 44-45, November 28/December 5, 1928, pp. 1133-1137 ; for the report *ibid.* No. 9-10, March 8/15, 1929, pp. 193-212.
[3] *Ibid.* No. 9-10, March 8/15, 1929, pp. 230-231.
[4] *Ibid.* No. 47, December 5, 1927, p. 1457.
[5] *Ibid.* No. 22, June 16, 1928, pp. 641-643, No. 23, June 23, 1928, pp. 661-664.

once more rejected the conception of " equivalence " between crime and measure of repression, and wished to eliminate fixed sentences from the code. Moral blame and retribution were concepts alien to Soviet law ; he proposed to rely on the principle of " practicality ". He advocated the sternest penalties, including the death penalty, for " socially dangerous " offenders, but wished to revise the corrective labour code for the benefit of casual criminals capable of being reformed.[1] In the debate Krylenko was criticized for under-estimating the rôle of deterrence in punishment, and for advocating indeterminate sentences, which were said to reflect the " corrective " theory of criminal law. Solts accused him of seeking to apply the decision of March 26, 1928, " mechanically ", and said that what was needed was not a good code, but " good courts which will work not mechanically, but creatively ". Krasikov, procurator of the Supreme Court of the USSR, also attached little importance to a new criminal code. Criticism was kept within bounds, but its abundance showed that Krylenko no longer enjoyed real authority, and that he had lost control over penal policy to more determined and less sophisticated men. The congress was content with a brief resolution instructing Narkomyust to work out a new code.[2]

Traskovich's theses on corrective labour policy were the most matter-of-fact of the reports. While he rehearsed again the criticisms and recommendations of the resolution of March 26, 1928, Traskovich offered a new and systematic classification of places of confinement, which fell into three basic categories — corrective labour institutions for convicted criminals, places of preliminary detention for accused persons under investigation, and reformatories for juvenile offenders. Corrective labour institutions were of several types : (1) labour colonies, designed for ordinary criminals, which should aim primarily at re-education through work ; (2) forced labour camps for criminals sentenced to forced labour for six months and upwards ; (3) isolators for " class enemies and

---

[1] *Ezhenedel'nik Sovetskoi Yustitsii*, No. 46-47, December 12/19, 1928, pp. 1176-1180 ; an explanatory article *ibid*. No. 7, February 20, 1929, pp. 146-152, was said to have constituted the substance of the report actually made by Krylenko to the congress, which was not included in the record *ibid*. No. 9-10, March 8/15, 1929, p. 219. Krylenko repeated his views in articles in *Izvestiya*, February 20, 24, 1929, while the congress was sitting.

[2] *Ezhenedel'nik Sovetskoi Yustitsii*, No. 9-10, March 8/15, 1929, pp. 219-221, 231-232 ; Solts was described by Krylenko as a man " who boasts that he spits at theory " (*ibid*. No. 7, February 20, 1929, p. 149).

declassed criminals ", designed to keep them isolated from the outside world, while employing them on work compatible with such isolation ; (4) concentration camps in remote regions, to which the less dangerous or incorrigible of those confined in isolators may be transferred.   In addition to these penalties, banishment was recognized as a proper punishment " chiefly for persons from class-enemy strata who oppose the Soviet power ", but also for some prisoners not socially dangerous enough to be kept in isolators.   It was clearly implied that all places of confinement should be under a single administration.   In the original version of the theses the claim was put forward that they should be transferred from Narkomvnudel to Narkomyust.   But this demand was evidently defeated ; and in an article published on the eve of the congress Traskovich reconciled himself to a commission to unify the work of the two commissariats.[1] Yanson had meanwhile already reached a settlement of this question. He reported that the proposal of Narkomyust could not be realized " in the immediate future " ; it was, however, proposed to hold " regular conferences " between representation of Narkomyust, Narkomvnudel and the OGPU, " for the purpose of coordinating all questions of the application of penal policy ", these conferences to be convened by Narkomyust.[2]

The proceedings of the congress inspired a fresh decree of the Sovnarkom of the RSFSR of March 23, 1929. Professedly based on the resolution of March 26, 1928, it reproached both Narkomyust and Narkomvnudel with their failure to implement that resolution, and the decree on corrective labour of May 21, 1928, with sufficient vigour.   It laid particular emphasis on the need for a further reduction of short-term sentences for minor crimes, and insisted that forced labour should be " one of the fundamental measures of social defence ".   Attention was to be given to the establishment of forced labour institutions for short-term prisoners, as prescribed in the decree of May 21, 1928, and to making them economically productive ; to re-educational work among young offenders and women prisoners ; and to the training of staffs of

----

[1] *Ibid.* No. 46-47, December 12/19, 1928, pp. 1194-1197, No. 7, February 20, 1929, pp. 152-155 ; these documents were said to form the substance of Traskovich's report to the congress (*ibid.* No. 9-10, March 8/15, 1929, p. 227).

[2] *Ibid.* No. 9-10, March 8/15, 1929, p. 210.

places of confinement. This last responsibility was placed on Nar-komvnudel, which thus by implication retained control of places of confinement. Narkomyust, Narkomvnudel and the repre-sentative of the OGPU attached to the Sovnarkom of the RSFSR were invited to expedite the preparation of a draft law introducing the penalty of banishment (ssylka); this and the provision for " regular conferences " of the three departments on questions of penal policy were the only mentions of the OGPU in the decree.[1]

The rapid extension of the powers of the OGPU reflected the climate of the period, and was the product of the tense economic and political situation rather than of any specific decision. The OGPU was at this time already in effective control of the principal isolators and concentration camps and of places of exile for those subject to banishment by administrative order, as well as of the Butyrsky prison in Moscow which was the main detention centre for those sentenced to deportation.[2] The line of demarcation between these places of confinement for those convicted of major state crimes and places of confinement for ordinary criminals under the control of Narkomvnudel was apparently not defined in any published order or decree. But it corresponded to the difference, maintained in Soviet criminal jurisprudence since 1924, between socially dangerous state crimes and other crimes which, owing partly to the nature of their consequences and partly to the status and character of the criminal, could not be regarded as socially dangerous; and it represented the last stage of the struggle be-tween the remedial view of penal policy inculcated by the socio-logical school of jurisprudence and the demand of the realists for maximum penalties in the interests of state security. At the end of the nineteen-twenties the former view, though still partly effec-tive in the minor and less spectacular proceedings of criminal law, was eclipsed in all major public utterances and acts of policy by the latter. The mood of the moment was represented by an article in a

[1] *Sobranie Uzakonenii*, *1929*, No. 37, art. 388.

[2] A report to the fifth Union Congress of Soviets in May 1929 recorded a recent inspection by the procurator of these " places of confinement under the control of the OGPU " (*SSSR: Ot S"ezda k S"ezdu* (*Aprel' 1927-Mai 1929*) (1929), p. 184); art. 20 of the foundations of judicial organization of 1924 prescribed that corrective labour institutions controlled by the GPUs of the republics should be subject to inspection by the procurators of the republics, but left the question of inspection of institutions controlled by the OGPU to be settled by the TsIK of the USSR.

leading legal party journal by the veteran jurist Stuchka. This proclaimed a " merciless class struggle " against " a prolongation of the senseless bourgeois *prison* system ", referred contemptuously to " pseudo-humanitarian phrases and goings-on ", and thought it right and proper that " the ' criminal ' part of our population should be included *in the ranks of workers* for our socialist construction ".[1] A corollary was that the character of offences, measured by the degree of danger which they presented to the social order, and therefore the penalties appropriate to them, changed with changing political and economic conditions.[2] The foundations of what afterwards became a vast network of concentration camps for forced labour under the direction of the OGPU were laid at this time. But its dimensions[3] were still small enough for it to be regarded by stalwarts faithful to the old party ideals as an exceptional expedient demanded by the harsh and transitory emergency of socialist construction in a backward country.

The changing attitude to law, and in particular the harsher sanctions applied to major transgressors, were symptomatic of the gradual erosion of the conceptions of NEP by those of a planned economy. The doctrine of law as a bourgeois instrument of equivalent exchange, which associated law with the survival of a market economy, and predicted the dying away of law (as well as of the state) when this was superseded by the victory of socialism, was convenient so long as NEP was in the ascendant; and the authority of Pashukanis, the inventor and most fertile exponent of the doctrine, was almost unchallenged.[4] When, however, the fifteenth party conference in October 1926 proclaimed that " the supreme historical task of building a socialist society . . . imperatively calls for a concentration of the forces of the party, the state and the

---

[1] P. Stuchka, *13 Let Bor'by za Revolyutsionno-Marksistkuyu Teoriyu Prava* (1931), pp. 196-197; the article originally appeared in *Revolyutsiya Prava*, No. 2, March–April 1929.

[2] *Ezhenedel'nik Sovetskoi Yustitsii*, No. 8, February 9, 1929, p. 174.

[3] An authority quoted in D. Dallin and B. Nikolaevsky, *Forced Labor in Soviet Russia* (1948), p. 52, gave a total of 30,000 prisoners detained in concentration camps in 1928, and a list of six camps (five in the north, and one in Kazakhstan) in 1930.

[4] For Pashukanis see *Socialism in One Country, 1924–1926*, Vol. 1, p. 86.

working class on questions of economic policy ",[1] the linking of
state with party and working class seemed to show that planning
for socialism would involve a strengthening, not a dying away, of
state power ; and, though no immediate conclusion was drawn in
the field of law, the foundations of current theory were impercep-
tibly sapped.   Stuchka, the only Soviet jurist whose authority
matched or surpassed that of Pashukanis, and who had at first
espoused his views, began to mark nuances of dissent.   In an essay
of 1927, while continuing to treat Pashukanis with great respect,
he referred to the " one-sidedness " of the equivalence theory,
which neglected the element of inequality inherent in bourgeois
law, " the law of the strongest ".[2]   Stuchka's main interest was in
civil law.   In the field of criminal law Pashukanis was far more
vulnerable.   Here his chief assailant, Piontkovsky, boldly asserted
that, since the aim of the law was to help the building of a communist society, nobody could be promised " equality . . . before the
criminal law ", and rejected the notion that " punishment is
merely retribution ".[3]

The turning-point came early in 1928, juridically, when Yanson succeeded Kursky as People's Commissar for Justice of the
RSFSR, and the resolution of March 26, 1928, heralded a stiffer
and more repressive penal policy for " state crimes ",[4] politically,
when the Right deviation in the party began to be branded as the
most dangerous obstacle to the uncompromising demands of
planned industrialization.   During the next twelve months, legal
theory and legal practice changed rapidly in several respects.   In
the first place, practical administrators asserted themselves at the
expense of sophisticated jurists and humanitarian idealists, whose
views were impatiently dismissed as survivals of a bourgeois and
liberal outlook.   Secondly, it was stressed that Marxism was a
philosophy of action, an instrument of change.   To be content
with explanation and analysis was to cultivate " spontaneity "
and " tail-endism ".   To plan was to overcome the spontaneity of

---

[1] KPSS v Rezolyutsiyakh (1954), ii, 195.
[2] P. Stuchka, Izbrannye Proizvedeniya (1964), pp. 563-564 ; two years later
Stuchka openly attacked Pashukanis for promoting the belief that " statutes and
the law are bourgeois and unnecessary for us " (id. 13 Let Bor'by za Revolyu-
tsionno-Marksistskuyu Teoriyu Prava (1931), p. 189).
[3] A. Piontkovsky, Marksizm i Ugolovnoe Pravo (2nd ed. 1929), pp. 45, 49-50.
[4] See pp. 364-365 above.

NEP; and law had to become a tool of planning.[1] Thirdly, and simultaneously with the declaration of a class offensive against the *kulaks*, renewed emphasis was laid on the class character of law. Law was an instrument of class rule; and, so long as classes existed, the notion of law as an expression of equality was a bourgeois illusion.[2] Purpose in law, wrote Stuchka, was " the conscious purpose of a class ".[3] Fourthly, this led to a new concept of " Soviet law " as " the law of the period of transition from capitalism to communism ", the law of a state where power was " in the hands of the proletariat in alliance with the toiling peasantry ".[4] This vindicated the authority of Soviet law by freeing it from any taint of bourgeois affiliations. Finally, the doctrine of the dying away of law, as well as of the state, was relegated to a still distant future when the transition to communism had been triumphantly achieved; meanwhile the weapons of state and law must be sharpened for the struggle. " Only through the Soviet state and Soviet law ", wrote an influential jurist in 1928, " will the dying away of law take place."[5] When Pashukanis, at the moment of the adoption of the five-year plan in April 1929, wrote that " the role of the purely juridical superstructure, the rôle of law, is diminishing ", and that " regulation becomes more effective as the rôle of law becomes weaker and less significant ",[6] he was still speaking the language of the first years of the revolution, now overtaken by the advent of planning. The grandiose five-year plan imposed on Soviet law the imperative obligation to support and enforce it.

[1] These points were made in A. Piontkovsky, *Marksizm i Ugolovnoe Pravo* (2nd ed. 1929), pp. 7, 37; for " spontaneity " and " tail-endism " see *The Bolshevik Revolution, 1917–1923*, Vol. i, pp. 15, 18. As early as 1925, Adoratsky defined the problem as being " how to use bourgeois legal forms for the creation of the communist society " (*Entsiklopediya Gosudarstva i Prava*, i (1925), 926, art. Dialektika i Pravo).

[2] The first reviewer of Pashukanis's *General Theory of Law and Marxism* in the journal of the Communist Academy pointed out that, since property-owning reflected relations of domination-subordination, private law must derive from public law, not *vice versa* (*Vestnik Kommunisticheskoi Akademii*, viii (1924), 363-364).

[3] *Entsiklopediya Gosudarstva i Prava*, iii (1927), 1485, art. Tsel' v Prave.

[4] *Ibid.* iii, 922, art. Sovetskoe Pravo.

[5] A. Stalgevich, *Puti Razvitiya Sovetskoi Pravovoi Mysli* (1928), p. 72.

[6] *Revolyutsiya Prava*, No. 4, 1929, p. 37; an editorial in the same issue (*ibid.* p. 6) spoke by way of contrast of " the creation of law in the interest of the socialist development of the national economy ".

In law, therefore, as in other fields of Soviet activity, the adoption, under the impetus of comprehensive planning for rapid industrialization, of more conscious, more active and more ruthless policies, coincided with the rejection of the Right deviation and the disgrace of Bukharin. The different themes were closely woven into the same pattern. Bukharin was discredited as a theorist in a period which called for men of practical experience. Bukharin was convicted of a " mechanistic " outlook which was concerned to explain reality rather than to change it. Bukharin had notoriously worked to play down class divisions in the peasantry at a time when the official line began to emphasize them. Most significant, Bukharin had been an early protagonist of the doctrine of the dying away of the state, and had clashed, both before and after the revolution, with Lenin's more cautious and more sophisticated views on the question.[1] In all these respects Pashukanis and his followers could be counted as conscious or unconscious disciples of Bukharin. When *Pravda* in January 1929 published Lenin's lecture of 1919, in which he argued that the proletarian state must for a time be kept in being as a weapon against the bourgeoisie,[2] the moment chosen for publication was generally regarded as a move against Bukharin. But what was said of the state was equally true of law, and sounded the death-knell of those who hoped to see a relaxation of the strong arm of the law in the critical years ahead. Legal theory was a peripheral topic, and no great haste was made to correct it.[3] But from 1929 onwards it was abundantly clear that legal enactments and legal administration would no longer be moulded by the ideals and purposes proclaimed by the party during the first decade of the revolution, but would be unreservedly and uncompromisingly geared to the ends of state policy.

[1] See *Socialism in One Country, 1924–1926*, Vol. 1, pp. 164-167.
[2] See p. 86 above.
[3] The first public attempt to associate Pashukanis with Bukharinism appears to have been an article in *Izvestiya*, October 6, 1930, which accused him of " slurring over Bukharin's errors about the doctrine of the state ", and advocating class cooperation at the expense of the class struggle; Pashukanis made a partial recantation in November 1930 (for a translation see *Soviet Legal Philosophy*, ed. H. Babb and J. Hazard (1951), pp. 237-238), and was eventually purged in 1937.

(d) Civil Law

The resuscitation of civil law, and the recognition, in art. 4 of the civil code of the RSFSR of 1922, of private rights, were strongly influenced by NEP and by the compromise inherent in it between the opposed principles of planning and of the market. In Marxist theory law, like the state itself, was an organ of class dictatorship and would have no place in the classless society; its retention was justified as a feature of the transitional period of NEP. Civil law was concerned with the private contractual relations which were still an essential part of the NEP economy.[1] But these would one day be superseded, as NEP would be superseded, by public regulation and planning; civil law would be replaced by what was sometimes called " economic law (khozyaistvennoe pravo) ", which consisted not of general laws, but of specific ordinances of the planning authorities. Some practical doubts soon began to be felt about this conclusion. In 1926 a commission was appointed by the Sovnarkom of the USSR to draw up " Foundations of Land Utilization and Land Consolidation " ; and these, after prolonged debates, were enacted by the TsIK of the USSR in December 1928.[2] On the broader aspects of civil law, however, deadlock was complete. In 1927 the Sovnarkom of the USSR set up a commission consisting of Drobnis, Kursky, Stuchka and other jurists to draft new foundations of civil law. The commission soon ran into differences of opinion about the extent to which the Union should impose on the republics laws regarding inheritance, marriage and the family, and did not get very far.[3] The continuance throughout the nineteen-twenties of the struggle between the two principles of planning and the market militated against any attempt by the USSR to promulgate foundations of civil law for the guidance of the republics, or by the RSFSR to revise its 1922 code.

The doctrine of the class character of law seemed more deeply embedded in civil than in criminal law. The famous art. 1 of the civil code undertook to protect private rights " except in so far as

---

[1] Kursky, in an article in *Izvestiya*, February 19, 1926, gave statistics of the rapid increase in civil cases coming before the courts after 1921.

[2] See Vol. 1, pp. 106-108.

[3] For an account of its initial stages by a member of the commission see *Ezhenedel'nik Sovetskoi Yustitsii*, No. 26, July 6, 1927, pp. 785-786.

they are exercised in contradiction with their social and economic purpose "; and art. 4 invited the court to exercise its functions, where no specific rule existed, " in accordance with the general principles of Soviet legislation and the general policy of the workers' and peasants' government ", and more explicitly " in the interests of the development of the productive forces of the country ".[1] Preobrazhensky argued at the time of the adoption of the code that art. 4 would permit the court to override the letter of the law where, for example, its strict application would favour the nepman against the worker.[2] This introduced a large element of uncertainty into the work of the courts ; Krylenko in 1926 — no doubt, by way of special pleading for an increase in the powers of the procurator — alleged that regional courts decided less than 50 per cent of civil cases correctly.[3] In the middle nineteen-twenties, with the reaction in favour of the well-to-do peasant and the campaign for revolutionary legality, stricter interpretations of legal rights were needed. Complaint was made of the frequent invocation by civil courts of arts. 1 and 4 of the code ; and in 1926 the supreme court of the RSFSR, quashing a decision of a provincial court, laid down the firm principle that art. 4 " does not give to the court a right not to apply the laws and enactments of the workers' and peasants' government in a particular case, where such exist ".[4] A few months later a detailed letter of instruction from the same authority showed how tenacious was the view that the worker, and the workers' state, enjoyed a privileged position in the interpretation and administration of the law :

> It cannot be denied that a dogmatic, exclusively formal, interpretation of the law is alien to the Soviet court. . . . The proletarian court cannot, of course, fail to imbibe current events which reflect the tempo of economic construction. . . . Where

[1] See *Socialism in One Country, 1924–1926*, Vol. 1, pp. 69-70, 79-80.

[2] *Vtoraya Sessiya Vserossiskogo Tsentral'nogo Ispolnitrel'nogo Komiteta X Sozyva* (1923), p. 48 ; see also the ambiguous reply of the *rapporteur, ibid.* p. 248. The same point was argued in a report by a prominent jurist to the fifth All-Russian Congress of Judicial Workers in February 1924 (*Ezhenedel'nik Sovetskoi Yustitsii*, No. 12-13, March 20/27, 1924, pp. 284-285).

[3] *III Sessiya Vserossiiskogo Tsentral'nogo Komiteta XII Sozyva* (1926), p. 252.

[4] *Ezhenedel'nik Sovetskoi Yustitsii*, No. 22, June 6, 1926, p. 701 ; the text of the ruling is in *Sbornik Deistvuyushchikh Raz"yasnenii Verkhovnogo Suda RSFSR* (1930), p. 166.

the interests of the workers or of the state imperatively demand this, it can openly go beyond the letter of the law, or, where the law is not sufficiently clear, or sometimes where the law has lagged behind the rapid stream of life, it can invoke the general principles of Soviet legislation or the general policy of the workers' government.

But any such appeal to art. 4 should be treated as " an exceptional measure " requiring specific justification on each occasion.[1] When, as late as January 1928, Larin proposed that a right of appeal from decisions of lower courts should be enjoyed by workers and employees, but not by Soviet economic administrative organs, Krylenko protested angrily against this attempt to draw a class line between the worker-defendant and the Soviet administration, i.e. an organ of the workers' state.[2] Ambivalent attitudes also prevailed towards the civil law rights of corporate bodies. The revised statute of trusts of June 29, 1927,[3] strengthened the recognition of the trusts, already accorded in the earlier statute of 1923, as independent entities capable of entering into legally enforceable contractual relations ; and, by allowing enterprises subordinate to the trusts to be placed on *khozraschet*, it paved the way for their recognition as juridical persons at a later date. But the statute also emphasized the obligation of the trust to fulfil the administrative orders of the higher planning organs and introduced the conception of the planned contract, thus effectively limiting the contractual freedom of the trust.   Administrative order had begun to replace contractual freedom.

The sixth congress of jurists in February 1929 was the occasion of a somewhat perfunctory review of the problem of civil law. Stuchka in a long report pointed out that labour law and agrarian law, and to a large extent food supplies and housing, had been removed from the purview of the civil code, and suggested that the time had come to prepare a civil code of the USSR.[4] The resolution which he had drafted, and which was adopted without discussion, expressed the view that the experience of the first six years had thrown sufficient light on " the legal character of property relations " to permit of the preparation of a new civil code ;

[1] *Ezhenedel'nik Sovetskoi Yustitsii*, No. 10, March 14, 1927, pp. 298-302.
[2] *Pravda*, January 8, 15, 1928.   [3] See Vol. 1, p. 372.
[4] *Ezhenedel'nik Sovetskoi Yustitsii*, No. 9-10, March 8/15, 1929, pp. 222-227.

that " the growing extent of the inter-organizational regulation of
production and exchange in the socialist sector of the economy "
justified the exclusion of these questions from the domain of civil
law ; and that the new civil code should be drafted in " simple and
popular language " intelligible to the workers who sat in the
people's courts.[1] But, after this demonstration, the question of
formulating foundations of civil law was once more allowed to
lapse. At the moment of the enactment of the first five-year
plan in May 1929, Pashukanis, then still a recognized authority,
attempted to formulate the consequences for civil law relations
of " the fusion of administration with legislation " inherent in
a fully planned economy :

> State regulation is characterized by a predominance of
> technical-organizational elements over formal elements. Legis-
> lative and administrative acts are transformed into operative
> tasks, and retain only a very slight admixture of juridical, i.e.
> formal, elements.[2]

The relations between the rôles of civil law contracts and of planning decisions long remained a conundrum for Soviet administrators and Soviet jurists.

Regardless of these theoretical uncertainties, and regardless also
of the constitutional prerogatives of the Union republics, the TsIK
or the Sovnarkom of the USSR continued from time to time to
issue specific decrees on the property or other rights of individuals
in the sphere of civil law.[3] Almost the only major field of civil law
which engaged the attention of the republics, and in which the
Union showed no inclination to intervene, was marriage law. The
marriage code of the RSFSR of 1918 had created equal mutual
obligations for both partners to the marriage, and had assimilated
the rights of illegitimate children to those of legitimate offspring ;
but, in substituting civil registration for a religious ceremony, it
had retained the conception of marriage as a civil law contract
creating rights and obligations.[4] Some early Bolshevik jurists

---

[1] *Ezhenedel'nik Sovetskoi Yustitsii*, No. 9-10, March 8/15, 1929, p. 232; the
resolution had been prepared well in advance of the congress (*ibid.* No. 6, February 14, 1929, pp. 122-123).

[2] *Revolyutsiya Prava*, No. 5, 1929, pp. 33-34.

[3] For examples see pp. 199–200 above.

[4] See *Socialism in One Country, 1924–1926*, Vol. 1, p. 29.

rejected altogether the contractual view of marriage, holding that rights and obligations flowed from the fact of cohabitation, and that registration of marriage was no more than a convenient record of an intention to cohabit, entailing in itself no legal consequences. After stormy debates in the TsIK of the RSFSR, this view, which obliterated the legal distinction between registered and *de facto* marriage, prevailed, and was written into the revised marriage code of November 1926.[1] It is significant that this precedent, the product of a consistent ideological repugnance to the conception of individual contract as a basis of social life, was not followed by the other Union republics, where ways of thought were less permeated by party doctrine and more by the established traditions of peasant communities. The Union authorities showed only an occasional interest in this period in questions of civil law. But their preoccupation with the strengthening of criminal law is unlikely to have made them sympathetic to the relaxation of legal forms in other branches of law, or to the kind of juridical thinking that lay behind the marriage code of the RSFSR of 1926.

[1] See *ibid.* Vol. 1, p. 37; for discrepancies between the marriage codes of the RSFSR and the Ukrainian and White Russian SSRs see *Ezhenedel'nik Sovetskoi Yustitsii*, No. 22, June 8, 1927, pp. 664-666.

CHAPTER 54

RELIGION

THE *détente* between the Soviet authorities and the Orthodox Church, which followed the death of Tikhon in April 1925 and the publication of his call for loyalty to the Soviet Government among his followers,[1] proved brief and precarious. The Living Church, created by the Soviet authorities in 1922 as a counter-weight to the Orthodox Church, and now commonly known as the " synodal " church to distinguish it from the " patriarchical " church of Tikhon's successors, was once more a disturbing factor. In November 1925 Metropolitan Peter, who had succeeded to Tikhon's functions as *locum tenens* of the patriarchate, was denounced by the cunning and ambitious Vvedensky, the head of Living Church, for complicity with counter-revolutionaries,[2] and exiled to Siberia. He was succeeded as *locum tenens* by Metropolitan Sergei, who had at one time some association with the Living Church, but had later been reinstated by Tikhon.[3] The cautious Sergei now sought to regularize the church administration by securing its formal registration with the People's Commissariat of Internal Affairs, and announced his success to the church in a long epistle of June 10, 1926. The church, wrote Sergei, having been assured of a legal existence, owed a corresponding obligation to the Soviet state :

> In the name of our whole Orthodox hierarchy and of our parishioners, I have taken it on myself to proclaim to the Soviet authorities our sincere wish to be law-abiding citizens of the Soviet Union, to be loyal to its government, and to hold ourselves completely aloof from political parties and from any enterprise that could harm the Union.

Relations between the Orthodox Church in the Soviet Union and the church abroad, which was frequently involved in anti-

---

[1] See *Socialism in One Country, 1924–1926*, Vol. 1, pp. 45-46.
[2] *Izvestiya*, November 15, 1925.
[3] W. C. Emhardt, *Religion in Soviet Russia* (1929), p. 320.

Soviet activities and propaganda, was evidently a delicate point. The letter explained that, while the church could take no ecclesiastical action against *émigré* clerics, it completely disavowed their political activities and declined any responsibility for them.[1]

This compromise brought reconciliation with the synodal church no nearer, and does not appear to have satisfied the Soviet authorities; for Sergei was in prison or exile in the winter of 1926–1927. But in the spring of 1927 he was released and took more decisive steps. In May 1927 he formed a " provisional holy synod " attached to the office of *locum tenens* of the patriarch.[2] On July 29, 1927, Sergei and the provisional synod issued a letter designed to be read in all Orthodox churches. It expressed devotion to the Soviet Government, now harassed by fears of blockade or attack from abroad, in terms far warmer than those of the epistle of July 1926:

> We wish to be Orthodox and at the same time to recognize the Soviet Union as our civil fatherland, whose joys and successes are our joys and successes and whose setbacks are our setbacks. Every blow directed against the Union, be it war, boycott, some public disaster, or simply a murder at a street corner like that in Warsaw, is felt by us as directed against ourselves.

The letter appeared to blame the church and its " insufficient consciousness of the full importance of what has been accomplished in our country " for past misunderstandings between the church and the régime, and it dealt more firmly with the issue of the *émigré* clergy. These were now required to give " a written promise of total loyalty to the Soviet power in all their public activity " — failing which they would be no longer recognized by the Moscow patriarchate. The publication of the letter in *Izvestiya* showed that its terms had been tacitly approved by the Soviet authorities.[3]

---

[1] The text of the letter was published in French in *Russie et Chrétienté*, ii (1947), 38-41.

[2] W. C. Emhardt, *Religion in Soviet Russia* (1929), pp. 151-153. The dual purpose of this move was apparently to provide a more effective counter to the claims of the synodal church, and to give Sergei a greater semblance of authority over Orthodox bishops and communities abroad; it was not conspicuously successful in either respect.

[3] *Izvestiya*, August 19, 1927. It was published in French in *Russie et Chrétienté*, ii (1947), 41-44, (misdated June 29) together with a letter of protest

After this understanding, the central administration of the church under Sergei was not again disturbed. Ecclesiastical dignitaries of the patriarchal church opposed to Sergei suffered the penalty of exile. Meanwhile, the synodal church retained a measure of support, though the Soviet Government took no sides in its controversies with the patriarchal church, and showed no sign of wishing to intervene in these disputes. Vvedensky continued to play some rôle in Soviet public life. In September 1925 Lunacharsky had two public debates with him on the questions " Christianity or Communism? " and " Idealism or Materialism? "[1] In September 1927 the French revolutionary writer Barbusse visited Moscow. He had just added to his fame by publishing two books entitled *Jésus* and *Les Judas de Jésus*, and writing an unperformed play *Jésus contre Dieu*, on the theme that Jesus was a revolutionary innovator whose teaching had been travestied and betrayed by the church. Lunacharsky greeted him with an article in *Pravda*, which celebrated Barbusse's other revolutionary activities, but referred only in parenthesis, without comment, to " his latest point of view about Christianity ".[2] On October 3, 1927, a public debate was held between Lunacharsky and Vvedensky on " The Person of Christ in Contemporary Learning and Literature ", in which Lunacharsky disagreed with the views of Barbusse, while Vvedensky upheld them.[3]

The Old Believers in the Orthodox church, and various Protestant sects, of whom the Baptists were the strongest, shared with the Russian Social-Democrats and other political dissidents the

of September 27, 1927, from a number of Orthodox bishops in exile at Solovki, who accepted the obligation of political loyalty to the Soviet Government, but objected to other parts of the letter (*ibid.* ii, 45-47); a number of Orthodox bishops professing fidelity to Tikhon and critical of Sergei met in Moscow from November 15-19, 1927, and issued a manifesto (*Orientalia Christiana* (Rome), No. 46 (1928), 65-68).

[1] For Lunacharsky's speeches see A. Lunacharsky, *Pochemu Nel'zya Verit' v Boga* (1965), pp. 67-96, 97-116. Lunacharsky's views on religion were always suspect in party circles owing to his association with Bogdanov and Gorky before the revolution; they were attacked by Skovrtzov-Stepanov in an article in *Bol'shevik*, No. 1, April 1, 1924, pp. 48-55.

[2] *Pravda*, September 10, 1927; A. Lunacharsky, *Sobranie Sochinenii*, v (1965), 508-510.

[3] The proceedings were not published; but extracts from Lunacharsky's speech are quoted *ibid.* v, 714-716, note 8, and Lunacharsky afterwards recorded that Vvedensky " defended " Barbusse (*ibid.* vi (1965), 281; see also A. Lunacharsky, *Siluety* (1965), pp. 324-325).

same persistent persecution at the hands of the Tsarist government, and a measure of sympathy was extended to them by the
early Bolsheviks. Not much could be hoped for from a creed as
primitive as that of the Old Believers. But the "sectarians "
(sektanty) — a name reserved for Protestant dissenters — were
often thought of as potential sympathizers or even converts.[1] A
dissenter addressed the eighth All-Russian Congress of Soviets in
December 1920 and offered his support to the régime.[2] As late as
1924, the thirteenth party congress drew attention to the " harsh
persecutions " which sectarians had suffered under the Tsars, and
hoped " by a bold approach . . . to steer into the stream of Soviet
work important economic and cultural elements to be found among
the dissenters ".[3] If the dissenters could not make good party
members, they might at least become good Soviet activists. Some
sectarians called Jesus " the first communist ", and sought to
" play down the incompatibility of religion with the revolution,
the dictatorship of the proletariat and communism ".[4] Dissenters
were often prime movers in the foundation of communes, *artels*
and other institutions based on a conception of communal life and
activity; it was even said that most members of agricultural
communes and *artels* were sectarians.[5] Mutual sympathy between
communists and dissenters was sometimes carried to strange
lengths. The story was told of the secretary of a Komsomol cell,
who was persuaded by the "evangelists " that Christianity had
been " distorted by the priesthood for the sake of gain ", and
that " the gospel is really socialism preached by Jesus Christ ";
the whole cell went to church, and the secretary read the
gospel.[6]

---

[1] V. Bonch-Bruevich, *Iz Mira Sektantov* (1922), p. 142, claimed that many
sectarians became communists.

[2] *Vos'moi Vserossiiskii S"ezd Sovetov* (1921), pp. 226-228.

[3] *KPSS v Rezolyutsiyakh* (1954), ii, 52.

[4] I. Bobryshev, *Melkoburzhuaznye Vliyaniya sredi Molodezhi* (2nd ed. 1928),
p. 41.

[5] F. Putintsev, *Politicheskaya Rol' Sektantstva* (1928), p. 246. A sectarian
commune in the Lower Volga region objected to the introduction of wages
(*ibid.* p. 392); a visit to an Evangelical commune on a former state farm in 1926
is described in K. Borders, *Village Life under the Soviets* (N.Y., 1927), p. 58.
For religious communities forming *artels* of building workers see Vol. 1, p. 460,
note 1.

[6] I. Bobryshev, *Melkoburzhuaznye Vliyaniya sredi Molodezhi* (2nd ed. 1928),
pp. 47-48.

In the spring of 1927 the atmosphere of apprehension and the reaction against policies of conciliation spread to the anti-religious front. The ambivalent attitude to anti-religious propaganda among the peasantry which had been adopted in 1923 prevailed throughout the period of conciliation of the peasant in the middle nineteen-twenties.[1] When, however, a revised statute of village Soviets was issued on September 26, 1927, " the supervision of the correct observance of laws on the separation of church from state and of school from church " was added to their functions.[2] Anti-religious propaganda was intensified. A resolution of the fifth Komsomol conference in March 1927 linked " the weakening of anti-religious propaganda among the young " with " a certain growth of the influence of religious and sectarian organizations (priests, Baptists etc.), and in the eastern national republics of the influence of the Muslim priesthood, on the young ".[3] *Pravda* wrote of a revival of ecclesiastical activities, and of 30,000 church councils consisting of " merchants, *kulaks* and well-to-do elements in general ", and drew a parallel between these and church organizations in the west which were engaged in a campaign against the Soviet Government.[4] Another writer asserted that Komsomol activities against religion were confined to sporadic campaigns at Christmas and Easter.[5] When a faithful Komsomol member applied to his cell for permission to marry in church to meet the wishes of his bride, it was granted by a large majority.[6] In September 1927 Stalin, in conversation with an American workers' delegation, had spoken with studied moderation of the party attitude to religion.[7] But at the fifteenth party congress three months later he noted " the weakening of the anti-religious struggle " as a " minus " in the current situation ;[8] and in 1928, following the grain collections crisis, an extensive campaign was

[1] See *The Interregnum 1923–1924*, p. 17, note 3 ; *Socialism in One Country, 1924–1926*, vol. 2, p. 317, note 4.

[2] *Sobranie Uzakonenii, 1927*, No. 105, art. 707.

[3] *VLKSM v Rezolyutsiyakh* (1929), p. 285.

[4] *Pravda*, April 1927 ; a report of the party central committee later in the year spoke of "anti-Soviet activity of ecclesiastics of all creeds and sects" (*K XV S"ezdu VKP(B)* (1927), p. 162). A total of 30,000 Orthodox churches was later claimed by Sergei (*Izvestiya*, February 19, 1930).

[5] I. Bobryshev, *Melkoburzhuaznye Vliyaniya sredi Molodezhi* (1928), pp. 15-16.

[6] *Ibid.* p. 53.   [7] Stalin, *Sochineniya*, x, 132-133.   [8] *Ibid.* x, 324.

waged to identify the church with the *kulaks*. The eighth Komsomol congress in May 1928 listened to a call to " unmask priests as defenders of *kulak* interests ".[1] *Kulaks* were said to " utilize religious institutions as the basis of their organizational work "; and priests and deacons, egged on by *kulaks*, controlled " Soviet work " in the village Soviet.[2] Examples were quoted of deacons appointed as presidents or secretaries of village Soviets, and of a priest directing a road-building project. During the elections of 1929 church councils acted as *kulak* electoral committees, and church festivals were arranged to take place on election days to lure away the voters. In the Muslim regions, religious ceremonies, including marriages and funerals, were timed to coincide with elections.[3] The opposition of priests to the kolkhozy was said to have intensified their " anti-Soviet activity ".[4]

The unexpected powers of survival shown by religious observances and beliefs inspired both disappointment and apprehension. Religion in the Soviet Union was extravagantly alleged to have the moral and financial support of such " high protectors " in the west as Rockefeller, Ford, Lloyd George and Coolidge.[5] The number of religious communities of all kinds was said to have doubled since 1923 ; the church now had 50,000 buildings and 250,000 persons engaged in the service of the cult.[6] In Zaporozhie priests were reported to have organized successful opposition to the closing of a church ; in Rostov priests and Baptists combined to defeat a proposal to close the cathedral.[7] Lunacharsky lamented that 30-40 per cent of school teachers held some kind of religious belief, including " more sophisticated forms of religion " like that of the " Tolstoyans ".[8] Sergei's letter of July 29, 1927,[9] had expressed the hope that " legal status will be gradually extended also to our lower church administration ". This hope was realized

---

[1] *VIII Vsesoyuznyi S"ezd VLKSM* (1929), p. 581.
[2] A. Angarov, *Klassovaya Bor'ba v Sovetskoi Derevne* (1929), pp. 23, 24.
[3] *Sovetskoe Stroitel'stvo*, No. 5(34), May 1929, pp. 124-125, 141-142, 154.
[4] *Na Agrarnom Fronte*, No. 11, 1928, p. 69 ; for the campaign of priests and Baptists against tractors and collectivization see Vol. 1, p. 212.
[5] I. Bobryshev, *Melkoburzhuaznye Vliyaniya sredi Molodezhi* (2nd ed. 1928), p. 38.
[6] *Trud*, February 7, 1929.
[7] *Izvestiya*, April 3, 1929.
[8] *Ibid*. March 26, 1929.
[9] See p. 383 above.

in a decree of the RSFSR of April 8, 1929, but in a form which revealed the determination of the authorities to keep ecclesiastical activities in a rigid strait-jacket. The decree recognized religious societies or groups consisting of not less than 20 persons aged 18 or upwards : such groups must register with the local Soviet executive committee or urban Soviet. Permission was required for congresses or assemblies of such groups ; and religious teaching might be given only in authorized religious seminaries. The main purpose of the decree appeared to be to restrict the functions of the church and its parishioners to the service of the cult. Social, cultural and recreational activities were firmly prohibited under severe penalties.[1] Another legislative act was significant of the keen preoccupation of the authorities at this time with religious influences on the peasant. The constitution of the RSFSR of 1925, like the original constitution of 1918, guaranteed to all citizens "freedom of religious and anti-religious propaganda ". The fourteenth All-Russian Congress of Soviets in May 1929 amended this article to read " freedom of religious beliefs and of anti-religious propaganda ".[2]

The rising hostility to the Orthodox Church, and fear of its counter-revolutionary influence, was extended also to the dissenters. In June 1927, *Pravda*, perhaps impelled by the international tension, published a weighty leading article under the heading-"Sectarianism and its Corrupting Role ". It was a misake, explained the writer, to think of the dissenters as " more or ltess pro gressive " merely because the Tsars persecuted them; Baptists, Evangelists and Adventists were all international organizations with a " democratic ", i.e. western-democratic, colouring. In the USSR they figured as traders, former factory owners, owners of mills and small private enterprises ; they included former Mensheviks and SRs. In the countryside they were often identified with *kulaks*. In founding communes and *artels*, they seized the initiative from the party, treating Jesus as " the first communist " and the gospel as " a work of *politgramota* ".[3] A current work on moods among young people continued the attack :

---

[1] The decree was published in *Izvestiya*, April 26, 27, 28, 1929.
[2] *S"ezdy Sovetov v Dokumentakh*, iv, i (1962), 140 ; for the constitution of 1925 see *Socialism in One Country, 1926–1926*, Vol. 2, pp. 253-255.
[3] *Pravda*, June 19, 1927.

Sectarianism is growing, in places quite menacingly. . . . The " Brothers in Christ " and their supporters enslave the toiling masses not only spiritually, but sometimes also economically : they try to extend their influence to the working class.[1]

The sects at this time claimed to have 975,000 members and three-and-a-half million people under their influence.[2] They were active among poor peasants and *batraks* and appealed especially to women.[3] At the eighth Komsomol congress in May 1928 Bukharin declared that Baptist and other sectarian youth organizations, coupled with the Orthodox League of Young Believers, had a membership almost as large as the Komsomol, and won support by promoting sound moral causes, e.g. campaigns against drinking and smoking.[4] But dissenters were sometimes pacifists who resisted the call-up for the Red Army. Presently repressive action began to be taken against them, though precise evidence is rare. In 1928 a commune established by an evangelical sect in the Ukraine is said to have been dissolved by the authorities on a charge of fostering counter-revolution.[5] " The drawing of religious communities into the class struggle, their active appearance as ' auxiliaries ' of the *kulak* ", was a feature of the Soviet elections early in 1929. Baptists held prayer meetings to coincide with election meetings ; and the class struggle was rejected in the name of " brotherhood in Christ ".[6] At a time when it was increasingly difficult to extract either grain surpluses or taxes from the peasant, it was reported with indignation that the Baptists in one region of Siberia had collected 8000 rubles for a prayer-house.[7] In the final campaign for a collective agriculture, toleration vanished from the scene ; and dissenters were as likely as the followers of any other religious cult to be denounced as enemies of the régime.

Signs of restiveness in the Red Army following the acute grain collections crisis of the first months of 1928 drew attention to the

[1] I. Bobryshev, *Melkoburzhuaznye Vliyaniya sredi Molodezhi* (2nd ed. 1928), p. 15 ; the writer specially notes sectarian influence on young girls (*ibid.* p. 50).

[2] A. Angarov, *Klassovaya Bor'ba v Sovetskoi Derevne* (1929), p. 32.

[3] *Sovetskoe Stroitel'stvo*, No. 5(34), May 1929, p. 142.

[4] *VIII Vsesoyuznyi S"ezd VLKSM* (1928), pp. 22, 25.

[5] F. Belov, *The History of a Soviet Collective Farm* (N.Y., 1955), p. 7.

[6] A. Angarov, *Klassovaya Bor'ba v Sovetskoi Derevne* (1929), pp. 32-35.

[7] *Trud*, January 17, 1929.

prevalence of religious sentiments and observances among the peasants who formed the bulk of the rank and file. In one regiment 45 per cent of the men were believers, and 43 per cent said that they would go to church when they returned to their village.[1] Soldiers commonly wore crosses under their uniform or hid them in their blankets. When debates were organized in soldiers' clubs between priests and spokesmen of the League of the Godless, audiences became impatient or applauded in the wrong places.[2] When " Bible-readers and evangelists " were admitted to one unit in order to " debate about texts ", the dissenters organized a mass meeting in the camp with " psalm-singing and religious rites ".[3] Such occurrences were publicized to drive home the need for policies of education and indoctrination in the Red Army.[4]

Anti-religious propaganda had always been a function of party work. Art. 13 of the party programme had set the goal of " the complete destruction of the link between the exploiting classes and the organization of religious propaganda " and " the liberation of the toiling masses from religious prejudices ", though care was to be. taken not to insult the feelings of believers. The journal *Bezbozhnik* had appeared regularly since the beginning of 1923 ;[5] and a society of friends of *Bezbozhnik* had developed into the League of Militant Godless, which held its founding congress, with a limited amount of publicity, early in 1925. Lunacharsky, who delivered the main report, recommended a certain caution in dealing with religion, which was to be attacked not by force, but by the " ideological weapon " ;[6] and the instructions issued by the league deprecated " mass anti-religious agitation which by its content and form sharply insults and ridicules the feelings of the sincerely believing part of the population, especially of the peasants ".[7] With the growing tensions of the winter of 1927–1928 such restraint was no longer acceptable. *Pravda*, in its anti-Easter article of 1928, complained that anti-religious propaganda

---

[1] *Krasnaya Zvezda*, June 1, 1928.   [2] *Ibid.* June 15, 1928.
[3] *Ibid.* December 15, 1928.   [4] For these policies see pp. 331-334 above.
[5] See *Socialism in One Country, 1924–1926*, Vol. 1, p. 40.
[6] For an abbreviated text of the report see A. Lunacharsky, *Pochemu Nel'zya Verit' v Boga* (1965), pp. 234-244.
[7] Quoted in M. Fainsod, *Smolensk under Soviet Rule* (1959), p. 432.

was left to " old fellows " who had once been worshippers of Tolstoy, Strauss or Renan, or to " connoisseurs of theological niceties
and biblical texts ". Propagandists preferred to remain in Moscow
rather than go out into the country, and pretended that " time and
the revolution are working for us ".[1] Resolutions of the eighth
congress of the Komsomol in May 1928 invited Komsomol members to " develop anti-religious propaganda ", and to " counter the
activity of ecclesiastical and sectarian organizations " by " drawing the peasant masses into social and political life and strengthening rural groups of the League of the Godless ".[2]   Christmas
day 1928 was celebrated with a solid leading article in *Pravda* on
the evils and dangers of religion, which treated the campaign
against it as an integral part of the class struggle.[3]   An article in
the journal of the party central committee equated lack of activity
on the anti-religious front with lukewarmness in the struggle
against the *kulak*, and pointed to the conclusion that " *the anti-
religious front is ceasing to be simply the arena of the cultural work
of the League of the Godless, and is becoming a sector of the political
struggle against all class forces hostile to us in town and country* ".[4]

In the spring of 1929, with the first five-year plan launched, it
was decided to hold a massive congress of the League of the Godless. *Pravda* alleged that the activity of religious organizations
was increasing and taking on " a more and more clearly marked
anti-Soviet character ". It complained that party committees
neglected anti-religious work, and that the sums allocated to it
were trivial.[5] Pressures tightened in other directions. Lunacharsky, in an article of March 1929, argued that " a believing teacher
in a Soviet school is an awkward contradiction ", and the authorities must " take every opportunity to replace such teachers by
others with an anti-religious outlook ".[6] On May 6, 1929 — the
date being apparently chosen to coincide with the Orthodox Easter
— *Pravda* delivered another broadside. Religious holidays were,
it declared, " the nodal point of religious propaganda ". The
sinister feature of religious organizations was that they were

---

[1] *Pravda*, April 13, 1928.
[2] *VLKSM v Rezolyutsiyakh* (1929), pp. 313, 335-336.
[3] *Pravda*, December 25, 1928.
[4] *Izvestiya Tsentral'nogo Komiteta VKP(B)*, No. 2-3(261-262), January 31,
1929, pp. 2-4.   [5] *Pravda*, April 18, 1929.
[6] *Ibid.* March 26, 1929.

" organically connected with the old petty bourgeois and peasant
life, and at the same time closely bound up with the political and
social life and activity of capitalist elements " ; they formed the
link between " the *kulak* in the countryside and the new bourgeoisie in the town ".   Religion was the enemy of socialist construction.   Drunkenness and absenteeism on religious holidays
cost the economy hundreds of millions of rubles.[1]   The second
All-Union Congress of the Godless opened on June 10, 1929.
Lunacharsky, who delivered the introductory speech and made the
principal report, pointed to three ways of countering religion —
by the building of socialism, which would destroy the foundation
of religion, by direct propaganda, and by administrative measures.
He did not exclude these last, since those who broke the law must
be " decisively punished ".[2]   Yaroslavsky claimed that membership of the league had risen from 90,000 in 1926 to more than
600,000 in 1929.[3]   But he admitted that it was weak in the countryside, and numbered only a handful of peasants among its members.
Major speeches by Bukharin and Kalinin testified to the political
importance of the occasion.   Bukharin described the struggle
against religion as " one of the *most important elements of the cultural revolution* ".   The familiar themes were laboured.[4]   The congress was plainly designed to keep party members up to the mark
and to dispel apathetic attitudes to this branch of party work.   But
there is little evidence that the league ever became a very effective
or popular organization.

Among the hated legacies of Tsarist Russia which the revolution was pledged to eradicate was anti-Semitism.[5]   Its constant

[1] *Pravda*, May 6, 1929.
[2] Lunacharsky's speech, his report and his concluding remarks are in A.
Lunacharsky, *Pochemu Nel'zya Verit' v Boga* (1965), pp. 329-343.
[3] *Pravda*, June 12, 1929.   The report of the party central committee to the
fifteenth congress in December 1927 gave two widely different figures for that
year — 140,000 including 30 per cent peasants, and 250,000, including 40 per
cent non-party peasants (*K XV S"ezdu VKP(B)* (1927), pp. 126, 162) ; not
much weight can be attached to any of these figures.
[4] The congress was extensively reported *Pravda*, June 12, 15, 1929 ;
Izvestiya, June 12, 13, 1929 ; *Bednota*, June 14, 19, 1929.
[5] Two famous documents of the first years of the régime were a decree of
Sovnarkom placing pogrom-makers and pogrom-agitators " outside the law "

use by Russian " whites ", and by some sections of foreign opinion, to discredit a régime many of whose leaders were Jewish had added urgency to the task. The returns of the 1926 census showed that, of Jews in the USSR (reduced from the 5 millions of the Tsarist régime to 2,601,000 by the territorial acquisitions of Poland, Lithuania and Rumania), 1,574,000 or 60·4 per cent lived in the Ukraine, 567,000 or 21·8 per cent in the RSFSR; White Russia had the highest proportion of Jews to total population (8·2 per cent). Of the Jewish population 82·4 per cent lived in towns; 14·9 per cent were classified as workers and 23·3 per cent as employers, most of the remainder being self-employed artisans or traders. The number engaged in agriculture was insignificant.[1] In the early days of the régime, Jews had played an extensive and powerful rôle in the party, though a high proportion of early Jewish members of the party had come over from the Bund or from the Mensheviks, and this created some prejudice against them.[2] A Jewish section of the party (Evsektsiya) had been established in Moscow since 1918, and had its subordinate Evsektsii in all important local party organizations in areas of large Jewish population, their purpose being to woo Jewish support for the party and the régime. Down to the end of 1926, the Evsektsii held regular congresses in Moscow.[3] The sixth and last congress, held in Moscow in December 1926, passed a resolution calling for the drawing

---

(*Izvestiya*, August 9, 1918), and a denunciation by Lenin of anti-Semitism recorded on a gramophone record in or about 1919 (Lenin, *Sochineniya*, xxiv, 203).

[1] For an analysis of the census returns of Jews see *Bol'shaya Sovetskaya Entsiklopediya*, xxiv (1932), 337; an analysis in *Sovetskoe Stroitel'stvo* No. 4(21), April 1928, p. 55, uses slightly different totals.

[2] The percentage of Jewish members of the party fell from 5·2 in 1922 to 4·3 in 1927; in the latter year only 3000 Jewish party members were former members of other parties (*Sotsial'nyi i Natsionali'nyi Sostav VKP(B)* (1928), p. 113). The percentage of Jews in the population was 1·8 (F. Lorimer, *The Population of the Soviet Union* (Geneva, 1946), p. 53).

[3] For sources for the history of the Evsektsii see S. Schwarz, *The Jews in the Soviet Union* (Syracuse, 1951), pp. 97-103; they were not dissolved till 1930, but from 1926 onwards lost their effectiveness. Kamenev is said to have told a Jewish group in 1925 that the Evsektsiya was the worst enemy of the Jews (quoted from a Yiddish source in *The Jews in Soviet Russia*, ed. L. Kochan (1970), p. 66), presumably on the ground that it kept them apart and hindered their assimilation into the rest of the population; according to a report in the Smolensk archives, local Evsektsii became a clearing-house for complaints of anti-Semitic activities (M. Fainsod, *Smolensk under Soviet Rule* (1959), p. 445).

of Jewish workers into branches of employment from which they
had formerly been excluded (railway workshops, coal-mining,
sugar factories etc.), for greater facilities for technical education,
and for settlement of Jews on the land.[1]

Anti-Semitism was, however, deeply embedded in traditional
Russian attitudes, especially in the countryside,[2] and was powerfully influenced by the incidence of changing Soviet economic
policies. In the middle nineteen-twenties, when private trade enjoyed a brief and conditional freedom, anti-Semitism began to re-
emerge on a scale which could not be ignored. The former Jewish
pale with its large concentration of Jews was a predestined focus
of anti-Semitism. A party report of 1925 on a village in Smolensk
province, of which half the population was Jewish, described the
Jews as having two preoccupations : religion and the flax trade.[3]
The gradual suppression of private trade in the later nineteen-
twenties, and reprisals against the nepman, bore with special
harshness on the Jews. In the larger towns (capitals of departments) of the White Russian SSR 8·8 per cent of the adult population were disqualified from voting in the elections of 1927 (4·5 per
cent in 1925–1926), in the smaller towns 12·8 per cent (7-8 per
cent) ; most of these were classified as traders or dependants,[4] and
a high proportion of them are likely to have been Jews.[5] A Jewish
American of Russian origin, visiting the Ukraine in the summer
of 1927, offered a broader diagnosis :

> The Soviet régime has liberated the Jew politically and
> socially, but has destroyed his chances for trade. He is forced
> into all kinds of occupations — bureaucracy, politics, manu-
> facture and farming. He makes himself felt wherever he goes
> by his cleverness and aggressiveness. Neither of these qualities

[1] *Izvestiya Tsentral'nogo Komiteta VKP(B)*, No. 13(186), April 8, 1927,
pp. 6-7.
[2] For symptoms of it in the early years of the régime see *Socialism in One
Country, 1924–1926*, Vol. 1, p. 41, note 1.
[3] M. Fainsod, *Smolensk under Soviet Rule* (1959), p. 441.
[4] *Sovetskoe Stroitel'stvo*, No. 8-9(13-14), August–September 1927, p. 72) ;
the proportion of those disqualified in the RSFSR did not exceed 6 per cent
(see Table No. 64, p. 487 above).
[5] In 1929, 80 per cent of those disqualified from voting in one White
Russian village (no doubt as traders or employers of labour) were Jews (M.
Fainsod, *Smolensk under Soviet Rule* (1959), p. 444).

makes him popular among gentile Russians, and there is a rising tide of anti-Semitism.[1]

An article in the journal of TsIK concluded that " the persistence of occupational habits and traditions is still great in the Jewish environment ", and that "*practical possibilities* of really purifying the social-economic structure of the mass of Jews are still *very limited* ".[2]

The spread of anti-Semitism could no longer be concealed. Both the census of December 1926 and the party census of 1927 recorded Jews as a national minority; and publication of the figures, even without comment, tended to draw attention to a proportion of Jews in privileged positions which was higher than in the total population. At the fifteenth party congress in December 1927 Orjonikidze quoted the percentage of Jews (as well as of other nationalities) among employees in public institutions in various parts of the Union, reaching 30 per cent in the Ukrainian and White Russian SSRs.[3] Kalinin in November 1926, having claimed that anti-Semitism could never penetrate deeply into the ranks of workers and peasants, admitted that " the Russian intelligentsia is perhaps more anti-Semitic now than it was under Tsarism ". This was because so many Jews, thwarted in other directions, occupied leading official positions, so that people asked : " Why are there so many Jews in Moscow ? "[4] The journal of Narkomyust recorded 38 cases of anti-Semitism which came before the courts of Moscow province (all but four of them in the city) in the year 1927–1928 ; most of these alleged verbal insults, but some involved physical assault. The " open outbursts of anti-Semitism in various corners of our Union " were regarded by the journal as " a reflection of profound economic and political processes taking place in the country ".[5] The Komsomol, which in the middle nineteen-twenties had a larger peasant component in its membership than the party,[6] was particularly subject to anti-Semitic

---

[1] A. Noe, *Golden Days of Soviet Russia* (Chicago, 1931), p. 152.

[2] *Sovetskoe Stroitel'stvo*, No. 2(31), February 1929, p. 138.

[3] *Pyatnadtsatyi S"ezd VKP(B)*, i (1961), 443-444.

[4] For this speech see p. 230 above.

[5] *Ezhenedel'nik Sovetskoi Yustitsii*, No. 4, January 31, 1929, pp. 83-85.

[6] Something had been done to mitigate the disproportionate prominence of Jews in the Komsomol, as in the party, in its earlier years ; at the fourth congress in 1921 18·3 per cent of the voting delegates were Jews, at the sixth congress in

tendencies. The fifth Komsomol conference in March 1927 issued a
warning against " anti-Semitism existing in certain strata of young
workers, peasants and students ".[1] A detailed contemporary study
of the prevalence of anti-Semitic moods and anti-Semitic utterances among the young appeared to justify a pessimistic diagnosis :

> Its growth is incontestable. It is well known that even some
> members of the Komsomol are infected with anti-Semitism.
> Does it always meet in Komsomol circles the decisive and swift
> rebuttal that a force hostile to the proletariat and to our organiza-
> tion deserves? No, not always.[2]

Christian organizations, Orthodox and Baptist, were named as
fostering anti-Semitic feelings among the young.[3] A mild form of
anti-Semitism is said to have been prevalent in the officer corps
of the Red Army.[4]

The revival at this time of a pervading sense of a national difference between Jews and non-Jews, which earlier party leaders
had ignored, may have been encouraged by the rise of Zionism ;
conversely, the growth of anti-Semitism was said to encourage
" propaganda of Zionists and other Jewish nationalists " among
the workers.[5] But other forces were also at work. The rise of the
opposition sharpened anti-Semitic tendencies. It was not altogether accidental that the principal opposition leaders — Trotsky,
Zinoviev, Kamenev — were Jews, and the most prominent defenders of the official line — Stalin, Bukharin, Molotov — were
not. Intellectuals commonly play a prominent rôle in oppositions ;
and in Russian conditions a high proportion of intellectuals were
Jewish. As early as March 1926 Trotsky, in a letter to Bukharin,
quoted a report from the secretary of a party cell referring to
rumours that " the Yids are making trouble in the Politburo ".[6]
When a small rural party group voted a resolution to exclude
Trotsky and Zinoviev from the party, one speaker remarked :
" Trotsky cannot be a communist, his very nationality shows that

---

1924 13·8 per cent, at the seventh congress in 1926 only 7 per cent (see table in
R. T. Fisher, *Pattern for Soviet Youth* (N.Y., 1959), p. 417 ; no figures were
available for the eighth congress in 1928).
    [1] *VLKSM v Rezolyutsiyakh* (1929), p. 283.
    [2] I. Bobryshev, *Melkoburzhuaznye Vliyaniya sredi Molodezhi* (1928), pp. 15,
18-36.
    [3] *Ibid.* pp. 12-13.   [4] *Krasnaya Zvezda*, November 29, 1929.
    [5] *Pravda*, February 19, 1929.   [6] Trotsky archives, T 868.

speculation is a necessity for him ".[1] Preobrazhensky, in a trenchant article of March 1927, attributed the recurrence of anti-Semitism to the nepmen, branded it as a symptom of counter-revolution, and called for a " stern war " against it.[2] An anonymous opposition report of the summer or autumn of 1927 identified " the growth of anti-Semitism " with " the rise of the Stalin-Vareikis ' theory ' of the building of a full socialist society in one country ", and protested against party toleration of " this shameful relic of mediaevalism and national chauvinism ".[3] Rakovsky, in his well-known letter from Astrakhan of August 1928, coupled the revival of anti-Semitism with the strengthening of religious activity, and attributed both to the growth of a bourgeois ideology stimulated by Rightist policies in the party.[4]

No party leader at this time failed to condemn anti-Semitism in the strongest terms. Stalin, at the fifteenth party congress in December 1927, noting the appearance of " some sprigs (rostki) of anti-Semitism ", not only among peasants, but among workers and certain sections of the party, declared that " this evil must be fought... with complete ruthlessness ".[5] At the eighth Komsomol congress in the same month Bukharin attacked the spread of anti-Semitism, though this criticism was not incompatible with the call for " a struggle against nepmen of all nationalities, Jews included ". Other speakers admitted that anti-Semitism " not only exists among workers, but is penetrating the Komsomol ", and ranked it with other " relics of the old way of life ", such as " religious humbug " and " a harsh attitude to women ".[6] A conference of workers' clubs prescribed three ways to counter anti-Semitism : not to idealize Jewish people as a whole, but to distinguish between " Jewish nepmen and Jewish toilers " ; to depict the Soviet attitude to Jews as a part of a general policy for nationalities in the Soviet Union ; and to apply economic measures designed "to bring health to the economic situation of the Jewish toiling masses, and to draw them into productive labour in agriculture and industry ".[7]

---

[1] Ibid. T 1006.   [2] Pravda, March 17, 1927.
[3] Trotsky archives, T 1001.   [4] For this letter see pp. 432-433 below.
[5] Stalin, Sochineniya, x, 324.
[6] VIII Vsesoyuznyi S"ezd VLKSM (1928), pp. 24, 90, 452.
[7] Kommunisticheskoe Prosveshchenie, No. 6(42), October–November 1928,
p. 79.

While party policy remained firmly opposed to anti-Semitism, symptoms of a covert hostility to Jews began to creep into official party pronouncements. Yaroslavsky, himself a Jew but a devoted follower of Stalin, was a pioneer in this field. In a report of February 1929 on the forthcoming party purge, he condemned anti-Semitism as a form of " Great Russian chauvinism ", but went on to remark that some Jews adopted " a rather exaggerated tone in their relations with non-Jews ", to whom they referred contemptuously as " goys ", and hinted that charges of anti-Semitism should not be too readily listened to.[1] A leading article appeared in *Pravda* deploring the spread of anti-Semitism among workers, especially those of peasant origin.[2] But in the same month the bureau of Jewish sections of the party issued a resolution on the attitude of Jews to the current Right deviation. It sharply dismissed the argument that Jews, being rarely engaged in agriculture, were not prone to this error. On the contrary, the fact that large numbers of Jews were craftsmen and artisans, members of the bourgeois intelligentsia, employees, traders or other kinds of middlemen, made them particularly liable to resist the advance of socialist principles. It was noted that Jews lived mainly in areas where industry was weakly developed (White Russia, the Ukraine west of the Dnieper), and did not therefore come under workers' influence. Jews were inclined to neglect class differentiation, and to under-estimate the dangers of chauvinism and nationalism, of religion and clericalism. The struggle against the Right deviation among Jews was therefore of outstanding importance.[3] The purpose of this pronouncement was apparently to make sure that no special indulgence was accorded to Jews in the forthcoming party purge. The resolution of the sixteenth party conference in April 1929 on the purge dutifully included " anti-Semites " as well as " concealed supporters of the religious cult " among those on whom the purge was to fall.[4] But the reservations of the bureau of Evsektisii seemed to foreshadow a weakening of the resistance hitherto offered by the party and its spokesmen to the gathering forces of anti-Semitism.

[1] E. Yaroslavsky, *Chistka Partii* (1929), pp. 42-44.

[2] *Pravda*, February 19, 1929.

[3] *Izvestiya Tsentral'nogo Komiteta VKP(B)*, No. 5-6(264-265), February 28, 1929, p. 20.

[4] *KPSS v Rezolyutsiyakh* (1954), ii, 611.

CHAPTER 55

THE POLITICS OF LITERATURE

THE literary front in the summer of 1926 was still clouded by the obscurity and ambiguity of the party line, the party leaders being divided between a determination to avoid involvement in literary controversy and to tolerate all writers not overtly hostile to the régime, and a vague ideological commitment to the proletarian writers organized in VAPP. Lunacharsky, as People's Commissar for Education, had some undefined authority over the world of literature. But his personal predilections were traditional and tolerant; [1] and this made him suspect to the Left. The ambitious Averbakh had enjoyed a windfall when his principal rivals in VAPP associated themselves with the Leningrad opposition, which suffered defeat at the fourteenth party congress in December 1925; and Averbakh emerged as the uncontested leader of the organization. [2] The journal *Na Postu* was wound up at the end of 1925, and the first number of its successor *Na Literaturnom Postu*, the organ of the reconstructed VAPP, came out in March 1926. [3] But attempts to extend the authority of VAPP over the whole field of literature were quickly checked. *Na Literaturnom Postu* made some profession of abandoning the political polemics of its predecessor, and devoted attention to the special credentials of proletarian literature, which was said to favour the transition from romanticism to realism, and from abstraction to concrete fact. After what was evidently a long struggle, and probably not without pressure from above, a joint meeting of literary groups was held on December 27, 1926, to found a comprehensive

[1] In 1926, in a discussion of Rimsky-Korsakov's opera *Skazaniya o Grade Kitezhe*, he argued that " even counter-revolutionary and mystical productions, where they have *a high artistic, cultural or characteristic quality*, should not be prohibited " (*Izvestiya*, July 27, 1926).

[2] See *Socialism in One Country, 1924–1926*, Vol. 2, pp. 86-87.

[3] *Na Postu* called itself on its title-page a " journal of literary criticism " ; its successor was described as a " journal of Marxist criticism " — a change in literary fashion rather than in substance.

Federation of Organizations of Soviet Writers (FOSP).[1] The decision seems, however, to have aroused little enthusiasm ; and it
was not till nearly a year later, on November 20, 1927, that Lunacharsky spoke at the opening ceremony of the new federation.[2]
    The loose and ample mantle of FOSP enveloped, in addition
to VAPP, the fellow-traveller All-Russian Union of Writers (VSP),
and a somewhat nebulous All-Russian Society of Peasant Writers
(VOKP),[3] as well as most of the minor literary groups of different
complexions which had proliferated under the tolerant régime of
NEP. The most conspicuous of these small groups were the
Futurists and technical innovators who drew their main strength
from Mayakovsky's prestige as the poet of the revolution. Their
journal Lef, which had petered out in 1925,[4] was revived in
January 1927 under the title Novyi Lef, and continued to challenge
with fading conviction the exclusive claim of VAPP to speak
for the proletarian writer. It received no encouragement from the
party, and was heavily attacked by Polonsky, editor of the eclectic
Novyi Mir, whose sympathies were with the fellow-travellers, in
two articles in Izvestiya entitled " Lef or Bluff? "[5] The most

    [1] Literaturnaya Entsiklopediya, ix (1935), 673-674. In August 1925, after
the party resolution of June 18, 1925 (see Socialism in One Country, 1924–1926,
Vol. 2, p. 85), several literary groups including VAPP had issued a joint statement that " the time has come to found a federation of Soviet writers " (Literaturnye Manifesty (1929), pp. 286-289 ; Oktyabr', August 1925, pp. 163-164) ;
and this is sometimes misleadingly named as the founding date of FOSP.
According to Lunacharsky (Izvestiya, October 1, 1927), the foundation of FOSP
was connected with a campaign to improve the material conditions of writers.
By a decree of September 30, 1927, writers were granted the same privileges as
regards housing as workers and employees (Sobranie Zakonov, 1927, No. 58,
art. 580) ; and an amendment was being sought of the decree on authors' rights
(for decrees on this subject see pp. 199-200 above).
    [2] For Lunacharsky's speech see p. 405 below.
    [3] Zhurnalist, No. 1, 1926, p. 16, gave the following figures of membership
for October 1, 1925 ; VAPP 2898, VOKP 709, VSP 360 ; all the others were
much smaller ; Gusev in 1927 gave the VSP 800 members (Pravda, April 30,
1927). By 1928 VAPP claimed 4800 members grouped in 30 national sections
(Izvestiya, May 6, 1928) : the total apparently included members of 80 regional
or local APPs (I. Rozanov, Putovoditel' po Sovremennosi Russkoi Literature (1929),
p. 335). The central council of VOKP held an " enlarged plenum " on May
15-17, 1928, and issued what was apparently its first manifesto (Literaturnye
Manifesty (1929), pp. 265-271).
    [4] See Socialism in One Country, 1924–1926, Vol. 2, p. 76, note 2.
    [5] Izvestiya, February 25, 27, 1927 ; the articles provoked a public debate in
which Polonsky, Mayakovsky and other literary figures took part (Literaturnoe
Nasledstvo, lxv (1958), 47).

anomalous position was occupied by the Formalists, originally an offshoot of Futurism (Shklovsky and Tinyanov, the most prominent of the Formalists, had both been contributors to *Lef*), who concerned themselves with literary techniques and aesthetic theory, not with revolutionary or proletarian themes; Bukharin, while recognizing their competence as " technical specialists ", denied that " form " in art could be divorced from its relation to social existence, and called the movement " antiquated " and " scholastic " and " a surrogate for knowledge ".[1]   Under the impetus of FOSP, the Formalists now drew nearer to the *Novyi Lef* group, and showed more interest in the social background of literature.[2]   The Pereval group, calling itself an All-Union Union of Worker-Peasant Writers, stood on a platform similar to that of the fellow-travellers.   It attached importance to the heritage of Russian literature and to the author's right to choose his subject, denounced an excessive addiction to form and style, and early in 1927 issued a declaration attacking both VAPP and *Novyi Lef*.[3] Constructivists aimed at creating a proletarian school of poetry, inspired by " love for statistics, for workaday speech, for citation of documents, for the workaday fact, for the description of the event ".[4]

Surrounded by these discordant voices, the fortunes of VAPP continued to prosper at the expense of its rivals.   But the hard core of resistance to its pretensions was provided by the fellow-traveller VSP and its journal *Krasnaya Nov'* ; and Averbakh's feud with Voronsky, dating from 1924,[5] had never been called off.   Averbakh celebrated the first issue of *Na Lituraturnom Postu* in March 1926 with a fresh assault on his adversary ; and Voronsky, now appraised of the imminent danger, retorted with an ironical article in *Krasnaya Nov'*, ending with a mock appeal to Lunacharsky :

> If I am to accept my end, may it not be at the hands of Averbakh. . . . To perish on the battlefield in open combat is a

[1] *Krasnaya Nov'*, No. 3, 1925, pp. 248-257.
[2] For a full account of this group see V. Erlich, *Russian Formalism* (The Hague, 1953).   [3] *Krasnaya Nov'*, No. 2, 1927, pp. 233-236.
[4] For a statement issued by them early in 1928 see *Literaturnye Manifesty* (1929), pp. 262-264 ; in 1929 they brought out a symposium entitled *Business*, the word being transliterated from English (*Na Literaturnom Postu*, No. 9, May 1929, p. 20).   [5] See *Socialism in One Country, 1924–1926*, Vol. 2, pp. 79, 81.

hard but honourable fate. But to be stifled by the " literary
exhalations " of Averbakh — may this cup pass from me.[1]

The invocation of Lunacharsky suggested that Voronsky had
friends in high places ; and Averbakh moved warily. At an " enlarged plenum " of VAPP which sat from November 27 to 29,
1926, Averbakh delivered his blows Right (fellow-travellers) and
Left (Lelevich, Vardin), spoke condescendingly of peasant writers,
gave a rather half-hearted blessing to FOSP, and maintained that
the hope for the cultural revolution lay in the proletarian writers
organized in VAPP.[2] But other pronouncements struck a different
note. Libedinsky reported on the need for a new platform " on
the basis of the teachings of Marx and Plekhanov ", and admitted
that the earlier platform had been tainted with the errors of Proletkult and with " communist boasting ".[3] A further resolution,
whose importance was underlined by its publication in extenso in
Pravda, specifically retracted the resolution adopted by the first
VAPP conference of January 1925 on a report by Vardin, on the
impossibility of peaceful rivalry between literary schools with
differing ideologies, and on the anti-revolutionary character of
fellow-traveller literature ; this was condemned for failing to
" take account of the changing forms of the class struggle in our
country ".[4]

[1] Krasnaya Nov', No. 5, May 1926, pp. 195-203. Averbakh had a capacity
for attracting intense personal antipathy ; Trotsky, originally one of his patrons
(see Socialism in One Country, 1924–1926, Vol. 2, p. 76, note 3), later referred
to " sharp-witted nonentities like Averbakh " who were " advertised as the
Belinskys of proletarian(!) literature " (Byulleten' Oppozitsii (fiaris), No. 11,
May 1930, p. 40). Averbakh also carried on a campaign against Polonsky,
editor of the eclectic Novyi Mir, whom he called " the old alter ego of Voronsky "
(L. Averbakh, Nashi Literaturnye Raznoglasiya (1927), p. 38) ; and Polonsky
penned a scathing indictment of the " opportunism and cliquiness, low level of
literary culture, . . . reckless and sometimes dishonest polemics " of Na Literaturnom Postu (V. Polonsky, Ocherki Lituraturnogo Dvizheniya Revolyutsionnoi
Epochi (2nd ed. 1929), p. 286).
[2] L. Averbakh, Nashi Literaturnye Raznoglasiya (1927), pp. 252-259 ; the
original report may have been written up for this volume.
[3] Izvestiya, November 30, 1926. For Proletkult see Socialism in One Country, 1924–1926, Vol. 1, pp. 48-50 ; the term " communist boasting " was a well-
known coinage of Lenin.
[4] Pravda, December 1, 1926 ; Trotsky, Sochineniya, xxi, 469-470 ; V.
Polonsky, Ocherki Literaturnogo Dvizheniya Revolyutsionnoi Epochi (2nd ed.
1929), pp. 222, 284-285. For the conference of January 1925 see Socialism in
One Country, 1924–1926, Vol. 2, p. 83.

If, however, the party leaders still sought to avoid a clash on the literary front, Averbakh was in no mood to spare his old rival Voronsky. As the struggle in the party against the opposition grew more acute, it became easier to implicate him in it.[1]   In March 1927 the rumour circulated that Voronsky was to be re-placed at *Krasnaya Nov'* by a new editorial board of three, in-cluding Gusev.[2]   Relations between the two largest constituent organizations in FOSP were now implacably hostile. VAPP was said to have been successful in securing two-thirds of the seats on the executive of the federation for its supporters; and Voronsky angrily exposed this manœuvre, calling the federation " a bureau-cratic enterprise ".[3]   On April 18, 1927, a meeting was held at the press section of the party central committee, at which the question of Voronsky's dismissal was " squarely put ".   He was fiercely criticized by Gusev, the head of the press section, as well as by Averbakh and other members of VAPP, and defended himself " not cleverly enough, but fairly firmly ".[4]   After the meeting, VAPP addressed a circular letter to all " organizations of prole-tarian writers ", detailing Voronsky's offences, and apparently announcing his removal from the editorship of *Krasnaya Nov'*.[5] The announcement was premature, and the struggle continued for a few weeks longer.   Gusev carried on the attack in an article in *Pravda* entitled " What kind of Writers' Federation do we

---

[1] See *Socialism in One Country, 1924–1926*, Vol. 2, pp. 80-83.   According to *Literaturnaya Entsiklopediya*, ii (1930), 313, Voronsky joined the opposition in 1925; he had been a signatory of the platform of the 46 in October 1923 (see *The Interregnum, 1923–1924*, p. 372).   He shared Trotsky's sceptical attitude to proletarian literature, and Trotsky in his autobiography briefly referred to Voronsky as " our best literary critic " (L. Trotsky, *Moya Zhizn'* (Berlin, 1930), ii, 316.)   He narrowly escaped being compromised in May 1926, when Pilnyak dedicated to him a story based on the death of Frunze (see *Socialism in One Country, 1924–1926*, Vol. 2, p. 111), and was arrested as a Trotskyite in January 1929 (see p. 417 below).

[2] Both Gladkov and Voronsky wrote to Gorky in this sense (*Literaturnoe Nasledstvo*, lxx (1963), 90; *Arkhiv A. M. Gor'kogo*, x, ii (1965), 51); on April 7, 1927, Gladkov reported that Voronsky's removal had been postponed (*Literaturnoe Nasledstvo*, lxx (1963), 93).

[3] *Krasnaya Nov'*, No. 4, April 1927, pp. 214-221.

[4] No record of the meeting was published, but references to it occur in letters from Gladkov, who was present, to Gorky (*Literaturnoe Nasledstvo*, lxx (1963), 90, 93-94, note 1) and in Voronsky's article cited in p. 404, note 2 below.

[5] Quoted from the archives in S. Sheshukov, *Neistovye Revniteli* (1970), pp. 208-209).

Need? ", which accused Voronsky of slighting the proletariat and making common cause with the opposition.[1] Voronsky replied in *Krasnaya Nov'* in the form of an " open letter " to Gusev, more moderate than his earlier articles in tone, though not in substance, in which he continued to attack Averbakh, but expressed willingness to work with VAPP " under another leadership ".[2] But this item, which appeared with a note of dissent from the other members of the editorial board, proved to be his swan-song. He was not formally dismissed or deposed, but declared himself unable to work with Raskolnikov and Friche, newly appointed to the board.[3] In November 1927 his name finally disappeared from the cover of the journal.[4] Individual fellow-travellers were at this time not directly penalized. But Zamyatin, whose novel *We* had been published abroad and enjoyed some success, was denounced in a long article in the journal of VAPP in September 1927 as " a back number ", who was playing " a harmful, reactionary, treasonable rôle ".[5]

The tenth anniversary of the revolution and the approaching fifteenth congress of the party inspired Averbakh to make a fresh bid for the hegemony of VAPP on the literary front. In the preface to a volume of his essays he boldly claimed that " VAPP is now the essential transmitter of the party line in *belles-lettres* ".[6] A leading article in the VAPP journal in October 1927 called for a further advance " on the path of the cultural revolution " ; and a month later Averbakh ingeniously distinguished between the literary views of the Trotskyite wing of the opposition, Preobrazhensky, Sosnovsky and Voronsky, and of the Zinovievite wing, Vardin and Lelevich, who had not fully grasped the basic hostility of the Trotskyites to proletarian literature and to the cultural revolution.[7] Other potential rivals were not neglected. At a

---

[1] *Pravda*, April 30, 1927,   [2] *Krasnaya Nov'*, No. 6, 1927, pp. 238-249.
[3] *Arkhiv A. M. Gor'kogo*, x, ii (1965), 67.
[4] Four instalments of his memoirs, relating to the pre-revolutionary period, appeared in *Novyi Mir*, Nos. 9-12, September–December 1928, and were then interrupted — no doubt, by his arrest (see p. 417 below).
[5] *Na Literaturnom Postu*, No. 17-18, September, 1927, pp. 56-65.
[6] L. Averbakh, *Nashi Literaturnye Raznoglasiya* (1927), p. 31.
[7] *Na Literaturnom Postu*, No. 20, October 1927, pp. 1-5 ; No. 22-23, November–December 1927, pp. 21-22.

literary discussion in Leningrad on the occasion of the anniversary, Averbakh, while himself refraining from direct criticism of Maya- kovsky, appears to have slyly encouraged an attack on him by Fadeev, another member of VAPP.[1] Meanwhile, the first issue of a new journal *Revolyutsiya i Kultura*, with Bukharin, Lunacharsky, Deborin and Pashukanis on its editorial board, appeared on November 15, 1927. The editorial manifesto, devoted to the cause of the " cultural revolution ", limited itself to a vague demand for " new forms of culture which correspond to the task of constructing a socialist society ". Lunacharsky still shrank from any commitment. In November 1927 an international conference of proletarian and revolutionary writers in Moscow provided him with a platform for a conciliatory speech on " Stages of Soviet Literature ", in which he mildly criticized the extravagances of the immediate post-revolutionary period, the excesses of the *Na Postu* group, and the lack of toleration for fellow-travellers, and looked forward to the rise of young proletarian writers ; and on Novem- ber 21, 1927, he spoke again in a similar vein at the long-delayed founding ceremony of FOSP.[2] On this occasion, FOSP issued a manifesto which, referring to the resolution of the party central committee of June 18, 1925, disclaimed any intention " to make the writer's work in any way mechanical or to simplify it in ac- cordance with this or that schedule ". On the other hand, the federation was conscious of the great " moral responsibility " of writers, and could not " remain indifferent to writers' work which artificially and systematically picks out the negative sides of our existence, distorting it and breeding pessimism in the masses of readers ". But lively discussion and mutual criticism between groups were welcome.[3]

All the evidence points to the continued reluctance of the party authorities at this time to engage themselves in the warfare of literary factions. The report of the press section of the party central committee to the fifteenth party congress in December 1927 briefly recorded the formation of FOSP into which all organizations of Soviet writers had entered. The " unhealthy

[1] *Literaturnoe Nasledstvo*, lxv (1958), 322 ; an article in *Na Literaturnom Postu*, No. 22-23, November–December 1927, pp. 61-73, while bestowing faint and conventional praise on Mayakovsky, described him as " a journalist (gazetchik)".   [2] A. Lunacharsky, *Sobranie Sochinenii*, ii (1964), 362-367, 646.
[3] *Literaturnye Manifesty* (1929), pp. 289-291.

phenomenon " which preoccupied the party authorities was the
publication by Gosizdat of " ideologically dubious works steeped
in moods of pessimism etc. "[1] The literary controversy made only
a fleeting and unsensational appearance at the congress itself.
Krinitsky, head of the Agitprop section of the party central committee, in a speech well stocked with quotations from Lenin,
made some conventional remarks on the cultural work of the party
and on the development of proletarian culture. He then abruptly
attacked Preobrazhensky for having spoken, at a session of the
Communist Academy, of " a crisis in Soviet culture ", and with his
name coupled that of Lelevich, who in a provincial journal had
written of " a crisis in the class content of Soviet culture ".
Lelevich, he remarked, " gave much the same definition of the
situation on the cultural front as the opposition had given in
economic questions ", and added emphatically that " all this is
nonsense ".[2] Krinitsky had supported the leaders of VAPP
against the Left opposition in its own ranks, but showed no signs
of wishing to intervene in the struggle between VAPP and its
rivals, or to import political issues into the struggle. Bukharin, in
a speech on January 24, 1928, the fourth anniversary of Lenin's
death, recalled Lenin's dislike of " chatter " about proletarian
culture, and of those who " dreamed of establishing proletarian
culture almost by some experimental laboratory method ".[3]

The next few months proved crucial. In the organization of
literature, as in other aspects of party and Soviet affairs, the rout
of the united opposition at the congress, the grain collections crisis
of the succeeding months and the unmasking of the alleged
Shakhty conspiracy, marked a period of acute tension and unrest.
A Union congress of proletarian writers was convened under the
auspices of VAPP at the end of April 1928. On the eve of the
congress, *Na Literaturnom Postu* in an unsigned editorial again
sought to equate opposition to VAPP with opposition to the party
leadership, and quoted a recent speech in which Stalin had insisted
on the development of " the cultural resources of the working
class " (the phrase, quoted from Lenin, was several times repeated)

---

[1] *K XV S"ezdu VKP(B)* (1927), pp. 223-224.
[2] *Pyatnadtsatyi S"ezd VKP(B)*, ii (1962), 1321-1327; for an account of
Krinitsky's career see *Voprosy Istorii KPSS*, No. 12, 1964, pp. 96-99.
[3] *Pravda*, January 27, 1928 ; for this speech see p. 454, note 4 below.

and on the need for a " cultural revolution ".[1]   More significant
was an article by Lunacharsky which appeared in the VAPP
journal as the congress opened.   Though slightly defensive in
tone, it was in effect an endorsement of VAPP's claims.   It was
a bourgeois habit, Lunacharsky remarked, to regard the writer
as " some kind of ingrained individualist ".   The charge against
VAPP that its leaders were too much concerned with organization
was misplaced.   He was sometimes shocked by " the rudeness of
tone, the unseemly mockery, the sharpness of judgment " exhibited in their criticism; but it was unfair to attack them as
" the new communist *chinovniks* of literature ".   The party knew
where " firm directives " were required, and where " to allow
wider limits and to leave some questions open to discussion ".
VAPP was right to adopt the line of " unconditional submission
to the directives of the party, readiness in all ways to become
100 per cent promoters of the ideas of the party ".[2]   Given Lunacharsky's previous restraint, it might well have seemed that the
party leaders had at length decided to cast their mantle over VAPP,
and make it the pivot and instrument of party control over
literature.

When, however, the congress met on April 30, 1928, with 230
delegates representing a VAPP membership of more than 4000, it
became clear that the victory of VAPP was neither uncontested nor
unconditional.   Krinitsky made the opening speech which was
intended to lay down the party line.   After much beating about the
bush, he harked back to the party resolution of June 18, 1925, as
" the fundamental political document ", and delivered three cau-
tions.   All forces of proletarian literature must be united, and
VAPP's " strivings for monopoly representation of the party line "
curbed; VAPP must " learn ", and refrain from " busy-body-
ing "; and better relations must be maintained with the fellow-
travellers.   Subject to these conditions, the party would " *help the
proletarian writers to win for themselves their historical right to
hegemony in our literature* ".[3]   Averbakh, in his report on the
cultural revolution, modestly admitted the need for " *learning and*

[1] *Na Literaturnom Postu*, No. 8, April 1928, pp. 2-6; for Stalin's remarks
see *Sochineniya*, xi, 36-38.
[2] A. Lunacharsky, *Sobranie Sochinenii*, ii (1964), 371-373; it was originally published in *Na Literaturnom Postu*, No. 9, May 1928.
[3] *Pravda*, May 5, 1928; *Izvestiya*, May 6, 1928, Accounts of the congress,

self-criticism ", but attacked the mass of politically unsound literature still being published. Rodov and Bezymensky spoke for the discredited Left wing of VAPP, but " failed to shake the congress ". Fadeev, continuing his feud with Mayakovsky, denounced *Lef* for falsely opposing its " factology " to the alleged " psychologism " of VAPP, and criticized the poem *Khorosho* written by Mayakovsky for the anniversary of the revolution.[1] Lunacharsky presented theses on the tasks of Marxist criticism, which were too theoretical to give any lead in current controversies.[2] While the congress was in session, *Izvestiya* published, as a discussion article, a fierce attack on VAPP and its leaders by Gorbov, a well-known critic and former contributor to *Krasnaya Nov'*. The hopes raised by the creation of FOSP, declared the writer, had been frustrated by VAPP, which had " practically dominated the federation from the moment of its birth ", and treated it merely " as a new form in which to realise its own ' hegemony ' ".[3]

After what was probably a stiff battle behind the scenes, the congress adopted resolutions broadly favourable to VAPP's ambitions. It ratified a decision, taken earlier by the council of VAPP, to create an All-Union Organization of Associations of Proletarian Writers (VOAPP) to coordinate the work of VAPP and the similar associations of the other republics.[4] The corollary of this was that VAPP was henceforth to be known as RAPP (" Russian " instead of " All-Russian ").[5] The main resolution of the congress

which lasted till May 8, 1928, appeared in *Pravda*, May 5, 9, 1928, *Izvestiya*, May 6, 8, 1928, and *Na Literaturnom Postu*, No. 10, May 1928, pp. 74-80, No. 11-12, June 1928, pp. 118-124, No. 13, July 1928, p. 5 ; but they are too fragmentary to give a clear picture of what took place. Some of the reports at the congress, including those of Averbakh and Fadeev, were published in *Tvorcheskie Puti Proletarskoi Literatury* (1929).

[1] Quoted in V. Pertsov, *Mayakovsky v Poslednie Gody* (1965), p. 226. *Khorosho* had already been attacked in *Na Literaturnom Postu*, No. 2, January 1928, p. 21, No, 5, March 1928, p. 54 ; Brik, an associate of Mayakovsky, retaliated with a caustic review of Fadeev's novel *Razgrom* in *Novyi Lef*, No. 5, May 1928, pp. 5-7.

[2] They were published in *Novyi Mir*, No. 6, June 1928, pp. 188-192.

[3] *Izvestiya*, May 6, 1928.

[4] The decision was announced in *Na Literaturnom Postu*, No. 6, March 1928, pp. 1-3, but does not seem to have been immediately effective ; the first meeting of the council of VOAPP was not summoned till January 1929 (*ibid.* No. 1, January 1929, pp. 7-12).

[5] *Ibid.* No. 10, May 1928, pp. 1-5. *Malaya Sovetskaya Entsiklopediya*, vii (1930), 175, gives this as the date of the foundation of RAPP. Other authorities

tactfully approved the "political line" of the VAPP administration, and found its work "in general satisfactory". But it
detected "a number of morbid phenomena and individual
shortcomings", which seem to have consisted of "an excessive
preoccupation with organizational affairs as such, a tendency
sometimes to replace real work by 'political agitation'". The
resolution nevertheless condemned in harsh terms both the Left
opposition in VAPP — "this pseudo-Left unprincipled opposition" — and the followers of Voronsky, whose "capitulatory
line" made them "a typical expression of bourgeois influence in
literature". A sinister passage indicated that one of the tasks of
VOAPP would be to inaugurate a "review" of the whole membership of associations of proletarian writers; this "self-purge" was
to be balanced by the recruitment of "young new creative forces,
especially workers from the bench".[1]

The victory was, however, still not unqualified. In March 1928
Maxim Gorky, who had been in voluntary exile since 1921, and
had recently shown symptoms of nostalgia for his native land,[2]
announced his approaching arrival in Moscow; and this news
had been hailed with enthusiasm by Bukharin in the columns of
Pravda.[3] Gorky had been one of the founders of *Krasnaya Nov'*
in 1921; and the initiated must have known that he numbered
Voronsky among his closest friends in Moscow.[4] On the other
hand, VAPP writers were notoriously cool in their appreciation
of Gorky, who had recently been described in their journal as
"a man without class consciousness, the ideologue of the
intermediate strata of society".[5] In April 1928, a week before
the VAPP congress was due to open, *Pravda* and *Izvestiya*
published a letter written by Gorky from Sorrento in which
he expressed himself as indifferent to the designation of "proletarian writer"; the title did not correspond to his conception

<hr>

(see *Socialism in One Country, 1924-1926*, Vol. 2, p. 84) date it from January
1925; but from 1925 to 1928 the abbreviation VAPP was still in common use.
    [1] *Literaturnye Manifesty* (1929), pp. 219-227.
    [2] Articles by Gorky on the occasion of the tenth anniversary of the resolu-
tion had appeared in *Izvestiya*, October 23, 30, 1927, *Pravda*, November 6-7,
1927.   [3] *Ibid*. March 29, 1928.
    [4] In February 1927 Gorky, apprised of the campaign against Voronsky
(see p. 403 above), had written to him praising his "service to Russian literature" and his "wonderful journal" (*Arkhiv A. M. Gor'kogo*, ii (1965), 45).
    [5] *Na Literaturnom Postu*, No. 4, February 1928, p. 94.

of writers " indispensable to the toiling world ". In a further article in *Izvestiya*, he quoted with disapproval passages from Mayakovsky and Bezymensky, another poet of the extreme Left, and mildly defended a Komsomol poet named Molchanov, who had been fiercely attacked by Averbakh.[1] At this moment, and from such a source, these pronouncements were embarrassing. The doyen of proletarian writers, the one unchallenged master of proletarian literature, does not appear to have been mentioned at the VAPP congress; and on the very eve of Gorky's return Averbakh replied sharply to Gorky's defence of Molchanov in an article headed " Vulgarity should not be defended ".[2] Gorky arrived in Moscow on May 28, 1928, being greeted by Bukharin, Lunacharsky, Enukidze and Orjonikidze at the train, and by large crowds waiting outside the station.[3] He spoke at a congress of the railwaymen's trade union, which happened to be in session, on May 29, and two days later was the hero of a mammoth meeting in the Bol'shoi Theatre, at which Lunacharsky delivered the principal speech of welcome.[4] But the RAPP leaders played no part in these proceedings;[5] and Astrov in *Pravda* attacked Averbakh and defended Gorky in an article entitled " Gorky and Communist Boasters ".[6] A few days later Gorky attended a reception in the editorial office of *Krasnaya Nov'* to meet writers associated with that journal. The speech which he delivered was unimpeachably orthodox. He spoke of " the new stratum of the bourgeoisie "

[1] *Pravda* and *Izvestiya*, April 21, 1928; *Izvestiya*, May 1, 1928; Averbakh's criticism appeared in *Komsomol'skaya Pravda*, October 2, 1927.

[2] *Na Literaturnom Postu*, No. 11, May 1928, pp. 13-17.

[3] A party headed by Skvortzov-Stepanov, the editor of *Izvestiya*, had met him at the frontier (*Izvestiya*, May 29, 1928).

[4] *Pravda*, May 27, 30, June 1, 2, 1928; Lunacharsky's speech is in A. Lunacharsky, *Siluety* (1965), pp. 229-244.

[5] A contemporary cartoon showed Averbakh, not very conspicuously, in a bevy of literary figures led by Lunacharsky to greet Gorky (*Literaturnoe Nasledstvo*, lxv (1950), 88-89).

[6] *Pravda*, June 3, 1928; Lunacharsky drafted an article expressing sympathy with Astrov's views and outspokenly condemning Averbakh's critical methods : " I have rarely met a man who has so many enemies ". The draft remained among Lunacharsky's papers annotated " *Izvestiya*, June 6, 1928 ", which appear to show that publication was planned (A. Lunacharsky, *Sobranie Sochinenii*, ii (1964), 374-378). But it never appeared. This was a tense moment in the party struggle, revolving in part round control of the press (see pp. 61-62 above) ; and to publish an article siding with Astrov against a professed champion of the Left might have been invidious.

arising on the basis of NEP as cunning, dangerous and " capable of taking the offensive ". It was stronger than the bourgeoisie of his youth, and " literature now must be even more revolutionary than it was then ". But the occasion marked a bond of sympathy ranging Gorky with the fellow-travellers of *Krasnaya Nov'* rather than with Averbakh and RAPP or with Mayakovsky and Lef.[1]

Nor had the leaders of RAPP, though they regarded themselves as the champions and promoters of proletarian literature, and in this capacity claimed a "hegemony" in the literary field, yet proclaimed the conception of a tight dictatorship over literature exercised by them in the name of the party. Art was referred to as " a mighty weapon of the class struggle ".[2] But the term " social command " was coined not by RAPP but by Mayakovsky, and the Lef doctrine that literary production was like any other form of production, with the implication that it was subject to the same processes of planning, was rejected by RAPP. The RAPP writers interpreted " social command " as an inner compulsion experienced by the writer to express his revolutionary faith in literature, not as a choice of subject imposed by a higher authority. Averbakh denied that an artist could be ordered to write on a particular theme:

> The class situation of the writer dictates to him directly the choice of themes and their treatment. . . . That the writer is conditioned in his free choice of themes is to a great extent the real content of the term " social command ".[3]

Libedinsky specifically retracted an earlier article which had seemed to invite a crude interpretation of the " social command ".[4]

[1] The reception and speech were reported in *Pravda*, June 13, 1928. Rykov's mention, at his trial in 1938, of conversations with Averbakh about Gorky " approximately from 1928 to 1930 ", implied hostility to Gorky (*Report of Court Proceedings: Anti-Soviet " Bloc of Rights and Trotskyites "* (Moscow, 1938), p. 627); and the conjecture in E. Zamyatin, *Litsa* (N.Y., 1955), p. 96 (a passage first published in 1936), that Gorky was responsible for the downfall of RAPP in 1932, though it cannot be substantiated, was symptomatic of relations between them.

[2] *Na Literaturnom Postu*, No. 13-14, July 1928, p. 4.

[3] L. Averbakh, *Kul'turnaya Revolyutsiya i Voprosy Sovremennoi Literatury* 1928), pp. 62-64.

[4] The original article appeared in the first issue of *Na Postu* in 1923, and was reprinted in *Literaturnye Manifesty* (1929), pp. 189-193 ; Libedinsky retracted it in his " platform " for the RAPP plenum of October 1928 (see p. 414 below).

Another writer protested against being told to write about socialist construction when he wanted to write about the civil war.[1]

The rapid transformation of RAPP into the blunt instrument of a narrowly conceived party policy of regimentation was due mainly to the economic and political pressures which led the party to clutch at every device to mould a restive and recalcitrant opinion, but partly also to the persistent ambition of the RAPP leaders to convert their undefined " hegemony " into a monopoly of power over other literary groups. The attack extended to *Novyi Mir*, whose editor Polonsky had already been bracketed by Averbakh with Voronsky as a patron of fellow-travellers.[2] In April 1928 Polonsky was replaced by Ingulov, an official of the party central committee.[3] The rising prestige of RAPP drew fresh encouragement from a break in the ranks of Lef. In August 1928 Mayakovsky abandoned the editorship of *Novyi Lef*, which was taken over by Tretyakov, the author of a sensational and successful play, *Roar, China!*[4] The reasons for the breach may perhaps have been largely temperamental. But Mayakovsky, addressing two meetings in September 1928 to launch a movement " to the Left of Lef ", alleged that Lef had " acquired the character of some kind of group eccentricity ", whereas " literary invention must become the expression of mass literary production ".[5] When interviewed a few days later by a Leningrad journal, he denied any " splits in Lef ", but claimed that the new movement " to the Left of Lef " stood for " still greater discipline in artistic work ".[6] His increas-

---

[1] *Oktyabr'*, No. 4, April 1929, p. 182. *Pechat' i Revolyutsiya*, No. 1-2, January–February 1929, pp. 19-75, published a symposium by various writers on " social command "; Polonsky, who introduced it, acutely observed that the phrase was the slogan of a " declassed intelligentsia ", whose members sought to make good their divorce from the working class, and that it was not a model for worker and peasant writers.

[2] See p. 402, note 1 above.

[3] One result of the change was that *Novyi Mir*, hitherto exclusively literary, began to carry articles on such topics as the chemical industry, disarmament, Dnieprostroi and Japanese imperialism; the other two, apparently inactive, members of the editorial board were Lunacharsky and Skvortsov-Stepanov. Polonsky rehabilitated himself, and his name reappeared on the cover of the journal from No. 9, September 1928, onward.

[4] Tretyakov had recently published an article attacking " pathos " and sentiment in literature, and calling for " business-like " writers (*Na Literaturnom Postu*, No. 4, February 1928, pp. 93-94).

[5] V. Mayakovsky, *Polnoe Sobranie Sochinenii*, xii (1959), 503-506.

[6] *Ibid.* xii, 183.

ingly incoherent utterances could be read as a move towards the party line of conciliation between the groups.

The centenary of Tolstoy's birth, celebrated in September 1928, provided the last common meeting-place for divergent literary schools. Lenin's slender contribution to literary criticism had been confined to four short articles on Tolstoy, all written before 1917; and, though his main interest had been in the social implications of the great novels, he had undoubtedly respected Tolstoy as a master of Russian literature.[1] Voronsky was an impassioned admirer of Tolstoy.[2] VAPP had been content to tread the same path. Averbakh in the spring of 1927 had proclaimed the need to learn, " first of all ", from Tolstoy;[3] Libedinsky, in his platform for the RAPP plenum of October 1928, used War and Peace and Anna Karenina as his models of style;[4] and the debt to Tolstoy of famous writers of the RAPP school, such as Fadeev and

[1] A curious and significant controversy had occurred earlier in the year. Olminsky, an old Bolshevik and a member of the editorial board of Na Literaturnom Postu, wrote an article in the magazine Ogonek criticizing the excessive adu ation of Tolstoy shown, among others, by Krupskaya and Lunacharsky; it was published with an editorial note pointing out that Lenin had written articles in praise of Tolstoy. Olminsky reverted to the matter in an article in Pravda, January 31, 1928, retorting that, if Lenin's articles were read in full, they revealed his profound disagreements with Tolstoy. Pravda, February 2, 1928, printed on its back page a large advertisement (of dimensions unusual in the Soviet press) announcing the forthcoming jubilee edition of Tolstoy's works and several books about Tolstoy. Two days later Pravda published an article by Olminsky under the title " Lenin or Lev Tolstoy? ", protesting against the "' American style' " and " indecency " of the advertisement; Lenin's works had received no such treatment. Lunacharsky, who was president of the commission for the jubilee edition, now took up the cudgels in an article in Pravda, February 10, 1928, deprecating the attempt to set Lenin's fame against that of Tolstoy. Olminsky replied in a further article in Pravda, February 16, 1928, complaining that Lunacharsky played down the fundamental opposition between Lenin and Tolstoy, and announcing that Na Literaturnom Postu would start a campaign of protest; but Olminsky was apparently at this time a lone wolf on the editorial board, since no campaign was launched.

[2] He wrote to Gorky in November 1927: " When I think of the literature of our time, I always have you in mind — Tolstoy and you " (Arkhiv A. M. Gor'kogo, x, ii (1965), 60).

[3] Na Literaturnom Postu, No. 10, May 1927, p. 16; a phrase used by Lenin to describe Tolstoy's method, " a tearing away of all, and all kinds of, masks ", was borrowed as a slogan by RAPP writers, but later condemned as an inducement to excessive introspection.

[4] For the platform see p. 404 below.

Sholokhov, whose *Quiet Don* began to appear in 1928, was
notorious. The Formalists were not behindhand in their devotion
to Tolstoy; Shklovsky, the most prolific of their publicists, celebrated the Tolstoy centenary with a pamphlet entitled *Form and
Style in L. N. Tolstoy's Novel " War and Peace "*. When on
September 10, 1928, a large concourse, including a bevy of distinguished foreign writers, assembled in the Bol'shoi Theatre to pay
tribute to the great master, it seemed for the moment that a common allegiance to literature transcended political divisions.[1]

The illusion was of short duration. In the autumn of 1928,
the quest for rapid industrialization and for maximum targets in
the five-year plan had reached an intense pitch, and the campaign
against the Right Wing in the party — Bukharin, Rykov and Tomsky — was about to be launched;[2] the strained atmosphere in-
vaded every sector of Soviet life. What was called the " first
plenum " of RAPP, which had been well advertised in advance,[3]
met on October 1, 1928.[4] The main document discussed at the
meeting was an " Artistic Platform of RAPP " prepared by Libedinsky. The platform was in form theoretical, distinguishing the
functions of art from those of science, but was not without political
overtones, which were emphasized in Libedinsky's speech replying
to the debate.[5] The occasion was clearly used to stake out RAPP's
claim to ascendancy over the whole field of proletarian literature.

[1] The meeting was extensively reported in *Pravda* and *Izvestiya*, September
12, 1928. The principal speech was made by Lunacharsky, but the text was
apparently not published; many foreign visitors added their tributes, and the
session, which included a Beethoven concert, lasted from 6 p.m. to 1 a.m. The
impending publication of the jubilee edition of Tolstoy's works (see p. 413, note
1 above) in 90 volumes had just been announced (*Pravda*, September 6, 1928); a
lecture delivered by Lunacharsky on September 30, 1928, on "Tolstoy and our
Contemporary World ", is in *Literaturnoe Nasledstvo*, lxix (1961), ii, 406-426.

[2] The discrediting of Bukharin, in particular, is likely to have made an impact on the literary scene; according to a book written in the summer of 1928
(its preface was dated September 1, 1928), " Bukharin, though he appeared little
and rarely in the press as a connoisseur of literature, enjoyed an immense authority in matters of literary policy " (I. Rozanov, *Putevoditel' no Sovremennoi
Russkoi Literature* (1929), p. 28).

[3] *Na Literaturnom Postu*, No. 15-16, August 1928, pp. 1-3, No. 17, September 1928, pp. 2-4.

[4] *Ibid*. No. 19, October 1928, pp. 1-3, No. 20-21, October–November 1928,
pp. 140-142.

[5] The platform was published *ibid*. No. 19, October 1928, pp. 9-19, No.
20-21, October–November 1928, pp. 6-14, the reply to the debate *ibid*. no. 1,
January 1929, pp. 26-29.

A leading article in *Na Literaturnom Postu* at the end of October 1928, lashed out fiercely on all sides. It significantly quoted, twice, Stalin's speech to the Moscow party committee of October 19, 1928, drawing attention to the Right danger ; and the writer (no doubt, Averbakh himself) discerned in literature the petty bourgeois trend which Stalin had denounced. *Krasnaya Nov'* in recent months, he observed, had both moved to the Right and declined in literary quality. The Tolstoy centenary had provoked " a peculiar idealization of Tolstoyism ", resulting in " an exaggeration of his revolutionary character and . . . an underestimate of his reactionary sides ". Pereval and Lef were both in a state of decay : the " ultra-Left theories " of Lef had " an almost openly reactionary character ".[1]   Much of the language was consciously borrowed from the political arena. A virulent campaign against Lef was waged at this time in *Na Literaturnom Postu*. One writer applied to Lef Proudhon's aphorism about prostitution : it was something not to be reformed, but to be abolished. Another called the members of Lef " utopians " who " pervert our literary policy ".[2]

This time the initiative, which had probably not been undertaken without party approval, proved fruitful. In the summer of 1928 the party central committee had re-entered the literary field with a resolution which opened by citing the resolution of June 18, 1925. This was said to " *maintain all its significance for the current period* " ; and the committee wanted " to draw the group of Left ' fellow-travellers ' nearer to the proletariat ". But other passages pointed in a different direction. War was declared on any " slipping away from proletarian class positions, eclecticism, or a favourable attitude to alien ideology ". Finally, the resolution proclaimed that literature, theatre, cinema, painting, music and radio must all play their part " in the struggle . . . against bourgeois and petty bourgeois ideology, against vodka, against philistinism ", as well as " against a resurrection of bourgeois ideology under new labels and a slavish imitation of bourgeois culture " ; and it called for a Union conference to consider these questions.[3]   When the

---

[1] *Na Literaturnom Postu*, No. 20-21, October–November 1928, pp. 1-5 ; for Stalin's speech see p. 77 above.

[2] *Ibid.* No. 22, November 1928, p. 23, No. 24, December 1928, p. 25.

[3] *Spravochnik Partiinogo Rabotnika*, vii (1930), 410-422. For preoccupation with undisciplined and petty bourgeois behaviour among the young at this

conference at length met on December 22, 1928, P. Kerzhentsev, deputy chief of the Agitprop section of the party central committee, made a report on party policy; and the principal literary figures of the day addressed the conference.[1] An article which appeared in *Pravda* while the conference was in session declared that the class war and the period of socialist reconstruction was only just beginning in art, and attacked Lunacharsky for his toleration of ideologically unsound productions.[2]

The resolution which issued from the conference, and was endorsed by the party central committee on December 28, 1928, " On the Provision of Books to the Mass Reader " was severely practical in tone, but revealed some impatience to make literature an effective instrument of party policy. State, social, cooperative and especially party organizations were exhorted to give attention to the publication and distribution of Marxist-Leninist literature, of mass literature on production designed to raise the technical knowledge of workers and peasants, of popular scientific works, and of *belles-lettres*, especially works on contemporary political themes or directed against bourgeois tendencies. It was declared " indispensable, in a greater degree than hitherto, to make mass literature an instrument for the mobilization of the masses around fundamental political and economic tasks ". Publishing houses were to submit their plans for consideration by party and other organizations and in the press, and to seek their authors among qualified communists and among workers and peasants.[3] The

---

time see pp. 168-171 above; the current work on the subject declared that " Bohemia in the milieu of the young literary generation must be given a sharp rebuff " (I. Bobryshev, *Melkoburzhuaznye Vliyaniya sredi Molodezhi* (2nd ed. 1928), p. 131). For the resolution of June 18, 1925, see p. 400, note 1 above.

[1] *Literaturnoe Nasledstvo*, lxv (1958), 83; of the speeches delivered only those of Mayakovsky appear to have been published. He praised Kerzhentsev for condemning the article in *Na Literarnom Postu* demanding the " destruction " of Lef (which suggests that the party attitude did not exclude elements of conciliation). He declared that the line should be " with Averbakh, with Fedin, with comrades from VAPP, with comrades from Lef, while rejecting Right fellow-travellers and standing up for fellow-travellers from Lef "; but he attacked the idea that " unemployed anarchists from *Na Postu* " should be allowed to " correct the communist ideology of Lef " (V. Mayakovsky, *Polnoe Sobranie Sochinenii*, xii (1959), 365-373).

[2] *Pravda*, December 25, 1928.

[3] *Izvestiya Tsentral'nogo Komiteta VKP(B)*, No. 2-3(261-262), January 31, 1929, pp. 10-11. The party occupied itself far less with the visual arts than with literature; but the Agitprop section received at this time a report from the party

resolution coyly refrained from naming RAPP, and the party may still have shrunk from placing too much power in its hands. But RAPP clearly expected to use its privileged position as the servant and instrument of the party and the state in order to assert its authority over other literary groups, now in a condition of eclipse or dissolution.[1] Weakened by Mayakovsky's defection, the journal *Novyi Lef* ceased publication at the end of 1928, and the movement made a last ineffective attempt to reorganize itself as a Revolution-ary Front (REF).[2] The Formalists, who had affiliations with Mayakovsky's group and were also threatened with internal dis-integration, attempted a rearguard action which was also a partial compromise with orthodoxy. Two of their leaders, Yakobson and Tinyanov, published in the last issue of *Novyi Lef* a programme which endeavoured to combine the linguistic approach to literature with a recognition of the social preoccupations of Marxist literary theory.[3] Most of the other groups fell gradually silent. A *coup de grâce* was administered to the surviving tradition of literary inde-pendence by the arrest of Voronsky as a Trotskyite in the first days of January 1929.[4] *Na Literaturnom Postu* celebrated the New Year of 1929 with a leading article entitled " The Class Crisis is Sharpening ", which once more identified RAPP's ambitions with the class struggle and with the party campaign against the Right. *Krasnaya Nov'* was attacked for opening its columns to " material not in the least of Soviet character " ; and FOSP was blamed for failing to produce any serious literature.[5] The party was drawn,

fraction in the Association of Artists of the Revolution, and issued a statement of policy. It considered that artists concentrated too much on rural life and on the civil war, and not enough on labour and on the proletariat : the town was " depicted exclusively at holiday moments ". Artists should concern themselves more with such subjects as industrialization, or the reconstruction of agriculture or the campaign against religion and alcohol (*ibid.* No. 4(263), February 15, 1929, pp. 14-15). The Lef movement looked forward to the replacement of painting by photography (*Literaturnye Manifesty* (1929), p. 256).

[1] When RAPP was dissolved in 1932, it was alleged that, instead of promo-ting " the broader mobilization of Soviet writers and artists round the task of socialist construction ", it had cultivated " group isolation " and " isolation from the political tasks of the day " (*Pravda*, April 24, 1932).

[2] *Literaturnaya Entsiklopediya*, vi (1932), 341.

[3] *Novyi Lef*, No. 12, 1928, pp. 36-37.

[4] *Annali, 1966* (Milan, 1966), pp. 648-649 ; for this round-up of Trotskyites see pp. 83-84 above.

[5] *Na Literaturnom Postu*, No. 1, January 1929, pp. 1-6 ; in April 1929, FOSP began publication of a journal *Literaturnaya Gazeta*, which in one of its

haltingly but inexorably, along the same path. Kerzhentsev in an article in *Pravda*, which once again avoided direct mention of RAPP, wrote boldly that " we shall strike back at bourgeois and petty bourgeois influence on art ". But he insisted on the continued need for a " cautious, comradely attitude " to fellow-travellers;[1] and Lunacharsky in an article of the same month struck the same restraining note.[2] Nevertheless, controls over literature were progressively tightened. A year after the resolution of December 28, 1928, a statement appeared in *Pravda* recognizing that RAPP followed a line in literature nearest to the line of the party, and calling for a consolidation of literary forces round RAPP.[3] Shortly after this summons, Mayakovsky dissolved what was almost the last independent literary group, joined RAPP, and committed suicide two months later.

first issues (May 27, 1929, pp. 1-2) announced a competition for sketches about socialist emulation (see Vol. 1, pp. 515-519). A first All-Russian Congress of Peasant Writers was held on June 3-8, 1929, and was addressed by Lunacharsky as representative of the party central committee (A. Lunacharsky, *Sobranie Sochinenii*, ii (1964), 412-425); but this was the least vital of all the groups.

[1] *Pravda*, February 22, 1929.
[2] A. Lunacharsky, *Sobranie Sochinenii*, viii (1967), 53-54.
[3] *Pravda*, December 4, 1929.

CHAPTER 56

THE NEW SOVIET SOCIETY

(a) The Structure of the Population

THE decision to take a census of the population of the USSR in December 1926 was recorded in a decree of September 3, 1926 ; the purpose was to ascertain not only the numbers of the population, but its " national, social and occupational composition ".[1] The only complete census of the Russian empire had been taken in 1897 ; later population estimates had been derived from incomplete enumerations and limited samples. *Pravda* on November 17, 1926, carried a head-line announcement of the census, now fixed for December 17, 1926, together with several articles on it. A leading article by Rykov explained that planning created a need for accurate information about resources and about the division of population by occupation and by social and national groups. Osinsky, the head of the Central Statistical Administration, emphasized the comprehensiveness of the census and its importance for such questions as employment or housing. A little later it was announced that a period of grace would be allowed for the completion of the census in certain outlying regions — a month in Turkmenistan, two months for the nomads of Kazakhstan and Kirgizia, three months in Yakutia.[2] On December 14, 1928, *Pravda* published an appeal of the government to the population on the correct filling up of census forms, and several reports on the preparatory measures in hand. On the day of the census itself, Osinsky had a front-page article on " The Census and the Struggle for Socialism ", describing the census as a

[1] *Sobranie Zakonov, 1926*, No. 59, art. 438.
[2] *Pravda*, December 10, 1926 ; in some Asian territories of the Union — in the Tajik ASSR, in parts of Turkmenistan, of the Kazakh ASSR and of the Siberian region, among the nomad peoples of the far north, and in one district of the Buryat-Mongol ASSR — it proved impossible to take the census till the summer of 1927 (*Vsesoyuznaya Perepis' Naseleniya : Predvaritel'nye Itogi*, Vyp. iii (1927), 3).

combination of a " cultural operation " and a " mass campaign ",
and claimed that " culture is being implanted in the wildest parts
of our country ".[1]

The census of December 17, 1926, returned the total population
of the USSR as 147,027,915.[2] Of these, 26·3 millions lived in
towns, and 120·7 millions in rural areas ; 77·8 millions were Great
Russian, 31·2 millions Ukrainian, and 4·7 millions White Russian.
Distribution of the population was uneven ; the RSFSR included
92·7 per cent of the area of the USSR and 68·7 per cent of the inhabitants, the Ukraine 2 per cent of the area and 19·7 per cent of
the inhabitants, Turkmenistan 2·2 per cent of the area and 0·7 per
cent of the inhabitants. Of the non-Slavs, the Turkic group was
by far the largest, but was marked by varying degrees of unity and
cohesion ; the Turkic peoples of Central Asia (including the
Kazakh steppes) accounted for 9·7 millions, those of the Volga
region for 3·3 millions, and those of the Caucasus for 1·9 millions.
Of other non-Slav peoples the largest were the Georgians with 1·8
millions and the Armenians with 1·15 millions.[3] The composition
of the population in certain respects reflected the experiences
through which it had passed since 1914. Of the population in 1926
37·2 per cent were under the age of 15 ; of those under 15 50·3
per cent were males, of those over 15 only 47·1 per cent.[4] The
returns showed 39·6 per cent of literates (50·8 per cent of males,
29·2 per cent of females) ; the census of 1897 had shown 22·3
per cent of literates. The highest rate of literacy (66·6 per
cent) was in the age group 20–24. Literacy varied directly with
density of population. In the Ukrainian SSR 44·9 per cent of the
population were literate, in the RSFSR and the White Russian
SSR 40·7 per cent ; the lowest rate (7·7 per cent) was in the Uzbek
SSR. The highest literacy rates (over 50 per cent) were found in
the Central Industrial (Moscow) and Leningrad regions and in the
Karelian and Crimean autonomous republics.[5]

---

[1] *Pravda*, December 17, 1926 ; one slogan appearing in this issue read :
" Whoever wishes to promote the growth of the USSR and the successes of
socialist construction — help the census ! "

[2] For the populations of the six Union republics see *Socialism in One Country
1924–1926*, Vol. 2, p. 231 ; for the populations of the autonomous republics and
regions see F. Lorimer, *The Population of the Soviet Union* (Geneva, 1946),
pp. 63-64.

[3] For tables see *ibid*. pp. 51, 55-61.   [4] For table see *ibid*. p. 142.

[5] *SSSR: God Raboty Pravitel'stva 1927–28* (1929), pp. 480-481.

The results of the census which excited the most anxious curiosity were, however, those relating to class and occupation. The paradoxes of a revolution victorious in a country where the proletariat was a small minority had led to the compromises of NEP; and the question whither these compromises were to lead not only preoccupied both theorists and critics of the Soviet régime, but constituted a central issue of policy. It was not only *littérateurs* like Gorky, or *smenovekhovstsy* like Ustryalov,[1] who saw in NEP a concession to the peasantry which threatened the socialist future of the régime. The cry that the revolution was in danger was constantly raised by the opposition, and found an echo in many party circles. Reassurance could be sought only in the undoubted fact of the growth of the proletariat, and in the beginnings of a migration from country to town which would gradually transform peasants into workers. Party men looked to the census to confirm this reassurance. The census returns classified the population by broad categories of occupation, giving both figures for those actively employed and totals for each category including dependants.[2] This did not, however, constitute a classification by class, or provide a firm basis for isolating the proletarian elements from other classes. Further investigation of this problem was required.

In May 1927, following the census, Sovnarkom appointed a commission to analyse and report on the social structure of the population. It comprised representatives of Narkomfin (Frumkin), Gosplan (Strumilin), the Central Statistical Administration (Pashkovsky), and the Communist Academy (Larin, Kritsman). The conclusions reached were confirmed by the commission on October 25, 1927, and embodied in an article by Larin in *Pravda*, November 6–7, 1927.[3] The commission classified the

---

[1] Gorky had written in 1922: "Almost the whole reserve of intellectual energy amassed by Russia in the course of the nineteenth century has been expended during the revolution and dissolved in the peasant mass. . . . The Russian peasants have risen again at the expense of the intellectuals and the working class" (M. Gorky, *Lénine et le Paysan Russe* (1924), pp. 182-183); for his later hope in an alliance of the workers with the intelligentsia to overcome the "illiterate countryside" see *Socialism in One Country, 1924–1926*, Vol. I, pp. 122-123. For Ustryalov see *ibid.* Vol. I, pp. 56-57.

[2] See Table No. 68, p. 491 below.

[3] Larin's article was reprinted, together with another article on rural overpopulation, in a pamphlet, Yu. Larin, *Sotsial'naya Struktura SSSR* (1928).

whole population on a class basis. The proletarian population amounted to 32·5 millions (employees were included in the category of workers and counted as proletarian[1]); of these 27·6 millions were urban, and 5·8 millions rural (batraks, Sovkhoz workers etc.). The peasant non-proletarian population (including poor and middle peasants and kulaks) was 104 millions. In addition, there were 6·8 million non-proletarian non-agricultural workers (artisans not employing labour, members of free professions etc.), and 3·5 million non-agricultural bourgeois (private employers of labour, traders etc.).[2] In the " proletarian " sector of the population, 13 millions were wage-earners — 4·6 millions as permanent, 1·8 millions as seasonal, non-agricultural workers, 3·1 millions as batraks and 3·5 millions as employees.[3] The rapid increase in the years from 1924–1927 of non-agricultural workers, regular and seasonal, had been accompanied by a somewhat less rapid increase of proletarian agricultural workers (mainly batraks) and of employees, and a decline in the number of poor peasants. The total peasant population had remained approximately stable in absolute terms in these years, the absolute decline in the number of poor peasants being balanced by a slight rise in the other two categories, but had declined relatively to the whole population. The towns and factories absorbed the whole natural population growth, both rural and urban.

These calculations, though fairly made on the principles laid down, were plainly designed to inflate the category of those classified as workers, and to generate faith in the rising proletarian element. The main conclusion announced by Larin was " the incessant growth in the percentage of proletarian population ".[4]   Few

---

[1] The classification of white-collar and other not directly productive employees as proletarian would not have been valid in capitalist society.   Marx in *Capital* distinguished sharply between " commercial wage-earners ", i.e. office workers, who become more and more numerous as industry develops, and productive workers who alone produce surplus value (Karl Marx, Friedrich Engels, *Werke*, xxv (1964), 310); and Engels in 1872 wrote that surplus value was " distributed among the class of capitalists and landowners, together with their paid servants from the Pope and the Kaiser to the night-watchman downwards " (*ibid.* xviii (1964), 214).

[2] See Table No. 68, p. 491 below, where corresponding totals are also given for 1924–1925 and 1925–1926.

[3] See Table No. 69, p. 492 below, where corresponding figures are also given for 1924–1925 and 1925–1926.

[4] Yu. Larin, *Sotsial'naya Struktura SSSR* (1928), p. 4.

of the classifications adopted were, or could be, rigid. The number of workers recorded by the commission was higher than the total labour force recorded in the census of December 1926 or for these years in later returns.[1] The commission appears to have classified as workers members of peasant households who spent several months of the year in seasonal employment in the towns, mainly in building; trade union resistance to recognition of seasonal workers may have accounted for the tendency of trade union and Soviet statisticians to classify them as peasants. Within the peasantry similar uncertainties of classification prevailed. Most *batraks* had a plot of land, however small, which contributed to their subsistence; most poor peasants from time to time received payment, in money or in kind, for work done for less indigent peasants. The peasant employer of labour might be a *kulak* regularly employing several hired workers or a middle peasant with a subsistence economy who in a good year employed one or two casual workers to help with the harvest. Any classification of the population by class relied on lines drawn at some indeterminate point between these categories.

The issue of the distribution between classes and categories of the population of the national income was exposed to similar ambiguities. At the Communist Academy in September 1926 Smilga, then still a leading figure in Gosplan, deplored the absence from the 1926–1927 control figures of a class analysis of the growth of productive forces : " we wanted to include this material, but could not ".[2] The omission was repaired in the control figures for 1927–1928, which attempted to establish both the total incomes of different sectors of the population and the respective contributions of private and socialized production. The figures revealed a steady, but uneven, advance in the economy. Income from agriculture was slowly increasing, but declined relatively ; in 1926–1927 for the first time it accounted for less than 50 per cent of the national income. Income from the socialized sector increased faster than from the private sector, from the cooperative sector most rapidly of all. The total income of wage- and salary-earners increased both absolutely and relatively to that of other groups. The total income of the bourgeoisie remained stationary,

[1] See Vol. 1, Table No. 21, p. 955.
[2] *Vestnik Kommunisticheskoi Akademii*, xvii (1926), 197.

and declined relatively.[1] In September 1927, shortly before these calculations were available, the platform of the opposition, quoting sample figures compiled by the economic institute of Narkomfin, alleged that in 1926 average income per head of peasants had exceeded that of 1925 by 19 per cent, of workers by 26 per cent and of traders and industrialists by 46 per cent. An attempt was made to draw up a balance-sheet of the past two years :

> The general national income increased, the *kulak* strata in the country enlarged their resources with enormous rapidity, and the accumulations of the private capitalist, the merchant, the speculator grew by leaps and bounds. It is clear that the share of the working class in the general income of the country has fallen, at the same time that the share of other classes has grown.[2]

This attack led to a bitter controversy in the " discussion sheets " issued by *Pravda* in the weeks before the fifteenth party congress of December 1927.[3] The principal result of the exchange was to show up the irrelevance of a comparison between figures based on income per head and figures based on the income of a class ; the rise in the total income of wage- and salary-earners reported in the Gosplan control figures reflected an increase in the number of employed persons — primarily, no doubt, of industrial and building workers — not in individual wages. It also appeared that the traders and industrialists whose income, according to Narkomfin statistics, had risen by 46 per cent in 1926, were confined to those in the highest category of tax-payers, and that their income was only 0·90 per cent of the national income. It might have been pointed out that the Narkomfin calculations on which the opposition relied had been compiled before the intensive squeeze on the private trader and *entrepreneur*, by way of price controls and increasingly progressive taxation, inaugurated in 1926-1927,[4] had had time to take effect. By the time the opposi-

---

[1] See Table No. 70, p. 493 below. The volume of control figures for 1927-1928 carried the publication date 1928 ; but the figures appear to have been available in the autumn of 1927.

[2] L. Trotsky, *The Real Situation in Russia* (n.d. [1928]), pp. 29-30.

[3] See articles by Kon in *Pravda*, October 30, 1927, *Diskussionnyi Listok* No. 1, and by Lifshits and Kon *ibid*. December 1, 1927, *Diskussionnyi Listok* No. 10 ; for the discussion sheets see p. 39 above.

[4] See Vol. 1, pp. 686-688, 748-750.

tion platform was circulated, capitalist elements in the economy had already suffered doughty blows. A Sovnarkom commission at the end of 1927 estimated that " capitalists " (i.e. employers of hired labour) formed 8 per cent of the population, and received 14 per cent of the national income.[1] But the main conclusion which emerged from all these calculations was the fluidity and ambiguity of the categories employed, and the impossibility of using statistics of national income as material for a class analysis of Soviet society; as the compilers of the control figures observed in a note, " the crude groupings of population given in the table are manifestly inadequate for an investigation of a distribution of the national income ".[2]

(b) The Class Analysis

Marx, in a famous letter of 1852, claimed originality for his discovery, not of the class struggle, which others had recognized before him, but of the fact that " the existence of classes is bound up only with particular phases in the development of production".[3] From the vantage-ground of the middle years of the nineteenth century Marx looked back to the struggle, now almost complete in the most advanced countries, though still incomplete elsewhere, which had resulted in the overthrow of the old feudal order by the bourgeoisie, and forward to the struggle, hardly yet begun, which would result in the overthrow of the bourgeoisie by the proletariat; and he attributed these revolutionary changes, past and to come, to the " development of production " resulting from the rise of capitalism and the industrial revolution. This brilliant diagnosis illuminated many aspects of nineteenth-century history, and inspired the great revolutionary upheavals of the twentieth century. But Marx's vision of the future failed to take account of two unforeseen factors. In the first place, the twentieth-century upheavals occurred not in the most advanced countries where bourgeois capitalism had won its greatest triumphs, but in backward countries where the bourgeois revolution was still incomplete, and where the class situation therefore failed to conform to the Marxist

[1] *Na Agrarnom Fronte*, No. 4, 1928, p. 116.
[2] *Kontrol'nye Tsifry Narodnogo Khozyaistva SSSR na 1927–1928 god* (1928), p. 497.
[3] Karl Marx, Friedrich Engels, *Werke*, xxviii (1963), 507-508.

pattern. Secondly, by the time the upheavals occurred, further
developments in technology and organization had altered the
character of production and of the class struggles bound up with it
in such a way as to cast doubts on the unconditional validity of the
Marxist class analysis. A Marxist party schooled in intellectual
analysis was doctrinally bound to conduct its analysis in these
terms, and to follow the *Communist Manifesto* in postulating a progressive division of society into " two great antagonistic camps, two
great classes directly opposed to each other : bourgeoisie and proletariat ". In the Soviet Union, both the calculations derived from
the census and the strictures of the opposition were based on the
assumption of a well-defined class structure. It was this assumption which was increasingly called in question by the course of
events.

    The definition of the peasantry in terms of class had long been a
crux in Marxist thought.[1] The Mensheviks, who had never believed that the situation in Russia was ripe for a proletarian
revolution, could treat the Russian peasantry as a homogeneous
group, and identify it with the bourgeoisie. Bolshevik insistence
on the alliance with the main body of the peasantry could be
reconciled with the orthodox class analysis only by postulating the
existence of a class division within the peasantry, of a small top
layer of indisputably bourgeois well-to-do peasants, and of a large
mass of poorer peasants and *batraks* who, whatever their technical
class affiliation (only the *batraks* could really be classified as proletarian), remained faithful to the alliance with the proletariat.
This conception, which was reflected in the policies of war communism and the committees of poor peasants, was relegated to the
background after the introduction of NEP. " Face to the Countryside " and " Enrich yourselves " were slogans designed to appeal
to the peasantry as a whole, and to attenuate class divisions in the
countryside. Here too the ambiguous appeal of socialism in one
country played its part. Kalinin, reflecting at a party conference
of the North Caucasian region in November 1927 on the importance of " the mass of our ordinary people", who are not " pro-
letarians in a huge industrial factory ", blurted out a truth which

    [1] See *Socialism in One Country, 1924–1926*, Vol. 1, pp. 94-99.

sophisticated exponents of the official line would have veiled in more discreet language :

You will, of course, never make revolutionaries of these ordinary people, or imbue them with revolutionary-Marxist spirit.

On the other hand, just as the English worker believed " that there is nothing better than England ", so these ordinary people should be impregnated with the idea " that Soviet society is the best society in the world, that nothing at all in the capitalist states can compare with it ".[1] Socialism is one country, with its marked national overtones, presupposed the conciliation of the peasant — even of the well-to-do peasant — and the recognition of a common interest in the building of socialism. " The untrue, petty bourgeois ' theory of socialism in one country ' ", in the taunting words of the opposition declaration of the 83 of May 1927, enabled the majority to turn a blind eye to " the class content of the economic processes which are taking place ".[2]

The theoretical embarrassments of the party approach to the peasantry found expression in the scholastic controversy that revolved round the term " thermidor ". On the ninth thermidor 1793, Robespierre had been haled to the guillotine, the revolutionary machinery of economic controls had been dismantled, and an interlude of liberal rule, flying the spurious colours of the Girondins, had paved the way for Bonapartist dictatorship. Émigrés had hailed the Kronstadt rising in March 1921 as a " Russian thermidor " ;[3] and Trotsky, in the first months of NEP, had seen current economic policies as " concessions to the thermidorian mood and tendencies of the petty bourgeoisie, necessary for the purpose of maintaining the power of the proletariat ".[4] Appease-

---

[1] M. Kalinin, *Voprosy Sovetskogo Stroitel'stva* (1958), p. 353.

[2] For this declaration see pp. 25-26 above ; Bukharin was later accused by the majority of ignoring class divisions in the peasantry (see Vol. 1, pp. 250-251).

[3] See *Socialism in One Country, 1924–1926*, Vol. 1, p. 57.

[4] L. Trotsky, *Between Red and White* (CPGB, 1922), p. 77 ; the Russian original has not been traced. Lenin, in notes made by him for his report to the tenth party conference of May 1921 on the tax in kind, wrote : " Thermidor? Soberly, *it may be*, yes? Will be? We shall see " (Lenin, *Sochineniya* (5th ed.) xliii, 403) ; but this speculation does not appear in the record of the speech. Bukharin later at the seventh IKKI in December 1926 attributed the use of the

ment of the peasant was the essence of the alleged Soviet thermidor. In the middle nineteen-twenties, when Bukharin's policies seemed in the ascendant, it was common for the opposition leaders to regard themselves as the true Jacobins and to brand the majority as thermidoreans. The controversy came to a head in the summer of 1927, when *Pravda* published an article by Bukharin's disciple Maretsky on " The So-called ' Thermidor ' and the Danger of Degeneration ", denouncing Trotsky's " unheard of, slanderous accusation ".[1] It was reflected in the exchanges between Trotsky and Solts at the party central committee in August 1927,[2] and in the resolution adopted at the end of the session, which taunted the opposition with having been " compelled to keep silent about the deliberately slanderous allegation of the degeneration of the leadership, of its so-called ' thermidoreanism '".[3] Three months later Joffe, in his letter to Trotsky on the eve of his suicide, observed that the exclusion of Trotsky and Zinoviev from the party " must inevitably be the beginning of the thermidorian period of our revolution ".[4]

The thesis did not lack plausibility. What falsified the prognostications built on it was a sharp reversal of policy which, after the expulsion of the opposition from the party, led to a return to the divisive attitudes of war communism, to the proclamation of a renewed offensive against the *kulak*, and to faith in the class struggle within the peasantry as a guarantee of support from the mass of poorer peasants for the party line. Throughout 1928 shrill denunciation of the *kulak* as a class enemy was a staple theme of official propaganda. But it also became clear that this target was far too limited. Even when the category of *kulak* had been broadened to include the " well-to-do " peasant, many — if not most — of those who fell indubitably into the category of middle peasants manifested the same hostility as the *kulaks* to the sacrifices demanded of them in the interests of industrialization; and

term to Martov (*Puti Mirovoi Revolvutsii* (1927), i, 118); he went on to claim that a thermidor was unthinkable where the major instruments of production were under state control (*ibid.* ii, 607-608).

[1] *Pravda*, July 24, 29, 1927; an intended third instalment apparently never appeared. An anonymous memorandum commenting on the article is in the Trotsky archives, T 878.

[2] See p. 28 above.

[3] *KPSS v Rezolyutsiyakh* (1954), ii, 380.

[4] For this letter see p. 44 above.

even the poor peasants and the *batraks*, whose class support had been taken for granted, were weak and unreliable allies. What invalidated the class analysis was the hard fact that, when it came to the crunch, the vaunted class division in the peasantry proved less real than its class solidarity in resistance to the régime. Kaganovich, in a report of October 1928 on the forthcoming Soviet elections, while reasserting the fundamental necessity of the alliance with the peasantry, admitted that there were " current contradictions ", and that the *kulaks* were supported by " a small top layer of middle peasants whose attitude is unstable ". But he claimed, on the strength of quotations from Lenin, that such waverings were insignificant " given a firm proletarian policy ".[1] A commentator in the journal of TsIK at the same period was less complacent:

> We must not for a moment forget that the vast majority of the population of our country is petty bourgeois.[2]

The increasing pressures applied in 1928 and 1929 to secure supplies of food for the towns and factories, and to hasten the process of industrialization, were dramatized as a struggle against the bourgeoisie, in which the bourgeois label was affixed not only to *kulaks* or well-to-do peasants, but to all who resisted the policies of the party and the government. Determination to press forward with industrialization at breakneck speed brought with it, from 1928 onwards, the now inescapable need to treat the peasantry as the main source of primitive socialist accumulation. What followed could fairly be described as a struggle between town and country, or between the régime and the peasantry. It was a straining of language to call it a class struggle directed against the bourgeoisie.

But by what class, or on behalf of what class, was the struggle waged? The question revealed both the limitations of the class analysis and the embarrassments of a theory of proletarian revolution in a country where the proletariat was conspicuously weak.[3]

---

[1] *Vsesoyuznoe Soveshchanie po Perevyboram Sovetov v 1929 g.* (1928), pp. 26–28.

[2] *Sovetskoe Stroitel'stvo*, No. 11(28), November 1928, pp. 11-12.

[3] See *Socialism in One Country, 1924–1926*, Vol. 1, pp. 99-105.

The seizure of power had been effected by a proletarian party under non-proletarian leadership with the support of the peasants ; and doubts were expressed from the first, by Rosa Luxemburg among others, of the proletarian credentials of the revolutionary régime. The reorientation of the party from the destructive mission of revolution to the constructive task of state-building called for the development within its ranks, or for the recruitment from outside, of administrative, managerial and technical skills which both affected its outlook and still further blurred its integral class character. Embarrassed attempts, buttressed by references to the alliance of the peasantry and of sympathizers from other classes who had imbibed the proletarian ideology, to maintain the proletarian character of the régime were matched by policies of recruitment for the party. Efforts were constantly made to refurbish the image of the workers' party by increasing the intake of workers by social situation and especially of workers from the bench.[1] But pressures to admit to the party members of whatever group or category who performed important services to the régime were unabated. The official doctrine of the party underwent a similar extension :

> Our party is not a caste, i.e. a closed group of workers. It is a political organization admitting to its ranks scions of other classes, if they have wholly and completely gone over to the ideological position of the working class, if they are sincerely ready to serve the cause of communism.[2]

Nor was the homogeneity of the party itself promoted by its rising members. The essence of the increase of the proletarian sector of the population, revealed by the census and proudly proclaimed by Larin, was the recruitment into its ranks of a reserve army of peasants. But the peasant did not become a class-conscious proletarian on the day on which he was drafted to a factory or a building site. Extensive wage differentials militated against any realization of an ideological uniformity and solidarity

---

[1] See pp. 104-111 above.

[2] E. Smitten, *Sostav VKP(B)* (1928), p. 18 ; of the 319,051 party members employed at the time of the party census of 1927 in Soviet, economic, cooperative, trade union or other public organs, 50 per cent were workers by social situation, 10·7 per cent peasants and 39·3 per cent employees ; of candidates so employed 61·1 per cent were employees (*Kommunisty v Sostave Apparata Gosuchrezhdenii i Obshchestvennytkh Organizatsii* (1929), p. 11).

of the workers.   Bukharin among others had drawn attention to
the changing face of the proletariat and the presence in it of very
diverse elements.[1]   At the Moscow provincial party conference in
November 1927 he admitted that " regroupings are taking place
within the working class ", due in part to technological changes, in
part to the fact that people were joining it " who enter a factory
for the first time " ;   a process was at work which " unmakes our
basic classes, depeasantizes the peasant and deproletarianizes the
proletariat ".[2]   Official doctrine preserved the class hypothesis of a
revolutionary proletariat only by an increasingly unreal identification of the proletariat with the party, and of the party with the party
leaders — a form of " substitutism " which Trotsky had long ago
exposed.[3]

The opposition, firmly wedded to the class analysis, was acutely
conscious of the apparent decline in the revolutionary potentialities
of the proletariat.   Trotsky in an unpublished memorandum of
November 1926 had noted disquieting symptoms :

> It would be incorrect to ignore the fact that today the prole-
> tariat is far less receptive to revolutionary prophets and to broad
> generalizations than at the time of the October revolution and in
> the first years after it. . . . The young generation just growing up
> is without experience of the class struggle and of the necessary
> revolutionary hardening.[4]

In a letter to the party central committee of February 11, 1927,
he faced the grim fact that " the proletariat as a class is not always
equal to itself ", and that " ten years ago our proletariat was far
more cultivated than at present ", and attributed the passivity of
the workers to the failure of the revolution to live up to their
hopes and illusions, or to provide them with a standard of living
higher than they had enjoyed before it.[5]   The hypothesis of a

[1] See Vol. 1, p. 456.
[2] *Pravda*, November 24, 1927 ;   for Bukharin's diagnosis of the influence of
the Red Army on this process see p. 533 above. A less favourable view was
taken by the opposition : the flow of peasants into industry was " nothing like
the proletarianization of the peasantry ", but " smacks of the peasantization of
the proletariat " (*Byulletin' Oppozitsii* (Paris), No. 11, May 1930, p. 23).
[3] See *The Bolshevik Revolution, 1917–1923*, Vol. 1, p. 33.
[4] For this memorandum see p. 18, note 3 above.
[5] Trotsky archives, T 3029 ;   *Pravda*, April 3, 1927, quoted this letter from
" a leading representative of the opposition " as a symptom of " the opposition's
lack of faith ".

mass of class-conscious workers ready, in response to the appeal of
the opposition, to drive home the victory of the revolution and
proceed to the building of the new socialist order proved as illusory
as the Stalinist postulate of a class-divided peasantry. The small
class-conscious factory proletariat of 1917 could plausibly be said
to have served as the spearhead of the revolution. Some workers
in the factories survived from this proletarian élite to carry the
dynamic of revolution into the drive for industrialization. The
remarkable achievements of Soviet industrialization are indeed
scarcely explicable except on the hypothesis that the enthusiasm
which inspired the planners and directors percolated to some
strata of the workers. But the mass of the proletariat in the later
nineteen-twenties, decimated by the impact of revolution and civil
war, diluted by the large influx of untrained peasants from the
countryside, cowed by years of unemployment, innocent of the
class-consciousness and solidarity bred in the struggle against
capitalism, lacked both revolutionary initiative and power of
resistance to authority. It was too oppressed by the needs and
hardships of the present to have any vision of a future that could be
fought for; and the appeals of the opposition fell on deaf ears.
When, at the anniversary celebrations of the October revolution,
the opposition failed, in spite of the ardour of a small band of
devoted supporters, to break through the apathy of the mass of
workers, Trotsky's worst fears must have been confirmed or exceeded. The expulsion and exile of the opposition, once more
without provoking any significant proletarian reaction, not only
put an end to public controversy, but made it clear that profounder processes were at work than a bureaucratic distortion of
party policy.

It was Rakovsky who, writing in August 1928 from his exile in
Astrakhan to another member of the opposition, offered the fullest
analysis of the problem of " the passivity of the masses, including
the communist masses ". He began with the classic parallel of the
French revolution. The third estate, having overthrown the
ancien régime, itself broke up. This was due not only to class
differences within it, but to functional differences. Once the revolutionary party had taken power, some of the victors became the
new rulers; difference in function set them apart from their
former comrades, and changed the nature of the party. The

participation of the whole third estate in government was a myth. Even before thermidor, power had passed " into the hands of a constantly decreasing number of citizens ". When a class seized power in a revolution, " a certain part of this class is transformed into agents of that very power ". The unity which the class possessed so long as it was a victim of oppression was broken. This was what had also happened in the Russian revolution. Members of the proletariat had risen to responsible positions, and had been the beneficiaries of a new " social, if not economic, differentiation " (" automobiles, housing, regular holidays etc. "). Such people had " changed to such an extent that they have ceased, not only ' objectively ', but ' subjectively ', not only physically, but morally, to be members of the working class ", so that " the Soviet and party bureaucracy is a phenomenon of a new order ". The political education of a new ruling class is a slow and difficult business : " no class is born with the art of ruling ". At the other end of the scale, account must be taken of the harsh experiences of the past ten years ; " *neither physically nor morally* " had either the working class or the party remained the same. What proportion of those now working in industry were workers before the revolution? What proportion of the new recruits represented a " semi-proletarian, semi-peasant element " — even a " semi-*lumpen* element " ? Below these, a large mass of unemployed lived in penury on small state subsidies, begging, theft and prostitution. The Lenin enrolment of 1924 had brought into the party and the Komsomol a mass of members who had " no conception of what the party régime formerly was ". " The Bolshevik of 1917 would scarcely recognize himself in the Bolshevik of 1928 ". Salvation could be found only in the birth of a new class consciousness :

> Formerly this class consciousness was acquired in the struggle against capitalism, now it must be acquired by participating in the building of socialism.

Rakovsky ended on a note of pessimism. The party bureaucracy made any such participation " an empty sound " ; and any hope of reform which depended on the bureaucracy was " a utopia ".[1] Trotsky himself, though so passionate and restless a

Rakovsky's letter, and Valentinov's letter to which it is a reply, are in the Trotsky archives, T 2206, 1895 ; the former was published in *Byulleten' Oppozitsii* (Paris), No. 6, October 1929, pp. 14-20.

politican could not share Rakovsky's cool intellectual detachment, appeared to accept this diagnosis when, after his expulsion from the Soviet Union early in 1929, he described the opposition as based on the principle of "ideological separation", not of "mass action", and added that "this corresponds to the character of our period".[1]

The ambiguous course of the revolutionary process in the USSR was due, in part, no doubt, to its Russian heritage,[2] but mainly to the changed character of the period. The criterion of class, defined in the Marxist sense in terms of relation to the means of production, provided a convincing analysis of the dominant rôle of the bourgeoisie in nineteenth-century society. Marxism was the product of the bourgeois revolution and of the relation of the state to society postulated by the doctrines of *laissez-faire*. The bourgeoisie became the economically dominant class, and in virtue of this predominance wielded political power. Politics were the superstructure on an economic foundation; the political supremacy of capitalism was incidental and subsidiary to its economic supremacy. Before the end of the century political antagonisms had begun to impinge on the picture. The economy was no longer — even to the extent to which this had once been true — a self-contained entity operating in abstraction from the state. Engels, towards the end of his life, became increasingly ready to admit that the "economic movement" was "affected by the reaction of the relatively independent political movement which it has itself started", and that economic relations, though "ultimately decisive", were "influenced by other relations of a political and ideological kind".[3] The aid of the state was more and more openly invoked to shore up and stimulate a faltering capitalist economy. Economic predominance could now be achieved only

---

[1] *Byulleten' Oppozitsii* (Paris), No. 1-2, July 1929, p. 20.

[2] It may be argued that the long-standing hypertrophy of the Russian state, explained by the weakness of the estates in the feudal period and by the weakness of the nascent bourgeoisie in the nineteenth century, was perpetuated, through the weakness of the proletariat, after the revolution; Trotsky wrote of the Soviet bureaucracy as having "risen above a class which is hardly emerging from destitution and darkness, and has no tradition of dominion or command" (L. Trotsky, *The Revolution Betrayed* (Engl. transl. 1937), p. 235).

[3] Karl Marx, Friedrich Engels, *Werke*, xxxvii (1967), 490, xxxix (1963), 206.

through the acquisition of political power. Lenin more than once emphasized the priority of politics in the achievements of the October revolution.[1] Trotsky wrote that " the predominance of socialist over petty bourgeois tendencies " was guaranteed only " by political measures taken by the dictatorship ", and that " the character of the economy as a whole thus depends upon the character of the state power ".[2] The economic concept of a ruling class was replaced by the political concept of a ruling party or group. The shift was symptomatic of changing attitudes and policies. Both in party purges and in the deliverances of the courts class shed some of its importance as a relevant criterion.[3] By the end of the nineteen-twenties the class analysis had, in all but name, been allowed to drop out of sight.[4] The party became the institutional form of the hypothetical dictatorship of the proletariat.[5]

(c) The Industrial Revolution

The Marxist hypothesis of the sequence of bourgeois and socialist revolutions had dominated all Russian thinking on the character of the coming revolution. The " legal Marxists " were able to regard themselves as Marxists because they looked forward to a capitalist revolution in Russia. Lenin had always been something of a pragmatist on the relation between the two revolutions.

We all treat the bourgeois and socialist revolutions as opposites [he wrote in 1905], we all insist unconditionally on the need

---

[1] See *Socialism in One Country, 1924–1926*, Vol. 1, pp. 130-131 ; Molotov in 1937 explained that " socialism was completely victorious in the *political* sphere already in the October days of 1917 " (quoted in *Sovetskoe Gosudarstvennoe Pravo*, ed. A. Vyshinsky (1938), p. 91).

[2] L. Trotsky, *The Revolution Betrayed* (Engl. transl. 1937), p. 237.

[3] See pp. 147, 378-379, above ; for the playing down of the class principle in the 1925 constitution of the RSFSR and in subsequent discussions of the Ukrainian constitution see p. 195 above.

[4] Stalin, in introducing the new constitution of the USSR in November 1936, explained that, " the exploitation of man by man " having been liquidated, " the *class structure* " of Soviet society had changed ; that Soviet workers and peasants now constituted new classes of a hitherto unknown type ; and that " the boundaries between the working class and the peasantry, as well as between these classes and the intelligentsia, are being effaced, and the old class exclusiveness vanishes " (Stalin, *Sochineniya*, xiv (Stanford, 1967), 141-146).

[5] For the controversy about the dictatorship of the party see *The Bolshevik Revolution, 1917–1923*, Vol. 1, pp. 230-232 ; *Socialism in One Country, 1924–1926*, Vol. 2, pp. 4-5.

to distinguish strictly between them, but can it be denied that in history separate partial elements of one and the other revolution are intertwined ?[1]

In a letter to Inessa Armand of December 1916, having declared that " the socialist revolution is *impossible* without the struggle for democracy ", Lenin concluded that it was necessary to " *combine* the struggle for democracy and the struggle for the socialist revolution, *subordinating* the former to the latter ".[2] When he arrived at the Finland station in Petrograd in April 1917, he greeted the Russian revolution as the prelude to a " world-wide socialist revolution ".   In the April theses he propounded to a hesitant party the view that the leadership of the Russian revolution must be assumed by the proletariat and by the Bolsheviks on its behalf. But the theses disclaimed the idea that the introduction of socialism in Russia could be an immediate task.[3]   The small class-conscious Petrograd proletariat served as the spearhead of the victorious coup in October.   But the revolution confirmed the peasant in the individual possession of the land which he tilled ; this was essentially a bourgeois ideal.   The initial pronouncements of the victors described it as a " workers' and peasants' revolution " ; and " socialism ", if the word appeared at all, was referred to as a goal of the future, not as a present achievement.   Thus, the October revolution, though led by the proletariat, contained both bourgeois and proletarian elements ; it had the dual function of completing the bourgeois revolution and making the transition to the socialist revolution.   This was as true in industry as in agriculture.   Lenin on the eve of the October revolution had described " state monopoly capitalism " — the latest and most developed form of capitalism — as " a step on the road to socialism " ; and in the spring of 1918 he was content to use the term " state capitalism " for the industrial régime established by the revolutionary government and to hail it as a " step forward " and a " victory ".[4] The building of a socialist order in an isolated, predominantly peasant, industrially backward country was unthinkable.   It could be envisaged only in the context of a " world-wide socialist revolu-

---

[1] Lenin, *Sochineniya*, viii, 85.   [2] *Ibid.* (5th ed.) xliv, 346.
[3] See *The Bolshevik Revolution, 1917–1923*, Vol. 1, pp. 78-80.
[4] See *ibid.* Vol. 2, pp. 88-95, 276 ; for the controversy whether NEP was a form of state capitalism see *Socialism in One Country, 1924–1926*, Vol. 2, pp. 70-73.

tion ", in which the advanced industrial countries, whose industrial revolution lay far behind in the past, would play the leading rôle. Industrialization was an essential pre-requisite of socialist revolution.[1]

The restraints imposed by these scholastic distinctions, however well grounded, were difficult to maintain in the turmoil of revolution and its aftermath. The dissolution of the Constituent Assembly, where the Menshevik Tsereteli denounced " attempts to introduce a socialist economy in a backward country ", the break with the Left SRs, who represented the petty bourgeois aspirations of the peasantry, and the onset of the civil war, which ranged the bourgeois capitalist governments of the west against the revolutionary régime, all hastened the division of the world into the two hostile and embattled camps of bourgeois capitalism and proletarian socialism ; and this division, which confirmed the Marxist prognostication, seemed to make a mockery of any bourgeois programme still embedded in the Russian revolution, and drove it forward at headlong speed on the road to socialism. Lenin in an unpublished note of January 1918 wrote of " the concretization of the first steps to socialism ".[2] In the spring of 1918 he optimistically declared that Soviet Russia " in a few months " had passed through stages of the revolution " in which other countries spent decades ", and that " capitalism has grown up into socialism ".[3] The civil war brought with it the collapse of the currency, and a régime of requisitions and rationing ; these dire necessities were hailed, in the desperate mood of the moment, as socialist achievements and dubbed " war communism ". When the committees of poor peasants were set up in June 1918 — a measure designed to promote the extraction of grain surpluses from well-to-do peasants — Lenin described this as the " October (i.e. proletarian) revolution " in the countryside, and triumphantly proclaimed that, in adopting this measure, " we passed the boundary which separates the bourgeois from the proletarian revolution ".[4]

The committees were soon disbanded. The end of the civil war was followed by the introduction of NEP ; the policies of war

[1] For the dual character of the revolution see *The Bolshevik Revolution, 1917–1923*, Vol. 1, ch. 5, *passim*.

[2] Lenin, *Sochineniya*, xxx, 368.

[3] *Ibid.* xxii, 375, 378.

[4] See *The Bolshevik Revolution, 1917–1923*, Vol. 2, pp. 53-55.

communism were abandoned and discredited. The conciliation of
the peasant, who was encouraged to exploit his holding for his own
profit, continued throughout the middle nineteen-twenties. In
theory, this retreat should have been marked by a return to earlier
assessments of the ambiguous character of the revolution. But
diffidence seemed now out of place. The victorious revolution
had beaten off the attacks of the international bourgeoisie and its
Russian agents. NEP, though formally a retreat, was in fact the
signal for a fresh advance ; and this could only be an advance into
socialism. To doubt the proletarian and socialist credentials of
the revolution now seemed captious and unworthy — a lapse
into Menshevism. Six months after the introduction of NEP,
and in preparation for the fourth anniversary of the revolution,
Lenin again attempted to define the relation between the two
revolutions :

> We solved the problems of the bourgeois-democratic revolu-
> tion as we advanced, in passing, as a " by-product " of our main
> and genuine, *proletarian*-revolutionary, socialist work. Bour-
> geois democratic transformations . . . are a by-product of the
> proletarian, i.e. the socialist, revolution.

The bourgeois-democratic revolution would " grow into " the
proletarian-socialist revolution:

> The struggle, and only the struggle, will decide how far the
> latter will succeed in outgrowing the former.[1]

It remained to give concrete content to the transformation. This
meant a conversion from small-scale individual to large-scale
collective forms of agriculture — an advance into socialism. But
it also meant, first and foremost, a process of large-scale industrialization, which had been an essential part of the bourgeois
revolution in western countries, and might in Soviet conditions be
regarded as a completion of the bourgeois revolution. In May
1921 Lenin firmly declared large-scale industry to be " the real
and sole basis for strengthening resources, for creating socialist
society " ; and a few weeks later he repeated to the third congress
of Comintern that " the sole possible economic foundation of
socialism is large-scale machine industry ".[2]

---

[1] Lenin, *Sochineniya*, xxvii, 26.   [2] *Ibid*. xxvi, 390, 461.

It was natural for Marx, writing in the middle of the nineteenth century and in western Europe, to think of the industrial revolution, the outburst of technological innovation and economic expansion in which industrialization was the cardinal factor, as uniquely associated with the bourgeois revolution, the transition from feudalism to capitalism, from a pre-capitalist to a capitalist economy. Marx towards the end of his life, under pressure from his Russian disciples, was prepared to admit that Russia, given favourable conditions, might have the opportunity " of avoiding all the ups-and-downs of the capitalist order ", and that " contemporary Russian land tenure may be a starting-point for communist development ".[1] But Marx did not pursue the argument ; and the problems of an industrial revolution in a country which avoided the stage of capitalism were not considered by any Marxist thinker. This lacuna the makers of Soviet policy were now obliged to fill. Since nobody — and least of all Marx — pretended that the socialist order could be built on a peasant economy, it was apparent that the industrial revolution must also be carried on and completed, with all the resources of modern technology, as a condition of the realization of socialism. The European and American experiences of the nineteenth century could and would serve as a model for Soviet industrialization. But the new industrial revolution and the socialist revolution could be seen as two facets of a single process, reminiscent of the process of " uninterrupted " or " permanent " revolution. Industrialization, hitherto conceived as a product of the bourgeois revolution, became part of the proletarian revolution. The two stages were telescoped. The dilemma of the dual character of the October revolution could be circumvented. The attempt to fuse industrial and proletarian revolutions into a single entity, and to treat the former as an integral part of the latter, had a certain plausibility. Industrialization meant more and ever more jobs for more and more workers, and was accompanied by incessant glorification of the workers' rôle in building socialism and of the bright prospects that lay ahead. It was notorious, however much the fact might be obscured by official propaganda, that industrialization had brought higher living standards to the workers of advanced industrial countries. The industrial revolution, as an adjunct of bourgeois revolution, had led

[1] See *The Bolshevik Revolution, 1917–1923*, Vol. 2, pp. 388-390.

to the supremacy of the bourgeoisie and the creation of bourgeois society. The industrial revolution, as an element of the proletarian revolution, would lead to the supremacy of the proletariat and the creation of a classless society.

The hypothesis which sought to equate the Soviet industrial revolution with the bourgeois industrial revolutions of the past was, however, vitiated by several fallacies. The foundations of the industrial revolution in western Europe had been laid in advance by the rising economic power of the bourgeoisie ; industrialization was only a further and decisive step in this ascent. Industry was the conscious creation of individual bourgeois *entrepreneurs* acting in their own interests. Soviet industrialization in the nineteen-twenties was a collective enterprise inspired by desire to catch up with the west, and to provide the USSR with means of defence to counter the superior military and economic power of the western countries ; in these respects it was a continuation of the policies of industrialization half-heartedly pursued by Russia before 1914. It was inspired by the conviction, rooted in Marxist doctrine, that a socialist order could not be built in a predominantly peasant country, that advanced industrial development was a *sine qua non* for the fulfilment of this task, and that, in this sense, an industrial revolution must precede the consummation of a proletarian revolution. In these conditions, industry was not the conscious creation of the proletariat as it had been of the bourgeoisie ; it would be nearer the mark to say that the proletariat existed for the sake of industry. In a speech of November 1925 Kamenev made the odd and revealing remark that the party did not support the proletariat " because we particularly love the proletariat or regard the proletariat as anointed with some special oil ", but because it was better qualified than the peasantry to participate in the building of socialism.[1]

It followed that the party which waged and directed the struggle pursued policies designed to strengthen the country politically and economically rather than to promote specifically proletarian interests. The polarization between bourgeoisie and proletariat promoted by the nineteenth-century industrial revolution was now replaced by a polarization between those who planned and directed economic activities and those who carried them out. Marx's

[1] L. Kamenev, *Stat'i i Rechi*, xii (1926), 510.

attitude to management in industry was ambivalent. He admitted that " all combined labour on a large scale requires, more or less, a directing authority ", and compared this function to that of an orchestra conductor. This was *per se* " a productive job which must be performed in every combined mode of production ". But he assumed that the exploiting and antagonistic elements inherent in this directive function were a by-product of capitalism and the class system, and that in a classless socialist society this control would lose its antagonistic and oppressive character.[1] In a discarded draft of *The Civil War in France* he wrote that what was needed was " a new organization of production or, more correctly, the liberation of social forms of production from the fetters of slavery, from their existing class character, within the existing organization of labour (created by contemporary industry) ".[2] And Engels looked forward to " a state of affairs in which every member of society will be enabled to participate not only in production, but also in the distribution and management of social wealth ".[3] Nothing in the growing complexity of modern industrial technology, or in the practice of Soviet industry, validated these sanguine expectations. As time went on, Soviet workers were no less subject than other sectors of the population to the harsh pressures of industrialization. The quip that the dictatorship of the proletariat had been transformed into a dictatorship over the proletariat was not without point.

Yet another fallacy lurked in the analogy between the two industrial revolutions. In western Europe, mercantile capitalism and the ways of life and thought associated with it had made extensive inroads on the old order of society before an industrial revolution was thought of ; this was notably true of Great Britain, the home of that first industrial revolution. The slow rise of the bourgeoisie had promoted the assimilation by it of the whole range of contemporary culture and administrative experience, and a progressive fusion between it and substantial elements of the old ruling class. The bourgeoisie needed no preparatory schooling either for political or for industrial revolution ; the necessary skills were already within its grasp. The Russian proletariat lacked every kind of preparation. If Lenin was right in believing that the

---

[1] Karl Marx, Friedrich Engels, *Werke*, xxiii (1962), 350, xxv (1964), 397.
[2] *Ibid.* xvii (1964), 546.   [3] *Ibid.* xix (1962), 104.

THE SOVIET STATE

proletariat could not make a revolution without an intellectual élite
to provide leadership and to imbue it with class consciousness, it
was even more certain that the proletariat, once its victory had
been proclaimed, needed similar and stronger reinforcements for
the exercise of economic and political power. Lenin declared, in
one of his last public speeches, that " years and years " would
have to pass before the proletariat would be able to raise its administration to " higher stages of culture " ;[1] when already on his
sickbed, he concluded that " the political and social revolution has
become the predecessor of a cultural revolution ".[2] In his last
published article he cautiously admitted that " we do not have
sufficient civilization to enable us to pass straight on to socialism,
though we have the political requisites for it ".[3] This did little to
support the analogy between proletarian and bourgeois revolutions.
The victorious Soviet proletariat of the nineteen-twenties lacked
the equipment which had enabled the victorious bourgeoisie of an
earlier epoch to consolidate its victory. It was not, and could not
be, a ruling class in the sense in which the bourgeoisie had been a
ruling class.[4] The dictatorship of the proletariat, which was to
occupy the interval till classes disappeared altogether, was a
political myth.

The third and most significant fallacy of the analogy was, however, its failure to distinguish between different historical periods.
The industrial revolutions of continental Europe, though inspired
by the example of the English industrial revolution, diverged from
it in significant respects. In England, the independent efforts of
a large number of individual *entrepreneurs* had built the formidable, but mainly haphazard, structure of English industry. But
this pattern could not be repeated. In mid-nineteenth-century
Europe, industrialization already called for more advanced technology, larger capital investment, and more complex organization ;
and this required a far greater measure of calculated, collective

---

[1] Lenin, *Sochineniya*, xxvii, 321.
[2] *Ibid.* xxvii, 397.
[3] *Ibid.* xxvii, 417.
[4] Bukharin at the fourth congress of Comintern in 1922 drew a sharp distinction " between the maturing of capitalism and that of socialism ", and
attacked " the stupid idea that we can mature in bourgeois society in the same
way as the capitalists did in feudal society " (*Protokoll des Vierten Kongresses
der Kommunistischen Internationale* (1923), p. 415).

planning, provided primarily by the banks.   In the incipient Russian industrial revolution of the eighteen-nineties a further stage was reached.   The motive of industrialization was not private profit, but national interest; it was the work predominantly not of individual *entrepreneurs*, but of large units; the main impetus came not from the bourgeoisie, or from any sector of it, but from the state.   The march of history had radically changed, and in some respects inverted, the original features of the industrial revolution.

When the Soviet leaders embarked on the task of industrialization, the notion of retracing the path of the bourgeois industrial revolution was no longer valid.   The desire of the " legal Marxists " to hasten the day when Russia would become ripe for the bourgeois revolution was misconceived and obsolete.   The world had passed beyond that stage, which could not be recalled or repeated.   Any analysis based on a comparison and contrast between the bourgeois concept of industrial revolution and the industrial revolution carried out in the Soviet Union which treated the latter as a distorted version of the former, and led to the conclusion that the strains of Soviet industrialization could have been avoided by a closer approximation to western models, was fundamentally misplaced.   Industrial revolution was now indissolubly associated with the conception of a national plan; and, since planning was an accepted and much advertised instrument of socialist, as well as of national, policy, the doctrine of socialism in one country provided a solid bridge.   The word socialism was, in fact, used ambiguously; and much of the controversy with the opposition about the building of socialism in the Soviet Union turned on this ambiguity.   The Soviet industrial revolution firmly rejected the bourgeois pattern of industrial revolution, and was based on the conception of central planning in the collective interests of the society.   In this sense its socialist credentials were impeccable, and the scepticism of the opposition was unjustified. But, in the sense in which socialism was identified with the aims or achievements of the proletariat, and proclaimed social equality as the goal, it could not be called socialist.   " The correct policy of the workers' state ", Trotsky observed, " cannot be reduced *only* to national economic construction ".[1]   This was not a proletarian

[1] *Byulleten' Oppozitsii* (Paris), No. 36-37, October 1933, pp. 2-3.

revolution — not merely in the sense in which the original industrial revolution was bourgeois, but in any immediately recog-
nizable sense at all. What Marx and Lenin meant by a proletarian
revolution, and what the Russian revolution failed to achieve, was a
process of human emancipation which would abolish exploitation,
not a revolution which would expose the masses to new forms of
inequality and new forms of bureaucratic organization and oppression.[1]

This new-style industrial revolution, therefore, though in some
senses socialist, could not be labelled either bourgeois or proletarian. The driving force which animated it was a politically
oriented and organized ruling group, whose core consisted of a
small circle of party leaders by whom major decisions of policy
were taken. In the later nineteen-twenties this circle found its
institutional centre in the Politburo, later in the personal entourage
of Stalin. But top political leaders, or even a single leader, cannot
function in isolation. They require not only the assured support
of army and police to maintain their authority against any threat
to order, but also the active cooperation of a ruling group, which
executes, interprets and supplements their decisions, and deter-
mines the day-to-day policy of the régime. As in any complex
society, the ruling group in the Soviet Union was necessarily
large, and was composed of men of very diverse skills and qualifications. It included not only those holders of key party and
Soviet posts, who were personally appointed by the central party
organs,[2] but administrators and managers, technicians and members of the professions, scientists and writers. Most of them were
not publicly known outside their special fields; and they were
united only in their determination to serve the régime, and to
direct those under their authority in the sense demanded by it.
These " leading cadres (rukovodyashchie kadry) ", who were not
always workers by social situation, and rarely workers by occupation, were the artificers of the industrial revolution and the leaders
of the society created by it. Standing beneath the top leaders, but
above the vast bureaucracy of clerical workers, the social status of

[1] Stalin in 1931, defending wage differentials, declared the " equalization "
or " levelling " (uraonilovka) had " nothing in common with Marxist socialism ", belonging exclusively to the highest stage of communism (Stalin,
Sochineniya, xiii, 118-119).
[2] See *Socialism in One Country, 1924–1926*, Vol. 2, p. 205.

this group had some analogies to that of a nineteenth-century ruling class.[1] But they were in no sense an economic class. It is true that they enjoyed extensive economic privileges. But an economically privileged situation was no longer, as in western bourgeois society, the foundation of political power. It was conferred by political power ; and some economic privileges were granted to rank-and-file members of the party and even to non-party " activists " — the reward earned by their loyal support of the ruling group.

The Soviet industrial revolution inaugurated under these auspices by the first five-year plan was comparable in magnitude with the industrial revolutions of the west, but was carried out in different conditions, by different methods, and at a more rapid tempo. It was an economic revolution directed by the political decisions and initiative of a ruling group. The laws of the market and the profit motive, which had served to set in motion the primitive processes of early industrialization, were no longer adequate to the scale and complexity of modern industrial technology ; planned investment from public funds was required for initial, but not immediately remunerative, projects. Consumer sovereignty — now a tarnished myth even in capitalist economies — was replaced by official planning. In a country where peasants living at subsistence level formed a large majority of the population, the integration of the peasant into industrial society was the work not of indirect economic compulsions, but of direct political coercion. The Marxist conception of the dying away of the political controls of the state, while economic controls were maintained and organized on a cooperative basis,[2] was thinkable only in a world where politics and economics appeared as separate or separable entities. It had no application in a world where economic ends were achieved by political dictates and political controls. A resolution of the sixteenth party conference of April 1929, which approved

[1] Somewhat fanciful similarities have even been detected in their aesthetic attitudes : a moralizing literature, a strictly representational art, and an ostentatious architecture.

[2] See p. 441 above. This assumption was rarely discussed in the Soviet period ; but Manuilsky told the sixth congress of Comintern in 1928 that only the political functions of the state would die away, and the " functions of social planning and control ", which had no counterpart in the capitalist state, would remain (*Stenograficheskii Otchet VI Kongressa Kominterna* (1929), v, 35).

the first five-year plan, oddly bracketed the state with the party and the proletariat as the new directors of economic policy:

The supreme historical task of constituting a socialist society, which confronts the dictatorship of the proletariat, imperatively demands the concentration of the forces of party, state and working class on questions of economic policy.[1]

Belief in a strengthening of state power for the achievement of economic ends was inherent in all planning.

After the end of the nineteen-twenties, the revolution fell easily into the pattern of " revolution from above ". The phrase appears to have been a coinage of 1848,[2] when a mass revolutionary movement was defeated, and revolutionary changes were effected from above. Marx in an article of 1859 embroidered the text that " reaction carries out the programme of revolution ", and concluded that Louis Napoleon had become " the executor of the revolution of 1789 ".[3] Engels in a letter to Kautsky of 1882 commented that " the *real*, not the illusory, tasks of a revolution are always accomplished as the result of the revolution ", and that Louis Napoleon, Cavour and Bismarck had been " the testamentary executors of the revolution ", in the sense that they had completed " the restoration of the oppressed and divided nationalities of central Europe, in so far as these were viable and specifically ripe for independence " ; the importance of this was that " an international movement of the proletariat is in general possible only

---

[1] *KPSS v Resolyutsiyakh* (1954), iii, 195 ; this prepared the way for Stalin's famous re-definition of the dying away of the state at the sixteenth party congress in 1930. For the coalescence of state and party institutions see pp. 130-131 above.

[2] See *Socialism in One Country, 1924–1926*, Vol. 1, p. 9, note 2.

[3] Karl Marx, Friedrich Engels, *Werke*, xiii (1964), 414 ; Engels remarked that " the very people who crushed it [i.e. the revolution] became — as Karl Marx used to say — its executors " (*ibid.* xxi (1962), 193). Marx elaborated in another context the same notion of a vicarious revolution from above: " England, it is true, in causing a social revolution in Hindustan, was actuated only by the vilest interests, and was stupid in her manner of enforcing them. But that is not the question. The question is, Can mankind fulfil its destiny without a fundamental revolution in the social condition of Asia? If not, whatever may be the crimes of England, she was the unconscious tool of history in bringing about that revolution " (*ibid.* ix (1960), 133 ; the same point is repeated *ibid.* ix, 226).

among independent nations ".[1]   In his critique of the Erfurt programme of the German Social-Democratic Party of 1891, he wrote
that the " revolution from above " of 1866 and 1870 must be
not reversed, but completed and extended " from below ".[2]   In
the last year of his life he reverted to the theme, with reference
to the period after the Bonapartist *coup d'état* of December
1851, in his preface to a new edition of Marx's *Class Struggles in
France*:

> The period of revolutions from below was concluded for
> the time being; there followed a period of revolution from
> above.

Bismarck in 1866 had, he concluded, imitated Louis Napoleon
with " his *coup d'état*, his revolution from above ", and " the
grave-diggers of the revolution of 1848 had become the executors
of its will ".[3]   It would be misleading to read into these passages
more than an acceptance of " revolution from above " as a temporary surrogate for " revolution from below " in a period when
the prospect of direct action by the masses had faded.   Marx, in
The Civil War in France, described the second empire as " the only
possible form of government at a time when the bourgeoisie had
already lost the capacity to rule the nation, and the working class
had not yet acquired that capacity ".[4]   Lenin, who set out to
revive and rehabilitate the revolutionary aspects of Marxism, never
lost his faith in the masses; and it may be significant that his only
reference to " revolution from above " was a quotation from the
passage in which Engels had envisaged it as something to be supplemented by a " movement from below ".[5]   It may be true that
Lenin's conception of the party vanguard which would instil revolutionary consciousness into the masses contained hidden seeds of
" revolution from above ".   But Lenin believed to the end of his
life that the benefits of a completed bourgeois democratic revolution could be reaped only through the process of a proletarian
socialist revolution.   Any notion of a latent incompatibility between them would have been firmly rejected.

In the later nineteen-twenties subtle changes occurred in the

---

[1] Karl Marx, Friedrich Engels, *Werke*, xxxv (1967), 269-270.
[2] *Ibid.* xxii (1963), 236.   [3] *Ibid.* xxii (1963), 516.
[4] *Ibid.* xvii (1964), 338.   [5] Lenin, *Sochineniya*, xxi, 419.

picture. The original concept, inherited by Lenin from Marx, of a
proletarian or socialist revolution from below, was insensibly
merged, and submerged, in the Stalinist industrial revolution from
above; and this process provides the key to the enigmatic period
of the first five-year plans, and to the rôle of Stalin as the representative figure of the period. The industrial revolution and the collectivization of agriculture marched hand in hand; it was to the
latter that Stalin incautiously applied the term " revolution from
above ".[1] Stalin's personality, combined with the primitive and
cruel traditions of Russian bureaucracy, imparted to the revolution
from above a particularly brutal quality, which has sometimes
obscured the fundamental historical problems involved. Stalin,
in driving forward the industrial revolution at breakneck speed, in
constantly urging the need to catch up with the west, proved a
more pertinacious, more ruthless and more successful revolutionary than any of the other party leaders: this certainly accounted
for the support he received over a long period.[2] But Stalin also —
and again more consistently and more callously than any other
leader — broke the accepted link between the industrial revolution
from above and the proletarian revolution from below. It was no
longer quite clear in what sense the régime stood for revolution at
all. Varga, franker and less cautious than any of the politicians,
blurted out the uncomfortable truth at the sixth congress of Comintern in 1928, at the moment when the first five-year plan was
taking shape:

> In capitalist countries we are *for revolution*; in the USSR
> we are *for evolution*, for internal peace, for peaceful develop-
> ment towards socialism.[3]

[1] The designation of collectivization as a " revolution from above " first
appeared in *History of the Communist Party of the Soviet Union: Short Course*
(Engl. transl. Moscow, 1939), p. 305, and was repeated by Stalin in his essay of
1950 on linguistics (*Sochineniya*, xvi (Stanford, 1967), 142).

[2] Recognition of Stalin's revolutionary rôle was the issue on which the
opposition split in 1928 (see pp. 67-68, 99 above). When Trotsky in 1926
called Stalin " the grave-digger of the revolution " (see p. 17 above), he had
perhaps forgotten the quotation from Engels in which the grave-diggers of
revolution become " the executors of its will "; but in a letter of May 9, 1928,
to his supporters in exile, he compared Stalin with enemies of revolution who
were none the less obliged to carry out parts of a revolutionary programme
(Trotsky archives, T 3112).

[3] *Stenograficheskii Otchet VI Kongressa Kominterna* (1929), v, 3-4.

In action, Stalin exploited the worker as mercilessly and as contemptuously as he exploited the peasant. He drove into opposition, crushed, and finally exterminated the old party leaders of the school of Lenin, who remained faithful to the ideal of proletarian revolution, and believed in industrial revolution as an integral, but subsidiary, part of it. The most conspicuous victims of Stalin's purges at all levels were old party men who could not stomach Stalin's flouting of their revolutionary faith. The purges had more of the aspect of a " white " than of a " red " terror ; their principal author stood out in the guise of a counter-revolutionary monster. Those who argued that no thermidor was conceivable in a country whose large-scale production was under direct state control [1] ignored the dual character of the revolution and the presence of thermidorian elements in the revolutionary state itself. Stalin presented to the Russian revolution, and presents to history, two contrasting faces : revolutionary and counter-revolutionary. This was the ambiguous character of the period. Engels's diagnosis of the historical rôle of Napoleon III, Cavour and Bismarck, who, by pursuing reactionary policies and by donning military uniform, brought to fruition the capitalist revolution in their respective countries, provided a curious analogy. The grandiloquence of Napoleon III, the cynical diplomacy of Cavour, and the blood-and-iron discipline of Bismarck were all reflected in the dictatorship of Stalin.

The ambiguous character of the revolution explained the marked differences in its impact on eastern and western countries. Lenin in his last published article detected the revolutionary potentialities of " countries drawn into civilization for the first time by the war, the countries of the whole east, the non-European countries ", and thought that Russia might be destined to mediate to them the revolutionary experience of the west.[2] When in the later nineteen-twenties the Soviet Union began to extend its influence in Asia, the impact was that of a vigorous nation in the throes of a process of industrialization, which might serve as an example and inspiration to less advanced countries eager to tread the same path. For these countries, where the prospects of a bourgeois revolution were illusory, and a proletarian revolution would have

[1] See p. 427, note 4 above.
[2] See *Socialism in One Country, 1924–1926*, Vol. 3, p. 612.

been a meaningless conception, an industrial revolution had a high place on the agenda. In advanced western countries with a developed and organized working class, where the Marxist scheme envisaged a proletarian revolution, the influence of the Russian revolution was different and largely negative. The conception, embodied in the Communist International, of leadership offered by the weak and backward Russian proletariat to the more prosperous and more sophisticated working classes of the west was foredoomed to failure.   In countries whose industrial revolutions already belonged to history, the appeal of the Soviet achievement was not to workers whose standards of life and civilization were far ahead of those of the indigent and relatively backward Soviet Union, but to economists, politicians and captains of industry interested in planning and productivity. Japan, the one Asian country to share the western experience of industrialization, conformed in its reactions to the Russian revolution to the western pattern. What impressed everywhere in the Soviet achievement was the new-style industrial revolution ; what misfired, and constantly tarnished the achievement, repelling those who had at first been impressed by it, was the illusory proletarian revolution.

The oddly distorted amalgam of bourgeois and socialist revolutions which issued in the Russian industrial revolution presented problems which might have proved insuperable even in a more propitious environment. The first bourgeois industrial revolution, also conducted without benefit of foreign capital, but dispersed and unplanned in its incidence, had also involved the widespread dragooning of a reluctant peasantry. Engels, in canvassing the prospects of a capitalist revolution in Russia, predicted to a Russian correspondent in 1893 that the horrors of this revolution would be even greater than those of the capitalist revolutions of the west :

> The passage from primitive agrarian communism to capitalist industrialism cannot take place without a terrible dislocation of society, without the disappearance of whole classes and their transformation into other classes ; and what enormous suffering and waste of human lives and productive forces that necessarily implies, we have seen — on a smaller scale — in western Europe.[1]

[1] Karl Marx, Friedrich Engels, *Werke*, xxxix (1968), 149.

The sufferings inflicted by a bourgeois industrial revolution could be attributed to blind economic laws or to unscrupulous individuals. The Soviet industrial revolution, shaped by modern technology and modern economic organization, seemed to owe its oppressive actions to calculated decisions by central planners and party leaders; and this, combined with the far harsher and more primitive social and political conditions in which the revolution took place, imparted to it its particularly bleak and inhuman character. At the end of the nineteen-twenties all that was left of the original revolutionary faith was the belief that intensive indus-trialization would in the long run increase material well-being in such a way as to mould a completely new society, which would assign to the former oppressed classes an enhanced and dominant rôle; and this appeal to the dual aim of this hybrid revolution — material progress and the emancipation of the oppressed — was fortified by appeals to the cause of national defence against the menace of hostile Powers and to the cause of backward peoples throughout the world. The outcome of the Soviet industrial revolution was remarkable enough to prevent the historian from dismissing this faith as wholly vain. It had brought, and would bring, to millions of men and women new ways of life, new oppor-tunities and new hopes for themselves and their children. Yet, at this very moment of its inauguration, the darkest period of Soviet experience was just looming on the horizon — the unremitting daily pressure on the lives of the workers, the ruthless war against the peasantry, the decimation of the intelligentsia, and the cruel and capricious personal dictatorship. Seldom, perhaps, in history has so monstrous a price been paid for so monumental an achieve-ment.

NOTE F

THE ACADEMY OF SCIENCES

DURING this period the prestige of the Communist Academy, notwithstanding its name and affiliations, was still overshadowed by that of the
old Russian (formerly Imperial) Academy of Sciences. Before the civil
war, and before the foundation of the Communist Academy, the cooperation of the Academy of Sciences, with Lenin's approval and encouragement, had already been sought for in the earliest stages of
planning.[1] Mutual suspicion stood, however, in the way of any lasting
link between the Soviet authorities and the academy, which carried on
its work in undisturbed, but ineffective, isolation till 1925. In that year
the academy was due to celebrate its 200th anniversary ; and, at a time
when the Soviet Government had begun to woo Soviet intellectuals, and
was also eager to conciliate foreign opinion, it decided to participate in
the projected ceremonies and to turn them to good account. In July
1925 a decree was published which recognized the academy as " the
supreme scientific institution of the USSR ".[2] Many Soviet notables
attended the celebrations in September ; and Zinoviev, before an
audience which included a large number of distinguished foreign guests,
delivered an oration hymning the glories of the academy and the prospects of Soviet science.[3] The laudatory article on the academy in the
first volume of the Soviet encyclopaedia, published in 1926, was written
by Oldenburg, an elderly scientist who had been permanent secretary of
the academy since 1904.[4]

This flattering recognition was bought at a price. The position of
the academy was plainly anomalous. At the time of the anniversary
celebrations Lunacharsky had expressed the view that, " as the academy
enters its third century, the question should be squarely put of some
kind of radical Sovietization". [5] Now that the policy of industrialization

[1] See *The Boslhevik Revolution*, 1917–1923, Vol. 2, p. 366.
[2] *Sobranie Zakonov, 1925*, No. 48, art. 351 ; " science ", in accordance with
European usage, includes all branches of learning.
[3] See *Socialism in One Country, 1924–1926*, Vol. 1, p. 122.
[4] *Bol'shaya Sovetskaya Entsiklopediya*, i (1926), 783-790 ; for an article by
Oldenburg on the services of the academy to the Soviet Union see *Izvestiya*,
October 22, 1927.
[5] *Novyi Mir*, No. 10, October 1925, p. 110.

had been proclaimed, all available resources must be harnessed to this task. The first intervention in the affairs of the academy took the form of a demand for an up-to-date statute to replace the long obsolete Tsarist instrument. The question was first mooted in the autumn of 1926 ; in February 1927 a commission of the academy drafted a new statute. This was discussed at a meeting of Sovnarkom on May 31, 1927, and approved by a general assembly of the academy a week later. It was issued in the form of a decree of Sovnarkom on June 18, 1927. This placed the academy under the direct authority of Sovnarkom, to which it was to submit annual plans of work and reports on its activities. A presidium was to be formed of the president, the two vice-presidents, the permanent secretary, and the secretaries of the two sections (mathematical-physical sciences and humanities) into which the academy was divided. The statute raised the number of members from 45 to 70 — an obvious preparation for the introduction of academicians more acceptable to the authorities.[1] In April 1928 the statute was amended by two further resolutions of Sovnarkom, the formality of approval by the academy being this time apparently omitted. The number of members was raised from 70 to 85 ; and 12 chairs were assigned to the historical sciences, four to the socio-economic sciences, and two to philosophy.[2]

The plan now was clearly to break the monopoly of academicians committed, almost to a man, to the traditions of the pre-revolutionary régime. Vyshinsky entered the fray with an article declaring that the academy must serve the cause of socialist construction, and condemning the *clichés* " that science is ' free ', that science cannot work to order, that ' social command ' is alien to the nature of scientific activity ".[3] The council of the newly created All-Union Association of Scientific and Technical Workers (Varnitso) criticized the academy for failing to coordinate the work of the two institutions, and for neglect of philosophical, social, economic and literary questions. It hailed the proposed increase in the number of academicians and chairs as " first steps . . . designed to bring the academy closer to Soviet public life ".[4] Protests appeared in the press against the failure of the academy to expel

[1] *Sobranie Zakonov, 1927*, No. 35, art. 367 ; for the events leading up to its adoption see L. Graham, *The Soviet Academy of Sciences and the Communist Party* (1967), pp. 82-85 — an account based on unpublished archives. The favour shown to the Academy of Sciences at this time in the form of grant of a million rubles to conduct scientific investigations in Kazakhstan and Yakutia provoked a jealous comment from Ryazanov on behalf of the Communist Academy (*Vestnik Kommunisticheskoi Akademii*, xxvi (2), (1928), 253-254).

[2] *Sobranie Zakonov, 1928*, No. 22, arts. 197, 198.

[3] *Izvestiya*, May 6, 1920.

[4] *Ibid.* May 25, 1928 ; for Varnitso see Vol. 1, pp. 583-584.

Struve, who had emigrated to Belgrade, and was engaged in bitter propaganda against the Soviet Government.[1] A writer in *Pravda*, repeating the same charge, pointed out that of all Soviet institutions " only the Academy of Sciences has preserved its former aspect without the slightest change ".[2] It was now decided to infiltrate a substantial number of communists into the academy at the forthcoming election of members. The struggle was carried on in the tense atmosphere created by the grain collections crisis, the increasing pressures of industrialization and the Shakhty affair. Early in 1928 the Politburo appointed a party commission to supervise the election. Since Leningrad was still the seat of the academy, the commission was composed of party members from Leningrad, and was apparently responsible to the Leningrad regional party committee. The number of vacancies in the academy was 42. " Social organizations " of all kinds were invited to propose candidates ; and in this way nominations were obtained for a number of prominent party figures.[3] In October 1928 all the nominations were considered by 11 commissions representing different branches of learning, in which members of the academy were joined by official Soviet delegates. The selection of the 42 candidates whose names were to go forward to the general assembly of the academy was a matter of hard bargaining. But the list eventually agreed on included all the party nominees.[4]

The hard core of old academicians, which had hitherto fought a delaying action, now had its last fling. The formal election took place

---

[1] *Izvestiya*, April 14, July 21, 1928.   [2] *Pravda*, October 18, 1928.

[3] *Izvestiya*, June 3, 1928, published a list of candidates, including Bukharin, Pokrovsky, the Marxist philosopher Deborin, the Marxist literary critic Friche, the chemist Bakh, the geneticist Vavilov, Ryazanov and the planners Krzhizhanovsky and Osadchy.

[4] *Izvestiya*, October 23, 1928 ; for an account derived mainly from unpublished archives see L. Graham, *The Soviet Academy of Sciences and the Communist Party* (1967), pp. 89-103. Enkidze was president of a commission of Sovnarkom for the affairs of the academy, and visited Leningrad in that capacity on October 1, 1928 (*Izvestiya*, October 2, 1928). Bukharin represented the party in these negotiations ; in a speech on " Lenin and the Problem of the cultural Revolution " delivered on the fourth anniversary of Lenin's death, he made a curious excursion into wishful thinking about the mood of the old academicians : " We have serious biologists among our elder scientists who enthusiastically discuss the question of the Marxist dialectic in the realm of biology. Physics, chemistry, physiology are overtaken by the same flood. The same must be said of reflexology, psychology, pedagogy. There is even a mathematical society which discusses the question of Marxist methods in mathematics " (*Pravda*, January 27, 1928). An account of the scientific activities of the academy in *SSSR: God Raboty Pravitel'stva 1927–28* (1929), pp. 484-487, made only the briefest reference to " the new elections of members of the academy, which had not been completed at the end of 1928 ".

in the general assembly of the academy on January 12, 1929 ; and, while most of the candidates got through, three party nominees — Deborin, Friche, and Lukin, a Marxist historian — failed to secure the statutory two-thirds majority. The fury aroused in party circles by this rebuff evidently frightened the academicians. The presidium hastily drafted a petition to Sovnarkom to be allowed, in derogation from the statute, to hold a fresh election ; and, after a heated debate, the sending of the petition was approved by the general assembly on January 17, 1929, by a majority of 26 to 9 with 4 abstentions.[1] The struggle was now over. When the three names were re-submitted to the general assembly on February 13, 1929, only one or two die-hards troubled to vote against them.[2] Later in the year an extensive purge of the staff of the academy was undertaken.[3]

The sequel of these events was surprising. The academy acquired the new prestige accruing to a Soviet institution without altogether losing the old prestige of its scientific eminence. In 1934 it transferred its seat to Moscow. The presence of two major academies in the same city was plainly an anomaly ; and by this time the Communist Academy, manned by stalwart party intellectuals of whom many had now fallen out of favour, was under a cloud. When in 1936 the decision was taken to merge the two academies, it was the All-Union (formerly Imperial) Academy of Sciences which retained its name and was clearly the senior partner in the amalgamation.

[1] *Izvestiya*, January 25, 1929.

[2] *Ibid.* February 14, 1929 ; L. Graham, *The Soviet Academy of Sciences and the Communist Party* (1967), pp. 110-114. The text of the petition and the decision of Sovnarkom to approve it were published in *Pravda*, February 6, 1929 ; for an indignant article protesting against the failure of the academy to keep up with modern scientific achievements, and warning it to " cease to be a state within a state ", see *ibid.* February 1, 1929.

[3] L. Graham, *The Soviet Academy and the Communist Party* (1967), pp. 121-127.

NOTE G

PEASANT COMMITTEES OF MUTUAL AID

THE problem of building up in the countryside organizations through which party and Soviet influence should be extended over the poorer strata of the peasantry led to further efforts being made to revive the unsatisfactory peasant committees of mutual aid (krestkomy or KKOV).[1] A decree of the RSFSR of March 29, 1926, provided that land should be placed at the disposal of krestkomy, without payment and for an indefinite period, for purposes of collective cultivation.[2] The fourth all-Russian congress of krestkomy in May 1926 recommended the collective cultivation of land with tractors and other machines as a source of revenue for the committees and as an example for the peasantry as a whole, and sought to end the practices of leasing land and hiring labour ; it also demanded the "dekulakization " of the committees. Another resolution of the congress described the committees as " an elementary school for that part of the population which is not yet in the cooperatives ", and called on them " to develop the independence of the peasants, and to aid the extension of collectivization in the countryside ". Krestkomy were to be organized by the village *skhod* ; this was apparently interpreted to mean that all members of the *skhod* should be automatically enrolled.[3] A long report on the committees at this time showed that their revenue came not from members' subscriptions, but from small industrial enterprises — local workshops producing implements or working up agricultural products : these were exempt from taxation. But party and Soviet leadership in the krestkomy was criticized as " thoroughly bad " ; and the impression remained that these were semi-moribund institutions.[4] A delegate to the session of the TsIK of the RSFSR in November 1926 spoke of the krestkomy in the North Caucasian region as small and neglected organizations which " help other bigger organizations in the restoration of agriculture and,

[1] See Vol. 1, p. 142 ; *Socialism in One Country, 1924–1926*, Vol. 2, pp. 466-467.
[2] *Sobranie Uzakonenii, 1926*, No. 28, art. 219.
[3] *Izvestiya*, June 1, 1928 ; *Bednota*, June 10, 1926 ; *Na Agrarnom Fronte*, No. 7-8, 1926, pp. 77-78, 84 ; *Sovetskoe Stroitel'stvo*, No. 8(25), August 1928, p. 78.
[4] *Na Agrarnom Fronte*, No. 7-8, 1926, pp. 72-97.

in particular, in aid to the poor peasants ", but were treated with contempt by *mirs* and village Soviets.[1]

The drive in the summer and autumn of 1927 for a more active agrarian policy was extended to the krestkomy. A decree of the Sovnarkom of the RSFSR and a resolution of the party central committee again demanded support for them from rural district executive committees and village Soviets, from poor peasants and party workers.[2] A further decree of November 1927 repeated the appeal to executive committees and village Soviets, but prohibited the president of a village Soviet from becoming president of the KKOV.[3] An article in *Pravda* defended the committees against attacks by the opposition.[4] But Kosior at the fifteenth party congress in December 1927 complained that they had " developed weakly ", and diagnosed a lack of clarity in mutual relations between krestkomy and land communities.[5] A resolution of the congress pronounced that, " while continuing to concern themselves with individual aid to poor peasants, it is indispensable that the krestkomy should direct their work more and more towards aid in collective production for the less well-to-do strata of the peasantry ".[6] This was followed up by an official spokesman at the TsIK of the RSFSR in April 1928 ; payments made to cover the expenditure of the krestkomy were to be replaced by " subsidies of a more or less economic character " to foster their economic activities. It was claimed without much conviction that the committees " play a most important rôle in the countryside ", though it was admitted that in many outlying regions they " can be counted only on paper ".[7] A report on the krestkomy issued in the spring of 1928 by the Rabkrin of the RSFSR gave a picture of stagnation. The committees had some importance as distributors of machines and tractors and of seeds ; but efforts to promote common cultivation had apparently been abandoned.[8]

The committees continued to exercise their original function of bringing aid to the poor peasant. In 1926–1927 aid was said to have been given in the form of subsidies and credits to a total of 3 million rubles, besides direct help in ploughing and harvesting. Schools, reading rooms, crèches, and institutions for the liquidation of illiteracy

[1] *Vserossiiskii Tsentral'nyi Ispolnitel'nyi Komitet XII Sozyva: 3 Sessiya* (1926), pp. 385-386.

[2] *Sobranie Uzakonenii, 1927*, No. 62, art. 429 ; *Spravochnik Partiinogo Robotnika*, vi (1928), i, 667-668.

[3] *Sobranie Uzakonenii, 1927*, No. 124, art. 832.

[4] *Pravda*, November 15, 1927, *Diskussionnyi Listok*, No. 4.

[5] *Pyatnadtsatyi S"ezd VKP(B)*, i (1961), 101.

[6] *KPSS v Rezolyutsiyakh* (1954), ii, 486.

[7] *Vserossiiskii Tsentral'nyi Ispolnitel'nyi Komitet XIII Sozyva 2 Sessiya* (1928), pp. 18-20.   [8] *Pravda*, April 7, 1928.

received 815,000 rubles.[1]   In 1927–1928, the total amount of aid
reached 3·5 million rubles, of which 400,000 rubles went to collectives
organized by the krestkomy themselves.[2]   A fifth all-Russian congress of krestkomy was convened on June 5, 1928, and was informed
that 79,000 committees now existed in the RSFSR against 55,000 in
1925 ; that 65 per cent of peasant households were enrolled in them ;
that their capital resources amounted to from 30 to 50 million rubles,
though only 10 per cent of members paid their dues ; and that they
owned 9000 enterprises of various kinds, 29,000 agricultural machines,
and 15,000 tractors.[3]   But an article summing up the results of the
congress admitted that nearly half the reported 79,000 krestkomy
" either exist only on paper or lead a purely unorganized existence ",
and called for more active leadership by Soviets and Soviet organs.[4]   A
complaint that those who worked in the krestkomy were " for the most
part illiterate ", and were " not clear enough about the tasks of the
committees ",[5] though it related specifically to the Transcaucasian
SFSR, is unlikely to have been inapplicable elsewhere. A report from
Azerbaijan described the committees as " very weak " and their
" social significance " as minimal.[6]   Official returns showed that the
membership of the committees consisted almost exclusively of middle
and poor peasants, with a sprinkling of members of the rural intelli-
gentia (no doubt, mainly teachers), and that the proportion both of
batraks and of well-to-do peasants was insignificant.[7]   Where the
committees were in any way efficient, their original purpose and character had been forgotten. Enterprises nominally organized by the
krestkomy were said to be run on commercial lines ; and protests were
heard against the penetration of the krestkomy by *kulaks*.[8]

---

[1] *Sovetskoe Stroitel'stvo*, No. 1(30), January 1929, pp. 31-32.

[2] *Ibid*. No. 9(38) September 1929, p. 122.

[3] *Pravda* and *Bednota*, June 3, 1928 ; the opening session of the congress
was reported in *Bednota*, June 7, 1928. For similar figures see *Izvestiya
Tsentral'nogo Komiteta VKP(B)*, No. 25(246), August 22, 1928, pp. 3-5, where
the weakness of party guidance and of financial resources was also admitted.

[4] *Pravda*, July 7, 1928.

[5] *Sovetskoe Stroitel'stvo*, No. 8(25), August 1928, p. 84.

[6] *Ibid*. No. 5-6(22-23), May–June 1928, p. 159.

[7] *Ibid*. No. 9(38), September 1929, p. 120.

[8] *Bednota*, February 8, 1929 ; November 3, 1929. On September 6, 1929,
the party central committee passed a resolution asserting that no serious attempt
had been made to carry out the injunction of the fifteenth party congress to
strengthen the krestkomy ; in many districts the elected organs of the krestkomy
were " contaminated with a *kulak* element ", and *batraks* were completely absent
from them. Concluding exhortations to do better in future carried little conviction (*Izvestiya Tsentral'nogo Ispolnitel'nogo Komiteta VKP(B)*, No. 26-27
(285-286), September 30, 1929, p. 29).

NOTE H

GROUPS OF POOR PEASANTS

BESIDES the peasant committees of material aid, another experiment, pertinaciously pursued during this period, but with equally small success, was the formation of a specifically " poor peasant " organization on a political basis. In October 1925 the party central committee, on a report by Molotov, had instructed local party organizations in preparation for the Soviet elections to convene special meetings of poor peasants ; [1] and the fourteenth party congress in December 1925 gave its approval not only to these meetings, but to the organization of " groups of poor peasants ", with the proviso that they did not imply a return to the kombedy or to the practices of war communism.[2] Memories of those dark days still evoked widespread mistrust in the mass of the peasantry, and among those party members who stood for conciliation of the peasant. When, on May 24, 1926, the Orgburo called for the formation of groups of poor peasants and batraks in Soviets, co-operatives, and peasant committees of mutual aid, it insisted that the groups must not turn themselves into independent organizations in competition with the Soviets, cooperatives etc., but must work within these organizations ; nor must any attempt be made to exclude middle peasants.[3] In spite of this warning, a correspondent of Pravda reported that the groups of poor peasants were trying to take the place of the village skhod, and that closed meetings were held from which middle peasants were excluded : this led " not to the strengthening of the alliance with the middle peasant, but on the contrary to the desertion of the middle peasant to the side of the kulak ".[4] In the summer of 1926 fresh attempts were made by party and Komsomol organizations to summon meetings of poor peasants in order to bring to light kulak

[1] See Socialism in One Country, 1924–1926, Vol. 1, p. 308 ; Vol. 2, pp. 347-349.

[2] KPSS v Rezolyutsiyakh (1954), ii, 199 ; for the kombedy see The Bolshevik Revolution, 1917–1923, Vol. 2, pp. 53-55.

[3] Spravochnik Partiinogo Rabotnika, vi (1928), i, 624-626 ; Izvestiya Tsentral'nogo Komiteta VKP(B), No. 26(147), June 30, 1926, p. 3 ; for a speech made by Molotov to the Orgburo, evidently on the occasion of the adoption of this resolution, see ibid. No. 29-30(150-151), July 26, 1926, pp. 1-2.

[4] Pravda, June 26, 1926.

evasions of the agricultural tax. But these proceedings once more provoked equivocal reactions among the middle peasants and at party
headquarters ;[1] and, in spite of encouragement to participate in the
groups, middle peasants took up a negative attitude to them.[2]

The Ukrainian committees of poor peasants (komnezamozhi), with
a longer history behind them, had more substance and vitality. The
reorganization of 1925, designed to deprive them of their political role,[3]
seemed at first to have dealt them a crushing blow ; and their membership fell in the next twelve months from 1,237,676 to 585,360.[4] Thereafter, as the tide of 1925 in favour of the well-to-do peasant began to
ebb, they revived. By October 1926, there were 10,517 committees
with 765,255 members, by April 1927 11,177 committees with 951,542
members, though only 39 per cent of these counted as poor peasants.[5]
The tenth Ukrainian party congress, meeting in November 1927 at the
moment of the inauguration of the " reinforced offensive " against the
kulak, was clearly concerned to revive the effectiveness of the komnezamozhi. It welcomed the increase in their membership, but censured
them for having done too little to promote policies of collectivization and
to defend the interests of poor peasants in the cooperatives.[6]

At the same moment, and under the same impulse of the renewed
emphasis on the class factor in party policy in the countryside, the
formation of groups of poor peasants elsewhere in the USSR was once
more taken in hand. Their number increased : " some hundreds " of
such groups were reported in 1926, and " some thousands " in 1927.[7]
But cautious attitudes still prevailed ; and care was taken not to evoke
the spectre of the kombedy of the period of war communism. At the
fifteenth party congress in December 1927, Molotov explained that
historical reasons accounted for the survival of komnezamozhi in the
Ukraine and of koshchi, which were similar organizations in Central

---

[1] Pravda, August 13, 1926.
[2] Vlast' Sovetov No. 7, February 13, 1927, p. 18 ; No. 19, May 8, 1927,
pp. 23-24.
[3] See Socialism in One Country, 1924–1926, Vol. 1, pp. 289-290.
[4] Sovetskoe Stroitel'stvo, No. 1(30), January 1929, p. 55.
[5] Izvestiya Tsentral'nogo Komiteta VKP(B), No. 4(225), February 13,
1928, p. 6. By June 1928 the number of members had risen to 1·5 millions ; of
these 89·1 per cent were Ukrainians and 91·5 per cent peasants (plus an insignificant 2·2 per cent of batraks) ; of the peasant members 32 per cent were middle
peasants, and 3 per cent (or more) well-to-do peasants (Sovetskoe Stroitel'stvo,
No. 1(30), January 1929, pp. 55-56 ; Na Agrarnom Fronte, No. 10, 1928, pp.
79-80).
[6] Kommunisticheskaya Partiya Ukrainy v Rezolyutsiyakh (1958), p. 414 ; for
the offensive against the kulak see Vol. 1, pp. 33-35.
[7] Pyatnadtsatyi S"ezd VKP(B), i (1961), 102.

Asia, and that these precedents did not justify the creation of similar committees of poor peasants in the RSFSR. The aim of the groups was to revitalize the Soviets and the cooperatives from within, and " not to isolate, to separate off, the poor peasants, in the form of a special organization, from the cooperatives and from the rural Soviets ".[1] The resolution of the congress instructed party organs " to organize and strengthen existing poor peasant groups attached to Soviets and co-operatives, in order from time to time to arrange meetings of these groups in villages and rural districts to share the experience of their work ", and to arrange " county and provincial conferences of poor peasant groups ".[2] The groups were, in fact, designed as instruments of the leadership and support of official policies which party fractions in rural organizations were too weak to provide.

Notwithstanding Molotov's warning, which was echoed in the journal of the party central committee,[3] the position of the groups, in the context of the renewed offensive against the *kulak*, was equivocal. In the critical grain collections of the first months of 1928, they were used, like the kombedy in the past, as instruments to extract grain surpluses from well-to-do hoarders ; and the provision to distribute a percentage of the confiscated grain to poor peasants [4] also followed the precedent of the procedures of war communism. Press and official reports drew a familiar picture of *kulaks* and speculators unmasked and brought to book through the activities of poor peasants ; [5] and a con-ference of poor peasant groups of the Moscow province demonstrated against the *kulaks* and in favour of collectivization.[6] On October 24, 1928, with local Soviet elections once more impending, the party central committee issued an instruction to local organs to conduct what was called " a review of groups of poor peasants " and to call confer-ences of the groups to stimulate their activity in the electoral campaign.[7] *Pravda* optimistically hailed them as leaders of the class struggle in the countryside and as " the *avant-garde* of the collective movement ".[8]

Both the hopes and the fears aroused by the groups of poor peasants

---

[1] *Pyatnadtsatyi S"ezd VKP(B)*, ii (1962), 1377-1378 ; in September 1927 Kiselev, a member of the presidium of the TsIK of the RSFSR, visited Frunze to preside over a congress of Kirgiz koshchi, and warned them to work in unison with the local peasant committees of mutual aid (*Izvestiya*, October 27, 1927).

[2] *KPSS v Rezolyutsiyakh* (1954), ii, 488.

[3] *Izvestiya Tsentral'nogo Komiteta VKP(B)*, No. 3 (224), January 30. 1928, pp. 1-3.   [4] See Vol. 1, p. 51.

[5] G. Konyukhov, *KPSS v Bor'be s Khlebnymi Zatrudneniyami* (1960), pp. 135-137.

[6] *Bednota*, April 10, 1928.

[7] *Pravda*, October 25, 1928 ; *Istoricheskie Zapiski*, xli (1952), 224.

[8] *Pravda*, November 2, 1928.

seem to have been misplaced. An investigation of the groups by
Rabkrin reported in the spring of 1928 that many groups had been
founded and attached to village Soviets, but that few of them worked.[1]
One weakness of the groups was said to have been that they were
convened from time to time to support specific campaigns, and then
allowed to die away.[2] A spokesman of the poor peasants remarked that
" the [party] cell and the rural district committee summon us only when
they need more votes for their candidates, and afterwards nobody is
interested in us, or does any work with us " ; " the groups of poor
peasants ", he concluded, " have not yet become a visible phenomenon
in the countryside ".[3] A conference of groups of poor peasants in the
Barnaul department of Siberia early in 1928 was said to have demonstrated its complete solidarity with the *kulaks* : " their heads are at the
disposal of the *kulaks* ".[4] Workers, returning to Moscow from summer
visits to the countryside in 1928, spoke freely of " ne'er-do-well poor
peasants " and the " wilful laziness of the poor peasants ", and found
them " at the beck and call of the *kulak* ".[5] Even in the Ukraine, only
50 per cent of the membership of the komnezamozhi consisted of poor
peasants ; and " practically no mass work " was carried on among the
members. Rumours were heard of " the contamination of the committees by bureaucratic, well-to-do and other elements ", which
formed 30 per cent of the membership.[6] A congress of komnezamozhi
at the beginning of 1929 laid down the rule — which can scarcely have
been enforced — that " members of the komnezamozhi who have been
transformed into middle peasants can remain in the organization on
condition that their holdings are converted to collective forms of
cultivation ".[7] A report on the " review " of the groups in the winter
of 1928–1929 indicated that their numbers had grown (though no figure
was cited), that most of them were attached to rural Soviets (a few also

---

[1] *Pravda*, April 7, 1928 ; the pages of *Izvestiya Tsentral'nogo Komiteta
VKP(B)* at this time contain many complaints of the ineffectiveness of the
groups (see, for example, No. 8(229), March 15, 1928, pp. 1-3 ; No. 33(254),
November 13, 1928, pp. 4-6).

[2] *Derevenskii Kommunist*, No. 15-16, August 15, 1928, p. 23 ; *Izvestiya
Tsentral'nogo Komiteta VKP(B)*, No. 7 (266), March 20, 1929, pp. 21-23.

[3] *Na Agrarnom Fronte*, No. 10, 1928, p. 79.

[4] Trotsky archives, T 1230 ; where, however, the poor peasants were not
organized, " the *kulak* exercises his influence through sub-*kulaks*, on the place
of collaboration, of hypocritical defence of ' poor peasant interests ' " (A.
Angarov, *Klassovaya Bor'ba v Sovetskoi Derevne* (1929), p. 42).

[5] Trotsky archives, T 2534.

[6] *Izvestiya Tsentral'nogo Komiteta VKP(B)*, No. 34(255), November 22,
1928, pp. 9-10.

[7] *Ibid.* No. 5-6(264-265), February 28, 1929, p. 21.

to krestkony or cooperatives), but that they were inactive except when mobilized for special campaigns, and that party leadership was poor.[1] Ambiguous attitudes were revealed at the sixteenth party conference in April 1929 about the rôle of the poor peasant groups. When Lominadze claimed, a little perfunctorily, that they had " almost everywhere of late begun to work better ", an interrupter asserted that they " exist, but do not work ".[2] Lominadze even proposed an addition to Kalinin's theses designed to strengthen their efficacy. But the amendment, though adopted by the drafting commission, was not accepted by the conference, apparently because it was associated with a further amendment, also put forward by Lominadze, condemning the admission of *kulaks* to the kolkhozy.[3] The final resolution of the conference noted that measures taken to organize poor peasants had proved " manifestly inadequate ", and must be strengthened, but did not specifically mention the groups.[4] Six months later, on October 20, 1929, when the grain situation was desperate, the party central committee adopted a resolution which provided for the admission of *batraks* to the groups, and described them as an " independent " organization of poor peasants and *batraks*.[5] This appeared to imply an independence of other organizations which had been specifically disclaimed at the moment of their foundation.[6] But there is no evidence that they played any active role in collectivization or in the liquidation of the *kulak*, and they do not appear to have outlived these events.

[1] *Ibid.*, No. 7 (266) March 20, 1929, pp. 21-23 ; for still more discouraging accounts from particular localities see *Derevenskii Kommunist*, No. 9 (105), May 12, 1929, pp. 21-23.
[2] *Shestnadtsataya Konferentsiya VKP(B)* (1962), p. 311.
[3] *Ibid.* p. 802, note 210 ; for Lominadze's amendment on the *kulaks* see Vol. 1, p. 178.
[4] *KPSS v Rezolyutsiyakh* (1954), ii, 589.
[5] *Derevenskii Komunist*, No. 23-24 (119-120), December 25, 1929, pp. 28-31.
[6] See p. 459 above.

NOTE I

"SELF-TAXATION"

THE *mir* had the time-honoured function of raising dues to meet communal needs, the *skhod* being the organ responsible for assessing and collecting them. Levies from member households were in practice compulsory, though neither the amounts exacted nor the basis of assessment were regulated by law. Such levies might include obligatory labour services for maintenance and repairs, hedging and ditching, road-making and so forth. This extra-legal authority, exercised by the *mir* in complete independence of the network of Soviets, and described by the question-begging term " self-taxation ",[1] seemed to the early Soviet leaders a disquieting anomaly. At the twelfth party congress in April 1923 Sokolnikov announced a policy of replacing self-taxation by local budgets ;[2] and the eleventh All-Russian Congress of Soviets in the following year coupled the proposed introduction of rural district budgets with the abolition of self-taxation.[3] Among the early decrees of the USSR were two insisting that self-taxation should be strictly voluntary and binding only on those households which voted for it.[4] The conference on Soviet construction which met in January and April 1925 wrestled with the dilemma ; but the desire of Narkomfin to abolish self-taxation or restrict it to labour services foundered on the stubborn resistance of the peasant delegates.

> However many laws comrade Kalinin may write here [said one], however many decrees he may issue prohibiting self-taxation, it exists, always has existed and will exist.

And another delegate declared that " you cannot go against life, and life will drive you that way ".[5] The conference adopted a weak compromise resolution proposing that self-taxation should be retained if voted by a majority of " the general assembly of citizens of the village ", but that

---

[1] The Russian term samooblozhenie literally means " self-imposition " ; the word for " tax " (nalog) implies an impost by governmental authority.

[2] *Dvenadtsatyi S"exd Rossiiskoi Kommunisticheskoi Partii (Bol'skevikov)* (1932), pp. 423-425.   [3] *S"ezdy Sovetov v Dokumentakh*, iv, i (1962), 23.

[4] *Sobranie Zakonov, 1924*, No. 6, art. 60 ; No. 8, art. 81.

[5] *Soveshchanie po Voprosam Sovetskogo Stroitel'stva 1925 g.: Aprel'* (1925), pp. 103, 107, 119.

a decision of the county or department executive committee was required in order to make it binding on the minority which had not voted for it.[1] Eighteen months later, it was reported that " the attitude of the peasantry to self-taxation tends to be favourable because it substantially eases the daily life of the peasantry (hire of shepherds, repair of bridges, keeping of wells in order, building of schools, maintenance of fire equipment etc.) " ; [2] and peasants continued to protest against a system of optional self-taxation as unworkable.[3] In some cases self-taxation was included in the village Soviet budget : this was recognized as an abuse. One of the aims of the introduction of village budgets was " to enforce revolutionary legality and liquidate all possible forms of self-taxation ".[4]

Party pressure against the system mounted during 1927. Unlike the agricultural tax, self-taxation levied by the *skhod* was not progressive. In 1927 poor peasants were said to pay in self-taxation 124 per cent of the amount paid by them in agricultural tax, middle peasants 71·2 per cent and rich peasants 23 per cent.[5] The journal of the party central committee drew attention to " *the equalization which bears sensitively on the interest of the poor peasant in the matter of self-taxation* ".[6] The " former customary law " of the *mir*, observed a commentator, was " the law of the economically strong ".[7] The sums raised by self-taxation were substantial. In 1925–1926 receipts from self-taxation in the RSFSR were estimated at 45 million rubles, and labour services performed were valued at a further 35 millions ; [8] in 1927–1928 self-taxation was estimated at 66 million rubles for the RSFSR, and 100 millions for the USSR, these figures apparently including some part of the money equivalent of labour services.[9]

Since a ban on compulsory self-taxation was clearly not enforceable,[10] attention was devoted to the need to legalize and regularize it. The

---

[1] *Ibid.* p. 184.

[2] *Izvestiya*, October 30, 1926 (art. by Kruglov).

[3] *Vlast' Sovetov*, No. 39, September 28, 1926, p. 5.

[4] *Izvestiya*, October 30, 1926 (art. by Tadeush).

[5] M. Rezunov, *Sel'skie Sovety i Zemel'nye Obshchestva* (1928), p. 13.

[6] *Izvestiya Tsentral'nogo Komiteta VKP(B)*, No. 29(202), July 30, 1927, p. 4.

[7] *Sovetskoe Stroitel'stvo*, No. 9(26), September 1928, p. 40.

[8] *Vestnik Finansov*, No. 4, 1927, pp. 58-60, 64.

[9] *Ibid.* No. 7, 1929, pp. 87, 90 ; in 1905 the revenues of *mirs* in European Russia were said to have totalled 78 million rubles (*Vlast' Sovetov*, No. 48, 1927, p. 6).

[10] It was pointed out that a ban would merely have the result of excluding the Soviets from participation in " the most vital issues in the countryside " (*Izvestiya*, October 11, 1927).

TsIK of the USSR, by a decree of August 24, 1927, allowed the *skhod* by a simple majority, provided half the qualified voters were present, to levy compulsory dues up to a maximum of 35 per cent of the agricultural tax, for social and cultural, though not for administrative, purposes. But these purposes were subject to definition by the authorities of the republic concerned ; the decision required the confirmation of the district or rural district executive committee, and the levy was to be administered by the village Soviet.[1] The ostensible aim of these provisions was to ensure that the proceeds would be used for public requirements, not for the benefit of the *mir* or of its members.[2] A decree of the RSFSR of January 7, 1928 listed the purposes to which the proceeds of self-taxation might be devoted : these were economic construction, health and education, road-building, fire protection, and services and amenities.[3]

Down to the end of 1927 attempts to secure control of self-taxation by legislative action were ancillary to the campaign to subordinate the *mir* to the authority of the village Soviet,[4] and had little practical result. The grain collections crisis of January–March 1928 not only introduced savage measures of compulsion into the countryside, but fundamentally changed the character of self-taxation by assimilating it to the " extraordinary measures " designed to meet the crisis. Its function, like that of other forms of taxation, was to mop up the surplus purchasing power of the peasant and to compel him to bring his grain to the market. It was now in everything but name a governmental impost ; and the official attitude to self-taxation changed abruptly from mistrust to fervent support. A decree of January 10, 1928, while formally maintaining the restriction on what might be raised by self-taxation to 35 per cent of the agricultural tax, provided that authority might be given to the executive committees of provinces and departments to exceed that limit, and removed the requirement in the decree of August 24, 1927, that self-taxation should be voted by half the qualified members of the *skhod*.[5] *Izvestiya* published a number of alleged statements by peasants

[1] *Sobranie Zakonov, 1927*, No. 51, art. 509.
[2] *Vlast' Sovetov*, No. 48, November 27, 1927, p. 7.
[3] *Sobranie Uzakonenii 1928*, No. 8, art. 73 ; a similar decree was issued by the Ukrainian SSR on January 2, 1928 (*Sovetskoe Stroitel'stvo*, No. 1(18), January 1928, p. 69).
[4] See pp. 239-243 above.
[5] *Sobranie Zakonov 1928*, No. 2, art. 29. The average rate of self-taxation for the RSFSR in 1927-1928 was reported to have been 36·4 per cent of the agricultural tax (*Sovetskoe Stroitel'stvo*, No. 9(26), September 1928, pp. 55-56 ; *Vlast' Sovetov*, No. 33, August 19, 1928, pp. 6-7) ; in January 1929 the *skhod* was authorized to raise the level of self-taxation to 50 per cent of the agricultural tax (*Pravda*, January 10, February 24, 1929).

in support of self-taxation, and in a leading article advocated its use for " constructive " purposes.[1] The party instruction of February 13, 1928, demanded that self-taxation should be made even more progressive than the agricultural tax at the expense of " kulak and well-to-do strata of the countryside ". The utilization of the sums realised by self-taxation was to be discussed and confirmed by the skhod, and carried out " under broad public control ".[2] Enforcement of self-taxation appears to have been one of the most common pretexts for forced levies from grain-holding peasants in the first months of 1928.[3]

It is not surprising that these draconian measures should have encountered stubborn resistance; kulaks were said to have described them as " a law against the peasantry ".[4] The journal of the party central committee admitted widespread peasant opposition to the new form of self-taxation.[5] In Smolensk province, " kulaks and well-to-do peasants conduct a fierce open struggle against self-taxation ", and one rumour was current that its purpose was to provide money for Comintern to send to China and England.[6] A survey by the Rabkrin of the RSFSR in 1928 disclosed great variations in local practice, both in the amounts charged and in the methods of assessment. In many areas the old practice of non-progressive imposition continued, and was attributed to the influence of the well-to-do households on village meetings ; elsewhere the level of tax on the well-to-do was said to be too high.[7] Kalinin promised that self-taxation would not again be imposed in the form of a " compulsory campaign ".[8] In the RSFSR a " firm prohibition " was announced on special campaigns for self-taxation, though these continued in some places ; and the amounts levied were reduced in many areas.[9] But the grain crisis of the winter of 1918–1929 was too grave to permit of any diminution of pressures on peasants who held the grain ; and promises of relaxation of the unpopular measures of the previous year served only as a cloak for more drastic exactions.

---

[1] Izvestiya, January 31, February 10, 1928.

[2] Stalin, Sochineniya, xi, 18-19 ; for this instruction see Vol. 1, pp. 51-52. The skhod envisaged in the instruction was the hypothetical " general assembly of citizens " established by the decree of March 14, 1927 (see p. 241 above).

[3] See Vol. 1, pp. 53-54.

[4] Bednota, January 11, February 14, 1928.

[5] Izvestiya Tsentral'nogo Komiteta VKP(B), No. 12-13(233-234), April 17, 1928, p. 4.

[6] See report of a meeting of the provincial party committee on April 28, 1928, in Smolensk archives, WKP 33.

[7] Vestnik Finansov, No. 7, 1929, pp. 85-87 ; for a complaint of its excessive incidence on the well-to-do peasant see Izvestiya, July 3, 1928.

[8] Pravda, September 23, 1928.

[9] Vestnik Finansov, No. 7, 1929, pp. 88, 90.

The article in *Pravda* of January 5, 1929, which signalled once more the disastrous failure of the grain collections,[1] while purporting to deprecate " extraordinary " methods, demanded " decisive measures " against speculators. The most popular device at this time for imposing forced levies was the so-called " Ural–Siberian method " (from its initial application in those regions) or " social action ", described by Stalin in April 1929 as " conducted on the principle of self-taxation ".[2] What is clear is that these methods of requisition had nothing in common with traditional self-taxation under the authority of the *mir*, and that the dismantling of the old machinery of self-taxation was a stage in the process of the decay of the *mir* and the liquidation of the *kulak*.

[1] See Vol. 1, p. 100.
[2] Stalin, *Sochineniya*, xii, 88 ; official reticence about the " Ural–Siberian method " was broken by some veiled allusions at the sixteenth party conference in April 1929 (see Vol. 1, p. 101, note 2).

NOTE J

WOMEN IN SOVIET WORK

A CAMPAIGN was mounted in 1927 to increase the participation of women in Soviet work. Statistics published after the Soviet elections of 1927 showed that, while women formed half of the qualified electorate, they rarely constituted more than one-third of those voting, or more than 10 or 12 per cent of those elected to village Soviets. The record for urban Soviets, especially in the RSFSR, was somewhat better ; here 40 per cent of those voting, and 20 per cent of those elected, were women. Of the deputies elected to the Union and All-Russian Congresses of Soviets in the spring of 1927, 8·2 and 9·0 per cent respectively were women. More women were also elected to the TsIKs of the USSR and RSFSR, though here too the proportion did not reach 10 per cent. A circular letter from the presidium of TsIK of July 16, 1927, complained of neglect of earlier directives, and called for more active participation by women in the work of Soviets and in current campaigns.[1] In August 1927 a Union congress of women workers and peasants was announced to coincide with the tenth anniversary celebrations of the revolution.[2] It met in Moscow on October 10, 1927, was addressed by Bukharin, Kalinin, Lunacharsky, Krupskaya and other party leaders and was widely publicized.[3] Ingrained prejudices, however, died hard.[4] A cartoon in *Pravda* showed an up-to-date young worker leading a woman to the Soviet and a *kulak* type behind dragging her away by the skirt.[5] Enukidze spoke of men jeering at women who came to vote or " simply pushing them out of the meeting " ;[6] and, according to another report, women who attended

---

[1] *Sovetskoe Stroitel'stvo*, No. 8-9(13-14), August–September 1927, pp. 116-117. [2] *Sobranie Zakonov, 1927*, No. 49, art. 503.

[3] For reports see *Pravda*, October 11–18, 1927 ; *Sovetskoe Stroitel'stvo*, No. 10-11 (15-16), October–November 1927, pp. 217-220. TsIK also organized a Union conference of " commissions for the improvement of working and living conditions of women of the east ", the purpose of which was to remove legal discrimination against women, and to draw them into economic and political life (*SSSR: Ot S"ezda k S"ezdu (Aprel' 1927–Mai 1929* (1929), pp. 150-151).

[4] See *Socialism in One Country, 1924–1926*, Vol. 2, pp. 317, 322, note 4.

[5] *Pravda*, February 1, 1927.

[6] *Vsesoyuznoe Soveshchanie po Perevyboram Sovetov v 1929 g.* (1928), p. 57.

meetings were greeted with jeers and " suffocated with tobacco smoke ".[1]
A typical peasant was quoted as remarking : " We did not make the
October revolution in order that our wives should be elected, and we
should sit at home." [2]

The proportion of women in Soviet organs gradually increased,
though the improvement may have been due more to pressure from the
centre than to initiative on the spot. After the elections of 1929 publicity was given to substantially increased percentages of women voters,
and of women deputies to rural Soviets (notably in the Central Asian
republics) and urban Soviets, and to district, department and regional
Soviet congresses and executive committees.[3] The most striking
successes were achieved by women in sections of a few urban Soviets,
notably in the regions of Moscow and Leningrad, where women were
sometimes in a majority.[4] But the authors of a statistical survey of
Soviet and economic institutions in the later nineteen-twenties noted
the low percentage of women employees, especially in highly qualified
posts ; and, " the further one goes from the cultural centres and great
cities, the number of women workers in our institutions systematically
diminishes ".[5]

[1] *Sovetskoe Stroitel'stvo*, No. 12(29), 1928, pp. 68-69.
[2] *Ibid.* No. 12(29), December 1928, p. 61.
[3] *Ibid.* No. 12(41) December 1929, pp. 9, 11, 15, 17 ; see also Table No.
64, p. 487 below.
[4] *Sovetskoe Stroitel'stvo*, No. 12(29), December 1928, pp. 68-69 ; a figure
of 84 per cent of women members was recorded in some sections of the Tver
Soviet (*ibid.* p. 15).
[5] *Gosudertasvennyi Apparat SSSR, 1924–1928* (1929), p. 7, cf. *ibid.* pp. 50-51.

NOTE K

COMRADELY COURTS

By way of relieving pressure on the people's courts an attempt was made towards the end of this period to breathe fresh life into an institution which testified to the persistent survival of early idealistic conceptions of administering justice. Lenin in December 1918, in an early draft of the revised party programme, had proposed " the introduction of comradely courts (for certain categories in the army and among the workers) " ; [1] and, though the proposal found no place in the programme adopted in March 1919, a decree of November 14, 1919, provided for the establishment of " workers' disciplinary comradely courts ". Attached to local trade union organs, and functioning in industrial enterprises, they were to consist of one representative of the administration, one of the trade union, and one of the workers. They were designed to deal with disciplinary and other minor offences ; and the penalties which they could impose ranged from a simple reprimand to dismissal or transfer to other work, or, in extreme cases of contumacy, transfer to a concentration camp.[2] At the time of the trade union controversy of 1920–1921 Lenin referred again to these courts, which he praised as a contribution to the cause of " producer democracy " ; [3] and after the introduction of NEP he enquired impatiently : " How many have been introduced, and when ? How many cases a month do they deal with ? " [4] But " comradely courts " were unpopular with the trade unions, and continued to languish till Rabkrin, in a resolution of September 10, 1927, mindful of the overloading of the people's courts with trivial cases, proposed to resuscitate them and to establish similar

[1] *Leninskii Sbornik*, xiii (1930), 85.
[2] *Sobranie Uzakonenii, 1919*, No. 56, art. 537.
[3] Lenin, *Sochineniya*, xxvi, 80, 127.
[4] *Ibid.* xxvi, 377. Similar " disciplinary courts " for minor offences or acts of negligence by officials and minor disputes were established in 1923 in state and public institutions in the RSFSR (*Sobranie Uzakonenii, 1923*, No. 54, art. 531), and a revised statute was issued in 1926 (*id. 1926*, No. 36, art. 294) ; but they were criticized as showing undue leniency to offending officials, and were abolished as the result of a decision of the fifteenth party congress in December 1927 (*KPSS v Rezolyutsiyakh* (1954), ii, 445). For an account of their working see *Ezhenedel'nik Sovetskoi Yustitsii*, No. 31, August 8, 1926, pp. 941-943.

courts in the villages.[1] The factory courts were criticized by the trade
unions as an attempt to set up a new judicial organ under procuratorial
supervision ;[2] and village courts were dismissed as impracticable.[3]
None the less Narkomyust in February 1928 worked out an elaborate
scheme for comradely courts in factories and state and public institutions, empowered to impose minor penalties, and conciliation courts
attached to village Soviets.[4] This received weighty support from the
resolution of the TsIK and Sovnarkom of the RSFSR of March 26,
1928, on penal policy, which advocated this method of relieving the
people's courts of the burden of dealing with minor offences.[5] Finally,
a decree of the RSFSR of August 27, 1928, ordered the establishment
of comradely courts in factories and in state or public institutions and
enterprises, by agreement between Narkomyust and the trade unions, to
deal with minor offences or disputes by such methods as public reprimand, the reconciliation of disputants, disciplinary action within the
factory or institution, or fines not exceeding 10 rubles payable to some
public or social fund. The " judges " in such courts were workers
elected for the purpose, and were bound by no formal rules of law.[6] In
the spring of 1929 30 courts were said to be at work in factories in
Moscow, Leningrad and Ivanovo-Voznesensk;[7] and a little later a
hundred such courts were said to exist, some of them against the will
of the trade unions, which steadily maintained that " trade unions are
not a judicial institution ".[8]

An experiment with village courts under the name of " conciliation
chambers (primiritel'nye kamery) " in counties of Moscow and Leningrad provinces in the summer of 1928 led an enthusiastic commentator
to hail it as " a first stage in the dying out of state control as an apparatus of constraint, and one more fresh step on the path of a society
which ' does not need the state machine ' ".[9] Such attitudes to the

---

[1] *Ezhenedel'nik Sovetskoi Yustitsii*, No. 10, March 14, 1928, p. 289.

[2] *Trud*, February 4, 5, 1928.

[3] *Ezhenedel'nik Sovetskoi Yustitsii*, No. 1, January 10, 1928, pp. 14-15.

[4] *Ibid.* No. 9, March 7, 1928, pp. 277-278.

[5] For this resolution see pp. 364-365 above.

[6] *Sobranie Uzakonenii, 1928*, No. 114, art. 707. According to Yanson the
original proposal was defeated in the Sovnarkom of the RSFSR by trade union
opposition ; and a recommendation was submitted to the TsIK of the RSFSR
to annul the clause of the resolution of March 26, 1928, on comradely courts.
This was, however, quickly reversed, and the decree adopted (*Ezhenedel'nik
Sovetskoi Yustitsii*, No. 9-10, March 8/15, 1929, p. 198).

[7] *Ibid.* No. 17, May 6, 1929, p. 377.

[8] *Pravda*, June 22, 1929.

[9] *Ezhenedel'nik Sovetskoi Yustitsii*, No. 28, July 31, 1928, p. 788, No. 11,
March 22, 1929, p. 246 ; Yanson remarked that comradely courts " in the

state and its legal institutions were already unfashionable and were soon to disappear. *Pravda* in June 1929 again drew attention to the need for comradely courts in rural areas, where the average distance from the nearest people's court was 35 kilometres.[1] But the paucity of information about either comradely or village courts suggests that they enjoyed only a modicum of success.

countryside are for the present called ' conciliation chambers ' " (*ibid.* No. 9-10, March 8/15, 1929, p. 197). The Kazakh ASSR " by way of experiment " established " conciliation commissions " in villages and settlements (auls) to deal with cases involving property to a value of not more than 15 rubles and certain cases of inheritance (*Sovetskoe Stroitel'stvo*, No. 2(31), February 1929, p. 156).

[1] *Pravda*, June 22, 1929 ; not till September 1930 was a decree of the USSR issued to set up " village courts " (*Sobranie Zakonov, 1930*, No. 51, art. 531).

TABLES

Table No. 52

Membership of VKP(B)
(from current party statistics)

	January 1, 1926	January 1, 1927	January 1, 1928	October 1, 1928
No. of Members	592,143	734,072	854,855	—
No. of Candidates	410,346	397,184	365,981	—
Total	1,002,489	1,131,256	1,220,836	1,456,696
		By Social Situation (in percentages)		
Workers	58·1	56·1	57·8	61·2
Peasants	24·6	26·3	22·3	21·1
Employees	15·5	16·2	17·9	16·3
Others	1·8	1·4	2·0	1·4
		By Present Occupation (in percentages)		
Workers *	40·8	38·1	37·6	39·9
Batraks	1·2	1·1	1·3	2·0
Peasants	14·8	15·4	14·4	12·5
(including Peasants Exclusively Engaged in Agriculture †)	(11·4)	(11·7)	(9·8)	(9·9)
Junior Service Personnel in Production ‡	—	—	1·7	1·2
Employees §	32·9	34·2	31·9	32·6
Junior Service Personnel in Institutions ‡	—	—	2·6	1·4
Military Personnel ‖	—	1·3	—	—
Artisans and Craftsmen	0·3	0·3		
Students	5·6	5·6	10·5	10·4
Unemployed	1·7	2·0		
Others	2·7	2·0		

* Defined as " Workers in factories and workshops, transport workers and other wage-workers ".

† Other categories of peasants were those combining agricultural work with administrative work, work as artisans or craftsmen, or labour for hire.

‡ The miscellaneous category of " junior service personnel " consisted of section-chiefs, charge-hands, storekeepers, watchmen, porters, firemen, attendants etc. ; a " new instruction " of the party central committee on the eve of the census required that they should be classified by occupation not as workers, but as employees (*Pyatnadtsatyi S"ezd VKP(B)*, i (1961), 110, ii (1962), 1627, note 87) ; a later order of the party central committee of March 13, 1928 (preserved in the Smolensk archives WKP 213), partially reversed this decision by re-classifying junior service personnel employed in factories as workers, those employed in institutions being still classified as employees.

§ Defined as " Workers in Soviet, party, trade union, cooperative and other institutions and organizations ".

‖ A circular of the party central committee of August 14, 1925, ruled that party members on military service should be registered no longer by the party authorities of the region from which they came, but by the political administration of the armed forces (PUR) (*VKP(B) v Tsifrakh*, v (1926), 5) ; this change did not take full effect till 1926 (*ibid.* vi (1927), 4).

Source : *VKP(B) v Tsifrakh*, v (1926), vii (1927), viii (1928), ix (1929).

The following revised figures (for January 1 of each year) were issued in 1930 :

	1926	1927	1928	1929	1930
No. of members and candidates	1,078,185	1,147,074	1,304, 471	1,532,362	1,674,910
Percentages (by social situation) of					
Workers	56·8	55·7	56·8	61·4	65·3
Peasants	25·9	19·0	22·9	21·7	20·2
Employees and Others	17·3	25·3	20·3	16·9	14·5

Source : *Bol'shaya Sovetskaya Entsiklopediya*, xi (1930), 553-556 ; For January 1, 1927, the figures quoted are those of the party census of that year, not the current statistics. Further slight discrepancies in official statistics of party membership are discussed in T. H. Rigby, *Communist Party Membership in the USSR* (1968), pp. 53-54. It was admitted at the fifteenth party congress in December 1927 that divergences occurred both in the data of the party census and in the current returns because " no general principle has yet been worked out for deciding whom to classify in what category or social group " (*Pyatnadtsatyi S"ezd VKP(B)*, i (1961), 133).

Table No. 53

National Composition of VKP(B)

Nationality	Percentage of party 1922	1927	Percentage of population 1926
Great Russians	72·0	65·0	52·9
Ukrainians	5·9	11·7	21·2
White Russians	1·5	3·2	3·2
Poles, Latvians and other Baltic peoples	4·6	2·6	0·7
Jews	5·2	4·3	1·8
Minority peoples in RSFSR	2·0	2·3	4·3
Transcaucasian peoples	3·4	3·6	2·5
Central Asians (incl. Kazakhs)	2·5	3·5	7·0
Others	2·9	3·8	6·4

Sources : This table has been compiled by T. H. Rigby, *Communist Party Membership in the USSR* (1968), p. 366. The 1927 figures are those of the party census (*Sotsial'nyi i National'nyi Sostav VKP(B)* (1928), p. 114) ; the 1922 figures are from *Izvestiya Tsentral'nogo Komiteta VKP(B)* No. 7-8(55-56), August–September 1923, p. 61 ; the figures of population are from F. Lorimer, *The Population of the Soviet Union* (Geneva, 1946), pp. 55-61.

Table No. 54

Admissions to VKP(B)

	1st half of 1926	2nd half of 1926	1927	Jan.–Sept. 1928
(a) Admitted as Candidates				
Total	95,344	71,840	176,180*	186,086†
Percentages (by social situation) of				
Workers	41·40	43·70	70·20	71·45
Peasants	25·50	24·35	23·90	23·34
Batraks	2·97	3·30	—‡	—‡
Employees	20·60	19·35	4·70	4·02
Others	9·53	9·30	1·20	1·19
(b) Admitted as Members				
Total	71,043	80,617	149,606	130,837
Percentages (by social situation) of				
Workers	59·50	51·51	54·3	63·6
Peasants	6·98	10·91	28·2	21·5
Batraks	0·83	1·39	—‡	—‡
Employees	24·47	28·10	15·5	13·5
Others	8·22	8·09	2·0	1·4

* More than half in the last quarter (the " October enrolment ").
† Nearly half in the first quarter (the " October enrolment ").
‡ Presumably included in " Workers ".

Source : *VKP(B) v Tsifrakh*, vi (1927), vii (1927), viii (1928), ix (1929) ; the percentages for 1926 have been calculated from absolute figures. An article in *Pravda*, September 2, 1927, quoted percentages of candidate admissions for 1926 both by social situation and by current occupation ; the classification by social situation gave higher percentages of workers and peasants, and lower percentages of employees, than the above table ; the classification by occupation gave percentages of workers and peasants (though not of employees) identical with those given in the above table for social situation — an instance of the confusion frequently prevailing in these statistics.

Table No. 55

Composition of Principal Soviet Organs in 1929

(in percentages)

	Worker	Peasant	Other	Party	Komsomol	Other
Village Soviets	8·7	84·4	6·9	10·0	6·4	83·6
Presidents of Village Soviets	8·3	88·3	3·4	32·3	7·3	60·4
Urban Soviets	53·4	4·5	42·1	46·1	7·6	46·3
RIK and VIK *	21·7	39·7	38·6	53·4	6·6	40·0
Presidents of RIK and VIK	26·3	41·2	52·5	96·3	0·8	2·9
OKRIK and UIK †	39·4	25·5	35·1	68·4	2·9	28·7
Presidents of OKRIK and UIK	38·8	14·4	46·8	99·7	—	0·3
Regional Executive Committees (RSFSR)	49·2	12·6	37·9	75·0	0·5	24·5
Provincial Executive Committees (RSFSR)	55·8	12·2	31·0	69·2	1·0	29·8
Executive Committees of Autonomous Regions (RSFSR)	21·8	33·2	45·0	70·8	1·9	27·3
Executive Committees of Autonomous Republics (RSFSR)	29·1	19·5	51·4	72·3	3·0	24·7
TsIK of the RSFSR	52·0	21·5	26·5	72·4	—	27·6
TsIK of the USSR	46·5	20·8	32·7	71·6	0·3	28·1

* Raionnye (district) and Volost'nye (rural district) Ispolnitel'nye Komitety.
† Okruzhnye (department) and Uezdnye (county) Ispolnitel'nye Komitety.

Sources: *Bol'shaya Sovetskaya Entsiklopediya*, xi (1930), 542; figures of party membership of village Soviets and rural district executive committees of the Union republics in 1927 were given to the fifteenth party congress in December 1927 (*Pyatnadtsatyi S"ezd VKP(B)*, i (1961), 448-449).

Table No. 56

Members Excluded from, or Leaving,* VKP(B)

	1927		1928 (first three quarters)	
	Excluded	Leaving	Excluded	Leaving
Totals	16,718	27,340	23,626	8,990
In Percentages :				
By Social Situation				
Workers	46·2	58·9	44·3	64·5
Peasants	29·5	34·2	29·1	16·0
Employees	22·3	5·1	27·8	6·9
Others	2·0	1·8	2·5	2·0
By Occupation				
Workers	29·9	52·1	26·6	56·0
Peasants exclusively engaged in agriculture	16·7	26·7	13·0	11·0
Other Peasants	5·4	2·9	3·5	0·6
Batraks	0·7	1·5	0·8	1·3
Employees	33·3	6·5	42·2	9·5
Junior Service Personnel	4·3	2·5	3·2	2·7
Artisans and Craftsmen	0·4	0·6	0·8	0·6
Others	9·3	7·2	9·6	7·4

* This rubric covered those "voluntarily" resigning and those "automatically" removed for failure to pay dues or to register ; the high number of those leaving in 1927 was doubtless due to the party census.

Source : *VKP(B) v Tsifrakh*, viii (1928), 28-31, ix (1929), 38-41.

Table No. 57

The Komsomol

	VII Congress (March 1926)	V Conference (March 1927)	VIII Congress (March 1928)
No. of Members	1,780,000	—	1,960,000
No. of full delegates	1,117	189	656
No. of non-voting delegates	285	367	—
Percentage among delegates of :			
Women	6·7	1	9·7
Workers	61·0	60·3 *	71·0 *
Peasants	19·8	15·9	11·0
Members of VKP(B)	88·0	97·0⎫	94·9
Candidates of VKP(B)	9·1	3·0⎭	

* Including *batraks*.

Source : *VLKSM v Rezolyutsiyakh* (1929), pp. 227, 281, 308.

Table No. 58

Rural Members of VKP(B)

(Party Census of 1927)

	No.	Per Cent
(a) By Social Situation		
Workers	65,691	24·9
Peasants	149,734	56·7
Employees	41,346	15·6
Others	7,284	2·8
	264,055	100·0
(b) By Current Occupation		
Workers	23,964	9·1
(including *batraks*	(13,226)	(5·0)
and other agricultural		
workers)		
Peasants	111,618	42·3
(including peasants	(84,880)	(32·1)
engaged in individual		
cultivation)		
Employees	105,229	39·8
Junior Service Personnel	5,492	2·1
Artisans and Craftsmen	3,923	1·5
Unemployed	9,409	3·5
Others	4,420	1·7
	264,055	100·0

Source : *Sotsial'nyi i Natsional'nyi Sostav VKP(B)* (1928), pp. 87, 89.

Table No. 59

Administrative Units of USSR

(on January 1 of the years named)

	1926	1927	1928	1929
Autonomous Republics	15	15	15	15
Autonomous Regions	14	14	14	14
Regions (Oblasti and Krai)	3	4	5	8
Departments (Okruga)	114	124	129	176
Districts (Raiony)	1530	1641	1854	2426
Provinces (Gubernii)	47	38	33	16
Counties (Uezdy)	442	419	343	198
Rural Districts (Volosti)	4428	4117	3564	1597

Source : *Administrativno-Territorial'noe Delenie SSSR* (8th ed. 1929), pp. 3, 11 ; for a classification of these units by Union republics see *ibid.* p. 12.

Table No. 60

Local Budgets

	1925–1926	1926–1927	1927–1928	1928–1929
(a) Revenue				
(in million rubles at current prices)				
Local revenues	500·3	640·9	716·3	877·5
State revenues transferred direct to local budget	316·6	411·9	443·6	121·9 *
Deductions from state budget	379·6	534·7	656·3	1240·3 *
Loans of local Soviets	41·3	81·0	105·2	104·2
Surplus from previous year	38·1	61·4	75·6	68·0
Total	1275·5	1729·9	1997·0	2411·9
(b) Expenditure				
(in million rubles at current prices)				
National Economy	251·8	456·4	575·1	649·4 †
Social and Cultural	467·4	620·4	769·3	992·5
Administration	343·5	364·8	327·6	367·9
Other Expenditure	140·3	211·4	268·6	294·8
Total	1203·0	1653·0	1940·6	2304·6

* The fall in " transferred " revenues, and rise in " deductions ", in 1928–1929 reflected a change in financial procedures (see Vol. 1, pp. 974–975).

† Expenditure on the economy was partly balanced by receipts, which were included under the item " local revenues " on the revenue side ; in 1925–1926 receipts exceeded expenditure, but from 1926–1927 this item showed a gradually increasing deficit which was carried on the budget.

Source : *Sotsialisticheskoe Stroitel'stvo SSSR* (1935), p. 675.

Table No. 61

Village Soviets and Inhabited Points (Seleniya)

	No. of Village Soviets	Average No. of Inhabited Points per Soviet	Average No. of Inhabitants per Soviet	Average No. of Inhabitants per Inhabited Point
RSFSR	55,340	9	1540	180
Ukrainian SSR	10,621	5	2300	c. 500
White Russian SSR	1,419	27	2900	110
Transcaucasian SSR	2,437	5	1875	368
Including :				
Azerbaijanian SSR	—	5	1539	292
Armenian SSR	—	2	914	387
Georgian SSSR	—	9	4100 †	454
Uzbek SSR	1,970	6	2000	340
Turkmen SSR	376	6	2427	440
Total	72,163	—	—	—

† The Georgian *temi* were equivalent to enlarged Soviets.

Source : *Administrativno-Territorial'noe Delenie SSSR* (8th ed., 1929), pp. 12, 21, 24-25, 28-29, 31.

Table No. 62

Village Budgets

	RSFSR	Ukrainian SSR	White Russian SSR	Uzbek SSR	Turkmen SSR	USSR
No. of Village Budgets						
1926–27	1,666	485	13	10	2	2,156
1927–28	3,411	687	34	7	3	4,142
1928–29	7,701	3442	84	85	—	11,243
1929–30	18,895	9981	520	75	10	29,846
Percentage of Total No. of Villages						
1926–27	3·0	4·5	0·7	0·5	0·5	3·9
1927–28	6·0	6·4	2·0	0·4	0·7	5·6
1928–29	14·0	32·1	4·8	1·3	—	15·4
1929–30	36·0	93·0	30·0	4·0	2·4	41·5
Average Budget (in thousand rubles)						
1926–27	9·3	—	—	—	—	—*
1927–28	7·2	10·3	8·3	10·9	—	7·4
1928–29	7·1	7·9	14·8	16·1	—	—
1929–30	8·5	18·3	—	11·8	26·4	10·2

* If Enukidze's figure of 2300 village budgets totalling 16 million rubles (see p. 246 above) is accepted for 1926–1927, this gives an average of 6·9 thousand.

Source : *Planovoe Khozyaistvo*, No. 6, 1930, pp. 94–95 ; no figures appear to be available for the Transcaucasian SFSR, where, as in the Uzbek and Turkmen SSRs, village budgets were virtually unknown before 1928 (*Sovetskoe Stroitel'stvo*, No. 4(21), April 1928, p. 37).

The total number of village budgets given for the USSR is not the exact sum of the numbers for the republics.

Table No. 63

Disfranchised Persons

(Classified by Grounds of Disfranchisement)

	1925–1926		1926–1927	
	No.	%	No.	%
Employment of Hired Labour	7,046	3·2	20,138	3·6
Living on Non-Working Income	37,609	17·0	43,388	7·7
Private Trade	125,230	50·7	219,015	38·8
Employees of Religious Cult	13,153	6·0	21,682	3·8
Members of Former Police	6,647	3·0	29,802	5·3
Condemned by Courts	7,135	3·2	27,574	4·9
Lunatics	4,402	2·0	14,062	2·5
Dependants of Disfranchised Persons	19,651	8·9	188,844	33·4
	220,933	100·0	564,545	100·0

Source : *Sovetskoe Stroitel'stvo*, No. 11 (28), 1928, p. 101 ; for a breakdown of the figures by republics and by urban and rural Soviets see *ibid.* No. 8-9 (13-14), August–September 1927, p. 22.

Soviet Elections, 1929
(Figures for 1927 in brackets)

		RSFSR	Ukrainian SSR	White Russian SSR	Uzbek SSR	Turkmen SSR
Percentage of those deprived of voting rights	Rural	4·2 (3·6)	4·5 (4·6)	1·8 (1·3)	6·5 (1·9)	—
	Urban	6·9 (6·0)	11·3 (9·0)	13·9 (12·8)	16·5 (—)	—
	Settlements of Urban Type	—	12·6 (13·1)	14·8 (14·0)	—	—
Percentage of Registered Voters Exercising the Vote	Rural	61·1 (47·5)	64·6 (51·6)	58·7 (46·3)	59·0 (46·3)	70·6 (40·0)
	Urban	73·2 (56·1)	75·7 (58·0)	72·9 (62·4)	58·3 (58·8)	62·2 (53·4)
	Settlements of Urban Type	—	73·2 (59·9)	63·5 (49·6)	—	—
Percentage of Registered Women Voters Exercising the Vote	Rural	47·3 (29·8)	—	42·4 (24·7)	43·8 (15·7)	59·1 (2·5)
	Urban	69·8 (49·7)	—	63·0 (59·0)	—	51·4 (43·7)
Percentage of party and Komsomol members and candidates in Soviets	Rural	14·9 (13·0)	16·7 (13·0)	16·8 (18·3)	17·6 (17·8)	20·9 (16·6)
	Urban	51·3 (51·0)	58·1 (52·1)	50·6 } (50·9)	—	56·4 (58·9)
	Settlements of Urban Type	—	38·5 (39·1)	34·4 }	—	—
Percentage of Women Elected to Soviets	Rural	19·0 (11·8)	17·5 (9·6)	19·6 (7·2)	25·3 (12·7)	20·2 (6·1)
	Urban	26·5 (21·1)	19·9 (17·6)	22·4 (12·7)	26·6 (18·0)	22·6 (27·8)
	Settlements of Urban Type	—	21·8 (14·8)	—	—	—

Sources: SSSR: Ot S"ezda k S"ezdu (Aprel' 1927–Mai 1929 (1929), pp. 127–141; SSSR: God Raboty Pravitel'stva 1927–1928 (1929), p. 32. The figures are based on incomplete returns, but the samples were sufficiently large to be representative; no corresponding returns were available from the Transcaucasian SFSR.

Table No. 65

Composition of Rural Soviet Organs in RSFSR

(in percentages)

	Village Soviets		Presidents of Village Soviets		Rural District Congresses of Soviets		Rural District Executive Committees		Presidents of Rural District Executive Committees	
	1926	1927	1926	1927	1926	1927	1926	1927	1926	1927
Peasants:	90·1	89·1	94·5	94·5	79·4	77·2	67·9	67·3	48·5	61·0
incl. peasants exempt from tax	8·4	16·1	6·9	15·5	9·3	18·1	8·6	20·6	3·5	25·2
Workers and *Batraks*	2·9	4·3	2·2	3·0	4·6	6·3	6·9	9·0	8·4	10·0
Artisans, Craftsmen etc.	0·8	1·1	0·4	0·4	0·7	1·0	0·8	1·0	0·1	0·4
Employees	6·2	5·5	2·9	2·1	15·3	15·5	24·4	22·7	43·0	28·6
Members of party or Komsomol	10·1	12·9	17·9	23·8	24·7	31·3	48·7	54·7	85·3	90·1
Elected for the first time	51·7	53·9	44·9	37·6	41·9	45·8	50·0	53·5	29·1	29·5

Source : *Sovetskoe Stroitel'stvo*, No. 8-9(13-14), August–September, 1927, p. 18 ; similar tables for the other Union republics showed no significant differences, except a somewhat higher percentage of " workers and *batraks* ", and of party or Komsomol members, at all levels (*ibid.* p. 21).

Table No. 66

Personnel of Soviet Institutions

	May 1, 1925	May 1, 1926	January 1, 1927	January 1, 1928
I. Administrative and Judicial	596,819	640,473	656,660	632,278
State Administration	436,049	469,959	474,556	437,520
Courts and Legal Personnel	36,724	38,889	39,743	38,899
Public Order and Security	124,046	131,625	142,361	155,859
II. Social and Cultural	829,935	949,416	1,060,925	1,166,947
Science and Education	528,512	582,861	656,272	720,847
Theatre, Art, Cinema etc.	14,668	17,959	24,857	28,394
Publishing	13,001	16,105	15,688	15,169
Health (incl. Veterinary)	257,330	312,173	342,239	381,830
Social Security	3,894	3,797	3,892	3,819
Social Insurance	12,530	16,521	17,977	16,882
III. Economic Institutions	185,579	208,808	200,310	185,372
IV. State Trade	119,312	162,000	156,403	131,737
V. Credit Institutions	29,123	38,272	35,554	33,060
VI. Transport	82,432	94,191	94,498	94,948
VII. Other	122,499	118,914	124,151	125,936
Total	1,965,699	2,212,074	2,328,501	2,370,278

Source : *Gosudarstvennyi Apparat SSSR, 1924–1928* (1929), p. 12.

Table No. 67

Party Members in Red Army

	1925		1929	
	No.	%	No.	%
Commanding Staff	18,106	31·4	45,419	48·8
Political Staff	14,115	24·5	11,266	12·1
On Courses or in Training Schools	11,909	20·6	10,774	11·6
Red Army Men (rank and file)	9,412	16·3	21,936	23·6
Other	4,105	7·2	3,578	3·9
Total	57,687	100·0	92,973	100·0

Source : *Bol'shaya Sovetskaya Entsiklopediya*, xi (1930), 542.

Table No. 68

Population of USSR by Classes

(in millions, including dependants)

	1924–1925	1925–1926	1926–1927
Proletarian * Non-Agricultural	20·4	24·6	26·7
Proletarian Agricultural	4·9	5·4	5·8
Total Proletarian	25·3	30·0	32·5
Poor Peasant	26·5	23·5	22·4
Middle Peasant	74·7	75·2	76·7
Kulak	4·5	4·7	4·9
Total Peasant	105·7	103·4	104·0
Working Non-Proletarian Non-Agricultural †	6·2	6·6	6·8
Non-Agricultural Bourgeois ‡	3·1	3·4	3·5
Declassed Non-Agricultural	0·5	0·6	0·6
Total Population	140·8	144·0	147·4

* i.e. wage-earners, including employees.
† Artisans, craftsmen, members of professions.
‡ Employers of labour, including artisans employing labour.

Source : Yu. Larin, *Sotsial'naya Struktura SSSR* (1928), p. 27.

Table No. 69

Proletarian Population of USSR

(in millions)

	1924–1925	1925–1926	1926–1927
Permanent Non-Agricultural Workers	3·6	4·2	4·6
Seasonal Non-Agricultural Workers	1·0	1·5	1·8
Proletarian Agricultural Workers	2·6	2·9	3·1
Employees	2·8	3·3	3·5
Total Employed	10·0	11·9	13·0
Dependants	15·3	18·1	19·5
Proletarian	25·3	30·0	32·5

Source : Yu. Larin, *Sotsial'naya Struktura SSSR* (1928), pp. 4, 7, 11.

Table No. 70

National Income

(in million rubles)

	1924–1925	1925–1926	1926–1927	1927–1928 (plan)
(i) By Categories of Population				
A. Agricultural (except wage-earners, included under B.1.)	8,592	10,375	11,122	11,871
B. Non-agricultural				
1. Wage- (and Salary-) Earners	3,760	5,607	6,623	7,131
2. Free Professions	66	76	80	86
3. Artisans and Craftsmen	527	569	610	650
4. Bourgeoisie	861	1,091	1,090	1,075
5. Others	570	757	864	896
Total	14,376	18,475	20,389	21,709
(ii) By Categories of Production				
A. Private				
1. Agricultural	8,592	10,375	11,112	11,871
2. Non-Agricultural	5,784	8,100	9,267	9,838
(Including Proletarian	3,700	5,607	6,623	7,131)
Total of A	14,376	18,475	20,389	21,709
B. Socialized				
1. State	992	1,415	1,700	1,942
2. Cooperative	57	172	251	307
3. Communal	164	190	220	250
Total of B	1,213	1,777	2,171	2,499
Total of A and B	15,589	20,252	22,560	24,208

Source: *Kontrol'nye Tsifry Narodnogo Khozyaistva SSSR na 1927–1928 god* (1928), pp. 494-496.

LIST OF ABREVIATIONS

(Supplementary to List in Vol. 1, pp. 985-91)

Agitprop = Sektsiya Agitatsii i Propagandy (Agitation and Propaganda Section)

Evsetktsiya = Evreiskaya Sektsiya (Jewish Section)

FOSP = Federatsiya Organizatsii Sovetskikh Pisatelei (Federation of Organizations of Soviet Writers)

Glavpolitprosvet = Glavnyi Politiko–Prosvetitel'nyi Komitet (Chief Committee for Political Education)

Gosizdat = Gosudarstvennoe Izdatel'stvo (State Publishing House)

IKKIM = Ispolnitel'nyi Komitet Kommunisticheskogo Internatsionala Molodezhi (Executive Committee of the Communist Youth International)

Istpart = Komitet po Istorii Oktyabr'skoi Revolyutosii Vsesoyuznoi Kommunisticheskoi Partii (Committee of the All-Union Communist Party for the History of the October Revolution)

Komvuz = Kommunisticheskoe Vysshee Uchebnoe Zavedenie (Communist Higher Educational Establishment)

Lef = Levyi Front (Left Front)

Politgramota = Politicheskaya Gramota (Political Instruction)

PUR = Politicheskoe Upravlenie Revvoensoveta (Political Administration of the Revolutionary Military Council)

RANION = Russkaya Assotsiatsiya Nauchnykh Institutov Obshchestvennykh Nauk (Russian Association of Scientific Institutes of the Social Sciences)

RAPP = Russkaya Assotsiatsiya Proletarskikh Pisatelei (Russian Association of Proletarian Writers)

Ref = Revolyutsionnyi Front (Revolutionary Front)

VAPP = Vserossiskaya Assotsiatsiya Proletarskikh Pisatelei (All-Russian Association of Proletarian Writers)

VLKSM = Vsesoynznyi Leninskii Kommunistischeskii Soyuz Molodezhi (All-Union Leninist Communist League of Youth (Komsomol))

VOAPP = Vsesoyuznaya Organizatsiya Assotisiatsii Proletarskikh Pisaltelei (All-Union Organization of Associations of Proletarian Writers)

VOKP = Vserossiskoe Obshchestvo Krest'yanskikh Pisatelei (All-Russian Society of Peasant Writers)

VSP = Vserossiiskii Soyuz Pisatelei (All-Russian Union of Writers)

ZSFSR = Zakavkavskaya Sotsialisticheskaya Federativnaya Sovetskaya Respublika (Transcaucasian Socialist Federal Soviet Republic)

INDEX

Abkhazian ASSR, 198
Academy of Sciences, 148n, 452-455 ;
  see also Communist Academy
" Activists ", 125-130, 145, 159-160,
  259, 261, 269n, 271, 277
Adiat courts, 355
Adoratsky, V., 375n
Adventists, 388
Agitprop, see under All-Union Com-
  munist Party (Bolsheviks)
Agrarian code, 136, 236-237, 242,
  245, 255, 261
Agriculture ; party members in, 179-
  180 ; income from, 423, 493 ; col-
  lectivization of, 438, 448 ; taxation,
  466-467
Ajarian ASSR, 198n
Aktiv, see " Activists "
Alekseev, 139
All-Russian Association of Proletarian
  Writers (VAPP, later RAPP), see
  Russian Association of Proletarian
  writers
All-Russian Society of Peasant
  Writers (VOKP), 400
All-Russian Trade Union of Agricultural and Forestry Workers
  (Vserabotzemles), 107-108, 110
All-Russian Union of Writers (VSP),
  400-401
All-Union Association of Scientific
  and Technical Workers (Varnitso),
  453
All-Union Communist League of
  Youth (Komsomol) : attacks united
  opposition, 11, 22, 24n, 33 ; opposition in, 40, 173 ; and young
  workers, 110 ; party activists in,
  125n ; and education, 151, 154-155,
  167-168 ; membership and composition, 161-165, 168n, 174, 177,
  179, 181n, 182-183, 230n, 433, 480 ;
  Bukharin's criticisms of, 163, 165n,
  167-168, 171, 174 ; and party
  membership, 164-165, 173, 176 ;

rôle of, 166-168, 174-175, 177 ;
  Stalin and, 166, 175-176 ; and
  trade unions, 166-167, 176 ; behaviour of young criticized, 168-
  172, 174, 177, 416 ; party control
  of, 172 ; criticized by opposition,
  172-174 ; purged, 177 ; and village
  Soviets, 253 ; and electoral commissions, 275 ; and 1927 elections,
  281 ; in campaign against bureaucracy, 297-298, 306 ; in Red Army,
  318, 321, 333 ; in Red Fleet, 332 ;
  and Osoaviakhim, 335 ; opposition
  to religion, 386, 389, 391 ; and anti-
  Semitism, 395-397 ; and peasant
  groups, 459 ; in Soviet organs, 478,
  488
  5th Conference (1927), 162, 164,
  166-167, 171, 297, 386, 396, 480
  4th Congress (1921), 395n
  5th Congress (1922), 177-178
  6th Congress (1924), 163, 395n
  7th Congress (1926), 161, 165,
  167, 396n, 480
  8th Congress (1928), 163, 165,
  171, 173-175, 177-178, 182, 298-
  299, 389, 391, 397, 480
  9th Congress (1931), 177
All-Union Communist Party (Bolsheviks) (VKP(B)) : membership
  and composition, 100-115, 116n,
  123, 125, 128, 165, 430, 433, 474-
  479, 481 ; 1927 census, 100-104,
  106n, 110, 157, 164, 179-180n,
  430n ; October enrolment, 100-112,
  164n ; party machine, 115-124 ; in
  government, 123-131, 444 ; discipline, 132-147 ; 1929 purge, 142-
  147, 188, 330, and education, 148-
  160 ; rural membership, 179, 187-
  188, 481 ; on kulaks, 183, 185-186 ;
  manifesto on 1929 election, 284 ;
  and administrative training, 306 ;
  and Red Army, 321-330 ; and
  writers, 416-417

496